D0871649

THE GREAT TASK REMAINING

BOOKS BY WILLIAM MARVEL

The First New Hampshire Battery, 1861–1865

*Race of the Soil: The Ninth New Hampshire
Regiment in the Civil War*

The Battle of the Crater (Petersburg Campaign)
(cowritten with Michael Cavanaugh)

Burnside

*The Battles for Saltville:
Southwest Virginia in the Civil War*

Andersonville: The Last Depot

The Alabama *and the* Kearsarge:
The Sailor's Civil War

A Place Called Appomattox

The Monitor *Chronicles: One Sailor's Account*
(editor)

Lee's Last Retreat: The Flight to Appomattox

Mr. Lincoln Goes to War

Lincoln's Darkest Year: The War in 1862

*The Great Task Remaining:
The Third Year of Lincoln's War*

THE GREAT TASK
REMAINING

*The Third Year of
Lincoln's War*

William Marvel

Houghton Mifflin Harcourt

BOSTON • NEW YORK

ISBN 978-0-618-99064-1

Book design by Melissa Lotfy

Maps by Catherine Schneider

PRINTED IN THE UNITED STATES OF AMERICA

Book Club Edition

For

Judge John L. Hurley

(1887–1962)

Bowdoin College

Class of 1908

A lifelong Lincoln scholar who bequeathed me his library and his fascination with that president; through him I shook the hand that shook the hands of John L. Sullivan and Joshua Chamberlain

Contents

List of Illustrations and Maps

Illustrations are from the Library of Congress unless otherwise credited.

MAPS

All maps are by Catherine Schneider.

Preface

The Civil War has fascinated me for as long as I can remember. By the time I was five my interest in it had already become so obvious that my mother started cultivating it, beginning with the day she introduced me to an ancient woman who, when she was five herself, had seen the Union army march into Savannah. My preoccupation with that epoch caught the attention of schoolmates and the yearbook staff at my high school, and despite the early lapse of my formal education I continued to study American history quite seriously, with special emphasis on that particular period. Like most amateur historians, I began with simplistic assumptions, including the belief that I needed only to memorize a long and complicated series of events and anecdotes to "learn" the war, much as cub riverboat pilot Sam Clemens "learned" the Mississippi River.

Such naive expectations should have withered before the competing images of the war as an altruistic abolition crusade and as a courageous struggle for agrarian survival, but then those partisan myths merged into a single nationalistic legend, bristling with an odd combination of religious and metallurgical metaphor. According to this compromise interpretation, the war served as a human sacrifice — a collective crucifixion, as it were, for the expiation of national sin — while the crucible of conflict forged a new and stronger nation from the wreckage of two antagonistic societies. That was the gospel of Lincoln, and it has become the New Testament of American history, crowding out the memory of other points of view that enjoyed considerable popularity and even validity in their day. Because those other viewpoints did not prevail, they tend to suffer at the hands of historians who are, themselves, indelibly influenced by the one that did triumph.

Today, the Northern war effort is generally viewed as a struggle of almost single-minded devotion to national unity by a majority of citizens, who were impeded by the obstructionism of a stubborn, deluded minority. Antiwar Democrats are usually vilified now as racially prejudiced, which was usually true enough, but so were most of the War Democrats — as well as many of the Republicans with whom they allied themselves. The peace faction is characterized as having operated on mistaken political premises, and that was often true, too, but the war party sometimes misjudged the political winds, as well. Through the distorted lenses of hindsight and presentism, though, Northerners who opposed the Lincoln administration are now seen as the villains of Civil War history, lurking like a fifth column to foil freedom, sustain slavery, and destroy the country.

The number of people who opposed the war at one time or another probably exceeds common impressions, for antiwar sentiment can now be found with increasing ease in burgeoning manuscript repositories. Attitudes about the conflict also changed frequently, and the degree of popular support fluctuated with each military defeat, or victory, and with each new, previously inconceivable federal intrusion into constitutional territory. The invisible constituency of women, who were not allowed to vote, provides some of the most virulent criticism of Lincoln's administration: many soldiers' wives showed dissatisfaction with the bloodshed, and with their husbands' subordination of family interests to a national devotion they did not especially share. From the beginning of the war to the end, for that matter, the soldiers themselves often revealed that love of country did not provide their principal motive for taking arms, if it motivated them at all.

The mercenary element in the creation of the Union army formed a significant theme in *Mr. Lincoln Goes to War*, which became the first in a projected four-volume reexamination of the entire war. The second volume of that tetralogy appeared as *Lincoln's Darkest Year*, in which the mercenary impulse accelerated as timid and vacillating leadership undermined Northern arms and prolonged the conflict. This third volume opens in March of 1863, as the Northern public reeled between two periods of abysmal morale: the useless bloodbath at Fredericksburg lay three months behind, and the disaster at Chancellorsville six weeks ahead. Spirits revived partially in the interim, only to plunge all the more precipitately after the second defeat, and by late June the peace movement had probably reached the peak of its wartime momentum. That momentum carried beyond even the Union victories of early July, which seemed briefly to foretell the collapse of the rebellion. Then Confederates in the East escaped annihilation after Gettysburg, resuming the offensive by October, while Confederates in the West recovered from Vicksburg and a summer-long retreat to trounce the Union army at Chickamauga Creek. The Northern citizen might be forgiven for wondering whether the war could ever be won, if the Confederacy could spring so vigorously back to life after such rare and signal Union triumphs.

The same phenomenon recurred after the sweeping victory at Chattanooga in November, which put the main Confederate army of the West to abject flight. The glow of that achievement was immediately dimmed when Robert E. Lee foiled a similarly promising maneuver in Virginia, and the following winter saw a series of Union defeats and embarrassments that again seemed to demonstrate the South's unlimited powers of rejuvenation. After all the successes won by the national army in the second half of 1863, by the spring of 1864 war-weariness and opposition to the administration had again reached critical levels, at least on the home front.

Toward the end of his life, the most eloquent historian of the Civil War, Bruce Catton, wrote that the Confederacy labored under "reduced circumstances" by the beginning of 1864.[1] That was certainly true, and we who now enjoy all the documentary sources from both sides clearly understand that. What we tend to forget is that those who lived through the war had no means of predicting the outcome, and little opportunity to accurately judge their enemies' conditions or attitudes. Many Confederate citizens lacked sufficient information to comprehend their own nation's desperate circumstances, and those who did might well have remained optimistic by recollecting the fluctuating fortunes of the American Revolution. The Northern observer could form no reliable impression of circumstances in the South, and sixty days filled with Union disasters wore heavily on the patience of the Northern public by the fourth week of April.

At both the beginning and the end of the war's third year, the majority party retained its hold on power as it had throughout the conflict, and as it would continue to, with as much repression as persuasion, and with a combination of electoral trickery and political manipulation. Executive proclamations often discouraged opposition candidates from effectively criticizing the administration, reducing many elections to sheer farce. The War Department regularly employed soldiers as both voters and ballot-box thugs to swing elections to the Republican Party, meanwhile punishing anyone in uniform who actively supported Democratic candidates. Deceit, dishonesty, and hypocrisy tainted the government at Washington as badly as they did the one in Richmond. Corruption permeated the war machine, fostering a tradition of graft that survived the war and blossomed a few years later into the most vendible Congress the United States had ever seen.

The citizens of that period had to balance their own values — rather than ours — to determine whether the evils attending the prosecution of Mr. Lincoln's war were worth bearing in order to achieve his goals. One of those goals became emancipation, and most Americans in the mid-nineteenth century failed to appreciate that ideal as thoroughly as their modern counterparts, for whom the end of slavery seems to provide abundant reason to justify all the death and destruction. Except for a determined minority of abolitionists, whose devotion to the Union faltered at least as much as that of any Peace Democrat, the Northern public's opposition to slavery showed more economic reasoning than altruistic philosophy. Many had long dreaded the competitive effect if the peculiar institution crept into the free states, while others now fretted over the labor glut if freed slaves migrated in the same direction. Then there were those who feared that making war on slavery would only stiffen the resolve of the most lukewarm Confederates, and others who scorned the sudden change in war aims as plain evidence of political trickery. On January 14, 1863, less than a fortnight after the effective date of his Emancipation Proclamation, Lincoln himself recognized that emancipation had saddled him with numerous political disadvantages.[2]

The less enlightened racial attitudes of those who voted for or against Lincoln made it easier for them to resist or resent the moral and political degradation that the war wrought, and the dangerous constitutional precedents that it produced. The real surprise, in light of that different perspective on the pivotal issue of race, is that a greater percentage of citizens did not vote against the administration. That might well have happened, had elections been allowed to proceed without the partisan intrigue of government officials — if, in other words, the administration that declared itself the defender of democracy had allowed untrammeled democracy to prevail when it was most important to know what the people wanted.

In his last book, historian Arthur Schlesinger cited two prominent Republicans for defending the First Amendment right to dissent in wartime. Schlesinger praised Senator Robert Taft for reminding the country, only days after Pearl Harbor, that "criticism in time of war is essential to the maintenance of any kind of democratic government." Any comfort that open debate might give to an enemy would be insignificant and transitory, Taft insisted, and would be outweighed by the benefits to the nation that preserved such freedom. Theodore Roosevelt also championed unfettered freedom of expression in the midst of the First World War, when Woodrow Wilson signed congressional legislation making it a crime to criticize the president or the government. Such statutory contradiction of the First Amendment, said Roosevelt, "is not only unpatriotic and servile, but is morally treasonable to the American public." Despite his passionate defense of free expression at all times, Schlesinger trod but lightly on Abraham Lincoln for his own suppression of free speech, although Lincoln often acted unilaterally and arbitrarily, and established some of the most momentous precedents in the way of wartime repression.[3]

In the same book, Schlesinger also remarked that there "are no more dangerous people on earth than those who believe they are executing the will of the Almighty."[4] By the end of his war's third year President Lincoln had begun to ascribe the duration and deadliness of the conflict to divine will: he wrote as much to a Kentucky newspaperman on April 4, 1864, and considered the concept in a private draft. Schlesinger was surely aware of that letter, for Lincoln's insistence in it that he was controlled by events became legendary. If the Lincoln-admirer Schlesinger failed to view Lincoln's argument on that point as another dangerous example of a political leader who thought he was serving God's will, it may be because the historian Schlesinger viewed the assertion as political rhetoric rather than as a statement of literal belief. So it appears to have been, too, however earnestly such statements may be seized upon as evidence of Lincoln's conversion from early skepticism. The salient clue in Lincoln's letter, which was devoted entirely to political defense, is that at that juncture he should have considered the results of the war a political liability to be disavowed, rather than an accomplishment to be claimed. A great many of the nation's citizens saw it precisely the same way, and in this account of our most turbulent era their perspective is neither forgotten nor dismissed.

PART I

WHEN PEACE WAS FAR AWAY

1

An Army Stretched Out on the Hills

✈ THE EXPANSIVE FITZHUGH farm, four miles northeast of Fredericksburg, Virginia, had been crawling with Union soldiers since the beginning of 1863. Dan Sickles, formerly a Tammany Hall politician of tarnished reputation and lately the commander of the Third Corps, had occupied the house as his headquarters through the latter half of that winter, but on the cold and lowery afternoon of March 12 he surrendered the grounds to a wedding reception for one of his junior officers. The groom had been unable to secure a furlough to be married, so the ceremony transpired in the camp of the 7th New Jersey, in which the groom commanded a company. Besides the betrothed captain, who hovered within a few days of his twenty-fourth birthday, the wedding party consisted of a bride not yet nineteen and nine adventurous bridesmaids, who had accompanied her on the steamer from Washington City. Chief among the guests stood Major General Joseph Hooker, who for the past forty-five days had commanded the Army of the Potomac. The entire regiment turned out under arms to form a hollow square around them all.[1]

The second week of March had alternated between luscious spring sun and soggy reminders of winter — but, unfortunately for the ladies in their light gowns, March 12 fell on the chillier side of that cycle. Raw winds reddened bare arms and chests, while foreboding Virginia skies demanded a canvas canopy to protect the nuptials. The New Jersey chaplain officiated while Daniel Hart and Ellen Lammond knelt before an altar of stacked snare drums to pledge themselves to each other, and when they arose as husband and wife the brigade band announced it with a blaring processional. Ladies, generals, band, and all then adjourned for a banquet and ball under tents raised in the yard of the Fitzhugh farm, where they prolonged the festivities into the evening. The brassy echo carried far across the hills of Stafford County, serenading thousands of envious soldiers sprawled in their camps above Fredericksburg.[2]

Weddings naturally prompt reflections on the future, but any such thoughts on this occasion could only have dampened the festive atmosphere. The shock of a bloody and lopsided defeat at Fredericksburg, only three months past, had not been forgotten. Just seven weeks before the wedding, a disastrous flank march had sent the dejected army into winter quarters, from which, inevitably, it would soon emerge for another attempt to subdue Robert E. Lee, his Army of Northern Virginia, and the rebellious states of the Southern Confederacy. Another seven weeks would find many of the participants dead, or seriously wounded. Captain Hart would be among the latter, and although he would survive his wounds he would never find successful employment outside the army; by cleaving to him, Nelly Lammond consigned herself to a dozen years on the barren plains of West Texas, sixteen years of widow's weeds, and an early grave.[3]

The celebrants therefore dwelt upon the present. Starved as they had been for distaff company, most of the soldiers doubtless found the present agreeable enough, with the bride's retinue to brighten the affair, and few men in that army appreciated female companionship more than Dan Sickles and Joe Hooker. So appealing were the bridesmaids to Sickles that he persuaded them to stay on another day — inviting them, the newlyweds, Hooker, and a host of Third Corps generals, colonels, and staff officers back to the Fitzhugh farm the next night to celebrate his recent promotion to major general. Detailed soldiers and servants festooned the yard with evergreen boughs and flags, and when the guests arrived that evening, Friday the 13th, the tents all glowed with the glitter of hundreds of candles. Even a couple of somberly clad chaplains sipped some wine and partook of the feast, though they stood aside for the dancing and departed before midnight.[4]

It was perhaps such contrived gaiety, more than the frequently dismal weather, that led one Yankee artilleryman to remark a few days later that their winter along the Rappahannock had been "uncommon pleasant," and the men wearing shoulder straps let no excuse for merriment pass. Saint Patrick's Day provided an opportunity for epic revelry, and as one might have expected, the Irish Brigade greeted it in that spirit. Outside their camp above Falmouth, enlisted men wielded shovels that their officers might play. On relatively flat ground they cleared a racetrack a mile long, complete with hurdles and ditches as wide as ten feet. Thomas Meagher, the hard-drinking brigadier, appeared in knee breeches, a cutaway coat, and a white stovepipe hat, reminding his troops of a circus ringmaster. He further cultivated that image by barking for donations to fund the frolic, although the facilities had all been produced by the labor of government soldiers. "Here is a large capacity," he apprised his assembled subordinates and superiors, holding the stovepipe hat upside down; "now *fill* it." The donations afforded graduated prizes for the three fleetest horses and riders, but much of that ended up in Meagher's pocket anyway: it was Meagher's Irish adjutant, dressed in bright jockey attire and astride the general's own little grey mare, who took first prize in the steeplechase after three heats. Following the main event Meagher opened the track to anyone else who wanted to ride, at a fee of five dollars dropped in his cavernous hat. That afternoon the reverberations of a heavy skirmish at Kelly's Ford, miles upstream, interrupted the entertainment in the middle of a sack race. "Get out of those bags," Meagher bellowed at the participants, and the brigade fell in to join the fray, but the alarm subsided before the first man stepped off.[5]

David Birney, commander of a division in the Third Corps under Sickles, refused to be outdone by the loudmouthed immigrant Meagher, and he scheduled his own festival for March 26, to celebrate nothing in particular. The same sports prevailed: horse racing, with and without hurdles; a greased pole; sack races; and "buckfights," in which men bound in a squatting position tried to knock each other over. General Hooker attended this gathering as he had all the others, and with him came the usual assortment of women. The bridesmaids had all returned to Washington, but scores of officers had brought their wives and daughters down to board at houses around the countryside, or to live with them in tents or stockaded huts, and that population obligingly submitted to corsets and crinoline. Garnering the most attention were the wives of two New York colonels. Both women inspired abundant occupation for the eyes and tongues of the troops, but it was the one who called herself Princess Salm-Salm whom everyone remembered. Formerly an actress under the name Agnes Leclerq, she had recently married Colonel Felix Prince Salm, a Prussian soldier of fortune who had come to America for this war. Princess Salm-Salm insinuated that she had seen only twenty-one winters, but an artillery officer who observed her that afternoon remarked that she and the other colonel's wife "have been very handsome women in their day." He considered them "still good-looking enough to stand very well in the eyes of General Joe," but Joe Hooker was nearing the end of his fifth decade. The day closed badly for the erstwhile Miss Leclerq: horses and riders showed less grace, with many a mount balking at the hurdles and numerous horsemen taking dangerous tumbles. Colonel Salm fell so hard that witnesses at first deemed his injuries mortal, but General Sickles gallantly consoled the princess while the surgeons saved her prince for death on another field.[6]

That near tragedy may have diluted enthusiasm for further orchestrations. Colonels were paid too well to have them lying about for months, recuperating from foolish accidents while lesser field officers oversaw their regiments. The Potomac army was growing short of officers that winter in any case, as many of those who had escaped the slaughter at Fredericksburg exercised the privilege of resigning their commissions, but the popularity of that avenue was not confined to the eastern theater. Lieutenants and captains from Maine to the Mississippi made their excuses as the spring campaigns drew nigh, or they dragged out convalescent furloughs for nebulous varieties of indisposition. "I don't believe the 'young patriots' will ever come back," said a Regular Army captain of some freshly appointed lieutenants on sick leave, "as they didn't come into the service except to draw their pay."[7] Some enlisted men who had just obtained commissions soon surrendered them for a discharge, and some applied for commissions precisely so they might exercise that very privilege. One of the senior captains in a Maine regiment found it difficult to resign because his services were deemed so crucial, and when ordered to rejoin his regiment he sought a presidential appointment as quartermaster so he could "get a Com[mission] to *resign*." Large numbers of men in the ranks had also decamped on the sly, choosing more informal and risky means of separation by overstaying their furloughs, disappearing into the army's byzantine medical system, or simply walking away from camp in a suit of civilian clothing. Sympathetic relatives filled the express trains with boxes of such clothing to help their soldier boys desert.[8]

One Connecticut colonel tried repeatedly during the winter to recover men who had slipped away from his command, but sometimes he gave up on them. After months of chasing several furloughed convalescents, he dropped them from the rolls of the regiment only to hear, soon afterward, that some of them had inveigled a surgeon into awarding them certificates of disability for their sundry ailments. The colonel ruled those tardy documents invalid, and declared the men deserters. Another private who appeared to enjoy good health left camp without permission and headed home, where he visited around enough that reports leaked back to regimental headquarters. He, too, attempted to absolve himself on a belated plea of illness, but the frustrated colonel would hear none of that, either.[9]

William Greene, of the 2nd U.S. Sharpshooters, typified this more casual deserter. After nearly a year of service, during which he had indignantly castigated those who failed to answer their country's call, Greene seemed to experience a conversion that became apparent late in the summer of 1862, when his regiment wandered into its first major battle at Second Bull Run. The sharpshooters fled the field and abandoned the battery they were supposed to support. Greene left the ranks soon thereafter because, as he explained it, he "got tired out," but that fatigue did not prevent him from walking all the way to Alexandria, where he sought a hospital bed. The surgeons sent him north to a hospital in Rhode Island. He schemed persistently for a discharge without success, but finally he left the hospital on a furlough and neglected to return. First he went home to southern New Hampshire, but over the winter he migrated to south-central Wisconsin. His sister and brother-in-law had moved out there to start a farm, and late in March he began working for them at $14.50 a month, plus keep. His infrequent letters bore no signatures, lest a prying postmaster report his whereabouts; it may have been fear of discovery that eventually prompted him to leave his sister's house and start drifting.[10]

A private in a new regiment from central New York appealed for a furlough, but his request was not among the few that his colonel granted, so he circulated the news that his mother was dying, or had died, and one of his comrades gave up his own furlough so the bereaved private might attend the funeral. No good turn goes unpunished, the generous comrade found, and late in March he remarked that the beneficiary of the sacrificed furlough "got on the wrong train" for the return trip, grumbling that "it took him to Canada instead of Washington."[11]

Soon after the glorified skirmish that served as his maiden battle, a Massachusetts shoemaker named Andrew Grover had inexplicably gotten himself captured in a locale completely dominated by the Union army. In July of 1862, as soon as the opposing forces agreed on a system of prisoner exchanges, Grover was released from Southern custody under the customary parole precluding him from bearing arms against the Confederacy until a rebel soldier of equal rank had been freed in formal exchange. He took that as license to return North, and like many former prisoners he simply stayed there, dodging the government's haphazard pursuit of such truants. In the spring of 1863 he was making his way northward from Massachusetts, supporting himself by selling bootleg liquor. He had just crossed the New Hampshire border into Fryeburg, Maine, when he ran into trouble, for Maine was a dry state and some abstemious resident turned him in. A transient miscreant of military age bore some investigation, with thousands of deserters roaming the country, and by the time the grand jury indicted Grover on liquor charges, his secret had been found out: at his court appearance an army officer took charge of him.[12]

Some men seemed to disappear into thin air. The previous autumn

Francis Richards had straggled behind the 11th New Hampshire during the march across northern Virginia, and when he failed to answer the roll call that evening, everyone supposed he had been scooped up by Confederate cavalry. Then the wife of one of his neighbors saw Richards at home and wrote about it to her husband, who served in the same company. The husband expressed considerable surprise that his comrade had deserted, but he revealed nothing like disapproval: he merely assured his wife that he would never abscond without consulting her first. By March of 1863, he added, desertion from camp had become almost impossible, so vigilantly did the perimeter guards and the provost details monitor the peregrinations of solitary soldiers.[13]

None of these men endured more than a taste of the battlefield: they may have forsaken their commitments over personal or political epiphanies inspired by a few months of service in the field. For thousands of other soldiers who had borne the brunt of the fighting, it was perhaps the sheer brutality of the conflict that had impelled them on clandestine journeys homeward, and especially from the Army of the Potomac, where stunning carnage seemed to produce the least tangible results. The previous December, waves of blue infantry had swept up Marye's Heights at Fredericksburg against raking Confederate artillery and a well-protected tier of blazing rifles, all without the slightest effect beyond depleting Southern ammunition. On the plain below Fredericksburg, William B. Franklin had sent out a feeble assault that nevertheless managed to crack Stonewall Jackson's line, but Franklin failed to support that breakthrough sufficiently and it was driven back with heavy losses. Well over a thousand Union soldiers had been killed on the field that bleak day, and the death toll neared three thousand after the worst-wounded had succumbed, but all those lives had not bought an inch of ground. Ambrose Burnside finally withdrew everyone to the left bank of the Rappahannock, and six weeks later, after deep mud doomed his last attempt to wield his unlucky army, he turned it over to Joe Hooker.

No wonder, then, that company clerks in the Army of the Potomac tallied such voluminous absentee lists. Winter conditions, poor food, political discouragement, and a burning desire to go home bred widespread dissatisfaction, leading to a mutiny in at least one Pennsylvania regiment.[14] By the end of January, 31 percent of the troops who came under Hooker's authority were absent for reasons mostly unknown: 85,000 all told, including many thousands who had deliberately deserted or who actively avoided duty on inventive pretenses. Hooker's reforms, including the introduction of regular, rotating furloughs, helped lessen the flight noticeably — suggesting that homesickness and unattended personal business also played a part in it — and by the end of February absenteeism

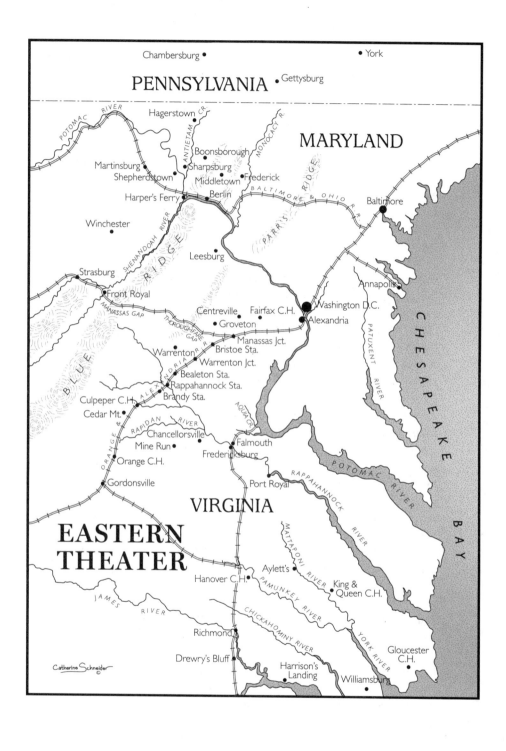

had been reduced to barely 27 percent. At the end of March it was down to 24 percent, but that was still higher than in other armies. The forces operating on the Mississippi River under Ulysses Grant began that same period with fewer than 21 percent of their men absent, and despite rampant disease, that proportion had risen barely half a percent by March 31. President Lincoln issued an amnesty proclamation on March 10, exempting all deserters who returned to their units by April 1 from any punishment beyond loss of pay for the time they were gone. A couple of weeks later, when newspapers published the official reports that had inspired Lincoln's act of combined magnanimity and desperation, an astonished public learned that 125,000 officers and men were absent from their commands.[15]

Wilbur Fisk, a Vermont private in that army who wrote occasional columns for a Montpelier newspaper, adopted what would become an enduring excuse for poor morale in the ranks: in a mid-March epistle he informed his readers that it was all the fault of civilian croakers, and especially those who denounced Abraham Lincoln's emancipation policy. "It is not the army that is demoralized," he asserted, "but the citizens at home." It required a generous measure of hypocrisy for Fisk to pontificate so self-righteously on the evil of desertion and its causes, but he may have felt a particular need to mitigate the responsibility of those who shirked their duty, for as he wrote that letter he had just returned from French leave himself. In his diary and his letters he tried to justify the excursion as a misunderstanding, but in fact he had pursued the same devious course as legions before him, leaving his unit without notice and finding his way home by way of a hospital and a convalescent camp. The principal difference in Fisk's case was that he courted and married a girl during his absence, and that required a return to respectability if he was to be able to support his wife.[16]

Private Fisk's self-serving opinion did reflect a growing discontent with Mr. Lincoln's war. Opponents had begun to make themselves heard in the summer of 1862, when Congress gave the president authority to demand levies of state militia from the governors. The announcement of the Emancipation Proclamation at the beginning of autumn sorely aggravated political differences, alienating many dedicated Unionists, and toward the end of the following winter Congress had empowered Lincoln to bypass the governors altogether and draft citizens directly. Such drastic departure from the democratic process alarmed some of the president's own closest supporters. By late March the dissenting chorus approached a crescendo.

Over the winter Isaac Welch, a state senator from Ohio, lamented to his counterpart in the U.S. Senate, Ben Wade, that the militia draft and the emancipation controversy had interposed a deep rift in the loyal population. "With a divided north," he wondered, "can anyone entertain a well grounded hope that we will ultimately succeed in putting down the rebellion: I think not." Democrats who had turned against the war, or had opposed it from the start, might soon gain enough control of state and federal governments to impede military efforts against the Confederacy, Welch warned, but the armies seemed to accomplish nothing as it was: Grant's ambitious campaign against Vicksburg lay stalled amid high water after successive failures, and William Rosecrans had burrowed his Army of the Cumberland into a Tennessee encampment after fending off a determined attack. The Army of the Potomac, which drew more than its share of attention, had disheartened the entire North with its last defeat. "If our arms are not attended with better success against April or May," Welch remarked, "especially the Potomac Army; how can we recruit the army?"[17]

Shortly after leaving his own seat in the U.S. Senate, and his role as President Lincoln's closest Washington confidant, Orville Hickman Browning listened to a depressing assessment of the war from an Iowa general who felt he was fighting not only against armed rebels but against a tide of incompetence in his own government as well. On the last Saturday in March this officer dropped into Browning's Chicago hotel room for an hour and painted the president as a political weakling whose pronouncement on slavery had galvanized Southern resistance. The secretary of the treasury, Salmon P. Chase, was bankrupting the country and depreciating the currency, he added, while the armies roamed almost wild, marauding against friend and foe alike without effective interference from their officers. The general could not see how the war would be won.[18]

George Templeton Strong — elitist New York City lawyer, advocate of vigorous war, and treasurer of the U.S. Sanitary Commission — had also begun to entertain serious doubts about the chances of victory by February. A month later his dejection lingered, although he noted an unaccountable "sanguine fit" among the Gotham gentry. "I can't tell why," he added, nor did there seem to be any reason for it. The war news continued to disappoint: Rosecrans's Tennessee army had stirred from its winter torpor just long enough to lose an entire brigade on what should have been a routine reconnaissance, and every few days a small band of Virginia cavalry would descend on the multitude of Yankees guarding Washington, with humiliating effect. Trouble was also brewing with England over British-built Confederate cruisers and parliamentary debate over recognition of the Confederacy. Some public satisfaction may have attended the adjournment of the Thirty-seventh Congress, which had earned a reputation for either reform or repression, depending on one's viewpoint. More likely, though, the sudden pulse of buoyancy among New Yorkers may have had something to do with a 20 percent drop in the price of gold over two business days, to $150 an ounce, which produced a flurry of enthusiasm on Wall Street.[19]

The course of the war weighed little on the personal lives of the wealthy, save when the resulting inflation shrank the value of their fortunes. Only collateral traces of the conflict flavored the diary of Lizzie Corning, the seventeen-year-old daughter of a well-heeled railroad administrator in New Hampshire's capital city. Her days passed in romantic reveries of stage actor John Wilkes Booth, afternoon visits from admiring young businessmen or government officeholders, and shopping for dresses selling at three times the monthly salary of a soldier, with the occasional surprise of a diamond ring from her indulgent father. On rare occasions she might accept a carriage ride through the camp of some regiment bound for the war, as a pleasant diversion from the ennui of her comfortable existence. Few of her male acquaintances faced military service even after the advent of conscription, and for her circle the divisive politics of the struggle appeared to provide little more than an engaging form of amusement.[20]

For those women who toiled more and frolicked less, the affairs of state inflicted a direct influence that provoked more passion. That passion diverged, however, over the ultimate merits of preserving the Union and (assuming that such an effort was worth the increasingly burdensome price) how it could best be accomplished. Daniel Coler had no sooner left New York's Chenango River valley for the war than his wife began deluging him with news of neighbors who had found a way out of uniform, and while she cast no overt aspersions on the cause, she implied that it hardly merited the personal cost to them. Emily Harris, whose husband had been gone over a year and a half, showed more of her teeth. She boiled with indignation over the government's inconsistent attitude toward secession: bumptious administration regents declared secessionists traitors and proclaimed it a criminal act to criticize Lincoln's war, she ranted, but they studiously ignored stinging invective from the more rabid abolitionists, some of whom still advocated secession themselves. Mrs. Harris deeply regretted and clearly resented her husband's decision to enlist, which left her flaying her fingers at shoemaking and other piecework to feed herself and her children at wartime prices. To her, the seceded states did not seem worth the sacrifices she and others were forced to make. "As a wife and mother," she told her stolid husband, "I should say let them go rather than have so many precious lives lost."[21]

The women who corresponded with Private Lewis Smith represented nearly the entire spectrum of opinion. His sister Lucy, a persistent Lincoln supporter, remained deliberately optimistic about the prospects for victory in the face of the worst news, and she damned the war's opponents up and down; sometimes she passed along the nationalistic comments of her husband, a mildly prosperous farmer who sat out the war at his village home. Smith's wife, Mary, who stayed on their hardscrabble hill farm with their six children, scorned those outspoken advocates of the war who lounged at home, and she hoped the new draft law would sweep those men into the army. His sister-in-law Hepsabeth, meanwhile, labored in a textile mill where cotton shortages frequently brought the machinery to a standstill. She urged Lewis to seek a discharge any way he could, so he might come home to his family and stop fighting for the "damed Negrows." By good fortune Smith, who had enlisted under the middling bounties of the previous August, entered a regiment that saw no action for more than two years. His family survived on the pay he sent home, supplemented by relief money from their community, and he made no appeal to go home.[22]

Plenty of his compatriots throughout the army did scheme for discharges, and squads of them bid farewell to each company that winter. The attrition naturally struck hardest among regiments in the field. The colonel of the 11th New Jersey described a stream of "miserable disheartning letters" from parents who begged for their boys' release — often at the instigation of their soldier sons, who knew that tales of hardship at home might do the trick.[23] A Pennsylvanian who desperately wanted out of the army hinted that letters documenting the impending death of family members might at least yield a furlough, but to his bitter disappointment such a ploy failed to free him from his regiment.[24] A Maine soldier who had served faithfully from the outbreak of the war conspired with his wife on how to get a furlough, admitting that if he could reach home he planned to persuade their local doctor to grant him a certificate of disability that he might parlay into a discharge.[25]

The rising clamor to get out of the army itself seemed to arouse administrative skepticism, and the War Department grew more reluctant than ever to part with its soldiers. A Pennsylvania captain who had lost his arm at Fredericksburg won presidential sanction for his attempt to raise a brigade of disabled men like himself, to perform light duty that would free others for the front, and that notion rooted quickly in government minds. The War Department gave medical officers authority to assign convalescents to hospital duty, and issued an order forming them into detachments for use as guards, clerks, and nurses; surgeons in need of stewards sometimes used that new authority to hold on to a good man long after even the convalescent thought he was fit to return to duty. The Conscription Act of early March had created scores of new provost marshals across the land, each of whom would need some troops to call upon, and partially disabled men seemed perfect for that duty, so Secretary of War Edwin Stanton formally established what he would later repent calling the Invalid Corps.[26]

The need for men to fill that corps abruptly slowed the migration homeward from the hospitals, and men suffering obvious, permanent disabilities waited interminably for official disposition. An Illinois private who had been wounded through the wrist in the December drive against Vicksburg languished in a hospital on Bedloe's Island five months later; his left hand dangled limp and useless, but he was told that no one who could walk would be discharged.[27] Another ailing soldier in Grant's Vicksburg force informed his father that the surgeons would spare only those who were too severely impaired to perform any duty, like those with discernible ruptures.[28] A middle-aged recruit in a new Pennsylvania regiment wasted away in the hospital for more than four months before army doctors relented.[29] The father of a fourteen-year-old runaway had to appeal to Senator Lyman Trumbull before he could liberate his son from the 14th U.S. Infantry, although the underage lad suffered visibly from Saint Vitus's Dance.[30]

Rumors purported that a substantial sum of money might convince army surgeons or contract physicians to declare individual soldiers unfit for even limited service. Few soldiers owned the resources to deliver a bribe, even if an accommodating surgeon presented himself, but if one served under sufficiently corrupt officers it was possible to buy a commission that one might then resign. A New York captain who constantly sought promotion for the money it would bring admitted to his family that he also promoted his men in return for favors, and that he would advance one man to the next vacant lieutenancy if the aspirant would "give me something handsome." A colonel in the Irish Brigade invited suspicion that he was selling commissions by finagling the appointment of officers from outside his regiment, some of whom had left dismal records under earlier commissions.[31]

Now and then a common soldier tried to buy his way out by means of a less furtive enticement. One member of the 40th Massachusetts who had served only five months on a three-year term offered three hundred dollars to a Connecticut fifer whose regiment was due to go home in the spring, proposing that the musician fulfill the last two years of his commitment as his substitute. With the scent of home in his nostrils the would-be substitute declined, but the arrangement would not have worked in any event: the provision for substitutes applied only to draftees under the new conscription law, and no longer could a Union soldier procure a substitute after he had begun his enlistment.[32]

Millions of letters flowed home from the Union armies that winter and spring. The vast majority of them were later tossed into stoves, fireplaces, and furnaces, but most of those that survive depict the authors as resolute, devoted to the basic cause of national union, and confident of ultimate success. Newspapers friendly to the administration tried to cultivate that confidence by dismissing defeats as insignificant, all the while emphasizing whatever optimism they could draw from events. When poor women went on a rampage in the Confederate capital, breaking into stores in broad daylight, Richmond newspapers characterized them as a greedy mob of base criminals. Efforts to conceal the incident from Union soldiers failed, and Northern papers exploited it as a bread riot that betokened a starving nation.[33] Combined with the steady trickle of hungry, promiscuously clad Confederate deserters drifting into Union lines, the story spawned the immediate impression that the Confederacy was about to implode. That in turn initiated another round of hopeful predictions that the war was nearly over, and that it would end in a ridiculously specific number of months, ranging from three to eight. Most who believed those bright forecasts seemed willing to stay on that much longer, and they assumed that similar good cheer flourished among all the troops around them.[34]

The patriotic tenor of such letters may have increased the odds that they would be preserved and made public by descendants, and discontent may have infected a greater proportion of the troops than the available fragment of surviving correspondence suggests.[35] Some of those more determined soldiers, in fact, inadvertently described an epidemic of disaffection. The volume of complaint had reached such a din by the spring of 1863 that some regiments tried to turn the tide by sending home resolutions of continued support for the administration, but sometimes those efforts backfired. A disappointed Iowa captain reported that his regiment flatly refused to adopt such a token, and Brigadier General James Garfield learned that his former regiment had drawn precisely the opposite conclusion, questioning the moral rectitude of the war as well as its political wisdom and chances of success.[36] A Maine private whose nine-month regiment was about to muster out after a tour of easy duty explained that many of his comrades shared his enthusiasm for the administration and the war, but he also heard a thunder of venomous denunciation: large numbers of his comrades vowed they would never serve under arms again, he wrote, "if the rebels came right into Maine," and plenty of other regiments harbored similar cynics.[37]

Thousands of soldiers who firmly embraced the cause of reunion anticipated that the new element of abolition would instill fresh spirit in the
Southern armies, and some of the more recent recruits felt thoroughly betrayed by the administration. A furious Massachusetts mechanic who had
enlisted two months before the Emancipation Proclamation gave a crude
example of that common expression when he told his brother that he had
enlisted for his "Cuntrey," and not "to fight for the damed nigers." "Old
Abe was pretty sharp — " snorted an Ohio soldier in a pestilential camp
on the Mississippi; "he never issued his proclamation until after he had us
all by the necks." This soldier assured his readers that he would never have
joined the army had he known the war was going to be bent toward such
goals. Wives vilified Lincoln's action, as well, like the Vermont virago who
shrank from the idea of her husband "becoming a sacrifice for the *devilish*
blacks."[38]

Edwin O. Wentworth, another recruit from the previous summer, corroborated the breadth of that feeling in the army with a letter to his
hometown newspaper, in which he alleged that the peace movement on
the home front had finally aroused the hopes of a dejected and disgusted
army. Soldier correspondents who portrayed rosy pictures of the war felt
safe enough signing their names to their newspaper submissions, but superiors usually pounced on those who submitted unflattering political
comments, and uniformed critics of the war soon learned not to identify
themselves. Wentworth injudiciously appended to the letter his distinctive initials and the number of his regiment, and a couple of weeks after
its publication the provost marshal appeared at his tent to arrest him.[39]

On village greens, the war had assumed a far more partisan tone since the
previous spring. In their zeal to crush the Confederacy and restore the antebellum Union, Abraham Lincoln and his secretary of war had trod
squarely and deliberately on numerous treasured elements of constitutional doctrine, and many of those who had once stood by him now recoiled at his methods. Foremost among the objectionable practices, perhaps, were the administration habits of ignoring due process and
usurping the authority of the congressional and judicial branches of government. That had led to thousands of arbitrary arrests, mostly of Democrats, at the whim of federal officials who were usually Republicans, and
some of the victims of those illegal arrests had spent weeks or months behind bars without charges, or on dubious accusations disguising purely
political motives.[40]

Then had come the Emancipation Proclamation, announced the previous September with an effective date of New Year's Day. By its nature that
document violated the U.S. Constitution in a manner that Lincoln him-

self had acknowledged, by overriding state sovereignty on the issue, and for many opponents that was enough. For most, it was the practical application of executive emancipation that stuck in the craw. If liberated en masse, as Lincoln's proclamation proposed, many of the South's four million destitute, illiterate slaves would inevitably flee to the North, creating a glut of cheap labor. Already, former slaves were making their way up the Mississippi and the Ohio looking for work, and military recruitment had stripped the Midwest of so much surplus labor that Ohio farmers snatched them up as soon as they appeared. One Quaker hired two such men, and sent one of them back downriver to retrieve his whole family.[41]

The proclamation had also swollen the "contraband" camps on the fringes of army posts. Thousands of slaves who had heard of the decree swarmed into Helena, Arkansas, from plantations on the Mississippi and Yazoo rivers. Some walked, some rode horses or mules taken from their masters, and some ferried in on U.S. gunboats. A small delegation of the U.S. Sanitary Commission tried to feed and clothe them all. Freedmen signed on as crewmen in the steaming ironclads, or took over the heavy labor formerly performed by soldiers: that soon extinguished a lot of the enlisted men's objections to emancipation, and drove home the advantage those same slaves had given the Confederates. Each slave's departure left an acre of some Southern plantation untilled, an Ohio surgeon ultimately calculated, and Confederate soldiers would eventually have to go home to keep their families from starving.[42]

Thus were some of the more prejudiced of the troops convinced of the wisdom of abolition as a means of hurting the enemy, or moved by pity for the abuse and outrages recounted by the newly freed slaves. Ironically, the presence of slaves still in bondage could exert the opposite influence. A Maine soldier serving in Florida declared himself and most of his fellow Yankees "converted" from their abolition principles after six months' proximity to the Gulf Coast variety of slavery. A captain from New Hampshire found the infamous institution much less horrendous than he had been led to believe, at least in loyal Kentucky, where the proclamation had no effect; slave men and women alike were dressed better than most New Hampshire farmers, he noted, and they seemed not to work nearly as hard as he and his brother did on their own farm. His description of Bluegrass slavery sounded so inviting that he felt constrained to add that he was not advocating it, but he doubted the enslaved population's condition would improve with freedom. The teeming contraband camps, meanwhile, peeled away any such illusions of lassitude and comfort.[43]

It took a little longer for the popular mind to embrace the concept of putting former slaves in uniforms and giving them guns: that proposal initially angered many of the same white soldiers whose burdens and dangers would have been lessened by the reinforcements. Border-state Unionists turned from the enterprise in high dudgeon, but the administration worried progressively less about popular acceptance, and a War Department desperate enough for troops to mobilize the army's cripples could not afford to ignore hundreds of thousands of healthy, unemployed black men. That spring individual regiments of freemen and freedmen were gathering under state designations outside Boston and on the South Atlantic coast. Edwin Stanton sent Lorenzo Thomas, the army's adjutant general, into the Mississippi Valley to recruit whole divisions of displaced slaves, if possible, under the authority of what would soon become the Bureau of Colored Troops, and to examine white soldiers willing to serve as officers in those new regiments.[44]

Recruits for the 54th Massachusetts consisted primarily of free black residents of the eastern half of the state. The regiment filled slowly at first, as did the white regiments raised early that year. One exceptionally literate new corporal from New Bedford credited the lethargy to the absence of a threatened draft and the resulting stinginess regarding bounties. "So long as patriotism was made a purchaseable article there were plenty of men to fill the ranks," he contended, "but now, when it is not a 'paying concern,' nobody cares much about going." James Montgomery, an old Kansas jayhawker, had better luck in the Department of the South. He exercised an informal draft of his own by simply forcing reluctant young men into his black South Carolina regiment, and he collected prospective recruits on forays from Hilton Head, South Carolina, all the way to Key West, where he enlisted 130 without resistance. Thomas Wentworth Higginson, a Harvard-educated abolitionist, shared with Montgomery in that coastal market, and by April his own novice regiment had completed its first amphibious campaign in Florida.[45]

One regiment at Helena, Arkansas, drew recruits from the great encampment of contrabands there. As elsewhere, white troops in the Mississippi basin largely frowned on the experiment, except for those who deemed it their only opportunity for commissions. "I do despise them," wrote the teenaged sergeant major of an Indiana regiment when he encountered an entire brigade of erstwhile slaves; "the more I see of them, the more I am against the whole black crew." The sergeant major might well have expected a captain's commission if he had been so inclined. Men applied by the hundreds — as many as fifty from a single Iowa regiment badly thinned by fever — and junior officers put their names in for field commissions. Some of those supplicants were merely trying to escape unpleasant relations with their superiors, and others disguised ambition for an office in which they might resign from the army, but to the disgust of many of their comrades most seemed motivated by the increased pay and prestige. "Excuse me from military honors," sneered an Illinois private, "if I have to go among the niggers to get them."[46]

In addition to these offenses to conservative sensibilities, Congress had armed the president with authority to collect internal revenue and to draft citizens at will, both of which circumvented state prerogatives and smacked of Old World autocracy. Many observers were pointing out both privately and publicly by early March of 1863 that Lincoln held firm control of both the purse and the sword: he could theoretically continue the war as long as he pleased, against the will of the people. As loyal a general as William Tecumseh Sherman had to concede that Mr. Lincoln had been granted unprecedented power — "he now is absolute Dictator," Sherman admitted.[47]

For those who envisioned the Republic less as a confederacy of states and more as the embodiment of democratic ideals, the accumulating executive usurpation constituted an ominous tilt toward centralized, authoritarian despotism. For those idealists, the Lincoln administration presented a more chilling threat to liberty and free government than the withdrawal of a few slave states. At the same time, alternative interpretations of the military map suggested a stagnation that seemed to confirm opposition warnings about the fruitlessness of coercion. For many who took that view, the war itself became the enemy, since it could bring no good and produced so much evil. Others still favored prosecution of the struggle, but without sacrificing the constitutional freedoms that distinguished the nation: rather than imposing a radical agenda and conscription on a reluctant population, they would have had Lincoln rescind the proclamations that had made the war so obnoxious to prospective recruits; rather than making war on Northern Democrats in and out of the army, they would have targeted the Confederate armies and government with the same nonpartisan spirit with which they had begun the conflict.

Democratic antipathy for administration methods seethed to overflowing that spring. In newspaper editorials, legislative debate, and party meetings from the pine forests of Maine to the plains of Iowa, Democrats raged at the war powers Lincoln had assumed and accepted, and at the Radical Republicans whose policies he appeared to favor. Disgruntled Democrats convened in central Illinois, a mere twenty-five miles from Lincoln's home, on March 14; the biggest political meeting that ever assembled in Crawford County, Wisconsin, met on March 26 to approve of speakers who belabored the war. Indiana had seen a spate of antiwar meetings since the beginning of the year, most of which had denounced the government's suspected aims on principle, but on March 20 a Wayne County meeting agreed that Lincoln's war measures threatened the very survival of constitutional government, and demanded an end to them. If

Lincoln used the new provost marshals to further his arbitrary arrests of citizens, the Wayne County men added, "blood will flow."[48]

A massive, boisterous assemblage filled the Cooper Union in New York City on the evening of April 7. The crowd spilled over into another impromptu convention outside, while inside the Great Hall speakers took the podium amid cheering and shouting silenced only by burly ushers' cries of "Order, God damn you!" Congressman Fernando Wood, the city's former mayor and a wily politician in his own right, disparaged Abraham Lincoln's presidency from the same stage where Lincoln had forged his campaign for that office barely three years before. Wood called for an immediate armistice and negotiations with the Confederacy — either overtly or covertly — and if the South refused to settle short of independence, then Wood proposed a binding referendum on whether the war should be resumed. He was followed by Senator John Carlile of West Virginia, a stubborn Unionist who had nonetheless considered the war unconstitutional from the outset. Lincoln loyalists who boycotted the event pronounced it a disappointing affair, but the attendance demonstrated surging power behind the new peace movement.[49]

Newspapers unfriendly to the Democratic view buried their coverage of the Cooper Union meeting behind pages of cheerier copy, including exaggerated, falsified, or perfectly apocryphal stories of brilliantly successful cavalry skirmishes, reports of military movements that had merely stalled, without retreating, and descriptions of invincible naval expeditions that had not yet been driven back, sunk, or captured. The most popular news of the day was the Republican victory in the Connecticut elections. Like the New Hampshire elections of March, the Connecticut races indicated that the opposition had reached a slight majority: not all Republicans prevailed, and those who did had to resort to manipulative or underhanded tactics.

New Hampshire Republicans had lobbied to bring home an entire regiment that had been raised in largely Republican districts, both to vote and to intimidate any opponents of the war. Most of the furloughed soldiers performed the former task and some attempted the latter, threatening to mob a Democratic newspaper as an earlier Granite State regiment had done. The most effective Republican strategy lay in splitting the Democratic ticket: the colonel of a regiment in the field, formerly a Democrat, ran as a "Union" candidate, stripping away several thousand Democratic votes. The legitimate Democratic nominee still outpolled the Republican, but he fell short of a majority, and New Hampshire law required a majority no matter how many candidates ran, so the election went to the Republican-dominated state legislature with predictable results.[50]

Connecticut governor William Buckingham had held office since 1858, but after a thorough canvass of the state in early 1863 he calculated that he would lose to his Democratic challenger by two or three thousand votes. A spoiler candidate apparently would have lent him no statutory means of foiling the popular will, so the Connecticut regiments became involved in a little plot to throw the election Buckingham's way. Resolutions denouncing the antiwar inclinations of Connecticut's Democratic Party went out to each of the state's military units with the ulterior motive of drawing out the individual soldiers' party loyalties. Officers in those units — every one of whom had been appointed by Buckingham — paid careful attention to which of their soldiers voted for and against the resolutions. The 14th Connecticut, for instance, considered its resolution on March 24. Of those soldiers who supported the statements, ten voting-age men from each company were selected to go home on furlough early in April with free transportation — and twenty men from the big heavy-artillery companies. No one who could not vote, or who had opposed the resolutions, was chosen to receive that precious gift, and at that time Connecticut fielded enough regiments and independent companies to have provided 2,920 soldiers at those quotas.[51] So ambitious a scheme could not have been accomplished without War Department complicity, and abundant testimony to the partisan furloughs implies that the government abetted them. Ultimately Buckingham survived with a majority of barely 2,500 votes: that was better than he expected, but he would probably have lost the election without the ballots of those handpicked soldiers. The ploy worked so well that Buckingham tried it again, successfully, the next year.[52]

More voting irregularities surfaced in an election at Indianapolis a few days later. Furloughed soldiers and Republican "rounders" reportedly descended on individual Democrats there, threatening them with bluster and numbers at first and finally persuading them to leave without voting: if their victims approached the polls, the bullies allegedly warned, they would be falsely reported to the sentries at the ballot box for "disloyal" remarks. In an atmosphere where government authorities habitually accepted unfounded accusations, that sort of browbeating proved somewhat effective.[53]

Victories won by such means only infuriated the opposition, and escalated tensions between Republicans and Democrats — or, as administration officials and their editorial friends began to characterize the factions, the patriotic "Union" and treacherous "Copperhead" parties — Copperhead being the slur applied to Peace Democrats and, eventually, to anyone who disagreed with the administration. Intimidation and retaliation had evidently become the order of the day. A prominent Connecticut Democrat claimed that in his state's industrial centers wealthy manufacturers sent their clerks to the polls as conspicuous registrars of local voting, both to pressure employees and purveyors into voting "the flag" and to establish an economic blacklist. The adjutant general of the U.S. Army personally intervened to punish a New Hampshire lieutenant for helping distribute Democratic ballots on Election Day, summarily dismissing him from the service "for circulating Copperhead tickets, and doing all he could to promote the rebel cause in his State."[54] Edwin Stanton, an apostate Democrat himself, had allowed soldiers of exalted grades to praise the war, the administration, and the Republican Party in myriad public venues; his War Department actively used soldiers (like the Connecticut faithful, and the troops who had "monitored" the Maryland polls in 1862) to bend state elections in favor of Republican candidates. Therefore the lieutenant's dismissal, couched in language implying the outright disloyalty of the entire Democratic Party, seemed to signify Stanton's declaration of war against mainstream Democrats. It also vindicated early critics who had perceived the war as little more than an exercise in partisan domination.[55]

Democratic rallies thus grew in frequency and rose in temper, especially after their strident objections attracted violent reaction. An indignation meeting in eastern Iowa in mid-April prompted a Davenport editor to howl about the "Scott County Disunionists," whom he described in viperous analogies. A similar demonstration a few miles farther down the Mississippi brought out wagonloads of armed Republicans who hooted and jeered the speaker before pelting him with eggs and at least a few stones. A New Jersey doctor paid a hundred-dollar fine for orchestrating the disruption of a purported Copperhead meeting and silencing the speaker in April. Democratic editors advised against reciprocal attacks, arguing that Union meetings merely degenerated into abolition harangues, but frustrated Democrats occasionally responded in kind. An army captain and a sergeant appeared at an April 19 meeting south of Indianapolis, ostensibly looking for deserters, where they were confronted by a group of Democrats who had brought their own guns. A scuffle ensued, and a former state representative killed one of the soldiers before he was shot, in turn, by the other. That same weekend, just west of Indianapolis, another meeting erupted in gunfire that left five men wounded, at least one of whom died.[56]

Pejorative nicknames like "Copperhead" and "Butternut" served to smear the peace faction to the ear of the war's supporters, for they conjured images of deadly snakes and dingy rebel uniforms (dyed with butternut extract), but those who professed that faction's principles took little umbrage at the slurs. Many conservatives reveled in the names: Samuel Medary, editor of the *Crisis* in Columbus, Ohio, advertised the

Copperhead emblem, or "Badge of Liberty," consisting of the head of Liberty neatly cut from a U.S. large cent, the prewar penny: this pin could be had for fifteen cents. An entire congregation of New Hampshire ladies showed up for church one Sunday wearing those political tokens on their breasts. Others cut a cross-section from a butternut and mounted it on their lapels.[57]

New Hampshire ran thick with antiwar sentiment, and that was especially true in the village of North Conway. That relatively affluent community provided only one volunteer during the entire war — a three-month man who enlisted in the hysteria after Fort Sumter — and the citizens openly embraced the name that was intended as an epithet. At the annual school meeting of District 8, just a couple of weeks after the state elections, the clerk recorded a decision to hire a female teacher, adding "that said teacher shall be a good Copper head."[58]

Still, Democrats shuddered at the ferocity of the names and threats cast their way — in print and in person. Soldiers who had never done much damage to the enemy boasted that they would "have a settlement" with those who opposed their war, up to and including returning home to "hang the whole concern." A Pennsylvania private imbued with equal portions of vengefulness and greed proposed stringing up the discontented element and distributing their property to the soldiers. General Sherman seriously considered the propriety of stripping the right to vote from men who did not support the war, including those who simply failed to enlist.[59] Perhaps forgetting that many of the war's worst critics had objected to it from the start, supporters and soldiers scolded the peace men for not abandoning their seemingly validated objections and helping the war party out of the very predicament those peace men had foreseen.

Some in the army made common cause with the peace movement, finding worse fault with abolitionists for bringing on the crisis, but even many of those soldiers who entertained their own doubts about the struggle appeared not to comprehend the similarities between their concerns and those of the antiwar element at home. Writing home from camp, many soldiers plainly refused to recognize any civilian's right to an opinion about a war he had not witnessed personally, while exaggeration and innuendo about Democratic aims and actions broadened the gulf between those in and out of uniform. Many soldiers credited the opposition with having prolonged the fighting, either by depriving the army of men and materials or by encouraging the enemy to hold out longer, and men who had taken up arms out of sincere national devotion held their critics in bitter contempt.[60]

Political differences frequently wrought sharp family rifts. Private Christopher McCracken, of the 20th Ohio, disowned his brother after an exchange of views on the war: "Sam need not call him Brother," explained a common friend. "He claims no connection with one who holds such opinions as Sam does."[61] A lieutenant in an Indiana regiment on the Rappahannock learned that spring that the Copperheads included his own brother, who promised that Democrats along the Wabash would resist the draft by force, if they had to, and that he would join them: the lieutenant and his fellow officers agreed that the draft should be enforced at all hazards, no matter who rose up against it. An Iowa woman divorced her husband after their antagonistic views on the war turned violent. In the Washington garrison, a nineteen-year-old Vermont sergeant jousted heatedly with his father, who fumed at the excesses of the Lincoln administration. The youth took his father to task for subscribing to the *New York Herald,* and hoped that on the way back to Vermont his regiment would stop to tear the *Herald* building to pieces. He dismissed his father's political complaints as "sneaking pretenses," and likened him to a traitor. Eventually the sergeant referred to himself sarcastically as "your scapegrace of a son," hypothesizing that their antithetical views could align them on opposite sides of a battlefield if the troops had to turn back to fight an internal uprising. Eventually the boy apologized for his insolence and reconciled with his father, at least temporarily, before borrowing money from him to buy his lieutenant's outfit.[62]

New York socialites like George Templeton Strong seldom stooped to insulting language. The glee of an obvious snub pleased his circle better, and few could inflict one more deftly than Strong. Taking his evening meal at the Century Club after its monthly meeting, Strong chatted with a number of New York's most esteemed citizens, but he pointedly turned his back on one Augustus MacDonough, who was believed to be the author of some minor reviews in the fiercely captious *New York World.* Strong justified the discourtesy with some high-minded nitpicking of his own. "No one in any degree accessory to the daily treason of that infamous paper," he wrote, "even as a mere contributor of opera and theatre criticism, should be cordially recognized by any loyal citizen of the United States."[63]

The battle lines lay at the edge of each faction's position, but it was the self-styled "loyal" citizens who seemed to guard their intellectual perimeter with the greater jealously, branding all who disagreed as traitors of the vilest stripe. Not that many weeks later, a New York colonel assessed the malicious impact of that relentless slander. "Copperhead" had become synonymous with "rebel sympathizer," the colonel recognized, and it incensed him that "the name is so freely applied to anyone who dares to have an opinion in the slightest degree of variance with those in power, that few have strength of mind enough to utter them." Name calling served as the first line of control for those who would accept nothing short of cheerful cooperation in their insistence on war; later conflicts would revive that tactic, producing pithy slogans designed to obscure the more substantive issues. Partisan pressure ultimately demanded such complete concurrence, the colonel observed, that Republicans had to tolerate some amusing inconsistencies to avoid contradicting or criticizing their leaders' actions.[64]

Unionists countered the welling opposition with rallies of their own, but those Unionists included firm Democrats who found Lincoln weak and his party corrupt. An enthusiastic convention of that loyal opposition met at Democratic Union Hall in New York City on March 9, and many of those Democrats participated in the formation of the city's first Union League chapter a few days later. For all their ardent prosecution of the war, their willingness to find fault with the president and the government irritated lockstep Republicans, who, when elections drew near, tried to stigmatize all Democrats as traitors. The keynote speaker at the Union Hall meeting, Ohio congressman George Pendleton, would become one of the principal targets of Republican traduction.[65]

The idea of an alliance between Republicans and War Democrats took hold nationwide. Brooklyn Academy filled to overflowing with a Union meeting on March 16, and others quickly followed in Toledo, Ohio, and New Haven, Connecticut, where another new Union League sprang to life. An event advertised as a "Union" rally drew a respectable audience to the German Theatre in Davenport, Iowa, on April 2, and that same evening New York's Union League sponsored another well-attended meeting at the Academy of Music, with speeches by major generals of national reputation, if not of particular genius. An activist coalition calling itself the Loyal National League sprang up in Portland, Maine, and others congregated under different names in most Northern cities of any size. A Union Club formed in faraway Brownville, Nebraska, complete with secret signs and passwords, and the commanding general in New Orleans provided space for a similar organization in that occupied metropolis.[66]

The Union League of New York planned an immense demonstration in the city for April 11 (which organizers mistook for the anniversary of the April 12, 1861, attack on Fort Sumter), and Washington officials hoped to amplify that observance with news of a substantive accomplishment by the navy. In mid-March, navy secretary Gideon Welles received a naval officer bringing dispatches from Admiral Samuel DuPont and the squadron off Charleston: the department had been planning to strike a staggering blow there, and had been collecting an armada of heavily armored monitors like the formidable, double-turreted monster called the *Keokuk*. DuPont and the local army commanders wanted to change the program from a massed assault of ironclads pushing straight into the harbor to a more gradual series of attacks on the batteries posted around the mouth of the harbor. Welles preferred not to wait, and President Lincoln, who stopped in at the Navy Department while the courier was still there, firmly agreed. Resisting delay in his naval commanders as he so often had in his generals, Lincoln sent the officer back to Charleston with orders to get on with it. Then Welles dashed up to New York in secret, returning the night of March 16. Two days later Senator Edwin Sumner, of Massachusetts, learned that a fleet of nine ironclads, some steam transports, and a number of troopships had left New York Harbor, headed for Charleston. The following day the *New York Times* announced to the world that preparations were nearly complete for an attack on the birthplace of secession, but more than two weeks passed without further news. Welles expected the fight to take place a few days into April, but he went to bed the night of April 6 still curious and anxious, fearing the reluctance of his senior officers as much as the chance of failure.[67]

For his reading material that evening Welles selected the first volume of the report of the congressional Joint Committee on the Conduct of the War, which had been released only that day by the Government Printing Office. The committee, chaired and dominated by Radical Republicans, had sprung from dissatisfaction and suspicion over the small but devastating defeat of Union forces at Ball's Bluff. The committee had already avenged itself on the commander there, Charles Stone, who had dared to criticize the congressmen's hypocrisy and had challenged their competence to judge strategic decisions: after six months of solitary confinement without charges and eight more months of enforced inactivity, Stone still sat idle at the Washington home of his father-in-law, awaiting an assignment in which he could use his considerable talents.[68]

In its final report from the Thirty-seventh Congress, the committee turned on its most coveted victim, George B. McClellan, who was gaining popularity as a potential Democratic champion. Democratic newspapers gave the report a hostile welcome, finding in it "abundant evidence of malice against Gen. McClellan," and indeed the evidence pointed to that bias. Although the committee had collected more testimony on other, earlier episodes of the war, the first volume focused primarily and pejoratively on McClellan and his command of the Army of the Potomac from July of 1861 until November of 1862, and most heavily on the operations of 1862. It began with the committee's very critical 64-page report and ended with 642 pages of testimony. By contrast, the committee's Radical majority supplied only four pages of strained flattery as a preface to the third volume of its report, which examined the chaotic and corrupt tenure of fellow Radical John C. Frémont as commander of the Department of the West.[69]

Private citizens, army officers, and government officials like Welles began devouring the report the moment it was released. The *New York Times* had already been publishing excerpts from galley proofs for a few days, warning of the document's intimidating bulk and announcing it, for those who preferred not to invest the time to read it, as a condemnation of McClellan's course. If anyone still doubted that assessment, the *Times* summarized the committee's jaundiced conclusions in an editorial blaming McClellan for virtually everything that had gone wrong while he commanded the army.[70]

The accumulated denunciation worked the desired effect: within forty-eight hours of the report's release even those who had heretofore kept an open mind now seemed persuaded of McClellan's incompetence, or even treachery. Secretary Welles himself recognized the intensely partisan nature of the committee, as well as its dubious fitness to appraise the decisions of military operations, but his initial browsing of the report moved him to regard it as more accurate than he had expected. A Massachusetts surgeon skimmed the committee's findings and came away convinced of McClellan's "weakness." A Maine lieutenant who had fought at Antietam under McClellan concluded, after reading the report by candlelight in his hut, that the committee had good reason to censure him.[71] Responding only to the headlines of those papers that embraced the report, Washington's commissioner of public buildings defended McClellan in a letter to his brother: "Poor McClellan was ostracized for not doing what nobody else seems able to do," remarked Benjamin Brown French, but then he dove into that first volume, the narrative portion of which consumed four hours alone, and a few weeks later he revised his impression. "I take back every word I ever said in favor of 'Little Mack,'" he confessed to his McClellan-hating sister-in-law. "I . . . have come to the deliberate conclusion that he is a mixture of coward, traitor, and imbecile, . . . It is now perfectly evident that, but for him, this war would now have been among the things that *were*."[72]

The committee report illustrated and aggravated the divergent public perception of the conflict that spring. With some cause, Democrats viewed the assault on McClellan as an attack on their party and its conservative principles. With equal partisan suspicion, Republicans saw the Democrats' defense of McClellan as an indication of deteriorating national loyalty in the opposition party. A similar rift had afflicted the Army of the Potomac for several months, beginning when McClellan was superseded by Ambrose Burnside, and McClellan's partisans among the generals had badly undermined Burnside's performance with their discouraging talk, hesitancy, and outright interference.

William B. Franklin fell into the vortex of that controversy. He had permitted two generals to leave the army on the eve of a major movement so they could lobby the president to countermand Burnside's orders, and Lincoln had injudiciously allowed their insubordination to succeed, thereby ending Burnside's effectiveness as a commander. Franklin's perfidy in that instance caused Burnside and others to look back on Franklin's lackluster performance at Fredericksburg and wonder whether he had not held back much of his strength to assure Burnside's failure there, too. In fact Franklin's relative lethargy on the left wing in the battle had originated in miscommunication between himself and Burnside, but political animosities had also played an indirect role through the excessive caution they prompted Franklin to exercise. McClellan's closest confidant, Major General Fitz John Porter, was then on trial in Washington on a thickly embroidered charge of battlefield disobedience that disguised his real crime of contempt for the Radical agenda: as one of Franklin's more dispassionate division commanders noted, in the event of disaster Franklin might have feared similar retribution if he had exceeded his orders. Republican papers used Burnside's committee testimony to blame Franklin for the defeat at Fredericksburg, and a letter promptly appeared telling Franklin's side of the story, including the not-quite-accurate explanation that he had failed to attack because he lacked any orders to do so. Waiting for orders in New York, Franklin hastily prepared a more extensive defense, publishing it a month after the report came out in a fat pamphlet with maps that demonstrated a slight, but critical, misunderstanding of the battlefield.[73]

The dispute with Franklin merely echoed the greater one over McClellan, and the reciprocating volleys of recrimination that spring ended lifelong friendships, like the one between McClellan and Burnside, each of whom felt betrayed by the other. Common friends strove to avoid the two generals' conflict — not always with success — and the controversy split the Army of the Potomac even more sharply than it did the public. The professional soldiers in particular still judged McClellan the best of the generals they had yet seen, cherishing "the greatest regard and admiration for him" long after he left the army.[74] Vast numbers of enlisted men hoped for his reinstatement, resenting both Lincoln's decision to remove him and the Radicals' campaign against him. The McClellan loyalists in the ranks included many whose politics clashed with the general's, but who remembered him as the man who had led them to their only semblance of victory. "Only give him back to us," wrote a private in the

Vermont brigade, where McClellan retained enormous popularity, "and we will follow him to the end of the earth if nead be."[75]

The improbability of McClellan's return bore less on his military competence than on his politics, for despite his fervent Unionism he failed to embrace the goal of emancipation so ardently sought by the Radical Republicans. The Radicals viewed that sort of disagreement as a disloyalty akin to treason, and the antagonism between their motivation and McClellan's defined an internal civil war that would plague the nation as long as the shooting lasted.

The main encampment of the Army of the Potomac sprawled across eighty square miles of Stafford County that April, from the Potomac to the Rappahannock and from Aquia Creek halfway to Port Royal. As the army awakened from its winter slumber General Hooker yearned to exercise it, to see if he had wrought well. Returning from a trip to Washington at the beginning of April, he commenced a series of reviews with the First Corps, farthest downstream, but the broken terrain there forced the divisions to form in separate locations. The next day Hooker moved on to nearby White Oak Church — a "miserable, insignificant structure, dilapidated and steepleless" — where John Sedgwick's Sixth Corps paraded more impressively with all nine brigades in full array.[76]

Hooker's visit to Washington had inevitably included an interview with the president. The two of them must have discussed Lincoln bringing a party down to see the resplendent new army, which Hooker was touting all over the city as the finest on the planet, and on April 3 Lincoln telegraphed Hooker with the details of an itinerary that seemed prearranged. Hooker replied in cipher that afternoon to confirm the accommodations, and at 5:00 P.M. on Saturday, April 4, Mr. and Mrs. Lincoln left the White House with their youngest son, Tad, Attorney General Edward Bates, and three citizens from the West Coast, including a newspaper reporter of Lincoln's acquaintance. A heavy snowstorm set in before they reached the Washington Navy Yard, but at sunset they boarded a steamer for Aquia Creek. The boat hove to in the river that night, so as to drop the party at Aquia Landing in time for breakfast, and Hooker had a train waiting to bring them to Falmouth Station. From there carriages whisked them through the blizzard to the house that served as Hooker's headquarters. Although he had posted the Lincolns' transportation anyway, Hooker had more than half-expected the storm to delay their departure from Washington by a day, and their fortitude in braving the weather gave him an awkward surprise. Some female company of indistinct relationship to the general and his staff lingered a little too long at his headquarters, and had to be hustled out the back stairs Sunday morning "in a most undignified way," as Dame Rumor portrayed it.[77]

The storm abated during the day Sunday, but several inches of heavy, wet snow precluded a planned review of the cavalry, which would have churned the parade field into a morass. The executive family could not be kept waiting indefinitely, though, and George Stoneman's corps of cavalry began gathering on Monday morning despite still-soggy ground. After receiving some of the senior generals, the presidential party adjourned to the Sthreshley farm, a mile east of the railroad, to witness the spectacle of more than ten thousand horsemen performing their sweeping maneuvers. A staff lieutenant from the Third Corps muttered about the cavalry's lank and feeble horseflesh, and an artillery colonel agreed, but another staff officer detected a more cadaverous aspect in Abraham Lincoln, whose gaunt face prompted a grim diagnosis in the age when consumption carried an irrevocable sentence of death. "The President looked very thin and pale," reported that lieutenant; "so much so that many people remarked that there was a fair chance of Hamlin being our President soon."[78] The most common adjective used to describe Lincoln on this sojourn was "careworn." "The President looks careworn and exhausted," thought Major General George Meade, who dined at the executive table, while a Vermont private thought him "thin and careworn," contrary to newspaper reports of his fine health. The winter had weighed heavily on Lincoln: to draw such comment, he must have wasted away beyond his national reputation for a long, lean frame.[79]

The army's cavalry had never paraded as a cohesive unit before, and that day marked the largest equestrian display in the nation's history. Every company not on picket fell in. Their front yawned out of sight across the landscape, and many ranks deep. Every officer who could borrow a horse came to watch, and some treated the event as another spring holiday: liquor flowed copiously in circles like the staff at Third Corps headquarters, where Dan Sickles spared no opportunity for a good time. Several carriages brought the different dignitaries. Attorney General Bates came in a coach-and-four, while Mrs. Lincoln arrived in an open carriage in the chill of early afternoon. Twenty-one consecutive guns bellowed a welcome as the president rode up alongside General Hooker, leading an escort of the 6th Pennsylvania Cavalry with scarlet pennants billowing from their distinctive lances, and they immediately began galloping up and down the assembled ranks. That circuit took them through three or four miles of ankle-deep slush, and when the last regiment had seen the commander in chief, he and Hooker pulled up with their lancers so the cavalry could pass in review. Mounted bands preceded each brigade: they pulled aside to serenade the passage of their comrades with brassy melodies, then swung into line as the tail ends of their units passed. Slouching troopers and undernourished horses spoiled the impression for those of a discriminating eye, but the civilians seemed impressed with the demonstration of four-footed power. So were the Confederates who stood atop Marye's Heights, beyond Fredericksburg, three miles away, staring through their binoculars and telescopes. Their bigger guns might have scattered the review, or inflicted some damage on the high command, but the informal truce that pickets had observed through the winter seemed to extend to the artillery.[80]

When the last squadron had trotted past, the mud-spattered multitude dispersed to distant camps to shake off the chill. For some, that chill no longer posed a discomfort: the surgeon of the 2nd U.S. Sharpshooters had drunk so deeply of General Sickles's hospitality that on his way back to the Thirds Corps he fell off his horse and tore his forest-green dress coat nearly off his back. Hundreds of infantrymen remained behind to hack away at brush and trees in adjoining fields, preparing ground for a much more massive infantry review, while the president and his entourage repaired to their quarters at Hooker's camp to host a dinner for the corps commanders. All came but Sedgwick, who was having acute eye trouble. General Stoneman brought his wife as a companion for Mrs. Lincoln.[81]

Mary Lincoln won the admiration of most of those officers. She struck General Meade, commander of the Fifth Corps, as "an amiable sort," and Sedgwick thought her "a gentle, kind-hearted lady." With the genuine sympathy of a woman who had lost sons of her own, she toured the hospitals and distributed little presents she had brought for the sick, all without any special notice of her identity. Those who saw her only at the reviews injected less affection in their descriptions, like the Massachusetts surgeon who described her as "a fat-faced, comfortable-looking woman."[82]

Tuesday gave the First Lady time for the hospitals. The day came off dry but still cold, and at noon Hooker took pity on his infantry, postponing the affair until the next day to give the mud more time to dry. Accompanied by Hooker, the president took the opportunity for a leisurely inspection of the troops, dropping in on Meade's corps along the railroad and, later in the afternoon, driving over to the Fitzhugh farm to prowl about the Third Corps. Not until Wednesday morning did the better part of the army — some seventy thousand men, give or take a few thousand — start lining up near the scene of Monday's exhibition. The damp, raw atmosphere persisted, aided by a thick cover of clouds, but the carriages again brought the ladies and the celebrities, and the cannon boomed another welcome for the chief magistrate, who cantered into sight beside Hooker. After them, in a strange and colorful uniform, rode a Swiss general to stir the curiosity of the serried troops. Lincoln's boy Tad followed eagerly on a pony. Behind these heralds trailed the medieval phalanx of lancers and, this time, a vast cavalcade of field officers.[83]

The army looked good, in part because the men with the shabbiest uniforms had been left in camp, but lusty cheers for the president bespoke renewed spirit. Rest, rations, and comfortable quarters had banished some of the gloom from the disaster at Fredericksburg and from Burnside's abortive Mud March, while furloughs and longer spring days had worked wonders on morale. The amnesty had brought back hundreds of deserters who had begun to dread the specter of firing squads or the opprobrium of their neighbors and comrades; officers and men were returning from leave, most of the last crop of wounded had either died or recovered, and with warmer weather, sick men were regaining enough strength to leave the hospitals. April had begun with nearly 164,000 men camped on the left bank of the Rappahannock, of whom more than 133,000 stood ready and equipped for battle. That formed an imposing host, even against the exaggerated numbers attributed to Lee's army, across the river. As everyone from Hooker to the greenest Yankee private understood, though, that sprawling force was going to shrink drastically over the next couple of months.[84]

In the opening days of the war, at the first inkling that Lincoln's call for three-month militia had augmented secession rather than cowing it, the War Department had begun demanding enlistments of longer duration. Doubting that many would respond to the Regular Army term of five years, Lincoln and his war minister settled on a three-year commitment that attracted many who supposed the conflict would end earlier than that. In the first weeks of that transition some governors had begged for permission to meet their troop quotas by completing their last ninety-day regiments, and the secretary of war acceded to a few of those requests, but he welcomed compromise proposals for two-year men with greater enthusiasm. Thirty-five infantry regiments had marched from Maine and New York for two years of duty, and all but two of them had found their way into the Army of the Potomac. Thirty-two of them remained with that army for the April reviews, one with barely a fortnight left to serve, and all of them — some 16,500 tough veterans — would be due for discharge by the end of June.[85]

Then there were the nine-month "militia" regiments, raised under the threat of a draft in the summer and fall of 1862. Ninety-two of them ultimately filled their ranks and mustered into service: all from the eastern states except two, from Wisconsin and West Virginia. Nearly three dozen of those wound up under Hooker's command. Because they had seen so little action and had endured so few hardships they were still the biggest regiments in the army, but they would begin going home in five weeks, stripping nearly 24,000 more men from the finest army on earth before the summer ended.[86]

The nine-month regiments significantly outnumbered the two-year men, but the army would not miss them half so much. Since the day they first arrived, the short-term, big-bounty men had borne the envy and contempt of both the veterans and the three-year recruits who had come out with them. A youth in the 17th Maine had served only fifteen weeks of his three years, and his first taste of hostile fire lay a couple of weeks in the future, when he learned that the 25th Maine had been assigned to the defenses of Washington for its nine-month tour. "Bully for the twenty fifth," he scoffed, from within sight of the enemy; "they marched four miles and luged their knapsacks one day and stood the march well and now they have gone into winter quarters." No matter where they went, scorn followed the nine-month regiments. A Massachusetts lieutenant said the three-year men simply hated them, complaining that they seemed to do nothing without calculating how much of their time remained, and a New Hampshire cannoneer noticed the same tendency among New Jersey militiamen who had been assigned to reinforce his battery for their final months.[87]

The nine-month militia levy had signaled another embarrassing administrative blunder for the Lincoln administration. Congress had authorized the concept with the Militia Act of July, 1862, but some very reasonable critics thought that simple arithmetic should have demonstrated the lunacy of immediately implementing that call: not only should it have been obvious that those militia would be leaving the army at the same time it was losing the two-year regiments, but the very timing of the militiamen's enlistment assured that they would be of no practical use in the field. "Any fool could have told them that the regiments would not be fit for service until last year's campaign was over," scribbled a disgusted colonel, "and that their time would be out just as this year's commenced." Indeed, as spring opened, the nine-month men were beginning to smell the greener pastures of home, and one of them conceded that his comrades were assiduously "shirking and playing off from duty." A subaltern in a nine-month Vermont regiment wailed that everyone seemed to hate them, including the public at home. "I suppose they would be perfectly satisfied if half of us could manage to get killed before our time is over," he wrote; "they seem to think . . . we have not any right to come home alive." Rebounding slurs caused a Connecticut man to bridle, too, and with healthy logic he reasoned that his regiment had done all it was ordered to do; it was not their fault if they had the good luck to miss any fighting.[88]

Even if the nine-month troops had not been champing to go home, their fruitless experiment meant that a total of 40,000 soldiers, or nearly a third of that 133,000-man army, was soon going to melt away. With all the respect the two-year men had earned on the battlefield, they, too, were closely marking the days until they could leave. Hooker's provost marshal, New Yorker Marsena Patrick, had been approached by his governor (the supposed Copperhead Horatio Seymour) in a scheme to reenlist the two-year regiments from their state into a new, grand organization of veterans. Winter rumors had told of early discharges coming for the two-year and even the nine-month men, in the hope they would enlist for three more years, and those rumors may have reflected part of the New York plan. General Hooker believed that the generous bounties of the previous year had killed any enthusiasm for reenlistment without substantial compensation, and with no pending draft call there were no state or local bounties available. A draft was likely soon, though, and men who had been on duty at the passage of the Conscription Act would be exempt, which made them eligible to serve as substitutes; Hooker suspected that most of the two-year men and militia would wait for that more remunerative opportunity. He proposed reenlisting them by whole regiments in return for an immediate furlough and the privilege of retaining their numerical designations and current officers, but that idea failed to interest a single company. "I am waiting anxiously for the advent of May," admitted Lieutenant Lewis Cleveland, of the 32nd New York, a couple of weeks before the review. He was to go early in June, and he would not be back.[89]

As the 32nd New York assembled for the review, Private James Albert Hard took his place in the ranks behind Lieutenant Cleveland. Hard had enlisted from the Upper Susquehanna Valley on May 31, 1861, a few weeks before his twentieth birthday. This youth had been much more fortunate than most of those who had succumbed to martial impetuosity in the first weeks of the war. Since its bloodless but exhausting experience at First Bull Run, his regiment had served on the Peninsula, in the Maryland campaign, and at Fredericksburg, but had waded into only two fights of any significance. Hard had missed the first of these, on the Peninsula, when a fever sent him to the hospital at Fort Monroe; the second, at Crampton's Gap, he had survived unscathed. At Antietam and Fredericksburg his brigade barely marched within range of shellfire. Still, this lad looked forward to shedding his uniform, and he clearly felt that he had done his part.[90]

Lieutenant Cleveland and Private Hard stood under arms for hours while Mr. Lincoln sped up and down the massed ranks doubled on their centers, taking his hat off for every regiment that saluted him until finally he left it off and took to nodding at each acknowledgment. As he approached the Third Corps, where Dan Sickles had arranged a signal, a bugle blew a sharp, clear note and sixteen thousand men snapped their weapons in front of their bodies in tribute. Not a word did anyone speak, nor a sound did the waiting men hear, until at last the sodden hoofbeats thudded nearer and the stream of horses fluttered past the rows of eyes riveted to the front. A fleeting glimpse and then he was gone, distinguishable only by the length of his frame on a horse too small. Presently the sun peeked through the clouds to brighten the austere, denuded landscape, and when the president had seen every rank he again led the procession to a halt so the troops could swing from line and pass before him, nearly fifteen dozen regiments strong with more than forty companies of field artillery in battery front. As each command reached the reviewing party, officers and men lifted their swords and rifles to a shoulder, in salute, and once past they broke into a double-quick to clear the way for those behind.[91]

For the majority of those marching men in blue, this would be the only connection they would have with the man whose army they composed. When, as old men with clouded eyes, they wrapped gnarled fingers over their canes and told the children of another century about the time they had seen Abraham Lincoln, they would be speaking of a review like this, on the ravaged hillsides of Stafford County or along the banks of Antietam Creek. For most of them, and for the last survivor of them, the memory would include this very day. In part it was for this that Lincoln had come down to the army, so the men who suffered the most to sustain his policies could see their leader, and know that he cared enough about them to spend hours in the saddle finding out how they fared. Not all in the ranks appreciated his effort. "[H]e looks as if he would soon go to kingdomcome," said an Irish corporal of the rawboned chief executive, "and there is few in this army who would be sorry if he was there." This man, whose wife supplemented his army pay by working as a maid, assured her that a visit from the paymaster would meet with more unsolicited enthusiasm than Lincoln did, besides doing the men more good.[92]

Lincoln had also come to escape the incessant pressures and anxieties of the capital, which had so drained him that everyone he passed remarked on his wan and withered face. The long days and hard riding tired him physically but invigorated him spiritually, and he seemed reluctant to return to Washington. Three corps had not yet been inspected by him, and he had not been seen by them, so he lingered two more days.

On Thursday, April 9, the First Corps turned out for him on a sloping plain with a magnificent view of the Potomac. The following morning Lincoln, Hooker, and Mrs. Lincoln's coterie started up the corduroy road toward Aquia Creek between lines of troops Sickles had sent out to cheer the president, but they dawdled along the way. At Stafford Court House

stood Oliver Otis Howard's Eleventh Corps, commanded until recently by
the expatriate German Franz Sigel and still heavily officered by other European refugees from the revolutions of 1848. With whole brigades of immigrant Germans and the sons of immigrant Germans fidgeting in formation behind him, the one-armed Howard waited so long that some of
the spectators started drifting away. Then, just as everyone began to suspect there had been a mistake, the guns barked their salute and out trotted Joe Hooker with the gangly civilian horseman in tow.[93] After a hurried
look at the men who had lately boasted that they "fights mit Sigel," the executive troupe proceeded to Henry Slocum's Twelfth Corps for an even
hastier repetition of the ritual. "The old fellow rode full tilt up & down the
lines with his hat off," a cavalry lieutenant recorded, "& looking as though
just so much riding had to be done & he was in a hurry to get through with
it." The ladies watched from army ambulances, but because of the terrain
the performance paled in comparison to all that had preceded it. Pine
thickets studded the undulating parade field, and encroaching vegetation
so constricted the maneuvers here that no regiment could spread itself
out with all ten companies in line of battle; instead they formed two-
company fronts, five ranks deep, depriving most of the rear companies of
any view as the cortege passed them.[94]

Alpheus Williams, who commanded one of Slocum's divisions, had
witnessed some of the earlier reviews, and he tended to agree with General Hooker's proud assessment of the army. The only blemish, as far as he
could see, was the diminished size of some of the older regiments. In his
own division Williams had three of those big nine-month regiments that
fielded upward of seven hundred men apiece, and if those three regiments
ever saw a battle, they would present a front a quarter of a mile wide. Williams also had four regiments of three-year men who had enlisted in the
summer of 1862, and they had lost quite a few to the hospitals and the
graveyard, but they each usually mustered a respectable number present
for duty. His eight regiments from 1861, meanwhile, had suffered terribly
under Nathaniel Banks in the Shenandoah Valley and at Cedar Mountain,
and then at Antietam, and they had been whittled down to veritable
skeletons. Even after incorporating recruits, the strongest of them could
barely put five hundred men under the colors by rousting every detailed
and detached man on the rolls. Those that had not been reinforced fell
far below that, and while they included the most trustworthy fighters
in the army, their parade line seldom stretched farther than a few hundred feet.[95]

That uneven alignment may have caught the president's eye, and
caused him to consider implementing another of Congress's more ludicrous proposals. In its parting blizzard of legislation, along with pro-

visions for national conscription and for retaliating against those who resisted or criticized that endeavor, the Thirty-seventh Congress had granted the president authority to consolidate the more attenuated units and discharge all the supernumerary officers. If exposure to disease and battle reduced the standard thousand-man regiment below five hundred, as was the case with many of those that were more than a year old, the ten companies could be compacted to five, resulting in the peremptory discharge of as many as ten lieutenants, five captains, one surgeon, the major, and the colonel, as well as forty corporals and twenty sergeants. Half of the most experienced commissioned and noncommissioned officers, who had survived the winnowing of incompetents, opportunists, and shirks, would thus be dispensed with — apparently in order to make way for another budget of novices and numbskulls, for that process manifestly contemplated the continued recruitment of entirely new regiments rather than fleshing out the old ones with new volunteers or conscripts.[96]

Within twenty-four hours at the beginning of April, the War Department had issued two orders that seemed to conflict by addressing both of those alternatives. On April 1 the adjutant general had called for a special muster for this very day, April 10, for the stated purpose of filling the old regiments up by draft call; that was made to look like an April Fools' Day prank when, the next day, the same office issued General Order No. 86, calling for the immediate consolidation of understrength regiments. That order was just filtering down to the field armies as Lincoln coursed the ranks of the Eleventh and Twelfth Corps, and the special muster of that day aroused the indignation of every officer from army headquarters down to regimental command. Edward Cross, the pugnacious colonel of the battered 5th New Hampshire, raged to former president Franklin Pierce that no enemy could have struck a more effective blow at the efficiency and morale of the army. Cross pointed out that the order would dismiss veteran colonels (like himself) from the line of promotion and leave only the commanders of the newest regiments to become generals, including the despised nine-month misfits. As self-interested in the matter as he might be, Cross made perfect sense, and he insisted that General Hooker concurred.[97]

The same order took a few days longer to reach Grant's army, above Vicksburg, but there it met with the same contemptuous reception. Like Colonel Cross, William Sherman characterized it as equivalent to a devastating blow from a mortal enemy. He informed his brother, the junior U.S. senator from Ohio, that two years of war had availed no greater advantage to the army than the education of company and regimental leaders and the weeding out of "Politician Colonels." Sherman postponed execution of the order to see if Grant would suspend it, but then he lost all patience and wrote directly to the adjutant general in Washington. Rather than destroy the army by depriving each of the most tempered regiments of seventy-eight of their best commissioned and noncommissioned officers, he pleaded, the department should recruit them all back to full strength with drafted men, all of whom should start their service as privates and learn their trade from the veterans. His solitary petition incorporated much of the same phrasing and every criticism of the order lodged in Cross's diatribe, written from a thousand miles away and from the far side of the political spectrum.[98]

Even the stubborn Edwin Stanton could not ignore the cacophony of complaint against Order No. 86, whether he perceived the madness of it or not. Without any conspicuous announcement to embarrass the secretary for supporting so preposterous a plan, army headquarters simply refrained for the nonce from enforcing the directive, but it remained an imminent threat during Lincoln's sojourn with the Potomac army. The specter of consolidation sorely troubled the more diminutive clusters of men standing on the rolling plateau near Stafford Court House. The wizened colonels of battle-shrunken commands must have been thinking, as president and general passed their upraised swords, that their glory days had come to an end, while upstart newcomers may already have been calculating their odds of rising to brigade command.

The passing thoughts of Abraham Lincoln, as he toured this most famous of his armies, never found expression on any scrap of paper. He clearly absorbed the air of collective might that the army presented, even considering the impending attrition, and he had composed a note imparting his opinion that Lee's army, rather than the city of Richmond, should be the target of that collective might in the next campaign. His messages to Gideon Welles, after the grand review of April 8 and the smaller one of April 9, betrayed his preoccupation with the Charleston expedition, for news of which he scoured the Richmond newspapers.[99] Yet surely in the many monotonous hours of scanning formations, certain striking faces or figures had provoked digressive rumination: a grizzled private older than himself; a soldier whose hand or cheek had been mangled by a bullet; a mere child with a snare drum strapped over his shoulder. The effects and impressions of these unavoidable vignettes he neglected to describe.

When the last soldier in the Twelfth Corps strutted past them, Hooker and Lincoln retreated to headquarters, plainly showing the wear of a grueling week. General Williams thought them both "greatly fagged" as they bid goodbye. The president had relished the respite from White House business, for all that it had exhausted him, but his executive duties demanded attention. The next morning he and his party slipped off for Washington, where he leaped instantly back into the administrative fray.

The grand army in Stafford County went back to its own work, packing up extra clothing and sending it back to Washington — where quartermasters eventually lost, stole, or sold much of it, to the ultimate expense of the soldiers who had entrusted them with it.[100] Two weeks later, the men Mr. Lincoln had inspected were preparing to move against the enemy. Within ninety days of that last review at Stafford Court House, more than ten thousand of them would be dead.[101]

2

The Road Unknown

➤ MR. LINCOLN HAD NO sooner returned to Washington than the newspapers started reporting on the ironclad fleet's progress against Charleston. The *New York Times* had spun its readers into a fever of expectation over the attack on that city when, days before the second anniversary of the outbreak of hostilities, it announced that the ironclads had been sent into Charleston Harbor on April 6 and had assailed Fort Sumter on April 7. The ships had given the symbol of secession as much of a pounding as they could, retiring finally "without definite result," as the *Times* put it. The attack was not renewed on April 8, boding ill for ultimate success, but nothing had been heard from Admiral DuPont. It all sounded like failure to those who had become accustomed to journalistic euphemisms for that all-too-common result. Still mistaking the date of the original Confederate attack on Fort Sumter in 1861, New Yorkers gathered April 11 for the long-planned anniversary rally at Union Square, but their enthusiasm benefited from no tidings of redemptive victory. Instead, pessimistic uncertainty left the gold market fluctuating madly.[1]

Of the eight mighty ironclads DuPont had sent inside the bar, five had been severely handled by the guns in Sumter, Fort Moultrie, and sand batteries on the islands that lined the mouth of the harbor. The Goliath of DuPont's armada, the double-turreted *Keokuk*, pulled away so full of holes that it sank the next day. Confederate fire put four other monitors out of action, jarring loose their pilothouses and jamming their turrets. Months of planning and weeks of anticipation evaporated in just a couple of hours. For the soldiers and sailors who watched and waited from afar, jubilation quickly festered into discouragement and anger. A seaman on the U.S.S. *Housatonic* tried to describe the battle and its emotional effect for his mother, but concentrating on the reverse drove him to such wrath that he flung the letter overboard, unfinished, and waited nearly a week to try again. "I am not in a verry good nature today and perhaps ought not to write," warned the colonel of an Ohio regiment outside Charleston, explaining that the "magnificent naval expedition" had "gone to the D[evil] *with flying colors*."[2]

The dejection reached all the way to Washington, arriving with the details of the fight. The president stalked about the War and Navy departments all day April 12, but no news came from Charleston until midafternoon, when the erstwhile commander of the *Keokuk* knocked on the door of Gideon Welles's house. The navy secretary had already grown morose in his presentiments of defeat, and the dispatches from DuPont only confirmed his mood. He took the papers to the White House and read them to Lincoln, whose spirits drooped with the disintegration of such cherished hopes. Wearing his bravest face and lauding the fleet for having withstood the South's most powerful artillery, the president wrote the admiral to put his ironclads back inside the bar, hoping to salvage an impression of ineluctable persistence. The monitors had failed only because of harbor obstructions that forced them into the vortex of enemy fire, Lincoln contended, and those obstructions could be removed before the next attempt. For all that confident talk, the inaugural effort in the springtime of promise had dissolved into impotent frustration.[3]

Faith in the ironclad fleet sagged despite a reflexive tendency to conceal how badly the ships had been damaged; by extension, hope flagged that Union military power could ever prevail against such determined resistance. Prepared as always to sustain the administration by mitigating any bad war news, the *New York Times* explained that the Charleston fiasco seemed worse than it was. Casualties among the crews only ran in the single digits, after all. From a military perspective the capture of that harbor meant little, claimed editor Henry Raymond — who had until then striven to portray Charleston as the Confederacy's second-most-precious city, the capture of which would probably strike the rebellion a fatal blow. "The absorbing interest felt by the country in the fight at Charleston led to an undue magnification of the value of the struggle there," concluded Raymond, as though chiding anyone who had credited his earlier coverage.[4]

For those perceptive enough to pierce the veil of propaganda, few headlines brought much solace. In every quarter, enormous investments of life and treasure ended in repulse or impasse. Confederates had encircled a Union brigade at Washington, North Carolina, and all attempts to relieve it had thus far failed: rumors of the town's surrender, complete with the department commander, made the front pages of the major dailies. Headlines announced that the Union footholds in Brunswick, Georgia, and Fernandina, Florida, were both going to be abandoned. Lee had detached two divisions under his principal subordinate, James Longstreet, toward Suffolk, Virginia, where Longstreet began laying siege to that outpost of occupied Norfolk. In the Virginia and North Carolina operations, the Southern troops had come primarily to discourage enemy incursions and to gather provisions, while their sieges served mainly as bluff and bluster, but Union generals at Suffolk, Norfolk, and Fort Monroe called frantically for reinforcements and artillery. Newspaper coverage of those backwater contests sharpened the apprehension of a public primed by stories of the greater failures.[5]

Among those greater failures, the so-called siege of Vicksburg, Mississippi, loomed conspicuous. Vicksburg sat on towering bluffs alongside the Mississippi, blocking the river and linking the eastern and western halves of the Confederacy. Its heavy guns bore down on any vessel that tried to pass, and more bluffs along the Yazoo River protected the city upriver. Every stroke against that citadel had ended in abject defeat.

Grant's first attempt had come in December, from the mouth of the Yazoo, with General Sherman's disastrous and fruitless attack on Chickasaw Bluffs; Grant was supposed to be creeping up on Vicksburg from behind, by the inland route, while Sherman hammered at the northern approach, but a raid on Grant's supply base had foiled his crucial part of the plan. Next had come an attempt to bypass Vicksburg's heavy river batteries by diverting the Mississippi through a canal cut across the sharp loop of the river that bent past the city, but after enormous effort the river refused to accept a new course — at least until the war was over, when the current ate through the hairpin peninsula and deprived Vicksburg of its riverfront trade. Two ironclad gunboats ran the Vicksburg batteries to raise havoc with a feeble Confederate naval presence, but the first ironclad was captured and used to sink the other. Grant designed another canal that was meant to revive the old course of the river, then known as Lake Providence, but spring floods inundated it prematurely, leaving underwater stumps to block the passage of gunboats and troop transports. In desperation Union engineers dredged another passage, far upriver from Vicksburg, cutting eastward from the Big Muddy to navigable streams that flowed down into the Tallahatchie River and thence to the Yazoo; ironclads took that route to reduce the Confederates' Yazoo batteries, but the boats found the rivers too constricted for adequate maneuvering and the enemy batteries too formidable to subdue. When they detoured to adjacent bayous, the rebels hemmed them in by dropping trees before and behind them, and swarms of Southern sharpshooters de-

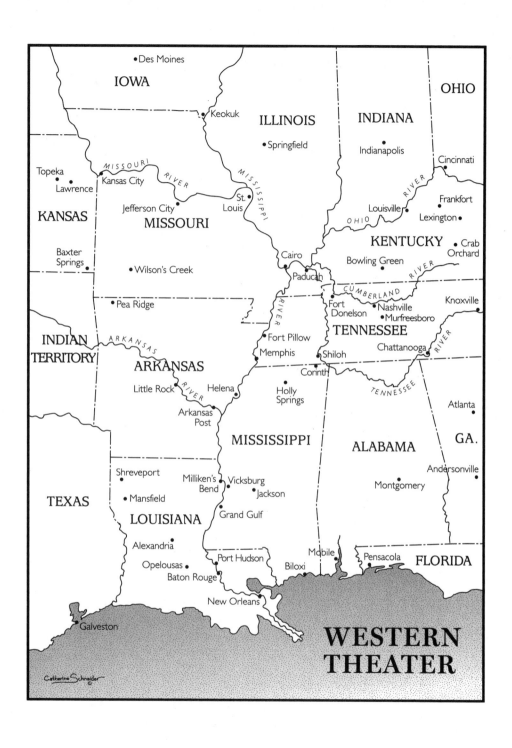

WESTERN
THEATER

scended on any who tried to remove the obstructions. Instead of clearing the way for the army, the navy ended up calling on the army for rescue.[6]

With each failure, Grant's friend Sherman lobbied for a return to the first plan, with the main army sweeping south from Tennessee and striking Vicksburg from behind, between the Yazoo and the Big Black River, while another force cooperated from the Mississippi River. That might have worked in December, Sherman conceded, if he had only waited until Grant could come up behind the city. Grant rejected that because it would first require moving the whole army, or the greater part of it, back upriver to Memphis, and that would seem too much like a retreat. With politicians and newspapers breathing down his neck for forward progress, the only direction he dared not take was back the way he had come. Now he decided to abandon all his canal projects, march his men below Vicksburg on the Louisiana side of the river, and cross them in transports that the navy would send down by running the Vicksburg batteries. Sherman cringed at the idea of putting the army on a single undependable road, railing at the political considerations that drove them to such perilous lengths, but because of that very vulnerability the thrust of the plan could not be shared beyond a handful of high-ranking officers on the river and in Washington. The country heard only that Grant had abandoned all his earlier projects, and that the Yazoo expedition had returned after forty-three days of wasted effort. "I hardly know what to think of Grant's *Do nothing* policy," complained one of his soldiers, languishing on a rare ribbon of dry land above the rebel bastion.[7]

Forty leagues south of Vicksburg, and twice that far by the winding Mississippi, sat the sister citadel of Port Hudson, Louisiana, where similar guns frowned down on the river from similar bluffs. Between those two points the river remained Confederate.

Port Hudson lay in the Department of the Gulf, where Nathaniel Banks had taken command from Ben Butler the previous December. With Banks had come an army thickly leavened with inexperienced nine-month troops who already considered their enlistments nearly half-finished, and he had found the headquarters city of New Orleans reeking of corruption. "Every body connected with the government has been employed in stealing other people's property," Banks conceded to his wife, adding that the enemy had been the object of open trade rather than active campaigning. Butler, whom local residents called "Beast," had insulted the population with crude proclamations like his promise to treat New Orleans ladies as prostitutes if they sneered at Union soldiers — but, Banks observed, Butler's subordinates had appropriated private homes and lodged actual prostitutes in them for off-duty entertainment. Such behavior was not likely to rekindle affection for national authority, and as he entered upon his new assignment Banks despaired of ultimate re-union. Within weeks the general's spirits revived as speculators desisted, or at least disguised their activities from his disapproving eyes, but Banks complained that his force remained too small to achieve any success in the field. His principal reports through March had described insignificant skirmishing in the bayous, his evacuation of Pensacola (a portion of which was left in ashes), and the complete capture of his freshly installed garrison at Galveston, Texas.[8]

Mosquitoes and contaminated drinking water felled Banks's men by the thousands through the nominal winter months. In their camps near New Orleans soldiers could find nothing to drink save from the muddy Mississippi, and they lay down to sleep in ankle-deep mud, "cofing and grunting all night," as one doomed New Hampshire private described it for his wife. Sickness so thinned the ranks that Banks's army lay essentially listless, and a telling blow against Port Hudson remained a treasured fantasy.[9]

"The Galveston disgrace was a shameful affair," snarled the Massachusetts captain of a loyal Texas cavalry company, "but I fear worse will follow if the present standstill policy is lived up to in this Department."[10] It was Admiral David Farragut of the U.S. Navy who finally proposed taking action against Port Hudson, asking Banks for nothing more than a distraction ashore. Banks forwarded some seventeen thousand troops to Baton Rouge early in March, and selected about twelve thousand of them to parade before the defenses of Port Hudson. Some of his greenest men took those marching orders as their death warrants, writing lugubrious "last" letters to their families and trembling at the ominous preparations in the hospitals, but their horror evaporated into embarrassment when they were asked to perform nothing more than a languid reconnaissance in front of Port Hudson on March 14. Farragut used that perfunctory diversion to steam up the river with four sloops of war and three smaller gunboats, firing ineffectually at the blazing bluffs and enduring a withering storm of iron. Only the two leading vessels passed the Confederate guns safely: Farragut's flagship, the twenty-four-gun *Hartford,* and the little *Albatross.* The rest of the fleet fell back downstream, more or less disabled, and the twenty-gun *Mississippi* ran aground, where shells plunged down upon it until it caught fire and exploded. The passage of the *Hartford* caused the Confederates some anxiety over the security of their Red River supply line, and General Banks took pains to emphasize such paltry advantages, but the admiral who threatened those supplies saw little success in the enterprise. The next day Farragut started a rough draft of his report, beginning with the admission that he must once again "report disaster to my fleet."[11]

Serial disappointments led to serious discouragement, and the armies under Grant and Banks showed a measure of the disaffection so prominent in the Army of the Potomac. Despite efforts by devoted officers, at least one of Grant's regiments refused to pass a simple resolution showing support for the war, while confidence in the government and in the chances of winning the war slumped sharply among Union troops in Louisiana.[12] Only in the Army of the Frontier, then ensconced in north Arkansas, and in the Army of the Cumberland, around Murfreesboro, Tennessee, did the general atmosphere seem reasonably cheery.[13] The little Arkansas force had triumphed in its last engagement, however, while the Tennessee army had taken the better half of a draw in its last fight — besides having the advantage of operating against the stubborn, cranky, and unimaginative Braxton Bragg. In every army, though, everyone seemed to understand that a burgeoning mass of the folks at home had grown sour on the war.[14]

If dismal progress in the field failed to discourage attentive Northern citizens that April, they could fret over the cultivated specter of vast, diabolical conspiracies to resist or even overthrow the government. Whether in paranoid reaction to the unpopularity of the draft and other governmental policies, or as an effort to demonize dissent, pro-administration editors and federal authorities had launched a campaign of publicity and prosecution against reputedly seditious secret societies whose members, they claimed, numbered in the hundreds of thousands. Most of the reports of these societies meandered inconsistently between alarming the public with wild estimates of the number of the conspirators and simultaneously implying the overwhelming unpopularity of their viewpoint. The arrest of four Germans as alleged conspirators in southeastern Pennsylvania triggered a protest by nearly three hundred German farmers at Reading: the Republican press approvingly reported that the Germans had been dispersed by mobs of enraged "patriots," who beat some of the protestors severely and threatened to lynch them, yet the routed farmers were said to represent a seditious network of a million and a half men.[15]

Then there was the latest crisis with England, all stemming directly from the war to suppress the Confederacy. The high-seas interdiction and seizure of British vessels had initiated the trouble, back in the autumn of 1861, when U.S. Navy captain Charles Wilkes removed two Confederate emissaries from the British mail steamer *Trent*. With a promotion to commodore as though to reward his inept handling of the *Trent*, Wilkes had begun demonstrating a preference for chasing prize money instead of Confederate cruisers, and in February of 1863 he had seized another British vessel by the name of *Peterhoff*. The British ambassador complained less about the *Peterhoff*, which a prize court quickly condemned as a blockade runner, than he did about the mail it had carried. Secretary of State William Seward had promised that the royal mail would not be disturbed, but the *Peterhoff*'s mailbags had been impounded.[16]

Southern commerce raiders made for more provocative discussion. Swift and well-armed cruisers like the *Florida* and the more famous *Alabama* had slid from the stocks at Liverpool and Birkenhead shipyards to ply the seas in search of Union merchant vessels, and British builders were already finishing the hulls of more formidable ships that might challenge the U.S. Navy, as well. British investors had also made heavy loans to the Confederacy, with which the South bought such weaponry, and by April Washington officials spoke more openly of the British government's passive complicity in these ventures as acts of war. Senator Charles Sumner wrote the pacifist John Bright, member of Parliament from Birmingham, that "it is now thought by many that the British Ministry mean war, since every body is supposed to mean the natural consequences of his conduct." Gideon Welles urged a firm tone from the more cautious Seward, and guessed the country could bear a war with England even while fighting the Confederates.[17]

The British prime minister, Lord Palmerston, did betray a tenderness for the patrician Southerners, and a bellicose tremor did course the island that spring, but it seemed to hinge more on anger at beastly Northern arrogance than on sympathy for Southern slaveholders. Civilized Britons recoiled in principle at descriptions (all too often accurate) of marauding Union soldiers, and resented in detail the unexplained or unjustified detention by United States naval officers of Her Majesty's subjects, who often proved innocent of any wrongdoing. Washington's indignation over the commerce raiders, which constituted a breach of Britain's own Foreign Enlistment Act, required considerable diplomatic sanctimony: United States shipyards had built vessels for the Russian navy to use against England during the Crimean War, and in the 1790s Americans had fitted out warships for the French in their war with England. For that matter, U.S. suppliers were outfitting French expeditions against the Mexican government even as the State Department objected to the British construction of Southern warships, and American arms suppliers happily profiteered from both sides in the Mexican imbroglio.[18]

The American pique over the cruisers reflected particular hypocrisy in light of obvious efforts by United States agents to violate the Foreign Enlistment Act for their own benefit. As Lord Palmerston later remarked, for instance, there seemed no difference between building ships for one belligerent and selling arms to the other. Secret United States agents were scouring Britain for rifles the same summer that the *Alabama* sailed from Birkenhead, working in competition against Confederate counterparts, and their progress reports to Washington included British newspaper clippings that were intended to incriminate the South for the same neutrality violations that those Northern operatives strove successfully to commit.[19] And while American diplomats ranted about the few score British sailors who had filled the crews of Confederate raiders, William Seward's State Department actively persuaded tens of thousands of Irishmen to come to America on the pretense of economic opportunities that consisted primarily of enlistment bounties. In February of 1863 Seward grew even more brazen, giving priority to males of military age and offering subsidies to those who agreed to enlist. Lancashire textile workers, unemployed because of the Union blockade of Southern cotton, began drifting to Canada for better prospects, but an oversupply of labor there — caused partly by draft-shy Americans — assured that they, too, would gravitate toward Mr. Lincoln's recruiters.[20]

While Parliament debated recognition of the Confederate States and Crown responsibility for the Confederate corsairs, the foreign minister complained formally of the hundreds of poor young Irishmen boarding steamers for New York each week on the promise of lucrative bounties. Charles Francis Adams, the American minister in London, blamed that Hibernian exodus on the labor shortage caused by his country's war: Adams, the son and grandson of U.S. presidents, replied that those indigent emigrants were probably responding to appeals from railroad corporations seeking employees who might be exempt from the draft. That may have been the blind, but during the 1862 militia draft, gangs of Irish "railroad workers" had served as handy pools of substitutes and volunteers against local recruiting quotas; in at least one instance their employers had bargained them away like so many slaves. With a broad new conscription law awaiting executive implementation, the demand for substitutes would soon enough revive, and most of those lads who took ship at the Queenstown quay would end up in blue uniforms — not always voluntarily. The alien draft exemptions that Adams had cited as the appeal of foreign laborers so frequently failed to save immigrants from the Union army that British Empire newspapers warned colonial citizens to resist the lure of employment in embattled America.[21]

The *Trent* affair had brought reinforcements of British Regulars to Canada, and had precipitated parliamentary action on Canadian defense, including copious shipments of arms and military stores for the Canadian militia. London enacted unpalatable military provisions for its possessions along the St. Lawrence, sparking the same sort of indignation and resistance that the imposition of frontier defense burdens had spawned in New England a century earlier. In the summer of 1862 the Canadians balked just as their Yankee cousins had in the early days of George III, rejecting the militia bill to the disgust of British gentry who lamented the Canadians' paltry contribution to their own protection. Canadians felt a certain fraternity with their neighbors to the south, not to mention a certain military inferiority, and most of them dreaded the idea of a war with the United States. That was especially true in Canada East and Canada West — the future provinces of Quebec and Ontario — where Americans provided the primary outlet for agricultural goods: in the predominately English Eastern Townships north of Vermont and New Hampshire, U.S. greenbacks constituted the only readily available currency, and the wartime depreciation of that new paper money also made the United States the most attractive place for Canadians to spend it. For all that good will and economic dependence, the tensions in the spring of 1863 prompted editors in those Eastern Townships to predict international "squalls," and the reluctant provincial population began vigorously organizing its militia, to the extent of drafting for those battalions that fell short of volunteers.[22]

"We drift fast toward war with England," mused George Templeton Strong, "but I think we shall not reach that point." Strong, who fretted over every arrhythmia in the stock market, looked down his long nose at "the shop-keepers who own England" and accused the entire realm of embracing a slave nation for the profits of building a few ships. Northerners had seemed admiring enough of the British Empire for eradicating its own slavery peacefully, a Canadian editor eventually noted, but they turned deplorably self-righteous over British disapproval of "abolition at the point of the bayonet." Strong predicted well, notwithstanding the bellicose vernal rhetoric. The *Peterhoff*'s mail went back into British hands unopened, and Anglo-American anxiety subsided for a few weeks, until the latest Southern rams neared completion at Birkenhead.[23]

However beneficial it may have been to national pride for Northerners to boast of taking on John Bull at the same time as Johnny Reb, it was well for United States interests that William Seward exercised a more conciliatory diplomacy. Sustaining another war would have posed an unenviable challenge to a government that was making so little evident headway against a starving new nation and its vastly outnumbered army. On the Rappahannock and on the Mississippi, Union armies fielded more than twice as many men as their opponents; in the Army of the Cumberland, William Rosecrans mustered half again as many soldiers as Braxton Bragg; overall the United States armies counted fifteen men under arms for every eight on duty in the Confederacy.[24] That powerful advantage in numbers, and the tremendous expenditures that had provided it, had not only failed to quash the rebellion but had — so far as many Northern citizens might have interpreted it — recovered relatively little territory. New Orleans would have been considered a desirable trophy, but its value diminished significantly with rebel artillery interrupting the Mississippi River. North Arkansas, west Tennessee, north Mississippi and Alabama, the thoroughly pillaged counties of northern Virginia, and the strip of scattered footholds on the Atlantic coast offered little solace against 150,000 dead Northern sons.[25]

For someone like Squire Strong, who lived among Manhattan's Roosevelts and Astors, the loyal state of Kentucky might have been added to the list of territory that was not worth saving for the Union, except perhaps for its strategic position and tobacco crops. Strong shuddered to learn that the patriotic ladies of Louisville had begun practicing their marksmanship with pistol and rifle, ascribing such shocking behavior to the barbarism that attended the presence of slavery. Abraham Lincoln put much greater stock in his native state, however, and garrisoned it with more than thirty thousand men against the exaggerated alarms caused by a few hundred mounted Confederates.[26]

To Kentucky, or rather to the Department of the Ohio, came Ambrose Burnside that spring. He arrived at the Cincinnati headquarters less than two months after his humiliating departure from the Army of the Potomac. The new command embraced most of the old Northwest, from the Straits of Mackinac to the Tennessee border and from Pennsylvania to the Mississippi. The Ninth Corps followed him there, traveling from Fort Monroe to Baltimore by steamers and thence to Cincinnati by rail. Train after train carried them over some of the steepest terrain the Eastern regiments had ever seen. Thousand-yard tunnels in the Alleghenies amazed them, and precarious mountainside railbeds terrified them; they gaped enviously at the fine, flat farms of central Ohio, where sheep and cattle had gone out to graze in the fourth week of March. From Harrisburg to Pittsburgh they never left the bone-jarring freight cars, but public dinners awaited them at the major stops. Citizens crowded the stations to witness the spectacle, cheering and waving flags or selling whiskey, as their sense of duty dictated. At Pittsburgh a twelve-year-old boy took the opportunity to exchange his impoverished home for a job as servant to a Yankee sergeant; he appealed to the sergeant's sympathy, alleging that his parents drank heavily, and when the soldiers repaired to their train the boy trotted eagerly along beside them, carrying some of his new master's equipment. As the troops arrived in Cincinnati Burnside fed them again before ferrying them below the Ohio River.[27]

In the Bluegrass they found pleasant campsites and no armed Confederates. The enemy lay, for the most part, along the fringes of the state, with the nearest sizable force in east Tennessee, which President Lincoln and General Burnside both longed to liberate from Confederate control:

there dwelt the heaviest concentration of Unionists left in the Confederacy, as well as the principal latitudinal railroad in the South. Burnside's old corps remained idle through the spring, however, and within weeks it began to look as though his responsibility consisted more of controlling the territory north of the Ohio than pacifying the territory south of it.

The plans for invading east Tennessee involved General Rosecrans, who still lingered at Murfreesboro after his narrow January victory near that place. Burnside assured Rosecrans that he would slide toward the Cumberland River and join metaphorical hands with him before proceeding into east Tennessee. They would protect each other's flanks, freeing whole divisions of guard details for front-line duty. It all sounded very promising, but tenuous supply lines across rugged terrain caused both generals substantial concern. For the present, Rosecrans satisfied himself with mounting a brigade of infantry on mules for an ambitious raid up the Tennessee River into Alabama and Georgia. Colonel Abel Streight left Murfreesboro with his own 51st Indiana and three other infantry regiments on April 10, taking two companies of Tennessee cavalry as scouts (and, perhaps, as riding instructors). The expedition would meet with disaster by the next full moon, serving mainly to deliver livestock, arms, and prisoners to the Confederates.[28]

More fortunate was a simultaneous foray by Colonel Benjamin Grierson with seventeen hundred Illinois and Iowa cavalrymen from LaGrange, Tennessee, southward across the entire length of Mississippi to Baton Rouge, but nothing was heard from Grierson after his departure in mid-April. Little could the cursory newspaper browser find of honorable accomplishment by national arms as the rebellion entered its third year. With the approach of May, attention increasingly drifted away from the great strategic prizes in the West to the more symbolic contest on the Rappahannock, where the huge blue army awaited the word of its popular new general.[29]

While Ambrose Burnside led the Army of the Potomac, Joe Hooker had criticized every strategic decision he made, and had evinced a certain satisfaction when the very elements foiled his commander. As Hooker discovered when he superseded Burnside, though, the juxtaposition of opposing forces on the Rappahannock posed a problem with a limited number of solutions. The public temper seemed to preclude any more changes of base, and administrative reluctance to admit a tragic mistake (or to concede the wisdom of George McClellan) discouraged that most logical transfer of operations back to the James River. That left only the turning of Lee's right flank, downstream, or his left flank, upstream, or the frontal assaults that had proven so deadly even before the Confeder-

ates had spent the winter perfecting their entrenchments. Hooker therefore considered every option he had ridiculed Burnside for pursuing,
and adopted as his most promising alternative an expanded version of
Burnside's last and most notoriously unsuccessful plan. Then, as though
in cosmic justice, the weather frustrated Hooker as completely as it had
his predecessor.

The day after Abraham Lincoln returned to Washington from reviewing Hooker's army, the general sent him the outline of a campaign that
appears to have represented an abrupt change in the plans he had conveyed during the president's visit. He was sending Stoneman's cavalry
corps, more than ten thousand sabers strong, way up the Rappahannock
past Kelly's Ford to the Orange & Alexandria Railroad, where it would
turn to the south and then swing east, threatening Lee's direct supply
line from Richmond. With provisions already reported to be short in the
Army of Northern Virginia, Hooker expected that this would prompt Lee
to abandon his fortifications on the Rappahannock and hasten southward, at which General Stoneman was to dig in across his path and delay
him until Hooker could pounce on him from behind.[30]

The cavalry cantered off on Monday morning, April 13, and the infantry prepared for a long, rapid march with vastly reduced supply trains.
While a doubtful Regular Army captain worried that they were only con-
fronting the enemy again "for the sake of the men whose term of service is
about expiring," paymasters distributed greenbacks to the troops, as was
their frequent custom on the eve of a bloody campaign. Each man drew
eight days' rations, instead of the customary three days' food that filled
the standard army haversack: the balance was to go into their knapsacks,
displacing most of the extra clothing a soldier usually carried. All sat waiting into Tuesday evening for orders to move, but after midnight rain
started pelting the canvas roofs of the old winter quarters and gusts of
wind began snapping them. Tents unprotected by stockaded walls filled
with water, washing the residents out and leaving their possessions afloat.
Insignificant rills ran like little torrents, and the Rappahannock began
climbing its banks. The storm continued through Wednesday, breaking all the unofficial records of the season, before settling finally into a
drenching downpour, and that night Hooker described every stream as
"swimming." Stoneman had reached Rappahannock Station, but he
halted his command in mid-crossing, when mud and high water stranded
his artillery on the north bank.[31]

At first Hooker tried to prod Stoneman forward without his artillery,
reasoning that muddy roads would prevent the Confederates from using
any against him, but in the end he called all the cavalry back and instructed Stoneman to sit tight until the rain let up. He supposed the en-

emy had already detected Stoneman's location, and might not take long to deduce his destination. Talkative Confederate pickets soon revealed that some information had indeed trickled over to them, but Hooker hoped that so audacious a plan would not seem probable. Periodic rains kept the river high for days, and President Lincoln telegraphed anxiously for news, fearing "another failure already" and implying that Hooker should have considered the possibility of inclement weather. "We cannot control the elements," Hooker replied, falling back on a defense he had not deemed satisfactory for General Burnside after January's Mud March.[32]

After three relatively dry days Hooker ordered Stoneman to resume his mission across the Rappahannock, but the river still ran too high, and within hours after the order arrived it started to rain again.[33] Lincoln impatiently gathered up his war lords — Stanton and General in Chief Henry Halleck — and steamed back down to Aquia Creek, where he summoned Hooker for a command conference on the nineteenth. Officially they passed it off as one more opportunity to review the troops, booming another of those twenty-one-gun salutes that informed the enemy of Old Abe's presence, but the tenor of his communications hinted that the president wondered whether Hooker meant to do anything at all productive between rainstorms. The general remained confident that the cavalry raid could still succeed, but whether from executive pressure or personal inspiration he leaned toward striking a more decisive blow against Lee by adding a powerful infantry movement to Stoneman's flank march. The nearest upstream crossings, at Banks's Ford and U.S. Ford, were too well protected for safe passage, but if he marched nearly as far upriver as Stoneman had he could barge more easily across Kelly's Ford. From there he might proceed to the Rapidan fords and lunge at Lee from right behind his left flank.[34]

Whatever he did, he knew he must do it quickly, for some of his two-year regiments were already beginning to slip away, and most of the others had grown alarmingly restive. A general order from headquarters answered the pressing question of when each regiment would be released, and a good many two-year men flew into a fury when they learned that they would have to serve several days or weeks longer than their own ciphering indicated. They had all enlisted under state authority, but only when their regiments filled up had they been mustered into federal service. Most men remembered the date in 1861 that they had left home to sign up, and that was the day in 1863 when they expected to return, but fewer of them recalled the date their regiments had mustered in, and that was when the War Department intended to let them go.[35]

The misunderstanding ignited some minor tragedies, and nearly launched a few of more massive proportions. John Chase, a sergeant in

the 24th New York who had enlisted from Oswego County in the first days
of the conflict, refused to do any more duty after the sun set on his second anniversary. When one of his officers confronted him, the sergeant
knocked him flat, throwing in a few more serious threats to boot. The
army could hardly be held together if that sort of behavior were allowed to
pass, and within hours Sergeant Chase found himself in front of a court-
martial that sentenced him to death by firing squad. President Lincoln
did not have it in his craw to kill so prompt a patriot, but the veteran of
Bull Run, Antietam, and Fredericksburg still went to prison with a ball
and chain for the rest of the war.[36]

Then a few mutinies flared. The enlisted men in one company of the
1st New York laid down their arms on April 22, claiming that their term
was up, and eight more companies followed suit the next day. According
to government reckoning, the entire regiment had not been mustered
into federal service until the tenth company joined them, fifteen days
later, and they were all expected to serve until May 7. The circulation of a
little whiskey increased the volume of the protest, but the provost guard
waded into the throng and collared the loudest of them, after which a
Maine regiment fixed bayonets and surrounded the mutineers through an
all-night rainstorm. The soaking, the bayonets, and the sobering off did
the trick: eventually most of the regiment went back to duty, however sul-
lenly, but a similar incident erupted in the Fifth Corps and a few days later
more than half of the 34th New York threw down their weapons. This regiment was to be discharged in mid-June, which seemed cruelly long to the
six early companies. Their brigadier, Alfred Sully, tried reasoning with
them, but they would not budge. The division commander, a Regular
Army officer named John Gibbon, brought out the 15th Massachusetts
and ordered them to load, whereupon he gave the mutineers five minutes
to align on their colors or be shot down. Once they had submitted, Gibbon
relieved Sully of his command.[37]

The army was not a place where dissent, however justified, was allowed to flourish, and this particular army may have been the most intol-
erant of all because of its proximity to the seat of democratic government.
Colonel Edward E. Cross, the conservative Democrat at the head of the
5th New Hampshire, reported the Army of the Potomac heavily infiltrated with "Abolition Spies" in the form of chaplains, tract distributors,
state agents, Sanitary Commission representatives, and reporters for the
more liberal Republican newspapers. The most casual remark might lead
a man to grief, and with some regularity valuable officers were summarily
dismissed for sins no more grievous than a private expression of disagreement with the administration. The commander of General Gibbon's division ambulance train, Captain John Garland, went home in disgrace on

the eve of the spring campaign because postal employees had opened his letter to a friend in Shanghai, finding in it what they interpreted as traitorous language. The most common examples of such language that spring consisted of nothing more shocking than disparaging assessments of Lincoln's Emancipation Proclamation, which General Hooker thought most higher-ranking field officers and generals opposed: some of the most loyal and competent officers believed that the proclamation had strengthened the enemy by uniting all Southerners, including the more obstinate Unionists, against an abolitionist North. Many felt that Lincoln had betrayed them with that document, and as a native of the fortified city across the Rappahannock, Captain Garland may have been one of them, but such sentiments could no longer be safely revealed.[38]

As if to impart a lesson to officers who were inclined to criticize their betters, Edwin Stanton supplied each regimental headquarters with several copies of Judge Advocate General Joseph Holt's summation in the court-martial of Fitz John Porter. Porter, one of the more promising major generals in the army, had technically been tried on a charge of disobedience of orders at Second Bull Run, but his real crime had consisted of his personal and political contempt for that onetime darling of Radical Republicans, John Pope. A court-martial carefully weighted with officers of Radical persuasion made their way far enough around the evidence to find Porter guilty, and he was summarily dismissed from the army after eighteen years of distinguished service. Presented in quantities sufficient for most regimental and company commanders to obtain, Holt's summary — the government's jaundiced version of the case — served both to justify the railroading of Porter and to intimidate those who might scorn their military or political superiors. The *National Intelligencer* offered the other side of the story, publishing the summation of Porter's defense attorney, but when a conspicuous shipment of that edition went out to Porter's friends in the army it was removed from the mail.[39]

Administration efforts to muzzle divergent opinion included preferential War Department treatment for newspapers that supported the president's policies, in concert with prohibitive restrictions on those, like the *Intelligencer,* that took more critical positions. No one illustrated government favoritism toward friendly newspapers better than George Wilkes, editor of the *Spirit of the Times,* in New York, which had specialized in sporting news until the war began. His unflattering coverage of George McClellan and his fawning accounts of administration pets had won Wilkes enviable privileges. Hooker effectively installed him as chief sutler at the headquarters of the Army of the Potomac, where Wilkes prospered surreptitiously under the authority of the nominal purveyor. Sutlers operated mobile variety stores for the regiments to which they were attached, selling dainty edibles and little luxuries to their captive customers at tremendous markups, but in his headquarters sinecure Wilkes enjoyed a more affluent clientele. Unlike common regimental sutlers, he also found it somewhat safer to engage in the illicit liquor trade. His two-star patron actually encouraged him in that line, thought Colonel Cross: besides raking in fat profits at the expense of soldiers and the government, Wilkes's headquarters duties seemed to consist primarily of plying the army's newspaper correspondents with whiskey, champagne, and positive information to "keep the Hooker sentiment up."[40]

When he came to Hooker's headquarters, Wilkes engineered an exclusive arrangement for the distribution of "truly Loyal" newspapers throughout the army. Newspaper agents would be allowed to sell only the most supportive sheets, like Horace Greeley's *New York Tribune* and John Forney's *Washington Chronicle,* which they would be allowed to hawk at five cents a copy despite the two-cent cover price. The vendors lived well under this pact, and the government enjoyed a better image, for peddlers were forbidden to sell any journals that offered more incisive interpretations of Mr. Lincoln or his war. The soldiers could only read variant viewpoints if the folks at home included those papers in private packages, and outright bans on the most contrary organs sometimes led to their confiscation when those packages were searched for alcohol and civilian clothing. Such venal and manipulative chicanery offended adherents of the subordinate party in and out of uniform, and disgusted those who clung to the ideal of an unfettered press. Unfortunately for Wilkes and his headquarters henchmen, one of those who found the bargain particularly odious was Marsena Patrick, provost marshal general of the Army of the Potomac. During the rainy days of late April, General Patrick learned of their liquor trade and arrested the lot of them.[41]

Joe Hooker demonstrated considerable tolerance for corruption and intrigue, so long as it worked to his own advantage, but few could fault his talent for lifting the morale of his troops. As he waited for the rain to stop, he implemented one last idea that had a more lasting impact on his soldiers than anything else he ever did. In March he had issued instructions and designs for badges to identify the different corps under his command, directing his chief quartermaster to supply the badges and ordering all inspecting officers to enforce their use. The badges arrived during the last week of April, and while the weather confined them to their huts, tens of thousands of amateur tailors unrolled their leather housewives to stitch the little scraps of flannel to the flat crowns of their caps. The badges all consisted of simple silhouettes two inches in diameter, or a little less. The circle assigned to John Reynolds's First Corps was the simplest of all. The Second Corps was represented by a trefoil, while the Third Corps had been wearing a lozenge since the days of Phil Kearny, now dead: Kearny had reportedly initiated the concept of badges by making the officers of his division wear one so he could identify them if they straggled away. Meade's Fifth Corps drew a Maltese cross, and John Sedgwick's Sixth the Greek cross. O. O. Howard's Eleventh Corps, inherited from Franz Sigel, would be identified by a crescent two inches tall, and Henry Slocum's Twelfth Corps — formerly that of Nathaniel Banks — by a star.[42]

The various badges were cut from red, white, and blue cloth, and in each corps the first division would wear red, the second division white, and the third division blue. At the time only one corps included a fourth division, and in that case the badges would be green. Any malingering or malfeasance on the march, in camp, or in battle would theoretically attract attention to these badges, assuming the soldier wore regulation headgear, and a single glance would suffice to determine the culprit's division. If the soldier also heeded the requirement to adorn his cap with the brass regimental numerals and company letter, it would be an easy matter to pick him out of a company formation. Good discipline provided the official purpose for this innovation, but it would inevitably yield the collateral benefit of esprit de corps. When they could be so easily identified, soldiers could not only be expected to behave and perform better but to develop the habit of competition with troops whose caps bore emblems of a different shape, or color. Toward that end, Hooker later expanded the idea to corps and division flags, and to the canvas covers of the baggage wagons.[43]

As the war progressed, corps badges spread throughout the national forces, but they originated on the Rappahannock in the spring of 1863, and the badges of that army became the most famous. Men who belonged to corps with distinguished battlefield records eventually embraced Hooker's simple insignia as personal symbols of valor, wearing them as pins on the breasts of their jackets. Those who survived the war would one day emboss the covers of their regimental histories with trefoils, diamonds, and the distinctive crosses; they mounted them prominently over the entrances to their reunion halls, designed their battlefield monuments in those shapes, and incorporated them on the faces of their gravestones.[44]

More than one officer wondered, as the men appeared at roll call with those fresh, bright badges on their forage caps, if it would ever stop raining. The river surged higher all the time, and the roads posed difficult passage for man or beast, let alone for tons of ordnance and wagons. An artillery colonel who had plodded up and down the Peninsula under McClellan during the monsoons of the previous spring took wry notice of those officers who had missed that campaign, but who still accused

McClellan of having dawdled needlessly there, although they now found the Rappahannock mud impossible to overcome.[45]

Then, at last, came three dry days, with enough wind to sift the moisture out of the roads, and Hooker decided to move. The Eleventh and Twelfth corps started first on Monday, April 27, marching up the Rappahannock toward Kelly's Ford and keeping well away from the river to avoid detection. Bulging knapsacks dug deeply into the foot soldiers' shoulders, and a hot sun soon raised enough dust to choke the trailing brigades. A winter's leisure had softened most feet, and over the course of fourteen miles rough brogans raised red welts that soon blossomed into blisters. The leaders covered half the distance to the ford by evening and went quietly into camp while the rest of the army bedded down with instructions to leave in the morning.[46]

That night's campfires filled the mailbags with the hopes and fears of the campaign now under way. A perennially optimistic young West Point graduate promised his mother a devastating defeat for the rabble across the river, and that confident air may have predominated. Heading his letter "The very last night in the old Camp," a Connecticut man assured his wife that the morning's movement could bring the war to a finish before his regiment came home, at the beginning of July, but a Regular Army captain whose division was heavily encumbered with such short-term militia did not feel so certain. "I can't say that I am at all sanguine about going into a fight with these nine month men," he confessed.[47]

On Tuesday morning the Army of the Potomac separated into two main bodies. The First, Third, and Sixth corps filed downstream under the temporary command of John Sedgwick, congregating clandestinely below the city behind the hills of the left bank. The Fifth Corps followed toward Kelly's Ford after the Eleventh and Twelfth, all under the general direction of Henry Slocum, while Darius Couch's fifteen-thousand-man Second Corps covered the lower Rappahannock fords, to keep the enemy from slipping between the halves of the divided army. General Hooker and his staff dashed off toward the Orange & Alexandria Railroad for a conference with Stoneman, whom Hooker still intended to send behind Lee's lines, and then he galloped after Slocum, whose column approached Kelly's Ford in a cold, drizzling rain that afternoon. Toward dark the engineer officer in charge of the crossing there sent a battalion over the swift-running river in boats to clear the way for throwing down a pontoon bridge; the Confederate pickets there resisted those few hundred Yankees by firing a single round, then fled without having seen the thirty-six thousand more who waited behind them.[48]

Meanwhile, below Fredericksburg, several hundred Maine woodsmen manhandled Sedgwick's cumbersome pontoons more than half a mile down to the riverbank in the darkness while the rest of his forty-five thousand troops slept without fires in the rain, all to maintain secrecy. With both halves of Hooker's army hidden, Lee was left wondering where the expected blow would come.[49]

Events on the morning of April 29 suggested a replay of the December battle of Fredericksburg. Sedgwick's Sixth Corps began crossing in the thick fog of predawn, its presence given away by the stentorian curses of the drunken brigadier who was to superintend the bridge work. Boatloads of infantrymen finally had to pole across in pontoons as others had in December, forty-five to a pontoon. "I felt a good deal like a man who is certain to see the last of this world and its follies," confessed Lewis Cleveland, the New York lieutenant whose enlistment was nearly out. They could hear the Confederate pickets' voices through the fog until a battery opened on them as the first boat touched the right bank, but the volley of canister flew high, over their heads, and Yankees leaped out of the boats into water waist deep, scrambling up the embankment. As bayonets burst from the fog ahead of blue uniforms, Southern pickets spilled out of their holes and sprinted for their main works.[50]

Sharper picket fire delayed the First Corps even longer downstream, until the rising sun began burning away the mists. Five Wisconsin, Indiana, and Michigan regiments known as the Iron Brigade took to the boats here, ignoring platoons of their fallen comrades in a desperate rush for the plains below the city, where the same regiments had fought less than five months before. Once a couple of divisions had tramped ashore on Lee's side of the river, that imposing force sat back and waited. Confederate pickets started sniping at their counterparts in blue, but some two-year New Yorkers shouted at them to stop: they were going home in three days, they said, and they didn't want anyone hurt. Such faint spirits notwithstanding, Lee thought Hooker "in earnest," for the crossing appeared to have plenty of strength behind it. From his cavalry, though, he also knew that O. O. Howard had crossed Kelly's Ford with at least fourteen thousand men, aiming to turn his left flank, and that Stoneman would probably race down the Orange & Alexandria to cut the railroads. He entertained no doubt that something big was in store for him (if he had, that day's *New York Times* would have removed any such doubt), so he called down to Port Royal for Thomas J. Jackson, the mighty Stonewall, to come up and confront Sedgwick.[51]

Slocum and Howard struck south from Kelly's Ford, sprinting toward Germanna Ford on the Rapidan. That afternoon skirmishers of the Twelfth Corps reached there and plunged in up to their armpits, with rifles and ammunition held high, seizing the ford along with a few companies of resident rebels, whose winter huts they appropriated that night

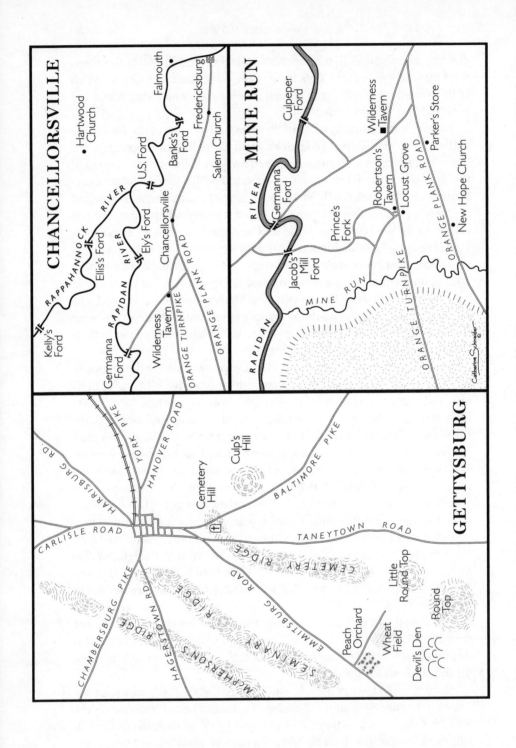

to escape the rain. Once George Meade had negotiated Kelly's Ford he veered east with his Fifth Corps and marched for Ely's Ford. A few hundred cavalry preceded each column, to scatter Confederate pickets and disguise the presence of the infantry. Both Slocum and Meade aimed for the rural crossroads known as Chancellorsville, where the big brick Chancellor home and tavern marked the junction of the Orange Plank Road and the old Orange Turnpike. From there they might have an open road to the rear of Lee's Rappahannock line.[52]

Late that afternoon the rain picked up, raising the watercourses just as Hooker had put a couple of difficult rivers between his supply base and most of his army. Now those eight days' rations made better sense, but they offered only marginal comfort. Tense officers under Sedgwick shuddered at a stillness one of them called "painful," and worried that Lee had planned an elaborate trap for them. He had to know of their presence by now, they assumed, and in their own ignorance of Hooker's plans they stared at those ominous heights behind Fredericksburg, anticipating another deadly disaster on the scene of their worst defeat.[53]

Lee was beginning to grasp Hooker's intentions by then, for his cavalry chief, J. E. B. Stuart, had told him about the Yankees taking both Germanna and Ely's fords. Finally, near midnight, Stuart forwarded Lee the results of his scouting north of the Rapidan, which had netted him prisoners from the Fifth, Eleventh, and Twelfth Union corps. Whether Sedgwick's crossing was a feint or part of a pincer movement, Slocum surely meant business with a circuitous march of so many, so carefully screened.[54]

The rain had subsided to occasional drizzle by Thursday morning, the last day of April, but the day dawned to a muggy mist. Now Hooker activated the next facet of his overwhelming concentration against Lee's left, crossing the Second Corps over the Rappahannock by U.S. Ford and starting Dan Sickles up from Sedgwick's downstream operation with his Third Corps. Their surplus rations and ammunition bore heavily on Sickles's sweating men, especially after the sun began blazing, and the more impulsive of them tossed aside their entire knapsacks to keep up. The better officers engendered appreciation and set good examples by taking some of the weaker men's rifles for a spell, but their first long march of the season nevertheless culled a few of them for ambulances to gather up, for no baggage wagons hampered this march. They pushed on into the darkness, collapsing after fifteen miles, still a couple of miles short of the ford.[55]

As the Union troops discovered when they approached Chancellorsville, the optimistically named tavern was the only building in that prospective village, sitting alone in the middle of a dense second-growth forest known locally as the Wilderness. The Orange Turnpike, the Orange Plank Road, and a few other byways traversing the forest offered limited communications and less maneuverability: only a handful of major clearings pocked the low canopy of that crowded brake. On May 1 Hooker moved in for the kill from Chancellorsville, sending out five corps in three files, but they had not yet emerged from the Wilderness when they met Confederate reinforcements coming head-on toward them: with an audacity that he was forced to assume, Lee had left only five brigades to guard the heights behind Fredericksburg and the plain below the city, directing the rest of his army toward Chancellorsville to face the greater threat. Fearing that his divisions would be chewed up faster than he could push them into line over those narrow tracks, Hooker fell back on the defensive, retracting his line to Chancellorsville and beyond, and ensconcing his battalions behind breastworks to meet Lee's attack. At the same time he ordered Sedgwick to prod the enemy below Fredericksburg, partly to determine how much force the Confederates had left there and partly to pose a threat that might convince Lee to withdraw some troops from the Chancellorsville fight.[56]

All remained quiet on Sedgwick's front. Some of his men ducked into the Rappahannock for a swim, and after more than a day of rain the off-duty men among the Confederate pickets lay along the riverbank to dry themselves out, reminding a Yankee quartermaster of "so many toads." When Hooker's instructions reached Sedgwick he trotted out most of the Sixth and First corps to show the enemy how strong he was, but then Hooker called everything off: after midnight he decided to put all his strength behind a drive from Chancellorsville. He told Sedgwick to take up the bridges on his front, and to send John Reynolds up to Chancellorsville with the First Corps. Reduced to his own Sixth Corps, Sedgwick would remain to deal with the enemy behind Fredericksburg.[57]

The dawn had not yet come on Saturday, May 2, when Lee and Jackson found a route to the rear of Hooker's Chancellorsville bivouacs. It would require Jackson to make a circuitous march south, west, and north, and would put him across the turnpike three miles west of Hooker's headquarters. Woods and distance screened him from any Yankee eyes (including those peering down from a balloon in Sedgwick's camp) until a division commander in the Third Corps caught sight of Jackson's column passing through an opening in the forest, a mile south of Chancellorsville.[58]

Dan Sickles sent a couple of brigades to investigate, and a brigade from Howard's Eleventh Corps unshouldered their knapsacks to follow. The 23rd Georgia hung back to shield Jackson's march, putting up a fierce fight in a cedar thicket around an old iron furnace. The 1st and 2nd U.S.

Sharpshooters, armed with breechloading Sharps rifles and still dressed mostly in forest-green uniforms, pinned the Georgians down with an accurate fire. Even the sharpshooters' chaplain took a belligerent hand in it, firing deliberately on a flag of truce when it popped out of a barn, but eventually the Georgia regiment surrendered and its colonel spurred away, into disgrace. About 360 Confederates filed out with their hands in the air. As the prisoners came shuffling back between bayonets on their way to the provost marshal, one of the sharpshooters noted that they seemed pretty well fed and clothed for the defenders of a starving nation. Those rebels boasted injudiciously that Jackson would be back with 75,000 men, but the Yankees took it as a bluff, and that lively skirmish allowed Jackson to proceed unmolested on his flank march. Joe Hooker rode back and forth around the Chancellor place, accepting roaring cheers from the troops idling about that intersection, perfectly oblivious to some 20,000 Confederates massing across the turnpike behind his right flank.[59]

Jackson's hammer fell late in the afternoon of May 2, hitting Howard's Eleventh Corps endwise as the troops relaxed along the Orange Turnpike. The onslaught came too quickly, and Howard's men — nearly half of them German, by birth or parentage — were too unprepared. Most of the Eleventh Corps crumbled, with every man for himself. Red, blue, and white crescents fled eastward down the turnpike toward Chancellorsville, carrying the panic with them. Officers bellowed in English and German, flailed with their swords, and even fired their revolvers at the wide-eyed fugitives, who dodged and bounded like so many sheep. Infantry and batteries on their way from U.S. Ford found the road near Chancellorsville jammed with battery wagons, runaway horses, pack mules laden with ammunition, and the often hatless, terrified refugees from Howard's regiments. Reinforcements rushing to the front to form a line against Jackson railed at "the dutch sons of bitches" who flew past them. A Pennsylvanian whose brigade was overrun by presumed Germans allowed that they "might have fought well with Sigel," but noted that "they did not fight worth shit under Howard."[60]

In the Third Corps it soon became obvious that the enemy had "squarmed around" the Union right, and Sickles brought his foremost brigades back from the site of its earlier scrap at the furnace, but Jackson's rapid advance isolated them. The last of Sickles's divisions, that of Hiram Berry, fell in beside the Twelfth Corps and slowed the assault in the twilight. George Meade threw the Fifth Corps in the way as the rebels neared roads that led to the fords; Meade's men built breastworks, but they had no entrenching tools so they hacked at the earth with their bayonets and tossed the loose soil into piles with tin plates or "enything that we could

get aholt of," as a Maine man recorded it later that night. There the Yankees settled in for the evening, with the dead and wounded lying between
them and the enemy. Hot sun had once again baked the moisture out of
the underbrush, and muzzle blasts lighted brush fires here and there that
burned some of the wounded alive. Their screams mingled with the rattle
of musketry, the roar of artillery, and the eerie shrieking of whippoorwills
as the forest sank into darkness.[61]

Thereafter, Hooker's campaign to destroy Lee's army deteriorated into
a fight for survival. Jackson fell during the night with wounds that would
help to kill him, and Lee put J. E. B. Stuart in command there. The next
morning five Confederate divisions pounded Hooker's Chancellorsville
position mercilessly in some of the most vicious fighting some veterans
had ever seen. Guns large and small clamored without respite from the
moment the sun rose until it reached its zenith, and a lucky Southern
gunner knocked Joe Hooker down with an injury that dazed him for
much of the day. That mishap and furious infantry assaults kept the
massive Union force on the defensive. Among those who fell, seriously
wounded, was Captain Daniel Hart, the seven-week bridegroom, whose
7th New Jersey ran out of ammunition while plugging successive ruptures in Sickles's line.[62]

With only his own corps and a spare division from the Second Corps,
Sedgwick had the job of coming to the rescue the hard way, taking
Marye's Heights by the same frontal assault that had failed so disastrously
in December. Sedgwick, though, had to face less firepower on those
heights than Burnside had, and he approached it a little differently. Most
of the Confederates behind the city had trudged off to join Lee, leaving
only nine regiments to defend the entire line, and Sedgwick prepared
six brigades to throw against them all at once, in three different columns. The troops who had sidled up behind the city itself piled their
knapsacks on the edge of town just as their ill-fated comrades had, five
months before, and at noon they started across a mile of open ground
where rebel artillery could play easily on them. That artillery and Mississippi marksmen offered only a fraction of the resistance that Longstreet's
entire corps had in December, and Sedgwick's Federals rushed in with the
bayonet without stopping to fire. The simultaneous, sprinting attack accomplished what Burnside's slow and piecemeal assaults had failed to do:
Union soldiers swept over Marye's Heights, sent a few hundred prisoners
to the rear, and surged on toward what was now the rear of Lee's army.[63]

Again Lee substituted audacity for strength, shifting a lone division
from his outnumbered Chancellorsville front to bring Sedgwick to a halt.
The leading Sixth Corps division met the first of these reinforcements at
the brick Baptist meetinghouse called Salem Church, four miles from

Fredericksburg's waterfront, where Sedgwick's advance brigades ran headlong into a trap. They had just blundered into thick woods on either side of the turnpike when, at a range of a hundred feet, the Southern line rose up and blasted a volley into their faces. Severely handled one after the other, Union regiments gave way as Confederates slipped around their flanks, forcing entire companies to wriggle out of their equipment straps and flee. Rail fences made better targets of some of them as they climbed over, while others tried to rally behind such paltry cover, but too few of them held to keep the rebels back. Those who hesitated too long soon heard the sharp commands of Confederate officers to throw down their arms and surrender, and scores of them complied. With sunlight waning, the Confederates let their prey slide back to a new position and brought up yet another division from Chancellorsville.[64]

Sedgwick backed up against a new pontoon bridge at Banks's Ford on May 4, waiting through the morning and the scorching afternoon. Lee spent the better part of the day arranging thirteen brigades to assail Sedgwick's nine here, and not until late afternoon did he send them in. Ten of Sedgwick's forty-seven regiments consisted of those nervous two-year and nine-month troops. One of the nine-month regiments, the 26th New Jersey, had been quaking since the battle opened, and in the previous day's assault of Marye's Heights those Jerseymen had melted away behind trees and stumps or into ditches to escape the bullets. Now they broke and ran when a Louisiana brigade tilted toward them, and that might have opened the belly of the Union perimeter if the 6th Vermont had not fixed bayonets and lunged into the breach, saving the day.[65]

Lee had withdrawn too many troops from before Hooker to mount another offensive there, and Hooker was waiting behind improved breastworks to deal him a bloody repulse, so Sedgwick's evening affair wrought most of the casualties for the day, and it did not end with sunset. In the darkness Lee hurled a new assault against the Sixth Corps, and Sedgwick drew back to the ford. He left a heavy guard of Maine and New York men to hold the riverbank while the rest of the corps retreated across the pontoon bridges, but the New Yorkers — some of them two-year men with a month left in the army — surrendered quietly and gave away the position of the Mainers, who fought fiercely to maintain their ground. In the end overcast and fog covered the retreat, and by daylight the last of the Sixth Corps was making its way to the safe side of the river.[66]

For Joe Hooker, that disappointment ended the campaign. To the astonishment, anger, and disgust of most of his senior officers and a good many men in the ranks, he gave instructions for the six corps at Chancellorsville to prepare for retreat. Marsena Patrick, the provost marshal general, could not imagine why Hooker would surrender the initiative in a fight against an enemy only half his size. The decision disheartened Patrick, and infuriated everyone he spoke with about it. Colonel Charles Wainwright, the commander of First Corps artillery, reported the same universal contempt, as well as the common observation that they would never have retreated from such a position if McClellan had been in charge. Disbelief, and even an open cry for McClellan, came from the headquarters of the Second, Fifth, and Sixth corps, as well. That afternoon a thunderstorm broke the heat, settling into a cold, somber rain as the army turned for the bridges. Hooker preceded everyone, and he had no sooner crossed than the rain lent an air of sagacity to his withdrawal, lifting the river so quickly that the bridges had to be extended to reach solid ground. With barely two weeks before they would start for home, the Penobscot lumbermen of the 2nd Maine drew the honor of covering the withdrawal at U.S. Ford. The last of the army rumbled over before daylight and the Maine men started backing toward the river, but no one followed them. After crossing the bridge they stacked their rifles and helped the engineers tear it apart.[67]

No one in Washington City knew, until the army plodded back to its old camps, which way the fortunes of battle had fallen. Favorable reports of the capture of Marye's Heights cheered the White House, but then Hooker telegraphed that Sedgwick had disappeared, reporting ominously that he "did not despair of success" just yet. On the afternoon of May 4 the dirge of a brass band echoed through the White House and an ambulance rumbled up Pennsylvania Avenue between files of infantry and cavalry with their banners draped in mourning, carrying the body of Major General Hiram Berry to the rail depot; the officer in charge of the escort whispered that the enemy had already retaken Marye's Heights. Forty-eight hours later the oscillating rumors of victory and defeat had given way to the unmistakable gloom of another failure.[68]

Hospital transports had already been disgorging the wounded at the Sixth Street wharf for a day or two when President Lincoln took ship for Aquia Creek to learn the details of the disaster. More than seventeen thousand men had been lost — nearly six thousand of them in prisoners — only to have the foothold on the opposite shore meekly surrendered. Between Burnside and Hooker, the Rappahannock River had cost the country thirty thousand men so far, and the army still sat where it had six months before. It was, the president admitted before Hooker's generals, a worse blow to Northern morale and international prestige than any of the war's previous defeats had inflicted. Hooker, the relentless critic of others, listed every excuse for himself: his subordinates had failed him; he had been stunned by a shell; the terrain had prevented him from maneuvering. Mr. Lincoln seemed to accept his explanations, blaming no one for the dispiriting repulse, but a government clerk dismantled Hooker's reasoning — noting, for instance (as Lincoln would once have reminded George McClellan), that Lee had no trouble maneuvering on the same ground where Hooker found it impossible.[69]

The significance of the more staggering Confederate losses, including Stonewall Jackson himself, would not become apparent to the average citizen for a long time. Sympathetic editors therefore ameliorated the more obvious bad news again, juxtaposing headlines about Hooker's withdrawal with outdated, optimistic announcements that Stoneman had ridden within five miles of Richmond. Mistaken by Virginia civilians for Stuart's cavaliers, a few of Stoneman's troopers had skirted the Chickahominy River, but they had tarried only briefly before galloping on to the protection of Union gunboats in the Tidewater. False rumors of Richmond's capture served merely to cast those communities that had celebrated the reports into deeper dejection.[70]

Perhaps the most effective response from the more hostile press came from the *Crisis*, of Columbus, Ohio. Editor Samuel Medary simply published Hooker's patently boastful congratulatory proclamation to his defeated army, word for word, right above the tasteful understatement of General Lee's own address to his victorious troops. Neither Hooker nor the Union cause benefited from the comparison.[71]

At home and in the army, personal opinion seemed to season individual reception of the news at least as much as it was influenced by it. Those who doubted the wisdom of the war doubted it all the more on hearing of Hooker's embarrassing rebuff, while those who most fervently supported the struggle recovered quickly from the shock and started looking for cause to hope. Walt Whitman, a middle-aged scribbler of poetry and a volunteer nurse in the Washington hospitals, found the first word of the army's retreat "very distressing," but within a few days he was arguing that Hooker had struck Lee's men "the heaviest and most staggering" blow they had yet received. It was actually McClellan who had done that, during the Seven Days battles of the summer before, but Whitman's erroneous interpretation helped sustain his will to continue the contest. From his rococo Manhattan study, George Templeton Strong more consciously took the same solace from his understanding that Lee had suffered more than Hooker. The army's optimists happily accepted that perceived advantage in lieu of victory, reveling in the grim calculation that Northern armies could better weather the attrition than their opponents. "The Rebels cannot stand more than one more such butchery," wrote a Wisconsin veteran of the fight. Halfway across the continent, a Massachusetts captain agreed with him, sagely predicting that the Confederates would "wear themselves out even by victories after a while."[72]

Those who refused to accept defeat selected or invented particular justifications. It was O. O. Howard's "cowardly rascals" who had caused the trouble, thought a First Corps soldier, who wanted the Eleventh Corps broken up and redistributed throughout the army. A Massachusetts chaplain blamed it on the preacher's perennial explanation, calling it "God's will" against a proud and avaricious nation.[73] Alonzo Cushing, a youthful battery commander who had spent April predicting a decisive victory from this campaign, raised Hooker as the culprit, asking his brother "is it not the man?" and charging that Hooker had handled the army badly. Partisans of McClellan or Burnside stifled their glee over Hooker's thrashing, and pinned the responsibility on him.[74] Absorbing the general exasperation at Fifth Corps headquarters, a clerk told his sister that the men had seen no need to retreat, speculating what a howl would have been raised against McClellan had he waited until April to advance, only to flee at the first contact. The *New York Herald* chastised Hooker with such unusual vigor that his chief of staff ordered every copy of that newspaper within the army confiscated and burned.[75]

The condemnation of Hooker provoked an exaggerated outpouring of support for him, both public and private, that may have revealed more enthusiasm than numbers. Soldiers in the ranks extolled Hooker for genius they could hardly have had an opportunity to measure, while higher-ranking officers praised him backhandedly for having even held his own against "the largest and best Rebel army." Senator John Ten Eyck of New Jersey wrote Hooker to assure him that he retained perfect confidence in the general. The two most prominent senators from the Committee on the Conduct of the War, Zachariah Chandler and Ben Wade, hurried down from their Great Lakes homes to inspect the army commanded by their new favorite. Their commitment to Hooker may have flavored their conclusion that the army still enjoyed fairly high morale.[76]

The oft-defeated Army of the Potomac did show remarkable resilience, but only after a little time had passed. Another Wade, a private in the 14th Connecticut, informed his sister upon returning to his old camp that he and his comrades "have got most awfully whipped." Assuming that Lee badly outnumbered Hooker, and that the men would refuse to risk their lives again after so many defeats, he believed they would be beaten all the worse if they tried it again. A Pennsylvanian who had run into the ambush at Salem Church concurred that the Army of the Potomac lacked the numbers to dislodge the enemy. A Maine man whose regiment had also taken a drubbing at Salem Church — after suffering severe losses in the assault on Marye's Heights only a few hours before — admitted to his sister nearly a month later that "I am not so sanguine as some of our ultimate perfect success."[77]

A great deal of confidence must have drained away with the departing regiments of two-year men in the days after the battle. Some of them had ducked the fight altogether through quirks in their enlistments, like most of the 10th Maine. In the summer of 1861 that regiment had been organized from the remnants of Maine's first three-month regiment, and the men had been allowed to reenlist for two years from the date of their mustering with the 1st Maine. On April 27, therefore, all but three companies of the 10th had headed for Washington and home while the 2nd Maine, which had served continually since early May of 1861, went into battle with Meade's Fifth Corps. The 2nd Maine was flailing away at rude breastworks with bayonets and bare hands just as the 10th Maine reached Portland. The tales of bloodshed among their former comrades wrung a blend of guilt and relief from the discharged veterans, but relief seemed to prevail. "I am heartily glad I was not in that scrape," admitted a discharged lieutenant as he visited around Portland.[78]

The 5th New York stayed with the army through the worst of battle, but before it was over the three hundred two-year men who composed nearly half the regiment turned for home. The three-year recruits shuffled off to join a new regiment elsewhere in the brigade, and that regiment's numeral was extinguished from the brigade casualty lists. Those three hundred, the "debris" of Abram Duryee's Zouave regiment, still dressed in the white turbans and baggy scarlet shintiyan of their original uniforms, marched up Broadway on Friday afternoon, May 8. Spectators lined both sides of the avenue, stood on balconies, and hung out windows to cheer and look for familiar faces. For those who had watched the eight-hundred-man regiment swagger down that same street two years before, the sight of the thinned ranks of bronzed veterans muted the joy of the homecoming with a touch of sadness. Looking down from the balcony of the Sanitary Commission headquarters, George Templeton Strong thought of the final movement of Beethoven's Third Symphony, the *Eroica*, with its ambivalent intimations of nostalgia, sorrow, and veneration.[79]

The 2nd Maine arrived in Bangor by steamer just three weeks after dismantling Hooker's last pontoon bridge on the Rappahannock. An immense throng on the banks of the Penobscot River threatened to spill onto the wharf, straining so eagerly toward friends and relatives in the disembarking regiment that a heavy guard detail had to hold them back. The local militia, the fire company, and several bands led the remains of the regiment down Bangor's own little Broadway, aflutter with flags and bunting, to the town square. A chorus of girls in bright white dresses greeted them with a song written for the occasion, and a host of dignitaries, including Vice President Hannibal Hamlin and the governor who had sent them off in 1861, belabored them with speeches. Afterward the town treated them to dinner in a nearby banquet hall, where the names of the regiment's ten battles had been painted on banners, as though to remind them of the scores of faces that had not come back with them. Once sated, the veterans turned in their muskets and cartridge boxes, shook hands with boon companions they might never see again, and started back to the lives they had left when their war was young and innocent.[80]

By the middle of May John Sedgwick calculated that the army was discharging a thousand men a day, and that hemorrhaging would continue for at least a month. "I presume they know in Washington where the reinforcements are to come from," he observed in mock confidence. He soon realized that no reinforcements were coming at all, and (as newspapers occasionally reminded an impatient public) any federal draft would have to await the effective statutory date of July 1. Those who remained were beginning to recuperate from the shock of Hooker's defeat, but the visible shrinking of the bulging divisions tinged that newfound morale with a sense of numerical inferiority.[81]

The last of the two-year regiments were still with the army when the earliest of the nine-month troops came due for discharge. When those militia regiments first arrived at the Army of the Potomac, a Maine cavalryman had groused that, after the war was over, no distinction would be made between the three-year men who did most of the fighting and the short-term militia who did little or none, and the homecoming celebrations of the nine-month men seemed to confirm that prediction. When they poured onto the wharf in Boston, the 916 fastidious and discriminating survivors of the 44th Massachusetts, who had buried only eleven combat casualties, met the same festivities as the 2nd Maine. Well-wishers lined their route from India Street to Boston Common, and when they filed under the arch at the corner of Charles and Beacon streets the mayor and city council heralded their glorious return from the jaws of death. The 5th Massachusetts Militia, which had not lost a man to hostile fire, landed on the other side of the harbor at Battery Wharf: there it waited two hours for an enormous ceremonial escort consisting of police, fire departments, home guard companies, and a two-page list of institute delegations and benevolent societies to form ranks and lead the way to Winthrop Square through a frothing sea of waving handkerchiefs and volleys of artillery fired from the Charlestown waterfront.[82]

Those delirious homecomings helped to spark rumors among three-year men who had enlisted in the summer or fall of 1862 that they had actually enlisted for only nine months, too. Similar stories circulated as far west as Kansas, although out there the source appears to have been Senator Jim Lane, whom many soldiers remembered having promised them the shorter enlistment. The collapse of such hopeful fantasies inevitably whittled away at the morale of every regiment that entertained them.[83]

The usefulness of those militia regiments that still had some time left suffered immeasurably from their very impatience. Schemers entering the nine-month regiments had tried to improve their bounties and cut their enlistments even shorter by joining their regiments late, but — as the two-year men had found — the government counted the entire regiment's time from the day it mustered into federal service, after the last man enlisted. Early recruits therefore underestimated their terms by as long as it had taken the regiment to fill up.[84] Even as they donned their first uniforms, those militia recruits had been trying to ascertain the day they would be discharged, but those calculations led to disappointment in April, when most of their comrades began making plans for their homecoming and learned of the merciless War Department mathematics. From the moment of that revelation every one of them, from the fifers to the field officers, began counting the days, and precious few of them entertained the slightest thought of ever returning to the front. Either in response to worried inquiries from home or in exasperated outbursts, many of them vowed they would never serve in uniform again, and most of them kept that promise. The nine-month experiment had raised the equivalent of two respectable armies, with all the associated expenses in provisions, pay, and pensions, but that costly venture had accomplished nothing of military significance. What it had done instead was to persuade the better part of ninety thousand able-bodied men that they never wanted anything more to do with the army.[85]

The two-year men felt much the same, which made their departure an even worse blow to the Army of the Potomac, because the army would miss them far more than it would the drafted militia. One of the first militia regiments to go home was the 127th Pennsylvania, which had disgraced itself in both of its only two engagements, at Fredericksburg and Chancellorsville: in the latter fight a good many in the 127th had loosed a volley into a friendly regiment before taking to their heels. In contrast to the flamboyant sendoffs accorded their brethren on the Carolina coast, these unappreciated militiamen went home to a humiliating chorus of jeers, jibes, and groans from the contemptuous veterans they left behind.[86] The commander of an Indiana regiment detected extreme apprehension of further action among both the officers and the enlisted men of the two nine-month New Jersey regiments that had doubled the size of his brigade: the two regiments had lost a hundred men in combat already, and that appears to have been a hundred more than they ever anticipated losing. When the hometown newspaper depicted the elaborate welcome given the 134th Pennsylvania, and described the regiment in glowing superlatives, one veteran of Fredericksburg reminded his family that poor discipline and filthy campsites had earned the 134th the utter disdain of fellow Pennsylvanians, who considered it the worst regiment from their state.[87]

New York had sent only two complete nine-month regiments, but it had supplied by far the most two-year men of any state, so New York City turned out again and again in May and June to welcome the regiments as they came off the troop transports or out of the railroad cars. The last of them — "or such poor fragments as war had left of them," as one sentimental reporter characterized them — reached the city on June 8. Making the traditional pilgrimage of honor up Broadway from City Hall through an adulatory gantlet of citizens, they passed finally beneath the balcony of the Madison Square Hotel, where General George McClellan stood waving to them. At sight of their old hero the soldiers themselves went wild, lifting hats, caps, and hurrahs in a delirium of spontaneous adoration that Joe Hooker would never hear from them again.[88]

Among the regiments mustered out of service the next day was the 32nd New York, which had enjoyed relatively good fortune throughout the war. All but ninety-nine of the men who had gone into camp on Staten Island in 1861 had lived to see this day, and fewer than four dozen of those ninety-nine had died in battle. The 32nd had fared particularly well in the final campaign with Sedgwick, supplying picket details and waiting in reserve during the fights for both Marye's Heights and Banks's Ford, where only one 32nd man had been killed. Lieutenant Lewis Cleveland had anticipated this moment with gnawing anxiety, for hostile superiors had tried to undo him until the last moment, attempting to smear him with accusations of cowardice when typhoid fever felled him in that last action at the ford. With a fresh court-martial acquittal in his luggage, the exonerated lieutenant bid the army a resolute farewell.[89]

Like Lieutenant Cleveland, Private James Albert Hard had served with the 32nd New York from that first colorful, confusing, and disastrous campaign to Bull Run. He, too, had missed one bloody battle from illness, but he had stuck with his company for most of the war. He had stood among the tens of thousands whom President Lincoln had inspected along the banks of Antietam Creek the previous October, and again on the rolling plateau above the Rappahannock in April. He had seen a great deal over the past twenty-four months; now he had enjoyed the sumptuous meal supplied by the Astor House chef to each of the returning regiments, and the stirring congratulations from the teeming sidewalks. On the morning of June 9 he collected the $20.72 the army owed him for his last hundred days' service, after clothing and equipment deductions, and he turned his back forever on the profession of arms. Not until old age would he wear anything like a uniform again, to convene with other veterans of his country's greatest conflict.[90]

Little did Private Hard suppose, as he headed for central New York with his paltry pay, that he would outlast every man who had accompanied him in the final parade up Broadway. As it happened, he would outlive every other soldier who had served in the Army of the Potomac during the four years that it trod the earth. Ninety years later, in fact, as he lay dying in a Rochester hospital, he would be the last survivor of all those millions who had carried a musket for — or against — the armies of Abraham Lincoln.[91]

3

The Clear and Present Danger
of Democracy

→ BETWEEN THE EXTREMES of political persuasion there dwelt many a heart that harbored grave doubts about the war that spring, even without the additional discouragement of more bloody defeats. Those disaffected citizens found much sympathy, but little in the way of representation, for the Republican machine had waged a relentless campaign to characterize disagreement with Lincoln's administration as disloyalty to the government, and to equate opposition to his war — or merely opposition to his means of pursuing that war — to outright treason.

Foremost among those who dared to differ with the administration was Clement L. Vallandigham, late three-term congressman from Ohio. Vallandigham had opposed the war from the first, believing the bayonet an odd instrument for restoring affection and loyalty in the seceded states, and he had become so strong a voice for the antiwar element that Republicans had bent every effort to defeat him the previous November. Thanks primarily to strategic redistricting, and partly to the nomination of a recently wounded general to challenge him, they had succeeded in unseating the incumbent in an election that otherwise went heavily against Ohio Republicans. In January, 1863, seven weeks before he left Congress and two weeks into the age of emancipation, Vallandigham had outlined his position in a speech that blamed the war on the Massachusetts brand of abolition agitation, rather than on the Southern reaction to that agitation, and he insisted that acceptance of slavery was "the price of the Union." He had believed from the start that the war had been initiated to abolish slavery, he said, "and you of the abolition party have now proved it to the world."[1]

That war had squandered the blood of hundreds of thousands, Vallandigham charged, and had ravaged the precious Constitution. It had pitched a solvent nation into "stupendous" indebtedness, to resolve which the government had imposed a system of new taxes he scorned as "the most onerous and unjust ever imposed upon any but a conquered people." All those lives and liberties had been lost, and all that treasure invested, yet the Confederate flag still flew below the Potomac and Ohio rivers. Better to call an armistice, he suggested, and consider the opposing argument, than to persist in so destructive and futile a war. With time, he predicted, and with appropriate concessions to the right of slaveholding, the South could eventually be won back to the Union. The civil wars of ancient Greece had not prevented their reunion for the repulse of Persian invasion, he noted — "nor did even the thirty years Peloponnesian war, springing, in part, from the abduction of slaves . . . wholly destroy the fellowship of those States."[2]

The perspective of nearly a century and a half seems to illuminate the flaws in Vallandigham's argument, which loses much of its modern appeal through the then-common racial attitude that underlay his patience with slavery. However subsequent generations might have felt about the old Union, it is now clear that the momentum for Southern independence in 1863 precluded a rapprochement within any period that fervent Unionists would have been willing to accept, and (as though corroborating Vallandigham's accusation of abolition motive) the tide of emancipation could not readily be stemmed once the dikes had burst. Those factors proved more difficult to gauge at the time, though, and political adherents aligned themselves with their respective factions more on faith and hope than on any reliable evidence. More tangible, and perhaps more relevant, were the costs of the war that Vallandigham had enumerated, and especially the dangerous precedents of constitutional infringement. Many of those who preached the doctrine of conciliation and compromise doubtless believed fervently that Southerners would respond, but others may have sensed the relative hopelessness of that avenue, at least as an immediate solution; for them, the rhetoric of compromise may merely have disguised a preference for sacrificing the slave states in order to salvage civil liberties in the remaining states.

Since Vallandigham's January speech, the new conscription law had augmented the ranks of the opposition and provoked seething editorial attacks on an administration that began to seem as much of a threat to liberty as the rebels in arms. Such vitriol had, in turn, angered and frightened proponents of the war, many of whom responded with violent rhetoric or action. There surfaced in the newspapers much talk of hanging those who disagreed, while the warnings about military despotism found a measure of justification that spring as mobs of off-duty soldiers attacked Democratic newspapers across the country. The failure to impose more than token punishment on those uniformed malefactors, if they were punished at all, left an indelible impression of official approbation or instigation, bringing still more moderates to the conclusion that the war was eroding the very rights its advocates vowed it would preserve.[3]

The Ohio River watershed saw a greater share of those constitutional infringements than most sections, perhaps because a larger proportion of the population there took a different view of Lincoln's war. Disturbing incidents regularly excited the public imagination, reported with alternating bias by an increasingly polarized press, but the demonstrated zealotry of government officials and their well-documented disregard for constitutional protections lends some credence to many of the more hostile interpretations. It was, perhaps, less important to critical citizens whether government officials had overstepped their authority in individual cases than that federal minions could usually do so with impunity in any instance.

An alleged local revolt to prevent the arrest of a deserter in Noble County, Ohio, was reportedly put down by a battalion of troops with artillery, but conservatives saw it differently: they recognized the "deserter" as a mere paroled prisoner whose anti-emancipation letter had been opened, while the "revolt" had consisted of a nonpartisan delegation of citizens who had confronted the arresting officials to demand fair treatment. The government looked even worse after troops disrupted a criminal proceeding in Clark County, Illinois, and arrested the judge. Two soldiers in the Indianapolis garrison had crossed the state line on the excuse of arresting deserters, leaving their jurisdiction and taking Illinois residents whose status as deserters also seemed uncertain. Judge Charles Constable found probable cause to bind the soldiers over for kidnapping, but an intimidating phalanx of troops from Indianapolis repaired to Clark County and prodded His Honor from the bench at the points of their bayonets — taking him into custody, instead. That example of militaristic insolence elicited the scorn of even the Canadian press.[4]

The author of that last outrage was Henry Carrington, colonel of the 18th U.S. Infantry. He was a rarity among the upper echelons of the Regular Army — a Republican and an abolitionist — and he had won his commission in 1861 through political connections rather than because of any demonstrated competence. He manned a desk in Indianapolis throughout the war, administering his domain as though it were under martial law. He sent alarming accounts of armed uprisings in the rural counties that he claimed to have suppressed with military force, and on the strength of a department order he prohibited the sale of firearms to Indiana citizens. He sent the president such wild, direct reports of a vast treasonous conspiracy that Edwin Stanton thought him imprudent, and warned Ambrose Burnside to look into his ravings as soon as he took over the Department of the Ohio. Henry Halleck was more blunt, warning Burnside that Carrington "has not sufficient judgment and brains to qualify him for the position."[5] In the face of all those administrative misgivings, Carrington still won a promotion to brigadier general of volunteers (after months of lobbying and hinting for a star), and he was given command of the entire district of Indiana, largely because of his presumed familiarity with the alleged disloyal conspiracy.[6]

Military discipline creates habits and expectations of obedience that can soon confuse notions about liberty. That may have been the case with Carrington, and it certainly appeared to be with General Burnside, whose devotion to a forcible restoration of the Union had persuaded him that contrary opinions on that subject amounted to treason. At such distance from democratic principles did Burnside blunder into his General Order No. 38, the final sentences of which prohibited the utterance of "sympathies for the enemy" on pain of exile to the Confederacy or a trial for treason. "Treason expressed or implied will not be tolerated," he warned. Abraham Lincoln had issued a similarly dictatorial proclamation the previous September, announcing his unilateral imposition of a measure of martial law across the entire nation, but it was for Burnside to demonstrate how flagrantly such decrees conflicted with the democratic process.

Vallandigham had already ridiculed Carrington's firearms ban in a speech at the courthouse of Butler County, Ohio. Pointing to the state line a few miles to the west, he reminded his audience that Carrington held authority only over U.S. soldiers within the borders of Indiana. It was the United States Constitution that governed private citizens, he roared, reading from the Second Amendment and Ohio's state constitution, which dealt simultaneously with the right to bear arms and the subordination of military power to civil authority. "Here, sir, are our warrants for keeping and bearing arms," he warned, " . . . and if the men in power undertake in an evil hour to demand them of us, we will return the Spartan answer, 'Come and take them.'"[7] Vallandigham's antiauthoritarian declamation surely found receptive listeners in southern Ohio, for the voters leaned as sharply toward Democratic candidates in the local elections of early April as they had the previous autumn. The state capital at Columbus and Vallandigham's home town of Dayton both chose Democrats for mayor, and Democrats swept every open seat in both cities.

Dayton Democrats celebrated in part by honoring Vallandigham for his contribution to the victory.[8]

Speaking to a great Union rally at the same Butler County seat where Vallandigham had taunted Carrington, Burnside implied that he, himself, held the authority to determine what did and did not constitute treason, and he made haste to enforce his Order No. 38. He ordered a Cincinnati bookseller not to carry Edward Pollard's *First Year of the War* because of the Confederate perspective that it promoted, and his subordinates arrested newspaper editors for publishing remarks too harsh to the administration. Before the close of April a military tribunal in Cincinnati condemned three Kentuckians to death for more serious violations of the order, and the same tribunal sentenced a Butler County man to four months at hard labor for alleged statements interpreted as voicing sympathy with the enemy.[9]

Having enjoyed such success with his denunciation of Carrington, Vallandigham made Burnside and the odious order his next target. The loss of his congressional seat freed him to campaign for other office, and he chose to seek the governor's chair. Democratic newspapers advertised his congressional record, including his speeches against most administration policies, in a volume more than two hundred pages long. A June 11 date for the Democratic state convention had no sooner been chosen than he organized five major appearances in Democratic strongholds between May 6 and June 4, but he began his campaign on April 29 with a three-day tour in the center of the state, excoriating Burnside for Order No. 38 in Somerset and on the steps of the state capitol.[10]

In his headquarters at Cincinnati Burnside soon heard of at least the speech in Columbus. His staff selected two captains from the 115th Ohio, which was doing provost duty in Cincinnati, and sent them to Knox County to record Vallandigham's speech; ten citizens went with them. The two officers left camp in civilian dress, leading some of their men to suspect they had resigned, but they boarded a train for the Democratic meeting at Mount Vernon, Ohio, on the first of May.[11]

Processions of Democrats from the different townships of Knox County started rolling into Mount Vernon shortly after 10:00 A.M. on May Day. U.S. flags alternated with homemade banners depicting butternuts; one warned that "the Copperheads are coming," in apparent parody of a Scottish folk tune called "The Campbells Are Coming." Butternut and Copperhead pins (or Liberty pins, as Democrats preferred to call them) abounded on dresses, lapels, and hats. Some towns accounted for more than eighty wagons, and Democratic observers seeking evidence of broad support estimated a minimum of fifteen thousand spectators. The entire cavalcade of wagons, including one behemoth carrying thirty-four girls to represent the unbroken Union, stretched nearly five miles and required more than two hours to pass in review. Vallandigham arrived on the eight o'clock train from Newark, and the local Democratic Club met him in a body to deter threatened violence; a couple of hours later the club returned for Congressmen George Pendleton and Samuel Cox, another pair of conservative, constitutional Democrats.[12]

The meeting opened in Mount Vernon's public square an hour after noon. Vallandigham spoke first while Burnside's two agents in mufti mingled in the crowd, waiting for the gubernatorial aspirant to say something contrary to the infamous order. They were not disappointed. Vallandigham castigated Burnside's military tribunals for dragging the Butler County man from his home "for an offense not known to our laws," and for consigning the Kentuckians to execution; he scorned such military trials of civilians as violations of the Constitution and "outrageous usurpations of power," adding that he saw no legal authority in Order No. 38 and had no intention of abiding by its strictures. As a free man, he asserted, he had no need to ask the permission of General Burnside to speak. One of the disguised officers scribbled hastily as the candidate gave Burnside one excuse after another to exercise his pretended authority. The other simply listened, and particularly noted the candidate's reference to "this unnecessary and injurious civil war," which he deemed an expression of sympathy with the enemy without recognizing it as a quote from one of President Lincoln's own proclamations. Vallandigham went on for over an hour, citing the Emancipation Proclamation and the Conscription Act as evidence that the war had not been initiated to restore the Union, but rather to suit abolitionists and to create a centralized despotism.[13]

His most damning indictment may have been an unintentionally overdrawn accusation, emanating from New York congressman Fernando Wood's specious interpretation of his correspondence with the president. Wood had written to Lincoln of his communication with allegedly credible men who were in a position to know that the South would return to the fold on condition of an armistice and a general amnesty. On the eve of Fredericksburg Lincoln had replied that he would certainly consider such an offer, but added that he doubted the accuracy of Wood's information; he also declined a cease-fire without more formal confirmation (though he may have rued those words a few days later, after Fredericksburg). Wood twisted that into the rejection of an overture for Southern submission, and so the story ran in Democratic circles. Such misrepresentations and exaggerations helped to darken an opposition view of Lincoln and the war that had already grown sufficiently dim on better evidence.[14]

Cox and Pendleton followed Vallandigham on the platform, holding the crowd rapt until five o'clock, but Vallandigham had to make the

4:00 P.M. train. Three nights later, toward eight o'clock on the evening of May 4, an unfriendly Dayton citizen spied on the house at 323 First Street and satisfied himself that Vallandigham was at home. From there he went straight to the telegraph office and notified General Burnside by a prearranged code that the would-be governor had not yet departed for his May 6 appearance at Norwalk, in the northern fringe of the state. Burnside thereupon sent Captain Charles Hutton to Dayton with scores of soldiers, and Hutton pounded on Vallandigham's door at two-thirty on the morning of May 5, shouting the homeowner's name with emphasis on the third syllable, rather than the second. Vallandigham responded that his name was not "Vallan*dig*ham," but Hutton replied that he cared less for the pronunciation than for the spelling, and demanded his surrender. While his wife and children cowered in another room, the candidate refused to oblige, backing through his house and locking doors until soldiers' boots had kicked them all down and he was cornered. By daybreak they had conveyed him to Cincinnati, where they locked him up in Kemper Barracks.[15]

The faithful of Dayton fairly exploded in fury at what they considered the kidnapping of their spokesman by Lincoln's legions. The *Daily Empire* fumed over the arrest, virtually calling for an uprising in headlines that asked whether free men would submit to such an outrage. "The hour for action has arrived," the editor announced. The *Empire* had earlier advocated the elimination of one Republican newspaper office for every Democratic organ destroyed by pro-administration mobs, and readers must have found such Old Testament justice inviting.[16] In short order a mob of a different persuasion descended on the president's most visible champion in Dayton, the *Daily Journal*, which had published some of the most venomous editorials against the government's latest political prisoner. The *Journal* went up in flames that day as so many Democratic offices had over the past two years, taking the surrounding block with it. A farrier's, a shoe and leather store, a saddlery, a tobacco warehouse, and a stove and tin shop added to the conflagration. Total losses exceeded forty thousand dollars. Incensed Democrats impeded the firemen who came to fight the fire, blocking the way and cutting the hoses they reeled off their wagons. Someone cut the telegraph lines, but word reached Cincinnati without much delay and Burnside sent Captain Hutton back with more troops to quell the riot, as well as to suppress the *Empire;* Hutton's men reportedly killed one citizen as he tried to cut a fire hose. Peace, if not tranquility, had been restored by midnight, but Burnside declared martial law in the city, and Captain Hutton acted as a temporary provost marshal, preventing further publication of the *Empire* on Burnside's order. Hutton arrested the *Empire*'s editor into the bargain, along with a number of other citizens.[17]

Predictably, the public responded to Vallandigham's arrest with contradictory outpourings of jubilation and indignation. Unquestioning supporters of the war welcomed it with expressions of relief and vengefulness, while critics and opponents saw in it the logical conclusion of the government's escalating assault on democracy. Most soldiers seemed to regard Vallandigham as something of a civilian mutineer, as though he owed the same strict obedience to Burnside's orders that was expected of them. An Indiana sergeant who earned extra money by arresting deserters from his Indianapolis camp hailed the arrest as "a good thing," and insisted that everyone "not tainted with treason" agreed with him. An officer with the Army of the Potomac measured his pleasure at the arrest against his fear that the president would not sustain Burnside. An Ohio corporal who claimed he had visited Vallandigham in his Washington hotel room months before suddenly found it important to report that the then-congressman had made numerous incriminating statements about a rebellion in the Northwest and the good it would do the country if President Lincoln were assassinated.[18]

Most Republican newspapers either assumed or implied that Vallandigham's arrest reflected actual evidence of his disloyalty, and relished the news as an opportunity to stigmatize Democrats within their own readership with treasonous innuendo. Democratic editors, on the other hand, even of the sternest pro-Union stripe, generally lambasted Burnside or the administration for doing such violence to the guarantee of free speech and the democratic process. The *Louisville Daily Democrat* abruptly ceased its praise of the new department commander, laying into Burnside without specifically naming him. Noting that it had never much agreed with Vallandigham, the *Detroit Free Press* described indignation and shock "that despotism has made so rapid strides under the republican regime," denouncing every step in his arrest and trial as a further violation of the Constitution. The day after reporting the arrest, the *Free Press* took up William Franklin's version of the Fredericksburg controversy to suggest that Burnside had tried to lie his way out of responsibility when he appeared before the Committee on the Conduct of the War. After the arrest of editors in Dayton and elsewhere, some sheets cloaked their criticism more discreetly, and the owners of the *Cincinnati Enquirer* suffered the additional intimidation of Burnside's personal warning. The *Cleveland Plain Dealer* simply remarked sarcastically, albeit at some length, on the "disloyalty" of editors who dared to question Union "victories" like Hooker's recent affair on the Rappahannock. Indignation meetings sprang up around the country, and most conspicuously in Albany, New York, where a mass meeting yielded resolutions censuring Lincoln for countenancing such highhanded action. Those resolutions were sent to the president on May 19, and foremost among the signatures on the letter that accompanied them was that of Congressman Erastus Corning. Even the Dutch ambassador turned up his nose at the arrest of an opposition candidate during an election campaign, writing home that "all the legal positions and guarantees are openly pushed aside and military dictatorship is recognized."[19]

Burnside's impulsive action, and Lincoln's implicit approbation of it, roused concern among the president's most loyal Republican friends, as well. Lyman Trumbull, the senior senator from Illinois, confessed to his former Senate colleague Orville Browning that he considered military arrests like Vallandigham's "unwarrantable," and thought they were "doing much injury." Like many Democrats, Trumbull feared that the civil system would be superseded by the military intrusions if they were not challenged, and that the government would thereby be "overthrown." Browning, who until recently had been one of Lincoln's firmest allies in the Senate, fully concurred.[20]

Ambrose Burnside saw none of that, and the embers of the Dayton fire had not cooled before the court-martial of civilian Clement Vallandigham began. It met in a room at the St. Charles Exchange, on East Third Street, at 10:00 A.M. on May 6. For judge advocate Burnside chose Captain James Madison Cutts, a young man of good pedigree but lascivious inclinations, who would soon be dismissed from the service for spying through a hotel transom on a married woman as she undressed. Eight officers sat to hear the case: four of them were members of Burnside's personal staff, and all were his dutiful subordinates. As was so often the case in the military tribunals of Lincoln's day, the accused entered the courtroom with little chance of escaping conviction for the allegations against him, even if they did not exist in any statute.[21]

Accused by court president Robert Potter of violating Order No. 38, Vallandigham refused to enter a plea: as he pointed out in an addendum to the trial, a military court had no jurisdiction over a citizen who was not a member of the land or naval forces of the United States, outside the theater of war, in a region not subject to martial law. Constitutional logic found a poor reception under the shadow of the bayonet, however, and Potter ordered a plea of "not guilty." The captains who had spied on the Mount Vernon speech constituted the two principal witnesses, and they described the Democratic rally there in terms that might have excited little comment from any but the most rabid Republican advocates of one-party rule. Apparently unconscious of the irony in prosecuting him for the remark, the first of those provost captains said he heard Vallandigham warn the crowd that the Conscription Act's broad network of provost marshals was intended as a political police force, to control and restrict the people. The second captain repeated Vallandigham's reference to the "unnecessary and injurious civil war," which the defendant explained he had couched in the words of Abraham Lincoln, observing that the president had not seemed to commit a disloyal act when he wrote them. The witness protested that Vallandigham had made the phrase his own, by which he seemed to imply that the loyalty of the statement depended upon who uttered it.[22]

This witness noted Vallandigham's claim that Lincoln had rejected a Confederate offer to return to the Union just before Fredericksburg, and Vallandigham asked for a subpoena to bring Fernando Wood to Cincinnati, with the letter from Lincoln that he believed would prove his claim. Cutts refused the subpoena, perhaps to avoid any embarrassment to the president, but, more likely, to hasten the trial to a conclusion, and in the end he dropped that single specification from the charges.[23]

Congressman Cox took the stand on the second day. Though the court probably viewed him as an ally of the defendant, and therefore not entirely credible, he actually opposed Vallandigham's gubernatorial nomination as an absolute detriment to the state party, and preferred a more moderate candidate. He nonetheless refuted many of the claims made by prosecution witnesses and insisted that the prisoner had advised no violence or resistance to legal authority. Vallandigham said he could produce a hundred or more witnesses who would corroborate Cox's recollection and contradict those of the two officers, and he asked for time to prepare an effective defense, but during a recess, Captain Cutts convinced him of the futility of the attempt. Without further ado the court received Vallandigham's hasty jurisdictional protest and offered the anticipated verdict of guilty on all the remaining specifications. They sentenced him to confinement in a federal facility for the duration of the war.[24]

Two days later Vallandigham submitted a petition for habeas corpus to the federal district court, enumerating the glaring shortcomings in Burnside's claim of jurisdiction and appealing to Judge Humphrey Leavitt for release. The court stalled, allowing Burnside a couple of days to object, and word of the petition reached Washington. To close that avenue of escape Edwin Stanton suggested to the president that he had better suspend the writ in that vicinity. Lincoln evidently considered it, but then he spoke to both Secretary Seward and Secretary Chase. Chase knew Leavitt, and predicted that he would not issue the writ, having refused a similar one before. Lincoln decided to wait, rather than appear to interfere (although he apparently would have interfered, if necessary), and his restraint bore fruit.[25]

Observing that his court had ceased intervening in military arrests, Leavitt opined that the rebellion was no time for the judicial branch to "embarrass or thwart the Executive." In what must be one of the most absurd legal opinions in American history, Leavitt ruled that the legality of Vallandigham's arrest did not depend upon Burnside's jurisdiction or lack thereof, but rather on the "necessity" of making it, and Abraham Lincoln bore the ultimate responsibility for deciding whether it had been necessary. The courts had no right to decide that "a co-ordinate branch of the Government" had acted unconstitutionally, Leavitt believed. The aging jurist revealed his political bias when he added that "there is too much of the pestilential leaven of disloyalty in the community," and that "there should be no division of sentiment" on prosecution of the war. He chastised the petitioner and his attorney for complaining of constitutional violations while they "look with no horror upon a despotism as unmitigated as the world has ever witnessed." Then, acknowledging that he was ignoring the rest of the legal arguments made in the case, he declined to issue the writ. Besides, he noted, even if he did issue it the federal authorities would probably humiliate his court by disobeying it.[26]

That hurdle surmounted, General Burnside chose Fort Warren, in Boston Harbor, as Vallandigham's Bastille. Caught between wishing to support the general whose leadership he had once helped to undermine and his desire to distance himself from the repercussions of Vallandigham's arrest, President Lincoln commuted the prison sentence to exile into the Confederacy. That seemed to condone the arrest and trial, but it afforded Lincoln an air of magnanimity while simultaneously associating Vallandigham with the enemy. Most important of all, perhaps, was the relief it would give from court and citizen petitions for the prisoner's release.[27]

The navy had just bought a sternwheel steamboat at Cincinnati called the *Exchange*, and Burnside asked to borrow it. He put his famous prisoner aboard, but kept him there at the dock for several days while he appealed to Washington, in vain, for reinstatement of the original penalty. On the night of May 21 Vallandigham's guards informed him where he was really going, and a few hours later the boat headed down the Ohio River to Louisville.[28] From there he went by train to the Army of the Cumberland, where he arrived late on Sunday, May 24. Rosecrans's provost marshal met him at the depot and fed him before escorting him five miles below Murfreesboro. At daylight Vallandigham followed his escort to the picket line, where an Alabama colonel demurred from making any formal acceptance of the celebrity. The colonel — who, as it happened, had but six weeks to live — sent back for permission to receive Vallandigham, but could not get it. Finally he agreed that the Union officers could leave their unwelcome guest just inside Confederate lines, where Vallandigham could come forward to present himself like any other citizen. The last the Union provost marshal could hear of the former congressman, he was introducing himself to the Alabama cavalry vidette as a citizen of Ohio and the United States.[29]

Braxton Bragg, commander of the Confederacy's Army of Tennessee, welcomed the outcast and gave him a passport for travel within his military department, but Richmond thought better of that and wanted him sent to the capital. Vallandigham acknowledged his continued allegiance to the United States, and revealed his expectation that he would be the next governor of Ohio. That forced the Confederacy to treat him as an alien enemy, requiring him to leave the South as soon as possible, but that was his wish in any case. Traveling to Virginia by rail, he spoke with Colonel Robert Ould, the Confederate agent for prisoner exchanges. In the course of that interview he supposed aloud that if the Confederacy could hold out for another year (until the 1864 election, presumably), Lincoln would be swept out of office; since Lincoln's election had precipitated secession, he supposed that Lincoln's defeat would offer an opportunity for reunion. That was one of Vallandigham's greater misunderstandings, as Jefferson Davis noted when he read Ould's report, but the Ohioan did offer one piece of wisdom that Davis would have done better to heed. Lee's army was just then on the march northward, his destination unknown even to many in the higher ranks. Vallandigham specifically cautioned against any invasion of Pennsylvania, "for that would unite all parties at the North, and so strengthen Lincoln's hands that he would be able to crush all opposition."[30]

Arrangements were made for Vallandigham to run the blockade through Wilmington, North Carolina, and he arrived at that port in mid-June. A day or two later he boarded a sleek paddlewheel steamer lying in the Cape Fear River, taking passage on it to Bermuda; from there a British vessel carried him to Halifax, on his way to exile in Canada West. Somewhere along the way he learned that the Ohio Democratic Convention had nominated him for governor by acclamation — precisely as he had told Rosecrans's staff officers that they would.[31]

Erastus Corning's May 19 letter to the president, conveying the Albany resolutions denouncing Vallandigham's arrest, provided Lincoln with his best excuse to publicize his version of the incident. Responding a few weeks later, and sending a copy to Horace Greeley's *New York Tribune*,

Lincoln asserted, incorrectly, that Vallandigham was arrested for "laboring, with some effect, to prevent the raising of troops, to encourage desertions from the army, and to leave the rebellion without an adequate military force to suppress it." This misrepresentation of the charges against Vallandigham led Lincoln to one of the more memorable sentences he wrote as president — which, like most memorable political rhetoric, appealed more to sentiment than to logic: "Must I shoot a simple-minded soldier boy who deserts, while I must not touch a hair of a wiley agitator who induces him to desert?" Speeches like Vallandigham's Mount Vernon address might have the effect of convincing a father to advise his soldier boy to desert, Lincoln contended, concluding that it would be more merciful to "silence the agitator, and save the boy."[32]

Lincoln was deliberately obscuring the point. "To say that he is disingenuous," remarked the *Detroit Free Press*, "would be to use a very mild term for a very strong fact." Lincoln failed to address the overriding question of how a democratic society could conduct an election campaign during wartime if challengers were effectively barred from criticizing the policies and actions of the incumbents. He did dispute the argument that wartime abrogation of constitutional guarantees would lead to the deterioration of those rights during peacetime, but he used a biological analogy that might suggest his own error. He claimed that his abrogation of free speech and habeas corpus during the rebellion could not weaken those rights "throughout the indefinite peaceful future," any more than "a man could contract so strong an appetite for emetics while temporarily sick as to persist in feeding upon them through the remainder of his healthful life."[33]

That comparison may have seemed more apt in an age before widespread consciousness about addictive drugs and behavior, but it revealed a telling deficiency in Lincoln's self-education. As well read as the sixteenth president was, he seemed largely unfamiliar with ancient history, and particularly Roman history. Dismissing the concept of a cultivated appetite for repression implied a real or feigned ignorance that increasing Roman tolerance for dictatorship during wartime had translated into peacetime application of illegal military force, which eventually crushed the Roman Republic. A measure of classical instruction might have heightened Lincoln's sensitivity to the dangerous precedents his administration had introduced.[34]

Toward the end of his letter to Corning and the Albany meeting, Lincoln hinted ambiguously that he might not have arrested Vallandigham. "I was pained that there should have seemed to be a necessity for arresting him," he admitted, adding that he would release him the moment he felt it safe to do so. That in turn prompted a visit from a committee of

Ohio's Democratic Convention, which presented a petition demanding the release of its new gubernatorial candidate. Contrary to Lincoln's assertion, the committee pointed out, Vallandigham was not arrested for, nor was he guilty of, discouraging enlistments or encouraging desertion: he had merely criticized the policies of Lincoln's war. If Lincoln's interpretation had been prevalent during the Mexican War (the committee implied), every political opponent of that war would have been subject to exile from the country — including Congressman Abraham Lincoln. Lincoln assiduously disregarded his self-serving mistake about Vallandigham's charges, simply insisting that his (and the committee's) opposition to the use of force against the Confederacy by itself encouraged desertion and draft resistance. He nevertheless indicated that he would consent to readmit Vallandigham if he behaved himself, and if the members of the delegation each signed a pledge to fully support Lincoln's war as well as funding and filling the army and navy that fought it. They unanimously and understandably refused, and the *Detroit Free Press* ridiculed the offer of "the great law breaker" to let the law-abiding Vallandigham return on the condition that he would "not disobey the laws."[35]

Vallandigham's exile gave apparent substance to the cacophony of treasonous accusation mounted by his political enemies. That made it easy in turn to characterize his faction's opposition to the war as antagonism toward the nation's troops, and most of the soldiers fell for that, including many who might have sided with the banished candidate in saner times. Trading jibes with rebel pickets on the outskirts of Vicksburg, an Iowa captain found it telling that his Southern counterparts expressed high regard for Vallandigham, and just when they had finally backed those rebels into a bottle.[36]

The sense of imminent victory that soldiers may have absorbed from their observations at the front took longer now to trickle back to Northern cities and towns. Thanks to repeated premature celebrations fueled by groundless rumors, even the official news of real successes took weeks to gain credence, and months to sink in. To the consternation of troops in the field, Northern church bells had already rung twice that spring for glorious military accomplishments that had never happened: the capture of Richmond had been falsely reported early in May, and a mistaken announcement of the surrender of Vicksburg circulated with amazing speed late in the month. All but the most gullible and eagerly optimistic eventually learned to look askance at introductory accounts of glorious triumphs, and to doubt rosy predictions of impending Confederate collapse.[37]

That spreading skepticism occluded any immediate perception of the promise that attended Ulysses Grant's great risk in the valley of the Mississippi, although it seemed obvious enough to Grant's men — including his perennially pessimistic friend, General Sherman. In three weeks Grant had managed what he had failed to do in three seasons, coming up behind Vicksburg and trapping most of its garrison in the city.[38]

While Grant marched most of his army down the Louisiana side of the river to their crossing below Vicksburg, Ben Grierson's cavalry raid the length of Mississippi lured Confederate attention to the northeast. Most of Lieutenant General John C. Pemberton's cavalry had been transferred from the Vicksburg region to Braxton Bragg, in Tennessee, and Pemberton had sent the rest into northern Mississippi to guard against raids there, so he had to detach infantry to confront Grierson, whose horsemen easily confounded and outdistanced everyone who pursued them on foot. To further confuse and alarm the Vicksburg garrison, Grant left Sherman's corps in the inundated bayou country north of the city, to feign another attack from the Yazoo River. With his other two corps Grant followed a looping course from Milliken's Bend along old, cutoff bends of the Mississippi to New Carthage, some twenty-five miles down the winding river. There he waited while the navy brought down gunboats, steamers, and barges to transport his infantry to the Mississippi shore. The flotilla that ran Vicksburg's batteries seemed too small to transfer the troops quickly enough, or to protect them during the passage, so Grant leap-frogged his men another couple of dozen miles downstream, where he could put the Big Black River between his crossing and the main body of Pemberton's troops.[39]

The name of the second rendezvous, Hard Times Landing, did not bode well for an army facing the broadest river on the continent, with sixty miles of treacherous road winding back to its last supply base, but General Grant took no stock in omens. Opposite Hard Times stood Grand Gulf, Mississippi, on another of those towering bluffs, which Confederate brigadier John Bowen held with a couple of brigades of infantry and dismounted cavalry from Arkansas and Missouri. Union gunboats bombarded the heights on April 29, but could not elevate the muzzles of their guns high enough to drive Bowen away, so Grant again slid downstream a few miles to Bruinsburg. There, on April 30, he crossed several divisions without resistance, flushing Bowen out of his works at Grand Gulf. Bowen marched down and put up a fierce fight between the river and Port Gibson, calling for reinforcements that Pemberton had held back in fear of Sherman's diversion, but after two additional brigades of worn-out infantry reached him, Bowen still had only seven thousand muskets to confront thirty thousand Yankees.[40]

Water and marsh had covered most of the terrain Grant's men encountered north of the Yazoo and in Louisiana, but below Vicksburg the Mississippi side consisted of a succession of deep ravines choked with underbrush and canes, where the roads ran along the spines of intervening ridges with only the occasional river or bayou to stymie the infantry. The Iowans skirmishing in Grant's advance quickly learned that anything but a head-on lunge at rebel roadblocks required considerable thrashing about in the underbrush on one side of the highway or the other. Thanks partly to the geography, Bowen's few thousand Confederates managed to hold the Yankees out of Port Gibson from just after midnight on May 1 until after dark that evening. Burning bridges as they fell back, including a sizable suspension bridge that caused their pursuers appreciable delay, they retreated first to Grand Gulf and then across the Big Black toward Vicksburg. Pursuing Federals eased into Port Gibson at daylight of May 2, just as Stonewall Jackson started his last flank march, a thousand miles away.[41]

The Confederate rear guard had left its dead behind, and a Norwegian lad with Grant's leading brigade told his family in the old language that some of the bodies were those of Negroes who had, he supposed, been persuaded to fight for their own slavery. This was the boy's first battle, and he may not yet have understood that the intense heat could darken dead flesh, or perhaps he had seen some swarthy Creoles from the 17th Louisiana who had died covering the Confederate retreat; this particular young man had enlisted more for the bounty than from any moral imperative, but even an errant rumor that slaves were taking up arms for their masters could not have pleased men whose labor and sacrifices had been bent toward emancipation by executive fiat.[42]

When the guns opened on Grand Gulf, Sherman dutifully made his way back to the bluffs above Vicksburg, where he had first struck against the city five months before. With gunboats he blazed away at the fortified heights, then pulled back and conspicuously unloaded his infantry from the steamboats while the outnumbered Confederates watched nervously. After dark he boarded most of the troops back onto the steamers, leaving a heavy skirmish line, but the next day he resumed the charade of preparing for an attack, renewing the bombardment for a few hours. That evening, having detained enough of the Vicksburg garrison to ease Grant's way at Port Gibson, he ordered the flotilla back to Milliken's Bend, whence Grant instructed him to hurry down the roundabout road to Hard Times Landing. All had gone well except the spontaneous and rather spectacular desertion of a soldier from one of the western regiments, who bolted from Union lines on horseback and galloped for the skirmish line of the 3rd Louisiana, cheering for "Old Kentucky" and returning the fire of his own pickets with a revolver. He was the only one of Sherman's men who stayed behind, sharing all he knew about Federal dispositions with the curious rebels who gathered around him.[43]

Grant had hoped to cooperate with Nathaniel Banks from Grand Gulf, suggesting the loan of a corps to reduce Port Hudson, after which they could turn back on Vicksburg together, but his coded mid-April message on that scheme had gone astray. By then Banks had undertaken a campaign to the Red River by way of Opelousas, through bayou country infested with alligators and enormous swamp serpents, where the water was too dark and dirty for bathing (though the general cavorted naked on the bank of one bayou for a time, trying to screw up the courage to immerse himself). Banks very much wished to join Grant, but not until he reached Alexandria, on May 8, did he learn of Grant's specific offer. Grant's message bore no date, though, and when he referred to sending Banks a corps by "the 25th," Banks assumed he meant May 25, rather than April 25. He agreed immediately to the proposal, and replied that he could reach the Mississippi above Port Hudson by that date, but during the three-week lapse Grant had crossed the Mississippi and started for the interior with his entire force. Under those new circumstances he asked Banks to bring his whole army up to join him against Vicksburg, but Banks lacked the steamboats to transfer his field force so far, and he feared leaving the Port Hudson garrison behind him with a clear road to recapture New Orleans. He replied that his best course would be to attack Port Hudson first and try to subdue the place.[44]

The lag in communication time between Banks and Grant precipitated much confusion that caused each general to suspect the other of a disabling impetuosity or territorial jealousy. Privately, at least, the commander at Memphis lambasted both Banks and Rosecrans for failing to aid Grant directly. Unfortunately for Banks, and later for Rosecrans, Grant was being shadowed by Charles Dana, a War Department observer who had quickly grown to admire Grant and took the general's side in most of his quarrels. Dana's reports went directly to Edwin Stanton, through whom their color influenced the reactions of General Halleck and the perceptions of President Lincoln.[45]

Grant's most frequent squabbles involved the next-ranking major general in his department — John McClernand. This political general had raised a good many of the troops in Grant's army, and he had shown some martial promise in early battles where Grant himself had erred notably. The repeated failures against Vicksburg had spawned concern about Grant's real capacity (thus Dana's presence), and the newspapers hinted so frequently at Grant's removal that General Sherman expected it, and that would have put McClernand in command. McClernand was therefore Grant's most prominent competitor when, less than a hundred hours into the fighting part of the campaign, Grant began remarking at headquarters that McClernand's "exceeding incompetence" had prevented him from capturing Bowen's entire force. Dana conveyed that observation to Stanton, who immediately wired back that Grant had the authority to relieve anyone who impeded his progress, and that he was expected to exercise that authority.[46]

By the time Banks decided to turn on Port Hudson, Grant had left the Mississippi behind and was working his whole army between Vicksburg and the state capital in Jackson, forcing Pemberton to scatter his forces to protect both places. Pemberton favored Vicksburg, and Grant followed the path of least resistance to the northeast, gleaning provisions from the countryside. Sherman had brought over ten dozen wagons that carried only basic rations and ammunition, while not even the field officers were allowed tents or personal baggage. All the way from the riverbank the troops had foraged indiscriminately from both livestock and crops ("we made chickens and mutton suffer," boasted an Iowan), but they had also plundered anything of value and burned or broke whatever they could not steal. Sheer envy at the riches accumulated by slave labor may have fueled some of the most senseless damage, as soldiers who hailed from modest or marginal homesteads encountered single plantations that matched the size and extent of their Northern villages. General Sherman himself shuddered at the wreckage of the first home he encountered, blaming it on the army's stragglers: he condoned the confiscation of anything needed to sustain the army, and admitted that he winked at the consumption of fence rails in campfires, but he complained to his wife that "this universal burning and wanton destruction of private property is not justifiable in war."[47]

The cornucopia of southern Mississippi spared the enlisted men from General Sherman's anxiety over provisions: as long as they kept moving, they could eat well. Victory seemed certain within days, they believed, and they appeared to credit Grant for it. In his last letter home, a few days before he was killed, a Wisconsin soldier described his weary division being called out of camp to cheer the commanding general as his entourage passed, but he said they followed the order "with a will." Grant's aversion to pompous display helped to win a touch of affection from his men, so many of whom had not come very far from their humble roots. He shunned braid, sword, and shoulder straps, and a Minnesota artilleryman who saw him nearly every day noted that Grant wore "an old hat that looks like he had slept on it all night." Westerners appreciated superiors

who put on no airs, and in the suffocating Mississippi heat, without tents
or toiletries, even those officers who cherished pretension could not easily
have cultivated it.[48]

Once Sherman came up, the army did keep moving, rolling through a
land redolent with blooming magnolias and plump, ripe fruit. Grant followed the old Natchez Trace across Hinds County, keeping his corps in
separate columns so as to glean as much of the countryside's bounty as
possible while preserving an assortment of strategic options. The Vicksburg & Jackson Railroad invited an attack, as Vicksburg's most direct
supply route, but Jackson itself now posed some danger. Several thousand
Southern reinforcements were gathering there, and Joseph Johnston, the
Confederacy's second-ranking field general, was coming to take charge.
As commander of everything between the Kentucky line and the Gulf of
Mexico he had the authority to bring in reinforcements from Bragg's
army and Mobile, but few enough could be spared from those points. A
small brigade started all the way from Charleston, on loan from P. G. T.
Beauregard, and another would soon follow, but when Johnston reached
Jackson he would have only six thousand troops. It did not help his management of the situation that Jefferson Davis had implied to Pemberton
that he should hold Vicksburg come what may, while Johnston was willing to sacrifice the city to save Pemberton's army.[49]

After calling up two brigades from Port Hudson, Pemberton might
have tallied forty thousand men within his jurisdiction. He waited behind the line of the Big Black River with three-quarters of them, keeping smaller detachments to the east, near Jackson, and it was those
smaller detachments that faced a sizable portion of Grant's fifty-five thousand troops at Raymond on May 12. A single brigade of Tennessee and
Texas infantry tried to bar the passage of James McPherson's corps, but
McPherson threw John Logan's division at them, amounting to twice
their number in mostly Illinois and Ohio regiments. After fighting for
most of the day, the Confederates fell back toward Clinton and Jackson.
Grant followed, intent on seizing the third Confederate state capital.[50]

McPherson's and Sherman's corps pushed on from Raymond early on
May 13, finding the enemy frenetically fortifying the roads into the city.
Pemberton came out from behind the Big Black with all the men he dared
to pull out of his entrenchments — fewer than seventeen thousand — and
started eastward along the railroad. First he hoped to find a secure position where he could force Grant to attack him, but then McPherson
appeared outside Clinton, just eight miles from the state capitol, and
Johnston urged Pemberton to strike him from the rear. Pemberton timor-
ously moved to obey (after the attempt turned to disaster he insisted it

had been against his better judgment), but Clinton was twenty-five miles away and Pemberton had not covered half the distance before Johnston's little force had to evacuate Jackson and leave it to the Yankees. The victors swept into town, stayed overnight, and in the morning promptly put the torch to every building for which there might be a military use, besides some for which no such use could be imagined. They tore up miles of track on the four railroads that converged in Jackson, firing the ties in pyres with the rails piled on top, to warp them against convenient reassembly. They burned all the city's numerous industries, iron foundries, and warehouses, a cotton factory, the railroad bridges, the main hotel, and the Catholic church, along with the rectory. Then they looted all the stores and private homes, again spitefully destroying whatever they could not carry or consume. Disappointed comrades, who gleaned no plunder because they had spent their entire sojourn in Jackson wrecking railroads, satisfied themselves with rifling the town of Clinton when the army turned back toward Vicksburg.[51]

No shirking stragglers sacked Jackson, despite General Sherman's wishful assumptions: these were main-line troops, present with their regiments or within range of the provost marshal. A British army officer, touring the South as a nominally impartial observer, found Jackson "a miserable wreck," and he evidently absorbed some of the Mississippians' contempt for Northern vandals, as well as for generals who would allow such demoralizing conduct. Disturbed even by a sanitized report of the looting, Sherman sent word back for his rear-guard commander to put a stop to it, but lower-level officers cast a blind eye on the thievery.[52]

Learning that Pemberton was coming from Vicksburg, Grant turned his entire army in that direction. A few miles short of the Big Black River he ran up against Pemberton, who was still trying to reach Johnston for a concerted attack on the invaders. With his back against Baker's Creek, Pemberton braced his three outnumbered divisions on a strong ridge across the Clinton and Raymond roads, anchoring his left flank on a prominent hill dominated by the plantation of the Champion family. Two successive Union divisions bent Pemberton's left backward, away from Champion's Hill; John Bowen's Missouri and Arkansas brigades counterattacked and recovered much of the lost ground, but a third Union division blunted Bowen's charge. Under heavy fire Pemberton's left started melting away as men drifted, and then trotted, toward the rear. A rearguard stand that cost the life of a brigadier allowed two of the Confederate divisions to retreat across Baker's Creek, but the third division could only get away by abandoning all its artillery and dashing cross-country to the south: Pemberton would never see that division again. The next day he made another stand at the Big Black River bridge, but the beating at Champion's Hill had discouraged his troops and many of them bolted away, leaving most of the rest of his field artillery behind. An engineer officer set the river's massive railroad and wagon bridges afire to buy more time while Pemberton's shaken and shrunken army scurried pell-mell toward the imposing defenses of Vicksburg.[53]

Grant gathered in well over two thousand prisoners at Champion's Hill, and many hundreds more at the Big Black. Among them marched a young man who represented an unexpected and little-known source of manpower for the Confederate armies. William B. Spoor, a dark, stocky private in the 2nd Missouri Infantry, had fought the Yankees at Pea Ridge, Corinth, Port Gibson, and now Champion's Hill — all losing battles, but he remained as fiercely defiant a rebel as he had been when he enlisted on the Missouri prairie in 1861. He scorned Northern freedom as hoax and hypocrisy, citing the repression of Vallandigham and other dissenters, while examples like the rapine at Jackson had fixed his impression of Union soldiers as ruthless vandals. Seven months would he spend in a Northern prison, and when he was exchanged he would go straight back to his regiment for more, and be captured again the next summer. Not until the war had clearly ended did he abandon the Southern cause.[54] Yet Spoor was a Yankee himself, born and raised in a farm community that straddled the Canadian border. In his mid-teens he had gone west while his family remained just inside Vermont, and when he arrived at his Maryland prison camp he learned that two of his younger brothers had come to Washington as bounty-rich recruits with a heavy-artillery regiment. He wrote to one of them asking for the loan of some U.S. currency, so he could buy vegetables, but the brother advised him instead to accept the "protection" of the federal government. Spoor wanted no part of such a government, spurning both the suggestion and the brother who had made it.[55]

Northerners of a conservative bent did not need to live long in the South to develop Southern sentiments, nor did they necessarily have to share the Confederate view of slavery. This seemed particularly true in border states like Maryland and Missouri, where Union military forces had preemptively overpowered the legitimate state governments in 1861, and Missouri had attracted the greater number of Easterners. All the emigrant males from one New Hampshire family quickly joined Missouri units aligned with the Confederate army, and one of them raised his own mounted company for guerrilla service. The Missouri regiments retreating into Vicksburg took with them a Pennsylvania native who had been educated at Yale and at Amherst College, in Massachusetts; his teaching career had included long sojourns in Illinois and Minnesota, but a few years' residence in Missouri had secured his loyalty to that state, and when the federal government declared war on Missouri he had marched south.[56]

Sometimes marital connections or mere political sympathy persuaded Northern citizens to cast their lots with the Confederacy. The hospital steward of the 6th Texas Cavalry came from Indiana. Two of John Pemberton's generals had been born in Indiana and New York, while Pemberton himself had been appointed to West Point from his native Pennsylvania. His Northern birth had created an epidemic of mistrust among his troops and the population within his military department, but Pemberton's competence should have sparked more doubt than his faithfulness to the cause. He and his subordinates had labored against superior forces in each of the battles of May, but by dint of nerve and ingenuity Robert E. Lee had achieved spectacular success in Virginia against worse overall odds, bluffing boldly in order to bring heavier battalions to critical contests. It was Ulysses Grant's good fortune to meet lesser generals than Lee through most of the war, and he encountered few of lower caliber than Pemberton.[57]

Grant's engineers quickly rebuilt the Black River bridge. By May 18 he had reached the outskirts of Vicksburg, where those deep ravines and steep ridges again dominated the landscape, and his three corps sealed off all escape. The next day Grant hurled Sherman's men against a fortified salient three miles northeast of the city. The defenders easily threw that hasty assault back, as they did a more ambitious three-pronged attack launched along the eastern perimeter in the enervating heat of May 22. Those two attempts cost Grant forty-five hundred men without any gain at all, so with his supply line once again secure to the Mississippi, he settled in for a siege, ringing Vicksburg with an eight-mile cordon of infantry and artillery.[58] Men on both sides dug like gophers all night long, every night, while Union mortar boats lobbed shells into the town. Rolling cotton bales or thickly woven bundles of saplings ahead of them as they extended their entrenchments, Union sappers could hear Vicksburg's women screaming after some of the explosions.[59]

Grant's men wearied quickly of spending every other day and night in the trenches, but with up to a third of their number down sick the Confederates had no relief at all from their own trenches. Less than ten days into the siege, discouraged rebels started slipping out to give themselves up, bringing stories of starvation rations and obstinate officers holding mutinous troops to their duty. In contrast there were those nighttime conversations between Iowa pickets and ferociously rebellious Northern-born

Confederates who swore they would fight until "hell froze over," but Joe Johnston caused the only real concern in the siege lines, gathering a relief force of thousands from all over Dixie.[60]

In unwitting exchange for some wonderful strategic opportunities, Nathaniel Banks helped to rob Johnston of part of his relief expedition. General Pemberton had scavenged Port Hudson for reinforcements, most of which ultimately made their way to Johnston instead, and as soon as Grant invested Vicksburg, Johnston called on the entire garrison to abandon Port Hudson and join him. Major General Franklin Gardner, yet another native of New York, still commanded six thousand Confederates inside Port Hudson, and six thousand reinforcements might have improved Johnston's capacity (and inclination) for aggressive action: given Grant's recent losses, Johnston and Pemberton together might soon equal him in numbers, if they could act in concert to harry him front and rear. While Johnston called for Gardner, Henry Halleck wired repeatedly from Washington for Banks to join Grant, mentioning for the sake of incentive that as the senior major general Banks would have command of the combined armies. Through a coincidence triggered by his slow and muddled communications with Grant, though, Banks was approaching Port Hudson with most of his army from above, via the Red River and the Mississippi, and with another column from below. The upriver column appeared outside Port Hudson on May 24, and the downriver contingent on May 25, closing off all Gardner's contact with the outside. As it happened, the courier with Johnston's last message to Gardner reached Port Hudson that same day, only to find every road to the garrison blocked by the enemy.[61]

Had Banks agreed to join Grant, Gardner would have been able to comply with Johnston's orders. Then both the armies at Port Hudson would have joined those contending for Vicksburg, and the Union advantage in numbers would have risen dramatically. The lower of the twin citadels would have fallen without a fight, and Grant — or rather Banks — would have had all the troops he needed without depleting other theaters of operation. In the absence of river transportation, that would have meant a long march overland for Banks, feeding his army off the land without even the few days' regular rations Grant had embarked with, but Gardner would have had to do the same. If Banks and his converging force from Baton Rouge had encountered only a couple of days' delay, Gardner would have escaped and no siege would have been necessary at Port Hudson.

Banks hoped to take the bastion by storm, and he wasted no time planning the assault. The ground equaled that of Vicksburg in difficulty, with deep ravines and tangles of felled trees lying under the muzzles of the

Confederate guns, but Banks arranged a coordinated attack that might have succeeded against the understrength garrison if only his division commanders had heeded his warning to act together. Musicians exchanged their instruments for hospital litters while batteries crept into position for an all-out assault on the morning of May 27, and volunteers spent the evening bundling cane stalks into fascines, which they would pile together in the ditches under the enemy parapets, to give the infantry a direct footbridge. More than one Union soldier spent the final hours of May 26 in nostalgic conversation with old comrades and antebellum friends, parting at last with long handshakes and meaningful glances into eyes that would never see another sunset.[62]

Before 6:00 A.M. on Wednesday, May 27, several brigades started through the snarl of impediments toward the north face of the fortifications. Under a shower of shells they drove in the Confederate skirmishers and closed in on their earthworks, but canister and musketry stemmed their momentum and drove them back to an adjacent hill. The divisions east and south of Port Hudson failed to support that vigorous thrust, and at noon Banks finally rode up to see what had happened to them. He found Brigadier General Thomas Sherman and his staff relaxing at their noon meal, with their horses unsaddled, and in a fury he relieved Sherman of command, replacing him with his chief of staff. Instead of calling the attack off as a lost cause, Banks sent the tardy divisions in at midafternoon, asking the battered troops on the north to resume their assault as well. Sherman saddled up and went in with his troops anyway, putting himself and his staff into the thickest of the fire by way of redeeming himself: he lost a leg, buying enough sympathy from Banks that his removal from command never made it into the official reports, but it all came to nothing. The Confederates shifted weight to meet each of the assaults, and the day ended in bloody defeat, with two Union generals and three colonels wounded and three colonels killed.[63]

The wounded came pouring into Baton Rouge at the rate of hundreds a day for several days. Litter bearers brought in all who had not ventured too near those blazing cannon, but those nearest the enemy works lay under fire throughout the night and into the next day. After their wounds had been dressed at the field hospitals, they started south in carts and wagons padded with confiscated cotton, lumbering along for eight miles before boarding steamers for the eighteen-mile journey to Baton Rouge. The injuries reflected every type of projectile, from a half-pound iron grapeshot that plowed through the shoulder of a Connecticut major to the bullets that shattered General Sherman's shin and punctured the arch of his aide's foot. A slab of shell sliced through the thigh of a man in the 8th

New Hampshire, leaving the leg looking like "a piece of beef steak" after attendants had washed it. A field surgeon resected Sherman's tibia and sewed up the gaping holes on either side of it, but infection later dictated amputation. Gangrene killed a fair crop of the wounded (including the 8th New Hampshire private), and, in some of the more serious amputations, too strong an application of ether left the patient dead on the operating table.[64]

Banks's sick list began to grow, too, as the grisly sights and terrifying sounds of the battle suddenly aggravated the endemic fevers. The 28th Connecticut had just arrived at Port Hudson from Pensacola the evening preceding the fight — timid, tender, and only ninety days away from discharge. The lieutenant colonel of the regiment, Wheelock Batcheller, began to feel ill at a distance of three miles from Port Hudson, and two hours before the assault was to begin he instructed a lieutenant of his old company to help him "get out of this." Batcheller climbed into an ambulance and rode down to the hospital, where he watched the bombardment while the lieutenant prepared a cotton-covered pallet for him in a slave cabin. He recovered briefly the next morning, but his health appeared to fluctuate all through June, and he drifted in and out of the hospital. At times he was the only sick man in his regiment, but he began to perk up toward the end of the siege, and when the Confederates marched out to surrender he finally felt well enough to leave the hospital and come up to watch the ceremony.[65]

Such delicate, discriminating soldiers posed a liability that Grant escaped. When Banks later saw the Union troops who had encircled Vicksburg, he envied their commander, whose men were obviously all "fierce-fighting" Westerners "in for work and in for the war." In a letter to his wife Banks grumbled that more than half of his own army at Port Hudson had consisted of inexperienced nine-month patriots who were, he knew, "determined not to run into danger." The extreme caution of the nine-month militia revealed itself most when Banks called for 1,000 volunteers for a storming party to lead the next assault. Whole platoons and companies stepped forward from most of the depleted three-year regiments for what they casually called a forlorn hope: 14 officers and 139 men came from the 13th Connecticut alone. Banks's four nine-month regiments from Connecticut, representing well over 2,000 men fit for duty, supplied the storming party with 2 lieutenants, a sergeant major, and 1 lone private. Six of the other big militia regiments engaged in the siege each contributed an average of fewer than 13 volunteers; five more produced 1 or 2 apiece, and six yielded none at all. As their terms drew to an end whole regiments of them started shirking duties that involved any potential for peril, and the 4th Massachusetts fell into open mutiny. One of Banks's division commanders asked for the summary dismissal of Colonel John Kingman, of the nine-month 15th New Hampshire, whom he accused of hiding in a ravine during the last assault on Gardner's works.[66]

Two three-year regiments volunteered to a man for that storming party, though their officers selected only a few score of their most reliable men. The 1st and 3rd Louisiana Native Guards, composed of free black enlisted men with some black officers and some white, had taken the extreme right of the May 27 attack. These regiments had originally been organized for militia service under the state government early in Louisiana's Confederate era, but the more color-conscious Confederate authorities had found the idea of black or mixed-race soldiers too repugnant to accept. In many cases the Native Guardsmen were property owners themselves (and even slave owners), and they showed as much willingness to defend their state under Union auspices as under Confederate. There had been some minor skirmishes beforehand, but May 27 marked the first pitched battle for black soldiers in this war, and those for and against the arming of freedmen had anxiously awaited the outcome of their inaugural trial. If the Native Guards left any official reports of their maiden engagement, they were never published, but word quickly circulated that they had conducted themselves surprisingly well before impregnable battlements. Despite his own conservative twist, General Banks described their conduct as exemplary. Good officers and careful discipline would make them "excellent soldiers," he predicted.[67]

The Westerners holding office in the national capital accorded the Mississippi River more strategic importance than it may have merited. As Vicksburg and Port Hudson went under siege, Attorney General Edward Bates assured the secretary of the navy that "this huge rebellion must, of necessity, live or die, triumph or be suppressed, in the Mississippi River." Abraham Lincoln felt much the same as Bates: for all the two men's adult lives, rivers had been the main corridors of commerce, and for their region of the nation, that commerce had culminated in the valley of the Mississippi. In the decade previous to the war, railroads had made tremendous inroads on that river traffic, finally shuttling as much or more of the prairie's produce east as the steamboats carried south, but the most astute politicians required years of such statistics to overturn their decades of observation and experience.[68]

The executive preoccupation with the river war easily filtered down to the general in chief, Henry Halleck, who had once commanded in that theater but whose ignorance of the communications lag and the complexities of Louisiana logistics left him baffled over Banks's failure to join Grant. Charles Dana aggravated Washington's annoyance with Banks when he telegraphed that Banks had declined to cooperate with Grant and had instead asked for reinforcements from the Vicksburg army. That brought President Lincoln to the wire, asking Grant where Banks was and where he seemed to be moving, and in the shadow of the president's displeasure Halleck defensively insisted that he had sent Banks "dispatch after dispatch" to join Grant, who was growing increasingly nervous about the troops Joe Johnston was collecting behind him. Finally Halleck gave up on Banks and appealed to two other department commanders, stripping their forces to assure Grant's success.[69]

From the Department of Missouri, Major General John Schofield sent Grant eight infantry regiments and three batteries of artillery, which he admitted left him "very weak," but so vital did the capture of Vicksburg seem to him that he offered to lend even more troops to the effort. Ambrose Burnside consented to supply thousands of his own troops, if necessary, but it could only be done at the cost of great disappointment. At General Halleck's own suggestion, Burnside had arranged his forces in Kentucky to cooperate with William Rosecrans by invading east Tennessee — an endeavor long cherished by the president — and Andrew Johnson had been lobbying Lincoln to let Burnside have the missing division of his Ninth Corps for that purpose. Burnside's army stood ready to march, and the order to reinforce Grant arrived at Cincinnati the night before Burnside intended to take the field himself. He replied that he could send eight thousand men or more if he abandoned the east Tennessee campaign altogether, concentrated his remaining troops, and went on the defensive throughout his department. Halleck, who had advised Burnside two weeks before that the best way to draw Johnston off Grant was to strike toward east Tennessee, now contradicted himself by telling Burnside to give up that mission and send the troops directly to Grant.[70]

Deep in Kentucky, five brigades of the Ninth Corps had stripped down for the long march over the mountains into Tennessee. Extra clothing had been sent away, quartermasters had whittled down the wagon trains, and, like Hooker's troops before Chancellorsville, the men had been cautioned to leave enough room in their knapsacks for five days' additional rations. They expected to move south, and it came as a surprise on the evening of June 3 when they started north instead, making a forced march late into the night under the bright glow of a moon just beginning to wane. After four hours of sleep, they leaned into the dusty roads again, reaching Nicholasville eleven hours later, and that night the leading regiments began crawling into freight cars that unloaded them on the banks of the Ohio at Covington. Ferries transferred the two divisions over to Cincinnati, where they packed into more boxcars, fifty to the car, and pulled out the next evening for Cairo.[71]

At Cairo — characterized by a passing Pennsylvanian as "the city of mud" — the Ninth Corps boarded a flotilla of steamboats for Memphis. Some of the wayfarers found time for a swim in the river, or to pull some fresh catfish out of it for dinner, but by the evening of June 8 the transports *Imperial, Express, Alice Dean, General Anderson,* and *Armada* began carrying away a regiment or two at a time; the last of them left the wharf by the evening of June 11. Commissioned officers took passage in the staterooms, but the enlisted men had to squeeze together on the rough decks that usually bore freight, fuel, and livestock; most rode on the hurricane deck, without protection from the rain, which began on June 9. The common troops were allowed into the dining halls in shifts once or twice a day, and they suffered their restrictions with the resignation of men habituated to privation, but ten dozen independent teamsters turned raucous on one boat, taking over the dining room and refusing to yield to a demanding contingent of would-be aristocrats in shoulder straps.[72]

From Memphis some gunboats took them under escort. Below the Tennessee line they began to pick out the charred chimneys of plantations standing along the riverbanks, marking the scene of Yankee retribution for guerrillas who had fired on earlier boats. Bales of hay and cotton surrounded the pilothouses of the steamers, and sometimes boiler iron, providing a breastwork against sharpshooters ashore; the *Armada* did hear a shot fired below the Arkansas River, but no one was hit. On June 14 they passed Milliken's Bend — where, with the help of Union gunboats, a little brigade of black Union recruits had driven away a rebel raid the week before, crossing bayonets with veteran Southern troops and crushing skulls with musket butts in a fight where neither side gave any quarter. The Ninth Corps finally disembarked a few miles below Milliken's Bend at Young's Point, within sight of fabled Vicksburg. Musketry and artillery rumbled portentously in the distance.[73]

The cantonment of black troops at Milliken's Bend had spawned a camp of contrabands at Young's Point that was populated mostly by women, old men, and children. They lived under rough canopies framed with sticks and sheathed in brush, eating well enough on government rations but clothed in rags. Curious Ninth Corps officers strolled among the refugees, and a Massachusetts captain stopped to talk with a nursing mother whose age he guessed as sixteen. She told him that her husband had been "pressed" into one of the Negro regiments, but she seemed indifferent to his fate; she might simply "find" another husband, she told the captain, although she specifically wished to avoid having more children. The captain also met a black soldier wounded in the fight at Milliken's Bend, whose dislike of combat was exceeded only by his hatred of slavery.[74]

A few more black recruits had established themselves nearby. Now and then white soldiers prowled their way to cause trouble, ridiculing the fugitives' efforts to drill or committing petty assaults that inflicted more humiliation than injury. The victims, who had been conditioned to recognize the striking of a white person as a capital offense, took the abuse with a patience that amazed witnesses. These were the first former slaves the veterans of the Ninth Corps had ever seen in uniform, and even the more bigoted of them began to speculate on the salary and benefits of obtaining a commission among the black troops. Sergeant George Upton, a conservative Democrat who had ranted wrathfully about being tricked into "fighting for the Niggers," had not spent a week in Mississippi before he considered applying for promotion in what he more moderately referred to now as a "colored" regiment.[75]

Grant ultimately sent the Ninth Corps up the Yazoo River, to Snyder's and Haines's bluffs, ten miles above Vicksburg. The Westerners in Grant's army sneered and harrumphed at them in a way that suggested they were neither welcome nor needed, but reports that Johnston had a sizable army behind him left Grant himself feeling more than a little vulnerable. In the most intense heat most of them had ever endured (they all came from New England, New York, Pennsylvania, and Michigan), Burnside's troops took up shovels and began digging earthworks facing to the east. Blackberries and wild plums abounded, and the landscape still blazed with magnolia blossoms and wildflowers, but the newcomers found the countryside inhospitable. Their camps teemed with lizards and four-foot rattlesnakes, while mosquitoes tormented them day and night. Except for a few springs, the water ran slow and stagnant. A week of drinking Mississippi River water on the steamers was starting to take its toll, and soldiers began stumbling in to the surgeon's call each morning, feeble and feverish. "If they keep us here long," worried a middle-aged man from the New Hampshire hills, "we shall die off by scores."[76]

Ambrose Burnside did not accompany his old corps to Mississippi. He specifically asked to go, pointing out that the transfer of the corps and the derangement of his plans left him with nothing to do, but Halleck thought it would be absurd for him to leave his department to a subordinate and go on campaign with less than a quarter of his troops. Burnside sent his chief of staff, John Parke, to command the two divisions.[77]

Burnside's enthusiasm for the battlefield, either in east Tennessee or in Mississippi, probably emanated from the dissatisfaction he had caused over the past month by way of injudicious administrative decisions. First there had been the arrest of Clement Vallandigham — which, because of his status as a campaigning candidate of the opposition party, had saddled the administration with a more maliciously partisan image than any arbitrary arrest the government had previously effected. Burnside had then aggravated that indiscretion by subjecting Vallandigham to trial by a biased military court that clearly lacked jurisdiction. These actions had merely imitated previous government infringements and threats, all of which seemed acceptable to someone like Burnside, who advocated abject nonpartisan loyalty to the central government in its hour of crisis. Subservience to the administration could hardly be viewed as nonpartisan, however, when the means of enforcing that loyalty posed the fundamental points of disagreement between the parties, and Burnside's repressive action against Vallandigham provoked an outcry that he met with still more repression. On the first of June, one week after Union officers carried out Lincoln's order to exile Vallandigham, Burnside issued Order No. 84, which included another arbitrary edict banning the *New York World* from his department and shutting down the stridently anti-administration *Chicago Times* altogether for "repeated expression of disloyal and incendiary statements."[78]

Warned of the impending suppression, *Times* pressmen locked up their forms and started their press at three o'clock in the morning, running off several thousand copies and sending them out as soon as they came off the folder. When two companies of the 65th Illinois burst into the office, they found only a few hundred copies, which they destroyed before sealing the building off with guard details.[79]

The Lincoln administration had trod on the First Amendment before, usually by refusing dissident newspapers access to the mail. So popular was the post office as a means of circulation that this partisan manipulation of a federal service served as a most effective muzzle: early in the war Postmaster General Montgomery Blair had forced New York newspapers to either change their editorial stance or close up shop. Administration officials had locked up conservative editors on numerous occasions, and had sat by in implied approbation when Unionist mobs demolished the print shops of opposition papers. Field commanders had forcibly closed the offices of critical newspapers before, as well, but the *Times* was the most widely read newspaper in the West, and Burnside's presumptuous order ignited a firestorm of rebuke from friend and foe alike.[80]

As might have been expected, Republican papers announced the suppression of the *Times* without criticism — but, conspicuously enough, most of them also avoided commendation. The foremost exception was Joseph Medill's *Chicago Tribune*, the bitter rival of the *Times* and its editor, Wilbur Storey, but the relative silence of other vigorously pro-Union sheets suggests a certain discomfort with the idea of the army officially shutting down a newspaper for its editorial opinion.[81]

Burnside's attempt to intimidate the more fervently critical journals nevertheless seemed to have the desired effect, at least initially, for some customarily outspoken Democratic editors also published the news with little or no comment. Samuel Medary, editor and publisher of the *Crisis*, got the story too late for inclusion in his acerbic weekly, but in its June 3 edition the *Cleveland Plain Dealer* had nothing editorial to say, confining itself to the bare announcement of the suppression and unadorned reports of public outrage and denunciation. In what bore the marks of a cunning, cautious test of how far the government might go to curb criticism, the following day the *Plain Dealer* published a front-page sketch of the life of Charlotte Corday. While the French Revolution descended from representative democracy into mob rule and Jacobin despotism, Corday had assassinated Jean-Paul Marat, who was widely viewed as the architect of the Jacobin takeover. Without printing a word about Ambrose Burnside or Abraham Lincoln, the *Plain Dealer* published an eerily similar account of a democracy that had fallen prey to military domination of the legislature, the destruction of opposition newspapers, and the arrest of dissident legislators. The seventieth anniversary of the Jacobin triumph had passed on June 2, allowing the *Plain Dealer* to deflect any charge of antiadministration motive on the excuse of historical relevance. Still, at a time when White House intimates themselves referred to Radical Republicans as Jacobins, the focus on Mademoiselle Corday hinted at an appeal to assassinate the enemies of American democracy.[82]

Senator Lyman Trumbull, Lincoln's frequent ally, roundly condemned the suppression in conversation with his former colleague Orville Hickman Browning. Browning, President Lincoln's close friend, likewise considered Burnside's order "a despotic and unwarrantable thing" that promised to pitch the state into a civil war of its own. The fear of violent reaction may have had some foundation, too: ugly gatherings of furious Chicago Democrats muttered that no other newspaper should be permitted to flourish if theirs was not, and a general at Cairo warned that factions in southern Illinois were ready to leap into open rebellion.[83]

Equally upset was Judge David Davis, who had managed Lincoln's election campaign. Perhaps cowed by the fate of Judge Constable in Clark County, Chicago judge Thomas Drummond hesitated to issue an injunction against Burnside's order when the petition first came before him. Judge Davis growled that he would have granted it on the spot, and at the request of the U.S. Attorney in Chicago, Davis started for that city himself, to sit with Judge Drummond on the case and lend him some spine. Senator Trumbull denounced the order, drawing a measure of protest from Unionists of an authoritarian stripe, but he found kindred spirits the breadth of the country. A mass meeting of prominent Chicago citizens, including the mayor, concurred with Davis and Browning that so flagrant a violation of the First Amendment would not have been expedient even if it had been legal, and that it could only do injury to the Union cause. They appointed a select deputation to petition the president on their behalf to rescind the order, and they were promptly seconded by the entire Illinois legislature: both houses called on Lincoln not only to overrule Burnside's order but to disavow it, warning that it was his only hope of assuring the American people that constitutional freedom "has not ceased to be."[84]

The Chicago court finally ordered the injunction, but by then it had become unnecessary. On the same day that the Illinois legislature condemned Burnside's intrusion into the civil affairs of the state, President Lincoln instructed the general to rescind his order. The *Times* immediately resumed publication, reporting on June 5 that a crowd of twenty thousand had convened to support free speech, and the *World* once again reached its subscribers below the Great Lakes. As though taunting Burnside now, the *Plain Dealer* ran a full-column advertisement for Confederate journalist Edward Pollard's *First Year of the War*, the sale of which Burnside had specifically banned.[85]

For seventy-two hours Lincoln's home state had threatened to erupt in open rebellion. He had quelled it with a stroke of his pen, but the actions he had undertaken or approved over the preceding two years indicated that he revoked Order No. 84 more in fear of public reaction than over any serious concern about constitutional integrity. Burnside's decree encouraged other department commanders to arbitrarily prohibit the circulation of unfriendly newspapers within their bailiwicks, the *Chicago Times* among them, and Burnside's humiliating executive reversal failed to abolish that dictatorial tendency. In the absence of pronounced public dissatisfaction over those later proscriptions, Lincoln saw no need to interfere on behalf of the Bill of Rights.[86]

The 150th Pennsylvania greets the spring of 1863 in formation on the main street of its smoky encampment at Belle Plain, Virginia, ten miles from Fredericksburg.

President Lincoln reviewing the cavalry of the Army of the Potomac on April 6, 1863, as drawn by Edwin Forbes.

Contraband labor at work on the Mississippi levee below Baton Rouge, Louisiana.

The 1st U.S. Colored Infantry, organized at Washington in the spring of 1863.

The Sixth Corps in rifle pits on the plain below Fredericksburg, holding the Union left during Hooker's flank march. This photograph was long misidentified as a depiction of troops waiting to assault Petersburg in the spring of 1865.

Fort Sumter after Union ironclads and land batteries had pounded it to rubble. The Confederate flag still flies over the gorge wall, at left.

Bringing the Chancellorsville wounded over the Rappahannock under a flag of truce.

Clement L. Vallandigham, the best-known critic of the Lincoln administration.

Frank Leslie's Illustrated portrays the attacks on Port Hudson: top, Admiral Farragut's costly bombardment; bottom, the bloody assault of the Louisiana Native Guards.

A cartoon lampooning Ambrose Burnside for arresting Clement Vallandigham and trying to suppress the *Chicago Times*, with some gratuitous insults added.

A primitive, but not inaccurate, engraving of Admiral Porter's ironclad fleet passing under the batteries at Vicksburg, April 16, 1863.

The Shirley house, near the Jackson Road outside Vicksburg, and the bombproofs of the 45th Illinois.

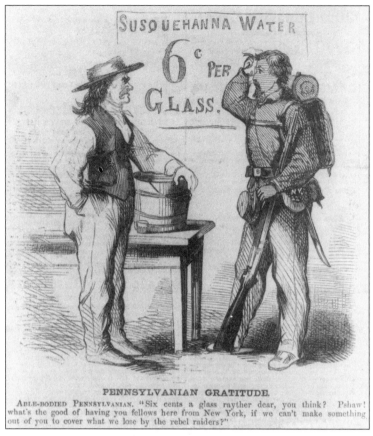

PENNSYLVANIAN GRATITUDE.

ABLE-BODIED PENNSYLVANIAN. "Six cents a glass rayther dear, you think? Pshaw! what's the good of having you fellows here from New York, if we can't make something out of you to cover what we lose by the rebel raiders?"

Satirical print of a Pennsylvania farmer gouging the New York militiaman who came to repel Confederate invaders. A good many Union soldiers remarked on the poor hospitality they met in the Keystone State.

The untended body of a Confederate soldier who was disemboweled by an artillery projectile on July 2 between the peach orchard and the wheat field south of Gettysburg. The remains of his severed left arm lie just below the propped rifle.

THE MEETING OF THE FRIENDS,
CITY HALL PARK.

A Republican cartoon depicts Governor Horatio Seymour as the idol of New York rioters, who in turn are caricatured as Irish thieves and thugs.

Edwin Forbes's sketch of the 118th Pennsylvania escorting five foreign-born recruits to their execution for desertion, carrying the coffins in which those men would soon be buried.

Encampment of the Army of the Potomac outside Culpeper, Virginia, in the autumn of 1863.

�֍

PART II

LONG, TOO LONG
AMERICA

4

Toward Getty's Town

→ OPPOSITION TO THE WAR had assumed numerous degrees of virulence since the outbreak of hostilities, from mild reservations to active antipathy. The increasing arrogance of those who controlled the bayonets had so aggravated the frustration and the rhetoric of constitutional advocates that much of the country had gravitated toward the conflicting poles of political opinion, especially since the summer of 1862, and as the spring of 1863 came to an end the specter of civil strife in the North haunted the sleep of many a citizen and soldier. Proponents of the war waxed hysterical, branding every dissenter as a traitor, and that condemnation seemed to arise as frequently from sincere conviction as from calculated partisan defamation. An Indiana officer with the Army of the Potomac so feared the gathering antiwar tide by June that he worried the "traitors at home" would burn his house down, and he regretted not having taught his wife how to handle a gun.[1] Wives and widows of soldiers complained of abuse at the hands of the "disloyal," while "loyal" newspapers freely blamed Copperhead miscreants for terrorizing soldiers' families, shooting into the windows of a home for invalid soldiers, and any other malicious incident that did or did not actually happen.[2]

Similar frenzy emanated from newspapers hostile to Lincoln's war. They angrily portrayed troops and artillery arrayed to intimidate peace rallies and indignation meetings, sometimes describing armed platoons of soldiers rushing the speakers' platforms. Democratic rallies were infiltrated by mobs of "abolition" thugs who hooted, hissed, and stoned antiwar orators, complained the opposition press. Editors insinuated, though apparently with some justification, that military authorities exaggerated or invented active resistance to federal authority to justify a crackdown on the civilian population. The only point on which Lincoln's supporters and opponents could seem to agree, observed one of the opponents, was that he could never win reelection without exercising "the most arbitrary power to suppress the freedoms of speech and action." Reasoning that elections descended into farce without free discourse, some Democrats seriously began to wonder whether the government would even hold any more elections.[3]

Ambrose Burnside's manhandling of the *Chicago Times* came as the popular outcry against the president's war reached its crescendo, and his misguided autocracy in the Department of the Ohio probably contributed more to that clamor than the actions of any other single person save Lincoln himself. On the very evening that he ordered the newspaper silenced, and before the country learned of it, as many as eight thousand concerned Philadelphians filled Independence Square to fulminate against arbitrary arrests for "crimes" of opinion, like Clement Vallandigham's, and against the growing impression that the country was sinking into a military dictatorship. Their complaints resonated agreeably even among the city's more moderate Unionists — which was natural enough, considering that Lincoln's cabinet all appeared to lament Burnside's authoritarian impulses, too.[4]

Late on the afternoon of June 3, while Democratic newspapers announced the suppression of the *Times* in strident headlines, and Republican sheets buried truncated versions of the story several pages deep, throngs of well-dressed citizens from all over New York began gathering at the junction of Sixth Street and Fourth Avenue to hear the advocates of peace make their case for an armistice. They filled the Cooper Union again and spilled out into several different gatherings outside, where judges and politicians and civilian celebrities reminded them that the chief magistrate owed as much obedience to the Constitution as the common citizen did. Banners inside enunciated the Democratic doctrine of "the Constitution as it is and the Union as it was," and calcium lights bathed the hall in a bright glow; the crowd alternately cheered for McClellan and Vallandigham or groaned for Lincoln and Burnside as speakers paused.[5]

These were Democrats who blamed Radical Republicans for commandeering the government and perverting it to their own uses from the very inception of the conflict. Radicals had scuttled peaceful compromise back in 1861, maintained those Democrats: even those who recognized Southern complicity in the commencement of hostilities could not absolve the Radicals for having assured that war would be inevitable, which only made the war party's constitutional infringements all the more distasteful.[6]

The New York meeting, characterized by organizers as a peace convention, seemed unanimously convinced that the Constitution's silence on the issue of secession made the war illegal, and there were those in Congress who hoped to restore peace by ceding territory through the executive and Senate authority to make treaties. Resolutions, passed by acclamation inside Cooper Union, asserted that the federal government had no right to force states to stay in the Union, that the assumption of unlimited dictatorial powers on the excuse of military necessity was "monstrous in theory and execrable in practice," and that "the dogma of unlimited submission to the will of the Executive branch is unworthy of an American citizen, and inconsistent with the principles of constitutional liberty." Then Congressman Fernando Wood, the former mayor of New York City, listed an assortment of reasons why the war should end immediately, most of which hinged on the threats the conflict posed to the Constitution. The vast expense to the treasury and the injury to international trade was galling enough, argued Wood, and he invited audience fury over Lincoln's reversal on the abolition question, but his most salient points included the charge that the war had become an excuse for "the most outrageous and damnable crimes against the liberty of the citizen." His most apt and angry imputation may have been that Lincoln's army was "a dangerous power, which already overrides the courts and the Constitution."[7]

Anxiety over military domination of the civilian population had intensified upon the passage of the Conscription Act, with its centralized network of provost marshals distributed across the nation, and it worsened when administration detractors realized how the new Invalid Corps would expedite such organized repression. In fact, the partially disabled soldiers who were being enlisted in that branch were intended precisely for such duty as the provost marshal's department might require.

The first regiments of that corps were just forming as June began, mustering in the curious sky-blue uniforms that the "invalids" themselves would soon grow to despise as much as they did the name the War Department had given them. Critics suspected it as a ploy to retain the loyalty of disabled men by keeping them at the public trough, and one veteran orderly sergeant who was forced into the corps found laziness the most conspicuous trait of his fellow invalids. If all the country's less severely crippled veterans joined that service it would amount to as many as 150,000 men, some estimated, and skeptics were already wondering what partisan use the administration was going to make of them. To some it seemed obvious: since those men were being paid all the benefits of their active-duty counterparts, without the same physical demands, the government appeared to be keeping them on retainer for some vital political duty. Their officers would be appointed by the president, rather than by state governors, and the government had already demonstrated a shameless hypocrisy in the dismissal of officers who campaigned for any but Republican candidates. Republican officials at the state and federal level had also shown no qualms about using selected groups of soldiers to carry close elections, so it seemed logical to suppose that the Invalid Corps might constitute a mobile voting reserve, to be assigned primarily in states where the Lincoln administration most needed electoral help. If that complicated manipulation failed to occur to administration faithful in the War Department or the White House, it was no fault of accusative Democrats, who had already seen enough to lend credence to such deep suspicion.[8]

Guileful as he was, Fernando Wood had concluded his speech to the Cooper Union peace convention with the accurate reflection that popular enthusiasm for the war had receded, as the failure of voluntary recruiting best illustrated. At the moment he spoke, it had probably sunk to its lowest ebb, and the sentiment for peace seemed ascendant. Wood insisted that the struggle could not be won, and immense numbers of people agreed with him. The most stubborn proponents of continuing the fight appeared to be administration newspapers and soldiers, but even the soldiers fell short of consensus. True, the spring riot in Richmond and the reduced rations of the Vicksburg garrison had misled more than the wishful thinkers of the army into a belief that the rebellion was about starved out: it would collapse with a little more pressure, thought many a correspondent at Sunday-morning campfires, and frequent Confederate desertions strengthened that argument despite relatively high Southern spirits. The ferocity of Southern attacks at Chancellorsville and elsewhere told another story, though, and hopeful Union soldiers who described plummeting Confederate morale on Tuesday might have to admit on Wednesday that the rebels fought like devils incarnate.[9]

The war party, meanwhile, adopted a strategy of vilifying the Peace Democrats. Perhaps partly in reaction to the rapid increase in the antiwar ranks, Republicans at home were damning all Democrats with a particular animus by the beginning of summer. Adherents of both factions tried to initiate debate with relatives and friends in the army by asking the soldiers for their personal opinions on politics; to encourage the desired response, the letters from Republican or "Union" correspondents often bristled with absurd accounts of Copperhead outrages.[10] In the camps, the perennial newspaper contest of mutual exaggeration and slander naturally redounded to the benefit of the Republican organs, because papers hostile to the administration customarily labored under greater circulation difficulties within the army than the more compliant and flattering sheets.

Other factors weighted the struggle for the soldiers' hearts and minds against the Democrats. The troops at Vicksburg, for instance, felt more optimistic about the prospects for victory than did the people at home who heard only of defeat and stagnation. Then, too, the peace advocates' hostility to emancipation, expressed through appeals to racial bigotry and economic apprehension, no longer found so eager an audience among soldiers as it did in the civilian laboring class. The men at the front were beginning to comprehend the value of slave labor to the Confederate war effort — and thus the value of freedmen's labor to the Union cause — as well as the impossibility of restoring slavery to the regions where Union armies had begun to banish it. The personal and military advantages that the contraband camps represented for the soldiers overcame some of their most deep-rooted prejudices. They still might not care whether the freed slave lived or died, but — insofar as it injured the cause of secession and removed the source of national rancor — most Union soldiers ultimately came to at least a grudging acceptance of emancipation.[11]

More decisive, probably, was the personal animosity for the peace party that Republicans fostered among soldiers, both by retailing preposterous tales of Democratic insults or abuse and by insisting that the Peace Democrats were undermining the war effort and thereby endangering those in uniform. Formal and informal proscriptions on Democratic literature in camp deprived most soldiers of any opportunity to see fantastic Republican accusations rebutted, or to read equally fantastic versions of Democratic counterclaims, or to learn the real details and direction of the opposition argument. Jaundiced interpretations of the peace platform by Republican newspapers and pamphlets prevailed, ultimately embittering a majority of the troops against Democrats who held opinions remarkably close to those that many of the soldiers had only recently expressed themselves. Unchallenged Republican invective that characterized the peace party as villainous and selfish enemies of the soldier and his family achieved remarkable success within the army, especially as mounting personal sacrifices made veterans increasingly reluctant to abandon the fight short of victory.[12]

Eventually, administration loyalists branded all Democratic opinion as mere Copperhead treachery, and — either from a sense of alienation or in fear of their comrades' sometimes-violent disapprobation — even the more receptive soldiers found it safer to spurn the dissident newspapers and literature that did leak into camp. Not long into the propaganda war men in the ranks started to credit the complaint that the peace faction was actually prolonging the fighting, and they alluded to the pleasure of coming home under arms to kill Copperheads.[13] Soon after Vallandigham passed through the lines of the Army of the Cumberland, a Minnesota lieutenant ranted about letters from kin who favored peace, complaining that Lincoln should have hanged Vallandigham — and anyone else who said or did anything that protracted the conflict.[14] Men from all ranks in the army, some of whom had previously entertained their own doubts about Lincoln's policies, eventually refused to listen to any rationale critical of the war or the administration. Some began to rebuke friends and relatives, including aging parents, for letters that revealed continued or increasing fealty to the same principles that the soldiers had once espoused. One New Hampshire soldier bickered constantly with his resentful wife over political principles that she accused him of having betrayed.[15]

The most effective propaganda probably consisted of the carefully nurtured myth of a vast Copperhead conspiracy, in collusion with Confederate operatives, to rise up behind the lines and overthrow the government. Colonel Henry Carrington, the commandant at Indianapolis, had essentially invented the Knights of the Golden Circle conspiracy in company with Indiana governor Oliver Morton. Basing his suppositions on a secret fraternity founded before the war by an enterprising confidence man, Carrington insisted in the spring of 1863 that as many as ninety-two thousand members of the order intended to rise against the government, and that within the past few weeks alone they had received thirty thousand arms. Morton's office arranged to have Carrington's delusions published in a little booklet, which was widely distributed by the Union League and other Republican-leaning organizations. Those groups peddled the exposé for as much as two bits per copy, and it whetted the fury of soldiers while offering would-be informants organizational details they could use for convincing testimony against recusant Democrats. Provost marshals soon started rounding up "dangerous traitors" and finding nests of the K.G.C. plotting disloyal activities, starting in President Lincoln's own home town of Springfield.[16]

By the time Congress passed the Conscription Act, the public seemed to have divided into two hostile camps, the one outraged that the federal government presumed to reverse the traditions of local control and personal liberty while the other deeply resented the dissidents' apparent betrayal of both the nation and the boys in blue. Thenceforward, political rallies frequently sparked violence and occasional bloodshed as disciples of one faction provoked those of the other.

Surviving accounts imply that it was more often Unionists who started the trouble, and those Unionists were usually soldiers. At least three significant incidents marred Saturday, April 18, 1863. At a Union meeting in Brown County, Indiana, on April 18, a soldier was shot to death after he wrested a rifle from a Democrat, who was then shot in turn by another soldier. That same day another rally exploded in gunfire at Danville, Indiana, and in Grandview, Iowa, a Unionist mob surrounded a Democratic rally, hooting and stoning the speakers, driving people away, and brandishing revolvers.[17] A couple of months later a woman was reportedly shot when she disrupted a peace meeting in Indiana. At a Democratic rally in Morrow County, Ohio, on the second Saturday in July, a soldier who tried to rip the butternut pin from the coat of a young man found himself underneath a pile of assailants, and that incident sparked a series of fistfights that continued throughout the afternoon. The strapping quartermaster of an Ohio regiment, who seemed to enjoy plenty of leisure at home in the summer of 1863, spent much of that time prowling around political rallies in Sandusky County, looking for fights with young Democrats, several of whom obliged him. Meanwhile, a group of soldiers in Mahaska County, Iowa, jumped a Democrat who had taken the precaution of arming himself, and he killed one of them.[18]

Even children suffered an occasional blow because of their parents' views on the war. A woman in eastern Iowa beset two little boys whose father was in the army, cuffing and cursing them when she heard them singing "We'll Hang Jeff Davis to a Sour Apple Tree," and she threatened their mother to boot. The young son of an Ohio soldier asked his father where he could get a pistol, after some other boys clubbed him, threw stones at him, and called their dogs to chase him, all the while taunting him about his father's service in the cause of abolition.[19] By the summer of 1863 partisan animosity had grown fierce enough to make or break marriages. The woman who intruded on the peace rally in Indiana was said to have been shot by her former fiancé: she had spurned him for his antagonism to the Lincoln administration, and when she burst into the meeting he supposedly emptied his revolver at her. While that tale stank of politically motivated embroidery, a young lady in Des Moines did specifically inquire into her suitor's politics before accepting his offer; his failure to join the army may have raised her suspicions, but she reported to a friend that she had inspected his head and found "Nary Copper."[20]

It required no belief in subversive clandestine societies to doubt that the draft could be implemented without much turbulence. The nation had never known universal compulsory service, which had always been regarded as an obnoxious trait of oppressive European monarchies. In their zeal to preserve the Union as the world's bastion of liberty, a great many Americans had ironically come to accept the concept of forcing men to fight a war, but those who lacked enthusiasm for the war retained the traditional image of conscription as an odious relic of feudal tyranny. The volatile emotions arising from theoretical conscription exploded as soon as provost marshals began appointing enrollment officers for their congressional districts.[21]

The draft law became effective on July 1, and by that date each district was supposed to compile a list of all eligible male residents between the ages of twenty and forty-five. Local citizens appointed by district provost marshals would conduct the enrollment under federal contract, just as census marshals had canvassed the countryside three years before, but these men could expect a hostile reception in many regions. In some districts, like southern Illinois, the inhabitants had turned so firmly against the war that whole communities harbored deserters, or rescued them if anyone tried to apprehend them, and the previous spring at least one reward-hunting citizen who arrested a deserter died at the hands of the friends who liberated his prisoner. Defiant residents of central Illinois openly wished every Union soldier dead, or boasted that they would resist the draft by force, fighting the Union army rather than the Confederates; some were suspected of having recruited companies for Confederate service. No one with eyes or ears retained much doubt that collecting the names and ages of potential conscripts could be a frustrating and perhaps dangerous task. Resistance might consist of nothing more than the passive refusal to state one's name, or giving a false name, both of which proved popular in New York City. That was enough to land a man in jail if the enrolling officer brought along a provost guard detail or could find a willing policeman, but the enrollment had not long been under way before provost marshals across the country began to hear that their appointees had been threatened, assaulted, or even murdered.[22]

The first noteworthy confrontation came in Holmes County, Ohio, between Columbus and Cleveland, but it may have had less to do with opposition to the draft than with the overbearing conduct of the government's enrolling officer. With stones and oaths, four workmen in an isolated hamlet chased away that official, one Elias Robinson, who had made himself obnoxious in the neighborhood with suggestive remarks to local women and slurs on the prevailing Democratic politics (the community lay twenty miles from Mount Vernon, the site of the huge May Day rally of five weeks before). When the district provost marshal arrived with a detail a few days later and arrested the four assailants, several dozen citizens surrounded them and compelled the soldiers to abandon their prisoners. The assistant provost marshal general in Columbus supposed that this represented the organized resistance promised by K.G.C. mythology, and he called for help to suppress the "insurgents," whom he calculated as several hundred strong; newspapers quickly inflated them to well over a thousand. Intending to deliver "an efficient lesson . . . to all rebels at home," the commander of the district of Ohio authorized a full-scale attack if the citizens refused to submit. On the morning of June 16 a mixed force of several hundred infantry and artillery, more than half of whom were prisoners just paroled from Abel Streight's ill-fated April raid up the Tennessee River, arrived in Holmes County to subdue the inhabitants. When they heard the troops were coming, some of the residents determined that they would arm themselves to protect their neighbors from the one-sided military justice meted out to Clement Vallandigham: they met the troops in a couple of skirmishes, but the soldiers never saw more than fifty of them. Prominent citizens interceded and persuaded the troop commander to let the suspects surrender for trial by civil authorities, rather than submit to the bias of military tribunals, and the provincials promptly disbanded.[23]

Trouble next surfaced in Milwaukee, Wisconsin, where enrollment officials came under attack from fiercely independent citizens including women who, according to rumor, flailed at them with cudgels and poured hot water on them from upper-story windows. The provost marshal there instinctively called for troops, but the department commander showed unusual restraint and insisted that the municipal police could handle it — which they evidently did. Women were also primarily responsible for obstructing and confounding the enrollment in Irish neighborhoods of New York's Thirteenth Congressional District, according to the provost marshal at Kingston. Maine militia responded to backwoods Franklin County, where a band of "deluded persons" had chased off an enrolling officer and done away with his papers. A Chicago enrolling officer was beaten so badly that he was not expected to live.[24]

The stiffest resistance arose across Indiana. In White River Township, just south of Indianapolis, enrolling officers were driven out by a group of men who, anticipating retaliation by troops from the capital, took to the woods with rifles and revolvers. In Fulton County, only sixty miles from Lake Michigan, angry Democrats berated neighbors who undertook the enrollment, and a mob of them pounced on one enroller, snatching away his lists. In Montgomery County citizens met in public and repudiated conscription, voting to prohibit the enrollment within their precincts; local decisions had no effect on federal law under the new centralized government, however, and even a dissident sheriff could never muster enough firepower to resist the government troops who responded to nearly every disturbance.[25]

On June 9 a marksman hidden in the woods of Rush County fired on a lone enrolling officer. He missed his target by so wide a margin that it appeared only to be a warning, but the deputy provost marshal for that vicinity concluded to accompany his enroller after that, taking along a couple of armed detectives. At noon on June 10 they rode up to a house near the scene of the shooting and the enrolling officer went inside to look for eligible male residents, whereupon some riflemen rose up from a nearby wheat field, killing the deputy provost marshal and one of the detectives with an unexpected fusillade. Within twenty-four hours three companies of infantry and cavalry repaired to Rush County, bringing in a couple of suspects, and the enrollment continued without further incident.[26]

On the same day as the Indiana murders, another enrollment officer was shot to death in the Allegheny Mountains of western Pennsylvania. In Monroe County, near the Delaware River, more gangs of draft resisters drove enrolling officers away with dire threats, and overpowered a squad that penetrated their neighborhood to arrest a suspected deserter, forcing them to release him and retire. One mob kicked and choked an enroller before destroying his lists, and they promised to burn out every Republican in the vicinity if the government tried to draft anyone in Monroe County. Informants claimed the disaffected citizens drilled regularly under arms in preparation for the inevitable fight with federal troops, but no such battle erupted despite recurring incidents. In certain areas no one at all could be found who would undertake the enrollment, and a nonresident who tried to enroll part of Greene County could not find one man who would give his name; he finally left town when idlers at a rural store threatened to hang him and produced a rope for the purpose. Provost marshals in the coal-mining regions of Luzerne and Schuylkill counties tried to answer the intimidation and assaults on their enrolling officers with brute force, responding first to tales of organized resistance by clandestine battalions of disloyal Irish. In Schuylkill County a judge released a suspected resister on a writ of habeas corpus, instead arraigning the deputies who had detained him, and the provost marshal asked for additional troops to crush the court. The provost marshal general, James Fry, replied that the court should not be allowed to override federal law, and he sent the troops.[27]

Accounts of resistance infuriated soldiers at the front, for whom such incidents seemed to signal the long-anticipated rising of Copperhead legions. One German resident of Schuylkill County who was serving in the 48th Pennsylvania swallowed the official insinuations that Irish miners were responsible for the violence (although the suspects there all had German names), and in company with his comrades he seethed over this apparent fire in the rear.[28]

Henry Carrington, self-appointed sentinel over the invisible Copperhead empire, still predicted significant guerrilla depredations in Indiana and Illinois for the latter part of June. Had the vast network of K.G.C.

"castles" actually existed, the violence would surely have been more intense and concentrated, but the bloodiest encounters involved the smallest groups. Larger mobs usually lacked the guns or the stomach for more than roughing up outnumbered opponents, and even armed contingents like the Holmes County minutemen gladly foreswore violence once they were assured their neighbors would not be subjected to the prejudgment of Ambrose Burnside's military courts. As frequent and widespread as enrollment resistance was, it demonstrated a conspicuous lack of central or even local organization. Analysis of those disconnected and spontaneous outbreaks should have served to discredit conspiracy theorists like Carrington, but no one had the leisure or the objectivity for such an analysis in 1863. The most obvious effect of resistance at the time was to further rile Union soldiers, who rapidly lost patience with the war's critics. In a revealing choice of regal vocabulary, the captain of a New York battery insisted that rigid enforcement of the draft was crucial to the concept that the government could now "*Command* her Subject."[29]

Echoes of the escalating dispute in the North reverberated in the South. In public discourse, conservative Northern Democrats implied that reunion would be a probable outcome if the government would only grant enough concessions to satisfy the Southern grievances of 1860. In their hearts some proponents of an armistice may have envisioned a much more gradual reconciliation, entailing years of negotiations, but many may simply have been disguising their desire to see the war ended whether the rebellious states resumed their allegiance or not. Responding to the implied offer, though, Southern editorials and correspondence, both private and official, suggest that the advocates of conciliation were entirely mistaken about the potential for peaceful reunion: the Confederacy would fight for outright independence to the bitter end. It was instead those who had originally opposed the war because it would require abject military subjugation of the whole South who could claim the better foresight.

Still, the division in Northern sentiment struck the South's most prominent soldier as a valuable opportunity. General Lee regretted the vociferous editorial condemnation of reconciliation, fearing it would undercut the antiwar argument in the North. Better to encourage the peace men, he felt, even to the extent of letting them think the South might consider reunion, than to neutralize their power to weaken Northern will. He may also have supposed that it would aid the peace party if Northern denizens had to endure the possibility of hostile armies traversing their territory, as the Southern population did, and that may have helped to convince him, early in June, to start pushing his army toward the Potomac again. By the time Northern enrolling agents began to feel the wrath of liberty-loving citizens, Lee had moved his headquarters and most of his army from Fredericksburg to Culpeper, on his way north.[30]

A Vermont corporal had worried, at the end of May, that the Army of the Potomac was going to have to bridge the Rappahannock again and pitch into Lee's army just to supply some interesting copy for the newspapers. A year later the corporal would cross that river once more, and sacrifice his life for more of those compelling headlines, but this spring General Lee had other notions. He slipped the rebel army away from Joe Hooker with little trouble, except for a spectacular clash of cavalry on June 9, a few miles from Culpeper. Brigadier General John Buford started the fight at daybreak, cantering over the Rappahannock with a division of Yankee horsemen and charging nearly to J. E. B. Stuart's headquarters at Brandy Station before the commander of the foremost Union brigade fell with a bullet through the head; his men were driven back with so many field officers down that a major brought that brigade out of the battle. Rush's Lancers, the 6th Pennsylvania Cavalry, went into the thick of the fray, having traded their lances for carbines, and they felled quite a few of Stuart's troopers before coming out even more cut up themselves, with their own commander missing.[31]

Brandy Station went down as the largest mounted action ever seen on the continent, or for that matter in the western hemisphere. It also marked the first instance in which Union cavalry held its own against Southern horsemen, but all the shooting and sabering exerted little influence on the operations of the Army of Northern Virginia. Three days later Confederate foot soldiers were plodding over the Blue Ridge into the Shenandoah Valley and turning down the Valley Pike, toward Maryland and Pennsylvania.[32]

The first obstacle Lee's army would encounter on the Valley Pike was the garrison of some seventy-six hundred men in and around Winchester. Abraham Lincoln had appointed many undeserving men to the highest grade the U.S. Army then offered, but not many exceeded the incompetence of Major General Robert Milroy, who commanded at Winchester. Milroy had shown himself a fool or a lunatic at Second Bull Run, and he was about to confirm the impression at Winchester.[33]

Among Milroy's infantry regiments was the 18th Connecticut, raised the previous summer; it had only recently arrived in the field after nine months inside Fort Marshall, in Baltimore, with its ranks still nearly full of men who had never seen an armed rebel. Major Ephraim Keech of the 18th resigned when the order came to join Milroy's division, and First Lieutenant George Kies, a neighbor of the major's who knew him well, remarked that Winchester must have been "too near the war" for Keech. Kies himself appeared to welcome the chance for action, which would have distracted him from his personal problems. He suffered from either a jealous wife or a wandering eye, and perhaps from both. He had accompanied the voting-age soldiers chosen for the hasty voyage home to reelect Governor William Buckingham (whom Kies scorned, privately, but in his position he may have known enough to conceal his conservative sentiments). His wife had gone to the local rail depot to greet him, but had somehow missed him, and he seemed to sense her doubt that he had even been there. That may have launched her suspicion that he was cavorting with other women in Baltimore, and his labored denials revealed that they had had similar difficulties before the war. As a junior officer Kies earned over a hundred dollars a month; his housing was free, and he drew a stipend for rations on top of that. Still, he sent home an average of only thirty dollars a month for the support of his wife and their surviving toddler. That was three times what most private soldiers could give their wives, but other officers frequently managed to do without half their pay, or more, and Mrs. Kies complained of shortages. Combined with hints gleaned from Major Keech's wife, Fannie Kies came to the conclusion that George was spending his extra pay on a woman in Baltimore, and perhaps several women. She even had the name of one, whose acquaintance he did not deny, but, alluding to their earlier episode, he replied that some third party was just trying to make trouble for them again. He pleaded for her confidence, buying her and their boy a round of expensive presents that mollified her for a time.[34]

Those gifts indicated that the lieutenant was holding back excess pay that he may well have been spending on female companionship, and if he was not, there were plenty of officers who were, for they could usually spare a lot more cash on such luxuries than privates who earned forty-three cents a day. Enlisted men's wives nevertheless suspected now and then that their husbands were being unfaithful, too. Infidelity afflicted the home front, as well, even in the face of severe community disapproval. Louisa Crafts, the wife of a nine-month man from Essex, Massachusetts, accepted the attentions of a local lothario within three months of her husband's departure for the lower Mississippi; he visited her home frequently, and sometimes stayed for days. One spring morning the two of them left her eight-year-old daughter with a black woman who lived nearby — evidently because no white neighbor was willing to mind the child — while they spent the day in Salem, having their photograph taken together. Tongues wagged mercilessly around town, but the pair made no effort to conceal their affair, and when her husband came home in the summer of 1863 it was to begin life as a single parent.[35]

Like many thousands of young men in the summer of 1862, one Vermont boy married a local girl just before he enlisted for what then passed as a generous bounty, but when he came home on furlough for the first time, well over a year later, she astonished him with a pair of twin baby boys born only days before his arrival. That soldier's reaction is not recorded, but in the northern New Hampshire town of West Milan, Private Frank Lang returned after an absence of a year and a half to find a newborn girl at his house. Lang had a reputation for violence, at least against his wife, and he extracted enough information from her to convince himself that Alvin Higgins, two farms away, had fathered the child. Swearing vengeance on Higgins (who slipped away from home when warned of it), Lang ostentatiously loaded a rifle; his wife, meanwhile, proceeded to the cellar and hanged herself from a floor joist with a skein of yarn. Higgins, who had a wife of his own, later returned home, but thereafter his family included an "adopted daughter" the same age as Mrs. Lang's misbegotten child.[36]

In the summer of 1863 William Paine, an assistant surgeon with the 21st Ohio, had his furlough spoiled by the discovery of a packet of love letters written to his wife by another man. He ejected her from the house before returning to duty, and the scandal spread far enough through their community that no one would board her, so she stayed at the hotel for a time, where rumor claimed that a man had left her room at two o'clock one morning. Her money ran out, however, and she had to take a job as a housekeeper for both income and lodging. More rumors had her pregnant by autumn, but no baby appears to have come to term. Eventually she and the doctor patched things up and spent another half century together, but they found it convenient to move to Iowa as soon as he left the army, and once there they changed the spelling of their last name.[37]

For every wife who consciously capitalized on her husband's absence, or who succumbed to temptation or the considerable vicissitudes of raising a family alone in an age of hand labor, there were several husbands who suspected infidelity, or feared it. A Vermont corporal who had often joked with his wife about her finding another man turned more serious about it when rumors filtered back from several sources that she was "sassing around all sorts" with anyone she could find. Surgeon John Rice, whose young wife self-righteously relayed the gossip about Doctor Paine, might well have wondered at her own giddy schedule of parties and balls. Frank Hubbard, a Vermont artilleryman with Nathaniel Banks in Louisiana, did ask, albeit tentatively, why his wife had stopped writing to him; as he was captured a few days later, and died in Confederate hands the following year, the chances are that he never learned the answer. A newly-wed musician in a New Hampshire regiment frequently related the dalli-

ances of his comrades or their wives in letters home, and after each report
he would hint broadly to his bride for confirmation that she abhorred
such behavior and would never betray him; when she failed to respond
with adequate clarity, he added that he would not want to come home to
such a woman.[38]

Certainly women who were left to fend for themselves and their children suffered unusual hardships, at least if their husbands went to war as
enlisted men. They not only shouldered all the traditionally male house-
hold burdens, in addition to their considerable housekeeping and child-
care duties, but they often had to provide for most of their own income
for long periods of time. The treasury could usually not simultaneously
cover its debts to contractors, offer inviting cash bounties to prospective
recruits, and pay the meager monthly salaries that were due the men
in uniform. To bridge that perennial shortfall, the administration that
portrayed itself as the true friend of the soldier simply let him wait for
months on end for his pay, since he could only refuse further service at the
risk of a firing squad. More often than not, therefore, the families those
men had left behind lived somewhere between marginal poverty and outright indigence. Their officers sympathized, and attributed much of the
demoralization in the ranks to the perception that the troops were neglected by the very government they strove to preserve. An Ohio captain
had to ask his father to pay the rent for one private's wife, noting that she
was about to be evicted for lack of funds, and he described many of his
men's families in dire need of food and fuel. Congress looked into it, and
tendered a joint resolution demanding immediate payment of the army
and navy by issuing more bonds and printing another hundred million
dollars in notes, but only at the beginning of May, 1863, was the secretary
of the treasury able to boast that he had discharged all the government's
outstanding debts. Even then he did so only by paying off the troops
through the end of February, and when he made that claim, another two-
month pay period was already overdue.[39]

The money the government printed to cover the pay arrearage only
sparked another round of inflation that was exacerbated by late April's
military stagnation, and when those devaluated dollars finally reached
the soldiers' families, they would not buy half what they had the year before. Canadian farmers along the border, who had balked at taking greenbacks at a discount of one-quarter in 1862, found the dollar so depreciated
in 1863 that many of them simply refused to sell to American markets,
which only further increased the cost of food in the States. The price of
gold coin had been dropping in March, and especially toward the end of
the month, but Treasury Secretary Chase's issue of virtual shinplasters to
the soldiers started bloating it again the moment it went into circula-

tion.[40] Prices rose for everyone the breadth of the country, eliciting sufficiently anguished comments from the fairly comfortable, but — as always — inflation wrought its worst damage on the humblest households.
Wages rose in partial reaction to the diminished worth of the currency
(and the shortage of labor), but not for those who had answered their
country's call.[41] Coal soared in New York in May, when decreased demand
should have been driving it downward, and provisions in Washington
seemed "enormously high" to the families of government clerks earning
more than ten times as much as an army private; single girls working as
copyists in the Quartermaster Department drew four times the salary of a
soldier.[42]

As though to worsen the plight of soldiers' families, once the backlog in
army pay had been nominally resolved, the Treasury Department immediately resumed ignoring its debt to the troops so as to satisfy the contractor and the recruit. That deliberate reliance on deferred pay for the troops
bore heavily on the families of those poorer soldiers who composed the
greater part of the army. Again came the plaintive letters from wives,
pleading that they had no money at all, that they had already gone deep
into debt, and that they were nearly out of food. A woman in western New
York was fortunate enough to have parents nearby who would take her
and her two small children in during those weeks when she ran out of
food altogether, but eventually she had to open a school in her home.
Soon she was teaching a couple of dozen children, all the while tending
her own two.[43]

Emily Harris, the mother of two young girls, endured four long years in
little Hampstead, New Hampshire, while her husband served in a war she
did not support. With no significant help from anyone, she kept and
maintained the modest house in which he had left her. Hampstead afforded her three dollars a week, and her husband sent a few dollars from
each month's pay when he received it, but that hardly covered food and
fuel. To supplement that inadequate support she fashioned bonnets, assembled shoes, knitted hoods, and took in whatever other piecework she
could find, completing it after the rest of her daily chores were done. For
all her labors, she always wrote regularly to her husband, although her
letters frequently lapsed into conservative Democratic diatribes against
the noble struggle in which Leander Harris saw himself so dutifully engaged.[44]

Like Mrs. Harris, Margaret Welsh had little success disguising how
much she resented her husband enlisting in the army — which had been
his whiskey-soaked solution to momentary insolvency. Apparently because she lived outside the state where he enlisted, she was never able to
draw the relief money he assured her she would get, so she lived with an

uncle and aunt on what her husband could send home. When he kept one entire payment for himself, she went looking for a job as a stitcher. Evidently she found her living arrangement unpleasant, as well, for she moved out of her uncle's home and into a boarding house. Tense lodging situations became a common problem for army wives. Long sojourns with the closest relatives frequently turned sour, as the wife of a Michigan soldier discovered when her own aunt began subjecting her to verbal abuse, and the only solution her husband could think of was to move her into his father's home.[45]

Wives begged their husbands to come home on furlough, particularly when a child was born or died, but the fare home often cost twice what a private earned each month, and the traveling ate up most of the few days' leave that a company commander could manage for them.[46] One Indiana private had to devote all but a dollar of his latest pay to the debts on his farm, so he could hardly consider spending another two months' salary on a quick jaunt back to the home he would never see again.[47] Sylvester Hadley, who had spent most of the winter and spring of 1863 sparking a fifteen-year-old girl during a lengthy furlough in New Hampshire, asked to go home again in the fall, when she delivered a baby. When he failed to gain permission, he simply walked away from the army and never returned, but relatively few soldiers subordinated the consequences of desertion to their familial duties.[48]

A Kansas cavalryman made repeated but clumsy efforts to calm his wife, who dreaded life alone on the prairie. He sent her money, for instance, but then he warned her to hide it in a belt around her waist. She wrote of her intention to sell their homestead and move elsewhere, but he told her to stay where she was and promised to send her money for a pony, presumably so she would not be so isolated. Raise some chickens and plant a garden, he suggested during another of her bouts of wanderlust a few months later, but he could not possibly get leave to come home. Eventually, in exasperation, he admitted that he had too many other things to think about, and that he was tired of her continual frenzy, but a furlough was still not possible. In the end he began to worry about her fidelity, implying that only her deception could destroy their "hapyness."[49]

Even when a man could find a chance to go home, the ensuing departure usually turned so heartbreaking that it seemed worse than not having come at all.[50] And then there were those instances, doubtless rare, in which the conjugal interlude itself disappointed the reunited couple. Benjamin Wells enlisted from Michigan during the war's first summer, immediately after taking a wife. They exchanged frequent letters to "Dearest Ben" and "Dearest Melissa," but two and a half years passed before he found an opportunity to return for a brief visit. When he announced that he could take advantage of a convalescent leave, his wife chided him that she would like a couple of hours' notice of his arrival, so he would not catch her "in the suds," but then she playfully added that she would not mind that, either. Their meeting proved strangely stilted, though: he seemed so taciturn that she feared she had offended him somehow, and his evident dissatisfaction with her housekeeping stung her deeply. After he returned to the army he wrote home less often, while her letters all bore a gingerly, apologetic tone. The furlough had accomplished little, apparently, beyond ending their thirty-month-long fantasy honeymoon.[51]

At least Lieutenant Kies was able to rekindle his wife's affection by dint of those enticing gifts. From Winchester he reassured her that he had not touched any woman since her, "not so much as to feel of her Leg." He longed only for her, he wrote, adding that he would certainly send her some more money the next payday. As it happened, though, there would be no more paydays for him for quite some time. The Confederate movement toward Culpeper posed a vague threat to the post at Winchester, but as late as June 10 Lieutenant Kies doubted the enemy would come that way. If they did they would be repulsed, he predicted, for Winchester was protected by ambitious earthen forts and General Milroy boasted confidently of holding his ground. Then, on June 13, Richard Ewell appeared south of Winchester just as Stonewall Jackson had, barely a year before, and he brought back many of the same troops. The results were also about the same as in 1862, except that Milroy made the mistake of lingering longer than Nathaniel Banks had, so his loss was that much greater.[52]

Early on June 14 a Southern division flanked the Winchester forts from the west. By midnight Milroy realized how heavily he was outnumbered, and decided to run. Leaving behind all their wheeled vehicles — supply wagons, ambulances, and every piece of artillery, besides mountains of supplies — the Yankees started stumbling toward Martinsburg under the final fragment of a disappearing moon. Ewell sent a division to intercept them under Major General Edward Johnson (known to his men as Allegheny Johnson), and before dawn he opened fire on Milroy's retreating column from the woods alongside the road, four miles north of Winchester. Milroy himself was nearby, and he threw his handiest regiments at the muzzle flashes in the darkness. Those regiments included the 18th Connecticut. Three times they lunged at an enemy they could not see, and once the Connecticut men blasted a volley into the backs of their own friends. The sky began to lighten just as their third assault stalled in front of a blazing railroad embankment filled with Confederate infantry and artillery. The dark blue line fell back in some disorder, with Johnson's Confederates in hot pursuit. After a few hundred yards a white flag went up from the rear of the fleeing mass, and the better part of three Union regiments surrendered. Lieutenant Kies would spend the next year and a half in the custody of his captors.[53]

The retreat continued toward the Potomac, with Milroy and his fleetest hangers-on leading it, but without instructions or directions some of the survivors went one way and some another, with fragments scattering to the winds. Milroy stopped at Harper's Ferry, but much of his command crossed into Maryland and continued their flight "like a covey of frightened birds," according to a witness on the Maryland side. Hundreds, apparently with the quartermaster employees and teams among them, never slowed down until they reached Franklin County, Pennsylvania, where for the next few days farmers along the turnpike watched their fields of timothy, wheat, and hay eaten up or trampled flat, while their fences and piled lumber vanished into campfires. A single regiment of their own men did more damage than five regiments of rebels, remarked a man who had seen the results of J. E. B. Stuart's cavalry raid the previous October, and he gauged those of Milroy's fugitives who camped unbidden on his property as "outlandish rascals."[54]

Ewell tallied four thousand prisoners, a couple of dozen pieces of artillery, and three hundred wagons full of provisions, besides abundant supplies of food and equipment. He had also inflicted more than four hundred casualties, and all at a cost of fewer than three hundred men. Southern sympathizers in Winchester rejoiced at their delivery from Yankee occupation (and especially from the much-hated, overbearing Milroy), while the town's Unionists sputtered in disgust over that general's stupidity. Here was yet another Southern victory, and a Union woman who watched it all wondered if it would always be thus. "If so," she mused, "much better to have peace now than to go sacrificing men & property."[55]

As soon as Lee's movements indicated that he might be striking north, toward the Potomac, Joe Hooker broached the idea of dashing across the Rappahannock with his whole army and marching on Richmond, which would either force Lee to come back south or allow for the easy capture of the enemy capital. Even after the disaster to Milroy's division, as many Federals lay ready for duty around Washington and Baltimore as Lee had in his entire army, and they enjoyed the added advantage of the intricate network of fortifications encircling those two cities. Richmond retained no such praetorian guard: other than A. P. Hill's three divisions, still lingering behind Fredericksburg, the only rebels between Hooker and the seat of Confederate government were two or three infantry brigades, a few battalions of heavy artillery, the provost guard, and gaggles of clerks from the various bureaus who could be armed for a haphazard emergency defense. A lowly cannoneer in a New Hampshire artillery battery envisioned that inviting opening and thought it called for an attack, but the commander in chief differed. Conscious as he was of the civilian paranoia about Washington, and particularly that of the Radical Republicans, Lincoln vetoed Hooker's notion and told him to follow Lee if he went north, keeping the Army of the Potomac between the enemy and the capital. Lee's army should be his target, the president still insisted, rather than Richmond. Halleck merely noted his agreement.[56]

This echoed Lincoln's fears from the spring of 1862. Richmond lay especially vulnerable, and plenty of troops stood by to close in on it, but a Confederate army crashing down the Shenandoah Valley so worried Lincoln that he dared not exploit the opportunity. D. H. Hill, the Confederate commander at Petersburg, remained to defend Richmond in an emergency, and he supposed he could repel forty thousand Yankees "without difficulty," but Hooker had more than twice that many. Had Hooker driven south, Lee would likely have turned back to hammer him from behind, which would have accomplished Lincoln's aim of protecting Washington while offering a fair chance to seize Richmond into the bargain. With the Army of Northern Virginia cut off north of Richmond, its odds for escape or survival would also have been sharply reduced, but when General Lee risked uncovering his own capital he relied on the reflexive timidity of his opponents. Those opponents included Mr. Lincoln, as well as General Hooker. Had the president owned less of a politician's caution and more of a soldier's audacity, like his counterpart a hundred miles to the south, he might never have been asked to compose remarks for the dedication of a national cemetery in Pennyslvania, and the capture of Richmond would have struck a more telling political and strategic blow than a battlefield victory over Lee. It was true that Lincoln had less reason for confidence in his general than did Jefferson Davis, but he may not have adopted so brazen a course even had Hooker demonstrated the skill and determination of Robert E. Lee.[57]

The troops who had spent most of the previous six months at Falmouth, Stoneman's Switch, and White Oak Church therefore broke up housekeeping and packed their knapsacks for another crossing of ground many of them had trod before. Dan Sickles started his Third Corps up the Rappahannock on June 11, after the cavalry. The First Corps followed the next morning, stopping for lunch near Berea Church, a little less than four miles northwest of Falmouth, and once everyone had finished his noon meal the drums beat for a very unusual event.[58]

John P. Woods, a soldier in his mid-twenties, had deserted from the 19th Indiana. His state had seen a great deal of desertion, including quite a few from his own regiment, and to help curb that practice his court-martial had decreed that he should be shot to death with musketry. Most men sentenced to die for anything but murder, treason, or rape could expect to escape the firing squad through either a mitigation of the sentence somewhere along the approval process or by the hand of executive clemency. President Lincoln was known to be dreadfully soft about executions, but he declined to interfere in this case (if anyone even approached him about it), and on the afternoon of June 12 the first division of the First Corps turned off the road into a broad field that sloped down toward a hollow. While the different brigades drew up into three sides of a square, an ambulance pulled up, disgorging Private Woods and a chaplain. A second ambulance delivered a plain coffin, beside which the pair knelt for twenty or thirty minutes. Then, though he protested that it was unnecessary, the prisoner's arms were bound behind him at the elbows and a handkerchief was tied over his face. While his comrades from the regiment looked on (including one whose cousin had just been sentenced to this same fate), six riflemen took position within ten paces of the coffin, where Woods was forced to sit. The commander of the squad held his hat out at arm's length, and the moment he dropped it the six rifles rattled their little volley. Woods fell back and thrashed a bit, so two more men stepped up to blow his brains out. With that the troops marched unceremoniously away while a fatigue detail remained behind to dig the obscure grave, which would never be marked or moved.[59]

General Hooker had evidently concluded that such gruesome scenes would be required with some frequency if they were to have any deterrent effect, and indeed few men in the army could remember ever having seen one of their own shot for any crime, let alone for so common an offense as desertion. Two Pennsylvanians in the Twelfth Corps tried to leave camp in civilian clothing when the army was ordered to move, and when courts-martial quickly condemned them Hooker refused to disapprove the sentences. A New Jersey soldier from the same division as the two unfortunate Pennsylvanians was brought back after a year's absence and he, too, was sentenced to die, so Hooker ordered all three of them shot together, in front of the entire corps. The executioners chose similar topography, with a gentle slope toward the gathered coffins, to increase the visibility for the assembled troops and to impose the most powerful impression on them.[60]

With such brutal lessons Hooker hoped to seal his army against further seepage, at least from desertion. He was already losing strength daily from the discharge of the short-term regiments, and that helped breed a belief that Lee was moving northward with a much larger force than the Army of the Potomac. Hooker seemed convinced of his own numerical inferiority, insisting that the Confederates had a hundred thousand men despite intelligence to the contrary. This misinformation filtered through the ranks, dampening morale in an army that had seldom been able to hold its own against equal or smaller Confederate armies. Lee's thrust toward the Potomac had already perforated Union morale to some extent, anyway, and not merely in Hooker's army: it appeared to officers in the Army of the Cumberland that the enemy was having his own way in Virginia, and New York observers foresaw another defeat. Persuaded by Chancellorsville, and by persistent rumors of Hooker's drunkenness, George Templeton Strong remarked that Fighting Joe was probably no match for Lee, "drunk or sober." Among the many who concurred may have been Hooker himself, who struck one close subordinate as afraid to fight Lee anymore, knowing now that the grizzled Virginian was "his master."[61]

Nevertheless the army pried itself from its familiar Stafford County camps and started after the foe. A tremendous thunderstorm on the evening of June 13 marked the first real rain in weeks: some troops went slogging and slipping into the night, but that was their last rain for days. June 14 began a five-day heat wave that left men gasping on the roadside: a good many fell dead from sunstroke, while others began to act "perfectly crazy." In the Sixth Corps alone hospital stewards and the provost guard picked up 400 men who had passed out with the heat. When he made camp north of Aquia Creek on June 15, a Minnesota veteran recorded more cases of sunstroke and heat exhaustion on that day's march than he had seen in two years of war. A Maine veteran referred to it as "that terrible Monday" in a letter home. A captain in a newer Maine regiment halted his company that evening with only 7 present out of 40, and the next day gave no relief: on June 16 the heat sent 180 men to the Second Corps hospital. Still more collapsed over the next two days, while the panic over Lee's drive down the Shenandoah Valley forced Hooker to demand ever-longer marches in suffocating dust, which lay in a fine, ankle-deep powder and swirled into rising clouds at the first footfall. Men tossed their extra clothing away rather than carry it. Walking alongside the column, junior officers again relieved the most exhausted infantrymen of their knapsacks, or rifles. A chaplain had to look closely through the reddish-yellow cloud to be sure he really saw two women trailing along behind their soldier-husbands, and one of them had shouldered her man's burdens.[62]

Most of the nine-month men spent that scorching third week of June preparing for the journey home, sitting alongside the roads while dusty comrades filed enviously past. Only one regiment of Pennsylvania militia remained with the First Corps, and one with the Eleventh Corps. A brigade of them — George Stannard's five Vermont regiments — had spent the winter along the Occoquan, and they waited for the army to pass. By the time they fell in to follow, thunderstorms had broken the worst of the heat, but still they considered the experience "harrowing" and could hardly believe that they were asked to cover twenty miles a day when other troops made thirty, or even thirty-five, in forced marches twenty-four hours long. Hundreds of them dropped out in what the veterans deemed "splendid" marching weather. They threw away half their belongings to lighten their loads, and complained bitterly of their sore feet. One of the Vermonters estimated that their brigade discarded five hundred dollars worth of apparel in front of their winter huts before they even started.[63]

Rebel cavalry ranged ahead of Lee's army, crossing the Pennsylvania line and charging into Greencastle as early as June 15. After stripping the town of horses and provender they sped on to Chambersburg, where they torched the railroad shops and the brand-new depot, built to replace the one burned in J. E. B. Stuart's October raid. Southern officers ordered the stores all opened, with everything to be paid for in Confederate notes. All that week rebels terrorized the prosperous Cumberland Valley. Outriders galloped ahead to Shippensburg, and then to Mechanicsburg, just across the broad Susquehanna from the state capital. Not far behind them came the infantry: on Friday morning, June 26, most of Richard Ewell's corps marched into Shippensburg, where a woman noticed that the one-legged general had to be strapped into the saddle, while a servant rode alongside with his crutches. With nothing but some timid militia to interfere with it, the Southern juggernaut pushed a vast caravan of refugees ahead of it. Men, women, and children fled with what possessions they could squeeze into their wagons, leading or herding thousands of fat, healthy horses that Confederate quartermasters would have coveted. Black residents mingled with the throng, including an elderly woman who staggered along in the company of her two grandchildren, whom she was bound to save from the slave catchers.[64]

The initial foray seemed like a small raid, and a lot of good soldiers in places high and low suspected it as nothing but a diversion for something else. George Meade doubted that Lee would attempt another invasion. No one in New York seemed to seriously believe that Lee would cross the Potomac until he did, whereupon the capricious civilian spectator again began to doubt the Union cause. To the soldiers, though, the possibility of another incursion seemed too good to be true, for in the army there flourished a widespread belief that a little invasion was precisely what Northern Copperheads needed to bring them into the war party. Soldiers across the country invited it as "good medicine" and "a fortunate occurrence" that might "wake up" the weary Northern will.[65]

The first reports of an enemy presence in Maryland and Pennsylvania did at least electrify the city of Harrisburg and the White House. Governor Andrew Curtin appealed to his citizens for a volunteer corps to protect the state, and the president authorized fifty thousand troops to serve for six months or less — "as if the nine months experiment was not disastrous enough," sputtered a Regular Army captain. To the surprise and disgust of everyone, very few Pennsylvanians responded to the governor's call, or to the president's: by June 22 only three regiments and a few scattered companies had mustered in for the defense of their own state, while the purportedly Copperhead governor of New York had forwarded eighteen regiments of militia to his counterpart in Harrisburg. In Pennsylvania, where enthusiasm for the war had worn so thin that citizens were fighting their own government's emissaries to keep themselves out of it, the latest round of proclamations and exhortations may have borne the shrill echo of weakness and defeat.[66]

When Ewell's Southern infantry began its march on Harrisburg, Curtin repeated and expanded his state levy, asking telegraph operators to distribute their communities' quotas to their leading citizens and have them read in the churches. Hundreds of untrained civilians did amble into Harrisburg each day, and as soon as they could be mustered into awkward militia regiments they marched to the banks of the Susquehanna to lie in the woods, but they were far outnumbered by the endless caravan of fugitives that rolled the opposite way night and day. Lincoln's proclamation for six-month service had apparently repelled more volunteers than it attracted, for thousands hung back, reluctant to commit to so long a period, and the governor had to remind his constituents that they would be released as soon as the emergency ended, just as they had been the previous autumn. Indignation at the apathy of the Keystone State festered in Washington, in New York City, and in many of the Pennsylvania regiments, but the response accelerated little until the Confederate army had pierced deep into the state.[67] A government clerk in Washington judged that people who would not defend their state deserved to lose their capital. Even Confederates commented on how many able-bodied men loitered about that prosperous valley — as though disgusted at the Pennsylvanians' failure to defend their communities, or astonished at the untapped manpower.[68]

Hooker's troops rested for a few days south of the Potomac while he tried to deduce Lee's whereabouts. The head of the Army of the Potomac camped at Leesburg, where commissaries and quartermasters reveled in the bounty of unmolested agriculture: one corn crib yielded seventeen thousand bushels of corn on the cob for the nourishment of Union horses and mules. The tail of the army lay at Wolf Run Shoals, on the Occoquan; one corps stopped near Centreville, spreading out over both the Bull Run battlefields — where, along the Warrenton Turnpike, the bones of soldiers killed the previous August poked from their shallow, eroded graves. Full skeletons lay here and there where they had fallen, picked clean over ten months. Curious soldiers wandered that uncharted cemetery near the railroad cut, reflecting on a fate many of them would soon share. Some, taxed too far by sun, exertion, and ailments they might have shaken off at home, died before their comrades took to the road again, filling their own graves in fence corners or among the roots of shade trees.[69]

With his army poised to either defend Washington or chase Lee northward, Hooker and his chief quartermaster rode into the capital. The general met with the president, who interrupted that interview to attend a brief cabinet meeting, where he seemed noticeably worried. Believing he wanted to resume the conversation with his army commander, the cabinet officers soon retired. That afternoon, Postmaster General Montgomery Blair told his sister that Lincoln had hinted at removing Hooker if, like McClellan, he allowed Lee to beat him in a race in which the Army of the Potomac held the shorter route. A few days later the president made the same remark to Gideon Welles.[70]

Thanks largely to J. E. B. Stuart's departure with most of his cavalry on a circuitous raid around the Union army, Hooker had deduced by then the direction of Lee's march and was moving his army over the Potomac at Edwards's Ferry, near Leesburg.[71] Once ashore on the Maryland side, the troops encountered a subtle but prominent change of atmosphere. In Virginia the long blue columns had met little but sour stares or studied frowns from the white population; even unmitigated Unionists like John Minor Botts of Culpeper County, who welcomed Union officers into his home, had not cared for the emancipation doctrine that followed in the footsteps of Lincoln's armies. The people of western Maryland entertained precisely the opposite proportion of sympathies from those of the Rappahannock region, with but few secessionists amid a preponderance of nationalists: it was no coincidence that the National Road bisected their domain. Old Glory hung in doorways and windows to advertise local loyalty, and bevies of girls gathered to wave lace handkerchiefs, sing national airs, or toss bouquets to young officers. Residents lined the roads in front of their houses with buckets of fresh water, pitchers of lemonade, or cans of milk. If a column stopped near a house, the owner's daughter might emerge with blackberry wine and pie for the officers, and occasionally a village squire would try to feed as many of the troops as his kitchen could serve before they moved on.[72]

The greeting invigorated the soldiers with a sense of righteous purpose they may not always have managed to maintain south of the Potomac. No longer need they feel the subliminal self-reproach that must often have attended their invasion and suppression of Virginia; now, when the enemy crossed an international boundary that their own government refused to recognize, they instinctively perceived themselves as defending their own homeland, and the knowledge fired their spirits as it had those of the Confederates on other fields. Depending as heavily as he did on the demoralization of his foe after the drubbings of Fredericksburg and Chancellorsville, General Lee may not have considered the powerful advantage the Yankees would glean from the elixir of fighting on — and for — home soil.

Neither did Lee appear to weigh the damage his campaign might do to the Northern peace movement, for which he had expressed such solicitude. For all the weak response of Pennsylvanians to appeals for militia, Democrats like New York's Governor Seymour, who had developed an intense aversion to prosecuting the war, did rally to the defense of home territory. In Baltimore, where impressed black laborers and unpaid white workmen lined public parks with entrenchments, those who volunteered to protect the city included a good many who had always been suspected of sympathy or collusion with secessionists. One former legislator who took refuge there, Josiah Gordon, had opposed the war from the start: he had spent six months in the bowels of a federal fort when Union troops arrested the state legislature over trumped-up fears of a secessionist plot. Gordon lived in Cumberland, and might have remained safely at home if, as his critics assumed, the rebels had really been his friends. As much as zealous Unionists declared otherwise, though, opposition to the war did not make a man a traitor to his own region, even if that antipathy included a willingness to let the Confederacy go its own way. Lee's intrusions into slaveholding Maryland had evidently not violated "Northern" territory in the minds of most of those from elsewhere, either in September of 1862 or in June of 1863, but the passage into Pennsylvania did. Many antiwar Democrats seemed anxious to see the invader driven from that free state — in spite of their grievances over the draft, arbitrary arrests, and the tyranny of generals who wielded the nation's soldiers against their own fellow citizens.[73]

Evidence that Lee had erred, politically, emerged from a Democratic press that had hounded Lincoln over his constitutional excesses. While praising the New York peace convention and hectoring the administration about conscription, dictatorial proclamations, and the abuse of military power, one Democratic newspaper on the upper Mississippi candidly remarked at this juncture that the vibrant "peace party" had disappeared the moment Confederate forces stepped into Pennsylvania. The observation may have been more premonitory than literal, for the peace faction had not entirely disappeared, even temporarily. Citizens opposed to the war still gathered in meetings large and small across the country, especially in the East, while Lee's ravenous legions scoured Pennsylvania for sustenance; one of the biggest peace rallies, with a reputed attendance as high as twelve thousand, took place on the banks of the Delaware River in Pennsylvania itself. Many Peace Democrats simply fathomed the injury their cause would suffer if Lee recast his heroic defenders of a beleaguered South as aggressors who finally posed the threat to Northern citizens that the war party had long claimed.[74]

After more than two weeks of relatively timid defensive maneuvering that may have reflected his dissatisfaction at Lincoln's strategic restrictions, General Hooker began to show signs of fight. Halleck had assured him that he had direct control of all troops between Baltimore and Cumberland, so Hooker made plans to pick up the ten-thousand-man garrison at Harper's Ferry, combine it with Slocum's Twelfth Corps, and cut off Lee's escape back across the river. Remembering the furor caused by the surrender of Harper's Ferry the previous September, the self-protective Halleck insisted that Harper's Ferry had to be held. Neither Hooker nor any other professional soldier on the scene could understand why: there was little there worth protecting, and the garrison was as vulnerable to capture as it had been the previous year. Besides, Hooker could put the men to better use elsewhere. In combination with Halleck's earlier denials of reinforcements, his behavior struck Hooker as calculated subversion. With his tactical plans foiled by Halleck and his strategic preferences vetoed by Lincoln, Hooker promptly asked to be relieved of command.[75]

If that request amounted to a challenge designed to loosen the restraints on his discretion, it failed. It went by telegram from Sandy Hook, Maryland, opposite Harper's Ferry, right after lunch on Saturday afternoon, June 27; before breakfast on Sunday morning, in his tent near Frederick, George Meade pulled on his spectacles to read the president's order placing him in command of the army. "You will not be hampered by any minute instructions from these headquarters," Halleck asserted in his accompanying letter, offering Meade the freedom to act entirely on his own judgment. Halleck even authorized him to remove the Harper's Ferry garrison if he deemed it necessary. Meade may not have known that Hooker had been promised similar latitude when he assumed command — as well as a promise that he would not have to report through Halleck, who despised him. The concluding weeks of Hooker's five-month tenure had illustrated how brief the life span of executive promises might be.[76]

As the news trickled through the army, it initiated more consternation than anything else. Few seemed to regret Hooker's departure, and the provost marshal of the army noted that Hooker left few friends behind despite having been the most "agreeable" of the four commanders he had known. The notion of again shuffling generals about in the midst of a campaign worried men in and out of uniform, and especially with a battle imminent.[77] In Washington the demise of Hooker reportedly brought rejoicing, but Halleck himself had to appeal to other generals for opinions of Meade — which he did after Meade had already been elevated to a command on which Halleck might have been expected to consult. Most soldiers outside Meade's Fifth Corps, and most of the civilian population, knew little about him, for he habitually avoided the self-promotion that seemed second nature to the Hookers of the army, but those familiar with his quiet competence and courage greeted the appointment with as much satisfaction as the circumstances permitted.[78]

The rest of the army, including at least one of Meade's greater admirers, could not fathom why, if the president was going to risk upsetting their leadership again at so crucial a passage, he did not restore McClellan. The commander of the 10th Vermont denied the newspapers' claims that the soldiers were happy with the change, and swore that they universally called for Lincoln to "give us back McClellan again." When the foot soldiers of the Sixth Corps passed through Littlestown, Pennsylvania, a couple of days later, they were greeted by a little boy sitting on a fence who held up a newspaper engraving of McClellan, and soldiers fell out of ranks to dicker with him for the portrait. Officers as far west as Grant's army could not understand Lincoln's seemingly partisan refusal to recall the only general who had ever led the Army of the Potomac to victory.[79] Civilians remained mystified, too. Refugees wandering ahead of Lee's army hinted at their own hope that Little Mac would return, and the governor of New Jersey, where McClellan's last orders had instructed him to reside, appealed directly to the president for the general's reinstatement — at least to the command of the army of New York, New Jersey, and Pennsylvania militia gathering at Harrisburg. Republican stalwarts numbered among McClellan's advocates, as well. Alexander McClure, Lincoln's staunchest advocate in Pennsylvania's Cumberland Valley, reported that he and other administration friends in Harrisburg were certain that McClellan would inspire volunteers and confidence, both of which were sorely lacking. None of this swayed the president, whose replies suggested that he feared the reaction of McClellan's Radical Republican enemies.[80]

Meade it would be, then, and he had not held his controversial new command six hours when J. E. B. Stuart's raid around the army threw Washington into administrative apoplexy. With three mounted brigades Stuart thundered through Fairfax Court House, less than twenty miles from the U.S. Capitol, veering north across the Potomac and striking a

wagon train bound for the Army of the Potomac at Rockville, only fifteen miles from Lincoln's summer residence at the Soldiers' Home. Rebel
troopers cut the telegraph lines for miles in either direction, severing convenient communications between army headquarters and the troops in
the field, and they took the last of the wagon train within five miles of
Washington City.[81] That sparked the usual frenzy, and soldiers started
marching hither and yon through the streets. Battalions of government
clerks and quartermaster employees replaced all the usual guards, and
provost marshals put the convalescents at Alexandria under arms, posting those from the eastern armies at the Long Bridge and those from the
western armies at the Chain Bridge.[82]

The last of Maine's nine-month men in the Washington garrison were
packing up to go home, and a Maine congressman approached them
about staying on a few days past their terms to protect the capital during
this latest emergency; the panic-prone Edwin Stanton went so far as to
order a Medal of Honor for any of them who submitted to a few extra days
of service. There were two regiments — the 25th and 27th Maine — and
both still had nearly full ranks: each had lost about a score of men to disease, and neither had ever seen an armed rebel, but fewer than three hundred of the nineteen hundred or so enlisted men agreed "to stop a while."
The rest boarded trains for home.[83] Their few counterparts with the Army
of the Potomac felt much the same, and with the crisis at hand the lieutenant colonel of the 12th Vermont consoled himself and his wife with the
reflection that the government "can't keep us but about four days more."[84]

Already Stuart had been delayed from rejoining Lee's main body
longer than he wished, so he rode due north with his booty. At ten o'clock
on Monday evening the harbingers of his column reached Union Mills,
five miles from the Pennsylvania line, where the adult children of William
Shriver invited them in; Shriver's daughters buttered the last two loaves
of bread in the house and started fires in the kitchen stove. The Shrivers
were some of the rare secessionists in the vicinity: three of the older sons
had gone South, leaving only a boy named Frank and seventeen-year-
old Thomas Herbert Shriver to be dazzled by the appearance of General
Stuart and Fitzhugh Lee, nephew to General Lee himself. The women
cooked for hungry Confederates through the night until, an hour or two
before dawn, Stuart waved his column back into the saddle and pounded
toward the Mason-Dixon Line. Young Herb Shriver rode along with him,
as both a guide and a prospective cavalryman.[85]

Correctly interpreting the various reports as another of Stuart's raids
around the Army of the Potomac, Meade remarked that he would have to
"submit" to it and turned all his attention to Lee's army. He circumvented
the telegraphic interruption by sending Halleck a detailed description of

his plans by separate couriers, one of whom was shot dead in an encounter with Stuart north of Glen Rock, Pennsylvania. Stuart's absence had allowed Union spies and cavalry a much better glimpse of Lee's whereabouts, and Meade started the army toward the Pennsylvania border to hunt him down. Two brigades of John Buford's cavalry division prowled ahead of the infantry, and on the morning of July 1 Buford's New York, Illinois, and Indiana troopers bumped into a stray division of Confederates on the turnpike from Chambersburg, west of Gettysburg.[86]

Both Lee and Meade expected to fight somewhere below the Susquehanna, each intending to choose the most advantageous ground, and Meade hoped that the hills around Gettysburg would offer prime defensive positions. Once it seemed certain that Lee would take the bait, Yankee infantry that had been easing toward Gettysburg began taking longer strides. Buford's two dismounted brigades delayed the enemy until John Reynolds galloped to the spot ahead of his First Corps and concluded that the terrain did, indeed, favor them. His leading brigades were just rushing onto the field when a rebel bullet knocked Reynolds out of the saddle, dead.[87]

Led by the Iron Brigade, which had earned its nickname in a brutal close-range clash ten months before, the first division of the First Corps formed across the Chambersburg Pike on McPherson's Ridge, a mile outside of town. They came at the double-quick, loading their rifles on the run, and plunged straight into a series of volleys that each dropped scores of them; the color-bearer of the 24th Michigan went down in the first flurry. A man in that regiment had shot a hole through his foot the day before to avoid precisely this duty, but no one faltered this morning. Confederate brigades were stacking up fast, though, once the sun passed its zenith, and under heavy pressure the blue line backed toward Gettysburg, but the Westerners of the Iron Brigade captured several hundred prisoners, including a brigadier general.[88] Most of the rest of the First Corps arrived, and then O. O. Howard's Eleventh Corps showed up with small numbers and the reputation of having run at Chancellorsville, but A. P. Hill's Confederate corps was pouring in from the west and Ewell's divisions were swarming down from the north. One-armed Howard, pious and obtuse, took command of both corps, directing operations from the cupola of the Adams County courthouse, but by four o'clock in the afternoon rebels were sweeping around the shrinking arc of Union resistance. Wounded, exhausted, or simply encircled by the overlapping Confederate lines as they dodged through the streets of the town, more than three thousand Union soldiers cast aside their arms and surrendered.[89] Barely a quarter of the 24th Michigan escaped: even their field hospital was overrun, surgeons and all. Here and there a man dove into an outbuilding or begged sanctuary in someone's cellar or attic. It was the worst day of the war for the Iron Brigade: an eighteen-year-old Wisconsin lad, two years a veteran, confessed to his parents that "I would as soon throw down my old musket & take a turn at farming as not."[90]

Meade sent Winfield Hancock, commander of the Second Corps, to take over the battlefield: Hancock was junior to Howard in date of rank as major general, but it was competence that mattered to Meade, and he obviously doubted Howard's capacity. Hancock arrived to find fragments of the First and Eleventh corps scampering back through Gettysburg; while he reinforced the battered brigades on Culp's Hill and Cemetery Hill, south of town, Meade pushed the rest of the army up from the state line.[91]

Blue uniforms rolled up the Emmitsburg Road, the Taneytown Road, and the Baltimore Pike all night and into the morning, and the rumors they encountered suggested that the army had met another Chancellorsville. The fifer in a Maine company confessed that the strategic situation indicated the rebels were "getting the best of us," and frantic runaways wearing the Eleventh Corps crescent on their caps told of whole brigades swallowed up or scattered to the winds.[92]

A thick fog shrouded the town early on Thursday morning. Both army commanders had reached the field, and the greater part of either army lay near Gettysburg or sped toward it by forced marches. Meade chose a horseshoe-shaped perimeter with his right grounded on Culp's Hill, his center on the hill where Gettysburgers buried their dead, and his left resting on the ridge running south from the cemetery. Lee focused on the enemy flanks, and much of that sultry day passed with Southern divisions creeping into position to assault the rocky, wooded crest of Culp's Hill and the low, seemingly vulnerable slope at the southern end of Cemetery Ridge. Most of the afternoon had passed by the time Ewell's corps had settled in before Culp's Hill and Longstreet's troops were in position to sweep across the Emmitsburg Road against the Union left.[93]

To the surprise of both George Meade and James Longstreet, by midafternoon the situation on the Union left had changed drastically. Dan Sickles, whose Third Corps had been posted at the lower end of Cemetery Ridge, on the extreme left, had taken it upon himself to push his troops out nearly a mile to a peach orchard along the Emmitsburg Road. His left flank trailed past a wheat field, resting near a glacial tumble of boulders known as Devil's Den, but his right dangled in the air on the road, and his unsolicited advance had uncovered the left flank of Hancock's Second Corps, back on the ridge. Meade noticed the gaping hole in his line and rode Sickles down to correct his blunder, but their conversation was interrupted by Longstreet's artillery.[94]

One of the first shells shattered the flagstaff of the 2nd New Hampshire and leveled a squad of men. The New Hampshiremen had been roused at 2:00 A.M. and marched until 9:00 to reach the battlefield, and since then they had changed position here and there to suit General Sickles. Finally they were ordered out into the peach orchard by the Emmitsburg Road, to support a battery near the modest home of a yeoman family named Wentz. Like the Culp house on Culp's Hill, the Wentz place represented the ease with which opposing political views migrated across state boundaries, for those two hardscrabble farms at either end of the battlefield had each contributed an itinerant boy to Confederate service. Both Henry Wentz and Wesley Culp, who had a brother wearing Union blue, had come back to fight the Yankees in their native town.[95]

Southern artillery decimated the brigades Sickles had distributed in such exposed positions, and Sickles himself went down with a shattered leg. Troops just coming up in support watched him ride by in a stretcher to the hospital, where his chaplain would hold the chloroform over his face while surgeons sawed off the tattered limb. Ultimately Longstreet's infantry knocked the ill-positioned Third Corps and its Second Corps reinforcements back toward Cemetery Ridge, sweeping over the peach orchard, the wheat field, and Devil's Den. The Army of the Potomac's provost guard formed several lines deep behind the battlefront, some on foot and some mounted, and their commander called it "hot work" to keep demoralized stragglers from slipping to the rear. With the division on his left, Longstreet hammered at the void Sickles had left between the two corps, and Hancock sacrificed the little 1st Minnesota in a desperate charge to stall the advance of an Alabama brigade. Nearly three-quarters of the Minnesotans fell in fifteen bloody minutes, but the Alabama brigade came no farther.[96]

Below Cemetery Ridge stood two rugged hills — Little Round Top and, farther south, Round Top. The smaller hill had just been timbered off, and some at headquarters started calling the stump-strewn knob Bald Top. These two peaks dominated the ridge, and if the Confederates could wrestle artillery up either of them they could enfilade Meade's entire line, taking the positions at Cemetery Hill and Culp's Hill from behind. Meade's chief engineer, Brigadier General Gouverneur Warren, spotted Longstreet's men veering toward Little Round Top, and he took the responsibility of diverting a brigade of fresh troops from the Fifth Corps to race over the top of Little Round Top and secure it. The four regiments of that brigade had hardly crested the summit when they looked down to see six regiments of Texas and Alabama infantry on the ascent, only a couple of minutes from the top. The rebels outnumbered and overlapped them, and only by furious firing and a bayonet charge did they sap the Confederates' momentum. Finally the Pennsylvania Reserves dashed in to their right, and part of John Sedgwick's dog-tired Sixth Corps trotted into line at the tail end of a thirty-mile march, driving the enemy back toward Devil's Den and eliciting shrill cheers from the surviving defenders of Little Round Top. That repaired the damage Sickles had done, and secured Meade's left once more.[97]

There still remained a couple of fierce fights to be waged on the Union right before the battle of July 2 ended. Dick Ewell had arrayed two divisions against Meade's right: Allegheny Johnson's before Culp's Hill and Jubal Early's in front of Cemetery Hill. Johnson struck first, with the sun drooping toward South Mountain. He enjoyed some initial success because much of the Twelfth Corps had shifted to the left of the line to shore it up against Longstreet's attack, but the remaining brigade of that corps had the advantage of intricate breastworks, and they held the hill until their comrades returned. Alpheus Williams brought his division back as Johnson's Confederates were giving up, and he pushed them well beyond the breastworks. By then it was dark, and Early had sent his brigades up Cemetery Hill, where they scattered more of those frazzled Eleventh Corps Germans and grappled with New York and Pennsylvania artillerymen right in their lunettes, evidently tasting how close they were to breaking the Yankees' line and severing their communications on the Baltimore Pike. A few of Howard's foot soldiers stuck by the gunners, crossing glinting bayonets in the moonlight. Then Winfield Hancock turned some of his troops back from Cemetery Ridge, and in the confusion of early night they pushed Early's men back down the hill. With that the roar subsided, except for an unexpected volley that sent the better part of the 145th New York bolting for the rear on the heels of its terrified colonel.[98]

At dawn of July 3 Lee still held the town, with his army still wrapped around Meade's horseshoe defense line — now elongated to a fishhook by the extension of troops to the Round Tops. All along that line, Union soldiers lay waiting, knowing the fight had not ended. Anticipating the potential for another bloody day's work, some scribbled hasty messages to apprise family of their safety so far, and their whereabouts, which a Maine private puzzled out as "Guiterville Pennsylvania." A Vermonter serving with the Regulars spelled it "Gettesburg," and thought they were all still in Maryland.[99]

Having failed to crush his enemy at either end, Lee intended to strike him in the middle with a massive infantry assault, and Confederate artillerists began aligning dozens of batteries in front of Seminary Ridge, which paralleled Cemetery Ridge a mile to the west. Lee wanted General

Ewell to distract from the main attack by moving on Culp's Hill again, but he had given the order too early and Ewell had already undertaken his part: at daylight Allegheny Johnson's division resumed its contest for the hill against a well-entrenched Twelfth Corps. A Pennsylvanian behind the breastworks thought the rebels lost ten men for every defender who fell, and in some lengths of the line the ratio far exceeded that, but in a counterattack some Union regiments suffered crippling casualties. Johnson's assault failed to carry any point, though, and by noon he pulled his brigades back to a respectful distance.[100]

The fire slackened on that front just in time to provide no diversion at all to Lee's principal effort. Around noon scores of Southern cannon opened what every witness seemed to agree was the loudest and most thorough shelling of their experience. Shards of iron sprayed the length of Cemetery Ridge, from the hills at the south to Cemetery Hill, at the north. A captain in the Eleventh Corps reported that "every species of projectile" tilled the ground around the intersection of the Emmitsburg Road and the Baltimore Pike, at the outskirts of Gettysburg, while men at the far end of Cemetery Ridge hid behind boulders to escape the fragments that flew all around them. A copse of trees stood near the center of Hancock's Second Corps, and there the rebel gunners concentrated most of their fire, though much of it flew wide. Hancock's troops huddled behind a low stone wall or in a shallow ditch. A field officer at the extremity of the Second Corps front estimated that twenty rounds a minute passed overhead, and he described a mighty hardwood reduced to a stump by successive shells. Abner Doubleday, commanding the First Corps now, in place of Reynolds, had endured the bombardment of Fort Sumter, and he pronounced it nothing compared to this.[101]

The guns fell gradually silent on Cemetery Ridge, where Meade's chief of artillery, Henry Hunt, learned that ammunition was running low. That persuaded Hunt's Confederate counterpart to slow his own rate of fire on the misapprehension that he had disabled all the Union guns, and finally the two opposing ridges assumed an eerie silence while Southern infantry deployed along Seminary Ridge.[102]

What followed was the defining spectacle of the war, and the most memorable hour in the life of every man who took part in it. They would call it Longstreet's Assault, but two-thirds of the troops came from A. P. Hill's corps. Virginians would embrace it as their own undertaking, renaming it Pickett's Charge, but George Pickett's division provided only three of the eleven brigades in that mile-wide formation: more regiments dressed ranks under the flag of North Carolina than under the seal of the Old Dominion. They came from South Carolina, too, and Tennessee, Ala-

bama, Mississippi, and Florida, and when they rose into sight with muskets gleaming and red banners streaming, their enemies muttered in
grudging admiration at the archaic pageantry. To the troops who waited
to receive it, the grand assault began with "a long brown line of men," followed by another, and then another, but those three lines evoked old ways
of war just as they represented old ways of life, and some in the Union
ranks could sense the obsolescence of both. "The moment I saw them
I knew we should give them Fredericksburg," wrote a Massachusetts major near the copse of trees, who had survived the bloody repulse before
Marye's Heights. "So did every body."[103]

The outdated tactics that had failed Lee at Malvern Hill and Burnside
at Fredericksburg might have worked one more time. Eleven brigades of
fresh Confederates (twelve thousand of them, give or take a thousand)
bore down on a point of Cemetery Ridge defended by only seven brigades
of Federals, many of whom had fought during the previous evening. That
was about the proportional advantage deemed necessary for the success
of an attacking column, but there entered that issue of the Union artillery,
most of which had not — as some Confederates supposed — been put
out of action.[104] Case shot and shell from those guns lacerated the front
line before it reached the Emmitsburg Road, and at closer range came
the canister. The first line all but disappeared. With an impetuous yell
three of the bulging nine-month regiments from Vermont swung out
perpendicular to the rebel ranks to rake them with a volley. Hancock's
brigades rose up from behind their stone wall and loosed a sheet of musketry point-blank into the second rank, driving it back to rally on the
third, which surged ahead over the stone wall. When they broke through,
Meade's provost marshal again called on the guard he had strung behind Cemetery Ridge to check a sudden rush to the rear, but too little remained of Lee's grand assault to widen the breach or hold the ground.
Men in blue came sprinting up from Culp's Hill, where Ewell no longer
occupied them, and those Southrons who made it over the stone wall
found themselves sealed inside Union lines. Their comrades, or what was
left of their comrades, saw the hopelessness of it all and bounded back toward Seminary Ridge.[105]

As the sun set on the worst day he had yet experienced as commander of the Army of Northern Virginia, Lee convened a council of war
at A. P. Hill's headquarters, on the Chambersburg Pike. Pickett's division,
which had been the one to break the Union line, straggled back to its old
camps with no semblance of discipline, and Ewell's topographical engineer scented a universal despondency among officers and men. When the
generals emerged from their council that evening, they had decided to

turn back for Virginia.[106] At least ten thousand men lay dead or dying. Perhaps that many more had been crippled for life, and most of those would find early graves or live for decades as impoverished pensioners of their nation or states.[107] Now the grand invasion was over, and with it had ended any immediate hope of dampening Northern will enough to bring the war to an end.

5

Uncle Sam Says You're the One

➔ THE FOURTH OF JULY in Washington City began with drenching showers, followed by the skirmish-like crackle of children lighting fireworks and grown men discharging revolvers and muskets into the air. Unsupervised boys as young as six loaded miniature artillery with black powder and touched off their little salutes. The first news from Gettysburg that morning told only of the repulse of the grand assault of July 3, with no suggestion that the enemy might retreat, but after nearly a year of setbacks, disappointments, and disasters, the loyal part of the population itched to celebrate the slightest hint of victory. A promiscuous collection of uniforms congregated in front of City Hall at midmorning, stepping off behind the U.S. Marine Band and a delegation of veterans from the War of 1812. A brigade of troops from the city garrison lengthened the parade of police and fraternal societies, churning the sodden streets into mud before a scorching sun could dry them, and after the procession had reached the big new Treasury Building came a fusillade of more formal pyrotechnics. The Marine Band turned into the White House grounds to serenade the commander in chief with national airs, and a reading of the Declaration of Independence initiated a round of speeches filled with hopeful assumptions about the military situation and the prospects for peace and reunion.[1]

From his perch on the White House portico, Postmaster General Montgomery Blair's little nephew, Blair Lee, found the display a little restrained. The boy's mother and grandfather — old Preston Blair, patriarch of an intensely political clan — shared the portico with President Lincoln, who showed a certain distraction with affairs in Pennsylvania. The Confederates had given up most of Gettysburg proper, Lincoln knew, but General Meade entertained doubts whether Lee intended to retreat: perhaps he was only drawing back to a more advantageous position, where he might force Meade to take the offensive. Even if the enemy did withdraw, the Army of the Potomac needed time to bring up rations, all of which appeared to worry the president. Since the first winter of the war, logistical explanations had been greeted at the White House as though they were merely excuses for inaction.[2]

At the same hour as the White House celebration, thousands of Democrats gathered in Concord, New Hampshire, to hear a different message delivered by Franklin Pierce, who had vacated the executive mansion precisely six years and four months before. With his friend Nathaniel Hawthorne seated near him on the dais, Pierce raged at Lincoln's war and at the damage he inflicted on the Constitution for the sake of that war. Brandishing a copy of Lincoln's oft-quoted letter to Erastus Corning, in which the president had equated Clement Vallandigham's campaign complaints to subversion and sedition, Pierce all but challenged the administration to arrest him, too.

"Who," Pierce wondered, ". . . has clothed the president with power to dictate to any one of us when we must or when we may speak, or be silent on any subject, and especially in relation to the conduct of any public servant?" What Lincoln had done to Vallandigham he might do to any of those present, the former president warned, but he urged his listeners to live "or if it must be, to die," as free men. The audacity that the administration had already demonstrated led Pierce and many others to suppose that Lincoln might even cancel elections if they seemed likely to result in Republican defeat, and in that event Pierce made a daring allusion to armed resistance. An assortment of Democrats of state and national renown followed him to the platform, broadening and refining the tirade against the unconstitutional and arbitrary exercise of power.[3]

With the public defection of a well-regarded former president, July 4, 1863, marked the high tide of Democratic opposition to the administration, and to the war. The invasion of Pennsylvania had capped such a long series of Union military defeats that opposition predictions of perpetual failure had begun to ring true, which only rendered the loss of civil rights pointless, as well as obnoxious. Furthermore, the imminent imposition of national conscription alarmed everyone of military age, especially among those who perceived the war as hopeless. All the uncertain reports emanating from Gettysburg on that eighty-seventh anniversary of Independence Day carried the same exaggerated assurances of success that had so often been transformed into calamity, with headlines announcing the deaths of Longstreet and A. P. Hill. Even ardent Unionists applied an instinctive skepticism to the tidings of overwhelming victory that came on

July 5, purporting the destruction of Lee's army and the flight of his fugitives toward Potomac River crossings that had already been seized by Union forces. The same overly sanguine reports continued on July 6, received by the prudent as "probably fictitious," but as the days passed a more credible tale of moderate triumph emerged, with Lee conducting a reasonably orderly retreat after a battlefield failure that seemed to surprise the Northern public as thoroughly as it did Lee himself.[4]

At first, half a victory proved quite acceptable, as it had after Antietam. With the cities of the eastern seaboard safe, newspapers began to rejoice, and the price of gold dropped to $1.38. "This ends the Rebellion," chattered optimistic businessmen on the streets of downtown New York, and fervent friends of the Lincoln administration mistook the natural winding-down of the Democrats' Fourth of July rallies for a stunned reaction to the first significant Union victory in many months. And then came the report that Vicksburg had surrendered to Grant.[5]

John Pemberton's illness-ravaged troops and the civilians who shared the siege with them were approaching starvation by the beginning of July. The Vicksburg *Daily Citizen* remained defiant as late as July 2, but so short was the city of all kinds of supplies that that day's edition came out on the reverse side of flowery wallpaper, some of which appeared to have been pulled from the walls of Vicksburg's battered homes. Early on July 3 a message came out from Pemberton asking for a commission of officers to arrange terms of surrender, but Grant insisted on immediate and unconditional surrender, while hinting that his terms might tend to the generous side. Pemberton agreed to a 3:00 P.M. meeting where the opposing works crossed the Jackson Road, and shortly after breakfast the guns fell silent all along the lines. The gunboats stopped firing, as well, once Grant could get a message to them. At 2:00 P.M. everything erupted again on McPherson's front, where the meeting was to transpire, but it soon subsided.[6]

Pemberton appeared on schedule and made a pitch for the European-style surrender of old, in which his vanquished army would emerge from his works fully armed, with colors flying, to march away in dignity and leave behind nothing but the captured city. Grant shrugged that off just as Pemberton must have expected he would, but he offered paroles instead of prison camps, and allowed the officers to keep their side arms. The Philadelphia Confederate took those concessions back to his headquarters to ponder with his own division commanders, and Union pickets primed their rebel counterparts that night with the delicious news that they would be allowed to go home on parole if their general accepted the terms. Shortly before dawn on July 4 Pemberton sent out his reply — accepting the terms if his men could march outside the works to stack their arms, instead of having the Yankees come inside to disarm them. White flags went up on the parapets at 8:00 that morning, and a couple of hours later about twenty thousand grimy and exceedingly spare Southerners filed out under a steaming sun to deliver their weapons. When the last of them marched back in, Union soldiers followed them, raising the Stars and Stripes over the courthouse where Confederate recruits had flocked two long years before. Inside, the victors found the houses riddled by artillery, the hills pockmarked with caves dug by shell-shy citizens, and the enemy camps in "a terrible plight," with thousands more rebels too sick to carry their weapons. Mingling freely with the occupation force, many of the defenders swore they would never fight again, and for some of them it was more than the hunger talking: most of the garrison marched away under their own officers to parole camps, but more than a dozen regiments crossed the Mississippi back to their homes in Arkansas, west Louisiana, and Texas, where Confederate authorities now posed less terror to the reluctant Southern soldier.[7]

That same Independence Day, Braxton Bragg's Army of Tennessee woke up south of the Tennessee River, having abandoned all of middle Tennessee to William Rosecrans and the Army of the Cumberland in a whirlwind, rain-drenched campaign without a major battle. Also, just as the Vicksburg garrison marched out to surrender, a strong Confederate division in Arkansas fell on the garrison at Helena. Weakened as it was by detachments to Grant, the place should have fallen, posing a threat to Grant's supply line, but in three hours the mismanaged attack was beaten back, with more than 1,500 casualties against fewer than 250 for the Federals. That marked the fourth major Confederate setback of the weekend, and five days later Port Hudson capitulated.[8]

The capture of Vicksburg left Port Hudson untenable, and made its defense unnecessary in any case. Had each of the two strongholds contained enough food, the sieges might have gone on indefinitely, for the undulating terrain served as a particularly sound impediment to infantry assault. That was especially true at Port Hudson, where Confederate pioneers had dropped trees into the ravines to form a tangle of trunks and tops, and their engineers had built imposing earthen parapets beyond that. General Banks had thrown a second assault against those works on June 14, but it had spent its momentum in the snarled timber and had been stopped altogether by a hail of bullets and buckshot, twenty yards from the rebel works.[9] After that Banks could find no volunteers to lead another attack, and had fallen back on a continual artillery bombardment to demoralize those on the inside. The Southerners simply carved holes into the soft embankments near their guns, burrowing in to avoid shrapnel and the glare of a sun that raised sweat even on idle men's brows by six o'clock in the morning.[10]

Once word of Pemberton's surrender drifted down the Mississippi, Banks relayed it to his counterpart inside Port Hudson, Franklin Gardner, and the echo of the final gun faded across the Mississippi on the evening of July 7. The next afternoon Gardner agreed to surrender, and on the morning of the ninth a division-long queue of Union troops filed into the stronghold with bands blaring patriotic tunes. Fewer than five thousand shabbily clad Confederates formed ranks to ground their weapons — some in the manner prescribed by the drill manual, which involved a deliberate genuflection before the conqueror, and some by casually dropping their arms or throwing them down in disgust and contempt. Relief seemed a more common sentiment among the ragged prisoners, with occasional evidence of outright satisfaction, and even their officers remarked gratefully on the kindly treatment of their captors.[11]

This latest of the many successes in a single week elicited another moment of factually imprecise eloquence from President Lincoln, who would remark with memorable exaggeration that the "Father of Waters again goes unvexed to the sea." To the relief of the president and all Westerners, the principal commercial corridor of his youth lay nominally open once more, though it would ever after carry a diminishing proportion of what its watershed produced. A Massachusetts man confessed to a Wisconsin friend that he considered any self-congratulation premature, adding "I wouldn't want to lead an excursion to New Orleans just now," but celebrations nevertheless erupted again in cities across the North. Bells rang, the hollow belch of cannon and blank gunshots echoed through the streets, flags fluttered over storefronts, and at nightfall the residents illuminated the windows of their homes, while boys organized torchlight processions.[12]

Elizabeth Blair Lee, the sister of Postmaster General Blair, the mother of Blair Lee, and the wife of a Union admiral, was chatting with a neighbor when the news of Vicksburg reached her home in Maryland. Another of Mrs. Lee's brothers, Frank Blair, commanded a Union division outside Vicksburg, but she suppressed her glee at the information because her neighbor had two brothers inside the city, with Pemberton. Sensitivity to her friend failed to blind her, though, to the sudden turn in the fortunes of Northern arms. The *New York Times* fairly crowed over such a "prodigious purification of the atmosphere within one brief week." A quartermaster detected a "glorious change" in morale among Louisville Unionists, and a heavy-artilleryman observed the same transformation among the men in the forts around Washington: Gettysburg had won the Army of the Potomac eternal renown, he admitted, but Vicksburg and Port Hudson were "the places that Count." The father of an Ohio soldier suspected that the defeats of July had struck the Confederacy its "death blow." Abraham Lincoln believed as much himself, asserting that if Meade could only crush Lee's army north of the Potomac, the war would be "over." The president's faith in imminent Confederate collapse could only have been strengthened by a letter that Jefferson Davis tried to send him through Lincoln's old friend, Confederate vice president Alexander Stephens. The letter addressed the issue of prisoner exchanges, but the public mistook it for a peace overture, and Lincoln's refusal to receive it allowed him to believe as much.[13]

While citizens of the North reveled in the long-unfamiliar glow of serial victories, those who had won them found little time to celebrate. The contest for Vicksburg had worn down the health and spirits of both the besiegers and the garrison, and for some of those in blue its capture brought little satisfaction. The day after the ceremony, a dejected Iowa cavalryman listed the death of one friend after another: in two weeks his entire mess had dissolved, with his brother and another man killed, his best friend dead of fever, and a fourth messmate sent to the hospital. To cap his misery, his regiment saddled up that very day and started down the road to Jackson after Joe Johnston, whose polyglot force had been hovering behind Grant with faint hopes of relieving the Vicksburg garrison.[14]

William Tecumseh Sherman followed the cavalry with his own corps and two others, throwing an impromptu log bridge over the Big Black River and pushing on to Jackson between miles of dense, mature cornfields and blooming cotton.[15] For a week Johnston made a stand west of the state capital, but with no more army for him to rescue at Vicksburg he saw little reason to risk his own makeshift command in a struggle for ruined Jackson. When he slipped away, some disappointed Southern patriot in his rear guard left a sarcastic message impaled on a stick, offering to fight the exultant Yankees at Meridian, another hundred miles to the east.[16] Sherman would take that invitation more seriously the following winter, but after pillaging Jackson once more the Federals turned back toward the Mississippi. They retired with unusual and inexplicable haste, especially in the borrowed divisions of the Ninth Corps, and in such oppressive heat that men began dropping in their tracks, just as Joe Hooker's had on their sprint after Lee. The temperature and humidity struck these men all the harder because so many in the column already bore the beginnings of fever in their blood, or had ingested the deadly microbes that lurked in river water. A train of ambulances rumbled out from the Vicksburg camps to collect those who had fallen prey to the sun, but some had already filled graves under the shade of live oak trees, where comrades had carved their names in the trunks.[17]

The height of summer brought pervasive sickness for the legions of Yankees sleeping on the fringes of the Mississippi River swamps, who were dying off three or four times as fast as Union soldiers in the eastern theater. Up and down the river, colonels whose regiments had suffered but little in battle reported barely half their men fit for duty. Baton Rouge hospitals bulged with four thousand sick from Banks's army, and a Massachusetts militiaman at Port Hudson predicted that if they remained there much longer there would be none of them left to send home.[18] After the surrenders, Grant and Banks both unburdened themselves of superfluous troops. Grant returned the men Burnside and Schofield had loaned him, shifted many of those he retained to more salubrious camps near Natchez, and started furloughing some of the more rundown men to recuperate at home, while Banks shipped all his nine-month regiments upstream for discharge. The northbound soldiers, and especially the short-term militiamen, died in droves all along the way. Comrades lugged them off the river steamers at every port, leaving them to recover or to manure unfamiliar soil, as fate might dictate, and hundreds of those who did survive the journey arrived at home in the final stages of the deadly diseases they had carried with them.[19]

Despite such appalling mortality, jubilation lasted all summer in the West, where Southern forces had suffered the most numerous and most devastating defeats. Gettysburg had seemed to lend most of the buoyancy to Eastern spirits. Vicksburg was all well and good, they seemed to say along the coastal states, but Gettysburg overshadowed it: it had been "the great battle of the war," decided a Maine officer whose brother had died a "glorious death" with the Iron Brigade on July 1. Gettysburg alone, insisted a Pennsylvanian in the Twelfth Corps, had transformed rebel confidence to "howling dispair."[20] Gettysburg may have attracted disproportionate attention more because it was so unexpected than for its strategic value, and the fragile foundation of that satisfaction soon began to crumble under the weight of ambitious expectations.

Immediately after the battle, most soldiers in the Army of the Potomac, and most citizens east of the Alleghenies, anticipated that the three days of fighting at Gettysburg merely formed the prelude to an apocalyptic struggle between Meade and Lee. Left behind to bury comrades on the battlefield after the Confederates departed, Union soldiers heard that William French held the Potomac fords with the Harper's Ferry garrison, and had destroyed Lee's pontoon bridge below Williamsport. The rain that began falling on July 4 would surely raise the river too high for an easy crossing, and with Meade bearing down on him from behind, Lee's doom seemed certain. He could draw no supplies from south of the river, reasoned a Maine cavalryman, and there seemed little chance of his army escaping in more than vestigial fragments. The principal army of the Republic strode south in supreme confidence, with men literally wearing the shoes off their feet so they could be in at the kill.[21]

The fable of Lee's hundred-thousand-man *grande armée* persisted, both around the campfires and in the mind of the commanding general. Even after estimating Lee's combat losses as high as thirty thousand, the more scientific gamblers in the Union ranks supposed that the Army of Northern Virginia still held a numerical advantage. Some units in Meade's army had been sorely reduced, particularly in the fighting of July 2, on the Union left: survivors in some regiments of the Third Corps reported as few as 150 or 120 men at morning musters. These remnants nevertheless joined the chase with a will: like their compatriots in less battered commands, they assumed from the plethora of caissons, ambulances, and wounded left in the Confederates' wake that, however many the enemy might be, Lee had tucked his tail firmly between his legs. A mountaintop encounter with seventeen hundred hungry and demoralized rebel prisoners helped to corroborate that impression.[22]

Keystone militia turned out with sudden valor, once the invaders had taken a sufficient thrashing. The volunteers began pouring in on July 4: five thousand of them milled about in Harrisburg by July 5, and thousands more came in the next day. A refugee in the Pennsylvania capital characterized those eleventh-hour volunteers as the foremost nuisance in the city, but after a few days of desultory drill they strutted down the valley after the rebels, complaining about rain, chest colds, and short rations. Some of them were already calculating how much money they might make during the campaign and wondering why they should not be eligible for enlistment bounties, all the while planning their next employment.[23]

Pecuniary considerations seemed to rule the Pennsylvania spirit. Since the Yankees had first crossed the state line they had detected a sudden withering of indigenous hospitality. Even as they had forged ahead to meet the enemy, drenched in sweat under a broiling sun, heavy knapsacks, and bulging cartridge boxes, the roadside buckets of water and milk had grown fewer and farther apart. The cheering and waving had continued as in Maryland, convincing native Pennsylvania soldiers of a grateful welcome, but most of their fellow citizens expected soldiers to pay — and to pay well — for any costlier expressions of appreciation. The people met their protectors with "a spirit of extortion & meanness," contended a Vermont major who paid a dollar for eighteen "miserable biscuits" smaller than a pocket watch. A twenty-cent loaf of bread went for fifty; eight ounces of half-rancid butter cost seventy-five cents, and a quart-and-a-half canteen of milk ranged from fifteen cents to twenty-five. Officers asking for a night of inside lodging were charged as much as a dollar to sleep on the floor. Many of the troops had just been paid, and spent their money so lavishly that residents found the gouging seductively easy. Some boasted to their neighbors of profits as high as two hundred dollars. More than one Federal remarked that Southern sympathizers in Maryland and Confederate families in Virginia often treated them with greater generosity than the niggling farmers of Pennsylvania.[24]

Any gratitude those farmers may have borne Union soldiers for expelling the Confederates failed to curb that mercenary impulse. They descended on the battlefield "in shoals" (grumbled an artillery colonel), selling pies to soldiers and engaging in ghoulish salvage operations — collecting valuables and marketable relics — while Meade's provost marshal had the devil's own time finding anyone among Gettysburg's largely antiwar population who would agree to bury the dead. Union soldiers had attended to many of their comrades' bodies, and to the enemy's as well, but Confederate corpses still lay about in abundance on July 6, and the bloated bodies of First Corps troops still littered McPherson's Ridge, west of the town, five days after they had been killed.[25]

To the relief of soldiers whose pocket money was already running out, the army soon saw the last of Pennsylvania profiteers. Only a day's march from Gettysburg lay Maryland, where Union columns again encountered verandas teeming with ecstatic young women who had adorned their hair with white wreaths, little girls fluttering tiny flags, and farmers' wives standing by to hand out butter and eggs.[26]

As usual the cavalry galloped ahead of the army, racing to seal off the river crossings from the left bank. John Buford led again, driving down to Frederick and then following McClellan's old route to Antietam, over Braddock Heights and South Mountain. Somewhere beyond Frederick, Buford's troopers picked up a man who had long been known for selling newspapers and maps in the camps of the Army of the Potomac. Deciding on the spot that he was funneling information on their movements to Southern forces, they hanged him early on the morning of July 6 — choosing a tree alongside the road leading down from Braddock Heights into the verdant Middletown Valley, about a mile short of that town. In a gratuitously cruel touch they first stripped him of all his clothing save his shirt, and Buford added a measure of gothic brutality with an order that the body should remain hanging for four days. Most of the Army of the Potomac traversed that very spot over those four days, passing almost beneath the bare feet and the buzzing flies, so the gruesome scene exerted more effect on loyal Union soldiers than on any potential spies.[27]

With his pontoon bridges gone and the river too swollen for ford-ing, Lee set his engineers to entrenching along a nine-mile front be-tween Hagerstown and a bend of the Potomac east of Williamsport, be-low the fords that were most likely to open first when the water receded. Union infantry diverged beyond Middletown on roads to Turner's and Crampton's gaps, toward Boonsboro and Sharpsburg. Meade's divisions trailed in over several days, taking up a line roughly parallel to Antietam Creek. His officers noticed that as soon as each of their regiments formed its line the men bent spontaneously to the task of building breastworks, which they improved with every passing hour. This was something new.[28]

There the antagonists lay through the second week of July, sparring and anticipating a battle to eclipse Gettysburg. Rain fell in torrents all morning on July 8, raising the Potomac fords even higher, and from his camp at Boonsboro that afternoon a Maine corporal lamented that they could end the war then and there if only enough men had come up. That was the same story his army had heard many times over, though: by the time every Union corps had come up, the Confederates were thoroughly dug in.[29] Meade suspected that Lee wanted another battle before he left Maryland, to ameliorate the humiliation he had suffered in Pennsylvania, and certainly the depth and breadth of his earthworks implied an inten-tion to linger indefinitely: later inspection revealed that the parapet of those nine miles of new works stood six feet thick at the top. Lee evidently wanted to receive the attack rather than deliver it, and a driving thunder-storm on the evening of July 12 kept the fords high, so Meade assumed he had time to spare.[30]

July 13 looked as though it might be the day, but the enthusiasm that had quickened the southward march of Meade's men had begun to fade. The rebels seemed too anxious to meet an attack, and their works looked too daunting. The Maine corporal who had wished for enough troops to make the attack on July 8 still thought they needed more on the thir-teenth, worrying that without reinforcements they would find Lee more than a match for them. It was, after all, the reverse of Pickett's Charge, ex-cept that the Confederates had much stronger works than had protected Cemetery Ridge. Most of Meade's generals felt the same way about a fron-tal assault, when he polled them on the night of the twelfth; they fretted over the likelihood of another Fredericksburg, which would neutralize all the political capital the army had just regained, and they were probably correct. Only one brigadier appeared to have any better idea: Joseph Bartlett agreed that the works were too strong in front, but he considered the extreme left of Lee's line vulnerable, near Hagerstown, where a corps or two might pry him out of his trenches and leave him with no other de-fensible position to fall back on. Bartlett's brigade occupied that part of the line near Hagerstown, with Sedgwick's corps, and he doubted that Meade had ever come up to examine that sector. Bartlett owned too little cachet to attend the council of war, so his pugnacious opinion was not represented at headquarters. Sedgwick himself opposed an attack, arguing that success was not sufficiently certain, while they could simply not afford defeat. Rather than risk giving Lee back all the prestige he had lost at Gettysburg, Meade decided to postpone any action for another day. Halleck, who had not seen the field, characteristically urged him to fight, but instead of striking at Lee on July 13 Meade spent that misty day trying to reconnoiter for a likely point of attack. Fog foiled that venture, however, and an afternoon downpour ended it.[31]

Orders nevertheless went out to advance against the Confederate works on the morning of July 14. The skirmishers rolled forward without resistance, though, and they soon ascertained that Lee had decamped, leaving only a rear guard and hundreds of his most seriously wounded men, who filled every house and barn his army had passed. Except for a clash between that rear guard and Union cavalry, the invaders slipped unmolested across a hastily improvised pontoon bridge and a chest-deep ford.[32]

The intelligence of Lee's escape reached President Lincoln in the middle of his cabinet meeting that same day. It was a spare gathering: Attorney General Bates was in St. Louis, Montgomery Blair lay sick at home, and Secretary Chase sat in his office at the Treasury Department writing a newsy and optimistic letter to the wealthy young man who proposed marrying his daughter, Kate. The navy secretary, Welles, was in attendance, as was Lincoln's new secretary of the interior, the oleaginous John P. Usher. Seward may also have been in the room when Stanton burst in and asked for the president's ear a moment; the two retired down a short hallway to the White House library, and when they returned a few minutes later Lincoln seemed so obviously distressed that Usher asked if Stanton had brought bad news. Stanton disingenuously denied it, but with a disapproving glance toward his war minister the president admitted that Lee had transported all or at least most of his army back into Virginia.[33]

That dissolved the cabinet meeting. Ambling with Welles across the gardens toward the department buildings, the president snarled something about "bad faith" in the failure to attack, as though crediting the old Radical Republican suspicion that a cabal of conservative generals sought to avoid absolute victory. For ten days, as congratulations for each success clacked in over the wire, Lincoln had envisioned the rebellion on the brink of disintegration. All that time, he had feared only this very misfortune to rob him of that triumph, and the blow knocked the legs from under him. He went into the War Department, belabored Halleck with his disappointment and frustration, and then stretched out on a sofa in Stanton's office, morose and oblivious as department heads and employees bustled about. Not for a moment did he seem to consider the consequences if Meade had suffered a bloody repulse. Halleck shared the president's unhappiness with Meade by telegram in a tactless tone of reproach, but Meade reacted as McClellan should have on numerous occasions, asking to be relieved from command if his performance failed to satisfy his superiors. Before the day was through Lincoln heard of that exchange, and he had recovered enough equanimity to appreciate the ingratitude his relayed remarks had shown for Meade's crucial victory at Gettysburg, so he composed a letter to Meade describing his state of mind. Whatever the circumstances of Lee's escape, it had quashed a magnificent opportunity to shatter the rebellion beyond continuation. "As it is," Lincoln mourned, "the war will be prolonged indefinitely." Although intended as a kindly explanation of an involuntary outburst, the president's letter still seemed accusative, and he never sent it.[34]

Welles thought the cigar-puffing Halleck bore a significant portion of the responsibility, since he might well have gone to the front himself if he thought the army could be maneuvered more aggressively. That was true enough, for Halleck played a largely passive role in the campaign. From his rejection of Hooker's planned sweep toward Richmond to his pressure for Meade to attack Lee's entrenchments, Halleck's communications with his field commanders often consisted of little more than passing along the president's wishes, translated into military jargon. Welles observed that Halleck had so completely failed to offer any innovative strategies that Lincoln could have handled the army himself — and much of the time he was doing just that, through Halleck. Halleck's disinclination to contradict or guide the president left the army hobbled by a commander in chief too preoccupied with political responsibilities and the safety of the capital to develop an effective offensive strategy.[35]

An Indiana officer in the Second Corps stumbled indirectly on an example of that preoccupation when, four days before Lee's escape, he criticized the army bigwigs for not bringing the forces from Fort Monroe and North Carolina up the south side of the Potomac to seal off Lee's escape for certain. That might well have impeded the crossing sufficiently for Meade to fall on the retreating enemy's haunches, but those troops could also have done some good had they concentrated against lightly defended Richmond while Lee frolicked in Pennsylvania. John Dix, the aging politician-general who commanded at Fort Monroe, supposed that Pickett's division still camped a few miles above the Confederate capital on June 25. He thought Pickett could draw on D. H. Hill's troops from Petersburg and the James River to defend the city, besides mobilizing government clerks and mechanics to muster a defense force as strong as Dix's own command. In reality Pickett had left to join Lee two weeks before, and a single brigade of twenty-five hundred remained where Dix saw an entire division of eight thousand; another Confederate brigade lay below Richmond at Drewry's Bluff, on the James, and a third at Petersburg, making seven or eight thousand men altogether. Dix, meanwhile, commanded four divisions, numerous independent brigades, and several scattered regiments totaling more than thirty thousand.[36]

Dix needed many of those troops to guard his base, but he should have been able to mount a troublesome attack on Richmond even without assistance from troops on the North Carolina coast. As early as June 14 Halleck lobbied him for such a move, but Dix allowed his initial expeditions to turn tail at the first sign of organized resistance. Then, when he gathered his surplus forces on the Peninsula at the end of the month, Dix — like Meade — held a council of war in which his generals argued against any offensive; as a token contribution he sent three brigades up the Pamunkey to burn some bridges and come scurrying back. By then the battle was raging at Gettysburg, and, rather than demanding the energy from Dix that he seemed to expect from Meade, Halleck instructed Dix to draw back on the defensive and send every spare man to protect Washington.[37]

Golden opportunities died on both the Potomac and the Pamunkey that July. When Meade followed Lee over the river, he chose a crossing well downstream, and many of his veterans noticed that they had occupied nearly the same location exactly one year before — and, in some cases, precisely two years before. That bred an air of futility, and men in the ranks echoed their president's fear that, once again, there was no end in sight for this war. Corroborating conservative suspicions that it was really Radical Republicans who wished to keep the war alive, Senator Charles Sumner confessed his actual relief that Lee had escaped, lest compromise attend any appeals for peace from the South before it had been completely conquered and humiliated by an army of freed slaves.[38]

As he led his horse south from Gettysburg, the colonel of the 5th Virginia Cavalry reflected that the foray into Pennsylvania "has done us no good." Lee himself, who owned a certain capacity for self-delusion, may have recognized the depth of understatement in that observation. If he had sent Longstreet's corps to Joe Johnston or Braxton Bragg in May, and had remained dug in against the cowed Hooker, the laurels of Chancellorsville might have been magnified by good news from the West. The tide of antiwar sentiment had so seriously dampened the war spirit above the Potomac through May and June, even as Grant moved inexorably toward

Vicksburg, that it seems unlikely Northern will could have readily sustained another major reverse. Instead, Lee's aggressive nature and overweening confidence in his army brought the Confederacy disaster in both the eastern and western theaters.[39]

During each of Lee's ventures across the Potomac, George McClellan and George Meade had tried to stimulate their troops with homeland imagery, accentuating the need to drive the invader from "our soil" in a manner that implicitly recognized the existence of a separate Southern nation. President Lincoln, who grew as nervous as anyone over those northward incursions, allowed the political implications of his generals' rhetoric to blind him to their inspirational intent, complaining that "the whole country is *our* soil." The president might carefully avoid any allusion to even temporary disunion, but the concept enjoyed tacit acknowledgment throughout the army. Colonel Rutherford B. Hayes hinted at it in a letter to his uncle, in which he denied any disappointment at Lee's successful withdrawal. "To get rid of him so easily is a success," Hayes contended, as though Lee had retired into a foreign realm.[40]

The same day that he wrote that sentence, Hayes observed that the enemy had undertaken a more modest and hopeless invasion of the Midwest. It happened to be coursing through his home state, aiming almost directly toward the town where his wife and children were living that summer, yet he only regarded it as further evidence of Confederate desperation. "Rebel prospects were never so dark," he assured his mother, "or ours so cheering."[41]

Hayes was talking about John Hunt Morgan, whom Braxton Bragg sent into Kentucky to threaten Louisville and wreck the railroads that supplied the Army of the Cumberland. Morgan took a couple of thousand cavalry and a four-gun battery, with instructions to recruit his Kentucky regiments and return as soon as possible — striking at the rear of Rosecrans's army if, in the meantime, Rosecrans should advance against Bragg. Morgan wasted a couple of days attacking Union outposts in south and central Kentucky and then spurred straight for Louisville, which was reported to be lightly defended. That city lapsed into the customary fright: martial law closed all businesses, and every man between eighteen and forty-five was ordered to report for military duty. By July 7 Morgan had passed through Bardstown, and Louisville shuddered at wild and contradictory rumors of his presence with tens of thousands of troops in any of several different locations, all converging on the city, but then he turned west of town toward the Ohio River and Indiana, whereupon Louisville relaxed.[42]

Completely ignoring his orders, Morgan commandeered a couple of steamboats at Brandenburg, Kentucky, and on July 8 started crossing his

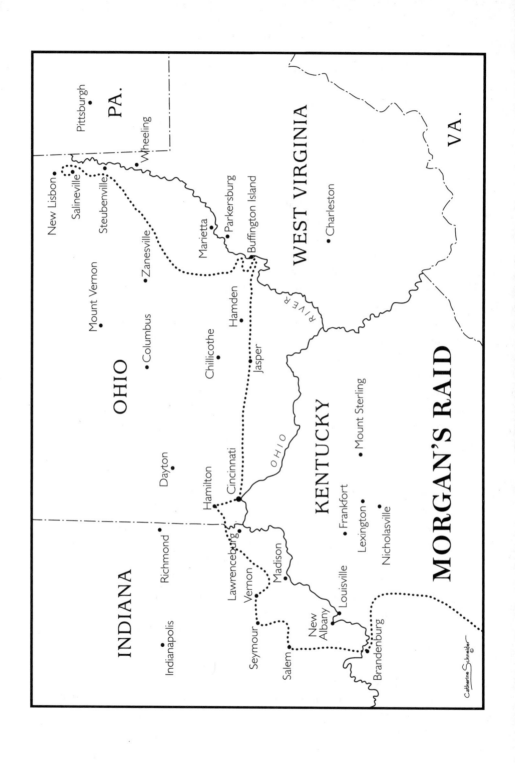

MORGAN'S RAID

INDIANA

OHIO

KENTUCKY

WEST VIRGINIA

PA.

VA.

Pittsburgh

Wheeling

New Lisbon
Salineville
Steubenville

Parkersburg
Marietta
Buffington Island

Mount Vernon
Zanesville

Columbus

Chillicothe
Hamden

Charleston

Jasper

Dayton

Mount Sterling

Hamilton
Cincinnati

Richmond

Lawrenceburg
Vernon
Madison

Frankfort
Lexington
Nicholasville

Indianapolis

Seymour
Salem

New
Albany

Louisville

Brandenburg

OHIO RIVER

Catherine Schneider

little division over the river piecemeal. The ferrying took all night; after daylight on July 9 the U.S.S. *Springfield*, a six-gun sternwheel riverboat, happened by and opened fire. Morgan's artillery sparred with the gunboat for an hour, but eventually the commander of the *Springfield* turned upstream to file an extravagant report of a sizable invasion.[43]

As the last of his troopers landed on the right bank they set fire to one of their stolen transports and rode due north, bringing southern Indiana to life and throwing Governor Oliver P. Morton into a dither over the safety of Indianapolis, which Morgan had intimated to one of the steamboat captains that he might target. Ever anxious about disloyal conspiracies, Morton and his executive coterie imagined that Morgan was headed for the arsenal in the capital, where he would find enough weapons to arm the massive phalanx of lurking insurrectionaries who were believed to populate the state.[44] Morton must have developed that specific apprehension unassisted by the Iago of his Copperhead chimera, Colonel Carrington, who had evidently gone off on a bender when the emergency seemed likely to drag him from his desk for service in the field.[45]

Indiana militia pecked away at the Confederate cavalry here and there, slowing Morgan's progress while two brigades of Union troopers under Edward Hobson trailed after him, a day or more behind. Paranoid predictions of a fifth column notwithstanding, with the exception of a fourteen-year-old runaway who tagged along as an orderly, no Indiana citizens appear to have joined the raiders, however alienated they may have been from the administration. Some did refuse to turn out for the governor's alarm, however, appraising the reports about Morgan as a Republican ruse to frustrate Democratic county rallies planned for that weekend. Robert Taylor, the clerk of Warrick County, refused to be bullied into service when his local home-guard captain waved the gubernatorial proclamation in his face. Declaring that the captain bore no legal authority to force men into his company, Taylor returned to his farm, fifteen miles down Pigeon Creek from the grave of Abraham Lincoln's mother. There he met an old acquaintance and former employee, now a deserter from the Confederate army, with whom he went to work planting tobacco.[46]

Quakers also resisted the governor's call. They sent their militia-age sons out of the raiders' apparent path to prevent them from being pressed into service, or moved their entire families out of endangered neighborhoods. One of the regular worshippers at the monthly meeting in New Garden Township, fifty miles north of Morgan's route, deemed it "very much crowded" with congregants from "away" during the week after Morgan's appearance. Harvesting their wheat well on the safe side of Indianapolis, meanwhile, farmers cringed and swore at the notion of Morgan pillaging freely in their state.[47]

Rumors painted a sinister portrait of Morgan: people seemed to believe that his men randomly shot women and girls in their doorways. More accurate were the reports that he appropriated all the best horseflesh as he advanced, leaving only winded nags for his pursuers to choose from, and his troopers ate very well from a lush landscape. A veteran telegrapher rode with him, sometimes splicing his portable key into the wires to confuse the pursuit and divert Union reinforcements with false reports.[48]

Then he turned into Ohio, stopping to rob post offices and private citizens when the opportunity offered. A feint toward Hamilton allowed him to pass without interference around Cincinnati, where the populace bridled at the martial law that kept most of them off the streets. Morgan sped steadily eastward once he had safely negotiated that city (where Burnside lay ill at his headquarters, trying to make sense of the reams of telegraphic reports). Perhaps Morgan entertained a grandiose scheme to join Lee's army in Pennsylvania after the longest cavalry raid of the war, terrorizing the North and gaining a reputation that might protect him from the court-martial his disobedience warranted. If so, he should have consulted a newspaper before crossing the Ohio, and he would have learned that Lee's chastised command had already turned back to Virginia.[49]

Now strength was gathering against the raiders, directed by wire from Ambrose Burnside's sickbed. Morgan's only safe haven lay south of the Ohio River, but a fleet of troop transports and gunboats plied that stream, picking up strays from his command as they tried to swim their horses across. The governor of Ohio backed his order for the mobilization of all able-bodied men with the threat of a six-month jail term for shirkers, so southern Ohio was soon crawling with clusters of variously clad men trying desperately to keep in step as they pulverized the grass on their town greens. Colonel Hayes's wife, who was visiting in Chillicothe, wrote her husband that the militia of all the adjacent counties had gathered in that town, and while Morgan was thought to be heading their way those "unarmed sheep" were lining up to be reviewed. The few who bore weapons were sent north of town, as far away from Morgan's anticipated entrance as possible. Roving scouting parties of those amateurs ran upon each other, each mistaking the other for Morgan's vanguard and taking to their heels in opposite directions, terrifying the country folk with wild alarms as they fled. Morgan bypassed Chillicothe in the end, but wherever he did encounter militia they generally surrendered with little or no fight; their greatest service consisted of detaining him by forcing his officers to scribble parole slips for all the prisoners to sign.[50]

Colonel Hayes did not immediately receive his wife's letter, for his regiment and several others had been pulled out of West Virginia to help intercept Morgan. Ten days and nearly four hundred miles after he first crossed the Ohio, the Kentuckian's eastward trajectory brought him back to it between Pomeroy and Portland. There the river turned a grand loop, the throat of which his command entered at a full gallop after losing a smart skirmish with two regiments under Hayes. The harried raiders struck for Buffington's Island, where shallows invited a crossing to Jackson County, in what Morgan would still have called Virginia. A good many of his exhausted cavaliers managed to swim to the other side, but Union gunboats came paddling upriver to stop them and Yankee soldiers started closing in onshore. Outgunned on all sides by naval ordnance and repeating carbines, two-thirds of Morgan's remaining horsemen and all his artillery surrendered under the command of his brother and brother-in-law while Morgan himself and several hundred stubborn desperadoes found a trail upstream. They tried the river a time or two below Parkersburg, only to be turned back by the gunboats.[51]

The fugitive column veered north and northeast, shedding weary and discouraged squads and individuals for another week as it wound toward Wheeling and crossed into the Department of the Monongahela. Thus it could be said — and was said — that Morgan had managed to ride completely through Burnside's domain, but by now the remnants of his division had been worn to a frazzle and cavalry from Burnside's department dogged them relentlessly. Thousands of militia from Pennsylvania and West Virginia, independent detachments of armed citizens, and Union cavalry blocked the way east above Wheeling. Like a wounded animal Morgan began circling aimlessly, finally clashing with Michigan cavalry at Salineville early on July 26 and losing more than half his remaining force. Along the banks of Beaver Creek, barely ten miles from the Pennsylvania border, he surrendered to Federal officers, who handed him over to incensed state authorities. The prisoners from Buffington's Island had been taken downriver and lodged in the Cincinnati jail, where they had been treated more like criminals than prisoners of war, and Morgan's contingent drew even worse accommodation. With his chief subordinates he entered the Ohio State Penitentiary in Columbus; the warden ordered them all shorn of hair and beards, like the other convicts, before throwing them in dank cells among the Buckeye State's worst felons.[52]

Within days Ohio Republicans began milking the raid for all the political capital it would yield. Noting Clement Vallandigham's passage through Bragg's lines one month before Morgan departed that army on his way north, the party's principal newspaper in Columbus offered the unfounded slander that the exiled Democratic candidate for governor had advised Morgan on his route through Ohio — which, cutting through the southern counties as it had, traversed the thickest of Vallandigham's territory. Like Governor Morton, the *Ohio State Journal* insisted that Morgan had intended to spark an uprising among antiwar Democrats, attributing the complete absence of such a rising to Morgan's mistake in stealing indiscriminately from both Copperheads and Unionists. The idea that disloyal Northern citizens had actively encouraged or invited the raid rooted quickly among the Republican faithful. A lieutenant colonel from Indiana firmly believed that Hoosier Butternuts were responsible for the raid, and General Lee's desire to curry antiwar sentiment just prior to his own invasion of Pennsylvania suggests that an indirect connection may have existed, at least in John Morgan's mind. No credible evidence ever demonstrated overt complicity, but Morgan's injudicious frolic (on top of Vallandigham's gubernatorial nomination) ultimately sealed the doom of Democratic prospects in Ohio.[53]

The last and worst blow to Peace Democrats' image that month originated with the orders to implement the draft, which became statutorily effective on July 1. On that date Provost Marshal General James B. Fry announced that conscription would begin immediately in ten selected congressional districts scattered across eight Eastern states. Fry obviously anticipated some resistance to the draft, and wished to begin slowly, lest the first exercise of this unpopular new federal intrusion should stir widespread revolt while so much of the nation's military forces were required in the field. He advised his assistants in each state to concentrate whatever troops they might be able to call upon wherever resistance arose, and to finish the process in one district before moving on to another. In the first set of instructions, issued on July 1, Fry made no call on states with militant Democratic majorities that promised the greatest likelihood of trouble, like Maryland, New Jersey, and New Hampshire, and he issued none in any state west of Pennsylvania, where antiwar sentiment festered; all those he postponed until some examples of peaceful conscription had been set.[54]

While the newspapers assumed that the president had issued another call for three hundred thousand men (his favorite increment, thus far), this first federal draft demanded one-fifth of the first class of enrolled men — that is, unmarried men between twenty and forty-five and married men up to the age of thirty-five. The initial lottery was held in Rhode Island, beginning July 7, without any formal proclamation from the president. By July 10 Governor James Y. Smith announced that it was going very quietly: the people accepted conscription almost as a duty, he said, as though hiring a substitute or paying the commutation fee were dishonorable. The governor badly misinterpreted his constituents' sentiments, however, by mistaking apathy for patriotism. One independently wealthy

Rhode Islander, who spent much of July examining diamonds to present to a prospective bride, made no mention whatever in his diary of either the nation's first public draft drawing or the receipt of his own draft notice; only in passing did he allude to dropping by the provost marshal's office in Providence to pay his three-hundred-dollar exemption fee, between diamond excursions. Of 1,259 men finally held to service in Rhode Island, 679 furnished substitutes and 463 paid commutation. Only 117 drafted men (one in thirty-seven) actually donned uniforms, and another 249 of those whose names were drawn failed to even show up for the physical examination.[55]

The lottery started in Boston on July 8. Attendants heard some fourteen hundred names called that day, and more on the ninth. Massachusetts, with its disproportionate share of militant abolitionists, bore the reputation of having helped to precipitate the war, and might have been expected to provide its quota without excessive prodding. Instead, a much higher percentage of Bay State draftees failed to report than in Rhode Island, and fewer (one in forty) submitted to conscription than in the neighboring state. Many a Brahmin slapped down three hundred dollars without hesitation for himself or his son, and sometimes for more than one son.[56]

Fry's July 1 orders included one district in New York, and five days later he added four other districts, with a combined initial quota of more than fourteen thousand names to be chosen for examination. The drawings began in the Ninth Congressional District, in New York City, on Saturday morning, July 11. Captain Charles Jenkins, the district provost marshal, opened the doors to his office on Third Avenue, at the corner of Forty-sixth Street, at precisely 9:00 A.M. to allow in as many as the building would accommodate of the thousand or more men who stood outside. There were, noted a reporter, "no men of mark there, or citizens of note; all were men of middle age and of the middle classes, whose interest in the scene before them was of the most painful intensity." The better classes, as the reporter might have characterized them, took no interest in such proceedings, which had no palpable, lasting effect on anyone with three hundred dollars to spare.[57]

An assistant turned a large tumbler, and another who had been blindfolded reached in to pull out a card bearing the name of William Jones, of Forty-sixth Street. Jones was not present to have his reaction recorded. Before the office closed that afternoon more than twelve hundred names had been drawn with no more interruption than an occasional muttered curse. The grumbling continued into the evening, though, and into Sunday morning, as the poorer working-class New Yorker began to realize that the federal government really intended to reach into his neighborhood and seize men like him for soldiers, even with a Democrat in the governor's chair. As they sipped their ales that Saturday night, the European immigrants among them may have reflected on the conscript armies and navies that had sustained the empires they had fled, or pondered the propriety of resisting such an imposition in the country that thought of itself as the land of liberty. Not a few of them probably mulled the prospect of being forced to fight for the freedom of a slave who might become his economic rival.[58]

Early on Monday morning, when they would normally have been at their jobs, a throng of workmen from railroad companies and iron foundries on the East Side gathered in the Twenty-second Ward on the half-developed greensward of Central Park. The New York Times of that day editorialized on conscription as "a Great National Benefit," but the men who met that morning clearly disagreed, and they planned a strike to express that disagreement. None of them, perhaps, recognized the irony that the park's principal designer, Frederick Law Olmsted, was an avid proponent of the draft — and of the commutation and substitute provisions that would allow men "of more value to the community" to escape service. The choice of Central Park as a rendezvous may have combined some transplanted Londoner's recollection of the free-speech tradition in Hyde Park with the need for a well-known public space of broad expanse to accommodate hoped-for thousands of protestors.[59]

Swelling their ranks with men persuaded to leave their own factories, the demonstrators rolled down Third Avenue several thousand strong toward Captain Jenkins's office, where the drawing had just resumed. Overpowering a detail of police, hundreds of men rushed the captain and his enrolling officers, several of whom they beat severely after preparing some tinder to set the place on fire. The police superintendent, John Kennedy, raced to the blazing building in a carriage just in time to take a savage drubbing himself. A contingent from the Invalid Corps came limping up Third Avenue in their conspicuous light-blue uniforms soon afterward, too few and too frail to make much of a fight, and the volley they fired only enraged the growing mob, which scattered them back down Third before they could reload. Then the victorious multitude (preponderantly Irish, according to most upper-class witnesses, but heavily salted with Germans and native-born "Americans") began drifting into adjacent streets to attack the homes of draft officers and federal officials. Some turned down Forty-fourth Street to Lexington Avenue, where they burned the brownstone homes of the city postmaster and a suspected associate of the provost marshal. The old Bull's Head Hotel went up in flames on Lexington by random brand or pure accident, but with greater deliberation the mob stalked along Forty-fourth until it reached the Or-

phan Asylum for Colored Children, sprawling the width of an entire block
on Fifth Avenue. The unfortunate inmates of the asylum represented for
most of the rioters the cause of the war, or at least the cause to which
it had been turned, and after much smashing of glass and furniture the
mob (which by then had begun to include women) set the huge building
ablaze, leaving hundreds of children homeless.[60]

Surly proletarians hovered in most of the city's public places, as though
waiting for action to come their way, and gangs of them merged with large
fragments of the mob that swarmed down Third and Fifth avenues. Turning west on Twenty-eighth Street, a sizable cohort found the provost marshal's office of the Eighth Congressional District, on Broadway, but the
drafting there had stopped at noon, when word of the trouble reached
that office. Suspension of the proceedings failed to discourage the rioters,
who burst into the undefended building and put it to the torch. Three or
four thousand people, mostly boys, surged to the corner of Second Avenue
and Twenty-third Street and broke open the doors of the armory there;
police fired on them, killing an Irish ironworker and wounding several
others. Next, a horde of angry working-class men surrounded the office of
the Fifth District provost marshal, setting fire to it and inadvertently destroying the adjacent buildings with it. Way up near Yorkville, on Eighty-
sixth Street, where no soldiers and only a handful of constables patrolled,
hundreds of intruders gutted the home of the Ninth District provost
marshal, and in the same vicinity another contingent (or the same one)
burned the Twenty-third Precinct stationhouse to the ground. Toward
evening more racial violence erupted in the Ninth Ward, near the West
Side docks, when hundreds of men and boys attacked a black drayman
and pummeled him senseless before hanging him from a tree on Clarkson
Street. He bore the same name as the first white man drafted at the Third
Avenue office — William Jones.[61]

United States soldiers on duty within reach of New York City numbered only in the hundreds. There were perhaps two thousand city police.
Most of New York's organized militia had gone south to defend Pennsylvania. The only other soldiers in the city consisted of the two-year men
who had been discharged over the previous ten weeks, and some of their
old officers began hunting them up to organize a defense. The collector
for the Port of New York advertised for a hundred of these men to serve as
temporary revenue aids with loaded muskets, and he called on the commander of the Navy Yard to supply a couple of dozen Marines and two
howitzers to defend the Subtreasury Building on Wall Street. Everyone
wanted guards by the dozen.[62]

Rain cooled the riot that evening, but the violence was rekindled with
greater fury on July 14. The day began with an attack on the mayor's resi-

dence, on Fifth Avenue, followed by a battle in the Upper East Side between a poorly armed mob and a combined force of police and soldiers. A couple of hundred police were battling the crowd with their nightsticks on Second Avenue, near Thirty-Fourth Street, when they encountered Henry O'Brien, the nominal colonel of a partially organized regiment. Bricks and stones rained on the police from the upper stories and rooftops of the buildings on either side, as well as from the crowd on the street. To the outrage of Irish neighbors who took sides with the mob, O'Brien had mustered some of his recruits and had brought along an artillery piece or two, with which he opened on the mass of people with canister. Most of the survivors scattered down side streets. O'Brien lived near there; with drawn sword and pistol he strode brazenly ahead to see what the mob had left of his home, and that was the last his men ever saw him alive. When he had ventured beyond the sight of his command, infuriated rioters felled him with stones, clubbed and stabbed him, tore his uniform from him, looped a rope around his neck, and used it to drag him about the streets. His mutilated corpse appeared at the dead house the next day.[63]

Governor Seymour rushed to the city and delivered an appeal for calm from the steps of City Hall, to no avail. Learning that the weapons from the Second Avenue armory had been moved to the Union Steam Works, four or five thousand people proceeded to Second Avenue and Twenty-second Street to storm that impromptu fortress. Women numbered prominently in that crowd, carrying rocks and clubs. Men with sledgehammers had forced their way in when about three hundred Metropolitan Police arrived and poured into the building. This squad carried revolvers as well as nightsticks, and they shot five men at the entrance. The others who were still inside had already spirited most of the guns out of the building, so the one-sided fight there left fourteen rioters dead, with the rest dropping from the second-story windows, and several were killed or seriously injured in the attempt. There appear to have been no police casualties at the steam works, but they failed to save the building, for after the detachment answered another call, citizens returned and burned the place flat. Flames rising from the Eighteenth Ward station house, on Twenty-second Street near First Avenue, added to that evening's glow on the Manhattan skyline.[64]

A little farther south, barricades started going up. Acting with the assistance of at least one returned soldier, residents began fashioning furniture, vehicles, and debris into breastworks on First Avenue at Eleventh and Fourteenth streets, as though preparing to defend the avenue against attack from the west. Gaps below Eleventh Street, on Twelfth and Thirteenth, and above Fourteenth rendered the barricades useless. At Thirteenth Street, instead of building a barricade, the mob destroyed a couple of new street-sweeping machines. On the Upper West Side, amateur saboteurs dismantled the horse-car tracks from Sixty-fifth Street to Sixty-ninth, while others set fire to Washington Hall, in Harlem. Houses were burning at random in the Twenty-second Ward. Such sporadic and hopelessly uncoordinated preparations left no doubt among military minds that the rampage had sprung to life spontaneously, without any central organization. As the afternoon wore on, it also became apparent that the politically motivated fury of the mob was giving way to wanton destruction and looting. All business had ground to a halt, idling thousands more who had taken no part in Monday's demonstrations, and reinforcements from that quarter lent the mob a mercenary flavor. In all precincts, women composed a far more conspicuous role in the unrest after midday on Tuesday.[65]

Bastille Day of 1863 seemed to inspire revolt. Perhaps taking their cue from the morning's news from New York, a couple of dozen men in Boston's North End jumped an official delivering one of the first draft notices to an employee of the gas works. A policeman came to his aid and the two ducked into a pharmacy, but their pursuers followed them in and began pelting them with bottles. The druggist persuaded the pair to leave, and they started toward the victim's lodgings at the Merrimac House, but the irate workmen overtook them, drove the patrolman away, and beat the provost agent over the head and shoulders until he broke loose and dove down a coal scuttle. Fearing the worst, the governor appealed for three companies of heavy artillery from Fort Warren, and he ordered a detachment of cavalry recruits to the State House on Beacon Hill. Some of the artillery occupied the Cooper Street Armory when, as the workday ended, men and boys started milling about in nearby Haymarket Square. A tall, strapping woman wandered among them, carrying a photograph of her son, who had been killed with the army, and she cheered the crowd on when they determined to attack the armory. Prying paving stones from Cooper and Endicott streets, they tossed them through the armory windows, whereupon the soldiers emerged, fired a volley of blank cartridges, and chased the crowd toward Charlestown Street with leveled bayonets. The troops returned to the armory but the mob followed, charging the building repeatedly and battering at the double front doors until they had knocked a hole in them. At that the artillerymen flung the doors wide open, and a gun crew opened fire with a charge of canister. The first volley killed one laboring man outright and wounded numerous others, but the civilians stood stubborn and defiant until a company of infantry stepped out and began shooting at them by platoons, killing and wounding young and old men, mere boys, some women, and one little girl.[66]

Retreating from the well-armed troops, the mob swept down Endicott Street to Dock Square and smashed open the door of a hardware store, where numbers of rioters armed themselves with muskets, shotguns, revolvers, and knives. Others were caught in the act of breaking into another shop by police, who shot one man and took him into custody along with several others. Boston had supplied hundreds of nine-month troops who had just returned from North Carolina, including the blueblood 44th Massachusetts and much of the 45th Massachusetts, and those recently discharged militiamen gathered at their private armories that evening; some of them reached the State House by 8:30. The presence of so many bayonets checked the outnumbered mob, which receded into the tenements of the dock district without further bloodshed, and the next morning the streets had fallen quiet, with soldiers patrolling by twos and threes.[67]

A sympathetic disturbance startled peaceful Staten Island on July 14, and New York officials saw signs of trouble in Brooklyn and Williamsburg. Provost marshals all across the city fretted over insufficient guard details, while New Jersey draft officials believed dissidents were preparing to offer resistance in any district where a draft might be held. The governor of Connecticut expected an attack on the Hartford arsenal. Residents of New Bedford, Massachusetts, imagined a preconceived plot of "the lower classes" from surrounding towns to attack and plunder their city, in conjunction with the New York riots. Federal troops on duty in most Northern cities started looking over their shoulders. Cincinnati citizens filled the sidewalk outside Burnside's headquarters, alternately groaning the general and cheering Clement Vallandigham, while inside the building Burnside's staff used loaded revolvers and carbines for paperweights.[68]

Draft selection was supposed to begin in Portsmouth, New Hampshire, on Tuesday morning. Warned of the New York riots by state agents in the city, and worried by citizen petitions for protection against an overweening federal government, minority governor Joseph Gilmore tried to stall for a more equitable apportionment of quotas. The riots in New York attracted federal attention more readily than citizen petitions or gubernatorial intervention, however, and — like his counterparts in New York City — the provost marshal for New Hampshire's First Congressional District announced Tuesday morning that the draft was being postponed one day. He put it off for another day on Wednesday morning, but that afternoon disgruntled workers from the shipyard and the harbor shops began clustering around the federal building at the corner of Daniel and Penhallow streets, cursing the provost marshal and calling out threats. After dark the crowd started throwing stones over the line of

Marines and volunteers who stood guard, one of whom fired a wild round when a rock bounced off his head. The rock throwers wandered away before dawn, but some who refused to leave were arrested the next day by Portsmouth police, and that transferred the trouble to the police station, where some of the agitators repaired to free their comrades. The police met the delegation with gunfire, and four of the protesting workmen fell with bullet wounds while their perceived leader was clubbed over the head and severely wounded; one officer suffered a broken wrist. Marines and the garrison of Fort Constitution came running, and the rest of the crowd of "cowardly, sneaking villains" (as the local Republican organ characterized them) retired. That ended the resistance in Portsmouth.[69]

Demonstrations, some of which grew violent, erupted in Jersey City, Brooklyn, Westchester County, and Troy. In Troy several hundred employees of the Rensselaer Iron Works and the Albany Nail Works marched through the streets on the morning of July 15, denouncing the draft and warning that none would be held in their city. They stopped before the Troy office of the *New York Times,* hurled stones through the windows, and finally burst in and tore the office apart. The *Times* reported that the protestors were dissuaded from racial violence by an Irish priest, turning instead to the local jail, from which they released all the prisoners.[70]

The weapons stolen from the Union Steam Works on July 14 gave some of New York's insurgents an edge on July 15. Confrontations that day developed into pitched battles, but the military began winning them. On Thirty-second Street, between Sixth and Seventh avenues, where another lynching had occurred on Tuesday night, a squadron of cavalry backed by artillery arrived about 9:00 A.M. to clear the street. Beleaguered by riflemen firing from upper windows and the tops of the houses, the artillery disgorged three quick volleys of canister into the mob, killing at least twenty-eight men and women — most of them Irish residents of Eleventh Avenue. Some Germans from Forty-second and Forty-third streets lay among the dead; seven soldiers were killed, and twenty wounded. In the afternoon another mob materialized in a tenement neighborhood on First Avenue, between Eighteenth and Nineteenth streets. A tiny battalion of veterans, recently discharged from two-year Zouave regiments, fell in for the emergency without their uniforms, and they also brought some artillery with them. Those guns raked First Avenue with ten rounds of canister, but the rioters showed more sense this time and took cover between discharges. They wounded a Zouave colonel, killed a few of his officers and men, and finally drove away the troops, who left some of their wounded behind. U.S. Regulars returned hours later, regaining the lost ground and retrieving the dead, after dispersing an equally combative mob that had swooped down on the more aristocratic residences of Gramercy Park.[71]

Navy gunboats took position to fire down the cross streets, if necessary. At last, troops began arriving from the Army of the Potomac. Henry Halleck had interfered with the return of most of the New York militia, despite their time being up, and had delayed the return of nine regiments by at least a full day. Edwin Stanton, making the best of Lee's escape over the Potomac, called his retreat an utter rout and declared that Meade's army could well spare a few thousand men to restore order in New York. His provost marshal general urged the immediate deployment of a force adequate to resume the draft, so as to assert federal determination and authority, and by Thursday morning, July 17, a semblance of order returned to most of the city while troops sought marauders door-to-door in the Upper East Side. By Friday the army had taken complete control. "I think 'Mr. Irishman' will have a heep of fun to resist now," smirked a Massachusetts man visiting in the city.[72]

Republicans cannily associated the political discontent that sparked the riots with the savagery and thievery that it produced, thereby stigmatizing all Peace Democrats and draft opponents. That seemed logical to Gideon Welles, who considered the rioters the partisans of Horatio Seymour; Welles held the governor responsible for encouraging the spirit that precipitated the mayhem, and, by forgetting Seymour's extensive deployment of his militia to defend Pennsylvania, Welles seemed to suspect him of permitting the riots to build and persist. Observing the simultaneous outburst of violence in so many different cities, an officer in an international marine insurance company concluded that "an extended political organization" must have guided the rioting, rather than the coincidental implementation of conscription in all those locations.[73]

Active-duty troops reacted venomously to the riots, frequently expressing a wish that they could return home and fight the enemy in their rear, whom they hated now more than the one in front. "If they resist," suggested a private who wanted to see heavy drafts of reinforcements, "dam them shoot them."[74] Even army doctors advocated slaughtering the protestors with artillery, and on reflection one surgeon proposed shooting any man who proved reluctant to support the government.[75]

Again, the notion of a disloyal conspiracy soon overcame all evidence to the contrary. An English tourist climbing Mount Washington learned that his fellow travelers fully believed the New York riots were specifically intended to initiate civil war within the Northern states, and Southern observers took pleasure in hoping the revolutionary impulse would spread to the Union army. Editors who harped on accusations of an active Copperhead plot found credulous readers, who eyed Democrats thereafter with intense animosity. Such perfect fodder did the riots offer Republican propagandists that a colonel with the Army of the Potomac, himself a Democrat who believed in stern war, half supposed that Republican provocateurs might have deliberately incited the mobs.[76]

The events of July had severely undermined the Northern peace party that Lee had hoped to encourage. After the invasion of Pennsylvania, the equivocating, self-interested citizen who might have held no firm feelings about the war suddenly regarded the slave South as an active threat to property and liberty in the free states. The war's advocates had tried to field that argument since before the fighting began, but it took a Confederate army on Northern soil for many to adopt that view, and once they did they usually accepted the more pejorative image of secession as an act of outlawry, rather than a bid for liberty. Morgan's raid and the draft riots only seemed to corroborate the impression of Southern brigands and dissenting Northerners as a demonic alliance, turning still more of the indifferent and the halfhearted into willing advocates of a vigorous war. Not only did success seem possible, at last, but the surest and fastest road to peace now appeared to be unrelenting aggressiveness on all fronts. The nation that had leaned sharply toward abandoning a losing cause on the last day of June narrowly missed winning that war in the middle of July, and ended the month much more determined, at least for the moment, to see it through to complete victory.[77]

For weeks following the riots, the dingy tents of Meade's veterans speckled New York City's numerous parks. Several Vermont regiments shared Washington Square and Tompkins Square with emaciated battalions of U.S. Regulars, quaffing rare fresh water from the Croton Reservoir and enjoying the "well dressed ladies" and "gay young women" who came — sometimes with motives of dubious propriety — to see the soldiers. These pleasures failed to compensate for the tardy rations, poor coffee, and inadequate shelter that some of the Vermonters recorded in their urban campsite, and there was nearly a riot among the soldiers when a summer downpour washed into their tents while the officers' and their horses escaped the flood with board floors and sheds. Strict discipline provoked another miniature mutiny when, in such civilized surroundings, officers ordered one of their men strung up by the thumbs for some minor infraction; the grumbling of his comrades assumed such a threatening pitch that the guards posted beside the trussed-up prisoner loaded their rifles.[78]

What the city-park garrison did not see in New York was any further sign of draft demonstrations. Late in July the governor of Pennsylvania diverted some of his tardier militia regiments to pacify fractious miners in the anthracite fields, but they met with no resistance there, either. The

close of July brought the end of violent resistance to the draft, anywhere
in the country. Even in Wisconsin, where the militia draft had produced
mob violence the previous autumn, a military presence and fortuitous de-
lays in implementing the draft muted any further manifestations of discontent.[79] The spirit of open defiance to tyranny, which orators had touted
as the nation's foremost legacy on the Fourth of July, gave way to the tactic
of practical evasion before August.

For that first draft levy, commutation posed the easiest and thus the favorite means of escape: of the 88,171 draftees who failed to win any of
two dozen types of exemption, 52,288 paid the three-hundred-dollar fee.
Many towns and cities held emergency meetings in the hope of convincing taxpayers to foot the bill, spreading the cost over the entire community. Where the checklist included a high enough proportion of voters
under the age of forty-five, such appeals met with more serious consid-
eration, apparently regardless of the political flavor of the community.
"There is scarcely a man about here to which the conscript law applies
that thinks it is right," a New Hampshire woman told her soldier husband.
The most prominent supporter of the draft in her town appeared to be the
young Congregational minister, an outspoken abolitionist whose occupation would have exempted him, and who (to the disgust of that soldier's
wife) thought himself too frail to enlist anyway. That town, like many others in New Hampshire, Maine, and elsewhere, voted to pay three hundred dollars to each man who was drafted — to use for commutation, as a
stake for hiring a substitute, or as his own enlistment bounty. Some towns
and cities paid lesser amounts, or created funds from which committees
would dole out varying subsidies to those who sought relief from conscription.[80]

That perennial phenomenon of war — the tendency of the most boisterous proponents to remain safely and comfortably at home — led plenty
of soldiers to applaud the draft as a means of bringing those bellicose
village-green patriots into the front lines. Thomas Brown, an impoverished Vermont farmer who had responded to the recruiting rallies and
bounties of 1862, confessed a fervent hope that the July call would bring
out a few of those who "stay at home and bark." Most of his comrades
would have concurred, but the commutation clause dashed those hopes:
as nearly everyone expected, most of the enrolled men who were "elected"
bought their way out. Commiserating with a drafted neighbor, Brown acknowledged that if he were a civilian again he would try to scrape up the
three hundred dollars, rather than be drafted, and again he probably expressed the prevailing view among soldiers, despite near-universal condemnation of a clause they found outrageously biased toward the rich. A
woman returning to her New York City home at the height of the riots

fully understood why the poor resented the commutation clause so bitterly: as a Massachusetts officer admitted to his family, it left only the
poor to do all the fighting after all those who could afford it paid for exemption.[81]

Earnest advocates of both war and draft tried to bend the inequities of
the commutation clause backward. It would keep the cost of substitutes
within reach of the poor, ran the spiel, otherwise the rich would bid the
cost of substitutes sharply upward. Who would spend more for someone
to go in his place if he could simply pay the fee? Lincoln himself saw it this
way: it was actually the provision for substitutes that favored the rich, he
reasoned, while the commutation fee only eased that objection. All the exemptions in the conscription law were meant to protect poor families, its
defenders insisted; with an irony that appears to have been unintended,
they often added that it gave the poor an opportunity for remunerative
employment, presumably as substitutes, and commutation simply represented another of those charitable concessions.[82]

Of course the remuneration the poor might realize would be that much
better if substitute prices rose well above the commutation fee, and indeed those prices did substantially exceed commutation within a few
weeks after the first draft notices had been delivered. If anything, the
three-hundred-dollar fee increased the cost of substitutes. Ten months
before, during the militia draft, a Pennsylvania woman thought her
neighbor did well to hold out for a hundred and fifty dollars before agree-
ing to go as a substitute when there was no commutation alternative at
all. Just before commutation, the top price for a substitute appeared to be
three hundred, which even desperate principals considered too high by a
hundred; afterward, that became the minimum, and as early as August of
1863 drafted men were paying four and five hundred dollars for a replacement.[83]

Imitating a common practice during the 1862 militia draft, men whose
age, health, and situations made them likely prey for the provost marshal
frequently banded together in private collectives, investing fifty to a hundred dollars apiece, or more, to insure themselves against having to pay
the entire commutation fee. This was the cheapest way out of the draft if
one's community failed to indemnify every enrolled citizen. The July draft
called for 20 percent of the enrollment, so only very bad luck would lead
to the conscription of more than four or five from a group of fifteen, and
with a hundred-dollar contribution apiece there would still be enough to
pay five commutation fees. With twice the investment, such self-insured
gentlemen could depend upon a three-year exemption from the draft by
hiring substitutes instead of paying the flat fee.[84]

Another 26,002 drafted men hired substitutes. A substitute freed the principal from all future draft calls until his substitute's term of enlistment ran out, and in 1863 most substitutes were expected to enlist for three years: by then, the majority supposed, the war would probably have ended, one way or the other. Recognizing the added security that his enlistment provided for a principal, the substitute nearly always demanded more than three hundred dollars, especially where the municipality was paying that much anyway, and they could easily bring five hundred or more. The prices quickly rose so high that they lured some soldiers from the path of duty: even with the army owing them six months' pay, some men at the front found it too inviting to desert and reenlist on behalf of a wealthy conscript. By the first of September such deserters were already being recognized at roll call in the various draft rendezvous.[85]

A substitute could not be liable to the draft himself, and the favorite sources of exempt, healthy males consisted of foreign citizens and youths under the age of twenty. The only son of a widow or aged parents could not be drafted, or the father of motherless children, so either could enlist as a substitute, but the price could escalate dramatically in regions where the quota exceeded the potential substitutes. That sent drafted men or their indulgent fathers roving farther afield, into towns where economic stagnation had already driven so many into the army that low draft quotas reduced the demand for substitutes, while continuing poverty increased the motivation.[86]

When a drafted man could present no disqualifying physical defect or one of the exempted familial situations, and if he could find no handy substitute, he might consult a substitute broker. In what had become a war to end slavery, the substitute broker very closely resembled the Southern slave trader. These entrepreneurs combed the cities for drifters, derelicts, or anyone else who seemed likely to need some ready cash, herding them back to smaller towns by the squad to satisfy prearranged contracts with drafted men or to vend on speculation. The standard commission for introducing an aspiring substitute to an anxious principal nominally hovered around twenty-five dollars, but from the very start a broker could skim a hundred or more from each prospect. Another year into the draft it would be hard to procure anyone but newly arrived aliens and black men for less than seven hundred apiece, and that often incurred the expense and subterfuge involved with transporting them across states that banned such human traffic, so the profits had to rise commensurately.[87]

Even civilians who had put their sons and their hearts into the war occasionally deemed the draft unfair, especially when legal technicalities combined to create intolerable individual hardships. Those unpleasant details of home-front conscription generally escaped the attention of soldiers, most of whom relished the imagined squirming of the "unlucky aged at home" and tended to frown on any who tried to escape service, by whatever means. Squeamishness and outright cowardice caused men to dread the army, as well as political aversion and economic self-interest, so Republican proponents of the war did as much of that squirming as anti-war Democrats, and a majority of both factions strove to avoid each levy. Colonel Charles Wainwright, the commander of an artillery brigade in Meade's army, spent a few days on leave at his home in New York right after the first crop of unfortunates had been selected. He scoffed at "rabid" Republican neighbors who initiated subscriptions to raise the commutation fee for "great hearty young men, who should under no circumstances be allowed to remain at home at such a time as this." Wainwright doubted that the draft would bring in many new troops.[88]

A Pennsylvania soldier remarked to one of his brothers that he held "a very poor opinion" of the brother's conscription-insurance club, but he promised to refrain from derogatory comment only because it was allowed under the law. Writing the same day to another brother in the club, he called it a "white-livered thing," and by the time he addressed a third brother that afternoon he was calling it the "Farmington Cowards Mutual."[89] Assuming (and asserting) that fear alone discouraged recruiting, a captain in the Pennsylvania Reserves insisted that any man who would not come into the army would not defend his own family against an assassin. One former captain, recently mustered out with his fastidious nine-month regiment and thus exempt from the draft, made disparaging comments about those who declined to serve — in the very letter in which he refused an offer to return to duty himself.[90]

Like Vermonter Thomas Brown, the same soldiers who hoped so eagerly for their political and personal antagonists to be drafted often grieved for their friends and relatives who suffered the merciless vicissitudes of the conscription system, advising them to pay commutation, find a means of exemption, or hire a substitute. A few months after insisting that all draft resisters should be shot, a New York private expressed great relief that neither of his brothers was drafted. A young man in the 17th Maine summarized this inconsistency in a single sentence that began with an admonition to his brother that he "must not come" if drafted and concluded with a jubilant "Bully for that" at the news that some of the local "copper heads" had been conscripted. Dismayed to learn that his brother had been drafted, one cavalryman developed a sudden conviction that one member of a family was enough to sacrifice for the army (the new law set the limit at two sons per family); he also lamented that two friends could have been drafted who had already been discharged from the service for physical disabilities.[91] Lieutenant Colonel William Henry assured his wife, back in Waterbury, Vermont, that her brother could never be passed by the examining surgeon, but when the surgeon did declare the brother-in-law fit, Henry offered three hundred dollars for the commutation fee out of his savings. A Maine corporal who had enlisted at the outbreak of war worried constantly that his brothers would be called into service: he advised the older one, who had a family, to pay the three hundred dollars and not be "foolish enough to come," but he betrayed intense glee when some of his antiwar neighbors had their names drawn.[92] The draft also filled impatient teenaged boys with romantic notions of going to war as substitutes, now that the army would take just about anyone, and soldiers with younger brothers lobbied them directly and through their parents to abandon such deadly nonsense, contradicting themselves and their comrades with assurances that no more men were needed.[93]

For those who could not afford commutation or a substitute — or whose fury at an increasingly intrusive federal government soured them against such compliant forms of avoidance — there was always migration. No sooner had the president signed the Conscription Act into law than bands of young transients started drifting northward or westward, into regions where provost marshals held no sway. Only days after passage of the draft law, a young man from Concord, New Hampshire, boarded a train that would take him to Stanstead, in Canada East. By the time the train reached Vermont's northern border, his car had accumulated two dozen more passengers of his age and motivation, and he learned that an average of thirty men a day were already crossing into Canada through that point. The hotels were overflowing with U.S. citizens, depressing the price of labor and aggravating French Canadians who already felt themselves oppressed by the English majority. Colonel Wainwright's gardener joined that exodus, guided by the North Star as fugitive slaves had been a decade before, and before long deserters began following the same route to avoid the network of domestic provost marshals.[94]

A Vermont saddler working in Frelighsburg, five miles over the Canadian border, took a prominent neighbor's advice to simply remain there once the draft lottery began, and he described an expatriate community crawling with draft evaders and army deserters, some of whom he knew from home. Plenty of Maine men also disappeared once their names were drawn, and many of them ventured toward Canada. With limited opportunities for work, those emigrants often had to seek alternative sources of subsistence, and newspapers in the Eastern Townships started documenting what became, for them, a significant crime wave. One of the Concord skedaddlers ran into trouble with the Compton constabulary soon after his arrival, when he was arrested with horses and wagons he had filched from families there. By autumn, Canadian editors were posting regular warnings for border residents to keep watch for thieves, and Vermont provost marshals had begun risking international incidents to lure absconders and deserters back into the state, where they could be arrested.[95]

Enrolled men who had access to enough money left the provost marshals even farther behind. With the draft under way in their state, the sons and nephews of two former Maine governors took ship for Buenos Aires, where sheep raising suddenly attracted them; a number of other potential soldiers from Oxford County joined them. The West also appealed to a lot of footloose bachelors who fell within the limits of military age. Conscription was going to be dreadfully difficult to enforce in sparsely settled Dakota Territory, for instance, and the threat from Sioux war parties had driven enough volunteers into cavalry companies to exceed the territorial quota. Just as the government tried to implement the draft, miners started flocking into the new gold fields of Idaho, where they could earn thirty-six dollars a week or buy into claims that produced hundreds of dollars in gold each day.[96] The older lodes of California still brought dreamers from the East, and with all the more frequency after the summer of 1863. Rising gold prices surely inspired some in that flood of new prospectors, but the idea of compulsory service in a bloody war just as surely lightened their steps westward.[97]

It was as Colonel Wainwright and many others had supposed. The commutation provision excused more than 52,000 potential soldiers, instead bringing in about enough revenue to keep the war going for another ten days. In all, 39,415 men failed to report for examination when called in that first draft. Fewer than 10,000 conscripts, reflecting barely 1 in 30 of those called, went into the army themselves. With the substitutes, that yielded 35,883 recruits to the armies — mostly to the Army of the Potomac.[98]

In Vermont, the poorest of the New England states, 1 in 16 drafted men chose active duty over commutation or a substitute. That was nearly double the national average: it was two and a half times the proportion in Massachusetts, and close to three times the rate in next-door New Hampshire. Reflecting that state's widespread poverty, fewer Vermont communities appear to have voted the funds to subsidize alternatives to personal service, and that left more Vermont residents with no choice when the provost marshal came around with his notices. When he reported at Burlington, a boy from Middlesex found the surgeons there passing almost everyone, except perhaps those who could afford a bribe. That helped to explain how Colonel Henry's frail brother-in-law was held to service, and probably also accounts for the suspension of the provost marshal and examining surgeon there, a few months later, for forwarding men unfit for service.[99]

Once declared sufficiently healthy, whether he really was or not, the conscript who confessed his inability to pay for either of his two major options was clothed in a uniform on the spot. He who lingered near home beyond his reporting date, as Edwin Horton did, felt the grip of a bounty-hungry sheriff or vigilante on his arm, and spent a few days under guard in Rutland or Brattleboro before heading to more formal confinement in New York and Alexandria on the way to the front. Street toughs from Boston, New York, or Philadelphia frequently dominated those dungeons, and a man without friends or a weapon seldom made it to the front with his money or watch. Even those who had reported conscientiously and indicated a willingness to serve sometimes landed in similar pens, and they always traveled under guard, like so many convicts on their way to serve long sentences.[100] During transport from one relay station to another, so many of the substitutes made a run for it that the officers in charge had to post double and triple guard details, sometimes with loaded weapons and orders to shoot, and occasionally a guard would kill one of them. From that first draft levy the various recruiting rendezvous became impromptu prisons. After July some officers habitually handcuffed contingents of conscripts and substitutes, including tried veterans who had finished their service in the two-year regiments and reenlisted with honorable intentions, only to regret reentering the service of a country that would treat them like common criminals.[101]

The Vermont conscripts included the first Quakers forced to bear arms for the Union. Some Quakers, especially in Vermont and the West, had already sufficiently disregarded their society's pacifism and the disapproval of fellow Friends to enter military service, and others felt ashamed that they could not, but now the army encountered three determined pacifists. With them, the draft law bred a religious version of the political paradox it had already created — of a war allegedly waged on behalf of liberty by coercing the unwilling into fighting it. The three Friends, all from communities along Lake Champlain, exercised passive resistance all the way from Burlington to the camp of the 4th Vermont at Culpeper, Virginia. Cyrus Pringle, Lindley Macomber, and Peter Dakin arrived at headquarters looking somewhat disheveled, for they had refused to don their uniforms voluntarily, and had had them pulled on by force. Their equipment had likewise been tied to them by others, and their rifles had been strapped awkwardly to their backs because they refused to handle them. Any of them could have drawn the commutation fee out of their savings, as they readily admitted, but they knew that the money would have been used to prosecute the war. The regimental commander distributed them through different companies in hopes of isolating them and weakening their resolve, but to no avail. Despite cruel punishments and the lecturing of a Quaker apostate who wore a sergeant's stripes, they refused duty day after day until the colonel relented and assigned them to the hospital. There, too, they declined to serve, evidently because their quarterly meeting had determined that even humanitarian work for the army would violate the peace testimony. The major of the regiment complained that the colonel had "babied" them, and he seemed to hope they would be shot, but before winter they would all be discharged for their especially conscientious objection.[102]

By September dubious new recruits were coming through Washington at the rate of several hundred every day, sometimes in shackles. Regiments whittled down by battle or disease mushroomed with the infusion of a hundred or two strangers in new, conspicuously dark-blue uniforms, but the morning muster formation soon started shrinking again as substitutes slipped away to try their enlistment ploy again in a new community. The recruits were nothing but a nuisance, declared a New Hampshire sergeant who had to tie them to trees for fighting and robbing each other, and within a few days a third of the hundred who came to his regiment had run off. Except for the Quakers, though, the major of the 4th Vermont judged the lot of conscripts and substitutes who replenished his regiment that summer the best recruits he had seen since coming to the war — better, even, than the volunteers. That may have resulted from the heavy proportion of actual conscripts in the Vermont levies, for Colonel Wainwright thought just as highly of the direct draftees who reached his battalion that August: they were an improvement over the avaricious bounty men of 1862, and especially over the rascals who had come out as substitutes, so many of whom never intended to do a day's service if they could help it.[103]

Yet many of the substitutes showed promise, too. Each lot contained numerous veterans, including nine-month men who still remembered their company drill and two-year soldiers who remained trained and tough. Among them lurked a few British soldiers, some of whom had served in the Crimea or India while others had just deserted across the Canadian border to earn relative fortunes as substitutes. The replacements all seemed seedy and undesirable enough when they first arrived (the "ugliest set of Devils that ever went unhung," reported a New Hampshire captain), but once seeded into a regiment many of them surprised their superiors. Substitutes predominated in each shipment, but men who had been with the army a year or two supposed, after looking them over, that most of them would make decent soldiers once broken to the yoke.[104]

Returning deserters added to the reinforcements, and especially in the Army of the Potomac. Those who had absconded now faced greater chances of detection because of the provost marshals whose subordinates scoured their districts for draft evaders. Willie Greene, the New Hampshire boy who had used a convalescent furlough to drop from sight the previous autumn, was still wandering from job to job in Wisconsin when conscription started sifting the population. He had been sparking a lovely young lady from Pardeeville, and was almost beginning to think of himself as a civilian again, but he would turn twenty in September and feared he would draw official attention. By winter someone turned him in, and guards soon delivered him to the camp of his old regiment, in Virginia.[105]

The consequences of desertion had escalated. So many faithless substitutes were slinking away by late August that headquarters resumed public executions to deter the trend, spreading them throughout the various corps for maximum effect. Immigrants made the favorite targets for the death penalty this time: as more than one American-born soldier noted, those unfortunates usually lacked a single relative in the United States to mourn their loss, which eliminated the more unpleasant political complications and reduced the chances of executive pardon. The first sacrifice was Thomas Jewett, an old soldier in Her Majesty's service who had decamped at Fredericksburg. His death, near New Baltimore on August 14, set the example for the Sixth Corps.[106] Next, five runaway substitutes from the 118th Pennsylvania, all Germans and Italians who spoke little or no English, endured hasty courts-martial without translators before they were condemned. Lincoln himself refused to intervene, and all five were shot by one mass firing squad at Beverly Ford on August 29, in front of the entire Fifth Corps.[107]

Willie Greene escaped the ultimate penalty. Besides the loss of pay for the year he had been gone, his punishment consisted of a fifty-dollar fine, but he returned to duty as the same malingering malcontent who had slipped away from the line of march immediately after his first battle. Just before that fight, Private Greene had self-righteously insisted that the government should draft any man who hesitated to enlist, but such sentiments never spilled from his pen again: within days of his court-martial and for the rest of his enlistment, he was constantly finagling for a discharge or some special duty that would take him out of the front lines.[108] He had apparently learned — as so many of those hesitant ones at home already realized — that war can be an exceedingly unpleasant proposition unless someone else is doing the fighting.

6

Take Increased Devotion

→ THE EUPHORIA OF early July had not lasted long. With so few of their fellow countrymen willing to join them in the struggle, those in uniform might have been excused for questioning the wisdom of their own devotion to Lincoln's war. Brigadier General John Geary, a division commander in the Twelfth Corps, remarked to his wife five weeks after Gettysburg that "there seems so little patriotism among the people at home, the country scarcely appears worth preserving." Geary was a Democrat, too, who went to war primarily to preserve the national unity.[1]

The only Americans who seemed willing to enlist that summer were not even citizens. Tens of thousands of fugitive slaves were pouring into Union lines at all points, creating a humanitarian crisis in contraband camps that lacked sufficient housing, clothing, food, or sanitary facilities. Freedmen had taken over much of the fatigue labor that had previously fallen to white soldiers, who stood gratefully aside, and the drudgery they saved helped to weaken the army's endemic racial prejudice. Some soldiers continued to balk at the sight of former slaves in uniform ("I do despise them," confessed an Indiana officer, "and the more I see of them, the more I am against the whole black crew"), but most of those who had once scoffed at the notion of emancipation also began to understand the disadvantages it posed for the Confederate army. One westering Maine man who had earlier scorned abolition attributed his conversion to the damage emancipation wrought on the Southern military machine: "every Nigger we take out of the field," he explained to his sister, "his place has got to be supplied by a Rebel soldier."[2] An Ohio surgeon figured that every slave who left a plantation meant another acre of land left untilled, and

Southern soldiers would eventually have to come home to keep their families from starving. Eventually the tolerance born of pragmatism developed into a grudging affection that emerged, albeit often crudely, in letters home. One officer who still harbored enough residual bigotry to refer to his laundress as a "Smoked American lady" liked her well enough to try to play a practical joke on her, and he seemed to enjoy it immensely when she turned it around on him.[3]

By the summer of 1863 Union soldiers were beginning to suspect, especially in the occupied portions of Tennessee and the Mississippi Valley, that slavery had withered beyond the point of recovery. In mid-August as staunch a Radical as Horace Greeley sensed freedom so near that he advocated readmission of the seceded states to the Union, and compensation of all slaveholding states in government bonds for the slaves they held in 1860, on no restriction save universal emancipation by July of 1864. Southern pride would have dictated rejection of Greeley's proposal had it been made officially, but it was not, and no offer that generous would ever surface again. Regarding the war now as little more than an antislavery crusade, though, Greeley confidently awaited an outcome he considered inevitable, regardless of setbacks, bloodshed, and cost.[4]

While benevolent agencies and individual volunteers strove to care for the women, the children, and the feeble who fled slavery, army administrators gleaned the healthy males for military service. Lorenzo Thomas's recruiting campaign into the Mississippi Valley had secured some twenty regiments of black volunteers — nearly as many troops (and ultimately better ones) than the July draft call produced. Massachusetts had mustered two black regiments, and two regiments of South Carolina, Georgia, and Florida contrabands had been organized into a brigade under quondam Kansas jayhawker James Montgomery. Thomas Wentworth Higginson, a Massachusetts abolitionist who had once assured John Brown that he was "always ready to invest money in treason," and who had hoped to incite a civil war that would separate the free states from the slave, took command of the 1st South Carolina in Montgomery's brigade; at the head of that regiment he proceeded to crush the same treason he had once espoused, and to force the seceded states back into the Union. George Stearns, another Bay State abolitionist who had helped fund and arm the murderous enterprises of Montgomery and Brown, accepted Secretary of War Edwin Stanton's appointment as recruiting commissioner for the new Bureau of Colored Troops, and set about enlisting both freemen and freedmen directly into federal service.[5]

In the spring President Lincoln had bet that "the bare sight of fifty thousand armed, and drilled black soldiers on the banks of the Mississippi, would end the rebellion at once." By the end of the year at least that many had been raised in the Mississippi Valley, though without the predicted result.[6]

The creation of so many new regiments brought hundreds of openings for promotion, for which thousands of veterans applied, and occasionally that opportunity dictated a soldier's sudden reversal on the matter of arming slaves. Lieutenant Frederic Speed, an ambitious Maine youth, had once turned disgrace into promotion by the application of his father's political connections and a little money. He lobbied repeatedly for further rank, and he overcame his scruples against Negro regiments when it appeared he might be able to take command of one, but the old contempt returned when that scheme fell through. A lieutenant earned about six times the pay of a sergeant, and the scent of such wealth lured middle-aged soldiers of modest backgrounds to consider the unpopular commissions, while others sought them to escape obnoxious superiors.[7] Especially in the vicinity of Washington, men from white regiments formed by squads for examination, and even in the field, officers complained that their best men would be lost if all their applications were accepted.[8] A certain opprobrium clung to a commission in the Colored Troops: one Illinois soldier sneered at his captain, who had applied for command of the 11th Louisiana, when "he . . . drew the prize, if prize it can be called."[9] Lieutenants and sergeants sometimes hung back as their captains sought field commissions in the Colored Troops, for that opened inviting vacancies in their own companies, but superior officers occasionally insisted that specific subordinates make their own applications — perhaps as a means of ridding themselves of difficult associates.[10]

The examination process weeded out some of the more obvious intellectual and educational deficiencies that had always afflicted officers in new white regiments, but plenty of poor material still seeped into the black units. Ten percent of the Massachusetts men commissioned in the Colored Troops were eventually cashiered, including one who was dismissed twice, and another 9 percent were discharged or mustered out prematurely — perhaps for administrative reasons, but possibly for inefficiency, incompetence, or corruption. Only two of Vermont's 104 Colored Troops officers had to be dismissed, but at least a dozen enlisted men who accepted such commissions resigned them within six months, adding some validity to the assertion that many used the new commissions as a way out of the army. Even among those who accepted the new positions in good faith, and served out their terms, there usually lingered an obvious condescension toward the men who served under them. An educated young Vermonter congratulated himself, after long pursuit of rank high enough to satisfy his self-image, that he had finally been given command of "a company of wooly headed gentlemen of the colored persuasion." Although they consisted mostly of freemen from the vicinity of Philadelphia, he seemed disgusted to find such widespread illiteracy among them that it was difficult to select the thirteen he needed for corporals and sergeants. Even Colonel Higginson, the abolitionist, betrayed a patronizing lilt in his most laudatory descriptions of the 1st South Carolina.[11]

Now and then, though, a black volunteer would bring conspicuous literary accomplishments into camp. James Gooding, for instance, was confined to the twin stripes of a corporal by the racial limitations on rank, but he wrote regular letters from the camp of the 54th Massachusetts to his hometown newspaper, revealing an eloquence that would have put many white captains to shame. He also revealed the common error of ascribing the most contemptible qualities to those with whom he disagreed politically, and he naively assumed that only "copperheads and traitors" harbored bigoted attitudes toward "*our* people." As Gooding might have inferred from the reduced pay Lincoln's government allowed black soldiers, Unionists in the most enlightened circles still subscribed to racial stereotypes as well, and a Boston reporter observed that Massachusetts troops joined freely in the hazing and harassment that white troops inflicted on the 54th.[12]

The 54th Massachusetts went straight to South Carolina, where Major General Quincy Gillmore had just taken command from the troublesome David Hunter. Gillmore had begun a new offensive against Charleston, adopting the piecemeal reduction of the place that Admiral DuPont had advised. From the second week of July he concentrated on Morris Island, below the main ship channel into Charleston Harbor. At the northern end of Morris Island stood the Cummings Point battery, which bore on both the channel as well as the weak side of Fort Sumter, and to protect it the Confederates had built a substantial fort across the island, naming it Battery Wagner. Gillmore took the southern tip of Morris Island on July 10, catching the rebels cooking their breakfasts, and he made a direct assault on Wagner the next morning, but the fort threw such a hail of lead and iron that the Yankees shrank from the job.[13]

A week later Gillmore made another stab at Wagner with the division of Truman Seymour, who had endured the 1861 bombardment of Fort Sumter as a captain in the garrison. Two brigades swept toward the fort at sundown, facing fierce artillery fire from Wagner, Fort Sumter, and other Confederate batteries within range. The leading brigade, which included the 54th, carried a portion of the battlements and held them for a long, dark hour, but the intense musketry and canister from the rest of the fort whittled away at the strength of the attacking column. So many officers fell, trying to inspire their men in the twilight, that discipline disintegrated in several regiments. Seymour himself was wounded, and both his brigadiers went down with fatal wounds. Seven officers died in the 7th New Hampshire alone, and that veteran regiment shed more than two hundred others killed and wounded that evening. The worst casualties came when the division lost its foothold and started to fall back across the narrow spit that connected Wagner to the rest of the island, where converging fire raked the frantic mass. As the newest and biggest regiment, the big 54th Massachusetts contributed 272 casualties to the total loss of more than 1,500, including Colonel Robert Gould Shaw, whose body was left behind in the retreat.[14]

Gillmore had lost a fifth of his entire infantry force in just eight days. As an engineer of the McClellan stripe, he shuddered at the cost of such frontal assaults, and reverted to the less barbarous siege warfare that his training prescribed. Through the rest of July and August, Union trenches and batteries crept toward Wagner. Confederate defenders lounged about their impregnable bombproofs wearing a kaleidoscope of variegated civilian attire, but if they owned no uniforms they did have plenty of ammunition, and they still held their fort at the beginning of September, denying the Yankees those Cummings Point guns within range of Sumter. As he inched toward Wagner, though, Gillmore also brought up long-range rifled guns that began to pock the brick walls of Sumter, and by the time the rebels evacuated Wagner on September 7, Fort Sumter had been pounded to rubble. Only a few score of stubborn Confederates still manned that foremost symbol of Southern independence, with all their artillery dismounted or otherwise disabled.[15]

Admiral DuPont, whose ironclad assault on Charleston had fizzled so abruptly in April, had also been relieved: the president had superseded him with a personal friend, Admiral John Dahlgren. As soon as the Confederates gave up Wagner (and with it the rest of Morris Island, complete with the vital Cummings Point battery), Dahlgren decided to take Fort Sumter by storm for the glory of the navy, before Gillmore could compel its surrender to the army. Dahlgren collected five hundred sailors and Marines from his fleet, put them in boats, and launched them toward the manmade island in the darkness of September 8, calling for cooperation from the army but insisting that it remain exclusively a naval operation. The commander inside Sumter armed eighty of his men with muskets, and detailed the other two dozen to light the fuses of shells and drop them from the ramparts. Dahlgren's boats landed piecemeal, and many failed to land at all. Armed with cutlasses and revolvers, the first few crews tried to climb the rubble, but the shower of lead, improvised hand grenades, and loose bricks drove them to cover, where the guns of Fort Moultrie threatened them with annihilation. Later boatloads either could not or would not endure that barrage; when those oarsmen pulled back to their ships they left a quarter of their comrades huddling under the ramparts of Sumter, where they surrendered in platoons to the Confederate garrison. Months later, those captured tars accompanied the first trainloads of prisoners into a big new Confederate prison camp at Andersonville, Georgia, where many of them would lay their bones for eternity.[16] The Confederate flag still fluttered over the crumbling fort in the middle of Charleston Harbor, mocking the confident besiegers who had celebrated so jubilantly over the victories of early July.

A thousand miles to the west, on the opposite end of the war, Union forces also bore the continued taunts of the Confederate banner — often at the hands of irregular troops who fought under no flag at all. The border country of Kansas and Missouri provided some of the most brutal tales to emerge from the Civil War. It was perhaps the most terrifying place in the country for civilians of any political tendency. For Union troops, however, the region had fallen incongruously quiet by the summer of 1863. John Schofield had sent Ulysses Grant such strong detachments from his department that he could pursue no offensive operations: as the Vicksburg campaign wound down, Schofield could field fewer than twenty-eight thousand men to defend Missouri, Kansas, the Indian Territory, Nebraska, Colorado, and much of what would become Wyoming. Those twenty-eight thousand included a significant number of Missouri militia in varying degrees of discipline, and he spread them through his sprawling bailiwick, mostly by companies, to act effectively (or ineffectively) as a police force. For some troops, duty in the department consisted of endless patrols and the occasional pursuit of roving guerrillas. For others it meant cruelly dull service in isolated outposts, while for the garrisons of certain towns the war had settled into a giddy routine of feasting and fandangos. Neosho, in extreme southwestern Missouri, must have been the most pleasant post in the entire department that year. Girls filled the town in an abundance that soldiers seldom enjoyed, working as cooks and laundresses for two cavalry companies of Missouri militia; the troops slept in a boarding house, and there was a dance every night.[17]

Rather than providing protection or diversion for the inhabitants, the soldiers themselves frequently posed a formidable threat. Drunkenness accompanied much of the off-duty frolics, leading large bands of armed soldiers into lawless behavior that the civil authorities dared not interfere with. Political prejudice and suspicion led some occupation forces to impose a violent oppression on their jurisdictions, to the extent of wide-spread murder, and a citizen of Missouri or Kansas could not always re-gard a military presence as a source of security, no matter what color uniform prevailed. In some districts the local commander might exert a draconian discipline to curb the marauding of soldiers — executing pick-pockets and petty thieves after drumhead courts-martial — but other commanders seemed to let their men run wild.[18]

It should therefore have initiated some alarm among the citizens of Johnson County, Missouri, when about three hundred mounted men, armed to the teeth, gathered along the Blackwater River just after the middle of August. On August 19 those horsemen started westward across Cass County under William Clarke Quantrill, keeping to the fringe of the Grand River watershed and picking up reinforcements along the way. Most of the band resorted to rough civilian garb, but many of them wore the blue uniforms of Missouri militia: they may well have been renegade militiamen, too, for deserters from those units were reported to be cast-ing their lots with Quantrill, but the company they were keeping that week persuaded them to skirt any militia outposts. Traveling in the after-noon and at night, they passed into Kansas early on the evening of August 20, slipping between Olathe and Paola and cantering briskly across the prairie in an upward arc toward the traditional home of free-state Kan-sans at Lawrence, fifty miles away, where many a slave-stealing raid had been planned into the very Missouri counties from which the raiders had come.[19]

Little border garrisons learned of the ominous column soon after it passed, and joined forces to undertake a tardy pursuit, but no one warned any of the towns that lay in their path. The only man who tried lived ten miles east of Lawrence, and he saddled up to spread the alarm during the wee hours of Friday, August 21, but his horse stumbled at a dead gallop in the darkness, killing both mount and rider. The inhabitants of Lawrence never realized that trouble was upon them until the heralds of that force thundered down Massachusetts and Tennessee streets, around 4:30 A.M., hollering loud enough to bring the people out of their homes. About fif-teen minutes later, at the tail of the column, older residents recognized a pale-eyed young man in a dark shirt, blue jacket, and broad black hat as their former townsman and border-war nemesis, Quantrill, who had come back with the most vicious band of cutthroats the war would ever produce.[20]

The outriders of Quantrill's horde made one pass down the three main thoroughfares to rouse the populace. When townspeople ran outside to see what had happened, the guerrillas reined about and came pounding back, shooting down every male citizen who came within range. But few of the bleary-eyed residents thought to bring weapons outside with them when they emerged, and those who did were all shot down before they could inflict any damage. Raiders who had evidently been coached by informants went straight to the homes of merchants to demand the keys to their stores and safes. Quantrill posted pickets along the woods south and east of town and on the hills just to the west — where the town fathers planned to establish the state university: even then a letter was on its way from Boston financiers to the mayor of Lawrence, George Collamore, authorizing fifteen thousand dollars for that purpose, but Collamore would never see it. The pickets kept him and most citizens from making their escape, except for a few who scattered into the brush bordering the Kansas River, north of town. Collamore correctly deduced that he would be near the top of any list to be captured or murdered, so he let himself down into the bottom of his well. His wife replaced the lid, shutting out the grey dawn glow that would be the last daylight her husband ever saw. He suffocated in the thin, dank air at the bottom of the darkened shaft.[21]

The Missourians sought out the town's Republican newspaper editors and killed them on the spot. Jim Lane, whom the assassins wanted most, escaped into a cornfield near his home and hid there while his wife tried to save their house; she stamped out or doused three successive fires lighted around or in it, but the arsonists persisted until finally the place went up in flames. A citizen tried to sound the alarm by ringing the bell at the Eldridge House, on Massachusetts Street. Guests there, including the provost marshal, Captain Alexander Banks, gathered downstairs, where they learned that there was not a single firearm in the building. As the senior army officer in the town at the time, Banks advised surrender, and from the front balcony he unfolded a white sheet. Eventually Quantrill rode by and accepted the surrender, promising safe conduct for the occupants, but his men robbed them of wallets, watches, and jewelry before bringing them to the Whitney House, which was owned by one of Quantrill's antebellum friends. Lacking weapons or officers, a handful of recruits from white and black Kansas regiments waited in their camps near town, powerless to help or flee, and by midmorning most of them had died under the guerrillas' revolvers.[22]

Gunshots and black-powder explosions echoed through the town as different bands within Quantrill's command gunned down the men they had robbed and blasted open bank vaults and safes. Once they had cleaned out everything of value in the banks, the stores, and the hotels, they started burning the business district, the courthouse, and the surrounding homes. Some went straight to the home of ex-governor Charles

Robinson, near the Kansas River, but before they could burn it they were driven away by a detachment of Kansas infantry on the opposite bank. After kindling most of downtown Lawrence, the guerrillas started shooting wildly at any man who showed himself, killing some as their wives and daughters clung to them by pressing the muzzles of their guns to their victims' breasts, between the women's arms. Quantrill and his senior lieutenants shielded the dozens of huddled prisoners in the Whitney House from the accelerating fury of the gunmen outside, eating a hearty if early lunch meanwhile, but finally the raider chieftan signaled that it was time to leave. As the last of his riders galloped out of town Quantrill took to the saddle himself, doffed his hat, and offered an Elizabethan bow to the ladies on the porch of the Whitney House before spurring his horse down Massachusetts Street the way he had come.[23]

The sack of Lawrence could not be counted as another Confederate victory because Quantrill carried no official connection to the Confederate army or government. Soon enough, local Confederate commanders would find his rapacious tactics too distasteful to tolerate, despite the results he achieved. Lawrence was, however, a significant embarrassment to Union officials in the West, where they began blaming each other down the chain of command for the disaster. Nearly two hundred buildings had been burned, scores of citizens and soldiers had been murdered, and untold thousands of dollars in cash, bonds, and valuables had left town in the saddlebags of desperadoes. The district commander, Thomas Ewing, issued an edict ordering all Missouri citizens to vacate their homes in the counties from Kansas City to below the Osage, supposing that depopulation might accomplish what his troops could not. For more than a month after the raid motley forces of civilians and soldiers followed the raiders out of Kansas and into Missouri, killing stragglers, but they never intercepted the main body or forced a pitched battle. Combined forces of Missouri militia and Kansas cavalry scoured western Missouri from the Grand River to the Ozarks, reporting great success in dispersing and killing bushwhackers whom they thought had taken part in the Lawrence raid, but six weeks later Quantrill was able to reassemble his loose battalion of allied gangs to inflict another overwhelming defeat against Union troops.[24]

This time Quantrill struck an isolated new encampment in extreme southeastern Kansas. Two partial companies of the 3rd Wisconsin Cavalry and about fifty men of the 2nd Kansas Colored Infantry had built a rude perimeter of breastworks near the Spring River at Baxter Springs, a couple of miles north of the Indian Territory. On the morning of October 6 almost a hundred men, black and white, slept in and around that makeshift fort, under the command of a Wisconsin lieutenant. At noon that day at least a couple of hundred of Quantrill's guerrillas rode in on them so fast that some leaped the breastworks before anyone could give the alarm, and they had to be driven out. The lieutenant wheeled out a little brass howitzer, manning it himself, and a few volleys from that gave the guerrillas a moment's pause: Few of Quantrill's men carried longer-range weapons than revolvers, so the carbines and rifles inside the redan kept them at a safe distance.[25]

Quantrill, who waited nearby with the rest of his command, detected a small wagon train approaching the fort under an escort of a hundred or more mounted troopers. Calling back the wing that had beset the garrison, he spread his entire command along the woods bordering the Spring River — every one of them dressed in Union uniforms this time — and swept down on the train with odds of at least two or three to one in his favor. The procession consisted of Major General James G. Blunt's headquarters family, including his staff, his brass band, and an artist for *Frank Leslie's Illustrated,* guarded by a company each of the 14th Kansas Cavalry and the 3rd Wisconsin Cavalry. Those two companies formed to meet the charge, but fired only one wild volley before bolting away with the guerrillas in hot pursuit. Blunt, the commander of that district, escaped with a dozen or fifteen men, but Quantrill's horsemen ran down most of the rest, and they took no prisoners: as fast as a man surrendered and dropped his weapons he was shot down, and most received the coup de grâce of a bullet in the head. Five or six who played dead managed to survive with several wounds, but the band perished to a man, as did Frank Leslie's artist and a twelve-year-old boy acting as servant to the bandleader. After chasing the last fugitives over the prairie for a few miles, Quantrill returned to demand the surrender of the fort, identifying himself as colonel of the "First Regiment, First Brigade, Army of the South," but the lieutenant commanding the earthwork wisely declined. Having already lost a few men, Quantrill chose not to assault a determined force behind its works and instead turned south, for Texas, incidentally capturing and murdering a party of Creek Indians who were scouting for Blunt between the Arkansas and Canadian rivers.[26]

Blunt made his way back to the little fort with a squad of men, but his tenure as district commander lasted only days longer. General Schofield removed him — not for military failures, because Blunt had actually achieved several modest victories in the past year, but for the "fraud, corruption, and maladministration" that flourished in Blunt's domain. The graft fell within the quartermaster and commissary departments, as usual. Schofield made it clear that he did not necessarily suspect Blunt of direct complicity, but Blunt did seem to cavort with characters whose dealings tended to the shady side. He had been an associate of John Brown when that charismatic mountebank began murdering his way toward martyrdom, and he was evidently friendly with Samuel P. Curtis — the general whose notorious cotton speculation had distracted him from his military duties in Arkansas. Blunt was also a close political ally and beneficiary of the senator and general Jim Lane, and that made him an enemy of both the past and present governors of Kansas — whose patronage Lane coveted and (with the help of both Edwin Stanton and Abraham Lincoln) occasionally usurped. Blunt had earlier tried to divert attention from his own mismanagement by charging Schofield, Governor Thomas Carney, and others with lying, thievery, and treason, and he sent a version of his diatribe to a distressed President Lincoln. According to Blunt, he was the victim of a conspiracy among "traitors, Government peculators, and Copperheads." It was the standard scoundrel's excuse for 1863.[27]

While the frontier fell into apparent chaos, both militarily and administratively, the Army of the Potomac lay relatively idle along the Rappahannock River. The enervating heat of July and early August, combined with the absence of large-scale fighting since the last crossing of the Potomac, had finally given George Meade's busy troops some extended leisure for nostalgic reflection, and that initiated sentimental reveries for comrades lost and living. When they weren't trotting out to see deserters branded on the cheek or riddled by firing squads, officers and men alike descended into an orgy of subscriptions to buy expensive gifts for favorite generals. The commissioned officers in the second division of the Second Corps pitched in for an inscribed sword, a saddle, and a horse for General Sedgwick, who had commanded that division in the old days of the war, before assuming command of the Sixth Corps. The Third Corps raised five thousand dollars to buy Dan Sickles a campaign carriage, team, harness, and other camp amenities so their impetuous chief could take to the field with only one leg. Not to be outdone, the Pennsylvania Reserves subscribed for an ornately engraved sword, belt, and sash from Tiffany & Co. for their former commander, General Meade, and soon afterward there surfaced a plan to buy a sword for Gouverneur Warren, the army's erstwhile chief engineer, who had taken over the Second Corps.[28]

The presentation of Meade's sword turned into the army's social event of the summer. As is often true with the rendering of tributes, the ceremony was designed as much for the promotion of the donors and the benefit of politicians as to honor the recipient, and it gave the ineloquent Meade intense embarrassment.

Soldiers from the Pennsylvania Reserves spent a couple of days trimming their camp in evergreen boughs and flags, building a rostrum, and erecting enclosed tents to keep that summer's bumper crop of flies off the planned banquet, but guards with fixed bayonets prohibited those same soldiers from approaching the scene when Pennsylvania's dignitaries arrived to bask in Meade's reflected glow. Samuel Crawford, the current commander of the Reserves and as ardent a self-promoter as ever donned a uniform, spread himself to deliver what one onlooker thought "a rather high-faluting speech," after which Meade focused on the accomplishments of his dead friend Reynolds and other fallen officers of the Reserves. Governor Curtin's chief aide had buttonholed Meade to ask for some flattering comments about Curtin, who was up for reelection in a few weeks, but Meade opted not to comply, so the *Washington Chronicle* obligingly inserted an imaginary accolade. The general concluded with the fast-fading hope that the war was about grinding to an end, and then Curtin himself took the stage to lobby for the soldier vote. A succession of lesser officeholders followed him to stump for their own reelection. At last hundreds of officers and politicos rushed for the dinner tents, and the evening ended with captains and colonels stumbling about, alternately gripping comrades' shoulders and the necks of champagne bottles with ferocious affection.[29]

One testimonial to an esteemed general perished prematurely. Savoring the camaraderie and appreciation of his onetime subordinates, John Sedgwick thought to offer a similar gesture of respect to General McClellan. Without suggesting what sort of token might be presented, he asked a couple of other corps commanders who had served under Little Mac if they concurred in his impulse, and if so how they might carry it out. A gathering of corps commanders at headquarters revealed that everyone from Meade on down thought it a capital idea, and they proposed offering the enlisted men a chance to get in on the tribute if they wished, with a ten-cent subscription rate for private soldiers and graduated contributions for higher ranks, up to twenty dollars for major generals. Each corps adopted the subscription, and a circular describing the planned testimonial spread through the veteran regiments.[30]

Carl Schurz, a Radical Republican and a dismal division commander in the ill-starred Eleventh Corps, relayed that circular to the secretary of the treasury, and Chase shared it with Edwin Stanton. Both men had come to dislike McClellan: Stanton detested him, and Chase considered the testimonial "an insult to the President." McClellan remained the most prominent Democrat in the country, and there were some crucial fall elections coming up in Pennsylvania and Ohio. At such a juncture it just wouldn't do to have the Army of the Potomac expressing its admiration for the deposed general, and especially with the reproach it would imply toward the president who had deposed him. This was more than the administration could stand, so Chase next took the circular to the president, who looked at it and promised to "see Stanton about it." Most Republicans in Washington City faithfully read the *Chronicle*, which had so zealously covered Meade's sword presentation for the benefit of the Republican Curtin, so everyone in the cabinet must have known about it, but no one had seen anything wrong with such a tribute. Now, though, the *Chronicle* vilified the McClellan testimonial as a scurrilous Democratic ploy, and with similar hypocrisy Lincoln conveyed his displeasure to Stanton. Thus did Halleck selectively invoke the authority of Paragraph 220 of the General Regulations, which prohibited anyone in the army from "conveying praise, or censure, or any mark of approbation against their superiors or others in the military service."[31]

That paragraph notwithstanding, the presentation of subscribed gifts to respected commanders remained a common and popular event in the encampments of Union soldiers. McClellan was the only commander whose subordinates were officially prohibited from showing their regard for him.

While the Yankees were busy expressing or suppressing veneration for their generals, the Confederates were shifting their weight to strike a powerful blow and recoup the prestige and momentum they had lost in early July. Humbled, perhaps, by his failure in Pennsylvania, Robert E. Lee seemed to relax his customary insistence about the importance of the eastern theater, and failed to exercise his usual jealousy over troops within his domain. Lee proposed luring Meade out to "crush his army while in its present condition," but he soon submitted to a counterproposal from his chief lieutenant. James Longstreet, who (according to Joe Hooker) supplied the real strength and brains of Lee's army, lobbied for transfer to the West with his corps, either as a replacement for Braxton Bragg or as commander of a force cooperating with Bragg. He predicted that the combined force could "destroy" Rosecrans's army, and his argument won the day. In early September he boarded two of his three divisions on trains for the roundabout journey to north Georgia. After more than a week's travel on rickety Southern rails through hospitable country, Longstreet arrived just in time to take charge of Bragg's left wing, stun William Rosecrans along the banks of Chickamauga Creek, and throw all but a portion of the Army of the Cumberland into full retreat.[32]

Rosecrans had demonstrated a capacity for gaining great success through maneuver, with little loss. He had pried Bragg out of his latest haven, below the Tennessee River, in the first week of September, forcing him to abandon Chattanooga and slip across the line into Georgia. Rosecrans followed on the assumption that his opponent would just keep running. As he pushed his scattered divisions south from Tennessee and eastward from Alabama, Rosecrans expected that he would enjoy the indirect support of a small Union army operating to his left, toward Knoxville. Now that Ambrose Burnside was done crushing free speech north of the Ohio, and now that the remains of his borrowed divisions were coming back from Vicksburg, he was finally organizing the expedition he had been hoping to lead into east Tennessee since the spring. After much delay in the gathering of horses, his infantry started into the mountains from Crab Orchard, Kentucky, on August 20. To the apparent surprise of some of his men, Burnside — commander of the second-largest department in the army — followed them the next day, togged out like a teamster in a checkered shirt, with his pants stuffed into the tops of his boots.[33]

The roads leading over the mountains into Tennessee were some of the worst in the country: mere unimproved tracks cut through native clay, and often straight up steep hillsides. One quartermaster spent seven hours of a September day worrying his trains up a single hill, and that was before the column reached the worst of the mountains. Burnside himself took two weeks to cover some 150 miles between Crab Orchard and Knoxville, riding into that unofficial capital of the Unionist enclave in east Tennessee on September 3 as the conquering hero. Rosecrans congratulated him and asked him to stretch his right flank down as far as the left of the Army of the Cumberland, and four days later Burnside's cavalry did reach Rosecrans's videttes, ahead of Halleck's instructions to do so. By September 9 Burnside had captured Cumberland Gap, complete with its Confederate garrison, and had deployed his seven brigades all the way from Athens, 60 miles below Knoxville, to Jonesborough, 100 miles above it. He left detachments at Cumberland Gap and toward the North Carolina border to guard against enemy forces there and in southwest Virginia, and he ordered the Ninth Corps to come down from central Kentucky, but the roads from that direction had not improved since Burnside's leading divisions churned them into soup.[34]

By then Rosecrans had started after Bragg, but he soon began to understand that his army would face an ambitious Confederate combination. Not only did advance news of Longstreet's movement convince him that he would soon meet those forces from Lee, but he learned that Joe Johnston had supplied Bragg with a couple of divisions from his Mississippi army. Halleck, Rosecrans, and later Lincoln besieged Burnside with appeals, advice, or instructions to go to Chattanooga and aid Rosecrans, but their messages each took several days to reach him. Worse yet, those telegrams either asserted or implied that Burnside should hold his line in east Tennessee, which required most of his force, but also send all his infantry to Rosecrans — or go to him with everything he had, which flew in the face of the president's long-cherished and just-realized dream of occupying east Tennessee. By the time Burnside received all that confusing and inconsistent correspondence, though, he had turned most of his strength toward the Virginia end of east Tennessee to face a threat from that direction, which seemed at first to be reinforcements from Lee's army.[35]

So Rosecrans saw none of Burnside's troops on the Chickamauga battlefield. By the time any of them started in his direction it was too late, prompting Rosecrans and his patrons to blame Burnside for all that followed.[36] Bragg caught Rosecrans with his three corps dangerously scattered on September 19, and spent most of that day and evening hammering at him. The first division of Longstreet's reinforcements reached Bragg that day: with Johnston's troops and those Burnside had pushed out of east Tennessee, that gave the Confederates a fair (and rare) advantage in numbers. Longstreet's arrival with his other division enhanced that advantage, and with it Longstreet piled into the Army of the Cumberland near noon on September 20. He broke through an injudicious gap in the Union line, and the Federals' right quickly crumbled. Two of the three largest Union corps fled the field, "every man for himself," admitted an Ohio soldier, and Rosecrans went with them. George Thomas, a Virginian whose loyalty had been questioned early in the war, stood fast and covered the retreat of the rest of the army with his own corps, three reserve brigades, and a division apiece from the other two corps. When night and bitter cold descended on the field, Thomas also turned for Chattanooga. Bragg let them go without further injury, instead posting his army on the heights overlooking Chattanooga to bottle Rosecrans up with his back against the Tennessee River.[37]

Longstreet's prediction about destroying Rosecrans's army had nearly struck the mark, and Chickamauga did effectively end Rosecrans's sojourn at the head of the Army of the Cumberland — although his removal hung in abeyance for a few weeks, until the chance of adverse political consequences abated. Here was a victory such as the Confederate army had never seen in the West, and while it came nowhere near compensating for all the defeats of July, it did announce that Southern forces had not been as thoroughly defeated and demoralized as so many had supposed. Soldiers in the oft-defeated Army of the Potomac could not help but suggest that the Western army had found Longstreet and his Eastern troops a little harder to handle. Casualties had been even heavier for Bragg than for Rosecrans, though, and back in New York George Templeton Strong consoled himself with the observation that the Confederacy could ill afford such costly victories.[38]

At the very moment Bragg was first crossing Chickamauga Creek to tear into Rosecrans, President Lincoln was considering the wisdom of imitating Longstreet's westward pilgrimage. Noting that Meade considered his ninety thousand men insufficient to overwhelm Lee's sixty thousand so long as Lee kept the advantage of the defensive, Lincoln wondered in a letter to Halleck why Meade could not reverse the arithmetic of military science: if he reduced his army to forty thousand and went on the defensive himself, it would spare fifty thousand men for use elsewhere. That logical deduction rather contradicted the president's renowned solicitude for the safety of Washington, which every commander of the Army of the Potomac had learned to heed at considerable cost in tactical latitude. Now Lincoln seemed to ponder an offensive that involved nearly as much risk to the capital as the plan he and Halleck had denied Hooker in June, back when Lee was taking his first steps toward Pennsylvania. Halleck called Meade to Washington on a whirlwind visit, and on the morning of September 23 he, Stanton, and the president grilled the general about cannibalizing his army. Meade resisted, however, and he left the capital with the understanding that nothing of the sort would be done.[39]

Escalating anxiety over Rosecrans, and the unjustified fear that Bragg would have the sense to attack him there before he could recover his balance, brought Lincoln's mathematical inquiry back to prominence in a rare nighttime cabinet meeting called by Stanton. Couriers roused Chase, Seward, and Halleck late on September 23, and John Hay, one of the president's private secretaries, rode out to the Soldiers' Home on Seventh Street to fetch Lincoln to the War Department. As they rose from their beds and came in by the glow of a three-quarter moon, they all worried that the ultimate disaster had befallen Rosecrans and his army, but Stanton set them at ease on that score: according to the latest telegrams, the army still clung to Chattanooga. The pressing question was what to do about relieving the place, and how quickly it could be done. Halleck offered optimistic estimates of how many men Burnside could bring down from Knoxville and over from Kentucky, and how quickly they could be marched to Chattanooga; he thought that reinforcements from Sherman could arrive no sooner from Mississippi via Memphis, despite the steamboat and railroad connections. No one could come to Rosecrans's aid in less than eight or ten days, they concluded.[40]

Encouraged by Lincoln's sudden willingness to consider stripping troops from Meade, Stanton proposed sending twenty or thirty thousand men — two or three corps — all the way from the Army of the Potomac to Chattanooga by way of Baltimore, Indianapolis, Louisville, and Nashville. The first units could be there in five days, he said, but Lincoln ridiculed that assertion; he doubted that a single corps could even be transported from the Rappahannock to Washington in five days, illustrating his argument with an amusing anecdote about some earlier troop movement. Stanton replied with a touch of temper that it was no time for jokes, but snorted that since the president seemed to disagree with his plan they might as well adjourn to the light supper he had prepared in another room.[41]

After the meal the secretary of state revived the idea of the troop transfer, lending it strong support. Chase also favored the idea. Lincoln's earlier inquiry on the subject notwithstanding, he now stubbornly resisted weakening the army before Washington, as did Halleck: both denied the symbolic or military value of the Confederate capital, yet both seemed preternaturally sensitive about protecting Washington as a symbol of national unity. Finally the president relented, though, and allowed the conference to conclude amiably with the typical politicians' solution of token concessions to each faction, thereby yielding a predictably diluted outcome. They decided to transfer two corps from Meade to Rosecrans, and to send them under the overall command of Joe Hooker, but they chose the Eleventh and Twelfth corps, which were the smallest and the least well regarded in the Army of the Potomac. The last monthly returns for the two corps, combined, had reported only 11,500 men present for duty, which (since Confederate divisions usually outnumbered Union divisions by 50 or 60 percent) would not even counterbalance the troops Longstreet had taken to Bragg. The Eleventh Corps still bore the army's blame for Chancellorsville, and had not completely erased that memory at Gettysburg. The Twelfth Corps had belonged to Nathaniel Banks, in the Shenandoah Valley and under John Pope, and, like the Eleventh Corps, it had always felt like a stepchild in the Potomac army. Their departure for the West would be so unobjectionable to the chosen troops and to the rest of the army as to suggest that Meade may have indicated, during his morning interview, which units he would most readily give up. As soon as Stanton had the president's assent he scribbled a volley of telegrams to the presidents and managers of the various railroads along the circuitous route, calling them to Washington as soon as they could come. Not until near midnight did he turn down the gaslights in his office and start for home, while Halleck remained behind to deal with the situation in Chattanooga and to warn Meade that he would be losing the two corps, unless he expected to move immediately against Lee's army.[42]

Once notified, the railroad men closed their roads to all competing traffic. From the main trunks and branch lines of Pennsylvania, Maryland, Ohio, and Indiana they collected more than a hundred passenger cars and fifty baggage cars at each relay station along the proposed route, anticipating that the transfer would be accomplished in three successive movements of three brigades each. Meade told Halleck he was waiting for reconnaissance reports that day to determine whether he would move against Lee, but upon seeing that equivocation Lincoln decided the matter himself. Halleck ordered Meade to prepare for the troop transfer immediately, but that message only reached Meade near noon the next day, after being delayed a couple of hours by a break in the telegraph wire. Thus the grand undertaking began with the loss of half a day. Meade further doubted that he could have the troops ready to leave before the following day.[43]

Half an hour after Meade had the word, he started bringing the off-duty elements of the Twelfth Corps in from their scattered camps and parking them around the nearest railroad depots; the First Corps, meanwhile, went out to relieve those who were on the picket line. Their movements were spotted by the enemy, so after dark most of the corps marched farther up the rail line to Bealeton Station. The Eleventh Corps lay near an inadequate rail line, and had to march to Manassas Junction. Once they arrived at their stations, too, it was not just a matter of putting the men on cars and shipping them off: the quartermasters had to turn in their teams and all the stores they had drawn, and as much as eight days' rations had to be cooked and issued. Someone had to decide whether to bring the corps artillery, of which Rosecrans had lost quite a bit, and if it was to go, there was the matter of transporting the horses, or drawing new ones in Tennessee. Once the order for Hooker's new assignment made the circuit of the pertinent commands, another complication arose when Henry Slocum, commander of the Twelfth Corps, refused to serve again under a general he considered neither an able soldier nor a worthy gentleman. Slocum submitted his resignation forthwith, and while the president refused to accept it he had to devise an arrangement that would keep Hooker and Slocum apart.[44]

When the troops were finally ready to board the cars, those managing the logistics discovered that there were far more of them than anyone had supposed. The Twelfth Corps, which had mustered 6,431 officers and men present for duty on August 31, numbered 10,600 according to the calculations at Meade's headquarters. Instead of the 5,145 men reported in the Eleventh Corps on August 31, O. O. Howard represented his command as 7,500 strong on September 24. That required dozens more passenger cars than anyone had anticipated, and the Twelfth Corps languished at

Bealeton Station until the wee hours of September 27 before transportation arrived. It came, finally, in the form of freight cars, with rough oak floors to jar bones and grate the skin until the first change of cars, more than four hundred miles ahead, and when those trains pulled out for Alexandria there were still more than 3,000 men left behind. The last stragglers from the Twelfth Corps left Meade's army early on Monday afternoon, September 28.[45]

The first two trains crawled out of Washington at 5:00 P.M. on September 25, hauling twenty-eight and twenty-seven cars respectively with 2,000 of the Eleventh Corps aboard. Four hours later they arrived at Camden Station in Baltimore, where yard hands had to disconnect some of the cars and put them behind a third locomotive, for the engines on the Baltimore & Ohio could pull no more than twenty-two cars over the precipitous Alleghenies on the way west. Traveling half an hour behind each other, those first three trains made less than ten miles an hour over "the roughest and most desolate country" one Pennsylvania soldier had ever seen. All three stopped in Martinsburg at midmorning on Saturday, the twenty-sixth, to take on wood and water while the troops ate breakfast at an impromptu banquet hall. After two more meals at mountain stations they arrived at the Ohio River below Wheeling just before noon on Sunday. The cramped and weary passengers scrambled out, ate another good lunch, and crossed to the Ohio side on a makeshift bridge of scows and barges before boarding the more comfortable passenger cars of the Central Ohio Railroad. From there the scenery improved, at least in the opinion of the farmers of the Eleventh Corps. They crossed the flatlands at about fourteen miles an hour: the first train passed through Columbus at three o'clock Monday morning, September 28, and pulled into Indianapolis at 3:40 P.M.[46]

A Quaker woman who spent that bright, clear day walking to her yearly meeting at Richmond, Indiana, kept to a highway near the railroad tracks most of the afternoon. She saw several trains pass filled with soldiers, some of whom must have taken advantage of their languid pace to exchange a few words with her, for even though this was the forefront of the supposedly secret mass movement, she knew exactly where they had come from — and that they were bound for "Chetanuga." By the time the Twelfth Corps started coming through, a couple of days later, crowds had begun gathering at many of the stations to cheer them as their cars crept past. The Confederates knew about them, too. A resident of Washington sent remarkably precise information across the Potomac as early as September 25, erring only in vastly exaggerating the strength of the troops Hooker was moving. Rebel cavalry monitored their passage across the foot of the Shenandoah Valley, reporting them as strong as twenty-five thousand, but Lee discounted that by half. Howard's and Slocum's were, he assured Jefferson Davis, "two of the smallest and most indifferent corps."[47]

One-armed General Howard ordered his leading regiments off the cars at Stevenson, Alabama, on October 2, eight and a half days after the executive conclave in the War Department. Most of the Eleventh Corps and part of the Twelfth came in that day and the next. Laggard troops had all departed Louisville by October 5, but for the next week and more the rails continued to ring with trainloads of horses, mules, ambulances, wagons, camp and cooking equipment, and personal baggage.[48]

Hooker beat any supporting troops from Sherman by weeks, and his arrival eliminated the need for Burnside to leave east Tennessee or weaken his position there, but the reinforcements might have done Rosecrans more good had they started when Washington first knew of Longstreet's westward journey. By late September they were not so vital to Rosecrans as Lincoln, Stanton, and the rest supposed: their real value would only be realized two months later.

The greatest protection for Rosecrans in early autumn lay in the person of Braxton Bragg. The Confederate commander wasted the precious days after Chickamauga preparing to besiege a beaten enemy whom he might have forced out of his lair by threatening his supply route above the Tennessee River. That, as James Longstreet suggested, should have pried Rosecrans loose and sent him flying back toward Nashville, for a more resounding and meaningful victory. It would also have put Bragg in a position to hasten up the railroad to Knoxville and flush a badly outnumbered Burnside out of east Tennessee, restoring direct communication between Richmond and Chattanooga.[49] Such movements in the three days after the battle would have nullified every Union success in Tennessee since Stone's River, in the first hours of 1863, and would surely have sent Northern morale plummeting once again.

The primary benefit the Lincoln administration achieved through the arduous shuttling of four infantry divisions was to offer reassurance that the armies of the West would be sustained: the bloody setback at Chickamauga would not likely be repeated or expanded upon, and the early summer's progress would resume. The people of Ohio and Indiana had seen an exaggerated token of the government's strength in the hundreds of crowded passenger cars carrying a fragment of the nation's armies through their communities, and people who lived along Hooker's route absorbed a measure of confidence from the demonstration. Confidence came precious to the administration just then, too, and particularly in the Ohio and Indiana counties through which those troop trains had run, where some important elections were scheduled for October 13. Of course, every election carried heightened importance during this war, and the party in power showed an exaggerated solicitude to win them all, by fair means or foul.[50]

In Kentucky, early in August, Ambrose Burnside had once again exercised his situational disdain for the fundamentals of democracy by declaring martial law in the state three days before the state elections. He did so, he said, because "Kentucky is invaded by a rebel force," the purpose of which he misinterpreted, probably deliberately, as disrupting the plebiscite and "forcing the election of disloyal candidates." The "invasion" came from a single brigade of cavalry bent on capturing remounts, arms, and cattle while creating a diversion in favor of John Morgan's raid, and by the time Burnside issued his edict the remains of that brigade were hurrying back through southern Kentucky for the safety of Tennessee. Burnside betrayed his ulterior motive by continuing martial law in the entire state through the election, long after the last rebel raider had escaped. Military sources also spread ludicrous rumors that thousands of "New York rioters" had been sent into Kentucky by Peace Democrats to sway the election, and that martial law had allowed the army to capture them and force them to work on the railroads. Federal soldiers controlled the polls in Kentucky counties 150 miles from the nearest armed Confederate, forcing suspected Democrats to swear to an obnoxious oath if they wished to vote, and arresting them if they declined. When that failed to prevent enough men from approaching the polls with Democratic tickets, provost marshals simply suppressed their vote entirely, refusing to allow any more such tickets in the ballot boxes.[51]

As some cynics predicted weeks before, troops were also employed to prevent any Democratic resurgence in Maryland. The military commander there, Robert Schenck, could contrive no excuse for martial law, but on the grounds that there were many "evil-disposed" and disloyal persons in the state he ordered provost marshals and other officers to arrest all such men who appeared at the polls. Like Burnside, he ordered a test oath administered as a proof of citizenship to anyone whose loyalty came into question, and the language of that oath could be conscientiously sworn to only by those who vigorously supported prosecution of the war. Schenck also authorized his military officers, rather than the judges of the elections, to decide who was or was not loyal: the loyalty of anyone who tried to submit a Democratic ticket might be challenged.[52] An incensed Governor Augustus Bradford issued his own proclamation declaring Schenck's order illegal, but Schenck refused to let the newspapers publish it. Bradford then appealed to President Lincoln, pointing out the likelihood that army officers would be especially prone to abuse the power of arrest, since some of them were themselves candidates for office; Schenck, for that matter, held a seat in Congress as a Republican. Lincoln modified that part of Schenck's order, directing military officers merely to prevent any "disturbance" at the polls, but he let the test oath remain and still required the election judges to impose it on those dragged out of line by army officers. The president sent his defensive reply directly to the Baltimore newspapers, where it appeared on election morning, while Bradford only received it later that day. With bayonets and partisan oaths to discourage them, and newspapers permitted to print only the administration view of such restrictions, Maryland Democrats lost any chance of the victory their numbers might otherwise have brought.[53]

Burnside and Schenck may have had good cause to worry about Republican candidates losing the election, but not to "disloyal" aspirants. Border-state Democrats had grown leery of the Republican partisanship that typified the superficially nonpartisan Union Party, and in fair elections the Republican or Union candidate might be vulnerable. Republican John Noell won reelection to Congress from southeastern Missouri in the fall of 1862, but his Democratic opponent, John Scott, brought charges of election fraud and unfair voting practices. The issue became moot when Noell died in office, however, and in a special election in the summer of 1863 Scott won the vacant seat with little difficulty. His party as a whole made substantial gains in that part of the state, as well.[54]

It was a different story in the North. There, Republicans had largely succeeded in their efforts to cast all administration critics as active opponents of the war, or as clandestine traitors. The victories of early July had restored the flagging confidence of many voters who had been ready to give up the struggle the previous spring, but it was the draft riots of mid-July that lent the taint of treason to political dissent. To the consternation of a young draftee who scorned both candidates as scoundrels, Vermont easily elected a new Republican governor that summer, choosing another of those railroad executives whose interests and influence led them to control state affairs. Maine gave a majority of thousands to a radical antislavery man who had only recently switched to the Republican Party in a campaign that saw the Democrat unjustly accused of Southern sympathies.[55]

The paramount contest that year came in Ohio, where the exiled former congressman Vallandigham and newcomer John Brough vied for the governor's chair. Voters hundreds of miles away watched this race anxiously, fearing that the shooting war would extend north of the Ohio.

Brough, another prince in the rising railroad aristocracy, had been a Democrat all his adult life, but he had supported the administration to the hilt since the beginning of the war, and as a Union candidate he could be expected to win the entire Republican vote as well as those of many former Democrats. Vallandigham's exile, meanwhile, had prevented him from using his considerable oratorical talent on the campaign trail, and it had stained his entire candidacy with an atmosphere of disloyalty, at least among those too dull-witted or stubborn to comprehend the political motivation behind his expulsion. That he had been tried for a crime that did not exist, by a jaundiced court that lacked jurisdiction, and that his very arrest and detention had violated the Constitution, did not occur to tens of thousands of citizens for whom it was enough to know that he had been convicted.[56]

Vallandigham campaigned by mail from Canada West, writing to political advisors, newspaper editors, and once or twice to the people of Ohio. He spent most of the summer in Niagara, near Buffalo, but late in August he moved to Windsor, opposite Detroit. Isolation left him a perfect target for the most outrageous slanders, and the Republican press let fly with a vengeance, abetted by the Union Leagues. Those semisecret organizations served mainly as propaganda organs during the campaign, harping persistently (and with exquisite cant) on the imagined network of secret societies that they claimed stood ready to join ranks with Confederates to overthrow the government. They cast Vallandigham as the leader of those societies in the North, accusing him of having orchestrated John Hunt Morgan's raid, Lee's invasion of Pennsylvania, and the New York draft riots. His opponents forged letters to "prove" his treachery, and partisan newspapers gladly published them as genuine. Even when the allegations did reach Vallandigham, he could seize no effective forum for rebuttal.[57]

A special effort to spread an impression of imminent military triumph represented another tactic in the campaign to beat Vallandigham, or any other candidate who questioned the war. Every season brought new predictions of victory close at hand, and the events of early July had given substance to such expectations, but that news was growing stale as the summer faded. Through the first half of September the Republican press nevertheless described recent setbacks as "alleged defeats," while giving headlines of "more glorious news" to every inch of gained ground, with occasional editorial allusions to the signs of impending collapse in the Confederacy. Soldiers, who habitually embraced such hopeful speculation, repeated it in letters home as though from personal observation. If the rebellion were teetering on the verge of defeat, then the quickest path to peace obviously lay in one last, overwhelming offensive, and those who could be convinced of the looming victory would surely sustain the war party once more. Executive aspirations to aid that illusion with more and greater victories before the Ohio election may have prompted Henry Halleck's urgent telegrams from Washington to Rosecrans, demanding an immediate advance in the movement that would lead to disaster on Chickamauga Creek. It may also have spurred James Garfield, who was at once chief of staff to Rosecrans and a member of Congress from Ohio, to the personal disloyalty of informing fellow Ohioan Salmon Chase that Rosecrans could and should advance immediately. "Let the nation now display the majesty of its power," Garfield concluded, "and the work will be speedily ended." With the war now costing two million dollars a day and the specter of insolvency growing, Chase certainly hoped for a quick victory.[58]

Good reason existed to doubt the sincerity, if not the accuracy, of all the verge-of-victory rhetoric. Gloom actually had stricken the South in the wake of the July defeats, but morale had begun to recover by late September. The advocates of any war usually insist at critical junctures that one more determined push will end the struggle, and justifiably skeptical Democrats saw the exaggerated optimism of late summer as a ploy to influence the Ohio election. The validity of that suspicion seemed confirmed when, after the disaster at Chickamauga spoiled that cultivated image of triumph, self-conscious Republicans charged in turn that the Confederates had thrown all their resources into that battle in order to exert a negative influence on those same Ohio elections. It was perhaps the desire to restore election-eve confidence, more than the hope of rapidly reinforcing the Army of the Cumberland, that dragged Joe Hooker's new command through the Buckeye State just before her citizens went to the polls.[59]

President Lincoln gave Vallandigham the only ammunition that came his way during the campaign. On September 15 he declared a nationwide suspension of the constitutional right of habeas corpus for prisoners arrested for aiding or abetting the enemy, as spies, as fugitive conscripts, or as deserters from the army or navy: it seemed that too many judges had been considering the release of prisoners for whose guilt little or no evidence existed. Vallandigham expected to reap much benefit from that latest leap in the Lincoln dictatorship, but the public showed little indignation. Desensitized by earlier invocations of a similar nature, a majority of citizens seemed oblivious to the potential for partisan abuse of the proclamation, viewing it instead as a threat only to the actual spies, collaborators, and deserters enumerated in the document.[60]

Small wonder, then, that Brough trounced his absentee opponent by the greatest majority of the war.[61] Ohio allowed its soldiers to vote in the field, and the outcome there fell so much more lopsidedly to Brough that Vallandigham may have been justified in his anticipation of fraud. Most soldiers had heard only the worst about "Villaindam," though, and they were developing a prejudice against any civilian who balked at the pretext of military necessity for federal intrusions, but the danger of retaliation, and perhaps violent retaliation, also shrank support for Vallandigham in the army. One Ohio soldier swore that no one in the Army of the Cumberland would dare vote for Vallandigham, lest his comrades "cut him to pieces." In the absence of secret ballots, that kind of intimidation assumed a more chilling note among men who at any moment might be thrown into the confusion of battle with those who had made such mortal threats. It could only have increased the Brough majority in camp elections where voting-age men were expected to make a choice one way or the other.[62]

More formal retribution awaited soldiers with the temerity to actually defend Vallandigham, as Benjamin Sells learned. Sells, a highly regarded captain in the 122nd Ohio and a veteran of the Mexican War, made no effort to disguise his principles, and that fall he was subjected to a court-martial. Superiors charged him with remarking that "the Administration has denied the freedom of speech to a man unless he is an abolitionist," reading and distributing Democratic newspapers, and asserting that Vallandigham was a loyal man for whom he and most of his company were going to vote. His regiment, meanwhile, was ordered into formation to hear the harangue of a colonel who excoriated Vallandigham, thereby proving the validity of Sells's charge of selective censorship. Sells won the commendation of his brigade commander in an action that took place while the court-martial was still deliberating, but he was convicted soon thereafter and dismissed from the service for his political opinions.[63]

Vallandigham's resounding defeat in Ohio, along with Andrew Curtin's reelection in Pennsylvania the same day, led to cheers, toasts, and torch-light processions from the East Coast to the prairies beyond the Mississippi. The moment it became certain that the Peace Democrats had been defeated, the war party could stop pretending that peace lay right around the corner. Illustrating that reversion from political sham to grim reality, President Lincoln immediately issued a new proclamation demanding yet another three hundred thousand soldiers from the country. It had long since become obvious that the July call would come nowhere near raising enough troops to compensate for attrition, let alone increase the army enough to achieve significant results, but a public admission of that deficiency before the election would inevitably have reinforced the argument of the peace lobby.[64]

Such devious methods drew plenty of editorial scorn from the losing faction, but right after the Kentucky elections, the *Louisville Daily Democrat* also questioned the motives of the president's firmest adherents. "If there is an Administration Party in this state," the editor scoffed, "it is that miserable mixture of abolition[ists] and contractors which carried the election at the point of the bayonet." Corruption among the most boisterously loyal supporters deeply tainted the Union cause, and a good example came right across the Ohio River from Kentucky, in Cincinnati. After months of insinuation and accusation from the Democratic press, Captain Francis Hurtt, half owner of the flagrantly Republican *Ohio State Journal* in Columbus, was quietly arrested in his capacity as Burnside's quartermaster for Cincinnati because of "irregularities in his accounts." Ultimately Hurtt was dismissed for using government money for his own personal purposes. Edwin Stanton's roving investigator, Charles Dana, found "various frauds" in the quartermaster's department at Louisville, too, including an "extensive swindle" involving the sale of two-year-old mules as full-grown.[65]

Almost everyone in the quartermaster and commissary departments seemed to have their fingers in the pie to some degree, from chief quartermaster Rufus Ingalls of the Army of the Potomac down to regimental supply sergeants. Ingalls supplied innumerable favors and government transportation for an overbearing sutler known as "Fat Andy," for whom he was generally recognized to act as a silent partner. For this and other dubious practices Ingalls occasionally ran afoul of his army's provost marshal general, Marsena Patrick, who expected eventually to catch him presenting injudicious endorsements. Ingalls, a native of western Maine, arranged appointments for several hometown friends as brigade and division quartermasters, and a corporal from the same neighborhood commented on the larcenous reputations of the men he had chosen. "You see how they get in to the quar. Masters dpt." the corporal observed; "they know where the money is to be made and they are bound to get rich out of this war." A Massachusetts quartermaster sergeant informed his mother that he routinely lifted goods from his regimental storehouse for his brother, and presumably for himself and other close friends. Rufus Mead, commissary sergeant of the 5th Connecticut, admitted to his family that he had gone into both business and housekeeping with the regimental sutler: Mead supplied their larder with provisions commonly obtained from the commissary department — fresh beef, coffee, sugar, bread, and the like — while the sutler provided the delicacies that such vendors usually stocked. Mead even drove the sutler's wagon on the march, congratulating himself on his choice of friends.[66]

In the spring of 1863 two brigade quartermasters conspired with a sly

New Yorker to skim grain and firewood from the Army of the Potomac's big supply depot at Alexandria, Virginia, and by December the junior partner in the scheme had stashed away thirty-one thousand dollars. That army also seemed rife with corruption among regimental quartermasters and commissaries. Soldiers' recurring complaints that they had been cheated in their clothing accounts often originated at least partially from the double-dealing of quartermasters at some level. Sloppy or slippery quartermasters, for instance, led to many a soldier paying for goods he never received, or for equipment lost in battle. Army contractors bore much of the blame for shoddy footgear and clothing for which the troops were charged twice the cost of high-quality civilian equivalents, but unit quartermasters who approved such substandard goods in return for part of the profits shared the responsibility for that injustice.[67]

Regimental quartermasters also usually escaped liability when they lost clothing and equipment belonging to their men, for which they should have been held directly accountable. Every spring, as the armies broke camp for the year's first campaign, orders came down to turn in all overcoats and extra clothing, which the quartermasters would transport back to Washington, Nashville, or St. Louis. As often as not those belongings were never returned to the troops, who were then forced to buy replacement articles at exorbitant government rates. The quartermasters who conducted those spring collections should have credited each man with whatever he was forced to turn in: after all, scrupulous accounting always attended the issue of new clothing or equipment, under any circumstances. Supply officers exercised no such care, however, when they took those goods back, and whole wagon trains full of soldiers' winter wardrobes vanished each summer, presumably through pilferage by those who shipped, stored, or guarded them, and the officers assigned to oversee every step of the process seldom paid the price for their negligence or dishonesty. Rarely did the question even arise, because the shortfall could be recovered so easily by charging it back to the victimized soldiers, who had no recourse but the capital crime of mutiny.[68]

Quartermasters reserved a special appreciation for hasty retreats, for in such cases supplies were usually destroyed en masse, without taking an inventory, and that settled everyone's accounts on the spot. When they could find no such opportunity to wash a suspicious imbalance from the record, charges would frequently fly, but through collusion with the post or regimental commander the malefactors often escaped prosecution or foiled their courts-martial, although superior officers occasionally fell from grace along with their conniving supply masters. There was General Blunt, in Kansas, who was relieved from duty for the widespread "inefficiency" in his department. In northeastern Missouri a militia general with the memorable name of Odon Guitar resigned some months after the appearance of an allegation that he was complicit in frauds perpetrated by the quartermaster of his former regiment. The most conspicuous case may have been that of Colonel Frederick D'Utassy, originally known as Frederick Strasser, who commanded the polyglot 39th New York; few in his regiment spoke English, which evidently allowed him to escape detection for two years while he swindled the government, stole from Southern civilians, and bilked his own men out of many thousands of dollars. More often than anyone probably realized, the officers of a regiment might pool their purses to cover a shortfall in return for an embezzler's resignation, to save the "honor" of the unit.[69]

Government employees and officials rivaled the knavery of profiteers in uniform. Henry B. Stanton, husband of women's suffrage pioneer Elizabeth Cady Stanton and an old antislavery crony of Secretary Chase's from the Free Soil Party days, had exploited that association for an appointment as deputy collector of customs for the Port of New York. In that office he began taking regular bribes to certify goods bound through the blockade, but this case, too, was kept under wraps until after the October election, although the officer who investigated it found similar corruption rampant in customs offices throughout New York, and it was evidently the same in the Vermont stations. The lesson failed to sharpen Chase's scrutiny of applicants for office: soon thereafter he appointed a treasury agent who had just been run out of the New York legislature for selling his vote, assigning him to Helena, Arkansas, where he became responsible for the contraband cotton that had corrupted so many others at that post.[70]

Not everyone who backed the president and his war stooped to larceny, but much of his support did rest among those who profited from the conflict, or from their adherence to the administration. Opposition newspapers lampooned the droves of postmasters, deputy marshals, tax assessors, enrolling officers, contractors, and government clerks who organized or dominated Republican rallies. Army officers, meanwhile, and civilians who held commissions or concessions from the government, often surprised themselves and their families with how much money they accumulated through regular service, legitimate enterprises, or mildly unethical arrangements. "I never done so well before," admitted a Vermont man who had resigned from the army to sell patent medicines to his former comrades; when he returned to duty with much higher rank and pay, he invested heavily (and covertly) with the sutler of his regiment, whose principal occupation consisted of charging his men several times the original price of the goods he sold. A petty dishonesty seemed to permeate the officer corps. The prim and proper commander of First Corps artillery grumbled disgustedly when he learned that most of his fellow officers signed false affidavits "on honour" so their purveyor's supplies could be transported safely, and at no cost to them, as government freight. "It is astonishing," he noted, "how few officers there are who consider it wrong to defraud the government in little matters."[71]

A purveyor catered to the officers of a brigade, or a division, much as a sutler served enlisted men. Each regiment was authorized one sutler, who operated a rolling general store for the troops in his concession. His wagon carried a surprising array of merchandise, including tobacco, candy, canned goods, cakes, jellies, butter, fresh fruit and vegetables when they could be had, pocket mirrors, playing cards, and camp gadgets like collapsible drinking cups. The assignment of their monopoly market required that they sell to the men on credit, since the paymaster generally ignored field regiments for months at a time, but when payday finally came the sutler's accumulated receipts had to be settled before the soldier drew a penny. They charged exorbitant prices reflecting a greed that was exaggerated by the risk involved in bringing goods through hostile territory, for guerrillas attacking a Yankee column would ride straight for any sutler's rig that came into sight. Even inside friendly lines no sutlers were ever really safe, both because they carried such coveted goods and because they were universally regarded as gougers and swindlers. When Union soldiers caught one of these peddlers driving to or from camp outside the view of higher authority they often pounced with all the fury of Confederate cavalry, surrounding the cart and tipping it over so the contents could be looted in relative leisure. A sutler who encountered idle troops under such circumstances often took the precaution of whipping his horses into a brisk trot, just in case.[72]

The most popular item a sutler carried was liquor, which he was permitted to sell only to officers, but at enormous markups he might slip a few bottles to the common soldier. Sutlers even managed to get their hands on comfort items that had been shipped to the army from charitable institutions with the intent that they would be distributed to the troops free of charge, and these they sold at similarly inflated prices. The profits of hawking goods so far from any competition could be staggering, compared to a private's pay, and when enterprising soldiers saw their sutlers clearing five thousand a year, they sought a way out of the service so they could get into the business themselves. A wise sutler would invite an enlisted man to share his luxurious living conditions and a fraction of the proceeds in return for someone to watch the store when the owner was sleeping or off collecting more stock. As Sergeant Mead of the 5th Connecticut learned, though, they preferred to hire men from the commissary or quartermaster departments, from which their avaricious apprentices might supply a portion of the inventory.[73]

The quartermasters and sutlers of the Army of the Potomac had to pack up their traps and get moving in a hurry on October 11 when, after two and a half months of relative inactivity, George Meade realized that Lee's army was loping around his right flank to intrude between the Union army and Washington. Lee may have hoped to disguise any weakness he suffered from the loss of Longstreet's corps, and he wished to discourage Meade from releasing any more of his troops to other points, so even with his customary disadvantage in numbers he took the offensive. He flung his remaining two corps, under Richard Ewell and A. P. Hill, in a wide arc around the upper fords of the Rappahannock, toward the Orange & Alexandria Railroad that fed Meade's army. Learning this almost too late, Meade hustled back up the railroad toward Centreville, giving up forty miles of ground to avoid being cut off. When Lee pounced, he fell on nothing but the Second Corps, under Gouverneur Warren. Warren lagged at the rear of the retreat with fewer than nine thousand men, his march having been stymied by the inexplicable delay of William French's Third Corps, ahead of him. With the enemy close on his heels Warren took cover in a railroad cut at Bristoe Station, shattering a hasty attack by Hill on the afternoon of October 14, taking several guns and hundreds of prisoners in a motley array of dusty grey and dirty brown uniforms, with a sprinkling of blue jackets or trousers.[74]

Meade turned about at Centreville, where high ground and old earthworks offered a safe haven, but Lee knew better than to attack a superior army in such a position. He wanted mainly to destroy the railroad north of the Rappahannock, assuring that no Union advance could move very fast until the road had been rebuilt, but for a few days he lingered in Meade's front to keep up the threat. When the Confederates finally did fall back, Meade recognized the real purpose behind Lee's gambit, conceding that "he has got[ten] the advantage of me."[75]

So the opposing lines began their gradual slide back toward the Rappahannock, averaging a couple of miles per day. November was well under way before the Army of the Potomac left its camps around Warrenton Junction and Morrisville with an eye to crossing back over the Rappahannock and reclaiming its camps of late summer. In the bitter morning chill of November 7, everyone threw off his blankets expecting to face another slaughter like Fredericksburg, and Meade may have been thinking of Ambrose Burnside's travails at that place as he arranged the Third Corps in front of Kelly's Ford and the Sixth Corps before Rappahannock Station. This time he caught Lee napping, though. At Kelly's Ford skirmishers of the 1st U.S. Sharpshooters — their forest-green ranks of two years before heavily daubed with regulation blue — splashed into the icy, waist-deep water and snared the entire guard detail. Leaving several dozen dead and three hundred prisoners, the rest of the Confederate force there took to its heels. A few hours later and a few miles upstream, a division from the Sixth Corps did even better in a furious dusk assault, bagging eight battle flags, six guns, and the better part of the Louisiana and North Carolina brigades defending that crossing. Some of the rebels put up a fierce hand-to-hand resistance, though, before they surrendered, and a private who had been with the 6th Maine from the beginning of the war claimed it was the toughest fight he had ever seen. In the next brigade the 5th Maine carried only three hundred men into its fifteen-minute portion of the affair, and lost nearly half of them.[76]

With the darkness came intense cold, and in their soggy pants and overcoats the victors made frantic efforts to build campfires. They had luxuriated in a profusion of worm fences around their recent bivouacs north of the river, mostly with rails of oak and chestnut that split nicely and burned well, but here in this camped-over vicinity they had to go a-roving for scraps and sticks. As they tried to dry their clothing and steal some sleep, they might have noted that four weeks had passed since they had fled their advanced lines at Culpeper Court House. Now they had recovered all but the last few miles of the lost territory, at what seemed by November of 1863 like a bargain rate of barely a thousand casualties.[77]

They pushed ahead a few more miles the next day. When they reached the camps they had vacated in such a hurry, around Brandy Station, they found that Lee's men had made themselves quite comfortable, as though expecting to stay for the winter. Log huts dotted the landscape, and shivering Yankees packed into them. Other cabins began springing up as the weather grew colder, reminding an Indiana colonel of "a primitive village in the far West." Rations came sporadically while engineers rebuilt the railroad and the bridge over the Rappahannock, and biting cold only sharpened the keen appetites of Meade's men, some of whom lapsed into insubordinate chants for more hardtack. Even the innovative sutlers could shuttle up little in the way of food, and the middle of November brought an ominous grumbling.[78]

Hunger had sharpened tempers in the Chattanooga garrison, as well. Confederates controlled the railroad and river traffic into that city, so provisions had to come in over bad, tortuous roads, and there had not been enough to eat for man or beast since the end of September. Late in October Grant opened the Tennessee River, but steamers could only manage partial rations of bread and meat, bringing no vegetable ration to speak of. Longstreet had left Bragg's army to strike for Knoxville, meanwhile, and he soon began to restrict Burnside's ability to gather food and forage: by November 17 he had driven Burnside into a perimeter around Knoxville, where a Michigan soldier described rations as "very short."[79]

There was no shortage of food at Salmon P. Chase's three-story brick mansion at the corner of Sixth and E streets in Washington, at least on the evening of November 12. At about seven-thirty carriages began dropping off a cavalcade of governmental elite, diplomats, and army officers to attend the wedding of Secretary Chase's stunning and calculating daughter, Kate, to Senator William Sprague of Rhode Island. The procession jammed E Street for nearly eight blocks. Attorney General Bates escorted his daughter, Matilda, and Secretary Stanton attended alone. Generals Halleck and Schenck came, and that first unlucky commander of the Army of the Potomac, Irvin McDowell, who brought his daughter. Dismayed by Chase's support of Radical plans for a punitive reconstruction of the Southern states, Montgomery Blair shunned the proceedings, and Chase noted his absence, but Blair's father and daughter arrived in the postmaster general's stead. Mary Lincoln also sent her excuses, but her husband descended from his carriage at eight-thirty and climbed the carpet that had been rolled down the two flights of stone steps, whereupon the wedding ceremony began. Kate swept into the parlor in a flowing white velvet gown, with her pixie face and a five-hour hairdressing ordeal hidden behind a lace veil. Sprague, fresh from the Ebbitt House hotel, wore a black suit with a white satin vest. The Episcopal bishop of Rhode Island joined them in marriage before five hundred densely packed guests, after which everyone adjourned to a sumptuous banquet and danced to the music of the Marine Band. Kate opened the ball. She selected the former consul to Rio de Janeiro as a partner rather than her new husband, who receded into the shadows from that moment, at least in the eyes of the capital's social sentinels. The bride, meanwhile, seemed to wear herself out competing for attention with the daughters of both General McDowell and the minister from Brazil.[80]

Some of the groom's Rhode Island guests incorporated the wedding into an extended tour of the city and the sites around it, and one woman assured her family and friends back home that she had "done" Gettysburg.[81] The site of the battle had become quite an attraction, for it lay in friendly territory, and — unlike Antietam — it could be reached conveniently by railroad. Lee had no sooner retreated than scavengers had swooped in to prowl for souvenirs, many of which ultimately stocked Gettysburg museums, and with a legion of humanitarian volunteers those relic hunters formed the first wave of tourists to besiege the town. Four days after the grand assault on Cemetery Ridge, a visitor from near Baltimore disembarked from the train at Oxford, ten miles out of Gettysburg, where he found the York Pike already crowded with pedestrians, horsemen, and an endless variety of conveyances. Most of those returning from the battlefield assumed a much more somber air than the convivial excursionists who had not yet seen the place, but at that early date the wounded had not yet ceased to scream, and the surgeons had not put away their saws.[82]

As late as the second week of August a British visitor still found the field littered with clothing and equipment, and it reeked from the stench of unburied horses; he also ran across three unburied Confederates in isolated spots. By November the wreckage of men and matériel at Gettysburg had been swept up. The dead, a majority of them Confederate, had been buried, but those Union soldiers whose bodies had not been claimed by relatives were being exhumed and carted to a new location on land bought by the federal government. There, near the bend of Meade's fishhook defense line and half a mile from the spot where Pickett's last fragments had surrendered, a local contractor prepared a national cemetery. Following the design of a landscape architect, laborers laid the moldering remains in a series of concentric semicircles, grouped by state, with a large section for those who could not be identified. Many wounded still lingered at Gettysburg, in hospitals on a large tract outside of town.[83]

The committee in charge of dedicating the cemetery fixed Thursday, November 19, for the ceremony, and invited scores of dignitaries, including the president. Edward Everett, the 1860 vice-presidential candidate on the Constitutional Union ticket, accepted the job of presenting the principal oration, while the president agreed to add a few approving remarks of his own. Lincoln's train left Washington at noon the day before, carrying his two personal secretaries, three cabinet members, the French, Italian, and Canadian ministers, and a number of hangers-on. At Baltimore they picked up General Schenck, and at Hanover that afternoon they met a trainload of governors coming down from Harrisburg. They pulled into Gettysburg at six that evening and all split up, with Lincoln taking a room in the home of the man who chaired the cemetery project, in the town center, known as the diamond. Thousands of strangers filled the streets, drinking whatever they could find in the way of alcohol. At night a crowd gathered in the diamond and called on the president and Secretary Seward at their side-by-side lodgings, asking for speeches but getting nothing much from the president and only an inaudible ramble from Seward.[84]

Fog blanketed Gettysburg the next morning as a squadron of cavalry, a regiment of infantry, and two batteries of artillery formed, with their van in the diamond, to escort the dignitaries to the cemetery. At ten General Darius Couch, formerly of the Army of the Potomac, waved the procession into motion, but it crept down Baltimore Street at an excruciating pace. The diamond lay only a mile from the cemetery even by a roundabout route down the Emmitsburg and Taneytown roads, but it was 11:45 before the troops delivered their charges to a substantial raised platform on what Meade and his generals had immortalized as Cemetery Hill.[85]

One of the guests from Washington estimated that the stand held 250 notables, including himself.[86] Governor Curtin was there, and Seymour of New York, and even dissident New Jersey's Joel Parker. Governor Bradford of Maryland, perhaps still aggravated at the military interference with his state's election, took a seat with them. So did Francis Peirpoint, chief executive of Virginia Unionists' rump government, as well as the present, former, and future governors of Ohio. They sat on the crest of the hill, looking down on the civilian dead to the east and the fresh graves of the Union soldiers to the west — "wedged in rows like herrings in a box," snorted an officer who had fought there, who cringed at the thought of low-bid contractors plucking the remains from sacred battlefield graves. Some 15,000 men, women, and children circled around, outnumbering the dusty horde that had burst out of the woods on Seminary Ridge twenty long weeks before.[87]

After a band had set the tone with a funeral dirge, the white-maned chaplain of the House of Representatives rose to open the proceedings with a prayer so long and lugubrious that he seemed to hope it might be mistaken for the oration of the day. The sun finally broke through during his attenuated obsecration, as though pouring forth a welcome from the heavens for Mr. Everett — who, after the band drowned the chaplain's echo with a hymn called "Old Hundred," rose to deliver the dedication address.[88]

Edward Everett had completed more than half of his seventieth year, and on that day he had less than fourteen months to live. He had served Massachusetts as a congressman, senator, and governor from the conservative wing of the Whig Party, scorning abolition as much as slavery, but secession had made him a fierce Unionist, and the words he uttered carried that flavor. Twenty minutes or more into his address, after the requisite classical allusions and preliminary homage to those who had stopped Lee at Gettysburg, he attempted to rekindle the collective hysteria that had sent the North into a war that secession itself had failed to provoke. The South did not seek independence, he declared: it sought domination of the North, or at least possession of the national capital. The clash at

Fort Sumter had been planned in the South to bring Virginia and North Carolina into the Confederacy, he charged, and that plan had been carefully orchestrated (apparently with the convenient but unwitting cooperation of Abraham Lincoln).[89]

From the observations of Union soldiers during and just after the battle, many a Gettysburg citizen would have disputed Everett's interpretation of the genesis of the war, but the aging orator launched uninterrupted into a forty-five-minute description of the battle, day by day and general by general. That finished, he filled the rest of his two hours with more political and historical argument. He who had praised the rebel patriots of Lexington, Concord, and Bunker Hill now denounced the rebels of the South as traitors who bore the sole guilt of bringing a dreadful war to the continent, yet he cast an image of future fraternity over the peace that would inevitably follow reunion with those errant-but-forgiven brothers. It had happened after the generation-long Wars of the Roses, he said, and after twenty years of civil war in England, and after the Thirty Years' War: antagonists of the most bitter civil conflicts had always resumed peaceful communion.

Waiting to speak behind Everett, the president may have winced to hear his audience reminded of wars that dragged on for decades, and to know that a war-weary nation would read that reminder in the morrow's newspapers. The exaggerated optimism of Eection Day had begun to subside again: hopeful and devoted Unionists might readily perceive the decline of Confederate fortunes and the attrition of Southern will, but cynics and conservatives saw only the withering of personal liberty, the bankrupting of the treasury, the endless slaughter, and the frustration of the massive Northern army, which lay contained at Chattanooga, stymied in Virginia, and just going under siege at Knoxville. Much of the nation wavered between those extreme impressions, and visions of years more of war would not endear them to his course. To be won over, they must be shown a worthy purpose, which he proposed to give them.

He opened by invoking the twin ideals of the civil religion, liberty and democracy, which had already begun to blend in the American mind as two halves of a mutually dependent whole. Then, having set a venerable foundation, he gravitated to a more tangible subject that could not fail to command the sympathy of his listeners: like Everett before him, and Pericles before them both, he embraced the image of the heroic soldier, wringing from it the personal pathos inevitably accorded to fallen sons, husbands, and fathers. He might have measured the success of his mechanism by the applause that erupted thereafter every time he mentioned "the brave men," and one reporter recorded "tremendous applause" after

Lincoln spoke of "what they did here." Four of his nine sentences appealed for devotion — not to the cause of liberty or equality, but to "these honored dead," or "they who fought here" — and all four times the crowd responded spontaneously, once breaking in at midsentence. Then, having wrapped the political cause of nationalism in the more personal emotion of compassion for the dead, he pleaded with the living to dedicate themselves to the "unfinished work" of those who had struggled there, and to "take increased devotion to that cause" for which they had died.[90]

In his brief and ingeniously efficient remarks he appealed to emotion rather than to the more critical realm of intellect. Many might have challenged the logic of his implied premise that liberty and equality could not be achieved except within the original boundaries of the United States: chief among those who disputed it had been the more fervent abolitionists among his current supporters, who had been so willing to accept secession to end the association with slavery. The president had obscured that deductive defect by speaking to the heart, and creating the impression that the value of those fundamental principles had been amplified by the blood already shed in defense of his debatable premise. Since many had already died in that effort, he seemed to say, then others should continue the struggle at the risk of their own lives.

As Lincoln asked for this renewed commitment, his only son of military age may have glanced once or twice out a window that opened on the Harvard quadrangle; Robert Lincoln would see no service until the last eight weeks of the war, when his father found him a safe spot on Ulysses Grant's staff. Edward Everett had three healthy sons between the ages of twenty-three and thirty-three, two of whom had been selected in the July draft, but both had escaped that levy and none of the three ever chose to take up arms. Meanwhile, in the anthracite regions north of Gettysburg, poor Irish miners continued their violent resistance to conscription even as the orators rose and retired on the stage, and when General Couch completed his duties as commander of the dignitaries' escort, he would send troops to suppress that recusant enclave. The more dangerous avenues for devoting oneself to the causes of liberty and equality, it seemed, could be left to others of lesser resources — even if they, too, were not willing.[91]

If such inconsistencies occurred to those wandering away from Cemetery Hill that afternoon, no record of their skepticism has come to light. Lincoln's carefully chosen words gratified those who still shared his dedication to preserving the Union, and persuaded many who had wavered to accept further sacrifice, lest those earlier sacrifices be wasted. Those who doubted his course continued to protest, but Lincoln's address had painted their most cogent criticisms as tasteless carping: now their opposition to the war not only insulted the struggle of the men in uniform, but belittled the sacrifices of the dead. Advocates of the war worked that ploy with diminishing subtlety until peace returned, by which time the sentimental plea Lincoln had employed at Gettysburg had deteriorated into the crude political bullying known as waving the bloody shirt.[92]

His mission accomplished, the president and his famished entourage rode back into town between the ranks of their escort. In the house on the diamond he received all who wished to shake his hand and compliment his eloquence until it was time for dinner, and afterward the marshals of the event arrived to take him to the Presbyterian church to hear one more speech before he returned to Washington. At six o'clock he and his secretaries made their way to the depot, and half an hour later his special train departed from Gettysburg Station.[93]

Virginia Unionist John Minor Botts and his family on the porch of his home near Culpeper. It was probably Isabella, at lower left, whom a Vermont soldier accused of excessive friendliness toward the guard who was posted at the house.

A sutler's shop in the camp of the horse artillery at Brandy Station during the winter of 1864.

The crowd gathered to hear the president speak at Gettysburg. Lincoln is on the rostrum in the distance at right.

The railroad depot at Chattanooga, with Lookout Mountain in the background.

Fort Sanders, in the defenses of Knoxville. Here Confederates met a bloody repulse.

Major General William H. French, who foiled Meade's plans below the Rapidan River.

Ford on the Rapidan River, which played a significant part in three major campaigns.

Brigadier General Henry Prince, whose indecision turned George Meade's likely victory at Mine Run into failure.

A cartoon of Columbia demanding her five hundred thousand sons from Abraham Lincoln, soon after he called for another half-million conscripts.

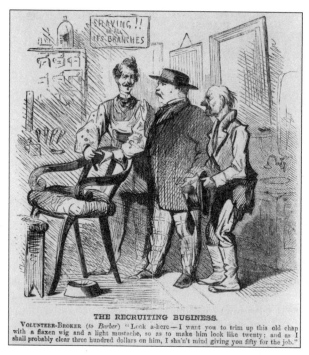

Another cartoon insinuating (with some justification) how the recent half-million-man levy would be met — by sending the old and the unfit.

William Waud's sketch, obviously based on secondhand information, of fresh contingents of Union prisoners entering the new Confederate prison at Andersonville.

Judson Kilpatrick at his Stevensburg headquarters, a few months after the death of his wife and a couple of weeks after his failed raid on Richmond, accompanied by his usual retinue of women and poseurs.

The exhibition hall of the U.S. Sanitary Commission's Metropolitan Fair, on Fourteenth Street in New York City.

The Grand Hall: inside at the fair.

The Red River campaign. Illustration of Taylor's Confederates attacking the Union wagon train at Sabine Crossroads.

PART III

MAKE NO PARLEY

7

Armies Like Ghosts on Hills

→ SINCE THE CAPTURE of Vicksburg and Port Hudson, the armies along the Mississippi had lain relatively inactive. Certainly there remained other Confederate bastions that needed taking, most notably at Mobile, but more than half of Nathaniel Banks's army had evaporated in July and August, when the nine-month regiments mustered out. That left him only twelve thousand effective troops for the entire Department of the Gulf, with its thousand miles of often-serpentine coastline from Pensacola to the Rio Grande. Banks concentrated most of his men between New Orleans and Port Hudson, necessarily ignoring all but a fraction of his territory, so provisions and supplies for Southern armies still flowed into Mobile and most of Texas with relative freedom, with only an occasional blockade runner lost to the thinly sprinkled U.S. Navy. Banks's enforced indolence also permitted the Texas rebels to strip their Mexican frontier of all but a skeleton force, the surplus from which they were able to employ elsewhere.[1]

Grant had returned the Ninth Corps to Burnside, as well as many of the troops he had borrowed of Schofield, from Missouri and Arkansas. Much of the remainder he scattered to more salubrious environs, with Sherman camping on the Big Black River and another corps steaming down the Mississippi to Natchez. Natchez seemed the most popular destination, perhaps because it had not yet been despoiled by the passage of Yankee soldiers, but now they came in abundance, accompanied by some early carpetbaggers from the discharged nine-month regiments. Grant and Banks corresponded at length on what to do next. Mobile seemed a likely target for them to combine upon, and, with orders from Washington, Grant set about sending a corps down to Banks for use in such an operation. Before anything could be done about Mobile, though, French forces in Mexico captured the city of Puebla and thousands of Mexican soldiers, whereupon they marched on Mexico City to impose an imperial government under an Austrian archduke. Washington's internal preoccupation prevented immediate enforcement of the Monroe Doctrine's proprietary provision, but it suddenly became desirable to reestablish some token federal presence in Texas to dissuade the French intruders from casting a covetous eye across the Rio Grande. Conveying Lincoln's wishes on that point, Henry Halleck informed Banks how vital it would be to plant the U.S. flag somewhere on Texas soil as soon as possible. That message nullified the Mobile operation, but the day he received it Banks replied that he hoped to be in Texas "within a week." That was August 15, and seven more weeks passed in preparations before Grant notified Banks that he would have to pull out of the Texas scheme in order to lend all the assistance he could to Rosecrans. James Longstreet's performance at Chickamauga had wrought all the far-reaching havoc with Union plans that he had predicted.[2]

Thus were the two armies that had opened the Father of the Waters allowed to languish for more than three months. George McClellan had been sacked for a forty-day pause after the bloodbath at Antietam, but in the intervening year the administration had evidently grown more patient, at least with its winning generals. Two weeks after William Rosecrans had outdistanced his army in the retreat to Chattanooga, Halleck wired Grant to come upriver for special instructions, and the circuitous, patched-up network of telegraph lines brought the message to Vicksburg on October 9.[3]

Grant left that same day, hobbling aboard the steamer on crutches. He had been badly hurt during a visit to New Orleans, five weeks before: his horse had reared up when the wheel of a passing cariole clipped its shoulder, but Grant managed to keep his seat and the horse had fallen heavily on him. Horses killed and crippled their riders every day, and for a lesser horseman it would have been easier to understand, but it was a curious accident for so renowned an equestrian as Grant. His history before the war gave disturbing substance to the explanation that he had had too much to drink, and General Banks ascribed the mishap to that very cause. Grant's friends and admirers found that charge difficult to accept precisely because of his antebellum reputation, although there had been rumblings of occasional drinking spells: a disgruntled quartermaster, for instance, had accused the general of going on a binge after the battle of Belmont. Several witnesses to the accident made no reference to intoxication, but their silence proved little, for that was an era when alcohol composed part of most army officers' regular diet, on duty and off. Enlisted men were seldom allowed to drink at all, but officers might be expected to take several bracers during the course of a trying day, and courts-martial were known to dismiss charges of drunkenness against commanders who had gone into battle little short of the blind staggers.[4]

When Grant reported from Cairo, Halleck sent him further instructions to proceed to Louisville, where he would meet "an officer of the War Department" with instructions for him. Still hobbling on a single crutch, Grant boarded a train bound for Indianapolis on the afternoon of October 17, and in that city he encountered the chief officer of the War Department, Edwin Stanton himself, who had just dashed out from Washington. Together they proceeded to Louisville, and along the way Stanton presented Grant with an order to command the new Military Division of the Mississippi, comprising his old Army of the Tennessee, Rosecrans's Army of the Cumberland, and Burnside's Department of the Ohio. With the new command came the choice of either keeping Rosecrans in charge at Chattanooga or replacing him with George Thomas, the loyal Virginian. Grant chose Thomas.[5]

In Louisville Stanton and Grant conferred with Quartermaster General Montgomery Meigs and with railroad managers to formulate a plan for getting enough food to the army at Chattanooga. They had not finished their second day in Louisville before word leaked down to Nashville and Chattanooga that they had arrived, followed almost immediately by the news their presence implied — that Rosecrans was relieved. Reintroducing himself to the saddle with a fifty-mile ride from Stevenson, Alabama, over miserable roads in a steady rain, a weary Grant arrived in Chattanooga on the night of October 23, establishing the headquarters of his massive new command in the field, with its most threatened army.[6]

The consolidation of the three departments made plenty of sense, combining under one head armies that might often have worked in concert with each other, but the size and complexity of the territory and the forces posed an intimidating challenge. As was his custom, Grant relied to a large extent on the aid of subordinates whose personal loyalty he could trust, and to whom he returned a stubborn fidelity of his own. The new command already included several old friends from his cadet days at West Point, including General Thomas, but the closest of those friends and colleagues by then was William T. Sherman, whom he asked for as his successor at the head of the Army of the Tennessee. Sherman had already started several divisions eastward across north Mississippi to help break the siege, but Halleck had ordered him to repair the railroad as he went, so he still lingered at Iuka, in Mississippi's northeastern corner, on October 28. Grant told him to drop everything and come on the run for Stevenson, to prevent the rebels from slipping west of Chattanooga to strike at the supply base in Nashville. Two days later, the advance guard of Sherman's relief column had sunk deep into Alabama.[7]

Grant also fretted over the possibility of Bragg sending a wing to interpose between Chattanooga and Knoxville, to threaten Burnside. There would be little he could do to prevent it, so bad were the roads, and that strategy had already occurred to Grant's best friend from the old army, "Pete" Longstreet. Based primarily on assumptions about Lee's attempt to slip between Meade's army and Washington, a mistaken warning also came down from Halleck that Lee had detached another corps — Ewell's, this time — to strike at Burnside from the northeast. Were it not for Grant's reluctance to yield territory, and the complication of supplies, it would have been better for Burnside to join Grant at Chattanooga, but Grant could hardly feed the men he already had there. Burnside's own supply line stretched all the way from the railhead at Nicholasville, Kentucky, over roads that were four times as long and at least as bad as Grant's wagon route from Alabama, and he could not even accumulate enough forage to sustain a march to Chattanooga.[8]

As it was, Grant calculated that ten thousand horses and mules had died bringing enough food over the mountains from Stevenson and Bridgeport to supply half rations, so if he was not going to evacuate Chattanooga he had to find a better way to feed the troops there. He and General Thomas spent several days scrutinizing the surrounding terrain, and all that time on horseback proved so therapeutic to Grant's injured leg that he disposed of his crutches. At the suggestion of Thomas's chief engineer, a contentious brigadier known as "Baldy" Smith, they settled on a shorter route for supplies than the fifty-mile mountain circuit Grant had had to navigate. It required a risky nighttime collaboration between the men in the besieged city and Hooker's two corps, downriver at Bridgeport.[9]

The Tennessee River took two long loops just below Chattanooga, carving out Moccasin Point on the right bank and curving around Raccoon Mountain on the left bank. In geological terms Moccasin Point represented the extension of Lookout Mountain, from which Confederate artillery frowned down on the city. Between Lookout Mountain and Raccoon Mountain lay Lookout Valley, the possession of which controlled the river as far as Brown's Ferry, on the far side of Moccasin Point. Complaining as always about the incompetence of his superiors, Joe Hooker crossed the river from Bridgeport on the morning of October 26 with most of Howard's Eleventh Corps and John Geary's division of the Twelfth, marching up the left bank toward Lookout Valley. From Chattanooga engineers prepared fifty pontoons as makeshift amphibious barges, and at 3:00 A.M. on October 27 some 1,350 officers and men

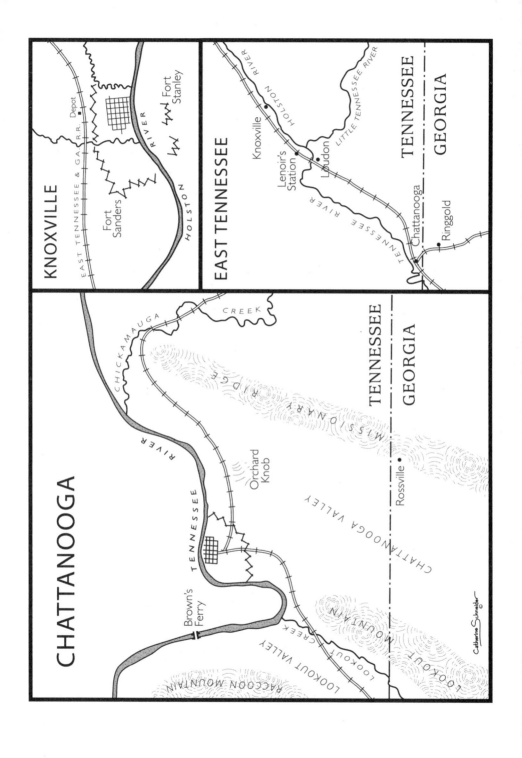

KNOXVILLE

East Tennessee & Ga. R.R. Depot

Fort Sanders

Fort Stanley

HOLSTON RIVER

EAST TENNESSEE

HOLSTON RIVER

Knoxville

Lenoir's Station

Loudon

LITTLE TENNESSEE RIVER

TENNESSEE RIVER

Chattanooga

Ringgold

TENNESSEE

GEORGIA

CHATTANOOGA

CHICKAMAUGA CREEK

TENNESSEE RIVER

Brown's Ferry

Orchard Knob

MISSIONARY RIDGE

Rossville

CHATTANOOGA VALLEY

RACCOON MOUNTAIN

LOOKOUT VALLEY

LOOKOUT CREEK

LOOKOUT MOUNTAIN

TENNESSEE

GEORGIA

Catherine Schneider

started downstream. The moon had turned full only a few hours before, but clouds and fog obscured their passage, and the only Confederate pickets to raise a murmur ultimately did nothing, concluding that the flotilla consisted of driftwood. At Brown's Ferry the passengers clambered out of their pontoons to seize a lodgment while the oarsmen pulled back to the right bank for two brigades that had come down by land. The rebels reacted quickly, but the boats ferried 5,000 Yankees over in an hour and they threw back a counterattack, taking hills that commanded their front and extemporizing some rough but effective earthworks.[10]

Hooker secured the downstream side of the oxbow that encircled Raccoon Mountain, then crossed to the Brown's Ferry side. He left Geary's division two or three miles behind, at Wauhatchie Station of the Nashville & Chattanooga Railroad, just across Lookout Creek from the base of Lookout Mountain. Peering down on the Federals from atop Lookout Mountain the next day, Longstreet and Bragg noted Geary's isolated position, and Longstreet proposed trying to cut him off after dark. One of Longstreet's divisions climbed the mountain during the night and scrambled down the other side under Micah Jenkins, who positioned most of it to hold Hooker back while John Bratton's South Carolina brigade assailed Geary. Without artillery, Bratton's six regiments hammered for nearly three hours at six regiments under Geary, who had the advantage of four guns from a Pennsylvania battery. In a stubborn defense Geary inflicted nearly twice as many casualties as he suffered, but, always the braggart, he reported to Hooker that he faced an entire division with only fifteen hundred men, and he increased the odds even further when he described the fight to his wife. Bratton claimed that he was making good headway against Geary's line (at one point his men broke into Geary's camp) but, in a misunderstanding that ignited an endless controversy, Bratton's supports pulled away and forced him to give up the contest. The Confederates all backed across Lookout Creek to the mountain. Despite losing his own son during the engagement, Geary boasted that he had achieved a complete triumph over the "veteran division of Hood," exaggerating Confederate losses by a customarily ambitious margin of 300 percent. Hooker echoed Geary's self-congratulatory tone.[11]

The battle of Wauhatchie saved Geary's division from capture, but there was never any danger that the rest of Hooker's troops could be dislodged from Brown's Ferry. The operation there opened the Tennessee River to within a two-mile wagon drive of Chattanooga, and a pair of steamers soon started plying between Bridgeport and Brown's Ferry with all the rations they could carry. That Cracker Line, as the men called it, seemed to relieve Grant's concern about malnutrition and actual starvation, but the troops continued to carp about their rations, and at least one voracious sergeant in the brigade that first seized Brown's Ferry remarked that he was still drawing half rations three weeks later.[12]

Until the little steamers could bring up enough provisions to increase daily rations and forage, Grant saw little hope of preventing any thrust by Bragg in the direction of Knoxville. No sooner had the Federals lifted the siege, though, than Bragg detached Longstreet for that purpose, reducing himself to a distinct numerical disadvantage now that most of Hooker's command had entered the amphitheater below Lookout Mountain. For that matter, Longstreet would be moving into east Tennessee to expel or capture a force under Burnside that exceeded his own, for Bragg allowed Longstreet to take only the nine brigades he had brought with him from Virginia — perhaps eleven thousand effectives, after the losses at Wauhatchie — along with a couple of Joe Wheeler's cavalry divisions. Burnside had brought about twenty-three thousand men down from Kentucky by then, but Burnside knew that Confederate general Sam Jones was gathering a force from different Allegheny Mountain commands at Abingdon, Virginia, to the northeast, which he feared might total fifteen thousand. Longstreet's advance from the southwest, with as many as twenty thousand between the infantry and cavalry, suggested they were planning to crush him between the two commands.[13]

When he learned that Longstreet had struck up the railroad toward Loudon, Grant sought to draw him back by attacking Bragg and trying to sever the Confederate supply line into east Tennessee. He urged Sherman to hurry his march through Alabama, and ordered Thomas to carry the northern end of Missionary Ridge and, once he had taken it, to drive toward the railroads that would feed Longstreet. Neither the teams nor the troops of the Army of the Cumberland had yet recovered from weeks of hunger, and discipline had suffered during the enforced inactivity, so Thomas found he could not undertake a significant offensive. As a result, Longstreet drove Burnside's pickets in south of Loudon and swept into that town on Friday, November 13, planting artillery on the riverbank opposite Burnside's southernmost infantry. Burnside's forces were scattered from Loudon nearly to the Virginia border, with other detachments at Cumberland Gap and out toward North Carolina; below Knoxville he could muster fewer men than Longstreet had, and far fewer than he supposed Longstreet to have. He concluded to lure Longstreet across the river toward Knoxville, ever farther from recall by Bragg, so Grant could handle the main Confederate army with better odds. Sandwiched between a known threat at Loudon and a more uncertain one at Abingdon, Burnside left his comfortable headquarters in Knoxville, where the posh home of a Southern sympathizer provided all the amenities of civilization, including an extensive library. While their chief hurtled south in a loco-

motive to delay Longstreet's advance, the portion of his staff that remained behind turned up the gaslights to write letters predicting they
would soon either retreat to Kentucky or wind up in Southern prisons.[14]

Burnside gathered a division of the Ninth Corps at Lenoir's Station to
meet his troops retreating from opposite Loudon, and with that combined command he started a Fabian retreat up the railroad before
Longstreet's two divisions. They pressed him at Lenoir's Station on November 15 and more particularly at Campbell's Station on November 16,
at both of which his rear guard discouraged too close a pursuit, but deep
mud and fatigue took its toll. In the 36th Massachusetts, Private Myron
Wood, a once-burly farm boy from the upper reaches of the Chicopee
River, felt so weak that during the first halt after Lenoir's he asked his sergeant if he could fall out of the ranks; perhaps he hoped to find an ambulance that would take him, but the retreat resumed almost immediately.
He never secured a ride or made it back to his company, and three months
later his parents were still trying to find out what had happened to him.[15]

Rather than continue his retreat back over the mountains into Kentucky, which would have given Longstreet his prize and convinced him to
break off the pursuit, Burnside pulled within the fortified perimeter of
Knoxville on November 17 with about twelve thousand organized troops
of all arms, besides a clot of loyal east Tennessee recruits and a host of
loyal refugees, whose excess possessions accumulated at the depot for soldiers to plunder. With picks and shovels Burnside's men started flailing at
the hillsides north and west of the city and on critical heights across the
river (here the Tennessee was then called the Holston River). Strong
earthworks rose through the night and into the next morning while Brigadier General William P. Sanders held Longstreet back with his dismounted cavalry. Sanders, a Kentuckian who had grown up in Mississippi, kept faith with his West Point oath, and his horsemen stood their
ground until Sanders himself fell, just outside the fresh fortifications.
They brought him back into the city through the big square redoubt that
formed the anchor of Burnside's line. When Sanders died the next day,
during President Lincoln's sojourn at Gettysburg, Burnside agreed to
name the big earthwork after him.[16]

From Chattanooga Grant telegraphed Burnside to hold on, promising
that he would soon draw Longstreet off him. Sherman had come up, he
said, and they did not intend to rest until they had either cut the enemy's
railroad or fought a major battle. Burnside replied that he felt safe within
the works, but that was his last wire from Knoxville before the lines went
dead.[17]

Grant issued instructions to General Thomas that same day to prepare
for an attack on Bragg's lines no later than November 25. Sherman would

march to the extreme left, four miles upstream from Chattanooga, cross the river, and with help from Thomas attack Bragg's right flank, at the northern terminus of Missionary Ridge. Rain slowed Sherman's column, but three of his divisions slogged across at Brown's Ferry, traversed the city, and proceeded north, hiding themselves well back from the river so Bragg might think they were chasing after Longstreet. One division lagged so far behind that Grant decided to leave it with Hooker, in Lookout Valley.[18]

Sherman's troops discovered that rations were still short at Chattanooga, and Yankees were not the only ones there with aching bellies. Some Confederates around the city fared as badly as the defenders, in the way of provisions. Squads of them crept into Union lines and surrendered daily, now that Grant had opened the Cracker Line through Brown's Ferry. They complained that they were half-starved on a pint ration of cornmeal per day, with a slab of pork, bacon, or beef tossed in now and then — about the same rations that Union prisoners would consider evidence of deliberate attrition, a year later — yet their supplies came straight from Atlanta by rail. One of those deserters came in on November 22 carrying a story that Bragg was withdrawing his army from the heights that commanded Chattanooga. That might foretell a wide sweep around Grant's right, through Alabama, to cut his rail connection with Nashville, or merely a retreat to more defensible ground, but in either case Grant wanted to catch him in midmovement, so he directed Thomas to force a fight ahead of schedule.[19]

Thomas sent out the better part of his army the next morning, along with Howard's Eleventh Corps. They marched as though in review, perhaps deceiving the enemy with that innocent ruse before deploying in line of battle to capture Bragg's advanced picket line on Orchard Knob, an isolated knoll in the middle of the plain below Missionary Ridge. It seemed that Bragg had no plans to go anywhere: the deserter had evidently misunderstood the withdrawal of two divisions that were meant to reinforce Longstreet. Thomas's foray into the valley caused Bragg to reel one of those divisions back in, but now he faced a significant threat from his well-reinforced prey with even fewer men than he had had the day before.[20]

On the morning of November 24, in a cold drizzle, Hooker undertook the next step in the program. Grant had left him three divisions from three different corps: one from Sherman's army, one from Thomas's, and Geary's division from Hooker's own Twelfth Corps. Studding Lookout Valley with artillery, Hooker belabored the Confederate entrenchments around the shoulder of Lookout Mountain while, under cover of heavy mist and fog that belted the mountain, Geary's men climbed unobserved off to the Confederates' left. The other two Union divisions occupied the attention of the rebels on the mountain with their work on bridges over Lookout Creek. When Geary had nearly reached the altitude of the entrenchments, he sideslipped across the mountain, passing unnoticed in the mist just beneath the noses of somnolent Confederates before springing upon the rebel pickets. Two brigades of Westerners had also been stealing up toward the fog-shrouded summit, including seven Missouri regiments, and when the shooting began they came lunging up the mountain to join Geary. Many of the rebels still huddled in the bottom of their works to avoid the fire of Hooker's guns, and never knew the Yankees were coming until they saw bayonets waving over their heads. Hundreds surrendered without pulling a trigger, throwing up their hands and hollering at their assailants not to shoot, "for God's sake," but then complaining about a Yankee trick as they filed down the mountainside.[21]

Within an hour the entire western face of the mountain had been cleared of the enemy. Hooker had directed his division commanders to advance no farther than the summit, lest they plunge into a trap, so the afternoon passed in desultory contest for possession of the crest, with rifles alone. The Federals could bring up no artillery, and the Southerners abandoned the few pieces they had dragged to the top. Judging from the casualties, neither side pushed very hard, and fewer than a hundred men died in what became known as the battle above the clouds. Inside the city, though, officers with telescopes caught a glimpse of their flag up there, and the perimeter broke into rippling cheers.[22]

As usual, Geary took all the credit for himself, assuring his wife that he had stormed and captured Lookout Mountain, turned Bragg's left flank, and forced him to retreat. In his official report he claimed that his division alone captured nearly two thousand prisoners on the mountain, yet the Confederates engaged there that day reported barely half that many of their men missing, altogether, during that day's fighting and the three that followed. General Thomas estimated Hooker's entire catch for the day as five or six hundred, at least some of whom had been taken by the troops who had come to Geary's assistance.[23]

However deadly or spectacular the battle was, and however much it may have been magnified by windbags like Geary and Hooker, it accomplished all that Grant needed to execute the rest of his plan. With Hooker atop Lookout Mountain, the Confederate left lay open to raking artillery fire and a flank attack, and the troops there instinctively swept back perpendicular to their line to face that danger. Seizing the mountain also opened a direct path between Lookout Valley and Chattanooga, allowing the wings of Grant's army to resume communications without two crossings of the river. Above the city, Sherman had ferried detachments over the river in pontoon boats before dawn that morning, to snare the Confederate pickets and secure the approaches for bridges. Not long after Hooker's men reached the top of Lookout Mountain, Sherman held the opposite end of Bragg's line, on Missionary Ridge. That night most of the mountain glimmered with the campfires of Hooker's men, while muzzle flashes still sparkled on the crest.[24]

Saturday, November 25, marked the deadline of Grant's schedule for his grand assault, and it began with Sherman slamming into Bragg's extreme right. He happened to encounter the best division commander in Bragg's Army of Tennessee, Patrick Cleburne, who put up an extraordinarily stout fight. Hooker was supposed to sweep down the eastern slope of Lookout Mountain into Chattanooga Valley, from which he was to turn north and roll up the Confederate flank on Missionary Ridge. Once Hooker's battle flags appeared on the ridge, Grant intended to send Thomas's army toward Bragg's center in a frontal assault. Conventional military wisdom would already have declared Bragg's flank turned with the loss of Lookout Mountain, and should have dictated retreat during the night (Cleburne had expected as much), but Bragg decided to fight it out. Crossing Chattanooga Creek cost Hooker several more hours than planned, so Grant withheld Thomas until the middle of that brisk and chilly afternoon, when he could see Southern troops leaving the center of their line to reinforce Cleburne. Sherman endured a vicious pounding, and men in his front line were beginning to look on the day as lost when Thomas finally saw a battery at Grant's headquarters blast the signal volley. He strung four divisions abreast — Westerners all, representing every loyal state from Ohio to Kansas, except Iowa. They sprinted toward the rifle pits at the base of the ridge, spilling rebel infantry out of them "like bees from a hive," and while Grant was trying to decide whether to continue the assault up the slope, Thomas's men decided it for themselves, pausing only to straighten their lines before lurching spontaneously after the fleeing rebels. A second tier of riflemen punished them briefly, but they, too, quickly joined the flight. As Grant and his astounded staff watched from Orchard Knob, and the remaining troops in Chattanooga stared spellbound, Thomas's broad front surged upward into point-blank fire from infantry and artillery on Bragg's final line, atop the precipice.[25]

As the late autumn light faded, the Stars and Stripes fluttered from different spots along the ridge. Hooker finally came into sight, rolling up the ridge from the south, and Confederates flooded down the eastern face toward the railroad, through the motley little villages of slab-sided huts where they had expected to spend the winter. Cleburne alone kept up the fight, backing toward Chickamauga Station under persistent pressure from Sherman, and smoke spiraled skyward from the mountains of supplies stored near the depot. The next morning Grant's staff strapped bedrolls to their saddles and followed most of the army south down the railroad, past smoldering mountains of cornmeal, bagged corn, and corn still on the cob. Artillery and piles of muskets lay forlorn and forgotten by the fugitives streaming toward Ringgold, Georgia, ahead of Cleburne's rear guard. By dawn of Monday morning, November 27, the only troops from the Army of Tennessee who remained in its namesake state were those with Longstreet and six thousand prisoners who were already on their way north, half of them so demoralized they seemed ready to give up the fight.[26]

Grant would have continued his pursuit much farther, bringing the war in the West closer to a conclusion, had he not had to turn his attention to Burnside's plight. As he told his wife that week, he did not intend to remain idle during the winter, but he had to divert a sizable part of his force from the operations in Georgia. Reminded via telegraph by General Halleck and the president himself to attend to his beleaguered subordinate in Knoxville, Grant detached Sherman to go to his relief with six divisions.[27]

Knoxville had been completely invested by then: Burnside's senior officer outside the city fretted at Cumberland Gap with a garrison of fussy six-month militia from Ohio, worrying all the while about those Virginia rebels under Sam Jones. Ten days' provisions remained in Knoxville when Hooker flushed the rebels from the sides of Lookout Mountain, although a trickle of food came down the river in rafts from loyal mountain folk. Burnside had thrown one sally out far enough to seize and burn some buildings where sharpshooters nestled, and Longstreet had reciprocated.[28] Longstreet certainly had information from prisoners that Burnside had cut rations in half to resist longer, and that another week's patience might yield him the city and the starving army within it, but indistinct information on the fighting at Chattanooga convinced him to make an attack of his own. The night of November 28 a disillusioned Michigan recruit named William Henry left his picket post and delivered himself up to the enemy, whom he regaled with all the details he could remember about Burnside's defensive network, complete with troop positions. Longstreet had already decided to throw a division at the earthen ramparts of Fort Sanders, and had postponed it only because of rain that day, but the turncoat's information told him everything he needed to know.[29]

The delay had worked to the advantage of the garrison in Sanders, consisting of about three hundred men inside the main work and another two hundred in adjacent rifle pits. They labored constantly on their fortress, finally piling cotton bales around Lieutenant Samuel Benjamin's big twenty-pounder Parrott rifles and the smaller rifles and howitzers. The parapet stood fourteen feet above the outside slope, but a six-foot-deep ditch surrounded it, leaving any who fell into it with a steep twenty-foot incline to scale. Before midnight on November 28 Confederates drove in the pickets around the fort, seizing a broad, deep swale that came within fifteen rods of the ramparts, and below the view of those inside. In the misty chill before dawn on November 29 some four thousand Georgians and Mississippians formed in that swale to compete with each other for the honor of being the first into Fort Sanders.[30]

Lieutenant Benjamin, who commanded the fort by Burnside's special order, expected an attack and had his men awake early. As the first glimmer of daylight filtered through the fog, Longstreet's artillery opened a twenty-minute fusillade against the fort, as did his infantry from its natural breastwork a hundred yards away. Benjamin kept his men down the whole time, but as soon as the rebel artillery subsided he waved them to their work. One of the four brigades rose over the swale and trotted toward the northwest salient, where the sharp corner of the work prevented placement of any guns. Only one of Benjamin's pieces bore on the assault, but it opened with charges of triple canister that mowed down swaths of men. Telegraph wire had been stretched between stumps before the fort, tripping men so they fell "in piles," but within two minutes the assailants had gained the ditch. As they flocked around the sides of the fort other guns could reach them, and began belching triple-loads of canister at close range. To escape this hail and try to climb the parapet they began leaping into the ditch, but most of those who went into it never came out. Some clawed their way up the precipitous face, but most were shot down or dragged inside as prisoners. Three reckless rebel color sergeants made it to the top with flags, but a Pennsylvania officer killed one with his revolver and a New York sergeant reached out to drag another inside, flag and all. Lieutenant Benjamin took case shot and shells in his own hands, had the fuses lighted, and lobbed them over the parapet into the ditch, where they wrought ghastly results and sudden panic. The first rebel brigade recoiled from such brutal punishment, losing heavily in the retreat, and a second wave suffered even more severely.[31]

In less than an hour it was all over, and the last Confederate shrank out of sight, convinced that the task was hopeless. More than two hundred men lay in the ditch several bodies deep, most of them dead or dying; another three hundred and more littered the field before the guns, and nearly three hundred had surrendered. When the survivors crawled out under a flag of truce, the blood had begun running into puddles in the ditch. While the two armies separated the dead and wounded, an injudicious pig wandered into their midst: a mixed platoon of Massachusetts and South Carolina riflemen pounced upon it, slaughtered it on the spot, and shared the quarters equally.[32]

Within hours, Longstreet learned that Bragg had been sent flying from Chattanooga, and soon he heard of Sherman's approach. Four foggy mornings after the attack, Longstreet began pulling his artillery back and reducing his picket line, while blaring bands covered the noise of his commissary herdsmen driving cattle northward. On the morning of December 5 he was gone, marching northeast toward — but not yet into — Virginia.[33] Sherman arrived right behind him, surprised that Knoxville had not been starved out yet, and the feast that the grateful Burnside's staff gathered for him spawned rumors that Burnside had exaggerated his distress. Long, muddy roads kept Union soldiers in east Tennessee hungry for months to come, in fact, but the region had been saved for the Union. The cost for that salvation may have included the survival of the Army of Tennessee — and with it that of the Confederacy.[34]

Nathaniel Banks had struck a symbolic blow to the Confederacy on November 2, finally restoring the flag to Texas soil as Henry Halleck had requested nearly three months before. With a convoy of transports and warships he landed a division on Brazos Island, at the mouth of the Rio Grande. A few days later infantry from Illinois and Maine marched into Brownsville to seize old Fort Brown, which a skeleton Confederate force had put to the torch before spurring their horses toward the interior. By the end of the month Union troops occupied Mustang Island, on Corpus Christi Bay, and controlled Pass Cavallo into Matagorda Bay. From those sunbaked havens they dispatched little reconnoitering expeditions all through the winter.[35]

In Virginia, November brought freezing cold nights followed by morning thaws, along with drenching rainstorms and snow that transformed the red clay into an amber mire: with his audacious October offensive Robert E. Lee had expended the best marching weather of another year. Betting that no general would risk the humiliation of repeating such a fiasco as Burnside's Mud March, veteran soldiers in the Army of the Potomac speculated that campaigning might have come to an end after they had resumed their old camps below the Rappahannock. Many of them had already constructed their huts in regimented neighborhoods, aligned on either side of broad company streets, with mud-and-stick chimneys and two or three shelter halves stretched over sapling ridgepoles and rafters. Winter visiting had even begun: a klatch of red-jacketed officers from the Grenadier Guards and the Scots Fusiliers had come down from Montreal to see how Cousin Jonathan made war, and some of Meade's generals treated them to reviews or mock charges by six thousand gleaming bayonets.[36]

Meade's friend Sedgwick observed that the commanding general had aged twenty years in barely twenty weeks at the head of the army: the strain of relentless and often unreasonable expectations was already beginning to tell. Notwithstanding the now-obvious danger of planning military movements around Virginia mud, the White House (and therefore General Halleck) still expected some late-year action from the eastern army — perhaps in residual frustration over Meade's failure to bag Lee in July, or to engage him in October. In a heavy rainstorm typical of the season, Meade made another dash into Washington on November 14 to meet with Halleck and Stanton about it, and as soon as he returned he warned his corps commanders to be ready to move their troops on short notice. While railroad crews repaired damage done by the storm, Meade's cavalry scouted the Rapidan River to determine which of Lee's flanks posed the greater opportunity. When he had chosen, Meade called in his former chief engineer, Gouverneur Warren, now commander of the Second Corps, and asked him to bring along Lieutenant Washington Roebling, of his staff. Roebling was an engineer who specialized in bridges, having been trained by his father, who built some of the biggest in the country, but just now Meade wanted maps and road builders.[37]

Lee had snuggled in behind the Rapidan River with — thought Meade — about fifty-five thousand infantry. Three weeks into November, two Southerners who had thus far clung loyally to the Confederate cause determined that the coming winter was going to turn off colder than ever, and rather than endure it on light rations they waded the river to trade information for asylum. Their calculation of the strength of Ewell's and Hill's two corps came remarkably close to the thirty-six thousand infantry Lee himself had reported on the last day of October; he could not have put fifty thousand officers and men into line with all his cavalry and artillery included. On that same day, Meade had tallied eighty-two thousand fighting men. Confederate defenses ran for thirty miles along the river, from an earthwork west of Orange Court House to more extensive entrenchments at Germanna Ford, with pickets behind rifle pits and cavalry videttes posted downstream from there until the Rapidan spilled into the Rappahannock. South of the river the old Orange Turnpike and the Orange Plank Road connected all the roads leading to the various fords, serving as Lee's trunk route through the second-growth tangle of the Wilderness and, east of that, to the well-remembered crossroads called Chancellorsville. Scouts and signal stations reported that those extensive works were fully manned for only half that distance: with his reduced strength Lee had condensed his long line, and the right wing of his main body camped below Morton's Ford, a good six miles west of Germanna Ford. It was this flank that invited attack. Meade hoped to swing his entire army around Lee's right, as Lee had done to him six weeks before, and force him to come out from behind those entrenchments for the fight everyone back at home wanted to see. He issued orders for a move at daylight on Tuesday, November 24.[38]

By some coincidence or collusion on the part of someone in the know, Washington newspapers bellowed the news of the advance the very day the orders were written. Still, at three o'clock on Tuesday morning the army's drummer boys (some of them fifteen years old and some fifty) began beating the assembly. Fat raindrops started pelting them before they had struck their tents or stripped the canvas roofing from their prized huts, and the roads started swimming before daylight, so Meade called a two-day delay. That brought the calendar to the day President Lincoln had proclaimed as Thanksgiving, but the men who left warm blankets to dismantle their shelters in the cold and darkness felt thankful for little, despite headquarters assertions that the army showed a sanguine spirit. Their officers primed them with the early news of Missionary Ridge, faced them to the left, and set them in motion. The army approached the Rapidan with a wide front: the First and Fifth Corps took the route farthest downstream, at Culpeper Ford, while General Warren led his Second Corps over Germanna Ford, five miles up the river. William French marched closest to Lee's flank with the Third Corps, followed by Sedgwick and the Sixth Corps, aiming for the deeper ford at Jacob's Mill. The next major crossing upstream was Morton's Ford, well covered by Confederate infantry and artillery.[39]

On Wednesday some rebels had been digging at rifle pits on the slopes running down to Germanna Ford, but Warren encountered no one when he reached there, a couple of hours before noon on Thursday. The Fifth Corps, under George Sykes, passed into the heart of the Wilderness through forests so thick that light alone seemed capable of penetrating it, but Sykes had a regiment over the river at Culpeper Ford by noon. Only at Jacob's Mill did anyone meet resistance. Southern cavalry guarded the ford, which had been running about chest-deep, and their bank of the river rose tall and almost sheer; a horseman could hardly climb it without dismounting. Some of French's infantry paddled over in pontoon boats, though, and as soon as they scaled the bluff and formed a skirmish line the cavalry cantered away.[40]

All three columns were supposed to cross simultaneously, but Warren had to wait two hours for the Third Corps to catch up. French's leading division commander, Henry Prince, had gone astray and had to double back; he was just beginning to build his pontoon bridge at 1:00 P.M., and the watches at French's headquarters ran twenty minutes behind those at Meade's. Not until 2:30 did French get most of his corps across the river, and Prince thought it was closer to 4:00. Meade demanded an explanation, and at first French seemed not to know what had happened. He could only complain that his camps had been four miles farther from the river than Warren's, which was true enough, but when he made his way to the front he discovered that his road was impassable for his artillery: the ford was simply too precipitous for wheeled vehicles. That bought him no indulgence, for he had been ordered to examine the route on Wednesday evening, and had delegated the responsibility to Prince. Prince in turn seems to have handed that duty off to staff officers, who had evidently inspected the wrong road. Meade ordered French to send his artillery back to Germanna Ford, adding detailed instructions that might have been insulting to a more competent and confident officer. Once Prince did cross the Rapidan he followed another bad turn until he ran across a mill on Mine Run, nearly stumbling into the enemy works. His skirmishers actually forded Mine Run before he faced his division about and marched it back again.[41]

The rest of the Third Corps sat down to wait while the vagabond division returned, and Sedgwick's entire Sixth Corps stood champing behind that, with every man wondering what the matter was as precious daylight faded.[42] Eight hours into the operation, French's control of his troops seemed to be slipping, and a Maine private in his corps blamed the day's errors on the bottle. A few weeks later a New Hampshire clergyman revealed to the *New York Tribune* that Meade told him French "was probably too drunk to know or do his duty" at Mine Run, and when French asked about it Meade only went so far as to say he had not "authorized" that observation; he did not deny saying it, and did not say he doubted it. The army's provost marshal thought French was "tight" during much of the campaign. As renowned a drinker as French was, though, Prince may have been the subject of that insinuation, as well: he had served in the army without much distinction for nearly three decades, suffering two wounds — the first in 1836 — and the second had left him with recurring pain that alcohol might have relieved. Meade, a West Point classmate of both French and Prince's, bore some troublesome old wounds of his own that added little to his patience. Over at Germanna Ford with Warren's column he grew furious, fearing that French's serial blunders would put them so far behind schedule that Lee would learn the extent of their operation and be fully prepared to meet it.[43]

Lee already knew that Meade was moving his entire army to the lower fords of the Rapidan, but at first he suspected a flanking movement toward Richmond. He planned a forced march toward Spotsylvania Court House to draw his army across Meade's front, but Meade moved too fast for him. If not for French, the whole Army of the Potomac would have been south of the river by sunset, and could have pressed on in the darkness until it came within striking distance of Lee's exposed flank. Any attack before 9:00 A.M. on November 27 would have fallen on a mere nine brigades of infantry, without any of the extensive entrenchments that added so much power to inferior numbers; until well after noon on that Friday, in fact, those nine brigades would see only Stuart's cavalry for reinforcements. But for French, victory should have been certain, and dual disasters to the Confederacy's two greatest armies might have crushed the Southern spirit.[44]

Such was the magnitude of the likely disappointment George Meade faced that Thursday night with the Sixth Corps, half of the First Corps, and all of French's and Sedgwick's artillery still stuck on the left bank of the river. At midnight some of the Sixth Corps was still climbing the sharp incline at Jacob's Mill, so everyone bedded down near their respective fords under the same full moon that lighted the headlong retreat of Braxton Bragg's army, five hundred miles to the southwest.[45]

Meade had wanted the whole army poised and ready to pounce that evening near Robertson's Tavern, on the turnpike, and at Parker's Store, on the plank road. He still thought there might be a chance the next morning, and issued orders for an early advance, but again French's corps delayed the program, with General Prince still in the lead. Enlisting a slave as his guide, Prince set off to connect with Warren's Second Corps at Robertson's Tavern, but he soon ran upon a fork in the road, and the need for a decision paralyzed him. His guide told him the left fork would lead him to the tavern, and he feared that the road to the right might lead him back into enemy lines. In an excess of caution Prince sent some cavalrymen down the left fork to find Warren, and down the right to look for the enemy. He soon learned that mounted rebel pickets lurked not far beyond the right-hand fork, yet he held his division idle at the intersection for two solid hours while he awaited an answer from the other direction. Confederate cavalry interfered with his return messenger, forcing him over a long detour back to the intersection, but at last Prince knew that he should have taken the left fork. The distance was less than four miles: had he initially followed his guide's advice and his own instinct, he would have been with Warren long before.[46]

By then it was nearly ten o'clock. Sykes had reached the plank road with the Fifth Corps, two miles south of the turnpike, and was moving west with the First Corps right behind him. Marching down the rough surface of the turnpike on a parallel course, Warren could at least see the

Fifth Corps off to his left, but he had only a general idea where French's left was when he ran into Robert Rodes's division of Ewell's corps. Rodes was coming out to test which way Meade intended to turn: he had already crossed Mine Run and felt his way a mile and a half beyond, to Robertson's Tavern and the little crossroads known as Locust Grove. Had General Prince not dawdled so indecisively he would have arrived there just about in time to crash into Rodes's flank, but Warren had to handle it all alone. Rodes had Edward Johnson's and Jubal Early's divisions behind him, while Warren's corps formed the weak center of the Army of the Potomac, for Sedgwick would not be able to bring up the Sixth Corps until French got out of the way, or closed the four-mile gap between himself and Warren. For the moment Warren filled most of it himself, stringing much of his strength out as a skirmish line for the whole front. Having learned from Prince's cavalry contact where the laggard division was, he expected it to come up on his right at any moment, but he would wait all day. Meade badgered French for hours, repeatedly ordering him to close up with Warren, and at one point Meade's irritable chief of staff sent French a dispatch bluntly asking, "What are you waiting for?"[47]

Prince's two-hour vacillation allowed enough time for Allegheny Johnson to catch him in the thick woods with that gaping void on his left flank. Cavalry videttes started pecking away at Prince's column, but then came skirmishers and a line of infantry, until Prince had to deploy both brigades of his division; French had detained (and then had apparently forgotten) Prince's third brigade, which was now stranded across the river. Warren dared press but little with three divisions in front of him, lest they barge ahead to overwhelm him and cut Meade's army in two, while French, perhaps smarting from his spate of embarrassments, resorted to more aggressive behavior. He wasted the rest of the morning in skirmishing, allowing the leading divisions of A. P. Hill's corps time enough to come to the rescue, and as those fresh troops stiffened the Confederate line that afternoon, French's real fight began. From two o'clock until four the bullets flew thick enough to suggest the common analogy of a hailstorm, but artillery could find no room to operate. In Prince's division, first one regiment would break for the rear and then another as the fire intensified or subsided on different parts of the line, and only the thick undergrowth prevented the Confederates from taking much advantage of those local triumphs. The inevitable tithe of timid began trickling to the rear, toward the fords.[48]

Joseph Carr's division sidled up on Prince's left, trying to grope toward Warren at Locust Grove, and when David Birney's division arrived late in the fight to relieve Carr, one of Birney's men claimed that General Carr's troops were "flying from the field," while the general himself was so ashamed of them that tears were rolling down his face. One of the new regiments that shouldered into line in place of Carr's men lost 13 percent in killed and wounded in the last hour before dark. Only when Sedgwick squeezed into line to bolster French did the Union right regain its footing, and join hands finally with Warren.[49]

About a hundred of French's men died on the field that day, and nearly seven hundred came back with bullet wounds. One small brigade in Carr's division lost more than ten dozen wounded, with only two surgeons to tend them. Those two doctors moved into half of the two-room house French had taken for his headquarters, operating through the night by candlelight on an unusual number of wounds to the chest and upper extremities: by this stage of the war soldiers had learned to do as much of their fighting as possible from behind some kind of cover. The disorganized French, whose staff could find no candles in their wagons, sent an officer into the impromptu hospital room to borrow one from the surgeons. Wrapped in a bloody apron, one of them glanced up from his table only long enough to refuse on the ground that they did not have enough for themselves, leaving the corps commander to read and write his orders by firelight.[50]

West of Robertson's Tavern the turnpike dropped quickly into a shallow valley before rising over a low ridge, and then it descended slowly again over mostly open ground for the better part of a mile to the banks of Mine Run. The creek ran fairly deep after a rainstorm, and it spilled into some marshy spots here and there, but beyond it the road climbed the long, steady slope of a broad plateau that offered defensive advantages reminiscent of Marye's Heights. When the skirmishers of the Army of the Potomac eased forward at daylight on Saturday morning they reached the first ridge without interference, prowling down the other side nearly to the creek before eliciting an admonitory volley from their counterparts on the other side. Lee had brought up the rest of his army, and had dug in along the crest of that intimidating slope with both corps. To those who had been there, it looked as formidable as the stone wall at Fredericksburg, with a moat thrown in to make it interesting. As they stood there staring in the cold morning air, the rain started falling hard and fast, and the troops who still had their rubber ponchos unslung their knapsacks to dig them out.[51]

After scouting their fronts through the downpour during the daylight hours, the generals convened after dark to ascertain where Lee's line might be weak enough to break. No one had found any sector that might have been described as vulnerable, so General Warren offered to take a strong detachment and circle around Lee's right flank far enough — twenty miles, if he must — to force a retreat from that imposing ridge

beyond the run. Warren may have been the junior-ranking corps commander, and the youngest, but he was the engineer who had saved the
army's left wing at Gettysburg, and at Bristoe Station he had severely
chastised A. P. Hill all by himself. Meade put tremendous confidence in
him, and had consulted primarily with Warren, and Warren's man Roebling, about all the engineering difficulties of this campaign. He therefore
approved the plan, adding one of Sedgwick's divisions to strengthen the
Second Corps, and at daylight on November 29 Warren set off. The rain
had stopped by then, leaving even the main thoroughfares oozing with
red mud, so Warren marched his column east, back up the turnpike to
Robertson's Tavern and around to the plank road, turning west there. It
was slow going after the tavern, for the plank road itself had softened up
quite a bit, but by early afternoon Warren struck rebel pickets and flung
out a couple of brigades to start driving them. Three miles later he ran
into the extremity of Lee's works, behind the headwaters of Mine Run,
and started edging his troops farther to his left; the enemy responded by
shifting troops to the right, where they still held high ground but had no
earthworks.[52]

The ground Warren took there looked so favorable for an attack that
instead of continuing his flank march he halted his command and returned to Meade's headquarters. He found that the other generals had decided to abet his flanking maneuver with a morning attack along Sedgwick's line, off to the right, and on French's front, in the center. Warren
reported his progress on the far left, and assured everyone that if his detachment was strengthened still more he could rout the rebels out of their
works in the morning, if indeed they stayed through the night with him
hovering on their exposed flank. Again Meade put faith in Warren's judgment, giving him two of the discredited French's three divisions, with instructions to make the attack at eight o'clock on Monday morning, November 30. When he attacked, Sedgwick would open with artillery and
follow up with infantry an hour later.[53]

The Virginia mud froze solid that night, and secrecy prohibited anyone
from building fires. Troops all along the line stacked their knapsacks in
the wee hours of the morning, and on Meade's right, where Mine Run
flowed three or four feet deep, they shivered at orders to charge right
through the stream at daylight. Rumors spread that some of the wounded
froze to death in their ambulances, and men complained of waking with
frozen fingers and toes while others spent the entire night walking back
and forth with overcoats on and blankets wrapped around them, stamp-
ing their feet. "I never suffered so much in my life," one man told his father.[54]

At the first glimmer of grey morning light, officers in Warren's wing crept from the ravine where he had hidden them to the brow of the ridge, glancing across another ravine to the plateau where the enemy still waited. The Confederates had spent the night working "like beavers," as General Lee's adjutant phrased it, and the lightly wooded slope now bristled with breastworks, artillery embrasures, and fallen trees, all of which had been dropped with their tops pointing downhill, toward Union lines; the limbs had been sharpened into makeshift abatis, to snag and delay any infantry assault while canister and musketry decimated it. At the bottom of the ravine, too, lay a troublesome fence and the marshy source of Mine Run, which Warren may or may not have seen in the dim light of the previous evening. Shuddering from the prospect of the work ahead of them as much as from the still-bitter cold, the men fell into ranks to listen to their generals' unconvincingly encouraging exhortations, but unusual numbers of them left messages and relics with their regimental chaplains to send to their families. Then General Warren took one last look before he signaled the assault, saw that the unprotected position of the previous day had been transformed into virtual impregnability, and — with as much courage as it would have taken to lead the assault personally — he called it off on his own responsibility. French's and Sedgwick's guns had already begun to sound, farther down Mine Run, so he sent Roebling galloping back to Meade's headquarters at the tavern, to warn of the change.[55]

Meade gasped at the news, lamenting that Warren had nearly half his army over there, but Roebling could only shrug his shoulders in sympathy. The message came just in time to withhold the attack on the right and center: a few men had already died in the initial skirmishing, including the well-regarded commander of one of the sharpshooter regiments, but fifteen more minutes might have seen a good deal more blood wasted. Meade dispatched his own son with one of the orders to cancel the attack, and in his haste the boy took a nasty tumble. Then the general rode over to look at Warren's front to see the field for himself. For all his disappointment, he had to agree that the younger man had chosen wisely.[56]

The chance had been lost the afternoon before, thought critics of less military training: if Warren had pressed his assault on the unprepared enemy with the force he had on Sunday, Lee could never have repulsed him. Perhaps, but without the rest of Meade's army ready to take advantage of his surprise, Lee might well have driven him back with an overwhelming counterattack while a fragment of his troops held that ominous ridge; he had done such things often enough before. As it was, Meade ordered all the gathered divisions back to the breastworks they had thrown together over the past two days, where they huddled for such warmth as they could find. Rather than convince Lee that he had given up the offensive, Meade continued the ban on campfires throughout the coldest day yet that year, and men grateful to have been saved from slaughter spent the day trying to avert frostbite. That night some of them moved back into the woods, built bonfires, rolled up in their blankets, and drifted into the deep sleep of exhaustion.[57]

The next day Meade came to a decision that matched Warren's for moral courage. As much as General Halleck, the Radicals, and much of the country might howl for action, however desperate and unavailing, Meade concluded that nothing more could be done. Lee had fortified his entire line: there was no room to flank him on his left, for there lay the river; to reach farther around his right would stretch the Army of the Potomac too thin. Supplies were running short, too, and it was no season of the year to bring over his heavy trains, for while the roads had frozen solid they would turn to soup as soon as they thawed. More men were said to have died of exposure in the trenches. A surgeon denied it, insisting they had only had some cases of frostbite, but a colonel among the Regulars claimed it was true. In any case, most of the men's hands were too cold to work their rifles. The only sound choice lay in retreat, and Meade ordered it on December 1, while Lee — undeterred by cold weather or imposing odds — planned an attack of his own.[58]

The First Corps started back toward Germanna Ford that afternoon, and at dark the rest of the army followed in stiff winds that drove numbing cold through flimsy overcoats. Few Union soldiers slept that night. They used every hour of the darkness to gain distance on the enemy, stumbling through the moonlight over the frozen ruts or standing motionless in the arctic wind as their columns crawled like an enormous inchworm toward the fords. Pontoniers laid the bridges back down, but at Culpeper Ford some had to splash through hip-deep water in a stiff current. Stragglers were still crossing early in the morning, spilling down the bank in terror at being left behind, and overloading the last pontoon boats so badly that some of them pitched into the icy water. Others appeared later still, plunging in to wade while the rear guard laughed at them, and a few fell far enough behind for rebel cavalry to scoop them up. Once across, most of the troops marched no more than a mile or two before falling out to build fires, change into any dry clothing that might remain in their knapsacks, and fall as soundly asleep on the frozen ground as if it had been a featherbed.[59]

The disintegration of his well-crafted plans put General Meade in a foul temper, for he fully expected to be made the scapegoat for failure, especially in the face of such intense demand for prompt, productive maneuvering. The president had warned him to fight a battle, whatever he did, and Meade said Stanton had told him it would be better to leave eighteen thousand casualties on the field than to come back without engaging Lee. After such bombast, few in the White House or War Department would appreciate how low morale would have sunk among both soldiers and civilians if he had insisted on making the assault of November 30 and been flung back as disastrously as Burnside had been, almost a year before. If such a debacle had not made a mockery of Lincoln's recent call for "increased devotion" it would at least have neutralized Grant's magnificent success at Chattanooga, for casualty lists, black crepe, and those ominous letters written in unfamiliar hands wrought far more distinct impressions at home than the intangible advantages of another alleged victory. Most would not notice that those misfortunes had been avoided, precisely because they had been avoided; all that would be counted was the failure. So certain did Meade feel of his pending removal that he left his staff at Stevensburg and rode ahead, alone, to Brandy Station, where he asked his old friend and classmate, General Patrick, if he could wait in his tent. There he unburdened himself of his morose expectations and the failures that had ruined his campaign.[60]

The public reaction came about as Meade had anticipated. The *New York Times* predicted that the nation would be "astonished and confounded" at another retreat without a test of arms, and more radical papers flayed Meade for it. Comfortable New Yorkers with little knowledge of the campaign called it "incomprehensible," and the wife of a conniving political general condemned it as "useless." Everyone expected that Meade's head would roll, if only to relieve the politicians or General Halleck of apparent responsibility, and dissatisfaction did prevail in Washington. One of the president's private secretaries, who wrote anonymous observations for a New York newspaper, revealed a measure of executive sentiment when he scorned the Army of the Potomac for "this eternal do nothing." In conversation with another of his secretaries Lincoln himself confirmed that frustration, remarking on what feats might be accomplished "if this Army of the Potomac was good for anything." The president also let it slip that he had considered replacing Meade with Grant, and only refrained from doing so because he and Halleck both thought Grant too important to success in the West.[61]

Meade, meanwhile, supposed that his discretion in avoiding inevitable and pointless carnage at Mine Run had earned him even more of the soldiers' respect than he had enjoyed previously. He had been roundly cheered and fairly mobbed by his men after chasing Lee across the Rappahannock in early November, and his capital did seem to be on the rise among the men. Colonel Charles Wainwright, chief of artillery in the First Corps, suspected that "his not fighting will do as much for him in gaining the confidence of the army as if he had won a victory." Company and field-grade officers hoped he would survive the politicians' anger, considering him as good a general as they were likely to get, and a Maine corporal who had served in the Army of the Potomac since First Bull Run assured his brother that "I like Meade better than any Genl who ever had command of this army."[62]

Neither Halleck nor the president, who had been so sympathetic to Burnside after the bloodbath at Fredericksburg, gave Meade so much as an encouraging word. For more than a week the general waited as though on a gibbet, suspecting with good cause that his fate hung on the availability of a replacement and on the determination of some error of his that might serve as an excuse for his removal. As much as the president wanted to depose him, the new congressional session had just begun and many a political battle waited to be fought, added to which the appointment of yet another new commander might emit the scent of weakness. Only through the administration's most friendly newspaper did Meade finally learn that, at least for the present, he would retain his command.[63]

The Army of the Potomac entered the third winter of its existence in the triangle between the Rappahannock and Rapidan rivers, just upstream from where it had spent its second and most miserable winter, and that was not lost on the veterans preparing their huts for cold weather. That, combined with the hardships and failure of the last campaign, produced an atmosphere of hopelessness and despair at the very moment when those who had begun counting down the final year of their service faced intense pressure to extend their terms for another three years.

Since Lee's army headed into Pennsylvania, the War Department had made desperate efforts to retain each crop of volunteers as their time expired. It had begun with the two-year and nine-month men, late in June, when the adjutant general announced that any who had completed nine months of service could reenlist for three years and earn a bounty of four hundred dollars, along with the traditional two-dollar premium for bringing in recruits. The bounty only represented an extra hundred dollars for the veteran's military experience, because the government had already tripled the standard federal bounty to three hundred. As additional incentives, however, the "veteran volunteer" could go home on a thirty-day furlough, have his choice of serving in any regiment then in the field, and sew a distinctive chevron on the cuff of his uniform coat to denote his prior service: this last privilege may not have seemed altogether trivial to soldiers who wore uniforms lacking the alluring adornments of European armies. Once the short-term regiments had all been discharged, the same offer was applied to all three-year men who had completed two years of their enlistments, and early in October regimental commanders started making that pitch at the evening musters. At first most appeared interested, and in some units majorities of the troops indicated that they would go along with it — especially if, as the officers claimed, their regiments could go home and spend three months recruiting to full strength. Most of those men recanted when they learned that the last part of the offer was only hypothetical.[64]

The rumors of going home to recruit arose from an idea germinating in Stanton's War Department. The secretary had exercised his perennial poor judgment about new organizations by extending the reenlistment benefits to any who enlisted in new regiments, as well as those in the field. That encouraged the creation of green units that had to be organized and trained before going into active service, which always appealed more to the service-wise veteran than staying in the front lines, but late in November Stanton tried to balance that error with a formal proposal to the most experienced troops. If three-quarters of a regiment or a company should sign up for another three years, they would go home in a body at government expense to reorganize and fill their ranks with new recruits. That would save them the cost of round-trip transportation and allow them to spend all thirty days of their furlough with their families, besides giving them two or three months of safe and relaxing duty in their home states. That latest order reached the Army of the Potomac just as Meade prepared to cross the Rapidan toward Mine Run, prompting some officers to use the impending campaign for persuasive leverage. On the day before the army left its camps, the officers of the 49th New York promised that any man who reenlisted would go home on a furlough that would probably encompass the rest of the campaigning season, rather than marching into the cold and dark with the regiment the next morning. That timely extortion produced quite a few veteran volunteers.[65]

Veterans would normally have composed the most difficult population to recruit. These were men who had seen all the insults, abuse, and impositions the government routinely inflicted upon its soldiers. From the "gift" of their first uniforms, which they were later forced to repay at exorbitant cost, to the deliberate practice of propping up a fragile treasury by deliberately withholding pay for half a year at a time, many of them had grown understandably resentful of their miserable treatment. Their most common initial response echoed their most common choice of words: "I can't see it."[66]

The regiments raised during the first months of the war included a great many men from the poorest families in their communities, who had chosen military service at least partly to escape from their poverty. Their failure in that attempt became manifest by the large number of those former hardscrabble farmers, workaday laborers, and slave-wage factory operatives who willingly considered the reenlistment offer primarily for the bounty it brought. From the first parade-ground reading of the War Department circular, men whose letters had always sympathized with their wives' enforced scrimping urgently solicited domestic advice on the prudence of committing to three more years of absence in exchange for another apparent opportunity for financial salvation. One unlettered Iowa soldier in captured Little Rock asked the mother of his six children what she thought he should do, and to illustrate the magnitude of the decision he reminded her that his regiment had already lost three hundred men. The same question came from a forty-year-old Vermonter who had given his wife permission to shoot their dog so she could avoid the new town dog tax — a tax levied to pay local war expenses like his own bounty. A humble Maine shoemaker of the same age, who resented the richer citizens' option of paying poor men like himself to fight for them, nonetheless asked his long-suffering wife's opinion about the opportunity before deciding to reject it. An itinerant printer who had come to disguise the economic motivation of his enlistment in a patriotic veneer suddenly reversed his long-standing opposition to reenlistment when he optimistically (and incorrectly) calculated that he could reap bounties of nearly a thousand dollars. Echoing the same unrealized prophecies with which he had rationalized his original decision to join the army, he assured his wife that he could buy a house and some land with such riches, but he promised to follow her judgment.[67]

Those who reenlisted often paid at least token homage to what Lincoln had called "the great task remaining before us." So did others who only considered reenlisting, and before Lincoln's suggestive eloquence. One Iowan guaranteed his cousin that Union success would assure "the continued progress of Freedom for all mankind"; if they failed, he cautioned, it would mean "a return to feudal times when the Few can set their feet on the necks of the Many, irrespective of color." More often did a desire for strict obedience to the government seem to drive those who stayed on, like the Michigan veteran who, as his term was about to expire, professed a determination to see the last rebel surrender "if I live," but such sentiments were surely not universal. Professional and economic opportunity appear to have constituted at least an equal motivation. The reassignment of men who declined to reenlist, along with earlier attrition and the incorporation of new recruits, created frequent opportunities for advancement. Experienced privates might see a chance for stripes and the exemption from fatigue duty that chevrons entailed, while sergeants entertained better prospects for commissions. Some enlisted in new units precisely for such promotions, but the cunning opted not to remain in regiments where too many officers already survived for the appointment of more.[68]

Financial considerations again clearly imposed an overpowering influence, as they had in 1861 and more obviously in 1862. For all the conscientious patriotism they professed, many hesitated to take another tour of duty if their home communities seemed stingy about additional local bounties. Others made the perilous assumption that such generosity would be forthcoming, and many signed their names only after confirming that their total compensation neared or exceeded a thousand dollars, besides monthly pay. Some refused more than that, and comrades sometimes viewed the reenlisted men as more mercenary than patriotic: a Vermont boy who considered reenlisting admitted that patriotism prodded but few to do so, conceding "it is I am afraid the money."[69] When the reenlisted veterans of the 23rd Massachusetts went home on furlough, the colonel insisted that "the fighting part" of the regiment was left behind. A private in the 23rd went so far as to remark that the men who reenlisted in it included the perennial loafers who continually ran down the army and the government, whom he expected to "shirk all they can" during their next three years, just as they had in the past two. As though in corroboration of that opinion, a sergeant in the same regiment admitted his aversion to the army and the war, but he confessed that so much money "looks big," and in the end he accepted another hitch, perhaps because of the series of rapid promotions that came his way; in spite of those advantages, though, he soon regretted the decision. That much money did look big at the end of 1863, despite wartime inflation, but its very profusion produced further inflation that quickly diminished the effect of the bounties.[70]

The prospect of going home for thirty days exerted nearly as potent an allure as the cash. Furloughs came seldom for enlisted men in the army, especially for those in the field, and almost never for more than a week or ten days at a time. Aside from those who partook of convalescent leave after a stay in the hospital, and those sent home with the ulterior purpose of having them vote, most Union soldiers served their entire terms without once visiting their families: ten-day leaves only translated into three or four days at home even for those near a rail connection, and travel cost two or three months' pay. As the politicians understood, a large proportion of homesick veterans would find the chance to spend an entire month with their families too attractive to turn down after an absence of two full years.[71]

John Wilmot, a young private in the 4th Vermont, faced both questions — about the bounties and about going home — from a peculiar perspective. During the haying season of 1861, as a teenaged farm hand in Vermont's Connecticut River valley, he had enjoyed a brief liaison with a twenty-four-year-old neighbor girl. Then he had enlisted, expressing unusual interest in the federal bounty of one hundred dollars, which he evidently expected to use as a personal stake when he came home; he assigned his seven-dollar monthly state supplement to his father, in return for permission to enlist. Not until he had been in uniform several months did his summertime seductress inform him that she was about to give birth to a child, asking him to sign his state stipend over to her. It was too late for that, he explained, but he sent her some of his pay whenever it came, and seven months after the child was born she resumed a fitful correspondence with him. When confronted with the reenlistment dilemma, he calculated that he would receive the federal bonus of $402, plus his original $100 bounty, along with Vermont's $125 state bounty, for a total of $627 even if the town of Thetford did not see fit to pay him a town bounty for enlisting against its quota. He had earlier hinted that whenever he did come home he would get married right away "if anyone will have me," so his appeal for guidance from an unwed mother left her no cause to discourage him when he added that reenlisted veterans would all go home for thirty days.[72]

Women lacking the embarrassment of fatherless children resisted the mercenary temptation far more stubbornly, and in most cases with profound effect. News of so many reenlistments drifted homeward that wives elicited vows from their husbands not to forsake them for another three years, but as the reenlistment fever spread, some feared their men might prove unfaithful to the promise. The pressure to reenlist increased as a regiment grew excruciatingly close to the three-quarter goal, but for a man in the 8th Iowa that failed to weigh more heavily than his wife's wishes; as he explained to his brother-in-law, "She Bade me not[;] then how Could I?" Other soldiers needed no coaxing from home to insist that they had done their part, and that their next duty lay with their families. A few begged their loved ones not to worry about them signing on again, implicitly acknowledging that they had erred by enlisting in the first place, when home should always have presented the more pressing obligation.[73]

Those who considered themselves kings of their castles paid little or no heed to importuning wives: a Michigan soldier chastised his for her "saucy" remarks about his inclination to reenlist. A Pennsylvanian who scorned his own brothers for hiring substitutes did not even give his wife a chance to voice her wishes. In southern New Hampshire Emily Harris, whose growing hostility to the war aggravated the economic difficulties she suffered because of her husband's absence, begged him not to reenlist, but he hesitated to promise. The bonus would provide "a nice little sum for us to start with after the war is over," he argued, adding that he had no intention of returning to his old, straitened living as a shoemaker. He mollified her with the concession that for her sake he did not "think" he would reenlist, as much as he wanted to, but before that letter even reached her he had done so, and she evidently knew nothing of it until he showed up at home, on his veteran furlough.[74]

Occasionally a man who refused the early reenlistment overtures with bitter sarcasm softened with persistent wheedling and reflection, and the conversion might require only a few days, or hours. Visions of imminent wealth and leisurely visits home brought thousands to the brink of the fatal decision, and self-deception often nudged them over the precipice. The Confederacy had already been beaten, ran one popular argument, and there would not be much more fighting: an Indianapolis woman found this belief especially prevalent among the reenlisted men from that city when they came home on their furloughs. Or at least the war was winding down, and everyone would be going home after the same third year they would have had to serve out anyway, turning all the bounties into a windfall for those insightful enough to realize it.[75]

The cajoling of officers and War Department grew more insistent as the last day of the year approached. Officers who preferred to go home when their enlistments expired in a few months faced a difficult dilemma, for they were expected to encourage their men to stay on, and that obligation fell heaviest on the colonels. The commander of an Indiana regiment asked his wife to understand how difficult it would be for him to refuse reenlistment himself if his regiment hovered near the magic three-quarter mark, and three-quarters of the original men in his old company had already reenlisted. Ultimately he did not sign on again, perhaps because three or four men who did so were rejected, throwing the regiment back below the minimum threshold and robbing it of the chance to go home as a unit.[76]

Official pressure included threats, as well as inducements. The reenlistment debate monopolized most campfire conversations during December, but any who disparaged the government's offer or ridiculed those who accepted it risked arrest on the now-serious charge of discouraging enlistments — although that failed to stop a good many critics. The winter-long refusal of furlough privileges to any but those who reenlisted may not have been the most effective trick, but it was certainly the most thoroughly resented. This restriction emanated partly from the danger that a large number of men would necessarily be absent on reenlistment furlough, and partly from the hope that many with pressing domestic problems would submit to the additional three years in return for a longer leave than was usually permitted. To turn the screws a little tighter, any member who failed to reenlist in his "veteranized" regiment would be re-assigned among strangers in a different unit when their comrades went home to recruit, while those with company-level warrants as musicians, corporals, or sergeants would be reduced to the ranks in those new com-mands. Then there was the ploy used in the 49th New York: those who re-fused to commit for another three years would be assigned to the field for active winter campaigning, while their comrades went home.[77]

Less coercion seemed necessary in the more successful Western armies than in the East. During the entire winter the Army of the Potomac se-cured 26,767 reenlistments in all branches of the service — one-fifth of the 136,000 who reenlisted throughout the U.S. Army — but somehow more of its regiments came up short of the three-quarter mark that as-sured organizational survival. In the same period, the smaller Army of the Cumberland — its morale soaring after the glorious triumph at Mission-ary Ridge — furloughed forty-five "veteran volunteer" regiments, a dozen batteries of artillery, and more than a score of individual companies. Maine, for instance, had supplied the Army of the Potomac with five three-year regiments in the spring and summer of 1861: a few dozen men reenlisted in each of those regiments, but in none of them did enough come forward to keep the organization alive after its third anniversary. In other armies, seven more Maine regiments became eligible to reenlist that winter, and all did so.[78] Only eleven of the twenty-six Massachusetts regiments that might have reenlisted did not, and all eleven of them served with the Army of the Potomac. Neither New Hampshire nor Con-necticut had any 1861-vintage infantry under Meade during the reenlist-ment hysteria, so in New England only Rhode Island (which had one such regiment) and Vermont (the poorest of those states, but the most gener-ous with subsidies) were able to retain all their old regiments in that army. In contrast, sixteen Iowa infantry regiments had organized early enough in the war to meet the guidelines for reenlistment, all of which served under Grant and Sherman in the West, and only two failed to take advantage of it; all five early Iowa cavalry regiments carried over, as well, and none of them were posted in the East. Five Minnesota regiments had the opportunity to reorganize as veterans, and the four in Western armies did, but the one battered Minnesota regiment in the Army of the Potomac could muster only a two-company battalion.[79]

By the third week of January, one of the only two cavalry divisions in the Army of the Cumberland had gone home on reenlistment furlough, leaving a single regiment of Regulars and a squadron of volunteers to do the duty of all. Western soldiers whose families thought they were coming home in the summer of 1864 had decided to stay on, leaving farmer-fathers to postpone sending their younger boys to school for a little longer. Whole companies reenlisted after two years of grueling campaigns and dreadful attrition in pest holes as deadly as Helena.[80]

There seemed no glaring reason why those west of the Appalachians should extend their terms more enthusiastically than those on the Rapidan. Grant's armies all required significant detachments from their main bodies to guard a much longer line of communications than the one that fed the Army of the Potomac, and his furloughed regiments included many that had spent months in relative ease on such duty, but just as many of the regiments that climbed Lookout Mountain and Missionary Ridge reenlisted, too. More than 85 percent of the regiments doing relatively pleasant coastal duty in the Department of Virginia and North Carolina had also recruited enough original members to avail themselves of veteran status, but easy duty alone could not have accounted for the greater popularity of reenlistment among those who served outside the Army of the Potomac. The Ninth Corps had spent most of the reenlistment season enduring short rations and the rigors of long marches on primitive roads, yet the commander of nearly every regiment old enough to be eligible for reenlistment had still convinced the requisite number of men to bind themselves over. Differing morale within the armies offers the only credible explanation, for if those other armies had not seen spectacular victories in recent weeks, neither had they seen as much defeat and frustration as Meade's soldiers had in the previous two years. Six months after its most glowing triumph, the Army of the Potomac had evidently regained much of its old pessimism.[81]

A Massachusetts man serving on the coast of North Carolina suspected that a desire to avoid the draft provided much of the impetus behind his comrades' reenlistment mania, assuming that staying in one's original unit was preferable to being forced into a strange one, but he was mistaken in his premise. The Conscription Act had exempted every man in the service at the time of its passage, in March of 1863, and that would have included any of the three-year men who were eligible for reenlistment.[82] The threat of a draft did, however, fuel some enlistments at home, where former and prospective officers were still trying to raise new regiments. The president's supplemental draft call of October aided them enormously in that enterprise, and the recruiting doldrums that had begun the year gave way to a certain eagerness as 1863 came to an end.

John Gould, formerly a lieutenant in the 10th Maine, opened a recruiting office in Portland in the middle of August, but he scared up no recruits beyond an "old man" of forty-five who had served with him in the 10th. Gould convinced the mayor and aldermen to post an extra hundred-dollar city bounty, but that brought him no new prospects, either, so within days Gould gave up the recruiting idea and started lobbying the governor for a direct commission in a new regiment formed around two skeleton companies of the old 10th. He even resorted to fervent prayer for the governor's indulgence, which he finally secured, but his new regiment progressed as slowly as his own recruiting had. Then came the October draft proclamation, and by the end of November more than five hundred men had signed the rolls. The draft deadline fell on January 5, 1864, after which bounties were to cease and the lottery was to be held, but by that date the new regiment had mustered well over nine hundred men. Gould expected quite a few more to join later, with their papers stealthily back-dated so they could have their bounties. Four weeks later they all took ship for Louisiana as the 29th Maine.[83]

Massachusetts also tried to raise a regiment called the 1st Veteran Volunteers during the summer of 1863, expecting to fill it with soldiers discharged from other regiments, but no one enlisted at all until after the October draft call. Men started coming early in November with some regularity as towns raised bounty money to protect their enrolled citizens. Early in January enough had enrolled to warrant the mustering of one field officer, but veterans numbered so few among the recruits that when the regiment reached its minimum capacity, late in February, it was simply designated the 56th Massachusetts. The state organized three other regiments at the same time, all on the strength of the draft threat and the bounties it produced. Vermont managed one new regiment under the same pressure, mustering in the first company on the very day of the deadline, and Connecticut produced two regiments, including one composed of black troops. Ohio also mustered a regiment of freedmen, but of white troops it could fill only one six-month regiment that summer.[84]

Soldiers who had seen the paltry results of the summer draft recognized how few of those at home wanted any part of the war. They doubted that a fraction of the desired three hundred thousand would materialize before the January draft date, but in late November, six weeks before the deadline, small towns began authorizing hundred-dollar bounties for volunteers, and that soon escalated to two hundred, as it had in the summer of 1862. By the end of December the going rate in the East appeared to be three hundred dollars (and four, five, or six hundred in particularly anxious towns), while rural counties in the West reached their recruiting goals at two hundred apiece.[85] Such prodigality by those desperate to avoid military service incensed men who had taken the field for those same home-front patriots two years before, in response to little more than promises of assistance to their families, only to find their communities faithless even to those vows.[86]

Panic gripped men who feared their names could not be missed a sec-

ond time, or who had just paid for commutation under the previous
lottery, but the combination of inducement and compulsion again accomplished much that the appeal to blind patriotism did not. From his recruiting station in Brooklyn, a political general who would come to grief
over bilking volunteers out of their bounty reported, on the last day of the
year, that business was improving dramatically, and he expected even
better results "after the holidays," when the draft deficiency fell due. As
the conscription deadline drew near, troops at the front began to notice a
leavening of neighbors and friends among the recruits who joined them.
Some of those townsmen admitted that they had only come for hefty
bounties and because they would have been drafted anyway, but for once
the officers hoped to find material for some good soldiers.[87] A squad of recruits for the 6th Maine included the colonel's son. On the brink of the
draft date one New Hampshire town raised three local volunteers against
its quota with the belated and begrudging approval of a three-hundred-
dollar town bounty, enticing two older family men of little means and an
equally strapped veteran; for its other twenty-one required recruits, the
community had to send its agents afield to ply strangers with still more
generous bounty offers.[88]

Those bounties took another leap once the deadline passed: two weeks
later a man in the hills of southeastern Ohio calculated that he was worth
six hundred dollars to his community, but he rejected that fortune in favor of a job at a logging camp. In some regions threats and bribery exerted
virtually no influence against a population almost unanimously opposed
to continued conflict: in President Lincoln's own domain of central Illinois, a provost marshal reported that recruiting efforts in four counties
up to the January 5 deadline had netted a total of fewer than twenty volunteers. New Jersey, still the Eastern state most hostile to Lincoln's war,
had to rely almost exclusively on new regiments to meet its quotas. Three
infantry regiments, two of cavalry, and three artillery batteries sought recruits in Jersey during the latter half of 1863 and early 1864, siphoning off
New York City's unemployed and recent immigrants by offering slightly
higher bounties.[89]

While recruits in new regiments could usually rest assured that field
service would be deferred through several months of organization and
training, they could also depend on eventually suffering the miseries and
dangers of the front — unless the war ended abruptly. Certain types of
service therefore attracted particular interest because they usually involved less risk and greater comfort, or both. A Pennsylvanian who had
spent much of the war making money as a sutler found, when his militia commission expired and he became subject to the draft, that the Signal Corps posed interesting challenges. With conscription hovering a

week away, a draft-age schoolteacher in Missouri wrote melodramatically about taking up the sword in a noble cause after he secured a safe and potentially profitable commission as commissary for a cavalry regiment. After a year of hardship and danger in the field without promotion, an Ohio lieutenant determined that he merited some special service, but when none came his way he resigned. The former major of a New York regiment, who seemed forever dissatisfied with his rank and pay, and who secretly dreaded the prospect of having to go back into battle, procured an appointment as lieutenant colonel in the Invalid Corps although there was really nothing wrong with him. In Iowa a man who could write a fine hand agreed to enlist with a company commanded by his neighbor if the captain would assign him as his clerk; another neighbor in the same company warned that the captain's promise would carry no weight once the regiment left camp to go on campaign, but the tenuous company employment translated into a permanent assignment at brigade headquarters, and the discriminating recruit never carried a rifle.[90]

Influential friends or relatives sometimes had to help orchestrate desirable appointments. In Vermont a young man who had considered himself unfit for service nonetheless passed his physical and had to pull some long strings to avoid the infantry, enlisting the aid of the governor to release him from the federal draft so he could accept a state assignment in the medical service. Thaddeus Stevens, the powerful Radical Republican congressman from Pennsylvania, intervened personally with the secretary of war to have his favorite nephew and namesake awarded a hometown vacancy in the provost marshal's department. An Indiana legislator who had secured his own plum as provost marshal chastised a son who had impetuously resigned a snug position as a brigade commissary, persuading him to keep the job.[91]

New Hampshire's chief executive recognized the lure of special service, and he exploited it to the best of his ability when his state faced a considerable shortfall in its quota on January 5. Instead of attempting to raise more infantry, Governor Joseph Gilmore used the reenlistment furlough of the state's only battalion of cavalry as the impetus for raising an entire regiment of that arm. The notion of riding to war must have seemed preferable to potential conscripts, as well as to boys afflicted with the idyllic visions of youth. Recruiting faltered in the spring, but Gilmore pushed through a special state bounty for the regiment, which he said would surpass the provost marshal's quota for the entire state by five hundred men if it could be filled to capacity. Gilmore eventually had even better luck with the heavy artillery. That was the favorite branch of service for those who did not want to sleep in the mud or brave the battlefield, and soldiers in the field advised their little brothers to seek it, if they must enlist. Wily veterans who knew better than to reenlist in their infantry regiments considered the heavy artillery an acceptable path to those generous bounties. The only new military force the Granite State had been able to complete in all of 1863 had been two companies of these "heavies," for duty at Fort Constitution in Portsmouth Harbor.[92]

Heavy-artillery companies, so called because their primary function consisted of working the heavy guns in permanent forts, averaged half again the size of their infantry counterparts, and their regiments included twelve companies rather than ten, giving them a complement of eighteen hundred men apiece, rather than a thousand. Each company required five officers, as well, instead of the three authorized for infantry. They carried rifles and trained as infantry, in case they had to defend their forts, but they enjoyed much better living conditions than the army's foot soldiers. Those who cast their lot with the heavy artillery expected to sleep in dry bunks inside heated barracks, with three cooked meals a day, and for the first three years of the war those expectations were usually met.[93]

Augustus Alvord, a finicky young New Englander who would have preferred a sinecure as chaplain (and later found one), chose the heavy artillery as a stopgap refuge when the draft fell on his town. John Pierce, a Massachusetts shoemaker who could barely support his wife and children at his trade, seemed to look on heavy-artillery duty in the next town as just another job, and accepted it on the promise of enough bounty and pay to let his family live well. A Connecticut man discovered that he could not enlist "to advantage" in the navy, so he opted for the heavy artillery to provide his wife with the bounty money and a six-dollar allotment from the state, but both he and Pierce found the money slow to come after they had been mustered in. John McCoy, a Canadian, also found the heavy artillery the most inviting employment available, but when his wife's foreign residency made it difficult for her to collect the state aid he lamented that "only for that I never would have joined the Army." William Garfield, a recruit in one of the New Hampshire companies at Fort Constitution, had a foster brother on duty with an infantry regiment who feigned wry sympathy when he learned that William had collected the same bounty as any other volunteer, slept indoors every night, and spent four days at home every three months.[94]

Several states capitalized on the popularity of heavy artillery to raise whole new regiments of that branch, or to convert existing infantry regiments into heavy artillery, which always entailed an opportunity for hundreds of new recruits and the appointment of numerous grateful new officers. Once the draft began, those new regiments filled with "a great rush," and everyone seemed to recognize the implicit promise that they would see only garrison duty, with never a battle to fight.[95] Competition

for commissions in the heavy artillery naturally ran higher than elsewhere, but political influence again carried as much weight as capacity,
experience, or previous performance. The captain of one of the companies
at Portsmouth, for instance, had resigned from the 5th New Hampshire,
but his erstwhile colonel considered him worthless, and pointedly refused
to recommend him for a commission in the Invalid Corps, let alone in the
heavy artillery.[96]

Through the spring of 1864 the heavy-artillerymen who ended up in
the forts around Washington came the closest of any in their arm to what
might have been called the front, and even they found their duty abun-
dantly pleasant. One man allowed his own young son to enlist in his company, so innocuous did the duty seem. Their polished boots and well-
brushed coats seldom saw mud or rain. They stood guard with little fear
of random shots from lurking enemies, and visited around the countryside among families who welcomed them to their tables. If they suffered
from the monotony of their existence, they had merely to compare it with
firsthand tales of misery and mayhem retailed by convalescents and furloughed soldiers from the Army of the Potomac, plenty of whom crowded
Washington as the new year began.[97]

8

The War Will Never Be Done

➔ FRANCIS BROOKS, A GENTLEMAN farmer from Medford, Massachusetts, closed his journal for 1863 with the hope that the new year would see the end of "this dreadful war," but not unless the flag had been restored to all its former territory, and treason had been eradicated. Mr. Brooks occupied the prime of life, just past his thirty-ninth birthday, and he was fit enough to have climbed hurriedly up and down Mount Washington in one afternoon the previous summer. He never considered military service, though, and never had to, for he could afford the full price of a substitute at peak rates. Restoration of the flag was no task for such as him.[1]

The grim duties of the battlefield seemed more appropriate to the likes of William Perkins, a lanky New Hampshire teamster who lived with his wife and son in his father's humble farm along the Saco River, 120 miles north of Medford. Perkins had just turned forty, and like Mr. Brooks he enjoyed good health, but he owned no property, and his wages gave him no prospects of acquiring any, short of inheriting his father's farm. Taxes on that farm — and on farms across the nation — were doubling annually from all the money spent to meet the draft quotas, while the cost of goods, provisions, and seasonal labor were skyrocketing, so on New Year's Eve Perkins made his way to Concord by stagecoach and train to be mustered into service. Two neighbors in similar pecuniary straits accompanied him, and their town agreed to give each of them three hundred dollars for their sacrifice. They changed into new blue uniforms, and a slick paymaster talked each of them into signing for a sixty-two-dollar advance on the federal bounty, which he never gave them.[2]

As those three volunteers headed south to the death they would all meet during the new year, they passed thousands of reenlisted men on their way north in more faded versions of those same uniforms. The veterans filled whole trains, using up several days of their furloughs on the trip from Chattanooga or Brandy Station or New Orleans to their home states. They left in such numbers that their army commanders half-expected the enemy to detect their absence, and take advantage of it. Some of them needed a week or more to reach their families, counting hours and miles that seemed never to pass, only to find that the days at home flew with lightning speed.[3] Up in Vermont, John Wilmot used the time to play with his alleged daughter and to marry the child's mother — who was never able to remember the day or the year of their wedding, and whose interest in her husband seemed linked to the government income he represented.[4] Other veterans who invested their bounty money in matrimony may have enjoyed more sincere affection and better luck than Private Wilmot, but a New York colonel discerned that the image of "four or five hundred dollars cash in hand set the girls wild after the men." As many as one-third or one-half the reenlisted men in some companies returned from their furloughs married, he recorded, while others just gave the bounty money to their pursuers without requiring a ceremony.[5]

The migration of so many men from disease-ridden armies back to their isolated rural communities inevitably introduced little plagues that ravaged certain hamlets, and the winter of 1864 brought complaints of more sickness than usual. In one Illinois prairie district a resident noted more illness than he had seen since he settled there. Indiana soldiers heard of an unusual incidence of sickness back home, too, while smallpox made its appearance in Chicago and struck Washington City in such volume that local officials established a requirement for mandatory inoculation that would have been difficult to enforce.[6] An outbreak of scarlet fever blighted Sturbridge, Massachusetts, in the spring of 1864. A soldier who came down with the measles in January of 1864 may have been the source of a rubeola epidemic that afflicted Meriden, New Hampshire, for the next two months. Diphtheria broke out in southern New Hampshire when the first of the reenlisted men came home. The same affliction killed dozens in the sparsely settled farming hamlets of western Maine, where it had been raging since the nine-month men came home, and smallpox appeared there, as well. "I can hardly realize that so many have died," recorded a Maine farmer whose diary alternated between visits from furloughed soldiers, neighbors falling deathly ill, and a cavalcade of funerals.[7]

The soldiers also brought an epidemic of intolerance home with them. Furloughed soldiers led or dominated mobs that attacked numerous Democratic newspapers that winter and spring, especially after a new draft call elicited another crop of critical editorials. They fell on opposition sheets with particular vehemence in Ohio, ransacking half a dozen offices in different communities across the state. As a grand finale before returning to the army, one group of soldiers in Darke County who had already destroyed a Democratic paper went on a more indiscriminate rampage a few weeks later, assaulting dissenting citizens on the street and in their offices. Furloughed soldiers discouraged a Democratic congressman from speaking at Paris, Illinois, early in March, but outraged citizens confronted them in a brawl that left three people wounded; near the end of the month a more serious riot erupted between soldiers and citizens in nearby Charleston, Illinois, producing a score of casualties including nine dead soldiers and citizens. Government officials used terms like "insurrection" to describe these incidents, implying that the violence consisted of organized insurgents assailing Union soldiers or citizens, but the soldiers themselves appear to have started most of the trouble. Usually, though, it was their civilian antagonists whom federal troops arrested.[8]

In political bellwether states like New Hampshire and Connecticut, the War Department's ploy of restricting furloughs to the reenlisted veterans assured that a more supportive portion of the army would come home to vote for Republican candidates, and Republicans in those two states used an assortment of stratagems to throw the soldier vote even more heavily in their direction. William Chandler, the crafty speaker of the New Hampshire House and son-in-law of Governor Joseph Gilmore, had helped manipulate military voting the year before, and now he enlisted the state's agent for New Hampshire soldiers in New York, Frank Howe, to help bring home a couple of hundred sound Republican voters from the forts in Portsmouth Harbor. Chandler suggested that Howe approach Major General John Dix, commander of the Department of the East, who kept his headquarters in New York, to give the captain at Fort Constitution authority to furlough most of the two heavy-artillery companies there. The men who had eluded the Conscription Act through that safe, soft duty were mostly Republicans, Chandler claimed: if their own immediate commander were able to select which of them to send on a ten-day furlough at election time, they would probably assure victory in several questionable towns while "the Copperheads and minors" stayed behind as a skeleton garrison. If Dix failed to accommodate New Hampshire Republicans that way, Chandler warned, he would go over the general's head to Stanton or "Old Abe."[9]

Someone — probably Chandler — asked a similar favor of Vermont's Republican governor, who arranged for all adult male residents of New Hampshire to go home on furlough from Vermont regiments. They had crossed the Connecticut River to enlist in considerable numbers during the first sixteen months of the war, for Vermont's seven-dollar monthly subsidy to soldiers' families had counted for much before the big bounties, and at the end of February they started packing for the trip home. Brigadier General Gilman Marston, a Republican congressman himself, served his party even more efficiently in his capacity as commander of the only New Hampshire brigade that ever came together during the war. Appealing to the colonels and captains of his three Granite State regiments at Point Lookout military prison, in Maryland, Marston assembled a list of the men who could be most readily trusted to vote Republican, and he sent all of those he could spare home on furlough. New Hampshire veterans whose reenlistment furloughs ran out in February saw them renewed by War Department order until March 10, two days after the state elections.[10]

Governor William Buckingham, of Connecticut, always found a way to allow his Republican soldiers to vote, and to prevent his Democratic troops from doing so. The previous year he had tricked the Democrats in Connecticut regiments into revealing themselves by orchestrating parade-field votes on a bogus pro-war resolution, but for the 1864 election he needed only to charge the hundreds of officers he had commissioned with handpicking voters from the Republican subordinates they had identified in the spring of 1863. With more War Department collaboration, Buckingham had about a hundred from each regiment (except the 29th Connecticut, the black soldiers of which could not vote) brought home free of charge on government transports; they took their arms and equipments, too, which would have allowed them to act as unofficial sentinels at the polls to discourage antiadministration electioneering. Even one of the Republicans, who was left behind as too young to vote, considered it a shabby trick that helped to corroborate all the Democrats' complaints about a military despotism.[11]

As an added precaution, Buckingham's henchmen also bought a few votes outright, when necessary. New Hampshire Republicans stooped to the forgery of Democratic tickets, with the gubernatorial candidate identified as Edward W. Harriman, rather than Edward W. Harrington. Had Democrats accepted tickets with the erroneous name and cast them as ballots, their votes would have been disqualified.[12]

Through such chicanery the elections in New Hampshire and Connecticut went mostly to the Republicans. Trickery might not have been needed at all, after the successes in the East and West during 1863, had it not been for another presidential proclamation issued on February 1. Basing his assumption on just such victories, and the belief that the Confederacy already lay in ruins, the provost marshal general suggested that now would be the time to summon another two hundred thousand con-

scripts beyond the three hundred thousand Lincoln had called for in October, and either through exuberance or misunderstanding the president
ordered a draft on March 10 for another half-million men, minus whatever volunteers came forward between February 1 and that date. Recalling earlier assurances of imminent Confederate collapse, which had
been followed by appeals for a few hundred thousand volunteers to finish
the job, jaded Democrats greeted the newest call on the eve of the election
as confirmation that a vote for Republicans represented a vote for eternal
war. Some suspected that Lincoln intended to raise another whole army
for an invasion of Mexico, to drive out the French.[13]

States and towns that had just surmounted their quotas under the last
call, or had not quite met those quotas, immediately faced onerous new
demands for volunteers from a resident population that had, in most instances, been culled of all but the unwilling. The desperate and destitute
in most communities had long since been absorbed into the army. Escalating bounties found increasingly fewer citizens like William Perkins
who would risk their lives to resolve acute financial hardships, especially
for a windfall of such rapidly decreasing value. Common laborers in the
cities and suburbs could demand thirteen dollars a week by the end of
1863, and before spring New England farm hands were getting forty and
forty-five dollars a month, plus their keep: a private soldier still earned
only thirteen dollars a month, and the inflation in wages sharply reduced
the attraction of bounties paid in town notes or in periodic installments.
After hearing what difficulties their home towns had overcome to satisfy
the government's last call, soldiers wondered how they could ever fill another quota so soon, and how much it would cost to try.[14]

Those who would present themselves to the examining surgeons
henceforth would more often turn out to be unfit for daily labor, either
through age or infirmity, and the surgeons seemed increasingly willing
to overlook the frail fodder they might have winnowed from a hardier selection. Gullible, adventure-hungry boys as young as fourteen posed as
adults, or wheedled permission from harried parents, and men with de-
bilitating diseases consigned themselves to the rigors of a service they
could never endure. Young soldiers who had already learned the miseries
of army life suddenly found that they had to dissuade still-younger brothers from going as substitutes for neighbors who fell within the limits of
draft age, and often their fathers threatened to enlist. Soon after the February proclamation a Maine cavalryman who had already lost a brother
at Gettysburg learned to his horror that his other two underage brothers
and their fifty-three-year-old father were all thinking of enlisting for the
money it would bring the family. At that same juncture, a Vermont corporal pleaded with his mother to dissuade his father, who had already served

in a ninety-day regiment and was periodically tempted by ballooning bounty offers: "if he does come again," warned the son, "he [will] wish him self in hell."[15]

Provost marshals, most of whom held their positions through political influence, usually carried enough authority to decide which recruits would be taken. They labored under growing pressure to provide more men, and that alone might have led them to ease the physical requirements even if it had not been for the tempting prevalence of bribery. Substitute brokers and town agents brought in most of the prospective soldiers as the era of the spontaneous volunteer came to a close, and the brokers collected up to twenty-five dollars as a legal premium for every man accepted, besides whatever they could skim or steal from naive youths and desperate immigrants with little English. The trade yielded enough money to warrant liberal gratuities to the provost marshals, who could either encourage their examining surgeons to relax their scrutiny on the plea of patriotic need or extend a portion of the brokers' bribes to the doctors.[16]

That scheme sprang spontaneously from the first contact between corrupt substitute brokers and venal provost marshals during the summer of 1863, and it spread through the system as soaring demand drove substitute prices and profit margins higher. Of thirteen men sent to one Indiana company in the autumn of that year, only three had the stamina to perform any duty. A New York colonel looking for recruits in his Hudson River district discovered that the provost marshal there accepted applicants in February whom he had rejected under the last draft because they were too old or too feeble to carry a musket. In western New York a fourteen-year-old boy who had been disqualified by both army and navy examiners as late as December for lung disease, a weak heart, and extreme youth, was accepted into a new cavalry regiment in January. The provost marshal and his examiner in Vermont's northern district were suspended in February for passing and mustering recruits who were clearly unfit for service, but those political appointees and most others under the provost marshal general held onto their sinecures no matter how much decrepit material they put into uniform. The provost marshal of Ohio's Second District was invited to resign, without prosecution, only when the governor complained that corruption infected at least half his state's local provost marshals, who were living far better than their salaries could account for.[17]

The quality of recruits that winter led a Vermont sharpshooter who had only enlisted the previous November to hope that new quotas would not be filled by more young boys and cripples. A Maine lad arrived in camp at Brandy Station that winter in the company of ten other recruits, one of whom went straight to the hospital with epileptic seizures, while another suffered from a stiff knee that left him barely able to walk, and a third — a boy of sixteen — had apparently brought a case of mumps to infect his new comrades. Negligence and corruption among the provost marshals and their surgeons might explain the blossoming of certain ailments in army hospitals early in 1864, as diseased recruits gravitated to surgeon's call instead of the duty roster. From December of 1863 to March of 1864, for instance, U.S. Army surgeons encountered a 95 percent rise in the incidence of inflammation of the lungs. Between January and April of 1864 the number of soldiers diagnosed with syphilis swelled 88 percent, at a time of the year when that disease was usually on the wane. Surgeons reported more cases of chronic alcoholism in March of 1864 than they did during any other month of the war. Treatment for "the itch" nearly doubled between December and March — partly from the close confinement of winter quarters, perhaps, but one surgeon reported in February that the pestilential warehouses and pens where volunteers and substitutes were housed were completely infested with lice, and they surely carried such parasitical livestock to the camps with them, along with scabies.[18]

Escorting recruits to his New Hampshire regiment under guard, Lieutenant Oscar Robinson lamented that his state would insult its soldiers by forcing them to mingle with "refugees from the penitentiaries and exiles from Canada." Neither he nor the politicians in Washington seemed to understand, or at least to acknowledge, that the declining quality of recruits reflected the limits of support for the war. With sufficient electoral knavery, Republican legislators, representatives, and governors might be continued in office, all of which implied a desire to pursue the conflict to a successful conclusion, but precious few of even the Republican voters would consider aiding that effort by taking up a musket themselves. After the first of the year most towns had to appoint selectmen or citizen agents to go bargaining for mercenaries in the cities or in the seedy dens where brokers housed prospective substitutes. They ventured as far as the winter quarters of hometown regiments, pleading for the reenlistment of fellow citizens who had long since decided against it — soldiers who openly jeered their plaintive municipal representatives for not reducing their town quotas by joining the army themselves. The local recruiters undertook a frustrating, expensive, and sometimes dangerous quest: the agent for Derry, New Hampshire, struck off with a French Canadian interpreter in search of volunteers, only to be found a few days later in a Massachusetts town, with an ax planted in his skull.[19]

Some of those agents, or substitute brokers seeking to fill orders for town agents, strayed across the border into Canada. The influx of American citizens on the run from the draft, as well as new waves of immigrants from Europe, had driven wages there so low that cumulative bounties of six or seven hundred dollars exerted more influence than they did in the United States, even when they were paid in Secretary Chase's depreciated greenbacks. Her Majesty frowned on foreign recruiters preying upon her subjects, though, and especially when they seduced the severely underpaid British soldier from his duty. Two Americans landed in jail in Canada West for soliciting the desertion of a private in the 63rd Regiment of Foot, and constables collared several New York recruiters who had crossed the St. Lawrence in search of volunteers. The hunting was good among the indigent, though, and with the exercise of a little discretion a broker might make a small fortune. So long as no contracts were concluded and no money changed hands, the Canadian authorities could hardly interfere: unlike in the United States, it had not become a criminal offense north of the border to simply discuss whether one should or should not enter military service. In the Eastern Townships, newly arrived and native-born Canadians by the score boarded trains bound for Vermont or New York, where they reported, often by prearrangement, to American recruiters.[20]

Boston followed more inventive avenues for meeting the various draft quotas. One idea may have sprung from a State Department circular advising ministers and consuls to encourage (and presumably aid) the immigration of European males between the ages of twenty-one and forty, professedly to offset the wartime labor shortage. Suspecting that it might be much cheaper than paying massive bounties for domestic recruits, the Board of Trade organized an ill-disguised vehicle for directly enlisting alien citizens against Boston's draft deficit. The Foreign Emigrant Society, as the enterprise was called, evaded neutrality laws by sending civilian agents to contract privately with Europeans on their own soil, giving them a hundred dollars and free passage to the United States in return for their promise to serve three years under any employer those agents might choose. By April several shiploads of eager German immigrants had arrived to reduce Boston's military obligation at wholesale rates for the municipality, since they collected only the three-hundred-dollar federal bounty.[21]

Later the mayor and board of aldermen retained broker Charles Burrill to find substitutes or other men who could be credited to Boston's quota at a price of $125 per man. Burrill identified 6,529 sailors in federal service who had given Boston as their residence when they enlisted, who should have been credited to the city, but they had entered the navy before the imposition of draft quotas and no one had bothered to count them. Congress finally recognized the excessive burden of draft quotas on cities and towns that had provided hordes of volunteers early in the war, and amended the law to allow those men to be counted retroactively, so Burrill pounced upon it. That gave him an existing trove of credits that drastically reduced Boston's obligation without a penny spent in bounties, but then the city balked at paying Burrill his agreed-upon price, arguing that the mayor had lacked the authority to consummate such a deal. The dispute over Burrill's claim for $816,125 lasted long after the anxiety over draft quotas had evaporated.[22]

Like the popular resort to commutation, technical solutions of that nature gave only temporary relief, for they provided no new men to fill the ranks and only led to new draft calls on the heels of the earlier ones. The recruits gathered from abroad, or from the sweepings of urban slums, often proved little more satisfactory than none at all. Contingents of recruits like the one Lieutenant Robinson had just delivered provoked the colonel of the 9th New Hampshire to wail that "for God's sake" he wanted no more like those, who came from "the Canadas, New Brunswick, Nova Scotia, Newfoundland, Prince Edward Island, Manilla, England, Ireland, France, Germany, Norway, Sweden, Choctaw Nation and quite a delegation from the furthest of the five Points. What an honor they are to the State." Language barriers and insincere motives often reduced the usefulness of such replacements to nothing, or worse, although every carload of new recruits brought some capable and conscientious men. The 9th New Hampshire drew two foreign-born recruits for every one who was a native of the United States, but more than a tenth of the new men would perish during a year and a half of service. Lieutenant Robinson's coffle, for instance, included William Perkins and his two neighbors, all of whom would leave their bones in national cemeteries over the next few months.[23]

For all the grousing about the quality of substitutes and volunteers, close observers in the West thought they detected an improvement in the quality of volunteers, or at least an improvement in the net worth of volunteers. The editor of the *Prairie du Chien Courier*, a Democrat in his mid-twenties who was conspicuously liable to conscription, remarked on the eve of Wisconsin's Third District draft that "the class of men who are volunteering now, are to all intents and purposes, *better men*, socially, mentally, and physically, than the mass who have offered themselves before." Translating the Victorian implications of "better men," this backhanded insult to the soldiers of 1861 and 1862 hinted that the combination of compulsory service and the resulting bounties was finally drawing recruits from families of more substantial means. "They have responsibilities, property, homes, families, and friends," he explained. "They are not needy adventurers." He was not describing the rich, but rather solid working-class and middle-class men who, when faced with having to pay several hundred dollars for temporary commutation, or several hundred more for a more permanent substitute, opted instead to pocket that same small fortune and take their chances in the ranks. As the *Courier* editor interpreted it, these men had simply been "prevented" from exercising their patriotic impulse to enlist for fear of stinting their families. Still, 546 of the men drafted in his district that month paid their three hundred dollars, and 4 more hired substitutes, leaving only 136 poor souls to show up at the draft rendezvous.[24]

Those recruits who did hail from relatively affluent families were usually the babies of their families. One well-to-do lawyer in Indianapolis endured his fifteen-year-old son's badgering all winter, but succumbed finally when an opportunity arose for the boy to join a ridiculously short-term regiment. A purportedly Copperhead town official in southwestern Wisconsin escorted two of his young sons to a recruiting station with permission to enlist, and he brought along a neighbor's. Across the country, it was young boys who showed the greatest enthusiasm for going to war. They tempted the recruiters in numbers sufficient to inaugurate official inquiries and federal legislation on the subject of adolescent soldiers, and a bureaucracy that initially rejected anyone but musicians before their eighteenth birthdays soon enough settled for a minimum age of sixteen, with parental permission. Regulations for the peremptory dismissal of officers who mustered soldiers under sixteen failed to stop the frequent induction of striplings a year or two younger than that, and usually without legitimate permission.[25]

Another dubious new source of manpower came to mind when Ben Butler, then in command at Fort Monroe, suggested recruiting from the Confederate prisoners in what had become the Union's largest military prison, at Point Lookout, Maryland. Even that seemed feasible to the president and secretary of war, and hours into the new year they approved the plan. Penitent rebels had been abandoning their cause and joining Union regiments for several months by then, most notably in Burnside's east Tennessee command, and prisoners of war had previously been allowed to switch sides if they swore, however falsely, that they had been forced into Confederate service. Now the Union army needed soldiers more desperately than ever, and that pretense about coercion went by the boards: any rebel willing to take the oath of allegiance could escape confinement by donning the blue uniform, no matter how eagerly he had originally entered Southern service. The prisoners at Point Lookout learned this just as they faced the worst of winter in the meager shelter of their stockade. To the hooting of their more devoted comrades, they started trickling out in pairs and squads to form the rudiments of what would become six full regiments of turncoats known as the Galvanized Yankees.[26]

Cold weather brought rebel recruits out of prison camps in the West, too. In the waning days of 1863 they began shambling out of Camp Douglas, in Chicago, and soon afterward the commandant at Alton, Illinois, reported numerous Confederate inmates who seemed "anxious" to enlist in the Union army. Several thousand loyal white Southerners, meanwhile, provided more reliable additions to Union arms in newly conquered Confederate territory. Two regiments each of Arkansas infantry and cavalry gathered at Little Rock that winter. Mississippi refugees in occupied Memphis filled a regiment of mounted rifles by March, and enough Texans volunteered to muster a regiment of loyal cavalry at the mouth of the Rio Grande. These new troops gave no immediate relief to draft-sensitive Northerners, and while they should theoretically have forestalled the demand for more troops, they did not reduce the quotas on the latest levy.[27]

Ambrose Burnside chose the old-fashioned method of raising troops, using his personal popularity to attract recruits when little else seemed to lure them except wads of money. The War Department capitalized on Burnside's appeal — for his star had risen anew after his successful defense of Knoxville (and, perversely enough, because of his unconstitutional arrest and prosecution of Clement Vallandigham). In the Ninth Corps, and especially among the regiments that had served with him since his days in North Carolina, there were few who failed to go wild at the sight of "Old Burn's" trademark whiskers. Edwin Stanton therefore relieved him of the Department of the Ohio and brought him east with orders to fill his old corps up to a strength of fifty thousand, "for such service as the War Department may specially designate." That phrasing constituted a shrewd piece of department salesmanship, for it not only suggested the "special service" that would pique the curiosity and stroke the pride of prospective soldiers, but it implied that the corps would not be consigned to the more common duty with the main armies, and especially not with the unlucky, unfriendly Army of the Potomac. Burnside located his headquarters in the Fifth Avenue Hotel, ordered handbills that went a step further toward promising the "special service" (which many supposed would restore him to the milder climate of North Carolina), and set off on a whirlwind recruiting tour, hoping to tilt wavering volunteers toward the enrollment tables by the mere force of his personality.[28]

In this enterprise Burnside found himself competing with Winfield Scott Hancock, who enjoyed similar esteem within his old Second Corps and who had nearly recuperated from a painful Gettysburg wound. They vied in particular for the population of Massachusetts, which had given Hancock a greater share of its 1861-vintage troops. The War Department had finally shown some determination to replenish those tough old regiments before accepting whole new levies of new ones, which gave Hancock the edge in Massachusetts at first, but by 1864 the greenest youth out shopping for a good spot knew that the safest bet was the heavy artillery, the cavalry, or a new regiment of any kind. That aided Burnside in turn, at least so far as numbers were concerned, for the Bay State's four new regiments all went to him. Burnside made the circuit of Boston's intelligentsia, appearing as the guest of honor at public parades and attending formal dinners with Governor Andrew, Edward Everett, and Oliver Wendell Holmes. His name and his famous face swelled his recruiting coffers with thousands of dollars from Union Leagues and individuals, and when Hancock followed him on a similar jaunt it stirred recruiting in general, helping to fill Burnside's new regiments.[29]

Without success, Burnside badgered the secretary of war for the third division of his corps, which had been detached a year before. With better luck, he asked for a whole division of U.S. Colored Troops, and the commanders of new black regiments petitioned specifically for assignment to his corps. So did the colonels of white regiments, old and new. As if to confirm rumors that the Ninth Corps would return to the North Carolina sounds — rumors that Burnside tried to cultivate into reality with proposed plans of action in that theater — one of Burnside's inspectors arrived in Annapolis to find room enough for the anticipated fifty thousand to camp. This had been the rendezvous for Burnside's coastal expedition, more than two years before, and the memory of those halcyon days revived the spirits of old soldiers who had seen the war turn brutal and bitter. The gaiety at Annapolis overcame even the dreaded conclusion of reenlistment furloughs, and men who had just left tearful bairns or brides still managed to frolic, stag, in the dance hall, or glean some fun from a rare snowfall along the Severn.[30]

Outside of the troops stationed in their home states, Burnside's men may have been the happiest in the Union army that winter, while the reenlisted veterans across the nation may have been the most forlorn. As soldiers soon learned, leaving home the second time is always worse than the initial departure, for the mysteries of the outside world had lost their luster by then, and the anguish of separation had grown all too familiar. A lieutenant colonel on his way back to his regiment from Michigan comprehended the phenomenon, recording on the day of his departure that "everybody who has been to the wars once knows what it is like to leave home for a second campaign." Husbands found they could hardly speak when the time came to go, or they struggled to conceal their sadness lest wives, children, and mothers explode in tears around them. The rueful wife of a stubborn Pennsylvania patriot could hardly contain her woe at bidding her husband goodbye, for the past thirty months had weighed so heavily on her that three more years seemed an eternity even if his life was spared — which it was not. Emily Harris, the New Hampshire woman who had failed to dissuade her husband from reenlisting, felt so desolate at the end of his fleeting visit that she almost wished he had not come, and her heartache seemed to wrack her with physical pain when she learned that his regiment had finally left the state to return to the battlefront. Knowing that he must return to the Army of the Potomac in a day or two, a musician in a Maine regiment counted the friends, relatives, and comrades gathered around the fireplace of his home and wondered where they would all be in a year; nostalgia enveloped him before he retired that night, and he scribbled in his diary "Remember the 17th day of Feb/64."[31]

Those going into the Union army for the first time soon regretted their decisions, as well, despite that still-vibrant curiosity about the country beyond their mountains. Exposure to cold, rain, and snow with little shelter and less firewood nurtured colds in the chest of every recruit. Bland, insufficient food left the body craving unidentifiable nutrients. Marching in knee-deep mud to their first campsite with the army, sleeping that night in puddles, and standing guard several nights in a row with cold, wet feet seemed to foretell an ordeal no one could survive, and those were the blissful days before they had seen their first battle. No wonder that many a young man who had recently succumbed to the allure of patriotism, adventure, and deceptive wealth moped about the army's camps that winter wearing an expression of profound remorse. The veterans themselves often showed similar dejection, for many had spent all their bounty money in grog shops and revelry. At that juncture they might have envied those calculating few who had used their reenlistment furloughs to effect an early departure from the army, and invested their bounty money to escape the States, either for Europe, Canada, or the territories, never to be seen by their comrades again.[32]

In his Department of Virginia and North Carolina, Ben Butler assumed responsibility for not only Point Lookout Prison but Aiken's Landing, on the James River, where the two armies periodically exchanged their prisoners. In July of 1862 Butler's predecessor, John Dix, had negotiated a system of exchange with his Confederate counterpart, Daniel Harvey Hill, that both governments had adopted for all their armies. The cartel decreed that each belligerent would deliver prisoners under a flag of truce to either Aiken's Landing or Vicksburg, where they would trade prisoners and lists of their names, which would be subjected to an excruciatingly monotonous matching process. If one side held more prisoners than the other the surplus would be paroled, making oath not to fight again until exchanged at a later time for opponents of equal rank, but once exchanged they would resume their places in the ranks.[33]

The Dix-Hill cartel had freed a lot of prisoners who had been held for as long as a year, quickly reducing prison populations by more than three-quarters, and it operated with little interruption or incident for nearly another year. On raids into Union-held territory, Southern troops paroled many thousands of Yankee prisoners without bringing them to the specified exchange points, but U.S. forces recognized most of those paroles anyway. The issue of black Union soldiers served as a burr under the saddle, especially after Jefferson Davis decreed that all such troops captured in battle would be turned over to state authorities, along with their officers, for prosecution under the laws governing servile insurrection. Slave states regarded that as a hanging offense, and while that mortal threat never became official practice, the Confederacy did refuse to exchange black prisoners, many of whom were either killed on the spot or delivered up to slave owners who claimed them as fugitives. Still, the two governments observed the cartel with occasional objections and exceptions until the summer of 1863, when the balance of prisoners swung abruptly and conspicuously to Washington's advantage. Only then did the cartel break down over a variety of disagreements, any or all of which may have offered mere pretexts for Edwin Stanton to retain a three-to-one superiority in prisoners that equaled an entire Confederate army.[34]

The first problem developed when Stanton decided not to recognize the thousands of paroles Confederates had extracted from Union prisoners in the field, on the argument that the rebels used such spontaneous releases as a convenient alternative to the burden of marching those prisoners back into permanent captivity. Army headquarters announced the repudiation of those paroles on the last day of the battle of Gettysburg, just as John Pemberton negotiated the surrender of his army, which Ulysses Grant paroled as a convenient alternative to transporting those prisoners upriver to Union prisons. A few days later Nathaniel Banks did the same with the Port Hudson garrison. More than thirty thousand Confederates had therefore been paroled under circumstances that Washington had just declared invalid, so further dispute arose when Confederate authorities declared the Vicksburg and Port Hudson prisoners exchanged, in part, against the field paroles of Union soldiers. Late in October Colonel Robert Ould, the Confederate commissioner for exchange, offered a complete swap of all prisoners, man for man, which seemed to abandon the issue of black soldiers, but the Union exchange commissioner suspected that Ould was merely skirting the issue semantically.[35]

The parole dispute seemed surmountable, unless Stanton's War Department was simply looking for some reason to cease prisoner exchanges. Cultural and political differences over the arming of black men, and especially runaway slaves, posed a less soluble problem, but Ben Butler questioned whether that provided the motive behind Stanton's reluctance. By the time President Lincoln left Washington for Gettysburg, conservative Democrats and Republicans were both beginning to wonder why an exchange could not be effected, so Butler attempted to negotiate directly with Colonel Ould. For a time it seemed they might find a way through the pettifoggery, but Butler made a personal enemy of his own government's commissioner of exchange, and his somewhat disingenuous communications ultimately failed to bridge the racial rift. Ould did seem intent on withholding at least those soldiers who were believed to be runaway slaves, so that became the nominal sticking point, and for some in the U.S. government that may have served as a righteous enough principle on which to suspend the cartel. The administration only adopted that position after gathering a vast harvest of Confederate prisoners, however, and subsequent events gave it the flavor of an excuse. The Union high command later revealed that it shunned exchanges to accelerate the attrition on Confederate manpower, but when long confinement produced frightening mortality and adverse public reaction, Union authorities consented to resume exchanges without the return of a single black captive.[36]

Existing prisons swelled with "fresh fish" through the second half of 1863, and several new ones sprang into existence. In July the first Confederate prisoners arrived at Point Lookout, Maryland, where the Potomac emptied into Chesapeake Bay, and by the end of November there were nearly 9,000 of them. At Camp Douglas, Illinois, the prison population grew from about four dozen on June 30 to nearly 6,000 on October 31. Between the end of May and the close of the year, Union prison facilities had swollen from ten sites housing 3,708 prisoners to twenty-two locations holding 35,549, and men who expected prompt exchange when they surrendered that summer instead had to while away as much as twenty months in confinement.[37]

Confederate prison keepers faced similar problems on a smaller scale, but with far more limited resources. As winter set in, some 13,000 Union prisoners huddled in Richmond warehouse prisons like Libby, or lived in tents on Belle Isle, in the James River. Their numbers challenged the vigilance of an inadequate provost guard, and the escape of nine dozen Union officers early in February threw the Confederate capital into consternation. Provisions for Lee's army often ran short because so much food was needed for the prisoners, who often went hungry themselves.[38] When it seemed obvious that the Lincoln government intended to end the cartel, the Confederate war department started looking for a more isolated prison site in a warmer and more productive climate. The choice fell on a tract of land in Sumter County, Georgia, near tiny Anderson Station, on the Southwestern Railroad. Local slave owners provided the labor to clear the site of its tall pines, the trunks of which formed a resinous stockade fence enclosing about sixteen acres. A few idle troops arrived there as guards and garrison for the new post, and by the middle of February the prison was nearing completion with an abundance of open space, plenty of slash for use as firewood, and a fine, clear stream running through it.[39]

The stockade still lacked gates and part of its walls when bedraggled Union prisoners started coming down from Virginia to fill it. The first contingent of 209 marched out of their Richmond quarters into bitterly cold air on the evening of February 17, filing into cattle cars between twin ranks of Virginia heavy-artillerymen. Their locomotive had "frozen up," according to one of the guards, so there they sat through the night. Finally the train rumbled off toward Petersburg, where they changed to other cars bound for Weldon, North Carolina. After a solid week on the rails and several changes of guards, the prisoners finally felt their train creak to a halt at Anderson Station on February 24. They crawled out into the warm Georgia air and hobbled half a mile on stiff legs to the still-incomplete stockade, but when they stepped inside they judged the place a vast improvement over the Richmond dungeons. A surgeon admitted two dozen of them to his tent hospital in a corner of the pen while the rest started collecting firewood and building materials in the enclosure, which some people were already beginning to call Andersonville.[40]

White Union prisoners would turn perfectly bitter toward a president they thought had abandoned them for the sake of their black comrades, and their families at home felt the same: the parents of a Vermont cavalryman who died at Andersonville engraved their anger at Lincoln's neglect on their boy's very tombstone.[41] The worst of that animosity would come later, but by the beginning of 1864 Lincoln already labored under widespread dissatisfaction, including the considerable opposition of conservative Democrats and the hostility of a sizable faction within his own party. He had been elected as a minority president, and a minority president he remained.

Governor Oliver Morton, of Indiana, warned Lincoln that "considerations of the most vital character demand that the War shall be substantially ended within the present year." Morton was alluding to the likelihood that Lincoln, and perhaps the Republican Party, might not hold the White House after the next quadrennial election, and perhaps not the Congress, either. For all the victories since the midpoint of 1863, opponents of the war gained gradual credibility in their cynical view of an endless, hopeless conflict. The worst disasters to Confederate arms wrought no damage to Southern will that Northern citizens could readily detect. Serial draft levies only illustrated that the more Confederate territory Union forces controlled, the more men it took to keep it, corroborating the relentless conservative warning that the war could only be won by complete domination and occupation of the seceded states. The war's most salient consequences to Northerners, besides the dead and wounded, were the erosion of civil liberties and a federal debt so enormous that it would bring "billion" into the American lexicon. When New York's Democrats convened in Albany before the 1863 elections, Governor Seymour had pressed the conciliatory policy once again, urging an offer for Southerners to return to their allegiance without the dreaded threat of emancipation. Use the summer's successes to demonstrate federal benevolence, he proposed, and he would only have advocated such a policy all the more fervently after the crushing triumph at Chattanooga. After all, asked a Detroit editor who liked Seymour's speech, were Union soldiers suffering and dying for reunion, or for abolition? Radical Republicans, who hoped to reduce the Southern states to conquered provinces until Congress could impose racial equality, saw the specter of a Democratic administration as the end of the fight for universal emancipation.[42]

Mr. Lincoln may have been thinking of Horatio Seymour's suggestion when, on December 9, he welcomed Congress back into session by announcing a proclamation for amnesty. It encompassed the magnanimity Seymour had championed for most Confederates except generals, political officials, and what another generation would call war criminals, but it hinged on acceptance of emancipation as Lincoln had declared it and as Congress might formalize it. He followed that proclamation for individual amnesty with a similar one for collective amnesty to the seceded states: if only one-tenth the number of men who voted in the 1860 election would take the oath of allegiance and elect a "republican form of government" for their respective states, he promised to recognize those governments and take the states under federal protection. He stopped short of restoring all the rights of statehood, but his offer portended it.[43]

Coming so soon after Braxton Bragg's astounding defeat at Chattanooga, Lincoln's announcement may well have reflected a belief that the Confederacy hovered on the brink of ruin, and needed only some avenue of escape for the common people to convince them to abandon the rebel leaders. It may also have been inspired by the recognition that he had but eleven months left before the next presidential election to convince enough American voters that his war actually did have a chance of restoring the Union. For a year and a half he had hoped for a loyal state government in Louisiana, with little success, but then a federal official from occupied Florida had come to Washington lobbying both Salmon Chase and Lincoln to give that state a chance. Only a week before Lincoln delivered his address to Congress, he had been advised by that Floridian, Judge Lyman Stickney, to allow every lawful voter "whose fidelity to your Administration and proclamation of freedom is unquestioned" to participate in an election for that southernmost state. Seven days later, Congress and the country heard the amnesty proposal.[44]

Conservatives could only appreciate that Lincoln's 10 percent solution to the reconstruction question lacked the punitive element — and apparently the determined egalitarianism — of the Radical Republican plan for territorial domination. Some immediately concluded that the president had deliberately designed the plan with such minimal requirements so he could establish puppet governments in enough seceded states to create the electoral votes he would need to decide the November election. If enough loyalists could not be found to match one-tenth of the 1860 voters, charged one Democratic editor, Lincoln's agents would probably count all the "soldiers, camp followers, and Negroes" to reach the magic number. To succeed, such a scheme would have required wonderful compliance in the occupied states, followed by cordial cooperation from Congress, but the editor's suspicion did not seem so far-fetched in light of the complex tricks Republicans had employed to throw other elections their way during this war.[45]

The reconstruction plan influenced the presidential selection even without any states taking advantage of it. The manner in which different people wanted to see the Southern states treated (assuming the Confederacy could be vanquished) determined which man they wanted in the White House to oversee the peace. A number of potential candidates lurked in the wings, some of whom wore generals' uniforms, but Lincoln's own secretary of the treasury stood in silent expectation as his main rival that winter. As early as January 6 Chase's unspoken desire for the nomination nearly interfered with the president's chances when New Hampshire — always the first to inaugurate the year's political contests — held its Republican state convention. Speaker of the House William Chandler entered the convention with a resolution to advocate Lincoln's renomination, but one of the state's more prominent Republicans tried to dissuade him for Chase's sake. Chandler ignored the overture and gave Lincoln the first coup in the party fight, but Chase remained an appealing choice among the more radical for many weeks thereafter. John C. Frémont, the 1856 nominee, hovered as another possible contender for that constituency. To the merriment of the Democratic press, Chase's ill-concealed ambition encouraged an editorial revolt among abolitionists that produced flurries of criticism and embarrassment for Lincoln. Chase pretended a

deliberate indifference to the nomination, but he made certain to dispar-
age the president in the course of his very denials, and through the winter
he kept up a voluminous correspondence with a young editor who was
writing an account of Chase's life that could, at any moment, have become
a campaign biography.[46]

While Radicals hoped for more than unadorned emancipation from
Lincoln, plenty of War Democrats and homespun conservatives who gave
themselves no political labels resented all the progressive ingredients of
the president's policies. A New York private betrayed the sentiments of
many when he complained that Lincoln and his supporters "have got the
Nigger on the brain rather to[o] much," adding "they want to make the
Nigger equal to us in everything Voteing and all." For that soldier and for
tens of thousands of other voters, many of whom articulated their reluctance less crudely, no one in the Republican Party exuded much appeal.
They would need someone more steeped in tradition — more devoted to
the social order and the rule of law.[47]

A suggestion of just such a person occurred to that portion of the
public early in February, when General McClellan's official report of his
tenure with the Army of the Potomac appeared from the Government
Printing Office as a bound executive document. His detractors judged it
nothing more than an unconvincing brief for the defense, but after its
appearance in the army, McClellan's numerous partisans thought they
detected a new surge of admiration for him, and indeed some previously
uncommitted soldiers began to show their deposed commander some respect. The official report amounted to something of a campaign biography itself, and Democrats supposed that Lincoln kept McClellan shelved
to reduce his presidential prospects. Were the general reinstated, his tremendous popularity would fill the Army of the Potomac with both recruits and confidence — or so charged a prominent New York Democrat
who believed that the president allowed McClellan to languish rather
than offend Radical Republicans and jeopardize his own nomination.[48]

If Lincoln could complete his reconstruction plan with one Confederate state, it might silence the critics within his own party, at least, besides winning laurels for the Union cause generally. The persistent Floridian Stickney had been peddling the latent loyalty of his adopted state
again through Lincoln's personal secretary, John Hay, and the president outlined his idea for Hay to go there to oversee the organization of a
"new" Florida. Commissioning the young man a major in the adjutant
general's department, Lincoln handed him a letter for Major General
Quincy Gillmore, commander of the Department of the South: leaping
completely around the chain of command once again, the president instructed Gillmore to cooperate with Hay's political efforts.[49]

Hay arrived at Hilton Head, South Carolina, on January 19, and he found General Gillmore already preparing to seize a portion of northern Florida. The country between the St. John's and the Suwanee rivers provided abundant timber and turpentine, Gillmore observed, besides the ever-valuable cotton, and the plantations there might disgorge some recruits from their slave population. Confederates in Georgia were also using the northern part of Florida as an immense commissary storehouse, where they pastured big herds of cattle that they drove north as needed; the quartermaster at Andersonville prison was shopping that region for beef cattle about then, as it happened. Gillmore also had information that Confederates were planning to rip up much of the Florida, Atlantic & Gulf Central Railroad west of Jacksonville, probably with the hope of depriving the Yankees of that line but also to salvage the rails and ties for a new road between Tallahassee and Thomasville, Georgia. When Hay added the president's wishes to the potential advantages of an occupation, Gillmore initially demurred with a litany of departmental shortages, fearing the undertaking would require him to control a larger portion of the state than the three or four counties he intended, but Hay gave him to understand that he would try to cultivate a loyal following in whatever fragment Gillmore could secure. Since he already had a foothold just inside the state, at Fernandina, Gillmore issued his own proclamation reiterating the president's, and had it posted in that town.[50]

From Hilton Head "Major" Hay, still dressed in his civilian tweeds and feeling as much like a secretary as a soldier, wrote to Nathaniel Banks for permission to scavenge for loyal Floridians in the Keys, which lay in the Department of the Gulf. Hay watched as General Gillmore organized a division for the invasion of Florida under Truman Seymour, the brigadier who had served inside Fort Sumter as a captain of artillery. General Meade, under whom Seymour had served, considered him "an excellent soldier, of good judgment, and courage," but Seymour had asked to be transferred from the Army of the Potomac to a warmer climate. Since then he had been with Gillmore in South Carolina, where he found things warm enough, and now he was going to Florida, where the heat may have been too much for him altogether.[51]

Seymour would leave with about six thousand men. Of his ten infantry regiments, five were white and five black. For reconnaissance he took Colonel Guy Henry's 40th Massachusetts infantry, extemporaneously mounted, and a few independent companies of cavalry from the same state, with three small batteries of artillery. He should get them all to sea before daylight on February 6, Gillmore adjured him, and arrive at the mouth of the St. John's by dawn the next morning, riding the high tide into the river to capture Jacksonville.[52]

John Hay, meanwhile, had steamed down on another vessel to Fernandina, where he consulted with Judge Stickney, had some broadsides posted with General Gillmore's proclamation, and opened his oath-of-allegiance business in a room over the town's principal store. To meet the 10 percent rule he needed only to collect 1,435 signatures in his oath book, but Florida had never been densely populated and the Confederate army had drained more men out of the state than had cast any variety of ballot in 1860. Many of the loyal people had decamped to safer climes, but Hay hoped to win over most of those who remained within reach of Union soldiers. That first day he enticed only a handful of Fernandina citizens, and those were men who had lived under occupation for two years, while one skeptic parsed the text of the oath so closely for recruiting trickery that Hay snapped the book shut in his face.[53]

Seymour landed his division at Jacksonville under only a few rounds of token resistance. The next day he sent out Colonel Henry with the cavalry to seize Baldwin, twenty miles to the west, where the Fernandina & Cedar Keys Railroad crossed the tracks of the Florida, Atlantic & Gulf line. Beyond that Gillmore did not seem inclined to go at first, except for a little dash to capture a train that was reported in the vicinity, and for some reconnaissance. Seymour reconnoitered with a peculiar enthusiasm, though. On February 10 he threw Henry's cavalry westward along the railroad again to Barber's plantation, on the south fork of the St. Mary's River, where a Confederate detachment waylaid the Yankee horsemen from their ambush on the west bank of the river. The rebels fled after inflicting a couple of dozen casualties. Seymour's mounted spearhead pressed on to sleep that night at Sanderson's Station, forty miles from Jacksonville, climbing back into the saddle the next morning and continuing toward Lake City, another twenty miles away. From Baldwin, with his main body, Seymour called on Gillmore for the 54th Massachusetts "without delay." Gillmore noted the insubordinate tone, but he sent most of the regiment.[54]

In Jacksonville, Hay continued his search for repentant rebels. At Gillmore's suggestion he tried the guardhouse, where nearly a hundred Confederate stragglers and a few of the more notorious secessionist citizens had been lodged, and there he made a great catch. Half the soldiers preferred taking the oath to going north to a prison camp and eventual exchange, and several of the civilians took that path out of confinement, especially after Hay promised that the Union garrison intended to stay in Jacksonville permanently. Five dozen signed his book that day, giving him nearly 5 percent of the names he would need for the "President's Tithe," as he called it. He found the population of Jacksonville exhausted and disillusioned by the war, and ready for peace at any price. Twenty miles away in Baldwin, Seymour reported precisely the opposite impression. The people showed no sign of giving up yet, he reported, and no slaves were flocking to the banner of freedom as they did when Union armies traversed other latitudes. In a rambling dispatch in which he lectured his department commander on strategy, Seymour asserted that Judge Stickney had evidently "misinformed" the administration about the loyal sentiments of the state, at least in the interior. He also complained that without a railroad engine or wagons he could hardly supply his men so deep in enemy territory, and he insinuated that the railroad was of too little use to warrant saving.[55]

Gillmore warned Seymour to bring his advance back to Sanderson's Station or the St. Mary's River if he met trouble, and then, with intelligence of ominous Confederate troop movements in Georgia, he ordered Seymour to pull everyone back even farther, to Baldwin. On February 13 Seymour drew his infantry and artillery back from Sanderson to Baldwin, coming into Jacksonville himself the next day to consult with Gillmore. In light of the poor response Seymour had encountered to both the amnesty proclamation and his recruiting among contrabands, Gillmore saw no advantage in further sallies into the interior. He only wanted to hold a broad fringe on the western bank of the St. John's River from Jacksonville to Palatka, he told Seymour, with infantry garrisons in and between those two towns and the cavalry roving where needed. With the river as a handy transportation corridor, he could resuscitate commerce there, convert the population to their national interests, and recruit for his existing black regiments and for a prospective new regiment of loyal whites. Useful though it might be to send raiders out to burn the Suwanee River railroad bridge, west of Lake City, Gillmore did not want him jeopardizing most of his infantry force on such a mission. As Seymour had mentioned in his discouraging evaluation of inland loyalties, a defeat on the battlefield would be disastrous to Gillmore's hopes for Florida, and for that very reason Gillmore gave him "positive orders not to get whipped."[56]

Then Gillmore returned to Hilton Head, leaving Seymour to command the contracted district. John Hay handed his local amnesty franchise over to a Massachusetts officer and sailed for St. Augustine, where he established another office and found nearly everyone ready to recognize the authority of the United States government. It was not the allegiance of Floridians that threatened the project with failure, but the sheer paucity of Floridians, and Gillmore may have been trying to build their numbers when he advertised that loyal refugees from the eastern part of the state might return in safety. For a little while that winter there seemed some hope that the president's 10 percent plan might really yield a nominal new government there.[57]

Unfortunately for those who hoped to win the state back, General Seymour appeared to succumb to the temptations of his first independent command within hours of his superior's departure. Gillmore might not have even reached Hilton Head yet when Seymour sent word to him, on February 16, that he intended to "move on." He neglected to say where he was going, but he did add another of those impertinent demands for reinforcements, as though Gillmore were nothing more than his adjutant general. The next day Seymour expanded on that sparse message, explaining that he aimed to penetrate some eighty miles into Florida, without supplies, to destroy the railroad near the Suwannee River, beyond Lake City, so the enemy could not disrupt the tracks east of that river. That violated Gillmore's instructions to stay where he was, and it flew in the face of Seymour's own earlier objection to wandering so far from his supply base without transportation, for he had still obtained no locomotive or wheeled transportation. It also conflicted with Seymour's expressed opinion of the railroad's insignificance, and, for a culminating contradiction, Seymour reversed his February 11 assessment of the civilian population, now insisting that the people were sick of the war and would readily come back into the Union with a little demonstration of benevolence. He admitted that Lieutenant General William Hardee was rumored to be in command at Lake City, which implied a significant Confederate force, but he asked Gillmore to divert attention from his ambitious raid by sending a naval demonstration up the Savannah River toward that city. That Gillmore would have to spend a day or two securing the assistance of the naval commander for that diversion seemed not to occur to Seymour, who noted in any case that his expedition would be under way by the time Gillmore even received the request.[58]

General Seymour appears to have undergone a sudden change of opinion on all those different topics in the two days between his last interview with Gillmore on February 14 and his first message of intent on February 16. Gillmore's abrupt absence may have introduced the principal ingredient in that transformation, in fact, for the ascension of a mere division commander like Seymour to control of a region as grandiosely exaggerated as the District of Florida could release the demons of megalomania in someone who carried that weakness. Certainly Seymour provided no evidence of any kind on which he might have justified such a complete turnabout, and his information about Hardee should have left him more reluctant than ever to range so far from his defensive perimeter.

Hardee had not come to Florida, though. The general in command at Lake City was Joseph Finegan, an Irishman who had spent the second half of his five decades in the northern part of the state. By the time Colonel Henry's mounted column first crossed the St. Mary's on February 10 and approached Lake City on February 11, Finegan pieced together a hybrid defense of fewer than five hundred infantry and barely a hundred cavalry from his own scattered troops and from the District of Middle Florida. These fragments could do little more than badger the advance of the Federals, but Henry fell back from Lake City without testing Confederate strength there, and soon thereafter reinforcements reached Finegan from Georgia that swelled his available force beyond two thousand men. The flat and featureless terrain between the St. Mary's and Lake City offered no advantages of position, so with his two thousand Finegan dug a line of entrenchments on the only defensible point that intervened, at Olustee Station on the railroad. To the north lay two-mile-wide Ocean Pond, while a cypress swamp protected most of his front and his right flank. General Beauregard detached a brigade from Charleston and sent it to Finegan under Alfred Colquitt, so by the middle of the month more than five thousand Georgians and Floridians manned the barricade at Olustee against any further incursion.[59]

Only when the Confederates had enjoyed enough time and respite to prepare themselves in this manner did Truman Seymour come to his decision to lunge forward with eight infantry regiments, his tiny cavalry brigade, and an assortment of field artillery to pursue what he had only recently considered a fool's mission. From Hilton Head an aggravated Quincy Gillmore composed a searing analysis of Seymour's contorted logic and blatant disregard for orders, implicitly commanding him not to lead the heart of his division into such danger for so little purpose, but by then it was already too late. That very day Seymour moved his headquarters from Jacksonville for Baldwin, where mountains of supplies had been accumulated on railcars drawn by horses and mules. The next morning he and his staff proceeded to Barber's plantation, where his infantry had been idling for nearly a week. His senior colonels — William Barton, Joseph Hawley, and the former Kansas jayhawker, James Montgomery — commanded three little brigades, and after breakfast on Saturday, February 20, they all formed in three columns and started west on or parallel to the main road from Jacksonville to Lake City.[60]

Henry's cavalry led the center column, followed by Hawley's 7th Connecticut and the 7th New Hampshire. The New Hampshire regiment labored under a burden of some three hundred new recruits, most of whom were substitutes, and they carried a measure of resentment as well, having just had half of their seven-shot Spencer rifles taken from them in order to better arm Henry's 40th Massachusetts. In return they had taken Springfield muskets, some of which had grown unserviceable from rust or missing parts in the hands of the mounted men. To the right of this column marched Barton's three New York regiments, and three black regiments took the left, under Montgomery. Three of the eight infantry units had little or no experience under fire. Barton's 115th New York had been captured at Harper's Ferry in its infancy, and had served mostly on garrison duty since, while only part of the 1st North Carolina (newly rechristened the 35th U.S. Colored Infantry) had ever so much as taken part in a field expedition. The 8th U.S. Colored, gathered that winter in Pennsylvania, had only left Philadelphia five weeks before, and hardly knew how to perform the evolutions of the company.[61]

The sandy road from Barber's plantation wound through miles of sparse pine barrens, the scent of which came all the stronger with so many of the yellow pine tapped for turpentine. Between the settlements at Barber's and Sanderson's they passed but few rustic cabins, largely dilapidated. At Sanderson's, about ten miles from Olustee, some of those turpentine farmers warned the Yankees that ten or fifteen thousand rebels waited for them at the next station, under General William Gardner. In fact Gardner, who had charge of Middle Florida, was on the scene with Finegan. He was senior to Finegan by date of commission, but he lacked any authority from Beauregard to interfere in Finegan's district and he was suffering from a recent operation on an old leg wound. The Olustee Confederates still numbered barely five thousand, though. Seymour had a few hundred more than that, but he had no means of confirming his informants' claims of Finegan's strength, and he had no reason to doubt that Finegan had dug in. He decided to keep going nonetheless, and he marched without flankers, never expecting to run into trouble until he reached Lake City, or at least Olustee.[62]

After Sanderson's Station the Yankees skirted the southern fringes of the great Okefenokee Swamp, and their course more often took them around sodden or inundated bogs thick with cypress and vines. The extemporized cavalry sauntered well beyond the column now, and the 7th Connecticut shuffled half a mile ahead of the rest of the infantry, but a couple of hours into the afternoon five Confederate videttes brought everyone up short about six miles beyond Sanderson Station. They traded a few shots with the Massachusetts horsemen, then reined to the rear in the evident hope of drawing Seymour's column into Finegan's ambush. Seymour, riding with the advance, instead halted his cavalry and allowed most of the men to dismount while they waited for the foot soldiers to come up.[63]

At first the general called on Colonel Hawley for two companies to spread out as skirmishers, and Hawley naturally took them from his own 7th Connecticut because it was the nearest. Like the 7th New Hampshire, the Connecticut regiment had been bolstered with recruits and substitutes the previous winter, and two of those men in Company D had soon grown bitterly antagonistic toward each other. They had scuffled a few weeks before the battle, and now the fortunes of war put them on the skirmish line together. Some men chose to settle their personal differences in battle, surreptitiously but permanently, although the customary targets of such vengeance wore shoulder straps: Hawley himself had observed, early in the war, that "both sides like to shoot officers" on the battlefield. At Olustee Private John Rowley used the opportunity to put a bullet through the head of his despised comrade, Jerome Dupoy, but in his haste for revenge he failed to make certain that no one was looking.[64]

Finegan, whose competence General Gardner grew to doubt during the next few hours, sent Colquitt forward to meet the enemy, and Colquitt arrayed a battlefront of Georgians across the railroad a couple of miles east of the Olustee barricade. Hawley sent up the rest of the 7th Connecticut, which was armed with more of those seven-shot Spencers, but the Georgians poured a hot fire into them and they soon started to fall back. Old fogies in army ordnance objected to repeating firearms because they encouraged the waste of ammunition, and the early fighting at Olustee seemed to prove their point. After driving Colquitt's line briefly with rapid fire, the Connecticut troops ran through their sixty-round-per-man issue in about forty-five minutes and started falling back, while Seymour hurried the 7th New Hampshire in to replace them. Hawley attended to it personally, running the New Hampshiremen in headlong in their marching column. As he neared the retiring line of his own regiment he ordered the Granite State colonel to deploy in line of battle on his eighth company, but in the noise and confusion, that instruction reached the companies inaccurately, and when Hawley tried to correct it the recruit-burdened regiment all but disintegrated. One company, and not one of those armed with Spencer repeaters, stood firm while the rest streamed to the rear.[65]

The only unit immediately available to fill the void was the perfectly raw 8th U.S. Colored. These recruits had practiced but little with their weapons, and one wing of the regiment had not yet loaded theirs when the regiment broke into a run to brace the left of the crumbling front. Colquitt swung his 6th Florida Battalion forward almost perpendicular to his line to enfilade this fresh Union reinforcement, and the black recruits came under as violent a fusillade as any veterans ever endured, but they filed awkwardly into position and held their ground for over an hour, until half their officers and 60 percent of the men had fallen dead and wounded. A particularly unlettered New Hampshire private attested that "thea fot desprat."[66]

Barton's brigade arrived, meanwhile, and Seymour threw those three New York regiments in on the right, extending that flank to Ocean Pond to foil a new menace there. Finegan pushed reinforcements forward to

both ends of Colquitt's front, and the fight persisted through the late afternoon, until thousands of empty cartridge tins littered the ground on
both sides. The belligerents fought at short range as some of the rebels
crept in close to make their smoothbores count, and a heavy proportion of
Seymour's casualties came from buckshot or round balls fired at low ve-
locity. After replenishing their own ammunition, the Southern infantry
on Colquitt's extreme left pushed the New Yorkers back from the pond far
enough to squeeze a pair of Georgia regiments between them and the
shore, and then those two regiments wheeled so they could rake the Yankees lengthwise, as the Floridians had done on the Union left. With both
flanks turned, the Union line could only fall back, and Seymour, finally
succumbing to the false rumors that he was badly outnumbered, brought
up his last reserves to cover a retreat.[67]

Those last reserves consisted of the two other black regiments. The
54th Massachusetts and the 1st North Carolina had held the rear, guarding the wagon train, but they threw off their knapsacks and Colonel
Montgomery prodded them into a double-quick. They arrived just as the
enemy overran a battery that had lost half its men and horses: the 54th
took the left of the line and the 1st North Carolina fell in on the right. Into
the evening they laid down a heavy fire, retiring slowly until most of the
wounded, stragglers, and fugitives had been started back toward Jacksonville, and then they turned to join the retreat behind a rear guard. Now
would have been the time for Finegan to slash at their column with what
cavalry he had, or board his infantry on the railcars that had delivered his
ammunition and reinforcements, but his pursuit ended two miles from
the battlefield. The shaken survivors of Seymour's folly escaped without
further punishment beyond that inflicted by their own terror: some of
Henry's Massachusetts men gave up their mounts to the wounded, and
they all dragged themselves twenty miles back to Barber's plantation,
sometimes throwing away everything they owned before finally collapsing in exhaustion and relief around midnight.[68]

Seymour retired all the way to Jacksonville, and enough of eastern
Florida remained open for Confederate commissaries to continue their
regular harvest of provisions and cattle herds. Much of that sustenance
started flowing into southwest Georgia for consumption by Union prisoners at Andersonville, where the captives from Olustee joined prisoners
taken in raids on other garrisons along the St. John's and the Atlantic
coast.[69]

The defeat only further dissuaded vacillating Floridians from renounc-
ing the Confederacy. For a few more weeks John Hay tried to distill some
loyal voters from the indigenous population, steaming as far south as the
pale-green waters of Key West, but by early March he gave it up for lack of

people. As Democrats had scoffed, he suggested that the residency requirements would have to be loosened quite a bit to secure even a tenth of the 1860 voters, despite the virtual unanimity of the few who did live within Union lines. A similar effort made more headway in Louisiana, where Union troops held the largest city in the Confederacy, and on February 22 a few thousand pledged loyalists there elected a new governor. A fragmentary constituency in Arkansas did the same, but in the end the 10 percent plan restored no seceded state to the Union. A Philadelphia resident who had spent much of the war in Mississippi insisted that most of the people there might take advantage of the president's amnesty if he extended it to everyone, without qualification. As he explained it to a neighbor, they did not wish to forsake their national, state, and local leaders, or see them suffer the traditional penalty for treason.[70]

Military authorities at Hilton Head tried to suppress the extent of the disaster at Olustee, holding back the disturbing report of the *New York Times* correspondent for nearly a week, but no one could ignore the transports full of wounded or the tales those men told. News of the Florida fiasco came on the heels of Democratic accusations that Hay's mission constituted another instance of the president's interference in military operations for partisan political advantage — that is, to spawn three more Republican electors from empty Florida districts for the November election. Administration friends disputed it, and denied any correspondence on the subject between the White House and General Gillmore, and in fact Seymour's impulsive thrust toward Lake City had not been part of the administration program, but Democrats weren't buying it. Senator Thomas Hendricks, a Unionist Democrat from Indiana, appealed for an investigation by the Joint Committee on the Conduct of the War. Chairman Ben Wade made the token inquiry for documents, but in the absence of a Democratic scapegoat and with the potential for Republican embarrassment, he and his Radical Republican majority lacked the curiosity to call so much as a single witness.[71]

The misadventure in Florida distracted public attention from the only other significant military activity in February, but perhaps it was just as well. William Sherman embarked on a railroad-wrecking spree in Mississippi that month, and he judged it a great success, but some of his men had developed a new habit of terrorizing the civilian population by hanging prisoners or beating them to death, and they managed to kill at least one woman. They had also destroyed crops and property liberally, and of that Sherman was aware. Such barbarity seemed unlikely to win back the Southern people, but Sherman had concluded that only the threat of complete devastation would end Southern resistance.[72]

Olustee also alleviated the Army of the Potomac's self-consciousness about repeated failures, if only temporarily. On their return from the Mine Run campaign, most of Meade's soldiers had scattered into huts that they or others had previously constructed. Some had to start anew, and in the First Corps the troops had already finished their winter quarters along the upper Rappahannock when orders came to move again, to Culpeper Court House. In the week of bitter cold surrounding Christmas, those reluctant transients huddled over minuscule fires fueled by what splinters of wood they could find, with firewood too distant for easy collection and the earth frozen too solid to sink tent pegs. By the first of the year everyone slept under a canvas roof in a tiny log, plank, or puncheon enclosure with two or more housemates — either two in a bunk, for warmth, or singly, to slow the exchange of lice. Four men might share a space seven feet wide and eleven feet long, with four feet of walls to the eave and a little standing room in the middle. In those muddy, damp, and smoky hovels they passed nearly every off-duty moment for as long as five months.[73]

No wonder, then, that they made the most of every opportunity for diversion. At Christmas one regiment in New York's Excelsior Brigade celebrated with such unwonted intensity that two other regiments had to fall in under arms to subdue them, and shots had to be fired before the revelers dispersed. Officers galore, and at least a few of the enlisted men, passed the time among the remaining civilian inhabitants, who came to tolerate their conquerors or even grew fond of them. After visiting private homes around his camp near Rappahannock Station, a Michigan soldier concluded that Virginia produced some lovely girls who liked Yankee soldiers "first rate," and similar opinions surfaced elsewhere in the sprawling camps. Tabor Parcher, a Vermonter in the Third Corps, camped at Brandy Station, reported to his wife that he knew three local girls who had gotten pregnant by Union soldiers, including the daughter of former congressman John Minor Botts. Botts's demonstrated Unionism had brought him occasional harassment by Confederate authorities, but while the Union army camped around Culpeper he enjoyed the protection of a permanent guard for his home. That appears to have been the undoing of his daughter, in fact, for Parcher claimed that the guard soon had her with child. "I wish it had been me," he flatly admitted, describing her as a pretty young woman of about twenty.[74]

Officers' wives swooped down on the sedentary army like a flight of starlings that winter, seasoning the camps once again with a taste of civilization and civility. They visited at the division hospitals, some of which had turned pine groves into garden spots, with log-cabin wards arranged around greens like a New England village and corduroy walkways bridg-

ing the mud. The presence of so many women naturally piqued the convivial instinct, and by late January — when the last chance of offensive
warfare had passed — the social season took wing. First came a disappointing affair in Joseph Carr's division of the Third Corps, at Brandy Station, where three hundred officers contended for the attention of no more
than thirty women. Apparently the decorations and refreshments in the
makeshift ballroom came up short, and a bevy of young women expected
from Washington did not appear. Worse yet, not enough of the women
who did come had been able to have their ball gowns sent down in time,
leaving perhaps too little décolletage for the hungry soldiers' eyes. One of
Mrs. Carr's close friends declined to attend for the very lack of a gown.
John Botts accepted his invitation, bringing one of the daughters whom
the invitation was surely meant to draw, but gossip along the fringes of
the dance floor failed to reveal whether she was the secret paramour
of the sentry at her front door. Her presence could not salvage the spirit of
the evening, in any case, and a young Maine major wrote it off as "a most
wretched time."[75]

The same could not be said for the Washington's Birthday ball sponsored by the Second Corps. The ballroom exemplified the resources General Warren and his officers invested in a deliberate attempt to over-
shadow the dismal Third Corps event. Lieutenant Roebling, Warren's
aide-de-camp and the son of the bridge builder, commandeered two local
sawmills for lumber and designed a hall ninety feet long by fifty feet wide,
with a spring floor to accommodate just enough buoyancy without collapsing. Alongside this he added a twenty-foot-wide saloon the length of
the building. The walls and floor alone consumed fifteen thousand board
feet of lumber, and details of soldiers spent weeks with axes and adzes,
hewing out hundreds of sills, joists, plates, and posts. The rafters, all "saplings" as long as twenty-nine feet, supported a canvas roof. To fill this ele-
gant space the better-connected officers invited every Washington celebrity and belle they could think of. Foremost among the latter was Kate
Chase Sprague, whose married name had not yet become habitual among
bachelors despite the presence of her husband. Vice President Hannibal
Hamlin arrived with his daughter, and Senator John P. Hale brought both
of his fetching girls. The unmarried corps commander contributed his
younger sister, Emily Warren, who traveled down from West Point especially for that evening. Governors, congressmen, and diplomats poured
into the ballroom bringing wives, daughters, and nieces, giving the men
their choice of two hundred or more dancing partners.[76]

General Warren asked Senator Hale's wife to the floor for the inaugural
dance, and a quartermaster from New Hampshire dashed in on the be-
witching Kate Sprague while his rivals stood gawking. Lieutenant Roeb-

ling became Emily Warren's captive from his first glimpse of her. One of the capital's better-known restaurateurs came down to cater the evening, and late that night the throng retired to Roebling's dining hall for a feast. General Meade, who had been fretting over whether he would be superseded as commander of the army, forgot about his standing with the War Department and squired Mrs. Hale to his table for the supper. The gaiety of that night infected even that sober and surly old soldier in the midst of his worst winter, and he wore an unaccustomed smile until after three o'clock in the morning.[77]

The success of the Second Corps ball inspired a host of imitations. Young Washington ladies, petulant over missing the grand event of the winter, shuttled down to Brandy Station by the carload for later, lesser versions, and for a brief and blissful interlude hoop skirts absolutely flooded the various encampments. The ring of the violin and the hollow clatter of prancing feet echoed through the bivouacs every night, moving a staff officer in the Sixth Corps to remark in the spring that he had attended so many informal dances and well-planned balls that he thought he might go into business as a dancing master after the war.[78]

Overshadowed as it was by the inexorable approach of another three seasons of slaughter, the gamboling persisted with a stubborn and deliberate ferocity, but as he shared the company of Mrs. Hale, General Meade was already plotting violence that would bring the brumal festivities to an abrupt end for many an unfortunate soldier. As he apologized to his wife for not bringing her down to the ball, he also explained to her the pressure he felt from Washington to liberate the prisoners at Richmond, at whatever risk, so the administration might be relieved of its increasingly embarrassing refusal to exchange prisoners. The War Department had already tried to recover the Richmond captives with a secret offer to sidestep its own administration's prohibition on exchanges, but the Confederates had not taken the bait. A Wisconsin senator had introduced a frivolous, frustrated resolution to raise a million-man army for ninety days to free Union prisoners, but his suggestion that fellow congressmen should adjourn their session and join that army did nothing to aid its passage. North and south, prison camps burgeoned out of control as Confederates deserted into the arms of the enemy to escape physical privations and as Federals fell victim to the battlefield blunders of both generals and politicians. Within a week of the first shuttle to Andersonville, captured Richmond newspapers had revealed the intention to transfer large numbers of Union prisoners from that city to Georgia, and policymakers whose stubbornness prolonged their imprisonment deemed it imperative to rescue them while they remained within reach.[79]

Meade's operation to deliver the Richmond prisoners would depart under the direction of Brigadier General Judson Kilpatrick, a reckless young blowhard with a comically large nose, a bigger ego, and a chronic flair for self-congratulatory falsehood. An aide on Meade's staff admitted that he could hardly cast his eyes on Kilpatrick without laughing out loud, and Kilpatrick's ridiculous image may have had as much to do with his pretentious carriage as with his intensely homely features. Planning for the raid began with a proposal from this Kilpatrick, who started yammering about it just before the newspapers reported on Union officers tunneling out of Libby; President Lincoln had called him to Washington to discuss his idea. Kilpatrick suggested taking his own cavalry division, heavily reinforced from two others, and striking south toward Richmond, wrecking railroads and distributing the president's amnesty proclamation along the way. He would detach a few hundred men to swing wide of Richmond to the west, destroying the James River Canal and crossing south of the river to cut the railroads below the Confederate capital. His main column would try to release their prisoners in Richmond, he added blithely, but if foiled in that attempt they could simply turn around and come back. He neglected to mention how the detachment below the James would escape, except to stipulate that it would "act as circumstances may require."[80]

Recalling the relative fruitlessness and considerable losses of George Stoneman's spring raid, and contending that those losses contributed to Lee's escape after Gettysburg, Meade's cavalry chief disapproved of the plan. The commanding general had been twice to Washington that week, though, and had absorbed the anxiety there over the prisoners: to him, they would pose the central target in such a scheme, rather than an incidental benefit to an otherwise unpromising incursion. After pondering the proposition for ten days, Meade authorized Kilpatrick to take nearly four thousand men — about half the army's cavalry — around Lee's right flank. Meade arranged for a sizable column of infantry and other cavalry to occupy Lee on his left, clearing a path for the raiders. Furloughs hung in abeyance, and commissaries doled out five days' rations.[81]

John Sedgwick marched the Sixth Corps through Culpeper Saturday morning, February 27, taking roads southwest toward Madison Court House. On Sunday parts of the Third Corps followed conspicuously, with bands blaring, and behind that came George Custer with some fifteen hundred cavalry. That threat had assuredly attracted the attention of the Confederates below the Rapidan, and after dark on Sunday Meade directed Kilpatrick to put his troops in motion. Before midnight Kilpatrick's advance guard of nearly five hundred men reached Ely's Ford, near Chancellorsville, and scooped up a dozen North Carolina cavalrymen on picket there before striking south. Between the river and the Virginia Central Railroad, the advance diverged from Kilpatrick's more direct route, and the two columns crossed the railroad ten miles apart.[82]

Colonel Ulric Dahlgren, the twenty-one-year-old son of Admiral John Dahlgren, led the smaller detachment. That fair and seemingly delicate young man kept to the saddle to compensate for a missing leg, lost in a skirmish during the pursuit of Lee after Gettysburg. In his pocket he carried the manuscript of an address he planned to read to his troops before they burst into Richmond, as well as lengthy instructions for the release of prisoners, the destruction of bridges, and the burning of arsenals and "anything else but hospitals." In his youth and zeal he had included in his address an admonition against allowing "the rebel leader Davis and his traitorous crew to escape." When it came to the orders to his men, he took his righteous wrath a step further, ordering that the city itself "must be destroyed and Jeff. Davis and cabinet killed." [83]

The murder of government officials doubtless exceeded any instructions Dahlgren had received, although one of Meade's staff joked that the raiders were meant to collect "all the rebel M.C.'s that are lying around loose." Dahlgren's principal duty was to slip into Richmond from below the James River, freeing the Union soldiers on Belle Isle and in the warehouse prisons along the river, while Kilpatrick pierced the works from north of the city. Dahlgren judiciously avoided a fight with rebels guarding the Virginia Central when he crossed it, but Kilpatrick charged an encampment at his crossing and alerted the enemy to his presence. Lee and the government in Richmond knew he was coming by Monday afternoon, February 29, and Kilpatrick learned of stronger resistance at the South Anna River railroad bridge near Ashland, about eighteen miles above the city. Dahlgren rode into the pitch-black night through drenching rain to reach the James River near Goochland Court House, twenty-five miles upstream from his goal. This was where he was supposed to cross the river, and the next day he nabbed a young former slave from the vicinity to show him the fords, but the river was running so high from the rain that even the horses could not wade it. Dahlgren turned furiously on his guide and, in a vicious moment consonant with the tenor of the murderous orders in his pocket, he ordered the boy hanged from a tree alongside the road.[84]

Thus Dahlgren approached Richmond from the left bank of the James, coming nowhere near Belle Isle and the majority of the prisoners. From Ashland, Kilpatrick pared off a few hundred men under a major to veer north and attack the South Anna bridge while he led the rest of the column south toward Richmond, and his skirmishers came closer to that citadel than McClellan's entire army had in 1862. The engineer colonel in charge of the city's defenses met them with heavy-artillerymen from the forts around the perimeter, sending them out on the Brook Turnpike as infantry. Like their Northern counterparts, those rebels had chosen heavy artillery for its reputation as a sedentary, comfortable, and relatively safe branch, but they had been in service for nearly two years and they maneuvered like veterans. Union troopers traded shells and then carbine fire with them, raising enough noise to carry into Jefferson Davis's office, but Kilpatrick found them too formidable for his suddenly sagging courage and after a few hours of skirmishing he put his command back in the saddle. He turned them for roads that ran between the Chickahominy and Pamunkey rivers toward the Peninsula, where Ben Butler's army waited to take them in. If only he had twice as many men, Kilpatrick wailed, he could have captured the enemy's capital, and his senior officers took up that apologetic chant.[85]

Late that afternoon, when Dahlgren heard the echo of Kilpatrick's fight on the Brook Turnpike, north of Richmond, he made a stab at the city from the west. The odds did not look good to the few hundred men behind him. A young Maine trooper felt, as they passed beyond the first line of fortifications, that he was entering a tomb, with the door slamming closed behind him. It was primarily local home-defense companies who met them, for the raid had brought out most of the resident militia, including many who remained secretly devoted to the Union: an attack on one's very home tends to blur political distinctions. Those inexperienced volunteers put up enough of a fight to discourage the young colonel, and as the drizzly dusk turned to darkness he gave up his mission and led his command north, in search of Kilpatrick.[86]

Kilpatrick had a good fifteen-mile start on Dahlgren, and with Confederate cavalry picking up his trail he showed no inclination to wait. The Yankees had kept to the saddle for as long as thirty-six hours at a time, stopping only to destroy property or fight, and they had begun to suffer from irresistible fatigue as well as from a veritable epidemic of hemorrhoids. They slept in the saddle now most of the time, but at every halt anyone who missed picket duty curled up for a nap. Three hundred North Carolina horsemen and artillerists came down from Hanover Court House and, in the midst of a midnight snowstorm, intruded on the bivouac of Kilpatrick's rear guard with close-range volleys of canister and a skirmish line, sending the exhausted Union column into headlong flight once more. In their haste they left their more seriously wounded comrades behind.[87]

From west of the city Dahlgren intended to lead his detachment in an arc north of it to rejoin the main body, but he set too brisk a pace in the darkness. Before long a gap divided the column, and riders who could hardly see their own horse's heads finally realized that they had lost the men ahead of them. The rain may have deadened the sounds that otherwise would have betrayed Dahlgren's route, and it had not yet turned to sleet, or the tracks might have shown the way. While Dahlgren wandered into the night with only a hundred men behind him, the balance of the column halted in confusion. The senior captain deduced the cause, and under him the greater part of the detachment found and fought its way through enemy territory, catching up with Kilpatrick among the old battlefields of the Peninsula, late on the afternoon of March 2.[88]

Dahlgren's part of the raid came to an end a few hours later. He had crossed both the Pamunkey and the Mattaponi rivers in a frantic hunt for a friendly haven, weaving aimlessly toward King and Queen Court House on another peninsula outside Union control. Near midnight of March 2 his weary little column wandered into an ambush consisting of a few dozen Confederate cavalrymen and a miscellaneous collection of local militia and home guards. Wedged between a fence on one side and a road cut through a hillside on the other, Dahlgren cantered out in front when he heard the challenge and drew his pistol, brazenly demanding the surrender of his antagonists. He was answered by a volley that knocked him out of the saddle, dead, and the rest of his followers bolted into the brush. The promiscuous mixture of soldiers and civilians came out to examine their kill, and a thirteen-year-old boy rifled Dahlgren's pockets — or so said his schoolteacher and militia captain, shortly afterward. In addition to some private plunder, the boy fished the hand-scribbled orders out of the dead man's coat. The motley command huddled there without campfires the rest of the night, but in the morning they found almost all the men who had followed Dahlgren to his doom, cowering in an adjacent field: only a few officers had made an attempt to escape, and they did not get far. In the daylight someone finally read the inflammatory prose of Dahlgren's intentions, and the incriminating documents went back to Richmond with the prisoners.[89]

There ensued a rancorous correspondence via flag of truce over the limits of civilized warfare. Union officials denied that any such orders had been issued or approved, while friends and relatives of Colonel Dahlgren charged that the papers had been fabricated by the Confederates themselves. Kilpatrick was the first to impugn the authenticity of the documents, in a letter that General Meade included with his response to General Lee's inquiry, but even Meade doubted Kilpatrick's veracity. Forgery seemed unlikely, given the semiliterate nature of the backwoods battalion that killed Dahlgren. Besides, an officer from the Bureau of Military Information who traveled with Kilpatrick conceded to General Patrick that the published version of the orders corresponded to the plans Dahlgren had outlined to him. The homicidal embellishments of the zealous young officer's manuscript orders may have had no genesis in official policy, despite the Dahlgren family's close friendship with President Lincoln, but that subtle difference sold with difficulty among Virginians who had barely avoided a mass prison breakout. That left the raid a political disaster as well as a military debacle, easily counteracting any fraternal sentiments the scattered amnesty proclamations might have resurrected.[90]

In Meade's army news of the raid's miscarriage met with a general dismissal, even among those who had earlier given great odds to its success. All had hoped to see the Richmond prisoners freed, but when the expedition came to naught the majority disparaged the effort as a fool's errand from the start. Such minor affairs exerted no impact on the war whether they succeeded or not, scoffed those who heard of Kilpatrick's retreat and Dahlgren's death. The same reaction met Seymour's rout in Florida. No matter what glorious prospects a foray might promise at the outset, its apparent relevance to the war as a whole always diminished in direct proportion to the degree of its failure.[91]

The army had more immediate and interesting gossip to digest, after all. Since December, General Meade had been pondering a comprehensive reorganization of the Army of the Potomac, and it started to come to fruition at the beginning of March. He sought to reduce the army from five corps to three, and to strew the fragments of the disbanded two throughout the other three. The concentration of divisions would theoretically leave the army more manageable, but corps commanders accurately surmised that Meade was looking for an excuse to remove certain unsatisfactory generals. As General Warren put it to Ben Wade's Joint Committee on the Conduct of the War, "It is more difficult to obtain five able and competent independent commanders than it is to obtain only three, and it is more difficult to manage five than three after you have got them." Chief among the unsatisfactory generals was William French, whose bibulous incompetence had figured so conspicuously in the failure of the grand opportunity at Mine Run, but there were others at corps and division level whom Meade wished to relieve. The consolidation idea occupied Meade more and more as February drew to a close, and word of it leaked into the ranks at the beginning of March, but the details remained secret and the execution hung fire for a few weeks, presumably in anticipation of congressional approval of new general officers.[92]

One general's appointment took precedence over all the others. Since George Washington, no American soldier had held a rank higher than major general except for Winfield Scott, who was elevated to the brevet, or honorary, rank of lieutenant general. Now, after congressional authorization, President Lincoln had appointed Ulysses Grant to the full grade of lieutenant general, passing him over the heads of all the other major generals who had preceded him. Grant's resounding victory at Chattanooga had brought him immense respect that made his victory at Vicksburg shine all the more brightly and completely overshadowed his early mistakes. His ascension to the command of all U.S. armies gave the best assurance Lincoln could offer of future competence and determination, and the three months of notorious failures that had followed Chattanooga had again left the president and his war badly in need of some good omen.

Grant's promotion also created abundant speculation in the Army of the Potomac, beginning with his introduction at one of Lincoln's fortnightly receptions. Halleck's nominal position as general in chief necessarily vanished when the third star appeared on Grant's shoulder straps, leaving army and department commanders to wonder whether Halleck might displace one of them. Halleck himself would have preferred returning to his old command in the Mississippi Valley, but most of those troops had been absorbed into Grant's Military Division of the Mississippi, which he left to his friend Sherman. Meade supposed that Grant might want someone he knew better in command of the Army of the Potomac, and Grant had served under Halleck early in the war. The unappreciated victor at Gettysburg was already under attack from generals he had removed or reprimanded, and from scheming subordinates who offered jaundiced testimony to Ben Wade's attentive Committee on the Conduct of the War. Meade's expectation that he would be relieved grew stronger when he learned that Grant came to Washington carrying the Western army's prejudice against Eastern commanders, whom they blamed for the serial defeats in Virginia.[93]

Observers in the army, in Washington, and in that part of the civilian population that did not subscribe to the concept of presidential infallibility agreed that Grant might do very well if he were allowed to act on his own judgment, without White House interference. Close and prolonged examination of the war's progress, or lack of progress, had convinced the more insightful that the administration had unwittingly foiled some of its more prominent generals in the past, and the same fate might well await Grant.[94]

In fact, the politicians may already have begun to undermine Grant before awarding him his promotion. In the middle of January he had sent Halleck a confidential proposal to abandon efforts against Richmond in favor of a campaign into North Carolina from Suffolk, Virginia, with New Bern and Wilmington as bases of supply. That would cut off provisions to Richmond, he argued, as well as allow Union armies to live off the land more and induce North Carolinians to desert. The terrain there offered fewer opportunities for defense, and the warmer weather would avoid months of financially and politically expensive inactivity each winter. It was a sensible and perfectly feasible plan, and rumors that it had been forwarded to Halleck probably initiated the rampant expectation in Burnside's Ninth Corps that he would return to the scenes of his former glory at New Bern. Inevitably such a strategy would have drawn Confederate attention and troops away from Washington, but the paranoia on Pennsylvania Avenue appears to have prevailed. Halleck objected on the grounds of the pet argument since Second Bull Run — that Lee's army, rather than Richmond, should serve as the target — so nothing ever came of that excellent idea, which closely resembled a combined effort McClellan and Burnside had pondered in 1862. The 1862 plan had not satisfied the executive branch, either: both Burnside and McClellan had instead been brought north to protect Washington, helping to drag the war into a third year. Now the fourth year was about to begin.[95]

9

God Alone Can Claim It

➔ "THE WAR LANGUISHES and makes no progress," complained George Templeton Strong as the spring of 1864 opened. "People naturally turn their thoughts, therefore, to questions of finance, taxation, and prices, and wonder whether gold will not soon be at 200 and butter a dollar a pound." With his extensive investments and cash reserves, Mr. Strong worried more about the price of gold and the effect of inflation on trade. Had butter risen to a dollar a pound he would simply have paid it. The majority of his countrymen might have thought twice about it, while the wives of most soldiers would not even have had to think: when prices rose, they simply bought — and ate — less. A New Hampshire woman feared that her husband's reenlistment bounty would disappear into thin air if she once started to spend it, but all the handwork that she could take in fell short of feeding her family. Prices were "abominably wicked," wailed a sergeant's wife from western New York, whose debts accumulated steadily while she prayed for Congress to approve an army pay raise that would translate to three of those overpriced pounds of butter per month.[1]

Everyone needed more money. The congressional session had hardly convened before congressmen started scheming for more travel expenses through "some hocus-pocus" to meet the soaring expenses in Washington. Railroad laborers in the West struck for higher wages, and strikes became so frequent in New York that the legislature tried to curb militant picketing. There was talk of giving soldiers raises, and eventually they would receive a pittance, but they would come last because they could be forced to wait.[2] Soldiers would often have been happy just to get the money the government already owed them, along with the stipends that their communities had promised, but the urgency of their families' plight troubled selectmen and senators far less after those recruits had bound themselves to service than before they had made that commitment. Wives therefore continued to borrow and beg for necessities that cost more than their husbands' pay would ever cover, if and when it did finally arrive. Army allotments brought a great deal of money into local economies — eight Maine regiments sent home over three hundred thousand dollars one payday that spring — but after that cash seeped into the towns it tended only to further reduce buying power there. Better-educated soldiers understood that paper currency fostered its own devaluation, as so many had predicted, and that the government would only print more of it to pay any additional compensation the troops might be awarded. Fiscal conservatives assumed that the administration was propelling the national economy toward inevitable collapse.[3]

To be sure, dreamers and drummers saw only opportunity in the midst of such turmoil, and Lincoln's old friend, former Illinois senator Orville Hickman Browning, returned to Washington to represent their entrepreneurial ilk before the Supreme Court, the War Department, Congress, and the president himself. Through the winter and spring Browning lobbied or litigated for railroads, contracting concerns, and individuals, once aggravating the harried Lincoln with his requests. Men of bold ambition sought fortunes in vast, risky enterprises, greasing palms and wheels at the state and national level to ease the passage of helpful legislation. The struggling little town of Kansas City glowed with candles in every window and echoed with the dull booming of blank cannon blasts one night in February, as residents welcomed the governor's signature on the Pacific Railroad bill. As the future terminus of a transcontinental railroad, the residents supposed, their town had found its financial deliverance. Then, a few weeks later, President Lincoln stipulated that the Union Pacific Railroad contractors would bring the eastern terminus of their line to the Missouri River at a point opposite Council Bluffs, Iowa, where he owned a quarter section of land. The road would bypass Kansas and Missouri altogether, reducing Kansas City to its former squalor while the luck of executive whim gratified a different band of promoters and convinced them of their own innate wisdom.[4]

Equally assured of their own wisdom were the well-heeled intellectuals who, like George Strong, had founded the Sanitary Commission at the outbreak of the war. Their organization purportedly existed to sustain the Union soldier's health and comfort with gifts of supplies and services, although soldiers complained that officers and Sanitary Commission agents consumed most of the food and delicacies. The senior members of the commission, meanwhile, appeared to cherish the more constant and sincere aim of sustaining and promoting their own political and social goals of nationalism, centralization, and liberal reform. It was no coincidence that most of the founders of the commission were also founding members of New York City's elite Union League Club. This was the genteel New Yorker's version of the Union League, the principal functions of which (as in most Union League spinoffs) were to provide members with a politically homogenous place of leisure and to produce blizzards of unconditional Unionist propaganda. Though nominally dedicated to the care of the troops, those who headed the Sanitary Commission generally turned a condescending eye on those who wore the nation's uniform, and on the masses from which they came. They maintained a largely practical concern for the soldier, as though he were primarily an expensive government resource whose greatest worth was concentrated in his trigger finger. Strong, who served as treasurer of the Sanitary Commission and as a member of its standing committee, alluded to the Northern soldiers quartered in the U.S. Capitol during the war's early weeks as "mudsills," and he betrayed more concern for the safety of the building's frescoes than for the welfare of its temporary tenants. In advocating that the government draft all the soldiers it needed, the Sanitary Commission's general secretary, Frederick Law Olmsted, defended a provision for substitutes because, as he argued without apology, a citizen's value to his community was measured by his income.[5]

Relying on the charitable inclinations and labor of tens of thousands of women, such gentry absorbed and controlled as much of the country's civilian relief work as they could, swallowing the Women's Central Relief Association and reducing it to a purely ancillary organization. The men obtained official sanction through their powerful connections, solicited significant contributions from their more affluent circle, and apparently luxuriated in the power and righteousness of their organization, but as usual it was the women who did all the work. Perhaps in frustration at their relegation to the political background, those women had begun to take more direct action by the autumn of 1863, and it was largely through their efforts that the first massive Sanitary Commission fundraising fair opened in Chicago that October. Partisan advocates of the war gathered the fair in a smothering embrace, shamelessly exploiting the deep compassion of the female organizers for political capital. The fiercely Republican *Chicago Tribune* extolled that city's fair as a public demonstration "against the poltroons and traitors who were enemies to the government, and opposed to the war." The Chicago event raised so much money that other branches of the commission held their own fairs in Cincinnati, Boston, Washington, and Brooklyn, until finally the women of New York City undertook one of their own.[6]

Ellen Strong, wife of the commission treasurer, became treasurer of the New York event. "Heaven help her!" responded her husband, but he gave his wife a great deal of advice and practical support for what would become a cumbrous enterprise. The male members of the commission took but little part in the planning of what everyone called the Metropolitan Fair, save to oppose the preferences of the women and to interfere with any decisions they made. The location posed the first point of contention, with the women leaning toward a big building at the corner of Broadway and Sixth Avenue while the men wanted the city to construct a new building on the Palace Garden lots west of Union Square, between Fourteenth and Fifteenth streets. The new building could later serve the 22nd New York State Militia as an armory, claimed its adherents, and Strong detected the scent of graft in one man's intercession with City Hall, but the Palace Garden site soon prevailed.[7]

By late January the fair dominated the lives of those involved in it. Committees and subcommittees of women scoured the country for material to fill the exhibition halls, appealing to the wealthy for cash, to artists for paintings and statuary, and to tradesmen for the latest innovations in their fields. The fabulously wealthy Alexander T. Stewart opened the donations with a check for ten thousand dollars, and so much money came in daily thereafter that the nation buzzed with suspicion of corruption within the Sanitary Commission. Firemen proudly delivered examples of their equipment; Albert Bierstadt brought some of his oil paintings of the Rockies, and a roomful of Indian artifacts, along with some Cayugas and Onondagas from upstate to pose in the regalia of their woodland brethren. The ladies paid a thousand dollars to a farmer beyond the Finger Lakes for the biggest ox New York City would ever see — a three-thousand-pound, pure-white Durham known as the Pride of Livingston County. Rush Hawkins, the wealthy colonel of a disbanded Zouave regiment, collected historic flags and cannon at the behest of the women's committee. The daughter of one of George Washington's cabinet officers accumulated a diverse array of antiques and pure junk for the fair's "curiosity shop," including Javanese idols, silver ostensibly used by Martin Luther, and candlesticks carved out of a cactus during the Mexican War. First the women, and later the men, spent weeks debating whether raising money by raffle came close enough to gambling to taint the reputation of the participants. Then the women began worrying about the amount of space the Fourteenth Street building had left them, which they considered inadequate by three-quarters. Strong saw the mayor about it, and another set of buildings was begun on Seventeenth Street, north of Union Square, but the delay contributed materially to a postponement of the fair by a week.[8]

The men (the "he-committee," in Squire Strong's journal) were supposed to act as auxiliary advisors to the women, as Strong did by consulting with the mayor, police, and fire department to assure the order and safety of the several sites, but by the time of the grand opening the women had been shouldered into the wings entirely. The mayor called a city holiday on Monday, April 4, and the male version of the fair committee took over from there, bending the opening ceremonies to their own purposes. The state's militia commander called out his first division, amounting to ten thousand nattily dressed patriots who had all found sufficient cause why they should not join the armies in the field. Twenty-seven marching bands mingled among them in a parade that began at the intersection of Broadway and Forty-third Street, where the head of the procession gathered beneath the flags of three black regiments raised under Union League auspices. A great banner of blue silk dominated the corner, bearing a gold-lettered demand for "Unconditional Loyalty." Robert Anderson, the ailing hero of Fort Sumter, occupied a place of honor with his family as the assemblage passed down Broadway toward Union Square that afternoon. The ticket booths opened at 6:00 to a crowd modest in numbers if not in resources, for the men's committee had imposed substantial entrance fees of two dollars a head for that first night, reduced to a dollar for the next day. Supplemental charges applied for admission to several exhibits, and the five-dollar "season ticket" could not be used for opening night. The families of workmen who had to worry about financing substitutes for the draft would find the event a little too pricey, and that may have increased the appeal of the fees to a committee of men who associated such plebian throngs with the mobs of the previous July.[9]

The inaugural ceremony began at 8:00 P.M., after the Great Hall had finally filled with a richly caparisoned crowd of what Mr. Strong considered the city's "best people." Bands blared "Hail Columbia" and "The Star-Spangled Banner," after which came the requisite lengthy prayer. Major General John Dix then took the stage and delivered his thanks to the ladies whose energy had driven the fair, but no lady stood by to offer the reply, for the women who had created it all had been left out of the program altogether. The male committee had offered the women one final humiliation by appointing one of their own men to come forward and make a response "on behalf of the ladies," leaving many of the women stifling tears of rage from the audience. In consolation the offended women were allowed a presence two nights later at the smaller opening ceremony for the Union Square building, where the men's committee afforded them "a little box of a room."[10]

Unvarnished nationalism permeated the sprawling exhibitions. To the left of the entrance sat Colonel Hawkins's Arms and Trophies Department, with a hundred-pounder Parrott rifle in the center of the room and an assortment of smaller guns and mortars surrounding it, including prizes of war taken from Burgoyne at Saratoga, from Santa Anna in Mexico, and more recently from the Confederates; conspicuous among the last was an English Whitworth rifle seized at Fort Pulaski, to remind visitors of Britain's arms sales to the rebels. Overhead hung the flag that had shaded George Washington as he took the oath of office as president, as well as thirty banners from the War of 1812 and the first U.S. flag to cross the border into Mexico. More than ten dozen regimental flags from the present war encircled the room, but Hawkins had also made certain to find twice as many captured Confederate banners to demonstrate the power of Union arms. One dubious and perverse trophy consisted of a drinking cup fashioned from a human skull: it was confidently identified as the cranium of a Union soldier that had been crafted into ghoulish utility by a fiendish Confederate, whom spectators were invited to loathe. The *New York Times* inadvertently impugned the accuracy of such labeling when it noted that the trophy room also displayed the original Bowie knife, with which Jim Bowie had allegedly killed a Nashville doctor in 1838 — two years after Bowie himself had been killed at the Alamo.[11]

In the center of the Great Hall between Fourteenth and Fifteenth stood the Floral Department — a thirty-foot-wide corral of tall supporting columns festooned in evergreen boughs, roses, lilies, violets, and wreaths of immortelle. Around the steeple of this impromptu cathedral hung the names of Union victories, emblazoned in reflective letters that sparkled as though aflame in the gaslights. On the western edge of the Palace Garden site stood the hundred-foot-long picture gallery, dominated by Emanuel Leutze's painting of Washington crossing the Delaware. The Hudson River school figured prominently, with Thomas Cole's *Catskill Creek* and Frederick Church's *Niagara* as the best examples. John Frederick Kensett, who supervised the fair's Department of Fine Arts, brought a taste of White Mountain art from northern New Hampshire with *Morning in the Valley of the Conways*. Eastman Johnson, called upon for a submission, provided *Working for the Fair*. The two-story restaurant on the Sixth Avenue end of the building seated a thousand people at a time and offered a menu modified from Delmonico's. Turtle soup could be had for fifty cents, and mock turtle soup for thirty-five. A porterhouse steak went for half a dollar, or for a dollar with truffles. Scrambled eggs were two bits, or four with ham.[12]

The Union Square buildings housed the International Department and a reconstructed colonial environment called the Knickerbocker Kitchen. The Music Department was housed there, too, offering an endless succession of concerts, and each evening these had to compete with a dramatic performance. Union Park itself supplied a playground for the amusement of children whose parents attended the fair: at one time or another during the three weeks that the fair endured, those children inevitably included a neighborhood five-year-old named Theodore Roosevelt and the toddler Edith Jones, who would become Edith Wharton. The livestock pens occupied Fifteenth Street, near Seventh Avenue, and there grazed the Pride of Livingston County, now fattened to an astounding thirty-six hundred pounds.[13]

The doors opened again at eleven on the morning after the inaugural. Thirteen thousand people traipsed through the exhibits on that first full day of operation, and by the time the drum corps sounded closing time, at ten that evening, the fair had produced forty-three thousand dollars in ticket sales alone. It was an especially affluent crowd that milled about the complex at a total admission of two dollars for every department. "We know that the poor, the honest and industrious poor, have not been there," observed the New York Times a week later. The editor certainly supported the fair and the patriotic inculcation that it strove to accomplish, and he attributed the costly tickets to an effort to reduce overcrowding, rather than to snobbery and greed, but he still lobbied for a reduction in price for at least a specific day. He hinted broadly at the underlying purposes of the fair, alluding to the need to "keep alive the flame of popular sympathy with the material and moral well-being of the National army," and he admitted that it was all well and good that the Sanitary Commission ministered to the needs of the sick and wounded soldiers, but it had also "done invaluable service as an agent for the recruitment of the army." Finally he added the economic argument with an element of unintended irony: most of the poor (unlike many of the rich, as he refrained from adding) had friends and relatives in arms, and they might be happy to tour the fair at a reduced rate, so they could buy some souvenir, "however small in intrinsic value."[14]

The administrators of the fair — that is to say the men's committee — did offer a reduced admission on April 7, having already realized seventy-three thousand dollars in gate receipts. The fair was supposed to raise even more money from the sale of goods than from entry fees, insisted the mandarins in charge, and they complained that the bargain rate of fifty cents led to such throngs that no one was able to buy anything. They insinuated that the sheer press of people impeded would-be buyers, but the actual source of their objection plainly originated with an influx of impoverished citizens from the lower precincts, as attested by the arrest of two suspected female pickpockets on that day, without specific charges. Thereafter the one-dollar admission was reinstated, along with the surcharge of a quarter for each of four "special" exhibits.[15]

One competition at the fair attracted interest out of all proportion to its potential as a source of revenue. Tiffany and Co. had donated two elaborate swords to the fair, one richly decorated in a naval motif and the other with engravings of artillery, cavalry, and infantry. They were intended as gifts to the officer in each branch whom fair attendants selected as the most deserving, and the cost for the privilege of casting a ballot was fixed at one dollar. For all their profligate spending, early visitors paid but little attention to the swords, but they preferred General Grant by a slim margin. On the day of the reduced prices, however, General McClellan surged ahead — thereby suggesting that the unpalatability of that day's crowd included political repugnance as well as pecuniary disadvantage, for the common members of the Sanitary Commission and the Union League cringed at any association with Democrats. To the irritation of New York City's Republican loyalists, including the *Times* editor and the commission squirearchy, McClellan held his lead for weeks. The *Times* did what it could in the way of subtle influence, publishing daily installments of McClellan's voluminous report with snide commentary, but two weeks into the fair McClellan still led Grant by 5,560 to 5,207.[16]

Then participants began casting more than one ballot apiece — the fair committee perhaps having changed the rules, for key officials of the Sanitary Commission had no intention of allowing McClellan to win. First one man paid $50 to give Grant that many votes, and in the final days the atmosphere of an auction prevailed. Grant pulled ahead by a few dozen on April 19, but the next day $12,824 went into the ballot box, to put McClellan back on top. The *Times* noted that James Gordon Bennett, editor of the rival *New York Herald,* put down $300 on McClellan, but the *Times* story failed to say how much its own management contributed on Grant's behalf. As the fair wound down, the *Times* invited everyone to join in the fray, professing that it mattered little who won the sword because the money would all go to aid the soldier, but to those who sponsored the fair it mattered very much indeed who won. Fair organizers actively conspired to deprive McClellan of even so harmless a measure of his popularity, withholding one massive contribution until the very last. In the final moments, August Belmont and another prominent Democrat entered $1,000 to expand McClellan's majority, but after they had departed, the contest was carried by one last infusion from the Union League, amounting to more than $17,000. Of the people who took part in the selection, a small majority, at least, appeared to favor McClellan — or so Treasurer Strong thought before the committee counted up all the donations — but General Grant won the prize with a final tally of $30,291 to $14,509.[17]

The Sanitary Commission made more than a million dollars from the

Metropolitan Fair, but the intense strain it laid on the women prompted their husbands to welcome the closing of the buildings. Two women who had given themselves over to the planning and operation of the fair died toward its conclusion: one of them collapsed at the fair itself, and both became martyrs to the cause of the soldiers. Mr. Strong, who fretted endlessly that his Ellen would break down under the long hours and severe stress of the fair, nevertheless doubted that the two ladies had perished from their own overwork, and they earned no accolades at the close of the festivities. The collaborative *Times* closed its coverage of the event with a few short paragraphs complimenting the men who had kept it orderly and efficient, without a word of the ladies who had brought it to fruition.[18]

During the first week of the Metropolitan Fair, Mr. Strong relished another partisan spectacle performed in the U.S. House of Representatives when an Ohio Democrat dared to reveal the extent of his frustration with the war. Alexander Long had come into Congress with a wave of Democrats after the election of 1862, and he vigorously opposed Republican war measures, including immediate emancipation, paper money, arbitrary arrests, and conscription. President Lincoln, who had begun issuing new draft calls every few weeks, called for another two hundred thousand men on March 14, with a deadline of April 15, and that may have been what impelled Long to a lengthy and bitterly critical speech in the House chamber.[19]

Long reminded his fellow members of the sharp decline in liberty since 1861, illustrating it with allusions to the deterioration of the Roman republic and the similarities between Lincoln's democracy and more recent imperial dictatorships. The loss of such freedom angered him all the more because he rejected the right of the central government to force a reluctant state to remain in the Union, and in support of that position he cited Congressman Abraham Lincoln's own 1846 House speech in defense of the right of revolution. In addition to that compounded objection, he claimed that the war was a failure. He characterized Lincoln's amnesty proclamation as "silly, absurd, and insulting" to the South. From a recent column in the administration-friendly *Washington Chronicle* he read that the Florida expedition had collapsed in failure, Sherman's expedition into Mississippi had "not been a success," and Charleston remained defiant while Lee's army still held the line of the Rapidan. As the war entered its fourth year, the rebels showed more vigor than they had ever been thought to possess. The struggle merely bore out the conservatives' warning from 1861, he insisted: the only alternatives were Southern independence or the "complete subjugation and extermination" of the Southern people. Of the two choices, he declared, he preferred the former.[20]

Republicans interrupted him repeatedly after that, but Speaker of the

House Schuyler Colfax knew a partisan opportunity when he saw one. Handing the gavel to fellow Republican Edward Rollins, of New Hampshire, Colfax stepped down to the floor and offered a resolution to expel Long from the House. The revelation that Long would prefer to recognize the independence of the Confederacy amounted to treason, Colfax maintained, and Long should be cast from their midst as a secessionist just as Jesse Bright had been removed from the Senate twenty-six months before. The charge in Senator Bright's case had been just as speciously exaggerated, Bright having done nothing worse than write a letter of personal recommendation addressed to Jefferson Davis as president of the Confederacy, before hostilities began. Republicans still ruled Congress, however, and they jumped on the proposal as a chance to expand their House majority by another seat — besides intimidating any other members from voicing their readiness to make peace.[21]

Benjamin Harris, another conservative Democrat from southern Maryland, chose that very moment to announce his own disaffection with the war. He shouted that he was a "radical peace man," inviting the Republicans to try expelling him, too. "I am for peace by the recognition of the South, for the recognition of the southern confederacy." House Republicans eagerly took him up on that dare, and the focus turned squarely on Harris for the rest of the afternoon on April 8. Late that day the vote was called, and a 60 percent majority supported the motion to expel Harris. House rules required two-thirds, however, so Republican Robert Schenck (who had beaten Clement Vallandigham, with the help of some strategic gerrymandering) promptly entered a new resolution to censure the gentleman from Maryland. That required only a simple majority, which the Republicans knew they already had, so they allowed no discussion and forced an immediate call for that vote. Shy of being lumped with peace men by the dominant party, some Democrats joined in the compromise for censure, and an overwhelming number of representatives agreed that for the opinions Harris had expressed he was "an unworthy member of the House." With that, they all went to dinner, including the unrepentant Harris.[22]

Congressman Long's fate remained to be decided, and Harris's self-sacrifice gave him time to muster some evidence for his defense. Speaker Colfax had based his resolution on the grounds that Long's remarks tended, and were designed, "to encourage the rebellion and the enemies of the Union." In the parlance of 1864 that was close enough to an accusation of treason, and Long lit upon Colfax's phrasing to highlight the Speaker's hypocrisy and illuminate his partisan motivation. He demonstrated that Colfax had been present in the House chamber on January 27, 1863, when Republican congressman Martin Conway voiced a similar

opinion. Conway, a Radical from Kansas, shared the abolitionist viewpoint that the slave states should be allowed to go their own way so the remaining states might be freed of the stink of slavery, and on that January
day of the previous year he had offered a resolution to cease all hostilities
and begin negotiations for recognition. The attempt to coerce the South
back into the Union was a failure, Conway had said, just as Long insisted
it was. Long pointed out that Colfax had made no attempt to have Conway
expelled for the same language that he now found so treasonable, but
then Conway had belonged to Colfax's own party and, furthermore, had
been a member of Colfax's Radical faction. The Speaker, whose career
would end in disgrace less than a decade later, acted so obviously from
impure motives that even the Republican *New York Times* chastised him,
remarking that his "zeal outruns his discretion." If every member were to
be expelled when his language encouraged the rebellion, suggested the
Times, the House would be left without a quorum.[23]

The entire House, or at least the Republican members, may have felt a
rare chill of embarrassment over so patently partisan an approach to the
suppression of free speech in the halls of democracy. Spectators jammed
the galleries to see the showdown, but no vote was ever called on Long's
expulsion. Instead, on the day after the *Times* criticism appeared, the resolution was amended to the same censure that had been imposed on Harris. Such a stricture carried no political impact save to suggest the unpopularity of Long's opinion, but in the face of public disgust with Republican
bullying, most Democrats found spine enough to defend their compatri-
ot's First Amendment rights. The amended resolution passed by a much
narrower margin, but right or wrong, the majority party was bound to
have something it could call a victory.[24]

Two months before he delivered his congressional screed, Mr. Long received a letter from a constituent who feared that Lincoln's rapid-fire calls
for troops portended an entirely new army, with which the president
hoped to invade Mexico. While French imperial ambitions in that country
did trouble the president greatly, the demands of a war at home prevented
foreign intercessions at the moment, even into a neighboring country.
Lincoln periodically encouraged military activity in Texas to blunt any
Napoleonic designs north of the Rio Grande, but Nathaniel Banks had
found it impossible to secure more than a few coastal lodgments. His September attempt to land a force at Sabine Pass, for operations against
Galveston and Houston, foundered under Confederate shore batteries,
and in his final weeks as general in chief Henry Halleck again suggested
the Red River as a logical route for the invasion of Texas. As always,
Halleck declined to issue explicit orders for which he might be held re-

sponsible, instead suggesting that Banks would be better off to consult with the commanders of adjoining districts, and with Admiral David Dixon Porter, of the navy's Mississippi Squadron.[25]

Banks did that. Frederick Steele, commanding Union forces in Arkansas, offered tentative support, and William Sherman, in Mississippi, seemed anxious to collaborate once he had completed his February raid in that state. Sherman had lived in central Louisiana just before the war, and cautioned Banks that he would be unable, in any case, to use the Red River as his supply line until it rose to twelve feet at Alexandria, which would not be until at least March.[26]

Banks, who had made political capital of his humble beginnings in Massachusetts textile mills, then wrote directly to President Lincoln on the subject of the enormous stockpiles of cotton that reportedly lay up the Red River. Louisiana, east Texas, and south Arkansas contained over two hundred thousand bales, he claimed, or a hundred million pounds, at a time when Northern manufacturers were crying for such raw materials. The blockade had driven the price extremely high, and Banks proposed buying that cotton from Confederate officers or loyal owners at pennies per pound. Not only would that start the looms working again in New England, and inject millions of dollars into a federal treasury that hovered on the brink of insolvency, but it would deprive the Confederate government of the value of that cotton and demoralize the officers who participated in the sale, besides slowing the considerable drain of gold to Confederate recipients through private speculation in cotton. These were evidently compelling arguments for pursuing an expedition up the Red River, on top of the additional territory an operation in that direction would bring under the control of Union forces and the population that could be mined for the amnesty proclamation.[27]

So thoroughly had cotton come to symbolize the corruption pervading this war that official correspondence bore little trace of Banks's reasoning, and when Henry Halleck took the stand before inquiring congressmen a year later he declined to repeat any of the "verbal statements" he heard uttered about the object of a campaign along the Red River. Banks's letter about buying Confederate cotton is not preserved in Lincoln's papers, and no reply to it survives. From the time Banks embarked on the expedition, he employed the same vague phrase to explain his authority, repeating that he acted on orders "from the Government," without specifying whether those orders came from army headquarters, the War Department, or the White House. Banks himself may have wondered where the actual directive originated, considering Henry Halleck's stubborn refusal to issue direct, positive orders. Alluding to previous dispatches in which he had conveyed the president's wishes for a campaign into Texas, Halleck

RED RIVER CAMPAIGN

told Banks that "it certainly was not intended that any of your movements should be delayed to await instructions from here." Halleck then approached Ulysses Grant about the plan (characterizing it as one devised by Banks and Sherman) with another indistinct proposal to send Sherman up the Red River with Banks; Halleck may have been the source of rumors that Sherman had initiated the idea, after it ended in disaster. James Wilson, a former staff officer of Grant's who was on duty in Washington, tried to divine the source of orders for the Red River expedition and failed, meeting with nothing but denials from every official authority. In describing a tendency toward executive interference in military operations, Wilson mentioned Lincoln's instructions to Gillmore about Florida, which had evidently left Halleck grumbling about orders issued over his head: that seemed to arouse Wilson's suspicions of a concept that one of Mr. Lincoln's more deceptive successors would cultivate as "plausible deniability."[28]

Banks secured a promise from Sherman to send ten thousand men up the Red River, escorted by Admiral Porter's fleet, for a rendezvous at Alexandria on March 17. From Little Rock, General Steele agreed (later than Banks would have liked) that he would march toward Shreveport with seven thousand men. Banks himself intended to collect seventeen thousand troops of the Thirteenth and Nineteenth corps under William Franklin in the vicinity of Brashear City and march them overland to Alexandria; from there he would pick up Sherman's troops on the Red River and start upstream for Shreveport. Franklin's troops had not yet concentrated by the time Banks expected him to start, on March 10, and Franklin knew he could never cover the 175 miles to Alexandria in a week, even in fair weather. As it was, a torrential rainstorm set in on March 9 and inundated the roads, so Franklin never budged until March 13, when the mud coagulated a little. The sun bore down fiercely after that. His attenuated columns wound through some of the richest land in the South, where columned mansions built by the proceeds of sugar production dozed in the shade of live oaks, and field hands by the hundred stopped to watch the Yankees pass. Franklin's advance detachment did not reach Alexandria until March 25, with the infantry columns following over the next couple of days in clouds of their own dust. Steele had only started from Little Rock by then with a portion of his force, struggling over primitive roads of his own with broken-down horses pulling most of his wagons.[29]

Porter's gunboats and Sherman's troops, led by Andrew Jackson Smith, reached the mouth of the Red River on March 11. Three days later they combined their resources to capture Fort DeRussy, downstream from Alexandria, with Smith circling behind the fort by land while Porter attacked it from the river. Transports carried the first of Smith's men into

Alexandria a full twenty-four hours ahead of the March 17 rendezvous Banks had proposed. The entire ten thousand men and the naval flotilla lay waiting there by March 18, as the first of Banks's cavalry came in on the road from Brashear City.[30]

When Banks and his entourage arrived at Alexandria they found the decks of the naval vessels filled with cotton bales. Caravans of wagons were coming in from the countryside between files of sailors and Marines, loaded down with more cotton that they had confiscated, along with thousands of dollars worth of other plunder, from horses and hunting dogs to paintings and furnishings. Porter himself allegedly appropriated some of the property his men brought in, including an entire stable of horses that he housed aboard one of his boats. Frank Howe, formerly the New York City agent for New Hampshire soldiers and now a special agent to the Treasury Department, likened Porter's looters to the mobs that had ransacked Lower Manhattan in July. Howe reported that Porter's sailors had burned thousands of bales of cotton, as well — fifty thousand, he guessed, while the Louisiana loyalists he met in Alexandria feared it was a hundred thousand. That much cotton would represent a loss to the treasury in the hundreds of millions of dollars. Secretary Chase relayed the complaint to Gideon Welles; Porter admitted collecting all the cotton he could as a prize of war — for which he would normally pocket a generous share of prize money — but he blamed the Confederates for burning the rest of it before he could seize it. Whoever had burned the cotton, Howe grieved especially for the example Porter's seizure would set for Confederates upstream: if rebel officers saw no chance to sell Union agents the cotton they controlled, they would probably destroy whatever they had as Banks advanced up the river, and all the economic advantages Banks had anticipated from the curious endeavor would go up in smoke.[31]

Also lost, as Howe understandably neglected to mention, was every opportunity for skimming the enormous profits of that trade, which he and an eager shoal of government-appointed speculators had depended upon. A few days later more cotton buyers came up the river and presented themselves to General Banks, handing him special authorization from the president himself, who directed the army and navy to give them all the transportation they needed to bring their goods downriver. Banks considered his suggestion of buying cotton from the enemy inappropriate enough to vigorously deny, later, that those men had any such authority.[32]

Alexandria, once a moderately prosperous little city of something over a thousand people, lay just below the falls of the Red River. Only at the highest stages of the river, in the spring, could deep-draft vessels negotiate those rapids. The river did rise on schedule, but not nearly to its normal level, and then it started falling again in the final days of March, just as Admiral Porter started working the shallowest-bottomed vessels of his flotilla over the falls. Pulling the eight-gun, seven-hundred-ton *Eastport* over without crushing its hull on the rocks required sixty hours of steady work. The dropping river forced Banks to establish a supply depot at Alexandria, so provisions could be unloaded from transports at the downstream side and reloaded on others above the falls. The depot in turn demanded a substantial guard, and Banks decided to leave a whole division there.[33]

President Lincoln elevated General Grant to the rank of lieutenant general and placed him in command of all Union armies on March 10, just as Porter's first gunboats had turned their prows toward the Red River, and Grant did not put much value in the expedition, or in Banks. He had not wanted Sherman's troops to join the venture in the first place, and now he wanted them back where they belonged so that, as soon as the weather permitted, Sherman could advance on the Army of Tennessee, now directly under Joe Johnston's command in north Georgia. At the same time, Grant was planning for Banks to move his troops against Mobile, to keep the rebels there from reinforcing Johnston even if Banks were unable to capture that port. This was all part of Grant's plan to strike the enemy simultaneously in as many places as possible, to prevent Southern forces from repelling attacks with troops stripped from unthreatened locations. Five days into his new command Grant wrote Banks with this idea, and instructed him to send back Sherman's troops if it looked as though he would need them "ten to fifteen days more time than Gen. Sherman gave his troops to be absent from their command," even if he had to give up the campaign to Shreveport. Setting the return date by Sherman's letter to Banks, in which he promised the ten thousand troops for "thirty days from the time they actually enter Red River," Grant was allowing Banks a deadline of about April 10, with a potential extension of "ten to fifteen days." That letter reached Banks on March 27, and while he might well have been confused about the exact date, he could not have misunderstood that he would not be able to keep General Smith's divisions for another full month.[34]

Banks ordered A. J. Smith fifteen miles upstream ahead of the transports, which might never have made it over the falls under the weight of the troops, and he sent Franklin after him on March 28. The Marine Brigade, a hermaphrodite fleet of soldiers who sailed on their own boats, could neither surmount the falls in their heavy vessels nor march by land, since they had no wheeled transportation, and at the request of the new commander of the Army of the Tennessee, Banks ordered them back up the Mississippi. That cost him three thousand rifles as well as any good will he might have engendered among the riverside residents of the state, for on their way down the Red River those volunteer marines stopped at every settlement to steal anything that could be moved. The division Banks left at Alexandria deprived the marching column of another three thousand men, so his army started up the river with about twenty-one thousand, plus a couple of thousand black engineers (which was to say laborers and train guards) from what Banks called his Corps d'Afrique, who came up from New Orleans to join the expedition. Banks himself lingered in Alexandria to oversee the president's project of collecting loyal voters, and to prepare for the local election of delegates to a constitutional convention.[35]

A raging thunderstorm greeted the troops as they crawled out of their tents that first day of the upstream march. Their path followed Bayou Rapides, a narrow channel running south of the Red River and parallel to it. The next day the most remarkable sight, for those who had traversed the flatlands from Brashear City and Opelousas, consisted of marching over an actual prominence in the topography — probably Henderson's Hill, at the upper reaches of the bayou. A lieutenant from Portland, Maine, who had served more than two years in southern Louisiana and along the coast of Texas, swore that this was the first hill he had seen since leaving home. As the column proceeded northwest, up the river, the terrain began to undulate a little more, while thick forests of tall pines must have helped make the Maine boys feel a little more at home. Lush cotton plantations lay between the hills, and the scent of smoke foretold the fate of cotton gins and warehouses at the hands of Confederates who fled before Banks's host.[36]

By April 2 General Franklin, who commanded the advance during Banks's absence, had concentrated the infantry at Natchitoches, nearly a hundred miles from Shreveport by narrow, roundabout roads. The town had never been blighted by the presence of either army, and as Franklin's weary columns rattled down its faintly foreign streets, the soldiers found the place unusually clean and well kept; trudging through on the lookout for a place to camp, they caught an occasional glimpse of nuns from Sacred Heart Convent. An old signpost pointed due west, indicating the first of the circuitous roads that would cross the Texas border fifty miles farther on. The town had grown alongside the Red River early in the eighteenth century, but then the river cut a new course four miles north, at Grand Ecore, leaving stately Natchitoches on a broad bayou known as the Cane River. Grand Ecore became the port for Natchitoches, developing into a modest little accessory community. General Banks arrived at Grand Ecore on April 3, and after a slow and difficult passage up the unseasonably low river, his flotilla gathered there, under towering bluffs. Nearby lay an old frontier outpost known as Fort Salubrity, where Brevet Second

Lieutenant Ulysses Grant had spent more than a year, nearly two decades before; from those bluffs he had begun his epistolary courtship of Miss Julia Dent.[37]

Banks seemed happy to rely on the professionals around him for the conduct of military operations. For his chief of staff he had chosen a West Point prodigy, Charles Stone, who would probably have shone much more brightly in this war but for the malicious chicanery of Radical Republicans in Congress; Stone could boast expertise in strategy, logistics, organization, arms, and other details, and his advice on those subjects would have been especially valuable to Banks. William Franklin had graduated first in his class at West Point, and Banks left him in control of the troops even after he reached Grand Ecore. Franklin kept the infantry encamped near Natchitoches, but he cast the cavalry far out on the road to Shreveport, to chase retreating Confederates.[38]

Those Confederates marched under Major General Richard Taylor, the son of the twelfth president and a Louisiana sugar planter himself. Taylor had been backing away from the Yankees since Porter and Smith seized Fort DeRussy, taking with him the two divisions that had held central Louisiana. The entire command amounted only to four brigades of infantry and dismounted cavalry from Texas, three Louisiana regiments, and more field artillery than he could conveniently support, amounting altogether to perhaps six or seven thousand men. He had lost nearly six hundred men to the advancing enemy, including his only regiment of mounted cavalry, which A. J. Smith's troops had captured with every man fast asleep. Spies inside Union lines provided Taylor with most of the information cavalry would have brought him, though, and he accurately gauged the combined corps of Banks and Smith at about twenty-four thousand; he even knew that Smith's divisions would be withdrawn before long. The lack of reinforcements from his own department commander, Kirby Smith, so angered Taylor by the time he abandoned Natchitoches that he regretted not having fought Banks near Alexandria, even if it had meant the destruction of his little army. They had given up "the fairest and richest portion of the Confederacy" without a fight, he fumed, and that paradise had now been reduced to a wasteland. The only response from department headquarters, in Shreveport, was the arrival of a couple of small Texas cavalry regiments and the promise of more.[39]

The only General Lee in the Union army commanded Banks's cavalry. Thirty-year-old Albert Lee had begun life as a lawyer, with no military training before the war, but he commanded all the cavalry in the Department of the Gulf and he had led the advance for Franklin all the way from Alexandria. Four little brigades composed his three-thousand-man division, most of which consisted of infantrymen who had been perched on horseback, and some of them had taken to the saddle only recently. With this improvised command Lee rode out nearly two dozen miles from Natchitoches to an intersection called Crump's Corners. There he ran against Confederate infantry that seemed at least a match for his entire division, although he drove it from the field in a nasty skirmish, but from prisoners or local inhabitants he learned that the enemy waited in even greater strength ten miles farther on, at Pleasant Hill. With that Lee drew back to Natchitoches, where the army and the fleet prepared for the final push toward Shreveport.[40]

The narrow, primitive road that curved west and north to Shreveport traversed vast stands of pine. The village of Pleasant Hill squatted around a crossroads on a plateau some thirty miles from Natchitoches, with the town of Mansfield nearly twenty miles beyond that. Two easy days' march past Mansfield lay Shreveport — a "very dilapidated" town of some four thousand souls that served as the improvised capital of Confederate Louisiana, the headquarters of Kirby Smith's Trans-Mississippi Department, and the reputed goal of Banks's campaign.[41]

Why Banks sought to capture Shreveport, and what he intended to accomplish on his last and most infamous trek as the commander of an army, later became a matter of serious question, and Banks himself seemed unable to answer that question satisfactorily. When the general came before the Joint Committee on the Conduct of the War, nearly a year later, Chairman Ben Wade asked him to explain it, and Banks claimed that he aimed for Shreveport because "the government" believed it was the quickest way into Texas. Driven by the perennial considerations of international diplomacy and by pressure from Texas Unionists, would-be Northern colonists, and speculating scoundrels, President Lincoln had long since asked for a military presence in the Lone Star State, and the previous summer he had notified Halleck that he wanted the flag reestablished there as soon as possible. Halleck had been badgering Banks for a major Texas operation ever since, apparently even after the president's anxiety about the state had dissipated. It was the general in chief's defensively nebulous persistence, and his hinting about the Red River route, that moved Banks to offer this initial response to Wade's question.[42]

After mentioning the Texas plan, Banks confused Wade's committee by testifying, next, that he expected to capture Shreveport and turn it over to General Steele, who was to come down from Arkansas with ten thousand men. That contradicted Banks's assertion about a campaign into Texas, and he only roused more curiosity when he argued that Steele could not have held Shreveport once it was taken. After the Army of the Gulf turned back downriver, he contended, Steele would have been surrounded, cut off, and captured. His correspondence at the time nonetheless bristled with confidence in the value and accessibility of Shreveport as a target, because as he advanced on that city he expected to keep pushing the enemy into Texas. His testimony to the contrary appears to have been influenced by instructions that he received later, from Grant: not until the middle of April would Grant's March 31 letter reach Banks, on his retreat to Alexandria, ordering him to abandon all movements toward Texas and leave Steele to garrison Shreveport, if indeed he had taken it.[43]

His outdated understanding of the wishes from Washington would explain why Banks still considered Shreveport a viable objective early in April. At least by March 27, though, he knew that Grant wanted the borrowed divisions under A. J. Smith returned to Sherman within about three weeks. If Banks expected Shreveport to be only the first prize in an extended plunge into Texas, he must have either planned on keeping Smith's troops against Grant's wishes or expected to pick up Steele's men to continue the pursuit, for he had already declared his own available field force too small to undertake an invasion along that route without substantial help from other departments. One year after he began the final advance from Natchitoches, he submitted a final report in which he implied that the thirty-day limit was too unreasonable to be taken seriously.[44]

Had Banks given up the campaign the moment he received Grant's first message, all would have been well. He might have taken his army to Mobile and greatly aided Sherman's planned movement toward Atlanta. He might even have satisfied the outer limits of Grant's schedule if he had turned back from Grand Ecore, although the river level would already have impeded the return of Porter's fleet. Instead Banks opted to press on to Shreveport, four or five hard days' march away if he were not resisted with much vigor, and by then it would be time for Smith's Westerners to start back for their own army.

The brief sojourn in Natchitoches gave the Yankees the most pleasant interlude in their campaign, and especially the foot soldiers of Banks's Thirteenth and Nineteenth corps, who had tramped nearly three hundred miles in the past three weeks. There had they found the diversion of a slightly alien civilization steeped in its French and Spanish heritage, and a rare taste of relaxation in a community unspoiled by war. The adjutant of the 29th Maine, John Gould, prowled the churches and played the organ in one, only to be displaced by a carousing captain from a Western regiment who pounded away for the amusement of his equally inebriated companions. Thrilled by a mail that brought six long-delayed letters from his wife, Sergeant William Winters of the 67th Indiana strolled the streets deep in nostalgic reveries of his boyhood home; in the cemetery he picked a few myrtle blossoms to send his wife with his answering letter.[45]

Two nights after his arrival at Grand Ecore, Banks directed Franklin to move out the next morning, April 6, and force the Confederates to fight a battle outside the defenses of Shreveport. The main body of the enemy waited at Mansfield, according to the intelligence Banks had gathered. He urged Franklin to move quickly, and to keep his divisions close enough together that they could support one another. Adjutant Gould, Sergeant Winters, and nearly twenty thousand other Union soldiers (including at least one stocky young woman passing herself off as a man) broke camp and packed their knapsacks. Richard Taylor waited for them a little over fifty miles away, with fewer than half as many muskets as Banks was sending forward.[46]

Lee's cavalry took the lead again that Wednesday morning, followed by two little divisions from the Thirteenth Corps under Thomas Ransom. Behind that came the only division of Franklin's Nineteenth Corps still with the expedition, commanded by William Emory. A. J. Smith waited until Thursday to leave Grand Ecore with his two divisions of the Sixteenth Corps, leaving behind his fragment of the Seventeenth Corps to protect the flotilla. Reenlistment furloughs left all those commands operating with reduced complements: the majority of some of the old regiments had not yet returned, and the remnants had been consolidated with other units for the duration of the campaign.[47]

The head of the column covered about half the distance to Pleasant Hill on Wednesday, with the cavalry camping ten miles ahead of that. The next morning the wagon trains bogged down in heavy rains, and Franklin finally put Ransom's trains behind the Nineteenth Corps, so the infantry moved a little more easily, but he insisted that Lee keep his own wagons right behind his cavalry. That left Lee all the more nervous as he felt his way into hostile territory, and on Thursday afternoon he met the first resistance in the form of Thomas Green's Texas cavalry. Green posted his men afoot on high, wooded ground about three miles beyond Pleasant Hill, with one of those rare open fields in front of his position. Lee dismounted one brigade and they skirmished with Green for over an hour. The Confederates charged them once, but when Lee brought up another brigade they started falling back toward Mansfield, trying to slow the Union advance until more reinforcements could reach Taylor. Into the steady rain that evening Lee pushed Green's Texans as far as Carroll's Mill, on Bayou San Patricio, ten miles past Pleasant Hill. There the stream and a Confederate battery stopped him for the night.[48]

Like Henry V at Agincourt and his own father at Buena Vista, Richard Taylor took the best ground he could find and prepared to fight against overwhelming odds. He made one last appeal for reinforcements to his own General Smith, at Shreveport, and Smith sent five thousand infantry from Arkansas and Missouri under Thomas Churchill, but those troops would still be on the road when the next battle ended. To contest Banks's army Taylor would have only the two divisions of infantry he had brought all the way up the river, and Green's cavalry. He settled the infantry in a couple of miles below Mansfield at Sabine Crossroads, where the routes from the Sabine River and Bayou Pierre converged on the stage road to Mansfield, arranging his battlefront on the woodline with open fields of fire before him. Green's horsemen continued to harass Lee's advance through the morning of April 8, and after breaking off their last delaying action they galloped back to cover Taylor's flanks.[49]

From information he had gleaned along the way, General Franklin doubted that the rebels would show any fight that day, and he remarked at least once on April 8 that they would see no battle there: he expected the enemy to make his stand closer to Shreveport. That conviction probably accounts for Franklin's negligence in pushing Lee's cavalry and the supporting infantry six or seven miles ahead of the rest of the army, while at the same time he again refused Lee's request to send his trains behind the infantry, with the rest of the wagons. Lee, Franklin insisted, must keep his wagon train closed up behind his cavalry. The army already stretched over that single, narrow road some twenty miles, from Lee's vanguard to the last of the infantry's wagons: Franklin worried that the straggling wagons would impede the march of his infantry if they were not prodded ahead, or that they would interfere with the progress of his own trains if allowed to drop behind with them.[50]

Lee stumbled into Taylor with two of his diminutive cavalry brigades, a brigade of infantry supports from the Thirteenth Corps, and a pair of artillery batteries. Banks's chief of staff, General Stone, rode along to lend the advance a measure of experience. At noon the cavalry strolled into the broad field, finding a Southern skirmish line stretched across a low hill. Lee halted on the edge of the woods and sent back for another brigade of infantry.[51]

The most precious commodity during the entire campaign may have been water, and thirsty troops had to choose from the least brackish bayous they could find. The brigadier commanding the infantry already with Lee noted that his men had not been able to fill their canteens since the previous night, when they were ordered up to aid the cavalry, and after marching most of the night and day they were "literally worn out." Franklin ordered another Thirteenth Corps brigade up to relieve them, and General Ransom went with it. With those reinforcements Lee started toward the imposing hill only to see the Confederates retire without a fight, but when he crested the hill himself he saw why: there sat Taylor's whole Confederate army — in front of him, off to his left, and far around his right flank — just waiting. Lee stopped again as General Banks came pelting up from the distant rear, and Lee told him they had better fall back if reinforcements could not be brought up quickly, for he generously estimated the enemy presence at fifteen to twenty thousand men. In fact Taylor fielded a lot fewer than ten thousand, but even with his borrowed infantry Lee might have mustered only four thousand.[52]

Banks evidently meant to accept the challenge anyway, and told Lee to stay where he was while he called on reinforcements from Franklin. Two hours later those reinforcements had not come, but neither had Taylor's, and with the afternoon waning Taylor could evidently no longer resist crushing the appealing morsel of the Union army in front of him. Outnumbered as he was, he could have asked for no greater gift than to have Banks move against him in such piecemeal fashion. Union watches read somewhere between 3:30 and 4:00 P.M. when Taylor opened fire and sent his line forward.[53]

Several times in quick succession the rebels charged. Union musketry and canister "mowed them down in files," and drove them back at first, said a Bay State artilleryman, but within half an hour the thin crescent of the Union front began to bend backward, and then the ends crumbled.[54] Lee ordered his artillery to limber up and get out, but so many horses had been killed in one battery that three guns remained where they were on the hillside. Most of the Union infantry turned and ran, but General Ransom galloped back and forth to rally a new line at the brink of the woods, until a bullet buried itself in his knee. Lee took over from there, holding the fringe of the clearing long enough for Ransom and many of the troops to escape, but then that front collapsed, too. Still shouldering its way up past the wagon train that all but blocked the road, the other division of the Thirteenth Corps met the fugitives surging toward the rear and, unable to push his men any farther, their commander deployed one brigade on either side of the road in the thick woods and struggled toward the clearing in line of battle. He reached there before Taylor's jubilant troops did, and stalled them for a time, but with barely a thousand-man front he soon found his own flanks giving way. Within an hour this division, too, turned and fled. Men, mounted and on foot, crashed through the woods with the crackling sound of wildfire. Retreat became panic as the last Union resistance fell silent, and the Confederates came swarming through the forest, rushing past abandoned guns and caissons until they fell upon Lee's wagon train. This booty may have distracted enough of the lean and hungry Texans who dominated Taylor's command to weaken his momentum, for another mile farther on the leading division of the Nineteenth Corps spread across an obscure intersection, five thousand strong, and stopped the onslaught cold, sparring into the evening until the moon rose.[55]

With no potable water nearby, Banks pulled all his troops back to Pleasant Hill that night and ordered Smith's two divisions of the Sixteenth Corps up to join him. The shattered Thirteenth Corps staggered back toward Natchitoches. That gave Banks about twelve thousand infantry against an enemy whose strength he imagined to be much greater, and the magnitude of the defeat at Sabine Crossroads seemed to corroborate the illusion of Confederate superiority. One corps commander and four brigadiers had been wounded in just three divisions, and one of the brigadiers was missing. Numerous regimental commanders, field officers, and staff officers were dead, or prisoners. Some two thousand men had been lost of six thousand engaged. Cyrus Stockwell, a private in the 77th Illinois, had stood alongside the guns in the center of Lee's first line; a half-spent bullet flattened itself against his hipbone, and he limped to the rear with the rebels right behind him, but he saw one neighbor dead on the field and he calculated that half the regiment had been either killed or taken prisoner. The 67th Indiana had occupied the other side of that same battery, and when the line broke it was every man for himself, so no one noticed what happened to Sergeant Winters. He may have turned to fire a last defiant round, or fallen behind his younger and more fleet-footed comrades, because no one who knew him saw him fall, and no list of prisoners ever carried his name. His letter bearing the myrtle blossoms arrived in due time at his wife's door, and that was the last she or anyone else ever heard from him.[56]

The next day, unaware that Banks had been reinforced by Smith, Taylor battered at the invaders again. He, too, had lost heavily in the clearing and in the final twilight clash with the Nineteenth Corps, but General Churchill had come up with those five thousand Missouri and Arkansas riflemen, bringing Southern ranks nearer to parity with their opponents. After a few hours' rest Taylor reconnoitered the Union line at Pleasant Hill and arranged for Churchill to make a sweeping flank attack on the Federals' vulnerable left, advising him to rely on the bayonet as a means of saving time and ammunition, which were both running short. Taylor waved his own two divisions forward on the left as Churchill started on the right, and Taylor's men broke through a weak point in Banks's line, throwing the Union right into confusion. Churchill failed by a furlong or two to envelop the enemy's left, instead swinging his own right flank in front of their line and inviting a counterattack by Smith's Sixteenth Corps that saved the day for Banks. Churchill had to fall back abruptly to keep his division from disintegrating, and that endangered Taylor's wing. The entire Confederate line finally faded into the woods, badly bloodied, to the echoes of Union cheering.[57]

Although he had won the day, Banks decided to continue his retreat all the way to Grand Ecore. In the darkness he left his dead and wounded on the field and slunk away, giving Taylor's assault all the earmarks of victory, and Kirby Smith ordered most of Taylor's troops back toward Shreveport so they could repel Steele's stalled corps in lower Arkansas. He left Taylor with a skeleton force of cavalry and infantry, but even with only a portion of his original command Taylor managed to send the amphibious invasion scurrying back down the river in relative panic. So ardently did he tail the foe that Banks saw at least five Confederate soldiers for every one Taylor could call upon. Porter, with the Seventeenth Corps troops, had tried to steam up parallel to Banks's advance, but an artillery attack from the bank of the river and news of the repulse at Sabine Crossroads sent the waterborne detachment scrambling back for Grand Ecore in the low water of a narrow, serpentine channel.[58]

Eventually the whole expedition turned back for Alexandria, lingering there for a fortnight to dam the river so Porter's gunboats and transports could lumber back over the falls. Taylor harassed them all the way, sinking trapped and crippled boats and trying, with the few men he had left, to block the escape of the larger but more demoralized army. To an older Wisconsin recruit with the flotilla, the enemy seemed like a cur snapping at their heels and barking every time the prey turned its back, but he allowed that "they done some tall barking."[59] Naval officers considered even the normally courageous Banks "awfully scared," and he seemed to have lost any respect that he may once have commanded among his own troops. A New York captain beating upstream to rejoin his regiment at Alexandria passed bodies floating in the river, and when he arrived he heard that the Confederates pressed them in such strength that they seemed "very audacious." Not until May 20 did the first of the Union infantry reach the Mississippi River, a month or more after Sherman was supposed to have his troops back and weeks after Grant's grand strategy required Banks to begin operations against Mobile.[60]

So it was all for nothing. Steele ultimately retreated back to Little Rock and the Red River remained Confederate, albeit with nearly every waterfront community ransacked and ruined and most of the valuable cotton destroyed. Banks, who met the successor to his command on his way back to New Orleans, could only congratulate himself that Kirby Smith had not let Richard Taylor retain enough troops to capture his army whole. The Northern public saw no subtle blessings of that sort, reflecting only that a national army reckoned at forty thousand strong and a powerful fleet of ironclads had embarked on an operation of ambiguous motive, only to be thoroughly trounced and sent packing in a backwater of the allegedly decrepit Confederacy.

"Oh it is *so* discouraging," wrote a New England soldier's wife when the news filtered back that Banks had been soundly defeated. "Heaven help the country," remarked an equally dejected George Templeton Strong.[61] Had Richard Taylor captured Banks's army — as he might possibly have done, if Kirby Smith reinforced him instead of sending most of his troops into Arkansas — Northern dismay would have echoed much more profoundly. As it was, the setback revived all the pessimistic warnings of the peace men.

The bumbling and apparently pointless expedition had upset more than the impending Atlanta campaign and any ambitions of seizing Mobile. Without A. J. Smith's troops to augment Sherman's garrisons in western Kentucky and Tennessee, Confederate cavalryman Nathan Bedford Forrest held high carnival there for a month with four mounted brigades. Forrest had just come up from north Mississippi, where he had soundly thrashed Union raiders numbering nearly three times as many as his own command. His escapades seemed almost gratifying to General Sherman, whose supply routes remained free from molestation while Forrest cavorted in territory of reciprocating loyalties, but the rebel's notorious depredations hardly inspired confidence in the effectiveness of U.S. forces in the region. While Union soldiers and sailors converged on Alexandria, Louisiana, for the drive toward Shreveport, Forrest diverted a fragment of his command to snare the five-hundred-man garrison of Union City, Tennessee. He threatened to raise the black flag at Union City if his demand for surrender were refused, and the place capitulated without a fight. Next he led his main body in a dash at Paducah, Kentucky, at the junction of the Tennessee River and the Ohio, and there he again threatened to give no quarter unless the town surrendered, but the Union colonel in charge of the garrison dared him to try it. Once they had pillaged the outskirts, though, the Confederates leisurely withdrew. Then, after roaming the country between the Tennessee and the Mississippi for another couple of weeks, Forrest turned his attention to Fort Pillow, fifty tortuous river miles above Memphis.[62]

Confederates had built this earthen battery on a bluff over the Mississippi in the first weeks of the war. They called it Fort Pillow in honor of the regional commander at the time, Gideon Pillow, whose reputation had disintegrated even before the place fell into Union hands the next year, but the name was to achieve greater and more lasting opprobrium in the spring of 1864. When Forrest first burst into west Tennessee, the fort was garrisoned by Major William Bradford's freshly raised battalion of loyal Tennessee cavalrymen and a section of the Memphis Light Battery. The battery was composed of black gunners, and had recently been re-designated Company D of the 2nd U.S. Colored Light Artillery. As in the Virginia theater, black troops in Tennessee and Kentucky had been assigned to garrison and occupation duty in backwater posts where they would not find much danger of open combat, but Stephen Hurlbut, commanding at Memphis, nevertheless sent more of them to Fort Pillow when Forrest posed a potential threat there. The 1st Alabama Siege Artillery, trained as infantry as well as on the big guns, had recently been transformed into the 6th U.S. Colored Heavy Artillery, and Hurlbut reinforced Bradford with a battalion of that regiment under Major Lionel Booth, who would take command as the senior officer.[63]

Hurlbut continued to worry about his outposts, but Major Booth — erstwhile sergeant major of a white artillery regiment from Missouri, and evidently a fairly tough customer — tried to ease the general's anxiety about Fort Pillow. "I do not think any apprehensions need be felt or fears entertained in reference to this place," Booth reported on April 3. "I think it, perfectly safe." This was his last communication with Memphis. That air of security prevailed for another week, but on April 10 Forrest decided to make Fort Pillow his next target. On the morning of April 11 he started that way from Jackson, Tennessee, taking two brigades of Tennessee and Mississippi troopers leavened with a few Missourians and Texans, all under Brigadier General James Chalmers.[64]

Three features of Fort Pillow drew Forrest there. First, it was isolated, posing little danger of reinforcement before his cavalry hit it and ran. Second, nearly half the garrison's complement consisted of black soldiers, most of them former slaves whose cash value at that period probably appealed to Forrest less than an opportunity to prove them ineffective as soldiers, and to terrify would-be recruits to their ranks. Finally, there was the original garrison of Tennessee Tories in Major Bradford's battalion: as cavalrymen they would have some horses worth capturing, and they offered a target for retribution as perceived traitors to their state and to the Confederacy, as well as for their willingness to serve alongside the black troops.

The last report that made it out of Fort Pillow tallied about 560 officers and men, of whom some 250 were black. Numerous civilians also lived in the little town alongside the fort, including men whom Forrest characterized as draft evaders, and a contraband camp had blossomed there. Daybreak had brought the first sounds of life to this little community when Confederate horsemen burst into sight beyond the outer works, having captured the pickets before they could fire their warning shots. The officers inside mistook the enemy's numbers, estimating them at 5,000,

6,000, or 7,000 strong, as all the frantic reports had claimed. In fact Forrest had brought fewer than 2,000 with him, and he might have lost a great many of those if he had tried to storm the fort from the outset. Instead, he sent in a demand for surrender under a flag of truce. Major Booth declined, and prepared to fight, but he withdrew his men from the outer perimeter into the tighter trenches around a big earthwork at the center. The barracks and other buildings lay between those lines, and around 9:00 A.M. a sharpshooter picked off Major Booth from that cover. Major Bradford took over, urging a steady fire from the battery and the infantry trench just outside it, and held his ground for four more hours. Early in the afternoon, Forrest sent in a second flag of truce, and this time he delivered another demand for immediate surrender with a threat that he would give no quarter if it were refused again. He allowed Bradford twenty minutes to consider it.[65]

Survivors inside the fort claimed that the rebels used that twenty minutes to creep closer. Southern troops did almost surround the place, closing every escape route except the river, and at least one regiment appears to have covered the slope of the bluff leading to the water. When the appointed time expired Forrest's men leaped to the attack without further warning beyond the blare of a bugle, enduring only a volley or two and scattered shots before they swept over the trenches, up the parapet, and into the fort. Hordes of them spilled into it with revolvers blazing, and the black soldiers fled down toward the river, most of them dropping their weapons. Bradford's Tennesseeans followed suit when they saw their foes shooting white men as well as black. Major Bradford, who may have suspected that Forrest was bluffing about raising the black flag, concluded that Forrest's men, at least, had taken it seriously. The major bolted after his fleeing troops, down to the riverbank. The Southerners who had positioned themselves in range of that route peppered the fugitives as they passed, either unaware or unconcerned that some of them were willing to surrender.[66]

General Chalmers complained, after the fact, that the garrison showed no sign of surrender. The U.S. flag remained at full staff until Confederates lowered it themselves, and he said he saw no white flags. Between Forrest's direct threat, their apprehension of Confederate racial retribution, and the indiscriminate firing when the enemy poured into the fort, the defenders probably anticipated the uselessness of such signals, and devoted every second to flight.[67]

A majority of them did not make it. Confederates chased them to, and into, the water, killing them as quickly as they could fire and reload. Almost none of the garrison still bore any arms by the time they reached the river, and the few who had revolvers surrendered them in the hope they might be treated as prisoners. Many of those who tried to swim away sank beneath the surface when shot, or drowned because they could not swim well enough. Of nearly 560 Union soldiers of all ranks who awoke at Fort Pillow that Tuesday morning, probably half were dead or dying by nightfall, and roving ghouls killed more of the wounded the next morning. Chalmers claimed that Union boats were allowed to land on April 13 and took away 69 wounded, at least one of whom was a woman; he also reported leading over 200 more prisoners away from Fort Pillow, with 40 black men among them, but a few of those wounded and prisoners were contrabands or white civilians. As many as 300 died at Southern hands on the spot — some in combat, more in the confusion of the precipitate retreat, and many after it became obvious that the fort had surrendered. Major Bradford was held prisoner for a few days and then shot, reportedly while trying to escape, but two eyewitnesses gave identical testimony that he had been murdered.[68]

Six days after the massacre, the Joint Committee on the Conduct of the War appointed Chairman Ben Wade and Daniel Gooch as a subcommittee to investigate the atrocity, and the next day they boarded a train for the Mississippi Valley, taking a recording secretary with them. In the hospital at Mound City, Illinois, they interviewed the surgeons and three dozen wounded survivors of the garrison, who were housed in three separate wards. The doctors offered evidence of an unusual number of close-range wounds, and their patients testified to mistreatment that ranged from unusual battlefield savagery to calculating cruelty, but some of it seemed too inventive to be true. Jacob Thompson, a runaway slave who worked at Fort Pillow as a cook, swore that he saw several black soldiers and two white ones nailed to buildings or logs by their hands and feet before they were burned to death, and he claimed that he could tell the difference between the charred remains because the white bodies "were whiter than the colored men." This same fellow obligingly, and obviously falsely, identified General Forrest himself as overseer of the slaughter, describing him as "a little bit of a man" whom he knew from before the war: Forrest is universally recorded as six feet, two inches tall, with a powerful physique. Other witnesses' excessively lurid claims could readily be attributed to the leading questions posed by the congressmen, or by the mere proximity of the patients' cots, since those who lay within earshot of each other's interviews might easily have corroborated or built upon earlier embellishments.[69]

Escalating exaggeration tainted most congressional investigations and government prosecutions of the period, for inquisitors often betrayed an eagerness to accept such invention and they seldom took the precaution of segregating witnesses. For all of that, medical treatment records and autopsies confirm the suspicious nature of many wounds, including severe saber cuts inflicted on a black soldier who lay sick in the Fort Pillow hospital at the time of the attack. Most of the wounded men resisted Wade's and Gooch's more suggestive questions, and the bulk of the testimony blended compatibly to portray a massacre of rapidly diminishing ferocity as the adrenaline settled. For twenty minutes or more after the surrender, Confederates inside the fort killed nearly every defender and denizen in sight, regardless of race, gender, or age. Some bodies were found inside burned buildings or tents; it was not clear whether they had been burned alive, but credible, corroborated testimony indicated that at least one man had been nailed to the floor of one of those buildings, although the nails were driven through his clothing and equipment straps. A sizable portion of Forrest's command continued the slaughter into the evening, with occasional objection or interference from Confederate officers, and by the next day those who would have stopped the mayhem seemed to have regained a measure of control, despite frequent instances of mostly surreptitious murder.[70]

However much of the brutality may have been blamed on the fury of battle, or whatever isolated acts of kindness or attempted intervention may have seemed to ameliorate the prevailing impression of savagery, the massacre was impossible to deny. The defeat at Fort Pillow therefore presented the Northern war party with some much-needed moral ammunition that spring. The humiliation Forrest's raid had caused the Lincoln administration and the blow Forrest had struck to the confidence of the Union soldiers who must oppose him were both neutralized by the barbarity on the banks of the Mississippi. The fruits of Forrest's successful raid instead accrued to his enemies in the form of soaring indignation at home and desperate determination at the front, among both the black troops who might face him and the white ones who served with them. When word of the butchery reached Memphis, the U.S. Colored Troops in that garrison fell to their knees and vowed never to ask for or give quarter if they met Forrest in battle.[71]

Half a continent away, Ulysses Grant was gathering all the troops he could strip from other theaters to wage his spring campaign against what the president considered his most appropriate target — namely, Lee's army. The idea appeared to have originated with Halleck, who had discouraged Grant's plan (or rather the plan of Grant's engineers) of operating against Richmond from the south, instead insisting on the president's perennial preference for keeping a massive force in front of Washington. Nearly two weeks before Lincoln promoted Grant to the top command, Halleck inquired of Quincy Gillmore how many troops he could spare from the South Atlantic coast for "operations against some other point." Gillmore calculated that he could shed seven to eleven thousand good veteran troops if he fell back on the defensive, especially if a few new regiments of Colored Troops were sent to replace them. The last significant actions in that region had been the sinking of the twelve-gun sloop *Housatonic* off Charleston by a homemade Confederate submarine, on February 17, and the Olustee disaster three days later. Those embarrassments had been sufficient, apparently, to discourage further efforts against the cradle of secession, and late in March Gillmore noticed that the furloughed troops of his command had been stopped in Washington by orders from headquarters. Correctly deducing the intent, he asked to have the rest of the Tenth Corps transferred from his department to join those veterans in the field, and he asked if he might lead them all. On April 4 he got his wish: Halleck, acting now as chief of staff to Grant, directed Gillmore to report with his corps to Ben Butler, at his headquarters in Fort Monroe.[72]

No troops were taken from the coast of North Carolina, but neither were any sent there to shore up Union garrisons against the portion of Lee's army that descended on the district under George Pickett. Between the remnants of his original division and the troops he absorbed in North Carolina, Pickett mustered about twelve thousand of all arms, whom he mobilized against scattered posts of Federals along the sounds. As January turned to February he orchestrated a three-pronged attack on New Bern, with assistance from sailors who planned to board and capture a sidewheel gunboat and turn it against the city. Crucial parts of the plan failed, and although the sailors did take the gunboat, they had to burn it to avoid recapture. Pickett finally had to give up the prize, but he kept troops in the vicinity through the winter to frustrate the occupation, advising against another attempt "till the iron clads are done."[73]

The ironclads Pickett referred to were the *Albemarle* and the *Neuse,* both in the stocks alongside upstream portions of navigable North Carolina rivers. The *Neuse,* on the river of the same name, might have given Pickett the best assistance in his attempt at New Bern, but the *Albemarle,* way up the Roanoke River nearly into Virginia, would have to pass the town of Plymouth if it were going to steam down to a useful career on Albemarle Sound. Commander James Cooke, of the Confederate navy, took the slender, heavily armored craft down the Roanoke on April 17, using his maiden combat voyage as a shakedown cruise to repair the earliest equipment failures. Two days later he confronted the two steamers that composed the primary Union naval presence at Plymouth, ramming and sinking one of them and chasing the other into retreat, along with the lesser vessels of the Plymouth flotilla. Then Cooke sent a boat ashore to confer with his counterparts in the army.[74]

From his headquarters in Petersburg, George Pickett had assigned Brigadier General Robert Hoke, a North Carolinian, to seize Plymouth, and Hoke went at it with more luck and success than Pickett had seen at New Bern. By April 19 his three brigades had already invested Plymouth and its garrison of nearly three thousand men, and he had captured Fort Wessells, the key to the town's defenses. General Henry Wessells, the Union commander in Plymouth, declined one invitation to surrender, but Hoke renewed the assault on April 20 while the *Albemarle* shelled the Yankees from the river. Rebel infantry overran another battery on the very edge of Plymouth, and the defenders fell into the earthworks around their central fort. Hoke made another demand for surrender, but Wessells asked to have his garrison paroled on the spot. Positioned as he was to overwhelm his antagonist, Hoke refused, so Wessells again declined, although he detected what he considered another of those veiled threats of "indiscriminate slaughter" if he did not submit. That foreboding impression appeared to emanate from the Union general's own apprehensions, though, for the bombardment had not long resumed when he ordered up the white flag, which Hoke immediately honored.[75]

Wessells probably asked for parole because his force included some recruits from among the contrabands and a couple of companies of loyal North Carolinians, a large percentage of whom had served previously in the Confederate army. The example of Fort Pillow may not have reached the Yankees at Plymouth, but they had their own reasons for anxiety. During his February operations General Pickett had captured numerous loyalists from the same regiment at Kinston, and had court-martialed the former rebel soldiers among them for deserting to the enemy: twenty-two had been convicted and sentenced to death, and Pickett had promptly hanged them. That led John Peck, the Union commander in North Carolina, to protest piously that the executed men had only belonged to the Confederate army because they had been the victims of the Confederacy's "merciless conscription," and he threatened retaliation against the prisoners in his hands. Peck's complaint rang a little hollow now that his own government had inaugurated conscription, and Union soldiers who deserted into Confederate service were routinely executed when they were recaptured. Both the Washington and Richmond governments had come to demand military service from their citizens with all the presumption of Eastern moguls, and the political sentiments of the conscript made no difference. Changing sides was one crime that neither belligerent would forgive during the height of hostilities.[76]

Most of the Tar Heel turncoats in the Plymouth garrison escaped by boat before the surrender, though, and Hoke evidently took no special action against the few dozen who remained. He assigned the 35th North

Carolina to escort the prisoners to their new life in prison, and those who kept a record of it remarked unanimously on both the courtesy and kindness of the guards who had, only hours before, bent all their energies toward killing them. By the end of the month hundreds of them had begun to arrive daily inside the stockade pen at Andersonville, where the squalor, smell, crowding, and rancid rations horrified their garrison-coddled sensibilities. Their bright blue uniforms and untouched knapsacks left them the richest denizens inside that palisade, and made them the most inviting targets of their desperate new comrades.[77]

Citizens in the North were just then reading of the Red River fiasco, including ominous signs that much of Admiral Porter's flotilla might be lost. The abject defeat of another Union fleet at Plymouth, and the unconditional surrender of an entire post, from the commanding officer and his staff down to the sutlers and contrabands, cast an unwelcome shadow over national prospects. Devout proponents of the war could not swallow such news neat. The *New York Times* assured readers that the barbarian rebels had summarily executed every black soldier and loyalist at Plymouth, meanwhile heavily underestimating the number of Federals taken prisoner and dutifully recording that the Confederate victory had come at enormous cost, alleging that Hoke had lost "fifteen hundred killed" when all of his casualties together appear to have footed up to fewer than four hundred.[78]

The capture of Plymouth convinced the Union district commander to abandon other nearby outposts, and long cavalcades of runaway slaves followed the evacuation in such frantic haste that several women had to drop out of line to give birth. The same newspapers that carried gratuitously varnished versions of this disaster announced in hopeful but unconvincing headlines that the Confederacy was "beginning to quake," but Southern journalists disagreed with understandable jubilation, after three solid years of resistance. "From the headwaters of the Red River to the coast of North Carolina," boasted the *Richmond Examiner*, "the horizon is fairly radiant with Confederate victory." Missionary Ridge, Vicksburg, and Gettysburg had faded into a legendary haze of ephemeral impediments to independence — precisely as Fort Donelson and Shiloh had after Second Bull Run, Fredericksburg, and Chancellorsville. Only five months had passed since Braxton Bragg's beaten troops had fled so shamelessly into Georgia, and until recently that army had been shedding dozens of deserters a day, yet Union forces seemed once again to have lapsed into impotence.[79]

The national army's most unequivocal triumphs that winter and spring came far beyond the Mississippi, with little fanfare and less cause for celebration. From Dakota Territory to the Mexican border, well-armed soldiers (who might never have worn uniforms if not for the sectional conflict) methodically harried, hunted, and killed native Plains tribesmen in their Stone Age encampments. The atrocities of Fort Pillow paled alongside some of the "battles" Union troops won in that theater, and Eastern newspapers that reviled Southern savagery toward black soldiers rarely mentioned victories that entailed even worse cruelties inflicted on helpless women and children by men wearing Union blue.[80]

Even while trying to ease the news of the disaster at Plymouth, the *New York Times* conceded that it really was a defeat, citing it as the latest example of a failed military policy. Editor Henry Raymond lumped the Red River expedition in the same inglorious category, charging that the army had spread itself too thin in an effort to occupy too much territory. Let the nation's legions concentrate and roll irresistibly toward vital points, urged Mr. Raymond, who appeared to applaud the anticipated program of General Grant. Raymond tried to fashion his argument as an indictment of George McClellan's own handling of the army, but McClellan had actually attempted the very type of overwhelming combinations proposed by the armchair strategist on Newspaper Row, only to have his main force depleted by civilian overseers in Washington. The unintended thrust of the editorial, for those who made that connection, was to illustrate the vacillation of administration policy three years into the war, and to insinuate that ineffective management had wasted hundreds of millions of dollars and tens of thousands of lives.[81]

In his Gramercy Park brownstone, George Templeton Strong turned long enough from helping his wife with the Metropolitan Fair to grieve over the economic wounds of the war. April brought "panic and smash" in stock market trading that reduced him to at least nominal and temporary insolvency, although he had no means then of knowing how long the crash would last. All the war news sounded bad: Plymouth and three thousand men were lost; the combined forces of the Western armies had been driven back down the Red River; it seemed clear that James Longstreet was sweeping back down the Great Valley into Virginia from Tennessee to join Lee, and perhaps to treat Meade as he had Rosecrans. In reflection of those gloomy prospects, the price of gold, which served in that era as the measure of public confidence in Secretary Chase's new paper currency, went soaring. Gold had been creeping gradually upward throughout the war, from barely more than par at the end of 1861 to $1.33 a year later and $1.52 on December 31, 1863. During the next three months the average price of gold rose eleven cents, but in April alone it climbed another seventeen cents toward Mr. Strong's dreaded two-dollar threshold. The term "inflation" came into vogue to describe the growth of speculative bubbles in the various commodities targeted for hoarding:

early in April butter had become the favorite article for exploitation, but as the month drew to a close it began to give way to coal.[82]

To a man like Strong, and many like him, the price of gold and goods mirrored the mind and will of the people. The fighting that would soon begin would be "fearful," he predicted, probably with unconscious emphasis on the Virginia campaign, and if it led to another disaster like the Bull Run battles, Fredericksburg, or Chancellorsville, he feared the worst. "What if we fail?" he asked his journal. "Has this people faith and virtue enough to persevere after another season of failure or even of *partial* success?"

It was a common apprehension that month. One of Senator Lyman Trumbull's Chicago correspondents warned him that "the people are not satisfied with the loose way in which the war is carried on." Everyone wanted a change, he was convinced, but there was no change in sight, all of which bore dark implications for the November election and, by extension, for the imminent Republican convention. "To be beaten now would end this government," the Chicagoan assured Trumbull, blending the interpretations of political and military defeat into one, as was the Republican wont.[83]

On the same day that Senator Trumbull's constituent alluded to the waning public patience, Lincoln himself attempted to soothe one of the most impatient factions of that public. In a letter dated April 4, 1864, to Albert Hodges, editor of the *Commonwealth*, in Kentucky's capital, the president tried to justify the Emancipation Proclamation and his decision to bring former slaves into the army: the latter action in particular had rankled Bluegrass State loyalists — and slave-owning Unionists everywhere, for that matter — as recruiting officers stripped their plantations of laborers. He had adopted those measures because he thought they were necessary to preserve the government, Lincoln wrote. Although he had always maintained that the president lacked any authority to act so unilaterally, he claimed that such "otherwise unconstitutional" decrees became lawful "by becoming indispensable to the preservation of the constitution, through the preservation of the nation." He tried to weld his duty to protect and preserve the Constitution to the preservation of the physical territory of the nation, just as he had in his inaugural address, with a metaphor that worked against him. On the steps of the unfinished Capitol, in 1861, he had employed the apt concept of divorce to characterize the secession movement, but then he had denied the comparison, insisting "we cannot separate." With Mr. Hodges he again conjured a fair comparison to the persistent rebellion of a province, remarking that "often a limb must be amputated to save a life," but to defend his reasoning he had to reverse the analogy somewhat awkwardly, insisting that "a life is never wisely given to save a limb." His original argument had depended on his assertion that the government belonged to all the people, which in turn had relied heavily on his debunked assumption that a silent majority in the seceded states still cherished the Union. He still adhered to the carapace of that defense when it was becoming clear that only a small fraction of the Confederacy's 1860 voters favored unconditional reunion, even after three years of intense suffering.[84]

That was where the logic continued to break down, especially for those who did not share Lincoln's preference for a powerful central government that could impose its will on any state or citizen. If others chose to leave, those critics contended, the Constitution might well be preserved in all its original purity among the states that clung to the Union. Still others simply doubted that force would ever prevail, believing that continued war only diminished the chances of ever achieving voluntary reconciliation, and that substantial faction may have been outnumbered by supporters of Lincoln's war who so despised his constitutional infringements at home that they felt their own government posed a worse danger to their liberty than did an independent Confederacy.

The final paragraph of Lincoln's letter to Hodges may have represented his attempt to address all such criticism collectively. "I claim not to have controlled events," he concluded, "but confess plainly that events have controlled me. Now, at the end of three years struggle the nation's condition is not what either party, or any man devised, or expected." None of this was his fault, he seemed to say, blaming all that had befallen the country during his administration on an all-powerful supreme being. He may have been pondering this glorification of his war — or this disavowal of responsibility for that war — for some time. He left an undated, handwritten note that his secretaries placed in September of 1862, proclaiming the probability that "God wills this contest, and wills that it shall not end yet," but that note might have been written at the time of his letter to Hodges, for both documents ascribe the carnage to supernatural intervention. "God alone can claim it," he assured Hodges, suggesting that the bloodshed thus far and the bloodshed that was to come amounted to divine punishment for the great wrong of slavery, as though national atonement required vast numbers of human sacrifices. Like a preacher straining for a trace of sacred influence in any tragedy, Lincoln reasoned that the sharing of the butchery, North and South, expiated the sins of both complicit sections, thereby offering "new cause to attest and revere the justice and goodness of God."[85]

Lincoln's followers tended to share his apparent confidence in ultimate success. At home and in camp, those observers welcomed another spring with some measure of hope. The valiant fight at Gettysburg, where North-

erners had finally wielded the moral advantage of defending home territory against an invader, seemed to demonstrate that the nation's principal
army had become a match for its foe. In the West, Chattanooga had similarly encouraged at least those who were disposed to be encouraged. For a
variety of reasons — chief among them, perhaps, a simple desire to salvage their own and their comrades' sacrifices from futility — many soldiers remained at least as determined to crush the rebellion as they had
the previous spring.

The men in the army expressed that determination with fluctuating
degrees of eagerness or resignation, however, and some of their assertions
carried more convincing tones than those of others. Significant numbers
of those who might contribute more of the human sacrifices began the
final year of the war wishing they had not committed themselves to it, and
doubting whether the struggle could ever accomplish the desired ends,
while others questioned whether those ends were even desirable. Soldiers
who had resented having their blood and toil turned to the cause of emancipation, a year before, now seemed less resistant to it, and most favored
the idea of black troops replacing them in the front lines, but some still
credited emancipation with stiffening Southern resistance and prolonging the war. The administration's increasing attention to freedmen and
their rights further aggravated many of those in uniform who had never
intended freedom to lead to constitutional equality: the nominal excuse
for the prisoner-exchange impasse incensed men who faced capture so often, and it dispirited those who, after spending months in squalid rebel
prisons themselves, saw their chances of release growing progressively
slimmer.[86]

One Quaker who had espoused the antislavery principles so common
to that sect, if not its peace testimony, underwent an abrupt change of
heart as a prisoner of war. Recovering from typhoid and diarrhea, a gaunt
and bitter Sergeant William Stevens denounced his government for allowing him to languish in enemy hands on the pretense of demanding
equal treatment for black prisoners. Stevens, who had enlisted during the
war's first summer, had evidently come to view contrabands as lazy and
indifferent to freedom, and he vowed that he would never suffer the experience again if it freed every slave in the South.[87]

Older hands, with better memories, scorned all the optimism about
the looming spring campaign as so much seasonal claptrap. A Vermont
captain who had served nearly three years dismissed all talk of Confederate collapse: it would take a lot more work than anyone guessed, he
warned, to overcome several hundred thousand desperate rebels fighting
on the defensive. "We have often thought we saw the end of the war almost before us," an Indiana colonel reminded his wife, three months be-

fore he was due to come home, "but when we grasped at it it vanished in air."[88]

Everyone expected that the imminent battles would be more brutal than ever, whether they ended favorably or not. Like the two-year and nine-month troops before them, therefore, the men whose terms were beginning to expire became especially anxious about fixing the day they would go home. Recalling the War Department's earlier response to similar inquiries, officers reminded their men that they would not be released until the third anniversary of their mustering date, which added several weeks to most three-year hitches. Men who had never shirked their duty took this as sheer treachery, and swore they would vote for the rankest Copperheads if Lincoln's War Department served them so faithlessly.[89]

April had not ended before the earliest volunteers in the Pennsylvania Reserves started clamoring for their discharges, and with another devastating clash likely any day some of them clamored a little too vigorously, ending up in the guardhouse. John Cuddy, who had only turned nineteen six months before, nevertheless calculated that he should be discharged from the 7th Pennsylvania Reserves on May 15. In every letter to his folks he assured them that he could not wait to get home and begin what he supposed would be a happy life, and had the War Department started counting from the day he enlisted he might have had a chance to do that. Instead, he marched with his regiment into battle ten days before he was to go home, fell into enemy hands, and died in a South Carolina prison the following autumn, a couple of weeks before his twentieth birthday.[90]

It was obviously financial plight that had sent Thomas Brown into the army in the summer of 1862, but he had enlisted in an existing regiment, which (he had been promised) would make him eligible for discharge with the original men in June. The war had clearly horrified him: he gave no hint of ever having embraced any of its reputed goals, and he admitted that he would accept any legal avenue out of the army. Through the winter and spring the tantalizing approach of his discharge made him desperately homesick, and when he heard what a productive sugaring season his sons had enjoyed back in the Upper Connecticut Valley he could hardly contain himself. He urged his family to plant as big a crop as they could, in the hope he could come home and help them harvest it, but three weeks later a bullet put an end to all those plans.[91]

William Stow, a corporal in the 2nd Vermont, had enlisted on May 7, 1861, but he had not been mustered in for another three weeks. As much as he had wanted a furlough by the end of 1863 he had declined to reenlist, evidently out of some dissatisfaction with an increasingly unjust and grasping government, so he told his parents he would have to wait until the end of May for a more permanent and satisfying homecoming. To his mother he revealed how ardently he longed for the peace of home, and on April 14 he reminded her that he had only forty-five days left: as it happened, he had but twenty-one days left, in the army and on the earth. In their final moments, men like Cuddy, Brown, and Stow probably never considered — as their president did — that their deaths might reflect "the justice and goodness of God." So comforting a thought undoubtedly occurred seldom even among those of more devout temperament, like Sergeant Stevens, who recovered his health and returned to the ranks in time to be killed just before his own enlistment ended.[92]

Peter Welsh, a color sergeant in the Irish Brigade, had enlisted at the end of a drunken spree and had spent most of the succeeding twenty months trying to justify that blunder to his wife, but he left plenty of evidence of his own lingering regret at the choice. In his last letter before the spring campaign, he cautioned his brother, who had just arrived from Ireland, "never for heavens sake let a thought of enlisting in this army cross your mind." Sergeant Welsh excused himself for having ignored his own advice with specious references to the duty owed by those who had lived in the United States for a few years, but a fortnight later he suffered a relatively minor wound that promised to send him home, and his glee belied those protestations of patriotic devotion. The festering wound ultimately killed him anyway, though, and if he saw the slightest justice or goodness in his own death, it was certain that his wife did not.[93] The fine sentiments President Lincoln had described for Mr. Hodges found more currency on the front page of a newspaper or on the floor of Congress than in a darkened parlor dominated by a coffin.

Epilogue

➔ DURING EACH of the war's four springs the administration had faced what it considered a military crisis, and each time it had responded by raising hordes of short-term troops. In the spring of 1864 the immediate danger came with less distinct visions of bristling bayonets: no rebel flags floated within sight of the White House, and no army under Stonewall Jackson or Robert E. Lee rolled down the Shenandoah Valley, sweeping all before it. This time the enemy Abraham Lincoln feared worst — the one he had attempted to allay on the hilltop at Gettysburg — had settled in the breasts of Northern citizens. Many had opposed his coercive course against the seceded states from the outset, and it was likely that their numbers had grown, but it was the weary and disillusioned who aroused more executive anxiety than the actively dissident. The conditionally supportive voter may have represented the largest of the nation's many constituencies, and the conditions of his support might seem too onerous if the South could remain so defiant and viable after such costly triumphs as the North had seen in 1863. With even greater determination than before, Lincoln insisted once again that the war could be won quickly, and in token of that perennial belief he accepted yet another proposal for an ephemeral army of amateurs — as many as a hundred thousand holiday hoplites, for a mere hundred days of service.[1]

Lincoln may have expected to conquer the Confederacy in a twinkling with these summer soldiers, just as he had anticipated thirteen months before that the appearance of fifty thousand black men with arms in their hands would bring all resistance to an abrupt end. These hundred-day men would draw no bounties, and they would theoretically man fortifications in the rear, freeing older troops for use on the battlefield, but the

War Department calculated that they would cost something like $25 million. Congress, with its enhanced powers of taxation, toyed with various methods of paying for that relative pittance as well as the rest of the government's burdensome military machine. First the nation's solons considered a substantial expansion of the income tax, followed by equally onerous taxes on stock trading, a 5 percent levy on the production of gold and silver, and as much as a 50 percent increase on import duties on everything except, for some curious reason, printing paper. Commercial banks faced a tax of one-half of 1 percent on their circulating currency, and one-quarter of a percent on their deposits.[2]

With those hundred-day men (and there would eventually be eighty-two regiments of them) the United States Army would comprise more than a million men. Nearly a third of the country's soldiers were absent from their commands for one reason or another, and a goodly number of expensive new recruits would soon be tossed out of the army because they were too young or infirm, but most of those men had to be paid, clothed, and equipped. Pay alone for that multitude accumulated at more than half a million dollars a day, and that was before Congress granted the soldiers their only raise since the first summer of the war. April produced the first splashes of green vegetation on the fringes of the well-trodden army camps, reminding each general and regimental commander that his troops must look their best for the reviews that inevitably preceded the opening campaigns, and that challenged the capacity of quartermasters to outfit hundreds of thousands of men.[3]

Part of the cost of new wardrobes could be wrung from the soldiers themselves, whose clothing allowance seldom covered the apparel they had to draw to replace contractors' shoddy goods, and for that reason mandatory issues of new uniforms inaugurated storms of protest and seething resentment. That was particularly true in the two regiments of U.S. Sharpshooters, which had originally worn forest green. Two years of grueling service had reduced the original garb to tatters: by the spring of 1864 most of the green uniforms had been replaced by regulation blue at the expense of the men themselves, but enough faded remnants of green remained to offend the eye of the field officers, who concluded that morale would only improve by reverting entirely to the distinctive green wool. Against the wishes of most of the men and many of the company officers, both regiments tossed off perfectly good blue blouses and trousers for the expensive new duds that made men stand out on the battlefield as the chosen marksmen with breechloading rifles.[4]

One-sixth of the nation's army had been invested in the Army of the Potomac. Major General John Sedgwick sneered that the government kept more soldiers in the loyal states than in rebeldom, but that statement reflected more of Sedgwick's disdain for the garrisons and provost details in the North than it did of statistical accuracy. It was true that two or three more armies might have been organized from the troops who lounged safely in barracks or permanent camps, waiting to quell the first public demonstration of popular dissent, but troops poured through Washington as never before.[5]

The march of Ambrose Burnside's Ninth Corps through the capital illustrated the vast expansion of the little struggle everyone had envisioned three years before. For weeks the corps had reorganized and recruited at Annapolis, providing diversion for the unexchanged prisoners at Camp Parole and for the sick and wounded in the hospitals that had taken over the naval academy and St. John's College. For many of those parolees and patients, and especially for those who belonged to Meade's army, this was their first glimpse of black troops — Burnside having accumulated his desired division of them.[6] At least one of his Michigan regiments provoked further comment with an attached company of sharpshooters composed of Winnebago and Wyandotte Indians. On April 23, that diverse corps started toward Washington on foot, for what purpose few of them were yet certain: the hopeful thought they might serve as garrison to the city, displacing the bandbox soldiers from their comfortable lodgings, but the more realistic and better-informed supposed they would join the Army of the Potomac. Burnside had not reached his recruiting goal of fifty thousand men, but his muster rolls did exceed twenty-seven thousand, so the columns that wound toward the Potomac as mere reinforcements for the country's principal army approached the size of the entire force Irvin McDowell had led to Bull Run in 1861.[7]

Much of the Ninth Corps had spent March tramping over the mountains out of east Tennessee, but this long, hot trip to Washington told on the thousands of new men and boys for whom this was the first of many — or, worse yet, not so many — punishing marches. Flurries of clothing, blankets, and ponchos littered their wake, to the delight of seasoned veterans who needed just this or that article to complete their kits. Then, on the third morning of the journey, they stopped on the outskirts of Washington, rested leisurely, and fell in again at noon, but when they faced toward the line of march this time, the officers paid unusual heed to their alignment, step, and intervals. People in the city took notice of them, for even there such massive processions came but rarely. They had followed the railroad most of the way from Annapolis, but suddenly they veered a mile away from their course until they struck Fourteenth Street, where each regiment wheeled to the left in column of companies.[8]

The balcony of Willard's Hotel hovered over Fourteenth Street just before it crossed Pennsylvania Avenue. There waited General Burnside to review them, and President Lincoln stood beside him with the trademark stovepipe hat in his hand, looking thinner and older than ever before. The officers called their men to the marching salute and lifted the blades of their swords to the brims of their caps, while the troops cheered lustily, but some of them missed the two men on the balcony as they surveyed the appreciative crowds lining the streets, windows, and porches. The throng swelled as word of the spectacle spread through the city. Walt Whitman, still volunteering in the Washington hospitals, waited on Fourteenth Street for three hours for the 51st New York to come along, with his brother in command. At sight of the brother he jumped out to march with him past the president, distracting Captain Whitman enough that he, too, forgot to salute.[9]

All afternoon the infantry and artillery of that single corps rolled past the hotel. They were still coming at 5:30, when John Hay saw them on his way from the White House to the Navy Yard. They were the finest-looking troops he had ever seen, Hay wrote a day or two later, but they reminded him of the early days of the war, when bright new regiments strode to Bull Run and the Peninsula "as if to a pic-nic." There was still much of that giddy, naive enthusiasm among the soldiers who strode past Willard's that day. Most of them had never laid eyes on their president before, or even watched a parade of such magnitude, much less taken part in it. A majority of them were still too new to this trade to realize what was about to happen to them: at least sixteen of the forty-four regiments in the corps, and the biggest of them, too, had never yet seen a shot fired in anger, and as many as half the men in the older regiments had only recently enlisted.[10]

First Sergeant John Jackson, of the 32nd Maine, may have typified the new man at this stage of the war. He had mustered in barely a month before, but he had more experience than most of his comrades in the Ninth Corps, for he was a veteran of the nine-month service. Those nine months of safe, sedentary, and rather comfortable guard duty had only confirmed his original expectation that army life consisted of generous enlistment bounties, bucolic retreats, and regular meals, so when his civilian work dried up again he resorted once more to the service, leaving behind no melodramatic declarations of patriotic intent. For all the young widows who moped about their home communities, and all the broken men who had come swinging home on crutches, or with empty sleeves, the easy money and the stirring sights still seemed to promise that this new undertaking might offer more of romance and adventure than of misery and peril.[11]

Beyond Willard's, the column traversed the muddy site of the unfinished Washington Monument, where stonemasons had ceased work for the duration and the grounds had been appropriated by quartermaster teams and their squalid stables. Among the men who had seen a little more of the war, the glimpse of that drab and dismal site registered more clearly than the celebrities on the balcony. The old-soldier descriptions of the day accentuated the miles they had marched and the landmarks along the way, rather than the luminaries who had simply watched them pass. Andrew Stone, a gruff, businesslike New Hampshire captain, elaborated little on the rare scene that others would cherish long after their illusions had been shattered. A few days afterward, he laconically informed his brother that they had marched three days, crossed the Potomac on the Long Bridge, and camped four miles into Virginia. Lincoln and Burnside appeared but incidentally in Stone's account, as though of no more importance than the unfinished monument. In the last letter his family would ever receive from him, the captain concentrated on the work that he knew lay only days away.[12]

Notes

ABBREVIATIONS

AAS: American Antiquarian Society
ALP: Abraham Lincoln Papers, Library of Congress
BGSU: Bowling Green State University
BL: University of Michigan, Bentley Library
BPL: Boston Public Library
CAHC: Camden Area History Center
CCHS: Chatauqua County Historical Society
CG: U.S. Congress, Congressional Globe
CHS: Connecticut Historical Society
CinHS: Cincinnati Historical Society
CL: University of Michigan, Clements Library
CWL: Basler, The Collected Works of Abraham Lincoln
DC: Dartmouth College
FHS: Freeport Historical Society
FPM: U.S. House of Representatives, Fort Pillow Massacre
GC: Gettysburg College
HL: Huntington Library
IHS: Indiana Historical Society
ISL: Indiana State Library
IU: Indiana University
KSHS: Kansas State Historical Society
KU: University of Kansas
LC: Library of Congress (Manuscripts Division, unless otherwise specified)
LSU: Louisiana State University
MEHS: Maine Historical Society
MHS: Massachusetts Historical Society
MNHS: Minnesota Historical Society
MOHS: Missouri Historical Society
MSSM: Massachusetts Soldiers, Sailors, and Marines in the Civil War
NA: National Archives
ND: University of Notre Dame
NH Archives: New Hampshire Division of Records Management and Archives
NHHS: New Hampshire Historical Society

NHSL: New Hampshire State Library
NSHS: Nebraska State Historical Society
OHS: Ohio Historical Society
OR: *War of the Rebellion: A Compilation of the Official Records of the Union and Confederate Armies* (all citations from Series 1 unless otherwise noted)
OR Atlas: Atlas to Accompany the Official Records of the Union and Confederate Armies
ORN: Official Records of the Union and Confederate Navies in the War of the Rebellion (all citations from Series 1 unless otherwise noted)
OR Supplement: Supplement to the Official Records of the Union and Confederate Armies
PEM: Peabody Essex Museum
PPL: Providence Public Library
RBHPL: Rutherford B. Hayes Presidential Library
RIHS: Rhode Island Historical Society
RJCCW: Report of the Joint Committee on the Conduct of the War (37th Congress)
RJCCW2: Report of the Joint Committee on the Conduct of the War, at the Second Session, Thirty-eighth Congress
RU: Rutgers University
SCL: University of South Carolina, South Caroliniana Library
SHC: University of North Carolina, Southern Historical Collection
SHSI-DM: State Historical Society of Iowa, Des Moines
SHSI-IC: State Historical Society of Iowa, Iowa City
SM: Sheldon Museum
UIA: University of Iowa Libraries
UNH: University of New Hampshire
UR: University of Rochester
USAMHI: U.S. Army Military History Institute
USG: Simon, *The Papers of Ulysses S. Grant*
UVM: University of Vermont
VAHS: Virginia Historical Society
VTHS: Vermont Historical Society
WHMC: University of Missouri, Western Historical Manuscript Collection
WHS: Wisconsin Historical Society
WRHS: Western Reserve Historical Society

Preface

1. Catton, *Reflections on the Civil War,* 111.
2. *CWL,* 6:56.
3. Schlesinger, *War and the American Presidency,* 73–74.
4. Ibid., 116.

1. An Army Stretched Out on the Hills

1. Messent and Courtney, *Twichell Letters,* 219; Sparks, *Patrick Diary,* 221; *Harper's Weekly,* April 4, 1863; Ninth U.S. Census of El Paso County, Texas (M-593, Reel 1583), p. 6, RG 29, NA.

2. Nevins, *Diary of Battle,* 171; Keiser Diary, March 10–12, 1863, USAMHI; *Harper's Weekly,* April 4, 1863; Sparks, *Patrick Diary,* 221; Robertson, *McAllister Letters,* 273.

3. Record of service and Pension Agency notice, Ellen L. Hart pension file, certificate 183101, RG 15, NA.

4. Messent and Courtney, *Twichell Letters,* 219–20; Meade, *Life and Letters,* 1:357.

5. Henry Beecham to "Dear Mother," March 16, 1863, WHS; Allen Landis to "Dear Father," March 20, 1863, LC; Chesson, *Dyer Journal,* 66–67; Kohl, *Welsh Letters,* 79.

6. Nevins, *Diary of Battle*, 175; Messent and Courtney, *Twichell Letters*, 223; Chesson, *Dyer Journal*, 68.

7. John Wilkins to "My dearly beloved wife," March 20 and 29, 1863, CL; John K. Fernsler Diary, February 12–25, 1863, USAMHI; Thomas Blanchard to "Dear Sarah," January 28, 1863, ND; George Thomas to "Dear Minerva," March 19 and 26, 1863, Thomas Family Correspondence, ND.

8. Daniel Kenney discharge, NHHS; Oliver Benton to Cora Benton, February 24, 1863, ND; Charles Barnard to "My Dear Maggie," March 11, 1864, MEHS; Josiah B. Corban to "Dear Wife and Children," July 1, 1863, CHS; *RJCCW2*, 1:112.

9. Griffin Stedman to "Sir," January 14 and April 13, 1863, CHS.

10. Ayling, *Register*, 978; Hastings, *Letters from a Sharpshooter*, 136, 146, 163, 166–67, 170.

11. Jackson and O'Donnell, *Clarke Letters*, 64.

12. *MSSM*, 2:807; *Oxford Democrat*, August 21, 1863.

13. Ayling, *Register*, 588; Ransom Sargent to "Dear Maria," January 18 and March 9, 1863, DC.

14. Henry Keiser Diary, February 19, 1863, USAMHI; John K. Fernsler Diary, February 21, 1863, USAMHI.

15. *RJCCW2*, 1:112; *OR*, 24(3):20, 163, and 25(2):15, 111, 180; *New York Times*, March 11 and 23, 1863. Leaves of absence were more freely granted in the winter, and Hooker's reforms were probably not entirely responsible for the gradual reduction in absentees.

16. Rosenblatt and Rosenblatt, *Fisk Letters*, 43–55; Fisk Diary, February 17, 1863, LC.

17. Welch to Wade, January 21, 1863, LC.

18. Pease and Randall, *Browning Diary*, 1:625.

19. Nevins and Thomas, *Strong Diary*, 3:295, 303; *OR*, 23(1):74, and 25(1):43–46, 65–73; Charles Greenleaf to "Dear Father & Mother," March 31, 1863, CHS; *New York Times*, March 5 and 6, 1863.

20. Eighth Census of Concord, N.H. (M-653, Reel 675), p. 157, RG 29, NA; Lizzie Corning Diary, February 9–June 6, 1863, NHHS.

21. Maria Coler to Daniel Coler, November 24, 1862, CL; Emily Harris to Leander Harris, April 7, 1862, February 20 and July 26, 1863, February 23, 1864, and undated fragment [but spring, 1863], UNH.

22. Houston, *Smith Correspondence*, 67–68, 71, 89.

23. Solomon Dodge to "Dear sister Eliza," January 17, 1863, NHHS; Robertson, *McAllister Letters*, 277.

24. Feargus Elliott to "Dear father and Mother and Brother," January 13 and March 14, 1863, USAMHI.

25. Marshall Phillips to "Dear Wife," February 6 and 27, 1863, MEHS.

26. *New York Times*, April 4, 1863; John Warner to "Dear Parents," April 8, 1864, UNH; *OR*, Series 3, 5:544.

27. Calvin Smith to "Dear Mother," March 14 and May 2, 1863, MHS.

28. Joseph Kohout to "Dear Father and Mother and Sister," March 31, 1863, UIA.

29. Alanson Miller to Frances Miller, December 17, 1862, February 11, 1863, and March 27, 1863, ND.

30. H. B. Cone to Trumbull, January 20, 1863, LC.

31. Albert Stearns to "Dear Sister," January 11, 1863, NHHS; Henry Vaughn to "Bub," July 24, 1863, Middlesex Papers, VTHS; Hughes, *Colby Papers*, 199; Kohl, *Welsh Letters*, 150.

32. James Law to "Dear Sister Agnes," March 18, 1863, CHS.

33. *Richmond Whig*, April 6, 1863; London *Times*, May 19, 1863; *New York Times*, April 8, 1863.

34. John Sheahan to "My Dear Father," April 8, 1863, MEHS; Kostyal, *Halsey Letters*, 64; George T. Chapin to John E. Chapin, February 17, 1863, IHS; Thomas Sterns to "My

dear Wife," April 5, 1863, UIA; John Foye to "Samuel," April 5, 1863, NHHS; James Giauque to "Folks at home," April 19, 1863, UIA; Thomas Cheney to "Dear Sister Melissa," April 8, 1863, UNH; James Brown to "Brother Thomas," April 6, 1863, MEHS; Meshack Larry to "Dear Sister," April 12, 1863, MEHS; Edward Davis to "Sallie," March 22 and April 16, 1863, UIA; Elisha Kempton to "Dear Folks at Home!" April 23, 1863, NHHS; David Seibert to "Father & All," April 12, 1863, USAMHI.

35. Descendants of soldiers who wrote disparagingly of Lincoln's government, or war, may have been more reluctant to release their letters, or less inclined to preserve them, because such sentiments came to be seen as treasonable; this might explain why more critical manuscript material seems to be surfacing as passions subside, and as wartime letters fall into the hands of generations unfamiliar with, indifferent to, or appreciative of their controversial content.

36. Gavin, *Pettit Letters*, 61; Williams, *Hayes Diary and Letters*, 2:397; Larimer, *Ritner Letters*, 147; Williams, *Garfield Letters*, 249.

37. John M. Jackson to "Dear Mother," April 11 and 28, 1863, ND; Jackson and O'Donnell, *Clarke Letters*, 65; James Shortelle to unidentified recipient, June 4, 1863, LC; William Stow to "Dear Father," March 14, 1863, UVM.

38. Nevins, *Diary of Battle*, 184; William Barrus to "Dear Brother," May 10, 1863, UNH; *Crisis*, March 25, 1863; Rien Tillison to "Dear Father," March 24, 1863, VTHS.

39. Wentworth to "My dear Wife," March 31 and May 12, 1863, and to the *Eastern Argus*, April 4, 1863, LC.

40. See Marvel, *Lincoln's Darkest Year*, 113–17, and Neely, *Fate of Liberty*, especially 51–65.

41. Clarkson Butterworth Diary, March 28 and November 11, 1863, Earlham; Sallie B. Miller to "Dear Brother Clason," May 7, 1863, CinHS.

42. Maria Mann to William Ropes, April 13, 1863, LC; John O. Crommett to "Dear Sister Cecelia," May 25, 1863, MEHS; Henry H. Seys to "Dear Hattie," August 20, 1863, CL.

43. James Miller to "Dear Brother," September 7, 1863, CL; *Portland Advertiser*, March 6, 1863; Sewell Tilton to "Dear Bro. & Sister," May 2, 1863, NHHS.

44. Mary Houston to William Coates, March 29, 1863, Yale; *Louisville Daily Democrat*, April 19, 1863; *OR*, Series 3, 3:100–101, 1111.

45. Adams, *Civil War Letters*, 13; James Montgomery to George Stearns, April 25, 1863, KSHS; *Boston Journal*, March 17, 1863; Looby, *Higginson Journal and Letters*, 105–23.

46. Sylvester, "Cox Letters," 64; Larimer, *Ritner Letters*, 157; Frederic Speed to "Dear Sister," April 6, 1863, and to "My Dear Father," May 26, 1863, CL; Charles Benton to Cora Benton, February 24, 1863, ND; Christopher Keller to "Dear Friends at Home," May 8, 1863, CL.

47. *Prairie du Chien Courier*, March 12, 1863; Simpson and Berlin, *Sherman Letters*, 418.

48. *Portland Advertiser*, March 7, 1863; *Illinois State Journal*, March 23, 1863; *Prairie du Chien Courier*, April 2, 1863; *Daily Gazette*, April 16, 1863; Terrell, *Report*, 338–42.

49. Nevins and Thomas, *Strong Diary*, 3:310; *New York Times*, April 8, 1863.

50. Sylvester Hadley Diary, March 10, 1863, NHHS; *Daily Chronicle*, March 12 and 13 and April 13, 1863.

51. William Church to Alexander Long, April 12, 1863, CinHS; Sears, *Fiske Letters*, 66; "Cousin Henry" to "Cousin Tim," April 5, 1863, Loomis Letters, CHS; *Crisis*, April 8 and 15, 1863. Dozens of Connecticut soldiers corroborated and protested this tactic in letters to the *Crisis*.

52. *New York Times*, April 8, 1863. A fervent Republican later confirmed (and condemned) this unseemly manipulation: see Robert Hale Kellogg to "Dear Father," March 25, 1864, CHS.

53. *Cleveland Plain Dealer,* April 11, 1863; *Crisis,* April 15, 1863, quoting the Indianapolis *Sentinel.*

54. William Church to Alexander Long, April 12, 1863, CinHS; George Towle to Charles Brewster, April 3, 1863, NHHS; *New York Times,* April 26, 1863.

55. *Cleveland Plain Dealer,* April 8 and 28, 1863; *Crisis,* April 29, 1863.

56. *Daily Gazette,* April 16, 1863; *Muscatine Courier,* April 18, 1863; *Prairie du Chien Courier,* May 14, 1863; *Boston Journal,* April 29, 1863; *Louisville Daily Democrat,* April 21, 1863; Terrell, *Report,* 351–52. Newspaper accounts of incidents like this inevitably flatter the faction favored by the editor, but most of the subsequent interpretive literature tends to accept government and government-friendly versions, when closer examination often suggests the culpability or contributory misbehavior of soldiers and other officials or supporters of the government.

57. *Crisis,* April 22 and 29, and May 6, 1863; *Daily Chronicle,* May 6, 1863.

58. "Records of School District No. 8, Town of Conway, Commencing April A.D. 1859," March 24, 1863, Conway Public Library. Even North Conway was not without its Unionists, however, and sometime after the meeting someone penciled in the parenthetical synonym "shit Hen" after "Copper head."

59. *Prairie du Chien Courier,* March 19, 1863; Charles Herbert to "Dear Parents," April 21, 1863, NHHS; Robert Hanna to "My Dear Wife," January 29, 1863, IHS; David Seibert to "Father and All," April 12, 1863, USAMHI; Simpson and Berlin, *Sherman Letters,* 419.

60. Joel Glover to "Dear Wife," March 20, 1863, UVM; William Barrus to "Dear Brother," May 10, 1863, UNH; William Smith to "Dear Parents & Sisters," March 12, 1863, CL; Nathan Gould to "Dear Mother," March 20, 1863, NHHS; Thomas Blanchard to "Dear Sarah," February 24, 1863, ND; Dan Mason to Harriet Clark, March 25, 1863, VTHS; Lucius Wood to "Dear Addie," May 23, 1863, WRHS.

61. Julius Wood to "Dear Parents & Sister," August 12, 1863, WRHS.

62. Elijah Cavins to "Dear Ann," April 9, 1863, IHS; Larimer, *Ritner Letters,* 136; George French to "Father," May 14 and July 18, 1863, to "Folks at Home," May 31, 1863, and to unidentified recipient, December 12, 1863, VTHS.

63. Nevins and Thomas, *Strong Diary,* 3:309–10.

64. Nevins, *Diary of Battle,* 281.

65. *New York Times,* March 10, 1863; Hammond, *Diary of a Union Lady,* 223; Nevins and Thomas, *Strong Diary,* 3:302–7.

66. *New York Times,* March 17 and 19, and April 3, 1863; *Daily Gazette,* April 3, 1863; *Portland Daily Press,* May 5, 1863; Union Club Minutes, NSHS.

67. *Washington Star,* April 3, 1863; Thompson and Wainwright, *Fox Correspondence,* 1:189–96; Beale, *Welles Diary,* 1:247, 262; Palmer, *Sumner Letters,* 2:152; *New York Times,* March 19, 1863.

68. Beale, *Welles Diary,* 1:262; *New York Times,* April 6, 1863; Marvel, *Mr. Lincoln Goes to War,* 273–78.

69. *Cleveland Plain Dealer,* April 7, 1863; *Louisville Daily Democrat,* April 7, 1863; *RJCCW,* 1:3–66, 113–754, and 3:3–6.

70. *New York Times,* April 2–7, 1863. For an expert look at the committee, see Tap, *Over Lincoln's Shoulder.*

71. Beale, *Welles Diary,* 1:262; Chesson, *Dyer Journal,* 69; Jordan, *Gould Journals,* 264.

72. Benjamin French to Henry F. French, April 8, 1863, and to Pamela French, May 3, 1863, NHHS.

73. *RJCCW,* 1:54–58, 717–18; Meade, *Life and Letters,* 1:358, 361, 362, 365–66; *Ohio State Journal,* April 14, 1863; Gurowski, *Diary,* 189; *Louisville Daily Democrat,* May 8, 1863; Franklin, *Reply.*

74. Meade, *Life and Letters,* 1:361, 362; *Correspondence of John Sedgwick,* 2:155.

75. Martin Davis to "Mr. Beckwith, Sir," April 1, 1863, UVM; William Stow to "Dear Father & Mother," February 23, 1863, UVM; William Hogan to "Dear thomas," February 18, 1863, VTHS; Rosenblatt and Rosenblatt, *Fisk Letters*, 58.

76. Andrew Young to "My Dear Susan," April 2, 1863, DC; Sparks, *Patrick Diary*, 229; Nevins, *Diary of Battle*, 176; William West Diary, April 3, 1863, MHS; Rosenblatt and Rosenblatt, *Fisk Letters*, 100.

77. *CWL*, 6:161; Hooker to Lincoln, April 3, 1863, ALP; Beale, *Bates Diary*, 287; Weld, *Diary and Letters*, 169; Meade, *Life and Letters*, 1:363; Sparks, *Patrick Diary*, 230; Nevins, *Diary of Battle*, 177.

78. *Correspondence of John Sedgwick*, 2:89; Weld, *Diary and Letters*, 169–70; Sparks, *Patrick Diary*, 231; Nevins, *Diary of Battle*, 177–78; George Marden to unidentified correspondent, April 7, 1863, DC. The *S* in "Sthreshley" is silent.

79. Meade, *Life and Letters*, 1:364; Rosenblatt and Rosenblatt, *Fisk Letters*, 64.

80. Weld, *Diary and Letters*, 169; Beale, *Bates Diary*, 288; Robertson, *McAllister Letters*, 282; William Speed to "My dear Lottie," April 12, 1863, CL; Nevins, *Diary of Battle*, 178; *Correspondence of John Sedgwick*, 2:89; Sparks, *Patrick Diary*, 231; O. Sandford to "Dear Mother," [April 6, 1863], SM.

81. Sparks, *Patrick Diary*, 231; George Marden to unidentified correspondent, April 7, 1863, DC; Weld, *Diary and Letters*, 169; *Correspondence of John Sedgwick*, 2:89; Meade, *Life and Letters*, 1:363.

82. Meade, *Life and Letters*, 1:363; *Correspondence of John Sedgwick*, 2:90; Chesson, *Dyer Journal*, 69.

83. Meade, *Life and Letters*, 1:363–65; Robertson, *McAllister Letters*, 282–83; *OR*, 25(2):180; Chesson, *Dyer Journal*, 69; Kostyal, *Halsey Letters*, 70; Rosenblatt and Rosenblatt, *Fisk Letters*, 64; Sparks, *Patrick Diary*, 232; David Seibert to "Father and All," April 12, 1863, USAMHI.

84. *Correspondence of John Sedgwick*, 1:90; Edwin Wentworth to "My dear Wife," April "7" [8], 1863, LC; Kostyal, *Halsey Letters*, 70; John Turner to "My Dear Daughter Virginia," March 31, 1863, Cumberland County Historical Society; Quaife, *Williams Letters*, 170; Scott, *Abbott Letters*, 173; Sears, *Dodge Journal*, 231; *OR*, 25(2):180; Meade, *Life and Letters*, 1:367.

85. Dyer, *Compendium*, 1219, 1222, 1405–18; *RJCCW2*, 1:219. The 36th New York should have mustered out in June, 1863, but was held until July 15, beyond its term.

86. Dyer, *Compendium*, 1014–15, 1018, 1226–27, 1249–51, 1263–66, 1352, 1363–64, 1467, 1469, 1613–15, 1619–22, 1635–36, 1653–54, 1666, 1687. A calculation of 23,586 nine-month men begins with *OR*, 25(2):243, 532, and *RJCCW2*, 1:219, which together tally 17,036 (the 133rd Pa. is duplicated, apparently in place of the 132nd, and the 135th Pa. is inadvertently listed as the "155th" Pa.). These two sources also overlook ten militia regiments that were with the army in April, and these are estimated at the average 655-man strength of the twenty-six listed regiments, or 6,550 for the ten and 23,586 altogether.

87. Daniel Brown to "Dear Brother Eph," November 30, 1862, MEHS; Horace Morse to "Dear Sis," March 28, 1863, MHS; Thomas Cheney to "Dear Brother," May 29, 1863, UNH.

88. Nevins, *Diary of Battle*, 184; Eben Calderwood to "Dear Wife," April 15, 1863, and Eben Roberts to "Kind Cousin," April 16, 1863, Calderwood Papers, MEHS; Nathan Gould to "Dear Mother," March 20 and April 4, 1863, NHHS; Joseph Spafford to "Dear Sister," April 19, 1863, VTHS; James Law to "Dear Sister Agnes," March 4, 1863, CHS.

89. Sparks, *Patrick Diary*, 228–29; George Bradley to "Dear friends at Home," February 20, "1862" [1863], Yale; Cleveland to "Dear Louise," January 9 and March 22, 1863, USAMHI; *OR*, 25(2):233–34, 243; *Daily Constitutional Union*, June 10, 1863; *Milwaukee Sentinel*, April 27, 1863.

90. Muster rolls of Company E, 32nd N.Y. Volunteers, Albert Hard military file, RG 94, NA.

91. Acken, *Inside the Army*, 219; John Wilkins to "My Dearly Beloved wife," April 8, 1863, CL; Nevins, *Diary of Battle*, 178; Meade, *Life and Letters*, 1:364; Wilbur Fisk Diary, April 8, 1863, LC; Weld, *Diary and Letters*, 170.

92. Kohl, *Welsh Letters*, 84.

93. Nevins, *Diary of Battle*, 178; Weld, *Diary and Letters*, 171; David Nichol to "Dear Sister," April 11, 1863, USAMHI; Friedrich P. Keppelman to "Dear Parents," April 10, 1863, USAMHI.

94. Albert Huntington to "Dear Father," April "9" [10], 1863, UR; Quaife, *Williams Letters*, 176.

95. Quaife, *Williams Letters*, 176; *OR*, 25(2):27–28.

96. *OR*, Series 3, 3:91.

97. Ibid., 109, 112; E. E. Cross to Franklin Pierce, April 14, 1863, Pierce Papers, NHHS.

98. Simpson and Berlin, *Sherman Letters*, 455–56, 458–59; *OR*, Series 3, 3:164–65.

99. *CWL*, 6:164–67.

100. Quaife, *Williams Letters*, 176; Kohl, *Welsh Letters*, 84, 139; Allen Landis to "Bro Will," April 18, 1863, LC; Hunley, *Young Letters*, 48.

101. A total of 5,131 Union soldiers were killed outright in the Chancellorsville and Gettysburg campaigns up to July 9 (*OR*, 25[1]:192 and 27[1]:193), and an estimate of 20 percent mortality among the 25,851 wounded would double that figure, besides the inevitable proportion of dead among some 12,000 missing (only 7,000 of whom were captured by the enemy) and more than a thousand who died of disease.

2. The Road Unknown

1. *New York Times*, April 11 and 12, 1863; Nevins and Thomas, *Strong Diary*, 3:310.

2. *ORN*, 14:3–8; William A. Campbell to "Dear Sister," April 13, 1863, MEHS; John Dillingham to "Dear Mother," April 14, 1863, FHS; Mushkat, *Voris Letters*, 114.

3. Beale, *Welles Diary*, 1:267–68; Laas, *Lee Letters*, 258; Palmer, *Sumner Letters*, 2:155–56; *CWL*, 6:170.

4. George Towle to Charles Brewster, April 13, 1863, NHHS; *New York Times*, March 19, April 8–10, and April 16, 1863.

5. *New York Times*, April 13–15, 1863; *Philadelphia Inquirer*, April 10, 1863; *Cincinnati Daily Commercial*, April 9 and 14, 1863; *OR*, 18:213–15, 600, 605–10; Lowry, *Swamp Doctor*, 149–61.

6. *OR*, 24(1):4–5, 18–24, 361–62; Larimer, *Ritner Letters*, 137; Puck, *Letters*, 50, 57. Ed Bearss's three-volume *Campaign for Vicksburg* details every episode of the struggle for that city, while Terrence Winschel's continuing series, *Triumph and Defeat*, is more accessible.

7. Simpson and Berlin, *Sherman Letters*, 420, 437, 453–54, 459–60; *OR*, 24(1):25–26, 29; *New York Times*, April 16, 1863; George A. Worster to H. B. Hill, April 5, 1863, Hill-Hudelson Family Papers, Earlham.

8. Nathaniel Banks to Mary Banks, January 15 and 22, 1863, LC; *OR*, 15:199–201, 233–34, 240–44, 698–99.

9. Gilbert Robie to "My Dear Wife," February 18, 1863, DC. For more on unhealthy conditions on the lower Mississippi see Anonymous Diary, January 30–March 16, 1863, Albert Austin to "Dear Mother," March 3, 1863, Andrew Farnum to "Dear Brother," February 18, 1863, Nathan G. Gould to unidentified recipient, April 4, 1863, and Charles Herbert to "Dear Parents," April 21, 1863, all in NHHS.

10. Edward J. Noyes to "My Dear Mother," February 5, 1863, Noyes Family Papers, MHS.

11. *OR*, 15:251–55, 272–75; Elias Wyckoff to "Dear Companion & Children," March 9 and 11, 1863, LSU; *ORN*, 19:665–702.

12. Henry Robinson to "My dear and affectionate wife and children," April 26, 1863, IHS; Larimer, *Ritner Letters*, 147; Sawyer, *Godfrey Letters*, 39, 40–42, 46–47; Eby, *Strother Diaries*, 164.

13. Edward Davis to "Sallie," March 22 and April 16, 1863, UIA; George Landrum to "Dear Amanda," May 15, 1863, and Marion Ward to "Home Friends," March 21, 1863, WRHS; Benjamin Bordner to "Mr. and Mrs. Hill," April 2, 1863, BL; Horace Hobart to "Dear Brother," March 2, 1863, IHS.

14. William Shaw to "Sister Emma," March 19, 1863, CL; Robert Moyle to "Dear Father & Mother," February 15, 1863, and Jim Giauque to Alfred Giauque, March 15, 1863, UIA.

15. *Daily Journal*, April 6 and 21, 1863; *Daily Gazette*, April 8, 1863; *Philadelphia Inquirer*, April 10, 1863.

16. Beale, *Welles Diary*, 1:266, 269–72, 304, 310; *ORN*, 2:100–101, and Series 2, 1:176.

17. Palmer, *Sumner Letters*, 2:153; Beale, *Welles Diary*, 1:250–51, 253–59.

18. Niven, *Chase Papers*, 4:17; Joseph Thurston to Richard Lathers, May 12, 1863, LC; *Eastern Townships Gazette*, April 17, 24, and May 21, 1863; *Advertiser*, April 30, 1863.

19. *Eastern Townships Gazette*, August 7, 1863; Marcellus Hartley to Edwin Stanton and to P. H. Watson, both August 2, 1862, quoted in Edwards, *Civil War Guns*, 73–74.

20. State Department Circulars No. 19 and 32, quoted in Balace, *Recrutements en Belgique*, 2; *Eastern Townships Gazette*, April 10 and May 1, 1863; Elvira Aplin to "Ever dear Son," March 16, 1863, CL.

21. *Eastern Townships Gazette*, April 24, 1863; *Crisis*, May 20, 1863; Sarah Fales to Edmund Fales, August 13, 1862, RIHS; Balace, *Recrutements en Belgique*, 7; *Advertiser*, June 4, 1863, quoting the *Daily News*.

22. *Advertiser*, July 31, August 7, 14, and 21, October 23, and November 13, 1862, April 2 and 9, 1863.

23. Nevins and Thomas, *Strong Diary*, 3:311; *Eastern Townships Gazette*, August 7, 1863; *CWL*, 6:183–84.

24. *OR*, 23(2):196–97, 733, 24(2):163, 702, 25(2):180, 696, Series 3, 3:179, and Series 4, 2:530.

25. Barnes, *Medical and Surgical History*, 1:146–51, 296–301, tallies 151,865 deaths from all causes among Union soldiers from July 1, 1861, to April 30, 1863. Nearly 10,000 died in April of 1863 alone. While the Union army actually occupied a significant portion of the Confederacy by then, raids into that occupied territory and a fluctuating battlefront obscured the degree of accomplishment for all but the more optimistic observers, and many of those underestimated how overwhelming a numerical superiority would be needed for complete conquest of the rebellious states. See, for instance, Augustus Paddock to "My Dear Cousin Mary," March 6, 1863, UVM; Claude Goings to Mary Goings, March 25, 1863, DC; Rien Tillison to "Dear Father," March 24, 1863, VTHS; Miller, *Whitman Writings*, 1:92, 99.

26. Nevins, *Strong Diary*, 299; *OR*, 23(2):198.

27. *Cincinnati Daily Commercial*, March 25, 1863; Lyman Jackman Diary, March 19–April 1, 1863, Albert E. Stearns to "Dear friends at home," April 3, 1863, and George Upton to "My Dear Wife," May 2, 1863, all in NHHS; Ransom Sargent to "Dear Maria," April 2, 1863, DC; Watson, *Hitchcock Diary*, 82–85; Loving, *Whitman Letters*, 90–91.

28. Williams, *Garfield Letters*, 255–56; *OR*, 23(2):224–25, 249.

29. *OR*, 24(1):521–22; Laas, *Lee Letters*, 258; Nevins and Thomas, *Strong Diary*, 3:315–16; Miller, *Whitman Writings*, 1:92; Burlingame, *Dispatches from Lincoln's White House*, 147–48, 149–50; Washington Roebling to John A. Roebling, April 15, 1863, RU.

30. *OR*, 25(2):199–200 [this April 12 missive is misdated April "11"]; *RJCCW2*, 1:113–15. See Sears, *Chancellorsville*, for an engaging study of this campaign and the events leading up to it.

31. Sparks, *Patrick Diary*, 232–33; Alonzo Cushing to "My Dear Coon," April 14, 1863, CCHS; John Wilkins to "My Dearly beloved wife," April 14, 1863, CL; Smith Bailey Diary, April 14 and 15, 1863, DC; Jordan, *Gould Journals*, 267; Nevins, *Diary of Battle*, 181; *OR*, 25(2):213–14.

32. *OR*, 25(2):214, 220; *RJCCW2*, 1:116; Nevins, *Diary of Battle*, 182; *CWL*, 6:175.

33. *OR*, 25(2):228–29; Jordan, *Gould Journals*, 267.

34. Sparks, *Patrick Diary*, 234–35; *Correspondence of John Sedgwick*, 2:90–91; Andrew Young to "My Dear Susan," April 21, 1863, DC; Joel Blake to "My Dear Laura," April 21, 1863, USAMHI; *RJCCW2*, 1:116.

35. *RJCCW2*, 1:116; *OR*, 25(2):233–34.

36. *CWL*, 6:189.

37. Racine, *Mattocks Journal*, 6; *OR*, 25(1):351–52, and (2):302; Chesson, *Dyer Journal*, 73.

38. E. E. Cross to Franklin Pierce, April 14, 1863, Pierce Papers, NHHS; Chesson, *Dyer Journal*, 71; *RJCCW2*, 112; Nevins, *Diary of Battle*, 184.

39. Nevins, *Diary of Battle*, 182; *OR*, 12(2, supplement):821–26, 1073–1109, 1112–33.

40. Sparks, *Patrick Diary*, 218–20; E. E. Cross to Franklin Pierce, April 14, 1863, Pierce Papers, NHHS.

41. Sparks, *Patrick Diary*, 220, 236; Racine, *Mattocks Journal*, 33; Scott, *Abbott Letters*, 173.

42. *OR*, 25(2):152; Jordan, *Gould Journals*, 269–70.

43. *OR*, 25(2):152, 470–71; Nevins, *Diary of Battle*, 208.

44. John D. Billings's wonderful *Hardtack and Coffee*, the most engaging and reliable reminiscence ever written by a Civil War veteran, includes an entire, illustrated chapter on corps and their badges (250–68).

45. Meade, *Life and Letters*, 1:369; Nevins, *Diary of Battle*, 183.

46. Jordan, *Gould Journals*, 270–71; *RJCCW2*, 1:116; *OR*, 25(2):269.

47. Alonzo Cushing to "My Dear Mother," April 27, 1863, CCHS; Alfred Talcott to Mary Talcott, April 27, 1863, CHS; John Wilkins to "My Dearly beloved wife," April 27, 1863, CL.

48. Sparks, *Patrick Diary*, 237; Meade, *Life and Letters*, 1:370; *RJCCW2*, 118–20; Quaife, *Williams Letters*, 179–81; Sumner, *Comstock Diary*, 241.

49. *Correspondence of John Sedgwick*, 2:111–12; Rosenblatt and Rosenblatt, *Fisk Letters*, 74–75; Nevins, *Diary of Battle*, 185; William West Diary, April 28, 1863, MHS; James Holmes to "My dear Sister Abbie," May 21, 1863, MHS; Blight, *Brewster Letters*, 220–21.

50. Weld, *Diary and Letters*, 187–90; William West Diary, April 29, 1863, MHS; Lewis Cleveland to "Dear Mother," April 30, 1863, and to "Dear Louise," same date, USAMHI.

51. William Speed to "Dear Lottie," May 10, 1863, CL; Nevins, *Diary of Battle*, 185–86; Hassler, *Pender Letters*, 233; Dowdey and Manarin, *Lee Papers*, 441–43.

52. Quaife, *Williams Letters*, 181–83; David Nichol to "Dear Father," May 8, 1863, USAMHI; *OR*, 25(2):293.

53. Sparks, *Patrick Diary*, 238–39; Andrew Young to "Dear Susan," April 29, 1863, DC; George Marden to unidentified recipient, April 30, 1863, DC.

54. Dowdey and Manarin, *Lee Papers*, 444–47; *RJCCW2*, 1:125.

55. Quaife, *Williams Letters*, 183; Nevins, *Diary of Battle*, 188; *RJCCW2*, 1:121–23; Meshack Larry to "Dear Sister," May 11, 1863, MEHS; Racine, *Mattocks Journal*, 8.

56. *RJCCW2*, 1:124–25; Acken, *Inside the Army*, 235–36; Quaife, *Williams Letters*, 186–87.

57. John Judd Diary, May 1, 1863, KSHS; Andrew Young to "Dear Susan," May 1, 1863, DC; William West Diary, May 1, 1863, MHS; Wilbur Fisk Diary, May 1, 1863, LC; *OR*, 25(1):558, (2):366; *RJCCW2*, 1:125.

58. *OR*, 25(1):408, 778, (2):353, 370, and Series 3, 3:314.

59. Anthony W. Ross to Sarah Emily Ross, May 13, 1863, OHS; Racine, *Mattocks Journal*, 10–11, 134; George Marden to unidentified recipient, May 4 and May 8, 1863, DC; Quaife, *Williams Letters*, 188; Meshack Larry to "Dear Sister," May 11, 1863, MEHS; Sparks, *Patrick Diary*, 241.

60. James T. Miller to "Dear Brother," May 12, 1863, CL; Quaife, *Williams Letters*, 190–91; *OR*, 25(1):483; David Leigh to Herman Drumgold, May 20 and June 1, 1863, DC.

61. Meshack Larry to "Dear Sister," May 11, 1863, MEHS; Styple, *De Trobriand Letters*, 98; Rufus Ames Diary, May 2, 1863, CAHC; Robertson, *McAllister Letters*, 322.

62. *RJCCW2*, 128–30; Henry Comey to "My Dear Father," May 5, 1863, AAS; Frank Collins to "Dear William," May 12, 1863, SHSI-IC; Horace Currier to Edwin Currier, May 27, 1863, WHS; *OR*, 25(1):479.

63. *OR*, 25(1):559, 599; James Holmes to "My dear Sister Abbie," May 21, 1863, MHS; William West Diary, May 3, 1863, MHS; Wilbur Fisk Diary, May 3, 1863, LC.

64. *OR*, 25(1):567–68; Jacob Haas to "My Dear Bro.," May 12, 1863, USAMHI; John Judd Diary, May 3, 1863, KSHS; James Brown to "Dear Brother" and to "Dear Sister Nell," both May 10, 1863, MEHS; Marshall Phillips to "Dear Wife," "April" [May] 4, 1863, MEHS.

65. *Correspondence of John Sedgwick*, 2:124; *OR*, 25(1):188–91; Rosenblatt and Rosenblatt, *Fisk Letters*, 78; Dan Mason to Harriet Clark, May 7, 1863, VTHS; Hosea Williams to Moses Parker, May 10, 1863, Parker Family Papers, UVM.

66. *OR*, 51(1):186–87; William West Diary, May 4 and 5, 1863, MHS; Wilbur Fisk Diary, May 5, 1863, LC; Weld, *War Diary and Letters*, 192–93.

67. Sparks, *Patrick Diary*, 242–43; Nevins, *Diary of Battle*, 201; Marshall Phillips to "Dear Wife," May 11, 1863, MEHS; Scott, *Abbott Letters*, 181; Edward Taylor to "My Dear Sister Lottie," May 7 and 12, 1863, BL; Quaife, *Williams Letters*, 201–2; William Draper to "My dear Wife," June 15, 1863, LC; Rufus Ames Diary, May 6, 1863, CAHC.

68. Burlingame, *Nicolay Letters*, 111–12.

69. Miller, *Whitman Writings*, 1:97–98; *OR*, 25(1):192; Meade, *Life and Letters*, 1:372; *RJCCW2*, 1:125, 128, 133–37; Gurowski, *Diary*, 221.

70. *New York Times*, May 8, 1863; Flavius Bellamy to "Dear Parents," May 4, 1863, ISL; John Sheahan to "Dear Father," May 9, 1863, MEHS; Lizzie Corning Diary, May 9 and 10, 1863, NHHS; Jordan, *Gould Journals*, 274.

71. *Crisis*, May 20, 1863.

72. Miller, *Whitman Writings*, 1:98, 99; Nevins and Thomas, *Strong Diary*, 3:318, 319; Horace Currier to Edwin Currier, May 27, 1863, WHS; William Draper to "My dear Father," May 17, 1863, LC.

73. Charles Parker to Edgar Van Hoesen, May 15, 1863, CL; Warren Cudworth to "My Dear Brother," May 9, 1863, AAS.

74. Alonzo Cushing to "My Dear Coon," April 13 and May 7, 1863, and to "My Dear Mother," April 27, 1863, CCHS; George Spencer to "Dear Mother," May 15, 1863, USAMHI.

75. Edward H. C. Taylor to "My dear Sister Lottie," May 7, 1863, BL; Sparks, *Patrick Diary*, 247–48.

76. Thomas Cheney to "Dear Brother," May 29, 1863, UNH; Williams, *Hayes Diary and Letters*, 2:410–11; Ten Eyck to Hooker, May 17, 1863, CL; Chandler to "My dear Wife," May 20, 1863, LC.

77. Edward Wade to "Dear Nell," May 7, and to "Dear Ellen," May 9, 1863, CL; Daniel Faust to "Dear Sister," May 23, 1863, USAMHI; James Holmes to Abbie Homer, May 30, 1863, MHS.

78. Jordan, *Gould Journals*, 272.

79. *OR*, 25(1):541, 543; *RJCCW2*, 1:219; Nevins and Thomas, *Strong Diary*, 3:320.

80. Rufus Ames Diary, May 26, 1863, CAHC.

81. *Correspondence of John Sedgwick*, 2:128, 129, 131; *New York Times*, April 18, 1863; *OR* Series 3, 3:90; James Brown to "Dear Friends," June 13, 1863, MEHS.

82. George Spinney to "Dear Sister," November 19, 1862, BPL; Haines, *Letters*, 119–20; Charles Woodwell Diary, June 26, 1863, LC.

83. Larimer, *Ritner Letters*, 133; Jones, "Bent Letters," 97; Robert Findlay to Robert Crouse, July 27, 1863, BL; *Kansas Chief*, March 12, 1863.

84. Robert Miller to "Dear Parents," November 2, 1862, and July 18, 1863, CL; Harrison Varney to "Absent One," June 6, 1863, DC.

85. Eben Calderwood to "Dear Wife," April 15, 1863, and Eben Roberts to "Kind Cousin," April 16, 1863, Calderwood Papers, MEHS; Leonard Valentine to "Dear Father and Mother," June 3, 1863, MEHS; Mark P. Waterman to "Dear Wife and Children," June 3 and 10, 1863, MEHS; James Law to "Dear Father," May 18, 1863, CHS; Roswell Farnham to "My Dear Wife," May 24, 1863, VTHS; William Allen to "Friend Benton," May 2, 1863, MEHS.

86. *OR*, 21:279, and 25(1):360; Wolf, "Taylor Diary," 348–49; Charles Goddard to Catharine Smith, May 24, 1863, Orrin Smith Papers, MNHS, quoted in Moe, *Last Full Measure*, 246.

87. Elijah Cavins to "Dear Ann," June 5, 1863, IHS; Gavin, *Pettit Letters*, 90.

88. *New York Times*, June 9, 1863; *Times* (London), June 22, 1863. The 168th and 177th New York were nine-month regiments, and the 176th New York, at least, was composed of both nine-month and three-year men.

89. Cleveland to "Dear Louise," May 3 and May 17, 1863, USAMHI; muster-out roll of Co. C, 32nd N.Y., Lewis F. Cleveland military file, RG 94, NA.

90. Muster rolls of May 31, 1861, through April 10, 1863, and muster-out roll of Co. E, 32nd N.Y., Albert Hard military file, RG 94, NA; *New York Times*, June 9, 1863.

91. *New York Times*, March 13, 1953; *Binghampton Press*, March 13, 1953. Hard was survived by several spurious Confederate veterans and one genuine Union drummer boy from Minnesota, Albert Woolson, who died in August of 1956.

3. The Clear and Present Danger of Democracy

1. *CG*, 37th Cong., 3rd sess., part 1, 165, and part 2, appendix, 53, 58.

2. *CG*, 37th Cong., 3rd sess., part 2, appendix, 55.

3. *Daily Gate City*, February 20, 1863; *Weekly Gate City*, February 25, 1863; *Nonpareil*, April 4, 1863; *Crisis*, March 11 and 18, 1863; *Cleveland Leader*, March 28, 1863; *Dayton Weekly Empire*, April 4, 1863; *Daily Chronicle*, April 13, 1863. As Mark Neely illustrates in *Southern Rights*, the Confederacy imposed similar infringements on traditional liberties. Southern repression met with somewhat less resistance, perhaps because the Confederacy was the invaded nation, but the question remains whether those infringements were altogether necessary to prosecution of the war on either side, and — if so — whether the need for such obnoxious precedents did not reduce the advisability of conducting such a war at all.

4. *Crisis*, March 25 and April 1, 1863; *OR*, Series 2, 5:367; *Eastern Townships Gazette*, April 10, 1863.

5. *OR*, 23(2):193–94, Series 2, 5:365–66, 52(1):342, and Series 3, 3:75–76, 79–81; Carrington to Abraham Lincoln, January 14, February 2, and March 2, 1863, ALP; Henry Halleck to Burnside, March 21, 1863, Box 11, Burnside Papers, RG 94, NA.

6. *OR*, 23(2):168; Carrington to William Cullen Bryant, November 14, 1862, ISL; Andrew Wallace to Burnside, April 29, 1863, Box 7, Burnside Papers, RG 94, NA.

7. *Dayton Daily Empire*, March 23, 1863, quoted in Klement, *Limits of Dissent*, 146; *Crisis*, April 8, 1863.

8. *Dayton Daily Empire*, April 11 and 18, 1863, quoted in Klement, *Limits of Dissent*, 147; *Crisis*, April 8, 1863.

9. *Ohio State Journal*, April 21, 1863; *Cincinnati Daily Commercial*, April 20, 29, and 30, 1863; Milo Hascall to Burnside, May, 1863, and J. R. Hawley to Burnside, May 19, 1863, both Box 7, Burnside Papers, RG 94, NA.

10. *Crisis*, April 29 and May 6, 1863; *Ohio State Journal*, May 2, 1863, quoted in Klement, *Limits of Dissent*, 151.

11. Daniel Larned Journal, May 5, 1863, LC; *Summit County Beacon*, May 14 and 28, 1863, quoted in Shankman, "Vallandigham's Arrest," 121–23.

12. *Crisis*, May 13 and 20, 1863.

13. Ibid. The Supreme Court later concurred in the illegality of the tribunals.

14. *Crisis*, May 13, 1863; *CWL*, 5:297. Lincoln actually encouraged the unauthorized peace proposal, rejecting only an immediate cease-fire (*CWL*, 5:553–54).

15. Daniel Larned Journal, May 5, 1863, LC; *Crisis*, May 13, 1863; *OR*, Series 2, 5:573–74.

16. *Dayton Daily Empire*, March 6 and May 5, 1863, *Dayton Weekly Empire*, March 14, 1863, quoted in Klement, *Limits of Dissent*, 144, 149, 160.

17. Daniel Larned Journal, May 5, 1863, LC; Sallie Miller to "Dear Brother Clason," May 7, 1863, CinHS; *Cincinnati Daily Commercial*, May 7, 1863; *Boston Evening Transcript*, May 7, 1863; *Louisville Daily Democrat*, May 7, 1863; *OR*, Series 2, 5:566.

18. James Adams to "Dear Father," May 7, 1863, IHS; Elijah Cavins to "Dear Ann," May 11, 1863, IHS; James Pike to David Tod, May 8, 1863, Box 7, Burnside Papers, RG 94, NA.

19. *Daily Gazette* and *Cincinnati Daily Commercial*, May 9, 1863; *Louisville Daily Democrat*, May 8, 17, 19, 20, 1863; *Detroit Free Press*, May 7, 8, 15, 18, 1863; Daniel Larned Journal, May 6, 1863, LC; *Cleveland Plain Dealer*, May 6, 1863; *Carroll County Register*, May 21, 1863; Nordholt, "Civil War Letters," 366.

20. Pease and Randall, *Browning Diary*, 1:630–31.

21. *Crisis*, May 13 and 20, 1863; *CWL*, 6:538–39.

22. *Crisis*, May 13, 1863; *OR*, Series 2, 5:633–38.

23. *OR*, Series 2, 5:636, 640.

24. *Crisis*, May 13 and 20, 1863; Cox to George McClellan, May 31, 1863, Reel 35, McClellan Papers, LC; *OR*, Series 2, 5:642–46.

25. *OR*, Series 2, 5:573–76; Lincoln to Stanton, May 13, 1863, Stanton Papers, LC.

26. *OR*, Series 2, 5:578–84.

27. Ibid., 608, 656–57.

28. *OR*, Series 2, 5:665–66; *ORN* 25:140, and Series 2, 1:81; Vallandigham to Horatio Seymour, May 21, 1863, Stillwell Papers, OHS.

29. *OR*, 23(1):569, 574, and Series 2, 5:705–6; John Crittenden to "Dear Bettie," May 27, 1863, University of Texas, Center for American History.

30. *OR*, Series 2, 5:958, 963–65, 966, 968–69; Jones, *A Rebel War Clerk's Diary*, 229–30.

31. Wiggins, *Gorgas Journals*, 70; *Crisis*, June 17 and July 8, 1863; *Eastern Townships Gazette*, July 24 and 31, 1863; Williams, *Garfield Letters*, 273.

32. *New York Tribune*, June 15, 1863.

33. *Detroit Free Press*, June 16, 1863; *New York Tribune*, June 15, 1863.

34. Although one biographer credits a claim that the young Lincoln read Gibbon's *Decline and Fall of the Roman Empire* and Rollin's *Ancient History* while lounging at his New Salem store (Beveridge, *Abraham Lincoln*, 1:135), Lincoln's prose and reasoning give little hint that he took much warning from the demise of the Greek and Roman models for American democracy. His better-documented reading material was largely confined to American history and biography, literature (including the Bible and religious literature),

and mathematics. His recorded borrowings from the Library of Congress, for instance, include no ancient history (Hertz, *Abraham Lincoln*, 1:369–71).

35. Ibid.; *CWL*, 6:300–306; *Detroit Free Press*, July 4, 1863.

36. Larimer, *Ritner Letters*, 174–75.

37. Jordan, *Gould Journals*, 275; Lizzie Corning Diary, May 9, 1863, NHHS; *Detroit Free Press*, May 26, 1863; William E. Putnam to "Friend Clarence," May 26, 1863, Fowler/Black Family Correspondence, PEM; Thomas Christie to "My Dear Sister," June 7, 1863, MNHS; Julia Leeds to "My dear friend," June 9, 1863, Duncan Letters, DC; Kohl, *Welsh Letters*, 98.

38. Simpson and Berlin, *Sherman Letters*, 470–73.

39. *OR*, 24(1):47, 252–53, 255; Simpson and Berlin, *Sherman Letters*, 465–66.

40. *OR*, 24((1):47–49, 655, 658, 663–65

41. *OR*, 24(1):48, 629, 677, and 24(3):268–69; William Rigby to "Dear Brother," May 4, 1863, UIA; John Jones to "Dear Parents," May 6, 1863, LC; Sylvester Bishop to "Dear Mother," May 4, 1863, IHS.

42. *OR*, 24(1):616, 631–32; Gilbert Gulbrandson to unidentified correspondent, May 3, 1863, USAMHI.

43. Simpson and Berlin, *Sherman Letters*, 466–67; Cutrer and Parrish, *Pierson Letters*, 194–95; *OR*, 24(1):576–78, and 24(3):268.

44. *OR*, 15:313–16, 24(3):192, 223–25, 247, 265, 276, 281, and 26(1):11; David Scott to "Dear Kate," September 10, 1863, IHS; Eby, *Strother Diaries*, 172.

45. Stephen Hurlbut to "Dear William," May 31, 1863, CL; *OR*, Series 3, 3:63.

46. Simpson and Berlin, *Sherman Letters*, 465; Charles Dana to Edwin Stanton, May 5, 1863, and Stanton to Dana, May 6, 1863, Stanton Papers, LC.

47. *OR*, 24(3):268; Larimer, *Ritner Letters*, 165; James Giauque to Alfred Giauque, May 15, 1863, UIA; John Jones to "Beloved Parents," May 10, 1863, LC; Christopher Keller to "Dear Friends At Home," May 8, 1863, CL; Simpson and Berlin, *Sherman Letters*, 468–69.

48. John J. Barney to "All at Home," May 9, 1863, WHS; Thomas Christie to "My Dear Brother," June 5, 1863, MNHS.

49. Simpson and Berlin, *Sherman Letters*, 470; *OR* 24(3):842, 850, 859, 870, 882, 883–84, 888.

50. *OR*, 24(3):249, 300, 846, 862; Howard Stevens to "My dear cousin Em," May 31, 1863, USAMHI.

51. Simpson and Berlin, *Sherman Letters*, 471; *OR*, 24(1):250–51, and 24(3):308, 310, 876, 877–78, 891–92; John Lester Diary, May 14, 1863, IHS; Larimer, *Ritner Letters*, 172.

52. Fremantle, *Three Months in the Southern States*, 109–10; *OR*, 24(3):314–15.

53. *OR*, 24(2):70–74, and 24(3):887.

54. *OR*, 24(2):82, 99, 112; muster rolls of Companies E and F, 2nd Missouri, roll of prisoners at Point Lookout, September 22, 1863, roll of prisoners paroled at Camp Douglas, February 13, 1865, and oath of allegiance, April 29, 1865, William Spoor file, Compiled Service Records of Confederate Soldiers Who Served in Organizations from the State of Missouri (M-322, Reel 111), RG 109, NA.

55. Eighth Census of Grand Isle County, Vermont (M-653, Reel 1318), pp. 38, 42, RG 29, NA; William Spoor to Austin Spoor, July 19, 1863, VTHS.

56. *New Hampshire Sentinel*, August 22, 1861; *Daily Chronicle*, November 23, 1861; Easley, "Cheavens Journal," 13.

57. *OR*, 24(3):439, and 52(2):468–69.

58. John Lester Diary, May 17–22, 1863, IHS; Larimer, *Ritner Letters*, 169, 171, 174; John Jones to "Dear and Beloved Parents," May 29, 1863, LC; Simpson and Berlin, *Sherman Letters*, 471–72; *OR*, 24(1):54–55, 59; William Christie to "Dear Father," May 31, 1863, MNHS.

59. George DeHart to "Dear Sister," July 2, 1863, SHSI-IC; "Brother Lyman" to "Dear Sarah," June 28, 1863, Richardson Family Papers, NSHS; Alonzo Jack to unidentified recipient, May 25, 1863, WHS.

60. Marquis Alonzo Hills to "Dear Father," June 8, 1863, KU; Charles Dana to Edwin Stanton, May 27, 1863, Stanton Papers, LC; Larimer, *Ritner Letters*, 175; Simpson and Berlin, *Sherman Letters*, 473.

61. *OR*, 26(1):12, 180, 494, 500, and 26(2):9, 10; Charles Dana to Edwin Stanton June 12, 1863, Stanton Papers, LC.

62. *OR*, 26(1):508-9; John Hammond Diary, "March 14," 1863, USAMHI; Sawyer, *Godfrey Letters*, 58-59.

63. Thomas Alexander Diary, May 27, 1863, ND; *OR* 26(1):509-11; Daniel Durgin to "Dear Sis," undated, Cram Family Papers, NHHS; Justus Gale to "Dear Sister," May 29, 1863, Gale-Morse Papers, VTHS; James Osborne Diary, May 26-28, 1863, MHS.

64. William Hayward to "My Darling Wife," May 28, 1863, USAMHI; Hiram Gregg Diary, May 29 and 30, 1863, DC; Daniel Durgin to "Dear Sis," undated, Cram Family Papers, NHHS; Barnes, *Medical and Surgical History*, 2:335, 8:494-95, 11:279, and 12:623, 845, 892, 894-95.

65. Jabez Alvord Diary, May 25-28, June 5-8, 10, 12, 13, 19-20, 24, 26, 28, July 1-3, and July 9, 1863, LC.

66. Banks to Mary Banks, August 1, 1863, LC; *OR*, 26(1):14, 57-65; William Dwight to Richard Irwin, June 27, 1863, Porter Collection, Yale.

67. *OR*, 26(1):45, 60-61, and Series 3, 2:436-38; Homer Sprague Diary, May 27, 1863, LC.

68. Bates to Welles, June 6, 1863, Lincoln Papers, Yale; Fite, *Social and Industrial Conditions*, 14-15.

69. Dana to Edwin Stanton, May 31, 1863, Lincoln to Grant, and Halleck to Grant, John Schofield, and Ambrose Burnside, all June 2, 1863, Stanton Papers, LC.

70. *OR*, 22(2):306-8, 23(2):384, and 24(3):325; Johnson to Lincoln, May 29, 1863, Stanton Papers, LC.

71. Henry Tisdale Diary, June 1 and 3-5, 1863, BPL; Gavin, *Pettit Letters*, 86-87.

72. Gavin, *Pettit Letters*, 87; Oscar Robinson Diary, June 8-11, 1863, DC; Henry Tisdale Diary, June 7-10, 1863, BPL; William Draper to "My dear Wife," June 15 and 16, 1863, LC; George Upton to "My Dear Wife," June 10, 1863, NHHS; *OR*, 24(3):395, 396, 404.

73. Oscar D. Robinson Diary, June 12-14, 1863, DC; Henry Tisdale Diary, June 12-14, 1863, BPL; *OR*, 24(2):446-48, 453-55; Charles Dana to Edwin Stanton, June 10, 1863, Stanton Papers, LC; Anson Butler to "My Dear Wife," June 14, 1863, UIA; Sewell Tilton Diary, June 15, 1863, NHHS; Hosea Towne to "Dear Friends," June 20, 1863, NHHS.

74. Sewell Tilton Diary, June 15, 1863, NHHS; William Draper to "My dear Wife," June 16, 1863, LC; Henry Tisdale Diary, June 15, 1863, BPL.

75. Henry Tisdale Diary, June 15, 1863, BPL; Upton to "My Dear Sarah," July 17, 1862, and June 19, 1863, NHHS.

76. Gavin, *Pettit Letters*, 89-90; Henry Tisdale Diary, June 17-18, 1863, BPL; Andrew Stone to "Brother Wes," June 18 and 28, 1863, NHHS; Lyman Jackman Diary, June 16-17, 1863, NHHS; Hosea Towne to "Dear Friends," June 20, 1863, NHHS.

77. *OR*, 24(3):384.

78. Ibid., 381.

79. *Chicago Tribune*, June 4, 1863; *Cleveland Plain Dealer*, June 3, 1863; *Crisis*, June 10, 1863.

80. For a few instances of earlier newspaper repression see Marvel, *Mr. Lincoln Goes to War*, 185-87.

81. *Chicago Tribune*, June 3 and 4, 1863; *Cincinnati Daily Commercial*, June 2, 1863.

82. *Cleveland Plain Dealer,* June 3 and 4, 1863.

83. Pease and Randall, *Browning Diary,* 1:632, 633; *Crisis,* June 10, 1863; Napoleon Buford to Jacob Ammen, June 4, 1863, OHS.

84. Pease and Randall, *Browning Diary,* 1:632, 633; *Crisis,* June 10, 1863; George Weston to Trumbull, June 11, 1863, LC; *OR,* 23(2):385; Resolutions of the Illinois Legislature, June 4, 1863, ALP.

85. *Cleveland Plain Dealer,* June 5 and 6, 1863; *Ohio State Journal,* June 6, 1863; *CWL,* 6:248; *OR,* 23(2):386; J. R. Hawley to Burnside, May 18, 1863, Box 7, Burnside Papers, RG 94, NA.

86. Racine, *Mattocks Letters,* 33; William Hamilton to "Dear Boyd," June 8, 1863, Hamilton Family Papers, LC; *Crisis,* July 1, 1863; *OR,* 34(2):363.

4. Toward Getty's Town

1. Elijah Cavins to "Dear Ann," June 12, 1863, IHS.

2. E. J. Runyon to "Governor Kirkwood," July 2 [1863], Disloyal Sentiments File, SHSI-DM, quoted in Wubben, *Civil War Iowa,* 115; *Dubuque Times,* July 23, 1863; *Dakotian,* June 23, 1863; *Oxford Democrat,* May 29, 1863.

3. *Prairie du Chien Courier,* May 14, 1863; *Crisis,* May 27, June 3, 10, and 24, 1863; *Detroit Free Press,* May 31 and June 5, 1863.

4. Wainwright, *Fisher Diary,* 453–54; Stephen Holt to "Dear Grandfather," June 4, 1863, DC; Beale, *Welles Diary,* 1:321; Niven, *Chase Papers,* 4:66.

5. *New York Daily News,* June 4, 1863; *New York Times,* June 4, 1863.

6. *Detroit Free Press,* May 29, 1863, articulates this position, claiming that the 1861 Crittenden Compromise would have satisfied every Northerner who had voted for John Bell or Stephen Douglas in 1860, as well as every Southerner — who, with Unionist Republicans, would have represented the majority of pre-secession U.S. citizens. Secessionists had overwhelmed the moderate element in the Gulf States, however, and formal organization of the Confederate States had drastically reduced any attraction the compromise might have had for Southerners, but it was primarily the Republicans in the U.S. Senate who killed that peaceful effort and prevented any test of its popular appeal. See, for instance, *CG,* 36th Cong., 4th sess., 1490–93, 1498–1519.

7. Draft resolution dated May 1, 1863, Crittenden Papers, LC; *New York Times,* June 4, 1863.

8. Nevins and Thomas, *Strong Diary,* 1:324; *OR,* Series 3, 3:205, 217; William Proctor to "Father & Mother," April 12, 1864, Fairbanks Museum; *Prairie du Chien Courier,* July 16, 1863.

9. Gustave Soule to "Cousin Hattie," June 3, 1863, USAMHI; Thomas Christie to "My Dear Brother," June 5, 1863, MNHS; Allen Landis letter fragment, mid-1863, LC; Wayne Morris to "My Dearly Beloved Companion," June 9, 1863, and to "Dear Brother," June 10 [1863], BL.

10. Hammond, *Diary of a Union Lady,* 241; John O. Rossetter to Robert Crouse, May 25, 1863, BL; John Foye to "Samuel," April 5, 1863, NHHS; Amanda Chittenden to George Chittenden, June 14, 1863, ISL; Mary Edwards to "Dear Uncle," August 20, 1863, Harrington Collection, RBHPL; Lucius Wood to "Dear Addie," May 23, 1863, WRHS.

11. Wells B. Fox to Robert Crouse, May 14, 1863, BL; John Crommett to "My Dear Celestia," May 25, 1863, MEHS; Edward E. Davis to "Dear Mother," June 16, 1863, UIA.

12. Milton Crist to "Dear Sister," August 7, 1863, IU; Nevins, *Diary of Battle,* 281; Sparks, *Patrick Diary,* 289; Solomon Hamrick to "Brother Charlie," April 17, 1863, IHS.

13. Houston, *Smith Correspondence,* 174; Anderson, *Geer Diary,* 125; Burgess, *Uncommon Soldier,* 37; William A. Smith to "Dear Parents & Sisters," March 12, 1863, CL; William Henry Shaw to "Sister Emma," March 14, 1863, CL; Dan Mason to Harriet Clark,

March 25, 1863, VTHS; George Hanson to "Dear Mother," April 5, 1864, KSHS; Myron Underwood to "My Dear Wife," July 26 and October 5, 1863, UIA.

14. John R. Beatty to Laura E. Maxfield, June 21, 1863, MNHS.

15. George Oscar French to "Folks at Home," May 14 and 31, 1863, and to "Father," July 18, 1863, VTHS; Stephen Pingree to "Cousin Augustus," August 2, 10, and September 7, 1863, Lyndon State College Collection, VTHS; Julius Wood to "Dear Parents & Sister," August 12, 1863, WRHS; Thomas Honnell to "Respected Friend & Adopted Brother," September 17, 1863, OHS; Emily Harris to Leander Harris, undated fragment [June, 1863], and Leander's reply of June 30, 1863, UNH. The Harrises fell into political dispute in almost every letter.

16. Jonathan Joseph to "Dear Sister," April 10, 1864, ISL; *OR*, Series 2, 5:363-67; Wayne Morris to "My Beloved Companion," May 27, 1863, BL; James Moses to Jacob Ammen, April 24, 1863, Ammen Papers, OHS. See also Klement, *Dark Lanterns*, 25-27. In *Copperheads* (25), Jennifer Weber notes that Klement's career-long investigation into the K.G.C. saga convinced him that it was an orchestrated myth, but she rejects his conclusion on the grounds that so many different people reported sincerely on disloyal secret societies, privately and officially, that their claims must have had substance. On the contrary, however, exaggeration, absurdity, and political or personal motive taint multitudes of those reports, and most seem only to reflect the prevailing hysteria. Weber seems unaware of Republican efforts to excite suspicion and encourage such reports. She alludes to McCarthyism, but overlooks that the Red Scare of the 1950s also produced blizzards of private and official reports detailing a vast nationwide conspiracy that simply did not exist. Her most chilling example of a seditious passage, meanwhile (*Copperheads*, 26), suggests that she, too, confuses contempt for administration policy with a desire to see the government overthrown.

17. *Louisville Daily Democrat*, April 21, 1863; *Prairie du Chien Courier*, May 14, 1863.

18. Amanda Chittenden to George Chittenden, June 14, 1863, ISL; unidentified correspondent to "Dear Brother," July 15, 1863, and "Miss Jane" to "Dear Friend," July 17, 1863, Kehrwecker Family Papers, BGSU; Jonathan Harrington to "Dear Parents," September 7, 1863, and Mary Edwards to "Dear Uncle," October 11, 1863, both in Harrington Collection, RBHPL; *Daily Gate City*, August 26, 1863.

19. E[liza] J. Runyon to "Governor Kirkwood," July "2" [presumably 1863], Disloyal Sentiments File, SHSI-DM, quoted in Wubben, *Civil War Iowa*, 115; William H. Rhoades to "Dear Father," December 20, 1863, Rhoades Letters, RBHPL.

20. Amanda Chittenden to George Chittenden, June 14, 1863, ISL; "Lottie" to Phebe Gale, November 16, 1863, Shaw-Gale-Noxon Family Papers, NSHS.

21. James Geary's *We Need Men* is the best of several books on the Northern draft.

22. Jacob Ammen to Samuel Curtis, April 18, 1863, A. Babcock to Ammen, April 23, 1863, Solon Burroughs to Ammen, April 24, 1863, and Hannah Thorne to Ammen, May 23, 1863, Ammen Papers, OHS; Jesse Handley to James Handley, June 29 (possibly 24), 1863, IU; *Cleveland Plain Dealer*, July 17, 1863; *New York Times*, May 31, 1863.

23. *Holmes County Farmer*, reprinted in *Crisis*, July 1, 1863; *OR*, 23(1):395-97 and Series 3, 3:403; *North Missouri Courier*, July 2, 1863.

24. Charles Branich to "Dear Brother in law and Sister," June 9, 1863, MNHS; *OR*, Series 3, 3:395-96, 490; *Oxford Democrat*, July 31, 1863; *Chicago Tribune*, June 26 and 27, 1863.

25. *Louisville Daily Democrat*, June 13, 16, and 18, 1863; Thomas Barnett Diary, June 20, 1863, Earlham.

26. *Daily Constitutional Union*, June 11, 1863; *OR*, Series 3, 3:338-41.

27. *OR*, Series 3, 3:330-32, 341, 351-52, 357, 372-73, 382, 421; Samuel Allen to Samuel Yohe, July 22 and 27, 1863, and Joseph Wetherwill to Yohe, June 11, 1863, Letters Received, Eleventh District of Pennsylvania, Nelson Bradford to James Bomford, June 22, 1863, Letters Received, Twelfth District of Pennsylvania, and Charlemagne Tower to

James Fry, June 26, 1863, Letters Forwarded, Tenth District of Pennsylvania, all in RG 110, NA, and all quoted in Palladino, *Another Civil War*, 105–11.

28. Henry Heisler to "Dear Sister," August 9, 1863, LC.

29. *OR*, Series 3, 3:410; Christopher Hoyt to "Dear brother and sister," July 27, 1863, NHHS; A. B. Long to "Dear Major," August 16, 1863, Duncan Letters, DC; George Anthony to "Kind Brother," August 15, 1863, CL.

30. Dowdey and Manarin, *Lee Papers*, 500–503, 507–9.

31. William Stow to "Dear Parents," May 30, 1863, UVM; Flavius Bellamy to "Dear Brother," June 12, 1863, ISL; Clement Hoffman to "Dear Mother," June 23, 1863, USAMHI.

32. *OR*, 27(2):440. The best single-volume account of the Gettysburg campaign, of which Brandy Station was the opening battle, is Sears, *Gettysburg*.

33. On Milroy at Second Bull Run, see Hennessy, *Return to Bull Run*, especially 418–19.

34. Kies to "My Dear Wife," April 11, 25, 29, and May 13, 14, and 26, 1863, CHS.

35. Cora Benton to Charles Benton, July 8, 1863, ND; Mary Burnham to "My Dear Son," March 29, 1863, PEM; *MSSM*, 4:449; Ninth Census of Essex County, Massachusetts (M-593, Reel 607), p. 31, RG 29, NA.

36. Tabor Parcher to "Dearest of all dear wives," April 9, 1864, UVM; *Daily Chronicle*, February 11 and 20, 1865; Ninth U.S. Census (M-593, Reel 839), p. 16, and Tenth U.S. Census (T-9, Reel 762, ED 35), sheet 20, RG 29, NA.

37. Sarah Rice to John Rice, July 21 and November 17, 1863, RBHPL; Thirteenth Census of Marshall County, Iowa (T-624, Reel 413, ED 138), sheet 4, RG 29, NA.

38. Edwin Horton to "Dearest Ellen," January 29, 1865, VTHS; Sarah Rice to John Rice, January 22, February 5 and 10, 1864, RBHPL; Frank Hubbard to "Dear Carrie," July 25, 1863, and Perry Parker to Asahel Hubbard, August 4, 1863, and November 28, 1864, Hubbard Family Papers, UVM; Ransom Sargent to "Dear Maria," January 14, 18, and March 6, 1863, DC.

39. Niven, *Chase Papers*, 3:358, 363–65, and 4:127; Mushkat, *Voris Letters*, 101; George Benson Fox to "My Dear Father," March 12, 1863, CinHS; *CG* 37th Cong., 3rd sess., 381; Beale, *Bates Diary*, 292; Kohl, *Welsh Letters*, 88.

40. Cora Benton to Charles Benton, August 30, 1863, ND; *Advertiser and Eastern Townships Sentinel*, July 31, 1862; Chancellor, *Thompson Diaries*, 53; *New York Times*, March 6 and April 1, 1863; Simon Stern to Edward Coxe, March 28, 1863, CL; *Milwaukee Sentinel*, April 27, 1863.

41. Kiper, *Dear Catherine*, 92, 121; Kent Diary, March 30, 1863, NHHS; *Daily Constitutional Union*, June 15, 1863; Sallie Miller to "Dear Brother Clason," May 7, 1863, CinHS.

42. Hammond, *Diary of a Union Lady*, 239; Moskow, *Emma's World*, 173; John P. Hatch to "Dear Father," April 10, 1863, LC.

43. Edward Hall to "Dear Susan," August 6, 1863, NHHS; Mrs. Elias Wyckoff to "Dear Companion," August 15, 1863, LSU (quoted in Doubleday Notes, LC); Cora Benton to Charles Benton, August 30, 1863, April 24, May 1, 4, and June 26, 1864, ND. One paymaster confided to a Massachusetts soldier that pay was being kept several months behind so that the money could be used to induce veterans to reenlist (Edwin Wentworth to "My dear Wife," April 17, 1864, LC).

44. Emily Harris to Leander Harris, July 13, 26, August 16, September 26, 1863, February 23, 1864, UNH.

45. Kohl, *Welsh Letters*, 17, 77, 87, 114, 147; Wayne Morris to "My Dear Companion," May 20, 1863, BL.

46. Delina Hopper to Daniel Hopper, July 13, 1863, WRHS; A. S. Boyce to "Dear Mary," April 19, 1864, BL; Thomas Harrison to Louisa Harrison, August 17 and September 6, 1863, IHS.

47. Henry Robinson to "My dear and affectionate companion," June 30, 1863, and to "My very dear and affectionate wife and children," August 17, 1863, IHS.

48. Sylvester Hadley Diary, October 22 and November 2, 1863, NHHS; Ayling, *Register*, 54.

49. William Haynes to "Dear Wife," May 8, 1863, March 10 and September 18, 1864, KSHS.

50. On this phenomenon see, for instance, Jacob Hunter to "Dear Wife," September 24, 1862, SHSI-DM; William Jackman to "Dear Nancy," April 9, 1864, RBHPL.

51. Wells to "Dearest Melissa," June 24, 1863, and Melissa Wells to "Dearest Ben," December 16, 1863, February 14, July 21, 22, and August 1, 1864, BL.

52. George Kies to "My Dear Wife," June 10, 1863, CHS; *OR*, 27(2):44, 440.

53. *OR*, 27(2):47, 118–19, 130, 137, 441; *OR, Supplement*, 5:69–73; *Record of Service*, 687.

54. *OR*, 27(2):46, 118–19; Josiah Gordon to "My dear wife," June 20, 1863, CL; Boyd Hamilton to "My dear Mother," June 26, 1863, Hamilton Papers, LC.

55. *OR*, 27(2):442; Mahon, *Chase and Lee Diaries*, 93–94.

56. *OR*, 27(1):34–35, and 27(3):242, 243, 909; Younger, *Kean Diary*, 76–77; Jones, *Diary*, 222; Thomas Cheney to "Dear Brother," June 17, 1863, UNH.

57. *OR*, 27(3):936; Sparks, *Patrick Diary*, 258. As the historian A. Wilson Greene so saliently pointed out to me, Joe Hooker's performance at Chancellorsville did not portend the sustained aggressiveness that the lunge toward Richmond would have demanded. Lincoln had urged McClellan to undertake a similar strategy in the fall of 1862, so his reluctance to repeat it may well have reflected dwindling confidence in Hooker.

58. *OR*, 27(1):141; Weld, *Diary and Letters*, 214.

59. Weld, *Diary and Letters*, 214; Elmer Wallace to "My Dear Parents," June 16, 1863, BL; Reid-Green, *Matrau Letters*, 58; Messent and Courtney, *Twichell Letters*, 239–42; C. C. Starbuck to Julietta Starbuck, May 10, 1863, IHS.

60. Mathias Schwab to "Dear Parents," June 22, 1863, CinHS; Blair, *Geary Letters*, 93; Quaife, *Williams Letters*, 216–17.

61. Sparks, *Patrick Diary*, 261; James Brown to "Dear Friends," June 13, 1863, MEHS; George Landrum to "Dear Amanda," June 20, 1863, WRHS; Nevins, *Strong Diary*, 3:325–26.

62. James Brown to "Dear Friends," June 18, 1863, MEHS; William White to "Dear Friend Jacob," June 14, 1863, VTHS; William West Diary, June 15, 1863, MHS; Wolf, "Taylor Diary," 355–56; Levi Perry to "Dear Sister," June 18, 1863, MEHS; Clinton Morrill to "Dear Carrie," June 23, 1863, Ingersoll Letters, MEHS; Racine, *Mattocks Journal*, 39; Kohl, *Welsh Letters*, 108; Matthew Marvin Diary, June 17 and 18, 1863, MNHS; Daniel Handy to "Jemima," June 17, 1863, RIHS; Messent and Courtney, *Twichell Letters*, 243. The Army of the Potomac suffered three times its proportionate share of sunstroke (Barnes, *Medical and Surgical History*, 6:854).

63. Racine, *Mattocks Journal*, 39, 44; James Brown to "Dear Friends," June 19, 1863, MEHS; Edwin Hall to "Dear Father," July 9, 1863, VTHS; Richard Irwin to "Dear Mother & Sister," July 4, 1863, UVM; Olney Seaver to "Dear Father," July 3, 1863, VTHS; Charles Manson to "Dear Mother," July 11, 1863, UVM; Kohl, *Welsh Letters*, 108–9; Seward Terry to Fred Barger, July 19, 1863, CCHS.

64. John Stumbaugh to "My Dear Son," July 9, 1863, C. B. Neeley to "Dear Parents," July 1, 1863, and Eunice Stewart to "My Dear Parents," June 24–July 2, 1863, all in USAMHI.

65. Henry Lyle to "Dear Mother," June 19, 1863, USAMHI; Meade, *Life and Letters*, 1:386–87; *Times* (London), June 29, 1863 (New York correspondent's report of June 17); Robertson, *McAllister Letters*, 325; George Marden to unidentified recipient, June 20, 1863, DC; Alexander Varian to "Dear Sister," June 18, 1863, WRHS; William Speed to

"Dear Lottie," June 18, 1863, CL; Horatio Taft Diary, June 29, 1863, LC; Wolf, "Taylor Diary," 356; Benjamin French to Henry French, June 28, 1863, NHHS.

66. *OR*, 27(2):211–12, 215, 217, 219; John Ames to "My dear Mother," June 21, 1863, USAMHI; *Daily Constitutional Union*, June 16, 1863.

67. A. L. Russell to "Operator, Norristown," June 27, 1863, CL; Pennsylvania militiaman to "Dear Wife," June 25, 1863, CL; Alex Hamilton to "My Dear Mother," July 5, 1863, LC; Nevins and Thomas, *Strong Diary*, 3:325; *OR*, 27(2):215–16 and 27(3):169; John Faller to "Dear Sister," June 25, 1863, USAMHI.

68. Horatio Taft Diary, June 29, 1863, LC; Emma Doyle Wilderman to "Dear Mother," August 1, 1863, Cumberland County Historical Society.

69. *OR*, 27(1):53; Rufus Mead to "Dear Folks at Home," June 21, 1863, LC; Levi Perry to "Dear Sister," June 18, 1863, MEHS; Racine, *Mattocks Journal*, 39; Alfred Ryder Diary, May 31, 1863, and John Ryder to "Dear Father," June 24, 1863, BL; Miles Beatty to "Dear Father," June 19, 1863, and George Soult to "John Beaty," June 21, 1863, UIA.

70. Sparks, *Patrick Diary*, 263; Beale, *Welles Diary*, 1:340, 344; Laas, *Lee Letters*, 276.

71. Alfred Ryder to "Dear Friends," June 28, 1863, BL; William Bryant Adams Diary, June 27, 1863, MEHS; William West Diary, June 27, 1863, MHS.

72. John Ames to "Dear Mother," June 28, 1863, USAMHI; William Evans to "Dear Father & Mother," July 1, 1863, USAMHI; Charles Johnson to "Dear Nellie," June 30, 1863, USAMHI; Racine, *Mattocks Journal*, 43–45; William Stow to "Dear Friends one & all," July 6, 1863, UVM; Sylvester Hadley Diary, June 27, 1863, NHHS; Wolf, "Taylor Diary," 359–60.

73. Charles Richardson Diary, June 23 and 28, 1863, LC; Bailey and Cottom, *Dunn Letters*, 6; Josiah Gordon to "My dear wife," June 20, 1863, CL.

74. *Prairie du Chien Courier*, June 25, 1863; *Portland Daily Press*, July 4, 1863; *Times* (London), July 18, 1863.

75. *OR*, 27(1):55, 59–60; *RJCCW2*,1:49–50, 173–74. For this episode and Halleck's duplicity toward Hooker, see Sears, *Gettysburg*, especially 30–32, 120–21, 123.

76. *OR*, 27(1):60–63.

77. Sparks, *Patrick Diary*, 265–66; Wolf, "Taylor Diary," 359–60; Nevins, *Strong Diary*, 3:326.

78. Samuel Heintzelman Diary, June 28, 1863, LC; Nevins, *Diary of Battle*, 227; John Ames to "Dear Mother," June 28, 1863, USAMHI.

79. Nevins, *Diary of Battle*, 229; William Wirt Henry to Mary Jane Henry, July 1, 1863, VTHS; William Stow to "Dear Friends one & all," July 6, 1863, UVM; John Proudfit to "Dear Sister," June 1, 1863, KU.

80. Boyd Hamilton to "My dear Mother," June 30, 1863, LC; *CWL*, 6:311–12.

81. *OR*, 27(1): 62, 66, and 27(2):692–96; Horatio Taft Diary, June 29, 1863, LC; Laas, *Lee Letters*, 278.

82. Benjamin French to Henry French, June 28, 1863, NHHS; John Judd Diary, June 28, 1863, KSHS; Edson Cheever to "Dear Aunt Bell," July 5, 1863, Marvel Collection.

83. Joseph F. Warren Diary, June 30, 1863, quoted in Pullen, *Shower of Stars*, 118; *OR*, 27(3):441, 637.

84. Roswell Farnham to "Dear Mary," June 29, 1863, VTHS.

85. Sarah Shriver to "My dear Lizzie," June "29" [30], 1863, LC; Andrew K. Shriver to "My dearest Mother," August 11, 1863, ND.

86. *OR*, 27(1):66–71, 27(2):696; Flavius Bellamy Diary, July 1, 1863, ISL. Buford had one regiment from Pennsylvania and one from West Virginia, but they were apparently held in reserve.

87. *OR*, 27(1):245, 927, and 27(3):416–17; Weld, *Diary and Letters*, 229–30.

88. Lyman Holford Diary, July 1, 1863, LC; Roswell Root to "Dear Grand Father," Au-

gust 23, 1863, USAMHI; letter fragment, Ryder Family Papers, BL; Reid-Green, *Matrau Letters*, 59; *OR*, 27(1):245.

89. Joseph Halbert to "Dear Sister Belle," August 10, 1863, Turner Letters, Cumberland County Historical Society; Flavius Bellamy Diary, July 1, 1863, ISL; Horace Currier Diary, July 1, 1863, WHS; Newell Burch Diary, July 1, 1863, CCHS; Weld, *Diary and Letters*, 230–31.

90. Elmer Wallace to "Dear Parents," July 5, 1863, BL; *OR*, 27(1):173; Roswell Root to "Dear Grand Father," August 23, 1863, USAMHI; Reid-Green, *Matrau Letters*, 60.

91. *OR*, 27(1):366, and 27(3):461.

92. William Bryant Adams to "Sister Dora," July 1, 1863, MEHS; Mathew Marvin Diary, July 1, 1863, MNHS.

93. Robertson, *McAllister Letters*, 332; *OR*, 27(1):115–16; Sparks, *Patrick Diary*, 267; Samuel Allen to "My dear Father," "June 3" [probably July 5], 1863, CCHS; Oeffinger, *McLaws Letters*, 195–96.

94. *OR*, 27(1):116; Messent and Courtney, *Twichell Letters*, 248.

95. Haynes, *Soldier Boy's Letters*, 107–8; Sylvester Hadley Diary, July 2, 1863, NHHS; Calvin Burbank to "Dear Cousins," August 10, 1863, DC; *OR*, 27(1):900; Mrs. E. A. Skelly to "My Dear Jackey," April 16, 1862, USAMHI.

96. Calvin Burbank to "Dear Cousins," August 10, 1863, DC; Henry Keiser Diary, July 2, 1863, USAMHI; Messent and Courtney, *Twichell Letters*, 249; Sparks, *Patrick Diary*, 267; *OR*, 27(1):371, and 27(2):618.

97. *RJCCW2*, 1:377; *OR*, 27(1):138, 653, 663; George Whitmore Diary, July 2, 1863, MHS; William West Diary, July 2, 1863, MHS; Henry Keiser Diary, July 2 and 3, 1863, USAMHI.

98. Quaife, *Williams Letters*, 229; Nevins, *Diary of Battle*, 245–46; *OR*, 27(1):372, 705–6, 800; George Benson Fox to "My Dear Father," July 4, 1863, CinHS; Charges and Specifications against Colonel E. L. Price, Samuel T. Allen Papers, CCHS. Captain Allen charged that Colonel E. Livingston Price traded coats with his orderly during the fighting at Chancellorsville and that he led the stampede at Culp's Hill; soon thereafter Captain Allen took over command of the regiment.

99. Marshall Phillips to "Dear Wife," July 3, 1863, MEHS; Lorenzo Miles Diary, July 3, 1863, VTHS.

100. *OR*, 27(1):775; Blair, *Geary Letters*, 98; James T. Miller to "Dear Brother," July 6, 1863, CL; Raab, *Willard Journals*, 197–200.

101. Frank Collins to "Dear William," July 31, 1863, SHSI-IC; George Whitmore Diary, July 3, 1863, MHS; Scott, *Abbott Letters*, 186; Charles Cummings to "My Dear Wife," July 6, 1863, VTHS; William West Diary, July 3, 1863, MHS.

102. *OR*, 27(1): 239, and 27(2):352.

103. Frank Collins to "Dear William," July 31, 1863, SHSI-IC; Charles Cummings to "My Dear Wife," July 6, 1863, VTHS; Scott, *Abbott Letters*, 188.

104. Decades later, two prominent Confederate artillerists seemed to take responsibility for having concluded that the Union guns had been driven away: see John C. Haskell to John W. Daniel, May 12, 1906, SHC, and Gallagher, *Alexander Recollections*, 259.

105. Frank Collins to "Dear William," July 31, 1863, SHSI-IC; Charles Cummings to "My Dear Wife," July 6, 1863, VTHS; Henry Dix to "Dear Father," July 9, 1863, VTHS; Sparks, *Patrick Diary*, 267; *OR*, 27(1):775.

106. Jedediah Hotchkiss Journal, July 3, 1863, LC.

107. The Union army reported 3,642 men killed during the campaign, and 16,576 wounded, besides 11,825 missing, many of whom were killed or wounded. Confederates apparently underreported their losses at 2,592 killed (Sears estimates 5,000), with 12,709 wounded and 5,150 missing. Many of the wounded died later: amputations of the leg in particular seemed to prove fatal more often than not during this war, and

one surgeon at Gettysburg reported that well over half the operations in his division hospital consisted of amputations, with more than half of those to the leg. See *OR*, 27(1):194, and 27(2):346; Sears, *Gettysburg*, 498; Barnes, *Medical and Surgical History*, 2:147, 255.

5. Uncle Sam Says You're the One

1. French, *Journals*, 424–25; Laas, *Lee Letters*, 282–83; *OR*, 27(3):515; Andrew Linscott to "Dear Parents," July 5, 1863, MHS.

2. Laas, *Lee Letters*, 283, 284.

3. *Daily Chronicle*, July 9, 1863; *New Hampshire Patriot*, July 8, 1863; *Crisis*, July 15 and 22, 1863.

4. Nevins and Thomas, *Strong Diary*, 3:328–29, 332; *New York Times*, July 5 and 6, 1863. Franklin Pierce retained abundant public respect at this juncture: his historical reputation deteriorated thereafter mainly because of the Republican animosity that this speech attracted. See Wallner, *Pierce*, especially 350–56.

5. Nevins and Thomas, *Strong Diary*, 3:330; *New York Times*, July 7, 1863.

6. *Daily Citizen*, July 2, 1863; Julius Wood to "Kind Parents and Sister," July 3, 1863, WRHS; *OR*, 25(1):59–60, and 25(3):460; John P. Jones to "My Dear Wife," July 8, 1863, CL.

7. *OR*, 25(1):60–61, and 25(3):460, 1059–60; Joseph Kohout to "Dear Father and Mother," July 13 and 16, 1863, UIA; Jim Giauque to "Brother Alf," July 4, 1863, UIA; James Proudfit to "Dearest Emilie," July 5, 1863, KU; Woodworth, *Winters Letters*, 63–65; John Lester Diary, July 4, 1863, IHS.

8. *OR*, 23(1):408, and 22(1):390–91, 407, 412; Alexander Varian to "Dear Father," July 18, 1863, WRHS; James Stewart to "Dear Cousin," August 10, 1863, Crawford Papers, NSHS; Cyrus Wheeler to "Father and Mother," June 29, 1863, BL; David Reynolds Diary, July 4, 1863, IHS.

9. Justus Gale to "Dear Sister Almeda," June 19, 1863, VTHS; Homer Sprague Diary, June 14, 1863, LC; William Stanton Diary, June 14, 1863, AAS; James Osborne Diary, June 15, 1863, MHS; Edward Belville to "Dear friends at home," June 16, 1863, Rutherford Papers, UVM.

10. Milton Bassett to "Dear Mary," July 18, 1863, CHS; William Simons to "Dear Sister," undated, CHS.

11. Banks to Mary Banks, July 6, 1863, LC; Thomas Alexander Diary, July 7 and 8, 1863, ND; John Hammond Diary, July 8 and 9, 1863, USAMHI; Homer Sprague Diary, July 9, 1863, LC; Jabez Alvord Diary, July 8 and 9, 1863, LC; William Shaw to "Sister Caroline and Family," July 25, 1863, CL; Milton Bassett to "Dear Mary," July 18, 1863, CHS.

12. *CWL*, 6:409; *Louisville Daily Democrat*, July 17, 1863; S. W. Jans to Henry Jackson, July 29, 1863, WHS; Clara Robbins to "My dear Friend," July 10, 1863, CL; Cora Benton to Charlie Benton, July 8, 1863, ND.

13. Laas, *Lee Letters*, 285; *New York Times*, July 9, 1863; William Spalding to "My Dear Miranda," July 16, 1863, BL; George Wheeler to "Dear Mother," August 1, 1863, NSHS; Davis, *Butler Family Letters*, 29–30; *CWL*, 6:314–17, 319.

14. Joseph Lester letter, August 20, 1863, LC; Asahel Mann to "Dear Mother," July 5, 1863, UIA.

15. *OR*, 25(3):475; Henry Tisdale Diary, July 7, 1863, BPL; Lyman Jackman Diary, July 4–10, 1863, NHHS.

16. Thomas C. Cross to "Dear Mother," July 14, 1863, BPL; Sewell Tilton Diary, July 17, 1863, NHHS; Andrew Stone to "brother Wes," July 17, 1863, NHHS.

17. Oscar Robinson Diary, July 18–21, 1863, DC; Sewell Tilton to "Dear Bro & Sister," July 28, 1863, NHHS; John H. Bailey Diary, July 7–11, 1863, USAMHI; Hosea Towne

to "Dear Friends," July 19, 1863, NHHS; Robert Rodgers Diary, July 10 and 11, 1863, USAMHI; Giles Thomas to W. P. and Margaret Thomas, July 16, 1863, Oblinger Papers, NSHS; George Upton to "My Dear Wife," July 25, 1863, NHHS; Dwight Darling to Charles Chase, December 21, 1864, NHHS.

18. David Reynolds Diary, July 11, 1863, IHS; Daniel Cilley to Ira Barton, August 3, 1863, DC; Joseph Smith to "Dear Mother," July 28, 1863, USAMHI; William Hayward to "My Own Darling Marry," July 4, 1863, USAMHI.

19. Marquis Hills to "My Dear Father," August 20, 1863, KU; Puck, *Letters*, 67. The twenty-one nine-month regiments in Louisiana lost an average of 111.4 men each to disease, against 32.2 men apiece among the seventy-three that served in the East.

20. Edson Cheever to "Dear Uncle" July 21 (or 27), 1863, Marvel Collection; Frederic Speed to "My dear Anna," August 4, 1863, CL; James Miller to "Dear Sister," August 2, 1863, CL.

21. Samuel Pingree to "My dear Parents," July 12, 1863, Lyndon State College Collection, VTHS; George Marden to unidentified recipient, July 5, 1863, DC; Charles L. Fales to "Dear Sister," July 6, 1863, CL; John Sheahan to "My Dear Father," July 5, 1863, MEHS; William Henry to Mary Jane Henry, July 7, 1863, VTHS; William West Diary, July 8, 1863, MHS.

22. Blight, *Brewster Letters*, 246; *RJCCW2*, 1:337; M. W. Harris to "Dear Father," August 13, 1863, NHHS; William Evans to "Dear Father & Mother," July 4, 1863, USAMHI; Lorenzo Miles Diary, July 4 and 5, 1863, VTHS; John Sheahan to "my Dear Father," July 6, 1863, MEHS; Joseph Rutherford to "My dear wife," July 7, 1863, UVM.

23. Robert Forrest Diary, July 4–6 and 10–14, 1863, USAMHI; Boyd Hamilton to "My dear Mother," July 9, 1863, LC; Bently Kutz to "Dear Mother," July 10, 1863, and to "Dear Parents," July 13, 1863, USAMHI.

24. Henry Keiser Diary, July 2, 1863, USAMHI; Stephen Pingree to "Cousin Augustus," July 18, 1863, Lyndon State College Collection, VTHS; Nevins, *Diary of Battle*, 228–29; Mathias Schwab to "Dear Parents," July 17, 1863, CinHS; Elijah Cavins to "Dear Ann," August 8, 1863, IHS; Sarah Shriver to "Dear Lizzie," July 3, 1863, LC.

25. Nevins, *Diary of Battle*, 254; Sparks, *Patrick Diary*, 268–69.

26. Andrew Hale Young to "My Dear Susan," July 12, 1863, DC.

27. Henry Morse Diary, July 6, 1863, CCHS; Weld, *Diary and Letters*, 239; Elijah Cavins to "Dear Ann," July 10, 1863, IHS.

28. Nevins, *Diary of Battle*, 258; David Nichol to "Dear Father," July 16, 1863, USAMHI.

29. Kohl, *Welsh Letters*, 112; Dan Mason to Harriet Clark, July 10, 1863, VTHS; Daniel Handy to "Jennie," July 11, 1863, RIHS; James Brown to "Dear Friends," July 8, 1863, MEHS.

30. Meade, *Life and Letters*, 2:133–34; Nevins, *Diary of Battle*, 261–62.

31. James Brown to "Dear Friends," July 13, 1863, MEHS; Meade, *Life and Letters*, 2:134; Nevins, *Diary of Battle*, 258, 260; Joseph Bartlett to "My dear Capt," August 12, 1863, LC; *Correspondence of John Sedgwick*, 2:135; *RJCCW2*, 1:336; *OR*, 27(1):92. See A. Wilson Greene's convincing defense of Meade's caution in "From Gettysburg to Falling Waters," in Gallagher, *The Third Day at Gettysburg*, 161–201.

32. *RJCCW2*, 1:381; William West Diary, July 14, 1863, MHS; Peter Abbott to "Folks at Home," July 12, 1863, VTHS; Blight, *Brewster Letters*, 244.

33. Beale, *Bates Diary*, 300; Laas, *Lee Letters*, 290; Niven, *Chase Papers*, 4:79–81; Beale, *Welles Diary*, 1:369–70.

34. Beale, *Welles Diary*, 1:370–71; Meade, *Life and Letters*, 2:134; Niven, *Chase Papers*, 82; *CWL*, 327–29.

35. Beale, *Welles Diary*, 1:370–71.

36. Elijah Cavins to "Dear Ann," July 10, 1863, IHS; *OR*, 27(2):306, 790, 793, and 27(3):450–54, 909, 933, 976, 984, 994.

37. *OR*, 27(2):818–19, and 27(3):111, 206, 412. See Greene, *Civil War Petersburg*, 144–45, on this episode.

38. John Marshall Brown to "Dear Nellie," July 20, 1863, MEHS; Rodney Ramsey to "Father: Sir," July 20, 1863, NHHS; Haynes, *Soldier Boy's Letters*, 113; John Sheahan to "Dear Father," July 19, 1863, MEHS; Palmer, *Sumner Letters*, 2:184.

39. Thomas Rosser to "My darling wife," July 7, 1863, Freeman Papers, LC. D. H. Hill made the postwar argument that a corps from Lee could have saved Vicksburg ("Chickamauga," 638–39). I must concur with Wilson Greene's observation that Confederate victory at Vicksburg would have required not only an infusion of new troops, but uncharacteristically astute and aggressive performances by John Pemberton and Joe Johnston. Longstreet's detachment to Braxton Bragg in September did lead to a signal victory at Chickamauga, but Bragg managed to transform it into an ultimately devastating defeat.

40. Burlingame and Ettlinger, *Hay Diary*, 62; Williams, *Hayes Diary and Letters*, 2:419.

41. Williams, *Hayes Diary and Letters*, 2:419; Lucy Hayes to "Dearest R," July 18, 1863, RBHPL.

42. *OR*, 23(1):817; *Louisville Daily Democrat*, July 7, 1863; William Spalding to "My Dear Miranda," July 10, 1863, BL.

43. *OR*, 23(1):708–10, 717; *ORN*, 25:242, and Series 2, 1:213.

44. *OR*, 23(1):659; *Cincinnati Daily Commercial*, July 11, 1863; undated letter fragment, early July, 1863, Larned Papers, LC; Davis, *Butler Family Letters*, 29.

45. Report of Brigadier General Milo Hascall, quoted in Klement, *Dark Lanterns*, 27. Klement (237) reveals that Morton's adjutant general suppressed Hascall's report of Carrington's drunkenness. Carrington never saw field service during the war, and his subsequent record on the Plains was punctuated by disaster.

46. *Richmond Enquirer* clipping in Moore, *Rebellion Record*, 7:453, 455; Wayne Morris to "My Dear Companion," July 9 (and 10), 1863, BL; Robert Taylor Diary, July 10–13, 1863, IHS.

47. Ruth Harvey to "Dear John," July 20, 1863; Francis W. Thomas Diary, July 18, 1863, and Thomas Barnett Diary, July 10–13, 1863, all at Earlham.

48. William Hoff to "Dear Father," July 31, 1863, OHS; Lucius Wood to "Dear Parents & Sister," July 16, 1863, WRHS.

49. A. S. Clarke to Burnside, July 29, 1863, Box 10, and Len A. Harris to Burnside, July 15, 1863, Box 9, Burnside Papers, RG 94, NA; Daniel Larned to "Dear Henry," July 26, 1863, LC. The *Louisville Daily Democrat* reported on Lee's retreat as early as July 7.

50. Rudolph Williams to "Dear Father," July 12, 1863, IU; Wayne Morris to "My Dear Wife," July 12, 1863, BL; Caroline Carpenter Diary, July 14, 1863, Earlham; Lucy Hayes to "Dearest R," July 18, 1863, RBHPL; *Crisis*, July 29, 1863; C. B. Lewis to Ambrose Burnside, July 28, 1863, Box 10, Burnside Papers, RG 94, NA.

51. Williams, *Hayes Diary and Letters*, 2:420; *OR*, 23(1):677, 776–80, 786.

52. *OR*, 23(1):673–75, and Series 2, 6:153, 174; James Cutts to Burnside, July 23, 1863, Box 21, Burnside Papers, RG 94, NA. My thanks to David Roth, of *Blue & Gray Magazine*, for pointing out that a fragment of Ohio lay in the Department of the Monongahela, which fact I missed while writing Burnside's biography.

53. *Ohio State Journal*, August 3, 1863; Elijah Cavins to "Dear Ann," July 13, 1863, IHS.

54. *OR*, Series 3, 3:323, 462–63, 467, and 5:625, 634.

55. *New York Times*, July 9, 1863; *OR*, Series 3, 3:482, and 5:625, 716, 730; William Chapin Diary, July 7–17, 1863, RIHS.

56. *Boston Journal*, July 9–11, 1863; *OR*, Series 3, 5:730; Charles Curtis to Charles Folsom, July 13, 1863, BPL.

57. *OR*, Series 3, 3:462; *New York Times*, July 12, 1863.

58. *New York Times,* July 12, 1863; *New York Herald,* July 14, 1863; *New York Daily News,* June 16, 1863.

59. *New York Times,* July 13 and 14, 1863; Olmsted to Preston King, July 9, 1862, ALP.

60. *New York Times,* July 14, 1863; *OR,* 27(2):899–907, 931; Nevins and Thomas, *Strong Diary,* 3:335–36. Iver Bernstein's *The New York City Draft Riots* offers a thorough and absorbing analysis of the riot. The site where the riot began, now a block-wide office building over a Third Avenue store called the Dress Barn, lacks any commemorative marking.

61. Nevins and Thomas, *Strong Diary,* 3:335; *New York Times,* July 14, 1863; Edwin S. Barrett to Joseph Gilmore, July 13, 1863, NHHS; Hammond, *Diary of a Union Lady,* 246; *OR,* 27(2):898–99; Helen McCalla Diary, July 17, 1863, LC.

62. Niven, *Chase Papers,* 4:84–85.

63. Nevins and Thomas, *Strong Diary,* 3:337, 338; *New York Times,* July 15 and 16, 1863; *New York Tribune,* July 15, 1863.

64. *New York Times,* July 15 and October 21, 1863; *New York Tribune,* July 15, 1863; Nevins and Thomas, *Strong Diary,* 3:338.

65. *New York Times,* July 15, 1863; *OR,* 27(2):897, 914, 917.

66. *Boston Journal,* July 15 and 16, 1863; *OR,* 27(2):890.

67. *Boston Journal,* July 15, 1863; Adelaide Fowler to "Dear Brother," July 19, 1863, PEM.

68. *OR,* 27(2):884, 890, 904–7, 930, 939; Joseph Ricketson to Deborah Weston, July 19, 1863, Chapman Family Papers, BPL; Daniel Larned Journal, July 22, 1863, LC.

69. Frank Howe to Gilmore, July 14, 1863, Executive Correspondence, NH Archives; Edwin S. Barrett to Gilmore, July 13 and 14, 1863, NHHS; *Daily Chronicle,* July 11 and 14–18, 1863; *OR,* Series 3, 3:805, 806; *Boston Journal,* July 18, 1863.

70. *New York Times,* July 16, 1863.

71. Ibid.; *OR,* 27(2):882; Nevins and Thomas, *Strong Diary,* 3:339.

72. *OR,* 27(2):884, 896, 916, 920, 921, 925, 926, 930; Helen McCalla Diary, July 17, 1863, LC; Nevins and Thomas, *Stong Diary,* 340; *New York Times,* July 17 and 18, 1863; John Parker to Richard Lathers, July 18, 1863, LC; S. W. Jans to Henry Jackson, July 29, 1863, WHS.

73. *Daily Chronicle,* July 17, 1863; *Boston Journal,* July 17, 1863; *New York Times,* July 17, 1863; Beale, *Welles Diary,* 1:372–73; John Parker to Richard Lathers, July 18, 1863, LC.

74. Isaac Gardner to "Dear Parents," July 17, 1863, USAMHI; Henry Heisler to "Dear Sister," August 9, 1863, LC; Thomas Cheney to "Dear Brother," July 30, 1863, UNH; Dan Mason to Harriet Clark, July 17, 1863, VTHS; Harris and Niflot, *Dear Sister,* 73; Christopher Hoyt to "Dear Brother," July 27, 1863, NHHS.

75. Henry Langdon to "My dear Sister," July 22, 1863, CinHS; Myron Underwood to "My Dear Wife," October 5, 1863, UIA.

76. Chancellor, *Thompson Diaries,* 52; Murray Mason to "My Dear Dr.," July 22, 1863, VHS; Nevins, *Diary of Battle,* 264.

77. Laas, *Lee Letters,* 295; Nevins and Thomas, *Strong Diary,* 3:335–36.

78. Rosenblatt and Rosenblatt, *Fisk Letters,* 139–40, 144; Albert Luther to "Dear Father," August 3, 1863, ISL; Peter Abbott to "Friends at Home," August 31, 1863, VTHS.

79. David Seibert to Christian Seibert, August 7, 1863, USAMHI; *OR,* Series 3, 3:544–45, 579–80, 592, 611.

80. *OR,* Series 3, 5:730–31; Emily Harris to Leander Harris, August 24, 1862 and July 26, 1863, UNH; Richard P. Kent Diary, August 6, 1863, NHHS; J. L. Barton affidavit, February 3, 1864, Cary Library; C. D. Longfellow to Charles Sherman, October 6, 1863, CHS.

81. Thomas Brown to Lydia Brown, August 17 and September 19, 1863, VTHS; Thomas Cheney to "My Dear Sister Melissa," August 16, 1863, UNH; Floyd Williams to

"Esteemed Friend," October 30, 1863, USAMHI; Hammond, *Diary of a Union Lady*, 246; Blight, *Brewster Letters*, 247.

82. Thomas Cheney to "Dear Brother," July 30, 1863, UNH; *CWL*, 6:447–48; *New York Times*, April 2, 1863; *Oxford Democrat*, August 7, 1863; *Boston Journal*, August 13, 1863.

83. Frances Miller to Alanson Miller, October 26, 1862, ND; Henry Robinson to "My dear and affectionate wife and children," April 26, 1863, IHS; David Nichol to "Sister Annie," August 10, 1863, and James Nichol to "Dear brother John," November 10, 1863, USAMHI; Kohl, *Welsh Letters*, 121. Substitute prices did eventually rise after revocation of the commutation clause in 1864, but those prices reflected further devaluation of the currency, a shrinking population of able-bodied, military-age civilians, and a steadily increasing aversion to serving in a war that grew deadlier by the month.

84. Nevins, *Diary of Battle*, 281; Clarkson Butterworth Diary, August 19, 1864, Earlham; Elvira Aplin to "Dear Son George," November 8, 1863, CL.

85. *OR*, Series 3, 5:730; Orlando Gilbert certificate of exemption, August 11, 1863, CL; Emily Harris to "Dear Husband," September 11 and 26, 1863, UNH; William Hamilton to "Dear Boyd," August 11, 1863, LC; *Portland Advertiser*, September 4, 1863.

86. Richard Kent Diary, October 30, 1863, NHHS; Solomon Grannis Diary, October 8, 1863, NHHS.

87. Charles Wilson, receipt to Charles Sherman, September 9, 1863, and C. T. Woodruff to Sherman, December 11, 1863, CHS; Frederick Bill to H. C. Holmes, August 2, 1864, CHS.

88. Elvira Aplin to "Ever Dear Son George," November 22, 1863, CL; George Hall to "Dear Father," March 20, 1864, UIA; Nevins, *Diary of Battle*, 281.

89. James T. Miller to Joseph, William, and Robert Miller, all September 7, 1863, CL.

90. Benjamin Ashenfelter to "Father Churchman," August 23, 1863, USAMHI; Alanson Long to Samuel Duncan, August 16, 1863, DC.

91. Harris and Niflot, *Dear Sister*, 73, 104; Daniel Webster Brown to "Dear Brother," July 28, 1863, MEHS; Augustus Paddock to "Dear Father," August 5, 1863, UVM; *OR*, Series 3, 5:731.

92. W. W. Henry to Mary Jane Henry, July 21 and August 5, 1863, VTHS; James Brown to Thomas Brown, September 4, 1862, and July 19, 1863, and to Lewis Brown, March 28, 1864, MEHS.

93. Charles Chace to "Dear Mother," October 19, 1863, and undated fragment evidently to William Chace, fall of 1863, UVM.

94. *Crisis*, April 15, 1863; Nevins, *Diary of Battle*, 289; Henry Vaughn to "Well our folks," March 1 [1864], Middlesex Papers, VTHS.

95. George Miles to Frank Miles, August 6, 1863, VTHS; *Oxford Democrat*, October 16, 1863; *Stanstead Journal*, September 10, October 8 and 22, and November 19 and 26, 1863.

96. *Oxford Democrat*, September 11, 1863; *Dakotian*, July 28, August 18, November 23, December 8, 1863.

97. N. B. Cobb to "Brother Walter," September 18, 1864, UVM; Josie Knowles to Moses Southard, November 20, 1864, and Thankful Southard to same, February 27, 1865, Moses Letters, MEHS; E. P. Feaster to "My Dear Nephew," March 9, 1864, Wadsworth Letters, WHMC.

98. *OR*, Series 3, 5:730.

99. Ibid.; Henry Vaughn to "Bub," July 24, 1863, Middlesex Papers, VTHS; *Stanstead Journal*, February 11, 1864. The same provost marshal and surgeon were eventually reinstated at that station.

100. Henry Vaughn to "Bub," July 24, 1863, Middlesex Papers, VTHS; Bradford Sparrow to "Anxious Parents & Brothers," August 28, 1863, and to "Father," September 1, 1863,

UVM; Edwin Horton to "Dear Wife," September 28, 1863, VTHS; Charles Chace, undated fragment evidently to William Chace [fall of 1863], UVM.

101. Samuel Howe to William Kineson, October 12, 1863, UVM; Marcellus Darling to "Dear Mother," September 2, 1863, and to "Dear Friends," September 15, 1863, UIA; Charles Coit to "Dear All," August 4, 1863, Yale; Stephen Green to "Dear Wife," August 8, 1863, CCHS.

102. William Stevens to Ann Stevens, October 21, 1862, and October 2, 1863, Robinson Family Papers, SM; Martha Talbert White Diary, December 24, 1862, IHS; Anna Starr to William Starr, May 31, 1863, IHS; Stephen Pingree to "Cousin Augustus," October 2, 1863, Lyndon State College Collection, VTHS; Henry Baker to Cyrus Pringle, August 4 and September 28, 1863, UVM; Peck, *Roster*, 119, 131, 133. Peck spells Pringle's name "Prindle."

103. Laas, *Lee Letters*, 307; Racine, *Mattocks Journal*, 63; Greenlief Foster to "Dear Brother," September 2, 1863, MEHS; John Jenks to "Dear Wife," November 8, 1863, UNH; Stephen Pingree to "Cousin Augustus," October 2, 1863, Lyndon State College Collection, VTHS; Nevins, *Diary of Battle*, 279.

104. Bradford Sparrow to "Anxious Parents & Brother," August 28, 1863, UVM; Andrew Stone to "Wes," September 27, 1863, NHHS; James T. Miller to "Dear Brother," September 7, 1863, CL; Rosenblatt and Rosenblatt, *Fisk Letters*, 136.

105. Hastings, *Letters from a Sharpshooter*, 166, 167, 170, 172, 174.

106. James Brown to "My Dear Friends at Home," August 10, 1863, and to "Dear Friends," August 16, 1863, MEHS; Marshall Phillips to "Dear Wife," August 10 and 19, 1863, MEHS.

107. Rufus Mead to "Dear Folks at Home," August 29, 1863, LC; William Hogan to "My Dear Son," September 5, 1863, VTHS; Greenlief Foster to "Dear Brother," September 12, 1863, MEHS; Levi Perry to "My Dear Sister," August 31, 1863, MEHS; Acken, *Inside the Army*, 333–36, 473–74; *OR*, 29(2):102–3.

108. Hastings, *Letters from a Sharpshooter*, 172, 188, 260; William B. Greene to "Dear Mother," December 17, 1863, UNH.

6. Take Increased Devotion

1. Blair, *Geary Letters*, 107.

2. Edward Davis to "Dear Mother," June 16, 1863, UIA; Maria Mann to William Ropes, April 13, 1863, LC; Sylvester, "Cox Letters," 64; John Crommett to "Dear Sister Celestia," May 25, 1863, MEHS.

3. Henry Seys to "Dear Hattie," August 20, 1863, CL; Sewell Tilton to "Dear Bro. & Sister," May 2, 1863, NHHS; George Hall to "Dear Father," January 15, 1864, UIA.

4. Wells Fox to Robert Crouse, May 14, 1863, BL; Horace Greeley to James Dixon, August 14, 1863, Wellington Collection, CHS; Greeley to Albert Gallatin Riddle, October 31, 1863, WRHS.

5. *OR*, Series 3, 3:1111–12; U.S. Senate, *Report of Harper's Ferry*, 226–27; Higginson to Brown, February 8, 1858, and to George Stearns, February 10, 1857, BPL; Looby, *Higginson Journal and Letters*, 91–97.

6. *CWL*, 6:149–50; *OR*, Series 3, 3:119–20; Dyer, *Compendium*, 1718–26, 1731–34.

7. Frederic Speed to "Dear Sister," April 6, 1863, and to his father, May 26, 1863, and August 28, 1863, CL; John Jenks to "Dear Wife," July 22, 1863, UNH; Haynes, *Soldier Boy's Letters*, 151, 155, 157.

8. Josiah Corban to "Dear Wife and Children," July 10, 1863, CHS; Larimer, *Ritner Letters*, 157.

9. Christopher Keller to "Dear Friends at Home," May 8, 1863, CL.

10. Cyrus Leland to "Dear Mother," December 13, 1863, KSHS; Stephen Holt to "Dear Grandfather & Mother," April 28, 1864, DC.

11. Higginson, *Massachusetts in the Army and Navy*, 2:484–98; Peck, *Roster*, 717–21;

Arthur Morey to "My Dear Cousin," February 4, 1864, UVM; Looby, *Higginson Journal and Letters*, 48–50, 53, 63.

12. Adams, *Civil War Letters*, 9, 13; *OR*, Series 3, 3:252; *Boston Journal*, March 17, 1863.

13. Robert Edwards to "Dear Annie," July 11, 1863, ND; John Dillingham to "Dear Mother," July 21, 1863, FHS; Onville Upton to "Dear Sister Mary," July 12, 1863, SCL.

14. Adams, *Civil War Letters*, 38–40; William Edwards to Helen A. Edwards, August 20, 1863, ND; Mushkat, *Voris Letters*, 130; Edward Hall to "Dear Susan," July 20, 1863, NHHS; *OR*, 28(1):201–2, 210; George Towle Diary, July 18, 1863, NHHS.

15. *OR*, 28(1):202–7, 727; Orra Bailey to "My Dear Wife," September 3, 1863, LC; Onville Upton to "Dear Sister Mary," September 14, 1863, SCL; John Marshall Brown to "My dear Nellie," August 28, 1863, MEHS.

16. *OR*, 28(1):725–27; *ORN*, 14:606–27; John M. Dillingham to "Dear Mother," October 8, 1863, and to "Dear Father," January 13, 1864, FHS; Hammer, *James Diary*, 35; Atwater, *Report*, 72–73.

17. "Mrs. Stillman" to "My Dear Brother," undated, WHMC; Sanford Bullock to Odon Guitar, September 9, 1863, WHMC; *OR*, 22(2):341–47; William Haynes to "Dear wif," May 8, 1863, KSHS; William Crawford to "Dear Brother," July 21, 1863, WHMC; Cyrus Leland to "Dear Mother," November 14, 1863, KSHS.

18. Julius Hadley to George W. Collamore, August 15, 1863, KU; William McIlworth to Odon Guitar, November 2 and 9, 1863, and R. S. Strahan and J. W. Jewett to Guitar, March 26, 1864, WHMC; Thomas Carney to Abraham Lincoln, June 25, 1863, KU.

19. *OR*, 22(1):579–80, and 26(2):225; James Hanway to "Dear John," August 30, 1863, KSHS; *Daily Times*, August 22, 1863; *Weekly Herald*, August 27, 1863.

20. *OR*, 22(1):583; *Daily Times*, August 23, 1863; Moore, *Rebellion Record*, 7:401.

21. Moore, *Rebellion Record*, 7:399, 401; Thomas Webb to Collamore, August 14, 1863, KU.

22. *Daily Times*, August 23, 1863; *Daily Missouri Republican*, August 23, 1863; Moore, *Rebellion Record*, 7:399–401; *OR*, 22(1):583. Banks was stripped of his commission a few weeks later (*OR*, Series 3, 5:909).

23. Moore, *Rebellion Record*, 7:400–401; *Missouri Daily Republican*, August 23, 1863.

24. *OR*, 26(2):348, 379, and 22(1):580–85; *Weekly Herald*, August 27, 1863; James Hanway to "Dear John," August 30, 1863, KSHS; Cyrus Leland to "Dear Mother," September 2 and November 14, 1863, KSHS.

25. *OR*, 22(1):698–700.

26. Ibid., 688–90, 695, 698–701; *Daily Times*, October 15, 1863; *Weekly Herald*, October 15, 1863; Charles Mumford to "Dear Wife," October 12, 1863, WHS; M. A. Vansickle to "Dear Father & Mother," November 1, 1863, KU.

27. *OR*, 22(2):319, 398–99, 595–97, and 53:565–67. See also Marvel, *Lincoln's Darkest Year*, 132–33, 301–2, 315. Curtis's son served as Blunt's adjutant, and was killed at Baxter Springs.

28. Rosenblatt and Rosenblatt, *Fisk Letters*, 132; Isaac Gardner to "Dear Parents," August 23, 1863, USAMHI; Schuyler S. Ballou to unidentified correspondent, November 22, 1863, USAMHI; Chesson, *Dyer Journal*, 112; David Nichol to "Dear Sister," September 18, 1863, USAMHI; *Correspondence of John Sedgwick*, 146–54, 156; Styple, *De Trobriand Letters*, 132; Agassiz, *Lyman Letters*, 25–26.

29. Nevins, *Diary of Battle*, 277–78; Isaac Gardner to "Dear Parents," August 23, 1863, USAMHI; William Hamilton to "My dear Mother," September 4, 1863, LC; Truxall, *Respects to All*, 47–48; Acken, *Inside the Army*, 333; Meade, *Life and Letters*, 2:145.

30. *Correspondence of John Sedgwick*, 155; Nevins, *Diary of Battle*, 282.

31. Niven, *Chase Papers*, 1:449; Nevins, *Diary of Battle*, 282–83; *OR*, 29(2):227, 261–62.

32. Dowdey and Manarin, *Lee Papers*, 594, 596; Burlingame and Ettlinger, *Hay Diary*, 83; *OR*, 29(2):693–94; Silver, *Moore Diary*, 164, 166–67; Oeffinger, *McLaws Letters*, 202; Cutrer, *Goree Letters*, 112.

33. Daniel Larned Journal, August 20 and 21, 1863, LC; Harrison Randall to "Dear Father," August 20, 1863, ND; Brun, "Fleming Letters," 25.

34. Daniel Larned Journal, August 21, 1863, LC; William Spalding to "My Dear Amanda," September 13, 1863, BL; *OR*, 30(1):34, and 30(3):333, 501.

35. *OR*, 30(3):617–18, 638, 655, 691, 717–18; *CWL*, 6:480–81. See Marvel, *Burnside*, 280–90, for this episode.

36. Orlando Poe to "My dear Wife," September 24, 1863, LC; Len Harris to Burnside, October 5, 1863, Box 12, Burnside Papers, RG 94, NA.

37. *OR*, 30(1):56–61; Reinhart, *Civil War Letters*, 154–58; George Hodges to "Dear Wife," September 25, 1863, WRHS; Richard Elder to "Dear Sister," October 3, 1863, OHS; Burlingame and Ettlinger, *Hay Diary*, 85–86; Horace Hobart to "Dear Brother," September 21, 1863, IHS; Williams, *Garfield Letters*, 296–97; Albion Tourgee Diary, September 20, 1863, CCHS. The most thorough account of Chickamauga is Cozzens, *This Terrible Sound*.

38. Nevins amd Thomas, *Strong Diary*, 3:358. Thomas Cheney to "Dear Brother," October 2, 1863, UNH. Bragg lost about eighteen thousand men, and Rosecrans sixteen thousand.

39. *OR*, 29(2):207–8; Halleck to Meade, September 22, 1863, Stanton Papers, LC; Meade, *Life and Letters*, 2:150.

40. Burlingame and Ettlinger, *Hay Diary*, 86; Niven, *Chase Papers*, 1:450–51, 453.

41. Niven, *Chase Papers*, 1:451–52, 454.

42. Ibid., 452, 454; Burlingame and Ettlinger, *Hay Diary*, 86; *OR*, 29(1):146, 29(2):118; Stanton to John Garrett, Thomas Scott, and S. M. Felton, September 23, 1863, Stanton Papers, LC. Chase and Hay timed the meeting from around midnight to about 1:00 A.M., September 24, but Stanton's telegrams to the railroad executives are all headed between 11:00 and 11:20 P.M., September 23.

43. John Garrett to H. J. Jewett, Dillard Ricketts, L. M. Hubby, J. M. McCullough, S. L. Hommidieu, W. H. Clement, and John Newman, September 24, 1863, Stanton Papers, LC; *OR*, 29(1):147–48.

44. Rufus Mead to "Dear Folks at Home," September 25, 1863, LC; Samuel Allen to "My Dear Father," October 12, 1863, CCHS; *OR*, 29(1):148–56; *CWL*, 6:486.

45. *OR*, 29(1):148, 154, 162, 166, 171, 172, and 29(2):118; Samuel Allen to "My Dear Father," October 12, 1863, CCHS; Rufus Mead to "Dear Folks at Home," September 29, 1863, LC.

46. *OR*, 29(1):158, 159, 161, 162, 167, 173, 178; James Miller to "Dear Brother," October 8, 1863, and to "Dear Mother," October 11, 1863, CL; Rufus Mead to "Dear Folks at Home," September 29, 1863, LC.

47. Margaret Jones Diary, September 28, 1863, Earlham; James Miller to "Dear Mother," October 11, 1863, CL; Davis, *Butler Family Letters*, 48; *OR*, 29(2):758–59, 769.

48. *OR*, 29(1): 184, 187, 191–95.

49. Ibid., 30(2):289–90, and 30(4):705–6.

50. Davis, *Butler Family Letters*, 43.

51. *OR*, 23(1):839–42, and 23(2):572; *Detroit Free Press*, August 14, 1863; Smith and Cooper, *Peter Diary*, 151; *Louisville Daily Democrat*, August 4, 5, and 7, 1863; *Cleveland Plain Dealer*, August 7, 1863; *Crisis*, October 21, 1863.

52. *Detroit Free Press*, August 14 and November 10, 1863; *OR*, 29(2):394–95.

53. *CWL*, 6:555–58; *Daily Missouri Republican*, November 4, 1863; Laas, *Lee Letters*, 317–18.

54. *Weekly Perryville Union*, March 13 and 27, and August 7 and 14, 1863.

55. Bradford Sparrow to "Parents & Brothers," September 9, 1863, UVM; *Oxford Democrat*, September 18, 1863; *Portland Advertiser*, September 8 and 9, 1863.

56. Thomas Barnett Diary, October 13, 1863, Earlham; *CWL*, 6:287; Mary Paxton to "Dear Cousin Fone," September 8, 1863, Harrington Collection, RBHPL.

57. *Crisis*, August 12, 1863; *Chatham Weekly Planet*, September 3, 1863, quoted in Klement, *Limits of Dissent*, 227; Vallandigham to Alexander Boys, September 1, 1863, OHS; Moore, *Rebellion Record*, 7:438-39; *Ohio State Journal*, August 3 and 27, 1863; *Cincinnati Gazette*, October 12, 1863; Vallandigham to Manton Marble, August 2, 1863, WRHS. See Klement, *Limits of Dissent*, 234-43, for the voluminous dissemination of defamatory propaganda by Republican newspapers, Union Leagues, and postmasters.

58. *Crisis*, August 19, 1863; *New York Times*, September 1, 7, and 11, 1863; *Detroit Free Press*, October 21, 1863; "Father" to "My very Dear Son," July 26, 1863, Rigby Papers, UIA; Puck, *Letters from the Front*, 70; *OR*, 23(2):592, 597; Williams, *Garfield Letters*, 289-91; Niven, *Chase Papers*, 4:102-4.

59. Meta Grimball Journal, August 4, 1863, SHC; Welker, *Garey Diary*, 102; Vallandigham to Manton Marble, August 13, 1863, WRHS; *Daily Gate City*, October 2, 1863.

60. *CWL*, 6:451-52; Vallandigham to Manton Marble, October 4, 1863, WRHS.

61. *Detroit Free Press*, October 15, 1863; Henry M. Weaver to "Dear Roll," October 20, 1863, Hurd Papers, WRHS; Leander Harrington to "Dear Brother," October 14, 1863, RBHPL.

62. John Vanhook to John G. Davis, October 29, 1863, IHS; Jonathan Harrington to "Father & Mother," October 14, 1863, RBHPL; Vallandigham to Manton Marble, October 4, 1863, WRHS; Clason Miller to "My dear sister," October 18, 1863, CinHS; Davidson, *Hartley Letters*, 56, 61; Mushkat, *Voris Letters*, 141; Thomas Honnell to "Respected friend," September 17, 1863, and to "Dear Brother Henry," October 26, 1863, OHS; Milton Crist to "Dear Sister," August 7, 1863, IU.

63. *Coshocton Democrat*, October 14, 1863; Charges and Specifications, Special Order No. 20, and farewell address, February 20, 1864, Sells Collection, WRHS; *OR*, 29(1):782; Davidson, *Hartley Letters*, 56.

64. Nevins and Thomas, *Strong Diary*, 3:304; Wainwright, *Fisher Diary*, 463; *Daily Gate City*, October 15, 1863; *CWL*, 6:523-24; *OR*, Series 3, 5:633-34.

65. *Louisville Daily Democrat*, August 4 and 7, 1863; *Cincinnati Daily Commercial*, April 23, 1863; *Crisis*, May 6 and July 29, 1863; Niven, *Chase Papers*, 4:210-11; Dana to Stanton, September 8, 1863, LC.

66. Sparks, *Patrick Diary*, 276, 331, 350; James Brown to "Dear Brother," April 13, 1864, MEHS; William Burbank to "Dr. Mother," December 7, 1862, CL; Rufus Mead to "Dear Folks at Home," April 29, May 9, and August 29, 1863, LC.

67. Pease and Randall, *Browning Diary*, 1:652, 657; Willard Templeton to "Dear Brother James," February 17, 1863, NHSL; Houston, *Smith Letters*, 128; David Nichol to "Dear Father," August 21, 1863, USAMHI; Kohl, *Welsh Letters*, 139.

68. Allen Landis to "Bro Will," April 18, 1863, LC; Edwin Wentworth to "My dear Wife," April 17, 1864, LC; Marshall Phillips to "Dear Wife," April 21, 1864, MEHS; Charles Hadsall Diary, May 16, 1864, NSHS; Rosenblatt and Rosenblatt, *Fisk Letters*, 71, 294-95, 305; Kohl, *Welsh Letters*, 139; Edward Taylor to "My dear Sister," September 13, 1863, BL; James Brown to "Dear friends at Home," December 30, 1862, and to "Sister Nellie," April 13, 1864, MEHS.

69. Elijah Cavins to "Dear Ann," October 20 and 25, 1862, and to "Dear Riley," October 25, 1862, IHS; Edward Hall to "Dear Susan," December 7, 1862, and May 26, 1863, NHHS; L. D. MacFarlane to John Schofield, November 23, 1863, and resignation dated August 31, 1864, Guitar Collection, WHMC; *Detroit Free Press*, June 14, 1863; Acken, *Inside the Army*, 222. See also Marvel, *Mr. Lincoln Goes to War*, 214, 253, and *Lincoln's Darkest Year*, 123 and 314-15, on corruption within the army's supply departments.

70. Niven, *Chase Papers*, 1:209 and 4:160–61, 289; Burlingame and Ettlinger, *Hay Diary*, 92; *Portland Advertiser*, December 30, 1863; *OR*, 41(4):387.

71. *Crisis*, August 26, 1863; "Father" to "My very Dear Son," July 26, 1863, and "Father & Mother" to same, February 2, 1864, Rigby Papers, UIA; William Henry to Mary Jane Henry, May 31, 1862, and January 11, 1863, VTHS; Nevins, *Diary of Battle*, 275–76.

72. David Seibert to "Dear Father," January 22, 1864, USAMHI; William Hamilton to "My dear Mother," April 11, 1863, LC; William Hogan to "Dear Son," November 16, 1863, VTHS; Elijah Cavins to "Dear Ann," August 8, 1863, IHS; Leopold Bürkner affidavit, June 30, 1862, Roll 2, Letters Received (M-494), RG 107, NA; Haynes, *Soldier Boy's Letters*, 100; Rosenblatt and Rosenblatt, *Fisk Letters*, 137–38.

73. Kohl, *Welsh Letters*, 128; Sparks, *Patrick Diary*, 236; William Hamilton to "My dear Mother," March 17, 1863, LC; David Seibert to "Dear Father," June 1, 1863, USAMHI; David Scott to "My Dear Wife," July 2 and 18, 1864, IHS; Charles E. Bates to "Dear Parents," April 24, 1864, VAHS; Rufus Mead to "Dear Folks at Home," August 29, 1863, LC; Merritt Stone to "Dear Sister Ella," April 24, 1864, VTHS. John Billings includes a section on sutlers in his memoir (*Hardtack and Coffee*, 224–30).

74. Ray, *Diary of a Dead Man*, 172; William Adams Diary, October 10, 1863, MEHS; *OR*, 29(1):9–10, 227–30, 241–43, 426–27; Dowdey and Manarin, *Lee Papers*, 607–9; Sparks, *Patrick Diary*, 299; Agassiz, *Lyman Letters*, 32.

75. Robertson, *McAllister Letters*, 343–44; Meade, *Life and Letters*, 3:153–54.

76. Agassiz, *Lyman Letters*, 42–44; Meade, *Life and Letters*, 2:155–56; Robertson, *McAllister Letters*, 355; *OR*, 29(1):556, 585–86, 626–30; Racine, *Mattocks Letters*, 77–80; Edwin Wentworth to "Dear Wife," November 11, 1863, LC; William West Diary [November 7, 1863, under "memoranda"], MHS; James Holmes to Abbie Homer, November 15 and 16, 1863, MHS.

77. Rosenblatt and Rosenblatt, *Fisk Letters*, 161–62; Elmer Wallace to "My Dear Sister," November 1, 1863, BL; *OR*, 29(1):250, 560, 561. Lee lost three times as many men as Meade: see *OR*, 29(1):428, 629, 630, 647.

78. Agassiz, *Lyman Letters*, 47; Davidson, *Hartley Letters*, 65–66; Elijah Cavins to "Dear Ann," November 18, 1863, IHS; *OR*, 29(2):439, 449; Rosenblatt and Rosenblatt, *Fisk Letters*, 163–65; Robertson, *McAllister Letters*, 362; Sparks, *Patrick Diary*, 306.

79. George W. Hodges to "Dear Wife," October 1, November 18, 1863, WRHS; Thomas J. Harrison to Louvisa Harrison, October 21, 1863, IHS; *OR*, 30(1):458; Conrad Noll Diary, November 23, 1863, BL.

80. *Washington Star*, November 13, 1863; *Washington Chronicle*, November 13, 1863; *New York Times*, November 15, 1863; Beale, *Bates Diary*, 314; Niven, *Chase Papers*, 4:196; Laas, *Lee Letters*, 310, 319; Charlotte Dailey to "Dear Lottie," November 16, 1863, PPL; Burlingame and Ettlinger, *Hay Diary*, 111.

81. Charlotte Dailey to "Dear Lottie," November 16, 1863, PPL.

82. Jaquette, *Hancock Letters*, 7–8; Beauchamp, *A Private War*, 70–71.

83. Edward Moseley to "My dearest Em," August 18, 1863, VAHS; Elizabeth Tuttle to "Dear Hattie," July 22, 1863, IU; Frank Stoke to "Dear Brother," October 26, 1863, Cumberland County Historical Society.

84. *New York Times*, November 18 and 19, 1863; Burlingame and Ettlinger, *Hay Diary*, 111–13; French, *Journals*, 433–34. The Gettysburg Chamber of Commerce reports that residents now call their midtown plaza the square, or the circle.

85. *New York Times*, November 20, 1863; Burlingame and Ettlinger, *Hay Diary*, 113; French, *Journals*, 434–35.

86. Wills, *Lincoln at Gettysburg*, 206, quotes an obvious underestimate of the size of the stand, but provides a fascinating and thorough (albeit almost wholly adulatory) analysis of the day's speeches and events.

87. French, *Journals*, 435; *New York Times*, November 20, 1863; Frank Haskell to

unidentified recipient, November 20, 1863, WHS. Although historians have accepted a change in the spelling of his name to "Pierpont," the provisional governor of loyal Virginia signed himself as "Francis Peirpoint" until long after the Civil War.

88. *New York Times,* November 20, 1863; Burlingame and Ettlinger, *Hay Diary,* 113; French, *Journals,* 435.

89. Except for an introductory sentence, Everett's speech is in the *New York Times,* November 20, 1863.

90. *New York Times,* November 20, 1863; *Detroit Free Press,* November 21, 1863; CWL, 7:17-23. The stenographer who supplied the *Free Press* copy obviously took down his own version of the speech, which varies conspicuously from the standard texts, beginning "Fourscore and ten years ago."

91. Chancellor, *Thompson Diaries,* 41; OR, 29(2):443, 451, 455, 476.

92. *Detroit Free Press,* November 26, 1863. Lincoln's invocation of the nation's martyrs differed from the actual or metaphorical flourishing of a blood-soaked shirt primarily in the elegance of the appeal: each aimed to exploit the sacrifices of the dead to secure political support and silence opponents.

93. French, *Journals,* 436; Burlingame and Ettlinger, *Hay Diary,* 114.

7. Armies Like Ghosts on Hills

1. OR, 26(1):651-52, 657.

2. USG, 9:137-38, 165-66; Simpson and Berlin, *Sherman Letters,* 515-17; Birt Scott to "Dear Brother," September 9, 1863, IHS; A. B. Long to "My Dear Major," September 9, 1863, Duncan Letters, DC; OR, 26(1):657, 672, 683, 686, 752-53, and 24(3):580-82, 672; Beale, *Welles Diary,* 1:385.

3. OR, 30(4):375.

4. USG, 9:260; C. C. Washburn to Elihu Washburne, September 5, 1863, LC; OR, Series 3, 3:770; Nathaniel Banks to Mary Banks, September 5, 1863, LC; statement of charges by William Kountz, January 26, 1862 (filed under February 12, 1862), Stanton Papers, LC.

5. OR, 30(4):403, 429; USG, 9:296-98; Stanton to Lincoln, October 16, 1863, Stanton Papers, LC.

6. OR, 30(4):434, 455, 478-79, and 31(1):706; USG, 9:305, 317.

7. OR, 31(1):713, 766, 789; USG, 9:353; Simpson and Berlin, *Sherman Letters,* 569-70. The most meticulous study of the Chattanooga campaign, if not the most recent, is Cozzens's *Shipwreck of Their Hopes.*

8. OR, 31(1):258-59, 687, 712; Meade, *Life and Letters,* 2:154.

9. OR, 31(1):77, and 31(2):29; USG, 9:334-35.

10. OR, 31(1):72, 77-80, 92-93.

11. Ibid., 41, 92-95, 113-17, 137-213, 217-18, 224-28, 231-33; Blair, *Geary Letters,* 131-32; Austin, *Bratton Letters,* 159. In his report of the battle (SCL), Jenkins also trebled Union losses in his estimate.

12. OR, 31(2):29, 31(3):38; George Hodges to "Dear Wife," November 18, 1863, WRHS.

13. OR, 30(4):765-66, and 31(1):258-59, 455-59, 680, 757.

14. Ibid., 31(2):258-59, 31(3):74, 88, 138; George Hodges to "Dear Wife," November 18, 1863, WRHS; Daniel Larned to Mary Burnside and "My Dear Sister," November 7, 1863, and to "Dear Sister" and "Dear Henry," November 14, 1863, LC.

15. OR, 31(1):332-25, 441; George Harwood to Mrs. Rice Wood, January 14, 1864, and Myron Wood to "Dear Father," February 12, 1864, MHS.

16. OR, 31(1):275, 296; Willard Templeton memorandum, "Thanksgiving morning" [1863], NHSL; William Draper to "My dear Wife," November 20 and December 1, 1863, LC.

17. *OR*, 31(3):177, 182.

18. Ibid., 31(2):31-33.

19. Simpson and Berlin, *Sherman Letters*, 572; Thomas Coffman to "Dear Jennetti," December 7, 1863, SHSI-IC; Mathias Schwab to "Dear Mother," November 13, 1863, CinHS; *OR*, 31(2):32-33, 126.

20. *OR*, 31(2):32-33, 90, 94-95, 745-46; Smith, "Journal," 33.

21. William Fordyce and W. C. Patton diaries, November 24, 1863, both in IHS; *OR*, 31(2):86, 170-71, 173, 315-17, 409, 607-9; William Swayze to "Dear Mother," December 3, 1863, IHS.

22. *OR*, 31(2):86, 173, 315-17, 409, 607-9, 691, 724; W. C. Patton Diary, November 24, 1863, IHS. The Union and Confederate units engaged on Lookout Mountain reported only 116 killed altogether during all the fighting of November 24-27.

23. Blair, *Geary Letters*, 142-45; *OR*, 31(2):90, 170, 173, 315-17, 409, 609, 691, 724.

24. *OR*, 31(2):33, 90; Smith, "Journal," 35.

25. *OR*, 31(2):34-35, 96, 318, 575, 748; Henry Robinson to "My very dear and affectionate wife," [December, 1863], IHS; Benjamin Bordner to "Brother and Sister," December 1, 1863, BL; Alexander Varian to "Dear Father," November 27, 1863, WRHS; Charles Caley to "My Dear Wife," November 27, 1863, ND; W. C. Patton Diary, November 25, 1863, IHS; Thomas Harrison to Louvisa Harrison, November 27, 1863, IHS; J. Dexter Cotton to "My dear wife," November 26, 1863, LC.

26. W. C. Patton Diary, November 25, 1863, IHS; Smith, "Journal," 36-38; *USG*, 9:478; Marion D. Ward to "Home friends," December 3, 1863, WRHS; Henry A. Robinson to "My very dear and affectionate wife," [December, 1863], IHS; Albion W. Tourgee to "Darling Wife," November 29, 1863, CCHS; *OR*, 31(2):35, 319, 576, 752-54.

27. *OR*, 31(2):25, 35; *USG*, 9:478.

28. *USG*, 9:438-39; James Nesbitt to "Dear Sister," November 27, 1863, WRHS; William Draper to "My Dear Wife," December 1, 1863, LC; Robert Rodgers Diary, November 23, 1863, USAMHI; Conrad Noll Diary, November 23 and 24, 1863, BL; Gavin, *Pettit Letters*, 119-20.

29. Conrad Noll Diary, November 23, BL; Cutrer, *Goree Letters*, 116; *OR*, 31(1):276, and (3):756-57; David Morrison to G. A. Hicks, November 30, 1863, Box 13, Burnside Papers, RG 94, NA; E. P. Alexander Diary, November 27 and 28, 1863, SHC. Sixteen-year-old William Henry had joined the 8th Michigan Cavalry two months before (muster-out roll of Company A, 8th Michigan Cavalry, William Henry personnel file, RG 94, NA).

30. Robert Rodgers Diary, November 25, 1863, USAMHI; Ransom Sargent to Maria Sargent, November 30, 1863, DC; Gavin, *Pettit Letters*, 121; *OR*, 31(1):299, 343, and 31(3):777.

31. *OR*, 31(1):276, 343-44, 353; William Draper to "My dear Wife," November 29, 1863, LC; Rudolph Williams to "Dear Father," December 11, 1863, IU; Gavin, *Pettit Letters*, 121; Robert Rodgers Diary, November 30, 1863, USAMHI; Blackburn, *Ely Diary*, 67.

32. *OR*, 31(1):344, and 31(3):777; William Spalding to "My Dear Miranda," December 6, 1863, BL; Ransom Sargent to Maria Sargent, November 30, 1863, DC; Blackburn, *Ely Diary*, 67; George Hawkes Diary, November 29, 1863, USAMHI.

33. *OR*, 31(3):758, 760; Charles Loring to Burnside, December 3, 1863, Box 22, Burnside Papers, RG 94, NA; Gavin, *Pettit Letters*, 121; William Draper to "My Dear Wife," December 2-4, 1863, LC.

34. *OR*, 31(1):278; William Draper to "My Dear Parents," December 22, 1863, LC; A. S. Boyce to "Dear Mary," January 29, 1864, BL; George Morgan to Austin Morgan, February 20, 1864, DC; Chauncey Mead to "Dear Kate," January 4 and March 4, 1864, WRHS.

35. *OR*, 26(1):397-401, 824-25, 847; *OR Atlas*, 43:8.

36. Rosenblatt and Rosenblatt, *Fisk Letters*, 163, 167; Sidney Burbank Diary, Novem-

ber 10, 1863, LC; *RJCCW2*, 1:402; Racine, *Mattocks Journal*, 81–82; Sparks, *Patrick Diary*, 307, 311; Agassiz, *Lyman Letters*, 48–50; Robertson, *McAllister Letters*, 360.

37. *Correspondence of John Sedgwick*, 2:162; *OR*, 29(2):449, 471, 473–74, 477, 478, 529, and 51(1):1125; Agassiz, *Lyman Letters*, 48.

38. *OR*, 29(1):13, 29(2):405, 475, 476, 480–81, 811, and 51(1):1126, 1128–29; Agassiz, *Lyman Letters*, 53.

39. Edward Bates to "Dear Jack," November 23, 1863, VAHS; *OR*, 29(2):481–82, 486–89; Rosenblatt and Rosenblatt, *Fisk Letters*, 167; Sparks, *Patrick Diary*, 312; *CWL*, 6:496–97; Agassiz, *Lyman Letters*, 50–51.

40. *OR*, 29(2):486, 487, 490–92; Acken, *Inside the Army*, 400; Roberton, *McAllister Letters*, 363–64; *RJCCW2*, 1:372; Rosenblatt and Rosenblatt, *Fisk Letters*, 169.

41. *RJCCW2*, 1:372, 385, 474; *OR*, 29(1):737, 744, 761; 768, and 29(2):485–86, 490–93.

42. *RJCCW2*, 1:321–22, 344, 385; *OR*, 29(2):491–92; Sparks, *Patrick Diary*, 313; Joseph Rutherford to "My dear wife," December 13, 1863, UVM; Rosenblatt and Rosenblatt, *Fisk Letters*, 169.

43. Meshack Larry to "Dear Sister," December 8, 1863, MEHS; *OR*, 29(1):747–48; Sparks, *Patrick Diary*, 313, 317.

44. Dowdey and Manarin, *Lee Papers*, 626; Tower, *Taylor Letters*, 92–93; *OR*, 29(2):847; *RJCCW2*, 1:385; *OR*, 29(1):817–18, 831, 838, 846, 876, 895, 897, 898.

45. Wilbur Fisk Diary, November 26, 1863, LC; *OR*, 29(2):480–81, 493–94; Agassiz, *Lyman Letters*, 52.

46. *RJCCW2*, 1:344; *OR*, 29(1):695, 762.

47. Sparks, *Patrick Diary*, 314; *OR*, 29(2):498–500. Chesson (*Dyer Journal*, 133) called the turnpike "flinty" that day.

48. Tower, *Taylor Letters*, 94; *OR*, 29(1):695, 763–64, 768, 29(2):500–503, and 51(1):1130; Davidson, *Hartley Letters*, 67; Robertson, *McAllister Letters*, 364–65; Joseph Rutherford to "My dear wife," December 13, 1863, UVM; Rosenblatt and Rosenblatt, *Fisk Letters*, 169.

49. *OR*, 29(1):763–64; Meshack Larry to "Dear Sister," December 8, 1863, MEHS; Racine, *Mattocks Journal*, 84–87; Webster Brown to "Dear Mother," December 4, 1863, MEHS; Sparks, *Patrick Diary*, 314; Edwin Horton to "Dear Ellen," December 4, 1863, VTHS.

50. *OR*, 29(1):682; Joseph Rutherford to "My dear wife," December 13, 1863, UVM. All but two of the amputations, excisions, or other major operations reported from that battle in Surgeon Rutherford's brigade, for instance, involved the arm or upper chest (Barnes, *Medical and Surgical History*, 8:506, 10:571, 676, 710, 722, 856, 877, 973, 12:455, 502, 723, 741–42, 781).

51. *OR*, 29(1):16, 696; Agassiz, *Lyman Letters*, 54–55; Charles Bowers to "Dear Lydia," November "27" [28?, 1863], MHS; Lorenzo Miles Diary, November 28, 1863, VTHS.

52. *RJCCW2*, 1:345, 386; *OR*, 29(1):696–97; Agassiz, *Lyman Letters*, 55–56; Edwin Wentworth to "My dear Wife," December 4, 1863, and to "Dear Father," December 5, 1863, LC.

53. *RJCCW2*, 1:345, 386; *OR*, 29(1):697, 740; Agassiz, *Lyman Letters*, 56.

54. Sidney Burbank Diary, November 30, 1863, LC; Scott, *Abbott Letters*, 235; Acken, *Inside the Army*, 405; Truxall, *Respects to All*, 51; Robertson, *McAllister Letters*, 367; Sparks, *Patrick Letters*, 316; Alfred Keith to "My dear Friend," December 4, 1863, VTHS; Charles Bowers to "Dear Lydia," December 4, 1863, MHS; Edward Wentworth to "Dear Father," December 5, 1863, LC. No reliable evidence of men freezing to death on this campaign has ever surfaced.

55. Robertson, *McAllister Letters*, 367–68; Scott, *Abbott Letters*, 235; Tower, *Taylor*

Letters, 94; Chesson, *Dyer Journal,* 133–34; Elijah Cavins to "Dear Ann," December 3, 1863, IHS; Sparks, *Patrick Diary,* 316–17; Agassiz, *Lyman Letters,* 56–57; *RJCCW2,* 1:386–87.

56. Agassiz, *Lyman Letters,* 56–57; Thomas Brown to "my Wife," December 5, 1863, VTHS; Meade, *Life and Letters,* 2:157, 159; Sparks, *Patrick Diary,* 316–17; *RJCCW2,* 1:346.

57. Chesson, *Dyer Journal,* 133–34; Scott, *Abbott Letters,* 234–35; Davidson, *Hartley Letters,* 67–68; Robertson, *McAllister Letters,* 369; Wilbur Fisk Diary, November 30 and December 1, 1863, LC. Almost all contemporary sources report extreme cold below the Rapidan that night.

58. *RJCCW2,* 1:346–47; *OR,* 29(1):16–17; Sparks, *Patrick Diary,* 318; Nevins, *Diary of Battle,* 305; Sidney Burbank Diary, November 30, 1863, LC; Agassiz, *Lyman Letters,* 58–59; Tower, *Taylor Letters,* 95.

59. Racine, *Mattocks Journal,* 87; Sears, *Fiske Letters,* 208–10; Robertson, *McAllister Letters,* 369–71; Henry Black to "Friend Fred," December 29, 1863, MEHS; Dowdey and Manarin, *Lee Papers,* 628; Edwin Wentworth to "My dear Wife," December 4, 1863, LC; Joseph Leighty to "Dear Sister," December 7, 1863, KU.

60. Meade, *Life and Letters,* 2:156–59; Nevins, *Diary of Battle,* 308; Sparks, *Patrick Diary,* 318–19; *RJCCW2,* 1:474–75.

61. *New York Times,* December 3, 1863; Nevins, *Diary of Battle,* 308–9; Nevins and Thomas, *Strong Diary,* 3:377; Joanna Lane to Benjamin Lossing, December 6, 1863, ISL; Elijah Cavins to "Dear Ann," December 19, 1863, IHS; Burlingame, *Dispatches from Lincoln's White House,* 193, and *Nicolay Letters,* 121.

62. Acken, *Inside the Army,* 393; Nevins, *Diary of Battle,* 309; Scott, *Abbott Letters,* 235; Sears, *Fiske Letters,* 215–16; James Brown to "Brother Thomas," December 16, 1863, MEHS.

63. Meade, *Life and Letters,* 2:160–61; *Washington Chronicle,* December 12, 1863.

64. *OR,* Series 3, 3:414–16, 785; Nevins, *Diary of Battle,* 285–86; Flavius Bellamy to "Dear Father," October 17, 1863, ISL; Jabez Burrows Diary, October 10, 1863, CCHS; James Brown to "Dear Friends," October 13, 1863, MEHS; Lucy Hayes to "My dear Mother," October 1 [1863], RBHPL; Blight, *Brewster Letters,* 261, 263; W. C. Patton Diary, November 15, 1863, IHS.

65. *OR,* Series 3, 3:486–87, 1084; Wilbur Fisk Diary, November 25, 1863, LC.

66. Augustus Paddock to "Dear Parents," December 10, 1863, and to "Dear Brother Eph," January 17, 1864, UVM; R. P. Mathews to George Aldrich, December 25, 1863, NHHS; Thomas Cheney to "Dear Brother," January 8, "1863" [1864], UNH; Levi Perry to "Dear Mother," November 3, 1863, MEHS; George Sargent to "Dear Mother," January 1, 1864, NHHS; Clement Hoffman to "Dear Mother," January 6, 1864, USAMHI; Marcotte, *Private Osborne,* 181; Martin Mericle to "Brother Boys," March 26, 1864, UIA; Chauncey Barton to "Dear Sister," April 14, 1864, LC.

67. James Nesbitt to "Dear Sisters," November 4, 1863, WRHS; William Barnes to "Dear Wife and children," December 9, 1863, SHSI-DM; Thomas Brown to Lydia Brown, October 22, 1863, VTHS; Marshall Phillips to "Dear Wife," February 27, 1864, MEHS; Edwin Wentworth to "My dear Wife," January 3, 17, and 31, 1864, LC.

68. Florian Giauque to "Cousin Alf," June 22, 1863, UIA; Charles Benson to Robert Curtis Ogden, April 5, 1864, LC; Charles Howe to "Dear Sister," March 30, 1864, NHHS; Floyd, *Owen Letters,* 19, 32; Edward Taylor to "My dear Lottie," September 29, 1863, and to "Dear Will," January 11, 1864, BL.

69. Nelson Chapin to "My Dear Wife," January 6, "1863" [1864], USAMHI; Rosenblatt and Rosenblatt, *Fisk Letters,* 186; Augustus Paddock to "Dear parents," December 19, 1863, UVM; Nevins, *Diary of Battle,* 309; Martin Clark to "Dier Friend Welthey," February 8 and March 6, 1864, Wealthy Field Letters, VTHS.

70. George Brigham to "Dear Sister," [January?] 22, 1864, AAS; Marcotte, *Private Osborne*, 181; Charles Maxim to "Dear Father," December 2, 1863, Sturtevant Letters, DC, and to "Dear Brother," July 31, 1864, CL.

71. Shannon, *Andrus Letters*, 69; Edwin Wentworth to "My dear Wife," December 16, 1863, LC; Brun, "Fleming Letters," 33; A. S. Boyce to "Dear Mary," April 19, 1864, BL; *OR*, Series 3, 3:1196.

72. James Nesbitt to "Dear Sisters," November 4, 1863, WRHS; John Wilmot to Sophronia Prescott, March 5 and November 12, 1862, September 26 and December 19, 1863, VTHS.

73. William Jackman to "Dear Nancy," December 24, 1863, RBHPL; David Werking to "Dear Becca," April 3, 1863, IHS; Lucinda Sisk to Thomas Poe, April 12 [1864], IHS; John Yowell to Caleb Core, December 3, 1863 and January 18, 1864, OHS; Cummings, *Day Diary*, 159; Rufus Mead to "Dear Folks at Home," January 4, 1864, LC; James Brown to "Dear Friends," January 9, 1864, and to "Dear Brother," January 21, 1864, MEHS; Peter Abbott to "Dear Mother," February 21, 1864, VTHS; Silas Sadler to "Dear Father and Mother," [ca. March, 1864], BL; George Sargent to "Dear Mother," January 1, 1864, NHHS; James Holmes to Abbie Homer, November 6, 1863, MHS; Thomas Cheney to "Dear Father," October 25, 1863, UNH; John Cuddy to "Dear Parents," November 29, 1863, Dickinson College.

74. A. S. Boyce to "Dear Mary," February 26, 1863, BL; Susan Miller to "Dear Parents," April 10, 1864, CL; Emily Harris to Leander Harris, December 6, 1863, and February 23, 1864, and Leander to "Dear Emmy," January 6 and February 7, 1864, UNH.

75. Rufus Mead to "Dear Folks at Home," January 4 and 7, 1864, LC; Charles Maxim to "Dear Father," December 2, 1863, Sturtevant Letters, DC; Edwin Wentworth to "My dear Wife," January 3 and 31, 1864, LC; Joseph Barton to "Dearest Wife," January 17, 1864, USAMHI; Davis, *Butler Letters*, 73; Gavin, *Pettit Letters*, 124. Mead changed his mind within three days of asserting his disinclination, and Maxim reenlisted on the same day that he wrote his father he would not; Wentworth's metamorphosis took a couple of weeks, but then he found that he was not yet eligible for reenlistment.

76. John Boyer to "Dear father and mother," December 31, 1863, USAMHI; John E. Luther to "My Dear Father," December 23, 1863, ISL; Elijah Cavins to "Dear Ann," December 23 and 28, 1863, IHS.

77. Cummings, *Day Diary*, 159-61; Basile, *Stearns Diary*, 28, 30-31; Pliny Jewett to "Dear Steve," November 2, 1863, VAHS; David Leigh to Herman Drumgold, February 1, 1864, DC; Edwin Wentworth to "My dear Wife," January 3, 1864, LC; James Giauque to "Brother Alf," December 31, 1863, UIA; John Cuddy to "Dear Parents," November 29, 1863, Dickinson College; *OR*, Series 3, 3:1084; Albert Luther to "My Dear Father," April 27, 1864, ISL.

78. *OR*, 32(1):16, 33:776, and Series 3, 5:651; James Brown to "Dear Friends," January 9, 1864, and to "Dear Brother," January 21, 1864, MEHS; William West Diary, December 29, 1863, MHS; Dyer, *Compendium*, 1219-25.

79. Dyer, *Compendium*, 1008-12, 1149-52, 1158-72, 1248-56, 1296-98, 1634.

80. Charles Bates to "Dear Parents," January 24, 1864, VAHS; "Father and Mother" to "Dear Son," March 30, 1864, Rigby Papers, UIA; Randolph Sry to Ith Beall, February 23, 1864, KU.

81. James Stewart to "Dear Cousin," January 24, 1864, Crawford Papers, NSHS; *OR*, 33:482-85 and 32(2):220; Gavin, *Pettit Letters*, 124; Blackburn, *Ely Diary*, 70-72.

82. Marcotte, *Private Osborne*, 181; *OR*, Series 3, 3:89, 133.

83. Jordan, *Gould Journals*, 287-92, 295; *OR*, Series 3, 3:892.

84. Weld, *Diary and Letters*, 257-59; Dyer, *Compendium*, 1016, 1267, 1549, 1654; H. C. Coy to "Dear Cousin," August 18, 1863, Arnold Papers, OHS.

85. Abel Gillett to Royal Cook, October 26, 1863, DC; Richard Kent Diary, November 27, 1863, NHHS; *Oxford Democrat*, November 27 and December 4, 1863; Robert Miller

Sr. to "Dear Son James," January 2, 1864, CL; Emily Thompson to "Dear Sister H,"
December 8, 1863, Aldrich-Thompson Papers, NHHS; Hiram Jones to "Dear Wife &
Children," December 28, 1863, Jones Papers, UVM; Thomas Barnett Diary, February 24,
1864, Earlham.

86. Woodworth, *Winters Letters*, 117.

87. Dudley Tillison to Charles Tillison, November 12 and 28, 1863, VTHS; Francis
Spinola to Edwin Stanton, December 31, 1863, LC; John Sturtevant to "Dear friends at
Home," December 27, 1863, DC; Meshack Larry to "Dear Sister Phebe," January 26, 1864,
MEHS; George Lyon to "Dear friend," February 6, 1864, VTHS; Byron McClain to "Dear
Father," February 13, 1864, UIA.

88. William West Diary, February 24, 1864, MHS; *Receipts and Expenditures*, 9–10.

89. Artemus Cook to "Friend Babbitt," January 3 and 21, 1864, RBHPL; C. C.
Sturtevant to Lyman Trumbull, January 9, 1864, LC; Robertson, *McAllister Letters*, 341;
Dyer, *Compendium*, 1353–56, 1364–66; Horrocks, *Dear Parents*, 23; Frederick Kronen-
berger Diary, December 2, 1863, GC, quoted in Frassanito, *Grant and Lee*, 31.

90. David Seibert to "Dear Brother," April 1, 1864, USAMHI; Amos Currier to "Dear
Father," December 28, 1863, SHSI-IC; Albion Tourgee to "My Dear Wife," August 23,
1863, and to "Dear Father," December 6, 1863, CCHS; Hughes, *Colby Papers*, 240–42;
Charles Cady to "Dear Brother," March 2, 1864, UIA; Larimer, *Ritner Letters*, 412.

91. William Austine to Henry Newell, October 3, 1863, DC; Thaddeus Stevens
to Edwin Stanton, December 19, 1863, LC, cited in Trefousse, *Stevens*, 267–68;
Richard Thompson to "My Dear Son," December 7, 1863, IU; *OR*, 33:809, and Series 3,
5:903.

92. *OR*, Series 3, 4:232; Henry Comey to "Dear Brother," July 14, 1862, AAS; Thomas
Aplin to "Dear Brother George," October 21, 1863, CL; Ayling, *Register*, 906–18.

93. For the easy life of the heavy artillery see, for instance, George Wheeler to "Dear
Mother," August 1, 1863, and April 28, 1864, and Charles Hadsall Diary for April and May,
1864, both in NSHS.

94. Alvord to "Dear friend," November 30, 1863, and to "My Dear Friend," March 7,
1864, DC; Pierce to "Dear Wife," January 3, 1864, and "My Dear Wife," June 23, 1864,
PEM; Frederick Hooker to "Dear mother and wife," February 4 and 10, 1864, and to "dear
mother," April 14 and 22, 1864, CHS; John McCoy to "Dear Martha," February 17 and June
25, 1864, DC; Jones, "Bent Letters," 139, 143.

95. *OR*, Series 3, 3:482; Dyer, *Compendium*, 1386–87, 1570–71, 1630; John Gallagher
to "Uncle Jonathan," June 12, 1863, PPL; Nevins, *Diary of Battle*, 319; Washington
Roebling to "Darling," May 21, 1864, Rutgers.

96. Holden, Ross, and Slomba, *Cross Writings*, 126, 140–41.

97. George Wheeler to "Dear Mother," April 28, 1864, NSHS; John Amadon to "Dear
Wife," January 16, 1864, UVM; George French to unidentified recipient, October 17
[1863], VTHS; Brun, "Fleming Letters," 32.

8. The War Will Never Be Done

1. Brooks Journal, July 13 and December 31, 1863, and June 29, 1864, MHS.

2. Ayling, *Register*, 463, 481, 495; Eighth Census of Carroll County, N.H. (M-653,
Reel 667), p. 27, RG 29, NA; Henry Winterstein to "Dear Clinton," December 15, 1863,
OHS; William Brown to George Chandler, March 13, 1864, NHHS.

3. John Lester Diary, February 6–13, 1864, IHS; Nathaniel Parmeter Diary, December 28, 1863, through January 5, 1864, OHS; Kohl, *Welsh Letters*, 149, 152; Nevins, *Diary
of Battle*, 315.

4. John Wilmot to "My Dear Ann," February 14, 1864, VTHS; Sophronia A. Wilmot
affidavit, August 13, 1864, and S. G. Heaton to Joseph Barrett, September 18, 1866,
Widow's Certificate 49014, Pension Applications, RG 15, NA.

5. Robert Cowden Diary, March 20–25, 1864, CCHS; Julius Whitney Diary, February 25, 1864, USAMHI; Nevins, *Diary of Battle*, 328.

6. J. H. Plimpton to Mary Richards, October 2, 1864, MNHS; E. P. Feaster to "Dear Nephew," March 9, 1864, Wadsworth Letters, WHMC; George Shanklin to "Dear Father & Caroline," April 22, 1864, IHS; *Prairie du Chien Courier*, February 18, 1864; Moskow, *Emma's World*, 194.

7. Lois Brocklebank to Mehetabel Loveren, March 20 and September 27, 1864, DC; Emily Harris to "Dearest Husband," January 10, 1864, UNH; Edgar Powers Diary, January 16–21, 29, and February 6–12, 1864, Bethel Historical Society; *Oxford Democrat*, April 8 and 22, 1864.

8. *Crisis*, February 3, March 9, and April 27, 1864; *Westfield Republican*, February 24, 1864; *Prairie du Chien Courier*, March 10 and April 7, 1864.; *OR*, Series 3, 4:148–53, 155; *New York Times*, March 30 and 31 and April 2, 1864; *Illinois State Journal*, April 4, 1864; Burlingame, *Nicolay Letters*, 128–29. President Lincoln kept the Charleston defendants confined for months, against both the law and the advice of his closest personal legal advisor. See Barry, "The Charleston Riot," and "'I'll keep them in prison awhile . . .'"

9. Chandler to Howe, February 17, 1864, Chandler Papers, NHHS. See also Chandler to Montgomery Blair, November 11, 1864, Blair Family Papers, LC.

10. Augustus Paddock to "Dear Father," February 25, 1864, UVM; Stephen Holt to "Dear Grandfather & Mother," March 21, 1864, DC; Lyman Jackman and Josiah Jones diaries, March 1–10, 1864, both NHHS.

11. Edward Bacon to "Dear Kate," April 6, 1864, AAS; "Lew" to "Dear Love," "March" [April] 6, 1864, Nettleton-Baldwin Family Papers, Yale; Robert Kellogg to "Dear Father," [March 25], 1864, CHS.

12. R. D. Lane to George Gilman, October 28, 1864, CHS; *New Hampshire Patriot*, February 1 and 17, and March 2, 1864; *Daily Chronicle*, March 9, 1864.

13. *OR*, Series 3, 4:37–59; *CWL*, 7:164; James Faran to Alexander Long, February 3, 1864, CinHS.

14. *Westfield Republican*, February 24, 1864; *Oxford Democrat*, March 4, 1864; Laas, *Lee Letters*, 326; *Stanstead Journal*, March 31, 1864; John Sturtevant to "Dear friends at Home," March 23, 1864, DC; George Jones to "Dear Friends at Home," February 7, 1864, UVM.

15. Cora Benton to Charles Benton, January 31 and February 12, 1864, ND; Rachel Aldrich to Asa Aldrich, April 29, 1864, and consent form signed by Elisha Aldrich, Brownson Papers, NHHS; James Easton to "Dear Brother," February 7, 1864, OHS; Charles Chace to "Dear Mother," October 19, 1863, and undated fragment to William Chace, UVM; George Parker to "My Dear sister Eliza," February 18, 1864, Calvert-Parker Papers, VTHS; Alonzo Cushman to "Dear Sister," April 28, 1864, and William Thompson to "Dear Father," January 2, 1864, both in Civil War Collection, AAS; William Weeks to "Dear Father," September 10, 1864, IU; John Sheahan to "My Dear Father," [February, 1864], MEHS; Philip Arsino to "Dear Mother," August 9, 1863 and February 16, 1864, VTHS.

16. C. T. Woodruff to Charles Sherman, December 11, 1863, CHS.

17. Flavius Bellamy to "Dear Parents," October 24, 1863, ISL; Nevins, *Diary of Battle*, 319–21; Cora Benton to Charles Benton, June 5, December 6, 1863, February 12, 1864, ND; *Stanstead Journal*, February 11, 1864; *OR*, Series 3, 4:1150, and 5:892, 901.

18. George Jones to "Dear Friends at Home," February 7, 1864, UVM; Edward Waite to "Dear Father," March 26, 1864, MEHS; Barnes, *Medical and Surgical History*, 1:452–55; Nevins, *Diary of Battle*, 320.

19. Oscar Robinson to "Dear Sister," January 9, 1864, DC; Nathaniel Parmeter Diary, April 9, 1864, OHS; Blight, *Brewster Letters*, 273; *Farmer's Cabinet*, January 12, 1864.

20. *Stanstead Journal*, December 3, 1863, February 4, March 24, and March 31, 1864. For recruiting in Canada, see Hamer, "Luring Canadian Soldiers into Union Lines."

21. Balace, *Recrutements en Belgique*, 2; *Boston Daily Advertiser*, January 6, 1864, and April 25, 1866; *Portland Daily Press*, March 28, 1864; *Portland Advertiser*, April 2 and 14, 1864. Michael Hager closely examines this scheme in "Massachusetts's German Mercenaries."

22. Contract of May 31, 1864, and brief dated April 3, 1866, Burrill Papers, MHS; *OR*, Series 3, 4:473.

23. H. B. Titus to Andrew Stone, January 18, 1864, NHHS; Elmer Bragg to "My dear Mother," January 9, 1864, DC; Oscar Robinson to "Dear Mother," January 5, 1864, DC; Ayling, *Register*, 512.

24. *Prairie du Chien Courier*, December 31, 1863, January 7 and 14, 1864.

25. Davis, *Butler Family Letters*, 72; *Prairie du Chien Courier*, December 24, 1863; Circular Orders 42 (1863) and 12 (1864), Ohio Provost Marshals Papers, OHS; *OR*, Series 3, 4:473. One of the more truthful claims in Frank Wilkeson's *Recollections* was that he was fifteen when he ran away from home to enlist.

26. *OR*, Series 2, 6:31, 768, 808, 1033–34, 8:993–95, and Series 3, 4:15.

27. *OR*, Series 2, 6:842; *Prairie du Chien Courier*, December 31, 1863; Scherneckau, *Diary*, 251; Dyer, *Compendium*, 997–1000, 1343, 1647.

28. *OR*, 33:362–63; William Boston to "Dear Aunt Rosa," April 10, 1864, BL; Daniel Larned to "My Dear Sister," January 8 and 10, 1864, LC; broadside copy, Box 20, and John Andrew to Burnside, January 25, 1864 (two letters), Box 15, Burnside Papers, RG 94, NA.

29. *Boston Evening Transcript*, February 2, 4, and 5, 1864; Charles Loring to Burnside, March 1 and 7, 1864, Box 16, Burnside Papers, RG 94, NA; Daniel Larned to "Dear A," February 4, 1864, LC.

30. Burnside to Edwin Stanton, January 26, 1864, Stanton Papers, LC; *OR*, 33:427–29; John Bross to Burnside, March 16, 1864, Simon Griffin to Burnside, March 2, 1864, Dorus Fox to Burnside, March 3, 1864, William Silliman to George Bliss, March 30, 1864, and William French to Burnside, March 16, 1864, all in Box 16, Burnside Papers, RG 94, NA; Julius Whitney Diary, March 21–23, 1864, USAMHI.

31. Sears, *Haydon Journal*, 343; Edwin Horton to "Dear Ellen," July 7, 1864, VTHS; William Jackman to "Dear Nancy," April 9, 1864, RBHPL; Susan Miller to "Dear Parents," April 10, 1864, CL; Emily Harris to "Darling Husband," April 17, 1864, UNH; William Adams Diary, February 17, 1864, MEHS.

32. Menge and Shimrak, *Chisholm Notebook*, 6–8, 107–9; Elmer Wallace to "Dear Parents," February 15, 1864, BL; Augustus Paddock to "Dear Friends at Home," April 21 and May 18, 1864, UVM; Chester Leach to unidentified recipient, February 21, 1864, UVM.

33. *OR*, Series 2, 4:266–68.

34. Ibid., 5:795–97, 6:75–76, 594–600, 8:986–95.

35. Ibid., 6:78–79, 401, 594–600.

36. Ibid., 6:532–34, 996, 1007–13, 7:606–7, 662, 8:122–23, 170; William Buckingham to Abraham Lincoln, November 18, 1863, ALP; *Detroit Free Press*, November 19 and December 17, 1863.

37. *OR*, Series 2, 8:990–94; Stephen Holt to "Dear Grandfather," December 6, 1863, DC; Archie Perkins to "My Dear Cousin," August 30 and December 25, 1863, March 10 and April 22, 1864, WHMC.

38. *OR*, Series 2, 6:438–39; Milgram, "Paulding Correspondence," 1132; Ryan, *Van Lew Diary*, 59; W. P. Kindreck to Abraham Lincoln, February 21, 1864, ALP; George Taylor to "My dear Ellen," September 27, 1863, CCHS; Newell Burch Diary, November 11, 1863, CCHS; John Dillingham to "Dear Father," January 13, 1864, Freeport Historical Society; Myron Woods to "Dear Father," February 12, 1864, MHS.

39. *Sumter Republican*, December 4, 1863, January 22, 1864; *Georgia Journal and*

Messenger, December 23, 1863; Richard Winder to Charles Armstrong, February 17, 1864, Winder Letterbook, RG 153, NA.

40. *Richmond Examiner,* February 18, 1864; John Whitten Diary, February 17–19, 1864, SHSI-DM; Amasa Isbell to "Dear Nannee," February 22, 1864, Calkins Collection; *Macon Daily Telegraph,* February 27, 1864; Register of Federal Prisoners Admitted to the Hospital, 1, RG 249, NA; U.S. House of Representatives, *Trial of Henry Wirz,* 687. For a history of Andersonville prison see Marvel, *Andersonville: The Last Depot.*

41. Joseph Brainerd epitaph, Greenwood Cemetery, St. Albans, Vt. For more rancor over the Lincoln administration's refusal to exchange prisoners see, for instance, Charles Colvin Notebook, April 30, 1864, Chicago Historical Society; David Kennedy Diary, May 9 and 20, June 9, 24, and 25, 1864, MNHS; Samuel Gibson Diary, July 2 and 16, 1864, LC; William Peabody Diary, July 16, 1864, USAMHI; Henry Stone Diary, July 16 and August 8, 1864, USAMHI; Kendrick Howard Diary, August 3 and September 2, 1864, VTHS; William Keys Diary, August 22 and 29, September 1 and 4, 1864, RU.

42. Morton to Lincoln, January 18, 1864, Stanton Papers, LC; *New York Times,* September 10, 1863; *Detroit Free Press,* September 18, October 7, and November 1, 1863; Palmer, *Sumner Letters,* 2:190–91. "Billion" was first defined by the French interpretation of a "thousand millions" in Webster's *American Dictionary of the English Language* in 1864 (122); previously it had denoted a million squared — the casual "trillion" of modern budgetary use.

43. *CWL,* 7:53–56.

44. Niven, *Chase Papers,* 1:438; Stickney to Lincoln, December 2, 1863, ALP.

45. *New York World,* December 11, 1863; *Detroit Free Press,* June 11, 1864.

46. Amos Tuck to William Chandler, January 6, May 5, 1864, NHHS; Burlingame and Ettlinger, *Hay Diary,* 141; Eleazer Hoar to "Dear William," February, 1864, CL; *Detroit Free Press,* March 3 and 6, 1864; Palmer, *Sumner Letters,* 2:229; Cyrus Wheeler to "Father and Mother," March 26, 1864, BL; John Stockton to "Dear Sir" [J. M. McKim], March 16, 1864, BPL; Chase to Albert Gallatin Riddle, March 11, 1864, WRHS; Niven, *Chase Papers,* 4:263–82, 323–58 passim.

47. D. L. Phillips to Lyman Trumbull, March 23, 1864, LC; George Wheeler to "Dear Mother," April 28, 1864, NSHS.

48. Nevins and Thomas, *Strong Diary,* 3:410; Chesson, *Dyer Journal,* 143; Sparks, *Patrick Diary,* 336; Clement Hoffman to "Dear Mother," April 16, 1864, USAMHI; Calvin Burbank to "Cousin Sarah," April 10, 1864, DC; Nevins, *Diary of Battle,* 330–31; Samuel Barlow to Montgomery Blair, April 26, 1864, HL.

49. Burlingame and Ettlinger, *Hay Diary,* 134–35, 144–45.

50. *OR,* 35(1):278, 295; *OR,* Series 2, 6:976–77; Burlingame and Ettlinger, *Hay Diary,* 145.

51. Burlingame and Ettlinger, *Hay Diary,* 146, 152; Meade, *Life and Letters,* 1:328–29.

52. *OR,* 35(1):280–81. The greater part of William Nulty's *Confederate Florida* is devoted to this single campaign and its aftermath.

53. Burlingame and Ettlinger, *Hay Diary,* 153–54; Burlingame, *Hay's Correspondence,* 77.

54. Moore, *Rebellion Record,* 8:394; Edwin Bearse to "Dear Mother," February 24, 1864, MHS; *OR,* 35(1):281–82, 286; Burlingame and Ettlinger, *Hay Diary,* 162.

55. Burlingame and Ettlinger, *Hay Diary,* 161–63; Burlingame, *Hay's Correspondence,* 75; *OR,* 35(1):282.

56. *OR,* 35(1):276–77, 282–84, 286; Burlingame and Ettlinger, *Hay Diary,* 162.

57. *OR,* 35(1):277, 481–83; Burlingame and Ettlinger, *Hay Diary,* 164–66; Burlingame, *Hay's Correspondence,* 77.

58. *OR,* 35(1):282–86, 482.

59. Ibid., 325–26, 331; Moore, *Rebellion Record,* 8:398–99.

60. *OR,* 35(1):285–86; Moore, *Rebellion Record,* 8:411–12.

61. Moore, *Rebellion Record,* 8:410, 412; *OR,* 35(1):303; Dyer, *Compendium,* 1449–50, 1472, 1725.

62. Moore, *Rebellion Record,* 8:396, 405, 409, 411–12; *OR,* 35(1):288, 326, 334.

63. Moore, *Rebellion Record,* 8:405–6, 409, 412; *OR,* 35(1):303.

64. *OR,* 35(1):303, 307; Hawley to Charles Dudley Warner, undated [but 1861] and September 2, 1864, Hawley Papers, CHS; Harriet Hawley to Jacob Eaton, May 4, 1864, Hoadley Collection, CHS. Rowley was hanged for this murder on September 3, 1864 (Record of Service, 307).

65. *OR,* 35(1):303–4, 307–8, 334, 343; Otis Merrill to unidentified recipient, February 26, 1864, quoted in Little, *The Seventh Regiment,* 222–23; Moore, *Rebellion Record,* 8:412, 415–16.

66. *OR,* 35(1):303, 311–12, 344; Norton, *Army Letters,* 198; Moore, *Rebellion Record,* 8:410; William Ford to "Dear Brother Jas," March 7, 1864, Knowlton Papers, NHHS.

67. *OR,* 35(1):289, 301–2, 332, 349–50; Barnes, *Medical and Surgical History,* 2:244, and 8:270.

68. Moore, *Rebellion Record,* 8:406, 413; *OR,* 35(1):315; Yacavone, *Stephens Letters,* 296; Edwin Bearse to "Dear Mother," February 24, 1864, MHS; William Ford to "Dear Brother Jas," March 7, 1864, Knowlton Papers, NHHS.

69. *OR,* 35(1):286–89, and Series 2, 6:1054; John Bartlett to "My Dear affectionate Sister," January 2, 1864, CHS; *Sumter Republican,* April 1, 1864; Archibald Bogle cash receipt, Confederate States Army Archives Miscellany, Duke University.

70. Burlingame, *Hay's Correspondence,* 77–79; *CWL,* 7:108, 243, 318, 418; Wainwright, *Fisher Diary,* 427.

71. *New York Times,* February 27, 1864; *New York Herald,* February 23 and March 1, 1864, and *Chicago Tribune,* February 29, 1864, quoted in Burlingame, *Hay's Correspondence,* 246–47; *OR,* 35(1):292.

72. Simpson and Berlin, *Sherman Correspondence,* 598–602; Stephen Werly Diary, February 9–13, 1864, WHMC. See Foster, *Sherman's Mississippi Campaign,* on this episode.

73. Nevins, *Diary of Battle,* 310–11; Edwin Wentworth to "dear Wife," December 16 and 29, 1863, LC.

74. John Willey to "My Dear Wife," December 25, 1863, USAMHI; Silas Sadler to "Dear Father and Mother," undated, BL; Tabor Parcher to "Dear Sarah," April 3, 1864, UVM; Robertson, *McAllister Letters,* 358–59. Parcher seemed to describe Isabella Botts, who was about twenty-two at the time, but whether she had a child that year could not be confirmed by census records.

75. Jaquette, *Hancock Letters,* 53–55; Elijah Cavins to "Dear Ann," March 13, 1864, IHS; Robertson, *McAllister Letters,* 383–86; Racine, *Unspoiled Heart,* 103.

76. Washington Roebling to "Darling Elvira," February 26, "1863" [1864], and bill for lumber for 2nd Corps ballroom, RU; Elijah Cavins to "Dear Ann," March 6, 1864, IHS; Meade, *Life and Letters,* 2:167.

77. Andrew Young to "My Dear Susan," February "22," 1864, DC; Washington Roebling to "Darling Elvira," February 26, "1863" [1864], RU; Meade, *Life and Letters,* 2:167, 168.

78. Laas, *Lee Letters,* 356; Elijah Cavins to "Dear Ann," March 21, 1864, IHS; Charles Whittier to "My Dear Addie," March 22, 1864, CL.

79. Meade, *Life and Letters,* 2:167–68; *New York Times,* February 10, 1864; *OR,* Series 2, 6:659, 691; *CG,* 38th Cong., 1st sess., part 1, 118–19; George Jones to "Dear Friends at Home," January 30 and February 22, 1864, UVM; Stephen Holt to "Dear Grandparents," February 14, 1864, DC; William Tritt Diary, January 7, 1864, USAMHI; Coco, *Bowen Letters,* 184; *New York Times,* February 24, 1864.

80. Agassiz, *Lyman Letters*, 76; *New York Times*, February 14, 1864; *CWL*, 7:178; *OR*, 33:172-73.

81. *OR*, 33:171-74; Meade, *Life and Letters*, 165-66; Washington Roebling to John Roebling, March 1, "1863" [1864], RU; Sparks, *Patrick Diary*, 341-42; Charles Greenleaf to "Dear Father & Mother," February 26, 1864, CHS.

82. Rosenblatt and Rosenblatt, *Fisk Letters*, 195; Agassiz, *Lyman Letters*, 77; George Lyon to "Dear Friend," March 6, 1864, VTHS; *OR*, 33:162, 175, 183, 194.

83. *OR*, 33:183, 194, 219-21.

84. Agassiz, *Lyman Letters*, 78; *OR*, 33:194-95, 221, 1200; Barnes, *Medical and Surgical History*, 2:178; Sparks, *Patrick Diary*, 343; Benjamin Fry to "Dear Friend," March 12, 1864, McFeely Family Papers, IHS.

85. *OR*, 33:184-85, 212-13; Jones, *Rebel War Clerk's Diary*, 345; William Wells to "Friend Anna," March 25, 1864, UVM, William Hills Diary, March 1, 1864, LC.

86. *OR*, 33:195-96; John Sheahan to "My Dear Father and mother," March 5, 1864, MEHS; Ryan, *Van Lew Diary*, 68; Jones, *Rebel War Clerk's Diary*, 343-44; Wiggins, *Gorgas Journals*, 94.

87. *OR*, 33:185, 201-2; John Sheahan to "My Dear Father," March 5, 1864, MEHS; William Wells to "Friend Anna," March 25, 1864, UVM; William Hills Diary, March 1, 1864, LC; Barnes, *Medical and Surgical History*, 2:178-79.

88. *OR*, 33:196; John Sheahan to "My Dear Father and mother," March 5, 1864, MEHS.

89. *OR*, 33:205, 208-10; statement of Henry E. Blair, dated August 22, 1874, quoted in Jones, "Kilpatrick-Dahlgren Raid," 537-40; statement of Edward W. Halbach, Pollard, *Lost Cause*, 504-6.

90. *OR*, 33:178, 180; Meade, *Life and Letters*, 2:190-91; Sparks, *Patrick Diary*, 347-48. Despite later books about the raid, V. C. Jones's *Eight Hours before Richmond* remains the best and most original account.

91. Robertson, *McAllister Letters*, 397; Agassiz, *Lyman Letters*, 79; *Correspondence of John Sedgwick*, 2:177; Nevins, *Diary of Battle*, 325; Meade, *Life and Letters*, 2:169, 170.

92. *Correspondence of John Sedgwick*, 2:168, 175; *RJCCW2*, 1:388; Meade, *Life and Letters*, 2:165-66, 169; Washington Roebling to John Roebling, March 1, "1863" [1864], RU.

93. Henry Halleck to Francis Lieber, March 7 and 14, 1864, HL; Meade, *Life and Letters*, 2:168, 169-70, 176; Charles Carroll Parker to "Darlings Katie & Mary," March 29, 1864, VTHS; *RJCCW2*, 1:359-76; *New York Tribune*, March 8, 1864.

94. Laas, *Lee Letters*, 355; John Roebling to Washington Roebling, March 21, 1864, RU; Eby, *Strother Diaries*, 216.

95. Grant to Halleck, January 19, 1864, CL; Sumner, *Comstock Diary*, 252; *OR*, 32(2):411-12. The main body of Grant's letter to Halleck was evidently written by one of the engineers [Simon, *Grant Papers*, 10:39-41]; I am obliged to Bryce Suderow, of Washington, D.C., for pointing this out.

9. God Alone Can Claim It

1. Nevins and Thomas, *Strong Diary*, 3:423, 429; Emily Harris to Leander Harris, February 23 and April 17, 1864, UNH; Cora Benton to Charles Benton, March 20, 1864, ND.

2. Joanna Lane to Benjamin Lossing, December 6, 1863, ISL; E. A. Miller to "My dear Child," April 16, 1864, CinHS; *New York Sun*, April 4, 1864; *OR*, Series 3, 4:448-49.

3. John Arnold to "Dear Wife and family," March 8, 1864, LC; Cornelius Nye to "Dear nephew," March 7, 1864, VTHS; *Oxford Democrat*, May 13, 1864; George Oscar French to unidentified recipient, January 31, 1864, VTHS; Racine, *Mattocks Journals*, 132; Sparks, *Patrick Diary*, 348.

4. Pease and Randall, *Browning Diary*, 1:658–65; George Miller to "Dear Father," February 11, 1864, KU; *CWL*, 3:397 and 7:228. See Bain, *Empire Express*, 163, for more on Lincoln's selection of Council Bluffs.

5. Willard Templeton to "Dear Brother James," June 24 and 25, 1864, and to "Dear Friends at Home," July 20, 1864, NHSL; Charles Cummings to "My Dear Wife," June 28, 1864, VTHS; Henry Bellows to Frederick Law Olmsted, August 13, 1863, LC; Nevins and Thomas, *Strong Diary*, 3:153, 292–93, 298, 307; Olmsted to Preston King, July 9, 1862, ALP. For an insightful, refreshingly frank examination of the Sanitary Commission and the ulterior motives of its founders, see Attie, *Patriotic Toil*.

6. Nevins and Thomas, *Strong Diary*, 3:273–74, 277, 379, 382–83, 406; *Chicago Tribune*, October 28, 1863; Pease and Randall, *Browning Diary*, 1:647–48; *Washington Star*, March 19, 1864. For the politics and ulterior impetus behind the Sanitary Commission fairs see, again, Attie, *Patriotic Toil*, especially 198–219.

7. Nevins and Thomas, *Strong Diary*, 3:373, 387, 421–22.

8. *New York Times*, March 24, 25, and 31, April 3, 4, and 5, 1864; Nevins and Thomas, *Strong Diary*, 3:396, 403, 406, 408, 412–13, 419; Nevins, *Diary of Battle*, 321–22.

9. Nevins and Thomas, *Strong Diary*, 3:411, 420, 421–24; *New York Times*, April 4 and 5, 1864.

10. *New York Times*, April 5, 1864; Nevins and Thomas, *Strong Diary*, 3:423–24, 426.

11. *New York Times*, April 4, 1864.

12. Ibid.; Nevins and Thomas, *Strong Diary*, 3:430.

13. *New York Times*, April 4 and 5, 1864.

14. Ibid., April 6, 11, and 12, 1864.

15. Ibid., April 7 and 8, 1864.

16. Ibid., April 6, 8, 9, 13, and 16–19, 1864.

17. Ibid., April 19–24, 1864; Nevins and Thomas, *Strong Diary*, 3:432.

18. Nevins and Thomas, *Strong Diary*, 3:427, 431–32; *New York Times*, April 24 and 25, 1864.

19. Nevins and Thomas, *Strong Diary*, 3:427; E. P. Bradstreet to Long, December 12, 1863, and James J. Faran to Long, February 3 and 7, 1864, CinHS; *OR*, Series 3, 4:636.

20. *CG*, 38th Cong., 1st sess., part 2, 1499–1504.

21. Ibid., 1506.

22. Ibid., 1515–19.

23. *CG*, 37th Cong., 3rd sess., part 1, 556–57, part 2 (appendix), 62–67, and 38th Cong., 1st sess., part 2, 1632; *New York Times*, April 11, 1864.

24. William Proctor to "Father & Mother," April 12, 1864, Fairbanks Museum; *CG*, 38th Cong., 1st sess., part 2, 1635.

25. James J. Faran to Long, February 3, 1864, CinHS; *OR*, 26(2):832–33, 871–72, and 34(2):15–16.

26. *OR*, 34(2):144–46, 149–50, 246–47, 266–67; Simpson and Berlin, *Sherman Correspondence*, 590.

27. *RJCCW2*, 2:354–56; Judson Bemis to "Dear Steph," October 17, 1863, MOHS; Johnson, *Red River Campaign*, 66, concludes that Banks never mailed his letter to Lincoln. Johnson's 1958 book is still the most thorough examination of this episode, as well as the most lucid, original, and entertaining treatment, notwithstanding subsequent works on the subject.

28. *RJCCW2*, 2:227, 384; *OR*, 34(1):181, 34(2):293, and 32(2):402, 410; Burlingame and Ettlinger, *Hay Diary*, 194; *USG*, 10:141–42. "Plausible deniability," a Central Intelligence Agency term denoting the ability of a chief executive to credibly deny knowledge of controversial government operations (even if he ordered them himself), entered the public consciousness during the disintegration of the Nixon administration.

29. *OR*, 34(1):659, 662, and 34(2):481, 491, 494, 542; William Rigby to "Dear Brother,"

March 12, 1864, UIA; *ORN*, 26:23; *RJCCW2*, 2:28-29; Jordan, *Gould Journals*, 309-16; Woodworth, *Winters Letters*, 118-20.

30. *OR*, 34(1):303-6; *ORN*, 26:24-31; *RJCCW2*, 2:57, 200.

31. Niven, *Chase Papers*, 4:361-63; Beale, *Welles Diary*, 2:26, 36-37; *ORN*, 26:292-93.

32. *RJCCW2*, 2:19, 74, 80-82, 177.

33. Jordan, *Gould Journals*, 316; *ORN*, 26:39; Niven, *Chase Papers*, 4:363; *OR*, 34(2):796-97; *RJCCW2*, 7-8.

34. *USG*, 10:200-201; *OR*, 34(2):494; *RJCCW2*, 2:14.

35. *OR*, 34(1):197-98, 34(2):735, 748, 768, and Series 3, 4:209; *RJCCW2*, 2:7-8, 24.

36. Jordan, *Gould Journals*, 318, 320-21; Kallgren and Crouthamel, *Dear Friend Anna*, 83; *OR*, 34(3):18-19.

37. *OR*, 34(1):420, and 34(3):20, 26; Woodworth, *Winters Letters*, 121; Henry Fike to "Dear Cimbaline," April 5, 1864, KU; Jordan, *Gould Journals*, 321-22; *USG*, 1:23-47. Improved roads appear to have shortened travel from nineteenth-century calculations.

38. *OR*, 34(3):20; *RJCCW2*, 2:57.

39. *OR*, 34(1):476-77 and 34(3):507, 513, 515, 518; Andrew Parsons to "Dear Wife," March 26, 1864, CL. Confederate returns are vague and incomplete.

40. *RJCCW2*, 2:57-58; *OR*, 34(3):17-18.

41. Moore, *Rebellion Record*, 8:546; Mrs. Robert J. Bell Diary, Parsons Papers, MOHS.

42. *RJCCW2*, 2:19-20, 227; *OR*, 34(2):46. See Johnson, *Red River*, 5-48, on the assorted factions lobbying for a Texas invasion, and on Halleck's part in prolonging the pressure on Banks.

43. *OR*, 34(1):11, 179-80; *RJCCW2*, 2:20.

44. Grant's March 15 letter to Banks, underscoring the deadline, is endorsed "Received Grand Ecore, 26th," but no Union troops had reached Grand Ecore by March 26. Banks claimed that he received it on March 27, "eight days before we reached Grand Ecore." See *OR*, 34(1):203-4, and 34(2):133, 610.

45. Jordan, *Gould Journals*, 322; Woodworth, *Winters Letters*, 121.

46. *OR*, 34(1):524-26, and 34(3):46; Jordan, *Gould Journals*, 323; Burgess, *Wakeman Letters*, 71-72.

47. *OR*, 34(1):256-57, 307; *RJCCW*, 2:201.

48. *RJCCW2*, 2:29, 32-33, 58-59; Jordan, *Gould Journals*, 323. Johnson, *Red River*, 128, identifies this water body as Ten Mile Bayou, but most Union reports and maps call it San Patricio Bayou.

49. *OR*, 34(1):227-28, 526; *RJCCW2*, 2:60.

50. *RJCCW2*, 2:23, 32-33, 56, 63-64, 69.

51. Ibid., 2:25, 60; *OR*, 34(1):290, 451.

52. *RJCCW2*, 2:25, 37, 60; *OR*, 34(1):291, 451; Francis Simpson to "Dear Mother," April 8, 1864, CHS. Much of Taylor's infantry consisted of dismounted cavalry. Lee's overestimate may have resulted from counting intelligence reports of those units as both cavalry and infantry.

53. *OR*, 34(1):182, 291, 456-57; *RJCCW2*, 2:61.

54. William Eastman to "Dear Mother," April 12, 1864, MHS; Francis McGregor to Susan Brown, April 12, 1864, OHS.

55. Moore, *Rebellion Record*, 8:541, 543, 547-48; *RJCCW2*, 2:61; *OR*, 34(1):182-83, 263, 273, 291-92; Jordan, *Gould Journals*, 323-25; Kallgren and Crouthamel, *Dear Friend Anna*, 86; Claude Goings to Mary Goings, April 18, 1864, DC.

56. *OR*, 34(1):182-83, 258-61; Cyrus Stockwell to "My Dear Wife," April 15, "1863" [1864], WRHS; Woodworth, *Winters Letters*, 127-29.

57. *OR*, 34(1):308-9, 527-29, 566-69; Jordan, *Gould Journals*, 327-28.

58. *OR*, 34(1):184–89, 309–10; *ORN*, 26:50–54, 71; Robert Edes to "Dear Betsey," April 19 and 30, 1864, MHS; Henry Fike to "Dear Cimbaline," April 12 and 16, 1864, KU; Mrs. Robert J. Bell Diary, Parsons Papers, MOHS.

59. *OR*, 34(1):189–93, 310–12; *ORN*, 26:54–56, 68–70, 71–77, 87, 92–95, 116, 130–34, 161; Henry Fike to "Dear Cimbaline," April 28 and May 1, 1864, KU; Andrew Parsons to "Dear Wife," May 23, 1864, CL.

60. Robert Edes to "Dear Betsey," April 30, 1864, MHS; Frederic Speed to "Dear Lotty," June 3, 1864, CL; Rufus Kinsley to "Dear Father," May 29, 1864, VTHS; James Fitts to "Dear Mother," April 26, 1864, UNH; *OR*, 34(1):312; Burlingame and Ettlinger, *Hay Diary*, 194.

61. Emily Harris to Leander Harris, April 17, 1864, UNH; Nevins and Thomas, *Strong Diary*, 3:443.

62. Simpson and Berlin, *Sherman Correspondence*, 626; *USG*, 10:285; *OR*, 32(1):251–54, 259, 34(1):509–11, 547–50, and 32(3):319, 329.

63. *OR*, 32(3):131, 177–78. On Fort Pillow see Ward, *River Run Red*, and Fuchs, *An Unerring Fire.*

64. *FPM*, 97, 99; *OR*, 32(3):770; Jonathan Harrington to "Brother," April 10, 1864, RBHPL.

65. *FPM*, 98, 104; *OR*, 32(1):596–97, 610, 611, 620–21.

66. *FPM*, 104; *OR*, 32(1):597, 621.

67. *OR*, 32(1):621.

68. *FPM*, 13, 104–14; *OR*, 32(1):519–40, 621–22.

69. *FPM*, 1–59, especially 1, 13–14, 30–31.

70. Barnes, *Medical and Surgical History*, 7:2, 19, 102, 107, 109, 8:268, 302, 9:136, 197, and 12:650; *OR*, 32(1):519–40; *FPM*, 15–53, 90–93.

71. Byron McClain to "Dear Brother," April 15, 1864, UIA.

72. *OR*, 35(1):493–94, and 35(2):23–24, 28–29, 34–37; *ORN*, 15:327–38, including *Charleston Courier* report of February 29, 1864.

73. *OR*, 33:93–94.

74. *ORN*, 9:656–58, 806.

75. *OR*, 33:298–99, 301–3; *ORN*, 9:657; Helmreich, "Lee Diary," 14; Samuel Gibson Diary, April 18–20, 1864, LC.

76. *OR*, 33:865–71.

77. Ibid., 299; Eliot, "Civil War Diary," 5; Asa Root Diary, April 21–23, April 29, and May 1, 1864, Barker Library; Ira Sampson Diary, April 30 and May 1, 1864, SHC; Helmreich, "Lee Diary," 15; Henry Adams Diary, April 21 and May 4, 1864, CHS; Robert Kellogg Diary, May 2, 1864, CHS; John Whitten Diary, April 30, May 1, 2, and 4, 1864, SHSI-DM; Oliver McNary Diary, April 21 and 30, 1864, KU.

78. *New York Times*, April 26, 1864; "Memorandum of Information," 22.

79. Charles Boyle to "Dear Home," April 29, 1864, CHS; *New York Times*, April 27, 1864; *Richmond Examiner*, April 27, 1864 (quoted in *New York Times*, April 29, 1864); Robert Moyle to "Dear father," February 28, 1864, UIA.

80. *Dakotian*, March 1 and 29, April 19 and 26, May 3 and 10, 1864; *OR*, 34(1):72–80, 880, 934–35.

81. *New York Times*, April 27, 1864.

82. Nevins and Thomas, *Strong Diary*, 3:423, 430–31; *New York Times*, January 1, 1862, January 1, 1863, January 1, April 1, April 28, and April 29, 1864. Although "inflation" had been used occasionally to describe currency devaluation before the war, *The Oxford English Dictionary* dates the first formal definition of that meaning from 1864. Webster's 1864 *American Dictionary*, incidentally, also included "income tax" among its new words for that edition (1315).

83. W. A. Baldwin to Trumbull, April 4, 1864, LC.

84. *CWL*, 4:269, 7:281; Louis Green to Alexander Calhoun, February 14, 1864, Guitar Papers, WHMC.

85. *CWL*, 5:403-4, 7:282. The similar phrasing and argument of the note and the letter are so striking as to suggest that they may have been composed much closer to each other than twenty months apart. Douglas Wilson suggests that Lincoln, an early religious doubter, came to disguise his skepticism to avoid scuttling his political ambitions (*Honor's Voice*, 308-13), and it would have been consistent for such a pragmatist to divert responsibility for a devastating war to an omnipotent supernatural power. As popular as it may be to interpret Lincoln's increasing use of biblical language during the war as evidence of his own continuing religious conversion, it is just as likely that he used it simply because it proved so persuasive; Christian belief would hardly have been the only doctrine he manipulated for polemical advantage.

86. James Uhler to "My Dearest," March 4, 1864, Cumberland County Historical Society; Charles Wilson to "My Dear Wife," April 28, 1864, NSHS; George Wheeler to "Dear Mother," April 28, 1864, NSHS; William Coe to "My dear Neine," March 19, 1864, LC.

87. William Stevens to "My dear Sister," March 26, 1864, SM.

88. Daniel Kenesson to "Friend Cobb," March 27, 1864, UVM; Elijah Cavins to "Dear Ann," March 6, 1864, IHS.

89. James Brown to "Dear Sister," April 28, 1864, MEHS.

90. Benjamin Ashenfelter to "Father Churchman," April 23, 1864, USAMHI; John Cuddy to "Dear Parents," January 10, March 29, and April 11, 1864, Dickinson College.

91. Thomas Brown to Horace Brown, May 19, 1863, to O. G. Morrison, December 30, 1862, and to Lydia Brown, February "30" and October 22, 1863, January 9, April 6, and April 20, 1864, VTHS; Peck, *Revised Roster*, 601.

92. William Stow to "Dear Parents," December 19, 1863, January 3, and February 24, 1864, and to "Dear Mother," April 14, 1864, UVM; Peck, *Revised Roster*, 52, 131.

93. Kohl, *Welsh Letters*, 155-56.

Epilogue

1. *OR*, Series 3, 4:237-39, 243.

2. *CWL*, 6:149-50; *New York Times*, April 27-29, 1864; *CG*, 38th Cong., 1st sess., part 3, 1953-55.

3. *OR*, Series 3, 4:465; Walter Shaw to unidentified correspondent, April 5-12, 1864, USAMHI; Abram Schermerhorn to "My Dear Mother," March 26, 1864, Lynde Family Papers, WRHS.

4. Racine, *Unspoiled Heart*, 112, 128; George Jones to "Dear Friends at Home," March 3, 1864, UVM.

5. *OR*, 36(1):198; *Correspondence of John Sedgwick*, 2:181; Henry Sanborn to "Kind Sister," February 25, 1864, NHHS; Charles Hadsall Diary, April 8, 10, and 25, 1864, NSHS; Ray, *Diary of a Dead Man*, 195; George French to "Dear Father and all," April 7 [1864], VTHS.

6. Merritt Stone to "Dear Sister Ella," April 24, 1864, VTHS; William Proctor to unidentified recipient, April 26, 1864, Fairbanks Museum; Harrison George to "Dear Parents," April 28, 1864, VTHS.

7. Harrison Randall to "Dear Father & Mother," March 22, 1864, ND; George Bates to "Dear Parents," April 27, 1864, CL; *OR*, 36(1):915; Harrison George to "Dear Parents," April 28, 1864, VTHS.

8. Charles Todd Diary, March 21-April 1, 1864, RBHPL; A. S. Boyce to "Dear Mary," April 26, 1864, BL; Weld, *Diary and Letters*, 280.

9. Frederick Swift Diary, April 25, 1864, RBHPL; Weld, *Diary and Letters*, 280; Charles Todd Diary, April 25, 1864, RBHPL; Hosea Towne to "Dear Friends," April 30, 1864, NHHS; Laas, *Lee Letters*, 372; Miller, *Whitman Writings*, 1:211-12.

10. Burlingame and Ettlinger, *Hay Diary,* 189; *OR,* 36(1):205–7.

11. John Jackson to Betsey Jackson, October 27, 1862, and November 15, 1863, ND; Rose Smelledge to "Dear Cynthia," June 10, 1864, Willey Papers, Conway Public Library.

12. Hosea Towne to "Dear Friends," April 30, 1864, NHHS; Frederick Swift Diary, April 25, 1864, RBHPL; Andrew Stone to "Wes," April 30, 1864, NHHS.

Bibliography

Manuscripts

American Antiquarian Society, Worcester, Mass.
    Edward W. Bacon Papers
    George Taylor Brigham Civil War Letters
    Civil War Collection
        Alonzo S. Cushman Letters
        William Thompson Correspondence
    Comey Family Papers
    Warren H. Cudworth Letters
    William L. Stanton Diary
D. R. Barker Library Historical Museum, Fredonia, N.Y.
    Asa W. Root Diary
Bethel Historical Society, Bethel, Maine
    Edgar Harvey Powers Diary
Boston Public Library, Boston, Mass.
    Chapman Family Papers
    Thomas C. Cross Letter
    Charles Folsom Papers
    Thomas Wentworth Higginson Papers
    George A. Spinney Letters
    John Stockton Letter
    Henry W. Tisdale Diary
Bowling Green State University, Bowling Green, Ohio
    Kehrwecker Family Papers
Christopher Calkins, Private Collection, Petersburg, Va.
    Amasa J. Isbell Letters
Camden Area History Center, Camden, Maine
    Rufus Ames Diary

Cary Library, Houlton, Maine
    J. L. Barton Affidavit
Chatauqua County Historical Society, Westfield, N.Y.
    Samuel T. Allen Papers
    Fred Barger Papers
    Newell Burch Diary
    Jabez Burrows Diary
    Robert Isaac Cowden Diary
    Cushing Family Papers
    Stephen R. Green Letters
    Henry H. Morse Diary
    George A. Taylor Letters
    Albion W. Tourgee Papers
Chicago Historical Society, Chicago, Ill.
    Charles M. Colvin Notebook
Cincinnati Historical Society, Cincinnati, Ohio
    George Benson Fox Papers
    Henry Archer Langdon Letters
    Alexander Long Papers
    Miller Family Collection
    Mathias Schwab Letters
Connecticut Historical Society, Hartford
    Henry H. Adams Diary
    John S. Bartlett Letters
    Milton H. Bassett Papers
    Frederick Bill Letter
    Charles A. Boyle Letters
    Josiah B. Corban Letters
    Julius and George Gilman Papers
    Charles Greenleaf Letters
    Joseph R. Hawley Papers
    Hoadley Collection: Harriet Hawley Letter
    Frederick Hooker Letters
    Robert Hale Kellogg Papers
    George Kies Letters
    James B. Law Letters
    Timothy Loomis Letters
    Charles E. Sherman Collection
    William H. Simons Papers
    Francis Simpson Papers
    Griffin Stedman Letters
    Alfred B. Talcott Letter
    Welling Collection: Horace Greeley Letter
Conway Public Library, Conway, N.H.
    Conway School District Records

Old Town Records
John N. Willey Papers
Cumberland County Historical Society, Carlisle, Pa.
Frank Stoke Letter
John Turner Letters
James Uhler Letters
Emma Doyle Wilderman Letter
Dartmouth College, Hanover, N.H.
Augustus Alvord Letters
Smith G. Bailey Diary
Ira M. Barton Papers
Elmer Bragg Papers
Calvin Burbank Letters
Royal Cook and A. M. Gillett Letters
Samuel Duncan Letters
Claude Goings Papers
Hiram Gregg Diary
Stephen H. Holt Letters
David Leigh Letters
Mehetabel Loveren Letters
George Marden Letters
John McCoy Letters
George Morgan Letters
Henry Clay Newell Correspondence
Gilbert J. Robie Letters
Oscar D. Robinson Papers
Ransom F. Sargent Papers
John W. Sturtevant Letters
Harrison W. Varney Letters
Andrew Hale Young Correspondence
Dickinson College, Carlisle, Pa.
John Taylor Cuddy Letters
Duke University, Durham, N.C.
Confederate States Army Archives Miscellany
Earlham College, Richmond, Ind.
Thomas W. Barnett Diary
Clarkson Butterworth Diary
Carpenter-Wright Family Papers
Hill-Hudelson Family Papers
Margaret Jones Diary
Student Records: John Harvey Letters
Francis W. Thomas Diary
Fairbanks Museum and Planetarium, St. Johnsbury, Vt.
William Henry Proctor Papers
Freeport Historical Society, Freeport, Maine
John G. Dillingham Papers

Gettysburg College, Gettysburg, Pa.
    Frederick H. Kronenberger Papers
Rutherford B. Hayes Presidential Library, Fremont, Ohio
    Charles Babbitt Letters
    Harrington Collection
    Rutherford B. Hayes Papers
    William Jackman Letters
    John R. Rhoades Letters
    John B. Rice Letters
    Frederick W. Swift Diary
    Charles D. Todd Diary
Huntington Library, San Marino, Calif.
    Samuel L. M. Barlow Papers
    Francis Lieber Collection
Indiana Historical Society, Indianapolis
    James A. Adams Letters
    Sylvester C. Bishop Letters
    Elijah H. C. Cavins Papers
    Chapin Family Papers
    John G. Davis Papers
    William F. Fordyce Diary
    Solomon Hamrick Papers
    Robert Barlow Hanna Papers
    Thomas J. Harrison Letters
    Horace Hobart Letters
    John F. Lester Diary
    McFeely Family Papers
    W. C. Patton Diaries
    Thomas B. Poe Letters
    Reynolds Family Papers
    Henry A. Robinson Letters
    David S. Scott Letters
    George W. Shanklin Letters
    Julietta Starbuck Letters
    William Starr Collection
    William A. Swayze Letters
    Robert Taylor Diary
    David Werking Letters
    Martha Talbert White Diary
Indiana State Library, Indianapolis
    Flavius Bellamy Papers
    Henry B. Carrington Papers
    Chittenden Papers
    Jonathan Joseph Letters
    Benjamin J. Lossing Letter
    James H. Luther Collection

Indiana University, Bloomington
    Milton Crist Manuscripts
    James Handley Manuscripts
    Richard W. Thompson Manuscripts
    Elizabeth Tuttle Manuscripts
    William C. and Harrison S. Weeks Manuscripts
    Rudolph Williams Manuscripts
Kansas State Historical Society, Topeka
    George Washington Hanson Papers
    James Hanway Collection
    William Casper Haynes Papers
    Judd Family Papers
    Cyrus Leland Letters
    George L. and Mary E. Stearns Papers
Library of Congress, Washington, D.C.
    Jabez Alvord Diary
    John Carvel Arnold Papers
    Orra B. Bailey Papers
    Nathaniel P. Banks Papers
    Joseph J. Bartlett Letter
    Chauncey E. Barton Letter
    Blair Family Papers
    Sidney Burbank Diary
    Zachariah Chandler Papers
    William P. Coe Correspondence
    J. Dexter Cotton Papers
    John C. Crittenden Papers
    Doubleday & Co. Notes
    William Franklin Draper Papers
    Wilbur Fisk Diary
    Douglas Southall Freeman Papers
    Samuel J. Gibson Diary
    Hamilton Family Papers
    John P. Hatch Papers
    Samuel P. Heintzelman Papers
    Henry Heisler Papers
    William G. Hills Diary
    Lyman Holford Diary
    Jedediah Hotchkiss Papers
    John Griffith Jones Papers
    Allen Landis Papers
    Daniel Reed Larned Papers
    Richard Lathers Papers
    Joseph Lester Papers
    Abraham Lincoln Papers
    Mary Tyler Peabody Mann Papers

Helen Varnum Hill McCalla Diary
George B. McClellan Papers
Rufus Mead Papers
Robert Curtis Ogden Papers
Frederick Law Olmsted Papers
Orlando M. Poe Papers
Charles H. Richardson Diary
James Edward Shortelle Papers
William H. Shriver Collection
Homer B. Sprague Diary
Edwin M. Stanton Papers
Simon Stern Letter
Horatio Nelson Taft Diary
Lyman Trumbull Papers
Benjamin Wade Papers
Elihu Washburne Papers
Edwin Oberlin Wentworth Papers
Charles H. Woodwell Diary
Louisiana State University, Baton Rouge
Elias Wyckoff Correpondence
Maine Historical Society, Portland
William Bryant Adams Papers
William A. Allen Letters
Charles Barnard Papers
Henry Black Letters
Daniel Webster Brown Correspondence
James Brown Correspondence
John Marshall Brown Papers
Eben S. Calderwood Papers
William A. Campbell Letters
John O. Crommett Letter
Greenlief P. Foster Letters
H. C. Ingersoll Letters
Meshack Larry Letters
Carl Knowles Moses Letters
Perry Family Correspondence
Marshall Phillips Correspondence
John Parris Sheahan Correspondence
Leonard Valentine Correspondence
Edward F. Waite Correspondence
Mark P. Waterman Letters
William Marvel, Private Collection, South Conway, N.H.
Edson Cheever Letters
Massachusetts Historical Society, Boston
Edwin W. Bearse Correspondence
Charles E. Bowers Papers

    Francis Brooks Papers
    Charles Burrill Papers
    William H. Eastman Correspondence
    Robert T. Edes Papers
    Holmes Family Papers
    Andrew R. Linscott Papers
    Frank C. Morse Papers
    Noyes Family Papers
    James Albert Osborne Diary
    Calvin Smith Letters
    William H. West Diary
    George Arms Whitmore Diary
    Myron Rice Wood Papers
Minnesota Historical Society, Minneapolis
    John Reed Beatty Papers
    Charles J. Branich (Karl Josef Breunig) Papers
    James C. Christie and Family Papers
    David Kennedy Diary
    Mathew Marvin Papers
    Mary E. Richards and Family Papers
    Orrin F. Smith Papers
Missouri Historical Society, St. Louis
    Bemis Family Papers
    Mosby Monroe Parsons Papers
National Archives, Washington, D.C.
    Record Group 15, Records of the Pension Office (RG 15)
        Pension Applications and Certificates
    Record Group 29, Records of the Bureau of the Census (RG 29)
        Eighth Census of the United States, M-653
        Ninth Census of the United States, M-593
        Tenth Census of the United States, T-9
        Thirteenth Census of the United States, T-624
    Record Group 94, Records of the Adjutant General (RG 94)
        Ambrose E. Burnside Papers
        Case Files of Investigations by Levi C. Turner and Lafayette C. Baker, 1861–
           1866, M-797
        Generals' Papers and Books
        Military Personnel Files
    Record Group 107, Records of the Office of the Secretary of War (RG 107)
        Letters Received by the Secretary of War from the President, Executive De-
           partments, and War Department Bureaus, M-494
    Record Group 109, War Department Collection of Confederate Records (RG
        109)
        Compiled Service Records of Confederate Soldiers Who Served in Organiza-
           tions from the State of Missouri, M-322
    Record Group 110, Records of the Provost Marshal General's Bureau (RG 110)

Tenth District of Pennsylvania, Letters Forwarded
Eleventh District of Pennsylvania, Letters Received
Twelfth District of Pennsylvania, Letters Received
Record Group 153, Records of the Judge Advocate General (RG 153)
    Richard B. Winder Letterbook
Record Group 249, Records of the Commissary General of Prisoners (RG 249)
    Register of Federal Prisoners Admitted to the Hospital at Andersonville,
    Georgia
Nebraska State Historical Society, Lincoln
    Harry Love Crawford Papers
    Charles Hadsall Diaries
    Uriah Oblinger Family Letters
    Richardson Family Papers
    Shaw-Gale-Noxon Family Papers
    Union Club Minutes
    George R. Wheeler Papers
    Charles Henry Wilson Letters
New Hampshire Division of Records Management and Archives, Concord
    Executive Correspondence
New Hampshire Historical Society, Concord
    Aldrich-Thompson Family Papers
    Anonymous Diary, 16th N.H.V.
    Albert T. Austin Letter
    Charles Gilman Brewster Letters
    Orrin Brownson Papers
    George H. Chandler Papers
    William E. Chandler Papers
    Charles Chase Papers
    Lizzie M. Corning Diaries
    Cram Family Papers: Daniel Veasey Durgin Letters
    Solomon Dodge Letters
    Andrew Farnum Letters
    John Harrison Foye Letters
    Benjamin B. and Henry F. French Correspondence
    Joseph Gilmore Papers
    Nathan G. Gould Papers
    Solomon Grannis Diary
    Sylvester Erwin Hadley Diary
    Edward F. Hall Letters
    M. W. Harris Letters
    Charles H. Herbert Papers
    Charles Emerson Howe Letters
    Christopher Hoyt Letters
    Lyman Jackman Diary
    Josiah N. Jones Diary
    Elisha M. Kempton Papers

Daniel R. Kenney Papers
Richard P. Kent Diary
James S. Knowlton Papers
Franklin Pierce Papers
Rodney Ramsey Letters
Henry M. Sanborn Papers
George H. Sargent Letters
Albert Stearns Papers
Andrew J. Stone Papers
Sewell D. Tilton Papers
George F. Towle Diary
Hosea Towne Letters
George E. Upton Letters
New Hampshire State Library, Concord
Willard J. Templeton Letters
Ohio Historical Society, Columbus
Jacob Ammen Papers
Lester Arnold Papers
Alexander S. Boys Papers
Core-Porter Papers
Joseph Easton Papers
Richard Newell Elder Papers
William Hoff Letters
Thomas C. Honnell Papers
Francis Norman Ross McGregor Papers
Ohio Provost Marshals Papers
Nathaniel Parmeter Diary
Sara Emily Ross Papers
James R. Stillwell Papers
Clinton B. Winterstein Letters
Peabody Essex Museum, Salem, Mass.
Mary B. Burnham Letters
Fowler/Black Family Correspondence
Fowler Family Manuscripts
John Pierce Letters
Providence Public Library, Providence, R.I.
Letters of Charlotte F. Dailey, Albert Dailey, and Walter E. Gardiner
John M. Gallagher Letters
Rhode Island Historical Society, Providence
William W. Chapin Diary
Edmund W. Fales Papers
Daniel A. Handy Letters
Rutgers University, New Brunswick, N.J.
William Farrand Keys Diary
Roebling Family Papers
Sheldon Museum, Middlebury, Vt.

Rokeby Museum Collection: Robinson Family Papers
Sanford Family Collection
William B. Stevens Letters
State Historical Society of Iowa, Des Moines
Adjutant General's Correspondence: Disloyal Sentiments File
William R. Barnes Letters
Jacob Hunter Papers
John Whitten Diary
State Historical Society of Iowa, Iowa City
Thomas Coffman Papers
Frank Collins Papers
Amos Noyes Currier Letters
George DeHart Letters
University of Iowa Libraries, Iowa City
Miles Beatty Collection
Anson Butler Papers
Charles Cady Papers
Marcellus W. Darling Papers
Edward E. Davis Letters
Giauque Family Papers
George Hall Papers
Joseph Kohout Papers
Mann Family Papers
Byron McClain Letters
Martin Mericle Papers
Robert Moyle Correspondence
William and Titus Rigby Papers
Sterns Family Papers
Myron Underwood Papers
University of Kansas, Lawrence
Ith S. Beall Collection
Marquis Alonzo Hills Collection
Kansas Collection
Thomas Carney Papers
George W. Collamore Papers
Henry C. Fike Papers
Joseph Henry Leighty Collection
Oliver R. McNary Diary
Josiah Miller Papers
John Kerr Proudfit Letters
John Henry Vansickle Papers
University of Michigan, Bentley Library, Ann Arbor
Benjamin F. Bordner Letters
William Boston Letters
A. S. Boyce Letters
Robert Crouse Papers

Wayne E. Morris Papers
Conrad Noll Diary
Ryder Family Papers
Silas W. Sadler Correspondence
Spalding Family Papers
Edward Henry Courtney Taylor Correspondence
Elmer D. Wallace Papers
Wells Family Papers: Benjamin F. Wells Letters
Cyrus B. Wheeler Correspondence
University of Michigan, Clements Library, Ann Arbor
George Tobey Anthony Letters
Aplin Family Papers
George Henry Bates Letters
Burbank Family Papers
Daniel Coler Letters
Fales Family Papers
Orlando M. Gilbert Certificate
Gordon Family Papers
Ulysses S. Grant Letters
Eleazer Hoar Letters
Stephen A. Hurlbut Letters
John P. Jones Letters
Christopher Keller Letters
Charles M. Maxim Letters
James T. and Robert E. Miller Letters
Charles Parker Letters
Andrew S. Parsons Papers
Pennsylvania Militiaman's Letter
Clara Robbins Letter
A. L. Russell Telegram
Henry H. Seys Letters
William Henry Shaw Letters
William Augustus Smith and Junius Smith Papers
William and Frederic Speed Letters
Simon A. Stern Letter
John Conover Ten Eyck Letter
Edward H. Wade Letters
Charles A. Whittier Letters
John Darrah Wilkins Letters
University of Missouri, Western Historical Manuscript Collection, Columbia
Henry C. and William H. Crawford Letters
Odon Guitar Collection
Archie Perkins Letters
Stillman Letters
Henry Wadsworth Letters
Stephen Werly Diary

University of New Hampshire, Durham
    Barrus Family Papers
    Thomas C. Cheney Papers
    James Franklin Fitts Papers
    William B. Greene Letter
    Leander Harris Letters
    John Henry Jenks Letters
    John W. Warner Letters
University of North Carolina, Southern Historical Collection, Chapel Hill
    Edward Porter Alexander Papers
    John Warwick Daniel Papers
    Meta Morris Grimball Journal
    Ira B. Sampson Diary
University of Notre Dame, Notre Dame, Ind.
    Thomas Benton Alexander Diary
    Benton-Beach Correspondence
    Blanchard-Walker Letters
    Caley Family Correspondence
    Robert Sedgwick Edwards Papers
    John M. Jackson Letters
    Miller Family Correspondence
    Harrison E. Randall Letters
    Shriver Family Correspondence
    Thomas Family Correspondence
University of Rochester, Rochester, N.Y.
    Huntington-Hooker Papers
University of South Carolina, South Caroliniana Library, Columbia
    Micah Jenkins Papers
    Onville Upton Letters
University of Texas, Center for American History, Austin
    John Crittenden Letters
University of Vermont, Burlington
    John Q. Amadon Letters
    Charles E. Chace Papers
    Cobb Family Papers
    Martin Van Buren Davis Letters
    Joel Glover Letters
    Hubbard Family Papers
    Richard J. Irwin Letters
    George M. Jones Papers
    Kineson Family Papers
    Chester K. Leach Papers
    Charles Manson Letters
    Arthur F. Morey Papers
    Augustus Paddock Letters
    Tabor Parcher Letters

Parker Family Papers
Cyrus Pringle Papers
Joseph C. Rutherford Papers
Bradford P. Sparrow Letters
William Stow Letters
William Wells Papers
U.S. Army Military History Institute, Carlisle, Pa.
John W. Ames Papers
Benjamin F. Ashenfelter Letters
John H. Bailey Diary
Schuyler S. Ballou Letters
Joseph Barton Letters
Joel Blake Letters
John Boyer Letters
Nelson Chapin Letters
Lewis F. Cleveland Letters
Feargus Elliott Letters
William J. Evans Letters
John and Leo Faller Letters
Daniel Faust Letters
John K. Fernsler Diary (in 96th Pennsylvania Collection)
Robert J. Forrest Diary
Isaac W. Gardner Letters
Gilbert Gulbrandson Letters
Jacob Haas Letters
John A. Hammond Diary
George P. Hawkes Diary
William Hayward Letters
Clement Hoffman Letters
Charles R. Johnson Letters
Henry Keiser Diary
Friedrich P. Keppelman Letters
Bently Kutz Letters
Henry Lyle Letters
George S. Lyon Letters
C. B. Neeley Letters
David Nichol Papers
William T. Peabody Diary
Robert W. Rodgers Diary
Roswell L. Root Letter
David Seibert Papers
Walter B. Shaw Letter
Skelly Family Letters
Joseph H. Smith Letter
Gustave Soule Letters
George A. Spencer Letters

Howard Stevens Letters
Eunice Stewart Letter
Henry Stone Diary
John Stumbaugh Letter
William Tritt Diary
Julius Whitney Diary
John S. Willey Letters
Floyd E. Williams Letters
Vermont Historical Society, Barre
Peter M. Abbott Letters
Philip Arsino Letters
Boardman and Miles Family Papers
Thomas H. Brown Letters
Calvert-Parker Papers
Charles Cummings Papers
Henry F. Dix Letters
Roswell Farnham Letters
Letters to Wealthy Field
George Oscar French Letters
Gale-Morse Family Papers
Harrison B. George Letters
Edwin C. Hall Papers
William Wirt Henry Papers
William Hogan Letters
Edwin Horton Papers
Kendrick R. Howard Diary
Alfred H. Keith Papers
Rufus Kinsley Papers
Lyndon State College Collection: Stephen and Samuel E. Pingree Papers
George S. Lyon Letters
Dan Mason Letters
Middlesex Papers: Henry J. Vaughn Letters
Lorenzo Miles Diary
Sylvester Nye Papers
Parker Family Papers: C. C. Parker Letters
Seaver Family Letters
Joseph Spafford Letters
William B. Spoor Letter
Merritt H. Stone Letters
Dudley Tillison Letters
William White Letters
John Wilmot Letters
Virginia Historical Society, Richmond
Edward Bates Papers
Jewett Family Papers
Edward Moseley Letters

Western Reserve Historical Society, Cleveland, Ohio
  George W. Hodges Letters
  Daniel D. Hopper Letters
  Rollin C. and Frank H. Hurd Papers
  George Landrum Letters
  Edward D. Lynde Family Papers: Abram G. Schermerhorn Letters
  Chauncey W. Mead Papers
  James Nesbitt and Isaac P. C. Raub Letters
  Albert Gallatin Riddle Papers
  Benjamin F. Sells Collection
  Cyrus H. Stockwell Papers
  Clement L. Vallandigham Papers (filed individually)
  Alexander Varian Letters
  Marion D. Ward Letters
  E. G. Wood Papers: Lucius and Julius Wood Letters
Wisconsin Historical Society, Madison
  John J. Barney Papers
  Henry J. Beecham Letters
  Horace Currier Papers
  Alonzo Gilbert Jack Letters
  Henry W. Jackson Letters
  Charles N. Mumford Letters
  War History Commission Records: Frank A. Haskell Letter
Yale University, New Haven, Conn.
  George Bradley Letters
  William Coates Papers
  Charles M. Coit Papers
  Abraham Lincoln Papers
  Nettleton-Baldwin Family Papers
  Thomas W. Porter Collection

Published Works

Acken, J. Gregory, ed. *Inside the Army of the Potomac: The Civil War Experience of Captain Francis Adams Donaldson.* Mechanicsburg, Pa.: Stackpole Books, 1998.

Adams, Virginia M., ed. *On The Altar of Freedom: A Black Soldier's Civil War Letters from the Front.* New York: Warner Books, 1992.

Agassiz, George R., ed. *Meade's Headquarters, 1863–1865: Letters of Colonel Theodore Lyman from the Wilderness to Appomattox.* Boston: Atlantic Monthly Press, 1922.

Anderson, Mary Ann, ed. *The Civil War Diary of Allen Morgan Geer, Twentieth Regiment, Illinois Volunteers.* Denver, Colo.: Robert C. Appelman, 1977.

Atlas to Accompany the Official Records of the Union and Confederate Armies. Washington, D.C.: Government Printing Office, 1891–95.

Attie, Jeanie. *Patriotic Toil: Northern Women and the American Civil War.* Ithaca, N.Y.: Cornell University Press, 1998.

[Atwater, Dorence.] *The Atwater Report: List of Prisoners Who Died in 1864–65 at Andersonville Prison.* Andersonville, Ga.: National Society of Andersonville, 1981.

Austin, J. Luke, ed. *General John Bratton: Sumter to Appomattox in Letters to His Wife.* Sewanee, Tenn.: Proctor's Hall Press, 2003.

Ayling, Augustus D., comp. *Revised Register of the Soldiers and Sailors of New Hampshire in the War of the Rebellion, 1861–1866.* Concord, N.H.: Ira C. Evans, 1895.

Bailey, Judith A., and Robert I. Cottom, eds. *After Chancellorsville: The Civil War Letters of Private Walter G. Dunn and Emma Randolph.* Baltimore: Maryland Historical Society, 1998.

Bain, David Haward. *Empire Express: Building the First Transcontinental Railroad.* New York: Viking, 1999.

Balace, Francis. *Recrutements en Belgique Pour Les Troupes Fédérales, 1864–1865.* Brussels: Center for American Studies, 1970.

Barnes, Joseph K. *The Medical and Surgical History of the War of the Rebellion (1861–65).* 15 vols. 1870. Repr. Wilmington, N.C.: Broadfoot Publishing, 1990.

Barry, Peter J. "The Charleston Riot and Its Aftermath: Civil, Military, and Presidential Responses." *Journal of Illinois History* 7, no. 2 (summer 2004), 82–106.

———. "'I'll keep them in prison awhile . . .': Abraham Lincoln and David Davis on Civil Liberties in Wartime." *Journal of the Abraham Lincoln Association* 28, no. 1 (winter 2007), 20–29.

Basile, Leon, ed. *The Civil War Diary of Amos E. Stearns, a Prisoner at Andersonville.* Rutherford, N.J.: Fairleigh Dickinson University Press, 1981.

Basler, Roy P., ed. *The Collected Works of Abraham Lincoln.* 8 vols. New Brunswick, N.J.: Rutgers University Press, 1953.

Beale, Howard K., ed. *The Diary of Edward Bates.* Washington, D.C.: Government Printing Office, 1933.

———, ed. *The Diary of Gideon Welles, Secretary of the Navy under Lincoln and Johnson.* 3 vols. New York: W. W. Norton and Company, 1960.

Bearss, Edwin Cole. *The Campaign for Vicksburg.* 3 vols. Dayton, Ohio: Morningside, 1985–86.

Beauchamp, Virginia Walcott, ed. *A Private War: Letters and Diaries of Madge Preston, 1862–1867.* New Brunswick, N.J.: Rutgers University Press, 1987.

Bernstein, Iver. *The New York City Draft Riots: Their Significance for American Society and Politics in the Age of the Civil War.* New York: Oxford University Press, 1990.

Beveridge, Albert J. *Abraham Lincoln, 1809–1858.* 2 vols. Boston: Houghton Mifflin, 1928.

Billings, John D. *Hardtack and Coffee; or, The Unwritten Story of Soldier Life.* Boston: George M. Smith & Co., 1887.

Blackburn, George M., ed. *With the Wandering Regiment: The Diary of Captain*

Ralph Ely of the Eighth Michigan Infantry. Mount Pleasant: Central Michigan University Press, 1965.

Blair, William Alan, ed. *A Politician Goes to War: The Civil War Letters of John White Geary.* University Park: Pennsylvania State University Press, 1995.

Blight, David W., ed. *When This Cruel War Is Over: The Civil War Letters of Charles Harvey Brewster.* Amherst: University of Massachusetts Press, 1992.

Bohrnstedt, Jennifer Cain, ed. *While Father Is Away: The Civil War Letters of William H. Bradbury.* Lexington: University Press of Kentucky, 2003.

Brun, Christian. "A Palace Guard View of Lincoln (The Civil War Letters of John H. Fleming)." *Soundings* 3, no. 1 (May 1971), 19–39.

Burgess, Lauren Cook, ed. *An Uncommon Soldier: The Civil War Letters of Sarah Rosetta Wakeman, Alias Private Lyons Wakeman, 153rd Regiment, New York State Volunteers.* Pasadena, Md.: Minerva Center, 1994.

Burlingame, Michael, ed. *At Lincoln's Side: John Hay's Civil War Correspondence and Selected Writings.* Carbondale: Southern Illinois University Press, 2000.

———, ed. *Dispatches from Lincoln's White House: The Anonymous Civil War Journalism of Presidential Secretary William O. Stoddard.* Lincoln: University of Nebraska Press, 2001.

———, ed. *With Lincoln in the White House: Letters, Memoranda, and Other Writings of John G. Nicolay, 1860–65.* Carbondale: Southern Illinois University Press, 2000.

Burlingame, Michael, and John R. Turner Ettlinger, eds. *Inside Lincoln's White House: The Complete Civil War Diary of John Hay.* Carbondale: Southern Illinois University Press, 1997.

Catton, Bruce. *Reflections on the Civil War.* New York: Doubleday & Co., 1981.

Chancellor, Christopher, ed. *An Englishman in the American Civil War: The Diaries of Henry Yates Thompson, 1863.* New York: New York University Press, 1971.

Chesson, Michael B., ed. *J. Franklin Dyer: The Journal of a Civil War Surgeon.* Lincoln: University of Nebraska Press, 2003.

Correspondence of John Sedgwick, Major-General. 2 vols. New York: C. and E. B. Stoeckel, 1902–3.

Cozzens, Peter. *The Shipwreck of Their Hopes: The Battles for Chattanooga.* Urbana: University of Illinois Press, 1994.

———. *This Terrible Sound: The Battle of Chickamauga.* Urbana: University of Illinois Press, 1992.

Cummings, Pamela, ed. *No Regrets: The Civil War Diary of David Day.* N.p.: Amber Quill Press, 2003.

Cutrer, Thomas W., ed. *Longstreet's Aide: The Civil War Letters of Major Thomas J. Goree.* Charlottesville: University of Virginia Press, 1995.

Cutrer, Thomas W., and T. Michael Parrish, eds. *Brothers in Gray: The Civil War Letters of the Pierson Family.* Baton Rouge: Louisiana State University Press, 1997.

Davidson, Garber A., ed. *The Civil War Letters of the Late 1st Lieut. James J. Hartley, 122nd Ohio Infantry Regiment.* Jefferson, N.C.: McFarland & Co., [1998].

Davis, Barbara Butler, ed. *Affectionately Yours: The Civil War Home-Front Letters of the Ovid Butler Family.* Indianapolis: Indiana Historical Society, 2004.

Dowdey, Clifford, and Louis H. Manarin, eds. *The Wartime Papers of R. E. Lee.* New York: Virginia Civil War Commission, 1961.

Dyer, Frederick H. *A Compendium of the War of the Rebellion.* 1908. Repr., with an introduction by Lee A. Wallace Jr. Dayton, Ohio: Morningside Press, 1978.

Easley, Virginia, ed. "Journal of the Civil War in Missouri: 1861, Henry Martyn Cheavens." *Missouri Historical Review* 56, no. 1 (October 1961), 12–25.

Eby, Cecil B., Jr., ed. *A Virginia Yankee in the Civil War: The Diaries of David Hunter Strother.* Chapel Hill: University of North Carolina Press, 1961.

Edwards, William Bennett. *Civil War Guns: The Complete Story of Federal and Confederate Small Arms; Design, Manufacture, Identification, Procurement, Issue, Employment, Effectiveness, and Postwar Disposal.* Harrisburg, Pa.: Stackpole Co., 1962.

Eliot, Ellsworth, ed. "A Civil War Diary." *Yale University Library Gazette* 16, no. 1 (July 1941), 3–13.

Fite, Emerson David. *Social and Industrial Conditions in the North during the Civil War.* Williamstown, Mass.: Corner House, 1976.

Floyd, Dale E., ed. *Dear Friends at Home: The Letters and Diary of Thomas James Owen, Fiftieth Volunteer Engineer Regiment, During the Civil War.* Washington, D.C.: Government Printing Office: 1985.

Foster, Buck T. *Sherman's Mississippi Campaign.* Tuscaloosa: University of Alabama Press, 2006.

Franklin, William B. *A Reply of Maj.-Gen. William B. Franklin to the Report of the Joint Committee of Congress on the Conduct of the War.* New York: D. Van Nostrand, 1863.

Frassanito, William A. *Grant and Lee: The Virginia Campaigns, 1864–1865.* New York: Charles Scribner's Sons, 1983.

Fremantle, Arthur J. L. *Three Months in the Southern States, April–June, 1863.* Edinburgh and London: William Blackwood & Sons, 1863.

French, Benjamin Brown. *Witness to the Young Republic: A Yankee's Journals, 1828–1870.* Hanover, N.H.: University Press of New England, 1989.

Fuchs, Richard L. *An Unerring Fire: The Massacre at Fort Pillow.* Mechanicsburg, Pa.: Stackpole Books, 2002.

Gallagher, Gary W., ed. *Fighting for the Confederacy: The Personal Recollections of General Edward Porter Alexander.* Chapel Hill: University of North Carolina Press, 1989.

———, ed. *The Third Day at Gettysburg and Beyond.* Chapel Hill: University of North Carolina Press, 1994.

Gavin, William Gilfillan, ed. *Infantryman Pettit: The Civil War Letters of Corporal Frederick Pettit.* New York: Avon Books, 1991.

Geary, James W. *We Need Men: The Union Draft in the Civil War.* DeKalb: Northern Illinois University Press, 1991.

Greene, A. Wilson. *Civil War Petersburg: Confederate City in the Crucible of War.* Charlottesville: University of Virginia Press, 2006.

Gurowski, Adam. *Diary, from November 18, 1862, to October 18, 1863.* New York: George W. Carleton, 1864.

Hager, Michael E. "Massachusetts's German Mercenaries in the Civil War." *New England Ancestors* 8, no. 2 (spring 2007), 20–24.

[Haines, Zenas T.]. *Letters from the Forty-fourth Regiment, M.V.M., A Record of the Experience of a Nine Months' Regiment in the Department of North Carolina in 1862-3, by "Corporal."* Boston: Herald Job Office, 1863.

Hamer, Marguerite B. "Luring Canadian Soldiers into Union Lines during the War Between the States." *Canadian Historical Review* 27, no. 1 (March 1946), 150–62.

Hammer, Jefferson J., ed. *Frederic Augustus James's Civil War Diary.* Rutherford, N.J.: Fairleigh Dickinson University Press, 1973.

Hammond, Harold Earl, ed. *Diary of a Union Lady, 1861-1865.* 1962. Repr., with an introduction by Jean V. Berlin. Lincoln: University of Nebraska Press, 2000.

Harris, Robert F., and John Niflot, eds. *Dear Sister: The Civil War Letters of the Brothers Gould.* Westport, Conn.: Praeger, 1998.

Hassler, William W. *One of Lee's Best Men: The Civil War Letters of General William Dorsey Pender.* 1965. Repr., with a foreword by Brian Wills. Chapel Hill: University of North Carolina Press, 1999.

Hastings, William H., ed. *Letters from a Sharpshooter: The Civil War Letters of Private William B. Greene, Co. G, 2nd United States Sharpshooters (Berdan's), Army of the Potomac, 1861-1865.* Belleville, Wis.: Historic Publications, 1993.

Haynes, Martin A. *A Minor War History Compiled from a Soldier Boy's Letters to "The Girl I Left Behind Me," 1861-1864.* Lakeport, N.H.: privately printed, 1916.

Helmreich, Paul C., ed. "The Diary of Charles G. Lee in the Andersonville and Florence Prison Camps, 1864." *Connecticut Historical Society Bulletin* 41, no. 1 (January 1976), 12–28.

Hennessy, John J. *Return to Bull Run: The Campaign and Battle of Second Manassas.* New York: Simon & Schuster, 1993.

Hertz, Emanuel. *Abraham Lincoln: A New Portrait.* 2 vols. New York: Horace Liveright, 1931.

Higginson, Thomas Wentworth. *Massachusetts in the Army and Navy during the War of 1861-65.* 2 vols. Boston: Wright and Potter, 1895.

Hill, Daniel H. "Chickamauga — The Great Battle of the West." In *Battles and Leaders of the Civil War,* edited by Robert U. Johnson and Clarence C. Buel. 4 vols. New York: Century, 1884–88, 3:638–62.

Holden, Walter, William E. Ross, and Elizabeth Slomba, eds. *Stand Firm and Fire Low: The Civil War Writings of Colonel Edward E. Cross.* Hanover, N.H.: University Press of New England, 2003.

Horrocks, James. *My Dear Parents: The Civil War As Seen by an English Union Soldier.* New York: Harcourt Brace Jovanovich, 1982.

Houston, Alan Fraser, ed. *Keep Up Good Courage, A Yankee Family and the Civil War: The Correspondence of Cpl. Lewis Q. Smith, of Sandwich, New Hampshire,*

Fourteenth Regiment New Hampshire Volunteers, 1862–1865. Portsmouth, N.H.: Peter E. Randall, 2006.

Hughes, William E., ed. *The Civil War Papers of Lt. Colonel Newton T. Colby, New York Infantry.* Jefferson, N.C.: McFarland & Co., 2003.

Hunley, C. Russell, ed. *The 14th U.S. Infantry Regiment in the American Civil War: John Young Letters.* Shippensburg, Pa.: Burd Street Press, 2000.

Jackson, Harry F., and Thomas F. O'Donnell, eds. *Back Home in Oneida: Hermon Clarke and His Letters.* Syracuse, N.Y.: Syracuse University Press, 1965.

Jaquette, Henrietta Stratton, ed. *South after Gettysburg: Letters of Cornelia Hancock from the Army of the Potomac, 1863–1865.* Philadelphia: University of Pennsylvania Press, 1937.

Johnson, Ludwell H. *Red River Campaign: Politics and Cotton in the Civil War.* Baltimore: Johns Hopkins University Press, 1958.

Jones, Bruce E. "The Letters of Lauren Elmer Bent." Master's thesis, Keene State College, Keene, N.H., 1976.

Jones, J. William, comp. "The Kilpatrick-Dahlgren Raid against Richmond." *Southern Historical Society Papers* 13 (1885), 515–60.

Jones, John B. *A Rebel War Clerk's Diary.* 2 vols. 1866. Repr. (2 vols. in 1), edited and annotated by Earl Schenck Miers. New York: Sagamore Press, 1958.

Jones, Virgil Carrington. *Eight Hours before Richmond.* New York: Henry Holt & Co., 1957.

Jordan, William B., Jr., ed. *The Civil War Journals of John Mead Gould.* Baltimore: Butternut and Blue, 1997.

Kallgren, Beverly Hayes, and James L. Crouthamel, eds. *Dear Friend Anna: The Civil War Letters of a Common Soldier from Maine.* Orono: University of Maine Press, 1992.

Kiper, Richard L., ed. *Dear Catherine, Dear Taylor: The Civil War Letters of a Union Soldier and His Wife.* Lawrence: University of Kansas Press, 2002.

Klement, Frank L. *Dark Lanterns: Secret Political Societies, Conspiracies, and Treason Trials in the Civil War.* Baton Rouge: Louisiana State University Press, 1984.

———. *The Limits of Dissent: Clement L. Vallandigham and the Civil War.* Lexington: University Press of Kentucky, 1970.

Kohl, Lawrence Frederick, ed. *Irish Green and Union Blue: The Civil War Letters of Peter Welsh.* New York: Fordham University Press, 1986.

Kostyal, K. M., ed. *Field of Battle: The Civil War Letters of Major Thomas J. Halsey.* Washington, D.C.: National Geographic Society, 1996.

Laas, Virginia Jean, ed. *Wartime Washington: The Civil War Letters of Elizabeth Blair Lee.* Urbana: University of Illinois Press, 1991.

Larimer, Charles F., ed. *Love and Valor: The Intimate Civil War Letters between Captain Jacob and Emeline Ritner.* Western Springs, Ill.: Sigourney Press, 2000.

Little, Henry F. W. *The Seventh Regiment New Hampshire Volunteers in the War of the Rebellion.* Concord, N.H.: Ira C. Evans, 1896.

Looby, Christopher, ed. *The Complete Civil War Journal and Selected Letters of Thomas Wentworth Higginson.* Chicago: University of Chicago Press, 2000.

Loving, Jerome M., ed. *Civil War Letters of George Washington Whitman*. Durham, N.C.: Duke University Press, 1975.

Lowry, Thomas P., ed. *Swamp Doctor: The Diary of a Union Surgeon in the Virginia and North Carolina Marshes*. Mechanicsburg, Pa.: Stackpole Books, 2001.

Mahon, Michael G., ed. *Winchester Divided: The Civil War Diaries of Julia Chase and Laura Lee*. Mechanicsburg, Pa.: Stackpole Books, 2002.

Marcotte, Frank B., ed. *Private Osborne: Massachusetts 23rd Volunteers*. Gretna, La.: Pelican Publishing, 2002.

Marvel, William. *Andersonville: The Last Depot*. Chapel Hill: University of North Carolina Press, 1994.

———. *Burnside*. Chapel Hill: University of North Carolina Press, 1991.

———. *Lincoln's Darkest Year: The War in 1862*. Boston: Houghton Mifflin, 2008.

———. *Mr. Lincoln Goes to War*. Boston: Houghton Mifflin, 2006.

Massachusetts Soldiers, Sailors, and Marines in the Civil War. 8 vols. Norwood: Massachusetts Adjutant General, 1932.

Meade, George. *The Life and Letters of George Gordon Meade, Major-General United States Army*. 2 vols. New York: Charles Scribner's Sons, 1913.

"Memorandum of Information as to Battles, &c., in the Year 1864, Called for by the Honorable Secretary of War." *Southern Historical Society Papers* 2, no. 1 (July 1876), 22–25.

Menge, W. Springer, and J. August Shimrak, eds. *The Civil War Notebook of Daniel Chisholm: A Chronicle of Daily Life in the Union Army, 1864–1865*. New York: Ballantine Books, 1989.

Messent, Peter, and Steve Courtney, eds. *The Civil War Letters of Joseph Hopkins Twichell: A Chaplain's Story*. Athens: University of Georgia Press, 2006.

Milgram, James W., ed. "The Libby Prison Correspondence of Tattnall Paulding." *American Philatelist* 89, no. 12 (December 1975), 1113–35.

Miller, Edwin Haviland, ed. *The Collected Writings of Walt Whitman*. 6 vols. New York: New York University Press, 1961–69.

Moe, Richard. *The Last Full Measure: The Life and Death of the First Minnesota Volunteers*. New York: Avon Books, 1993.

Moore, Frank, ed. *The Rebellion Record: A Diary of Events with Documents, Narratives, Illustrative Incidents, Poetry, Etc*. 12 vols. 1861–69. Repr. New York: Arno Press, 1977.

Moskow, Shirley Blotnick [ed.]. *Emma's World: An Intimate Look at Lives Touched by the Civil War Era*. Far Hills, N.J.: New Horizon Press, 1990.

Mushkat, Jerome, ed. *A Citizen-Soldier's Civil War: The Letters of Brevet Major General Alvin C. Voris*. DeKalb: Northern Illinois University Press, 2002.

Neely, Mark E., Jr. *The Fate of Liberty: Abraham Lincoln and Civil Liberties*. New York: Oxford University Press, 1991.

———. *Southern Rights: Political Prisoners and the Myth of Confederate Constitutionalism*. Charlottesville: University Press of Virginia, 1999.

Nevins, Allan, ed. *A Diary of Battle: The Personal Journals of Colonel Charles S. Wainwright, 1861–1865*. New York: Harcourt, Brace, & World [1962].

Nevins, Allan, and Milton Halsey Thomas, eds. *The Diary of George Templeton Strong*. 4 vols. New York: Macmillan Company, 1952.

Niven, John, ed. *The Salmon P. Chase Papers.* 5 vols. Kent, Ohio: Kent State University Press, 1993–98.

Nordholt, J. W. Schulte. "The Civil War Letters of the Dutch Ambassador." *Journal of the Illinois State Historical Society* 54, no. 4 (winter 1961), 341–73.

Norton, Oliver Willcox. *Army Letters, 1861–1865.* Chicago: privately printed, 1903.

Nulty, William H. *Confederate Florida: The Road to Olustee.* Tuscaloosa: University of Alabama Press, 1990.

Oeffinger, John C., ed. *A Soldier's General: The Civil War Letters of Major General Lafayette McLaws.* Chapel Hill: University of North Carolina Press, 2002.

Official Records of the Union and Confederate Navies in the War of the Rebellion. 31 vols. Washington, D.C.: Government Printing Office, 1894–1927.

Palladino, Grace. *Another Civil War: Labor, Capital, and the State in the Anthracite Regions of Pennsylvania, 1840–68.* Urbana: University of Illinois Press, 1990.

Palmer, Beverly Wilson, ed. *The Selected Letters of Charles Sumner.* 2 vols. Boston: Northeastern University Press, 1990.

Pease, Theodore Calvin, and James G. Randall, eds. *The Diary of Orville Hickman Browning.* 2 vols. Springfield: Illinois State Historical Library, 1925 and 1933.

Peck, Theodore, comp. *Revised Roster of Vermont Volunteers and List of Vermonters Who Served in the Army and Navy of the United States during the War of the Rebellion, 1861–66.* Montpelier, Vt.: Watchman Publishing, 1892.

Pollard, Edward A. *The Lost Cause; A New Southern History of the War of the Confederates.* New York: E. B. Treat & Co., 1867.

Puck, Susan T., ed. *Sacrifice at Vicksburg: Letters from the Front.* Shippensburg, Pa.: Burd Street Press, 1997.

Pullen, John J. *A Shower of Stars: The Medal of Honor and the 27th Maine.* 1966. Repr. Thorndike, Me.: G. K. Hall & Co., 1999.

Quaife, Milo M., ed. *From the Cannon's Mouth: The Civil War Letters of General Alpheus S. Williams.* Detroit: Wayne State University Press, 1959.

Raab, Steven S., ed. *With the 3rd Wisconsin Badgers: The Living Experience of the Civil War through the Journals of Van R. Willard.* Mechanicsburg, Pa.: Stackpole Books, 1999.

Racine, Philip N., ed. *Unspoiled Heart: The Journal of Charles Mattocks of the 17th Maine.* Knoxville: University of Tennessee Press, 1994.

Ray, J[ean] P. *The Diary of a Dead Man.* [Conshohocken, Pa.]: Acorn Press, 1979.

Receipts and Expenditures of the Town of Conway for the Year Ending March Eighth, 1864. Laconia, N.H.: J. B. Batchelder, 1864.

Record of Service of Connecticut Men in the Army and Navy of the United States during the War of the Rebellion. Hartford, Conn.: Case, Lockwood & Co., 1889.

Reid-Green, Marcia, ed. *Letters Home: Henry Matrau of the Iron Brigade.* Lincoln: University of Nebraska Press, 1993.

Reinhart, Joseph R., ed. *August Willich's Gallant Dutchmen: Civil War Letters from the 32nd Indiana Infantry.* Kent, Ohio: Kent State University Press, 2006.

Report of the Joint Committee on the Conduct of the War. 3 vols. Washington, D.C.: Government Printing Office, 1863.

Report of the Joint Committee on the Conduct of the War, at the Second Session,

Thirty-eighth Congress. 3 vols. Washington, D.C.: Government Printing Office, 1865.

Robertson, James I., Jr., ed. *The Civil War Letters of General Robert McAllister.* 1965. Repr. Baton Rouge: Louisiana State University Press, 1998.

Rosenblatt, Emil, and Ruth Rosenblatt, eds. *Hard Marching Every Day: The Civil War Letters of Private Wilbur Fisk, 1861–1865.* Lawrence: University Press of Kansas, 1992.

Ryan, David D., ed. *A Yankee Spy in Richmond: The Civil War Diary of "Crazy Bet" Van Lew.* Mechanicsburg, Pa.: Stackpole Books, 1996.

[Sawyer, Candace, comp.]. *Civil War Letters of Captain John Franklin Godfrey.* Portland, Maine: [Candace Sawyer], 1993.

Scherneckau, August. *Marching with the First Nebraska: A Civil War Diary.* Norman: University of Oklahoma Press, 2007.

Schlesinger, Arthur M., Jr. *War and the American Presidency.* New York: W. W. Norton and Company, 2004.

Scott, Robert Garth, ed. *Fallen Leaves: The Civil War Letters of Major Henry Livermore Abbott.* Kent, Ohio: Kent State University Press, 1991.

Sears, Stephen W. *Chancellorsville.* Boston: Houghton Mifflin, 1996.

———. *For Country, Cause & Leader: The Civil War Journal of Charles B. Haydon.* New York: Ticknor & Fields, 1993.

———. *Gettysburg.* Boston: Houghton Mifflin, 2003.

———, ed. *Mr. Dunn Browne's Experiences in the Army: The Civil War Letters of Samuel W. Fiske.* New York: Fordham University Press, 1998.

———, ed. *On Campaign with the Army of the Potomac: The Civil War Journal of Theodore Ayrault Dodge.* New York: Cooper Square Press, 2001.

Shankman, Arnold. "Vallandigham's Arrest and the 1863 Dayton Riot — Two Letters." *Ohio History* 79, no. 2 (spring 1970), 119–23.

Shannon, Fred Albert, ed. *The Civil War Letters of Sergeant Onley Andrus.* Urbana: University of Illinois Press, 1947.

Silver, James W. *A Life for the Confederacy, as Recorded in the Pocket Diaries of Pvt. Robert A. Moore.* Wilmington, N.C.: Broadfoot Publishing, 1987.

Simon, John Y., ed. *The Papers of Ulysses S. Grant.* 30 vols. Carbondale: Southern Illinois University Press, 1967–2008.

Simpson, Brooks D., and Jean V. Berlin, eds. *Sherman's Civil War: Selected Correspondence of William T. Sherman, 1860–1865.* Chapel Hill: University of North Carolina Press, 1999.

Smith, John David, and William Cooper Jr., eds. *A Union Woman in Civil War Kentucky: The Diary of Frances Peter.* Lexington: University Press of Kentucky, 2000.

Smith, William Wrenshall. "Holocaust Holiday: The Journal of a Strange Vacation to the War-torn South and a Visit with U.S. Grant." *Civil War Times Illustrated* 18, no. 6 (October 1979), 28–33, 35–40.

Sparks, David S., ed. *Inside Lincoln's Army: The Diary of Marsena Rudolph Patrick, Provost Marshal General, Army of the Potomac.* New York: Thomas Yoseloff, 1964.

Styple, William B., ed. *Our Noble Blood: The Civil War Letters of Regis de Trobriand.* Kearny, N.J.: Belle Grove Publishing, 1997.

Sumner, Merlin E., ed. *The Diary of Cyrus B. Comstock.* Dayton, Ohio: Morningside, 1987.

Supplement to the Official Records of the Union and Confederate Armies. 100 vols. Wilmington, N.C.: Broadfoot Publishing, 1994–2001.

Sylvester, Lorna Lutes, ed. "The Civil War Letters of Charles Harding Cox." *Indiana Magazine of History* 68, no. 1 (March 1972), 24–78, and no. 3 (September 1972), 181–239.

Tap, Bruce. *Over Lincoln's Shoulder: The Committee on the Conduct of the War.* Lawrence: University Press of Kansas, 1998.

Terrell, W. H. H. *Indiana in the War of the Rebellion: Report of the Adjutant General.* [Indianapolis]: Indiana Historical Society, 1960.

Thompson, Robert Means, and Richard Wainwright, eds. *Confidential Correspondence of Gustavus Vasa Fox, Assistant Secretary of the Navy 1861–1865.* 2 vols. New York: Naval Historical Society, 1918–19.

Tower, R. Lockwood, ed. *Lee's Adjutant: The Wartime Letters of Colonel Walter Herron Taylor, 1862–1865.* Columbia: University of South Carolina Press, 1995.

Trefousse, Hans L. *Thaddeus Stevens: Nineteenth-Century Egalitarian.* Chapel Hill: University of North Carolina Press, 1997.

Truxall, Aida Craig, ed. *Respects to All: Letters of Two Pennsylvania Boys in the War of the Rebellion.* Pittsburgh, Pa.: University of Pittsburgh Press, 1962.

U.S. Congress. *Congressional Globe.* 36th and 37th Congresses.

U.S. House of Representatives. *Fort Pillow Massacre.* 38th Cong., 1st sess. H.R. 65.

U.S. House of Representatives. *Trial of Henry Wirz.* 40th Cong., 2nd sess., 1867. Ex. Doc. 23.

U.S. Senate. *Report of the Select Committee of the Senate Appointed to Inquire into the Late Invasion and Seizure of Property at Harper's Ferry.* 36th Cong., 1st sess., 1860. S. Rep. 278.

Wainwright, Nicholas B., ed. *A Philadelphia Perspective: The Diary of Sidney George Fisher, Covering the Years 1834–1871.* Philadelphia: Historical Society of Pennsylvania, 1967.

Wallner, Peter A. *Franklin Pierce, Martyr for the Union.* Concord, N.H.: Plaidswede Publishing, 2007.

War of the Rebellion: A Compilation of the Official Records of the Union and Confederate Armies. 128 vols. Washington, D.C.: Government Printing Office, 1880–1901.

Ward, Andrew. *River Run Red: The Fort Pillow Massacre in the American Civil War.* New York: Viking, 2005.

Watson, Ronald, ed. *From Ashby to Andersonville: The Civil War Diary and Reminiscences of George A. Hitchcock, Private, Company A, 21st Massachusetts Regiment, August 1861–January 1865.* Campbell, Calif.: Savas Publishing, 1997.

Weber, Jennifer L. *Copperheads: The Rise and Fall of Lincoln's Opponents in the North.* New York: Oxford University Press, 2006.

Webster, Noah. *An American Dictionary of the English Language.* Springfield, Mass.: George and Charles Merriam, 1864.

Weld, Stephen M. *War Diary and Letters of Stephen Minot Weld, 1861–1865.* Boston: Massachusetts Historical Society, 1979.

Welker, David A., ed. *A Keystone Rebel: The Civil War Diary of Joseph Garey, Hudson's Battery, Mississippi Volunteers.* Gettysburg, Pa.: Thomas Publications, 1996.

Wiggins, Sarah Woolfolk, ed. *The Journals of Josiah Gorgas, 1857–1878.* Tuscaloosa: University of Alabama Press, 1995.

Wilkeson, Frank. *Recollections of a Private Soldier in the Army of the Potomac.* New York: G. P. Putnam's Sons, 1893.

Williams, Charles Richard, ed. *Diary and Letters of Rutherford Birchard Hayes, Nineteenth President of the United States.* 5 vols. Columbus: Ohio State Archaeological and Historical Society, 1914–26.

Williams, Frederick D. *The Wild Life of the Army: Civil War Letters of James A. Garfield.* East Lansing: Michigan State University Press, 1964.

Wills, Garry. *Lincoln at Gettysburg: The Words That Remade America.* New York: Simon & Schuster, 1992.

Wilson, Douglas L. *Honor's Voice: The Transformation of Abraham Lincoln.* New York: Alfred A. Knopf, 1998.

Winschel, Terrence J. *Triumph and Defeat: The Vicksburg Campaign.* 2 vols. Mason City, Iowa: Savas Beattie, 1998, 2004.

Wolf, Hazel C., ed. "Campaigning with the First Minnesota: The Diary of Isaac Lyman Taylor." *Minnesota History* 25 (1944), 11–39, 117–52, 224–57, 342–61.

Woodworth, Steven E., ed. *The Musick of the Mocking Birds, the Roar of the Cannon: The Civil War Diary and Letters of William Winters.* Lincoln: University of Nebraska Press, 1998.

Wubben, Hubert H. *Civil War Iowa and the Copperhead Movement.* Ames: Iowa State University Press, 1980.

Yacavone, Donald, ed. *A Voice of Thunder: The Civil War Letters of George E. Stephens.* Urbana: University of Illinois Press, 1997.

Younger, Edward, ed. *Inside the Confederate Government: The Diary of Robert Garlick Hill Kean.* Baton Rouge: Louisiana University Press, 1973.

Newspapers

Advertiser and Eastern Townships Sentinel, Waterloo, Canada East

Binghampton (N.Y.) *Press*

Boston Daily Advertiser

Boston Evening Transcript

Boston Journal

Carroll County Register, Ossipee, N.H.

Charleston (S.C.) *Courier*

Chatham (Canada West) *Weekly Planet*

Chicago Tribune

Cincinnati (Ohio) *Daily Commercial*

Cincinnati (Ohio) *Gazette*
Cleveland (Ohio) *Leader*
Cleveland (Ohio) *Plain Dealer*
Coschocton (Ohio) *Democrat*
Crisis, Columbus, Ohio
Daily Chronicle, Portsmouth, N.H.
Daily Citizen, Vicksburg, Miss.
Daily Constitutional Union, Washington, D.C.
Daily Gate City, Keokuk, Iowa
Daily Gazette, Davenport, Iowa
Daily Journal, Indianapolis, Ind.
Daily Missouri Republican, St. Louis
Daily News, London
Daily Times, Leavenworth, Kans.
Dakotian, Yankton, Dakota Territory
Dayton (Ohio) *Daily Empire*
Dayton (Ohio) *Weekly Empire*
Detroit (Mich.) *Free Press*
Dubuque (Iowa) *Times*
Eastern Townships Gazette and Shefford County Advertiser, Granby, Canada East
Farmer's Cabinet, Amherst, N.H.
Georgia Journal and Messenger, Macon
Harper's Weekly
Illinois State Journal, Springfield
Kansas Chief, White Cloud
Louisville (Ky.) *Daily Democrat*
Macon (Ga.) *Daily Telegraph*
Milwaukee (Wis.) *Sentinel*
Muscatine (Iowa) *Courier*
New Hampshire Patriot and State Gazette, Concord
New Hampshire Sentinel, Keene
New York Daily News
New York Herald
New York Sun
New York Times
New York Tribune
New York World
Nonpareil, Council Bluffs, Iowa
North Missouri Courier, Hannibal
Ohio State Journal, Columbus
Oxford Democrat, Paris, Maine
Philadelphia Inquirer
Portland (Maine) *Advertiser*
Portland (Maine) *Daily Press*
Prairie du Chien (Wis.) *Courier*
Richmond (Va.) *Examiner*

Richmond (Va.) *Whig*
Stanstead (Canada East) *Journal*
Summit County Beacon, Akron, Ohio
Sumter Republican, Americus, Ga.
Times, London
Washington Chronicle
Washington Star
Weekly Gate City, Keokuk, Iowa
Weekly Herald, St. Joseph, Mo.
Weekly Perryville (Mo.) *Union*
Westfield (N.Y.) *Republican*

Miscellaneous

Joseph P. Brainerd gravestone inscription, Greenwood Cemetery. St. Albans, Vt.

Sources and Acknowledgments

This book is documented largely by the impressions, opinions, and attitudes prevalent during the Civil War. In order to avoid the imperceptible foibles of memory and the insidious distortions of political or personal motive, I have relied almost exclusively on thoughts and statements recorded at the time. That has entailed months of poring over manuscripts with faded ink, tiny script, or atrocious orthography, most of which contain little more than monotonously similar renditions of personal needs and wishes. The tedium of that practice is occasionally repaid with the discovery of a remarkable observation or a cryptic reference that means little by itself, but completes a puzzle when juxtaposed with other equally obscure clues. Only by diving into the ocean of extant letters and diaries from that period can one reliably fathom the varied viewpoints of the era. Immersing myself in that material in a chronological progression through three of the war's four years has forced me to reassess conclusions that I had supposed were becoming fairly settled after so many years of serious study.

Unlike academically affiliated historians, I have no university to thank for leaves of absence, no department head to acknowledge for lightened teaching loads, and no foundations to credit for research fellowships. I have, however, always been grateful for the Lincoln Prize at Gettysburg College, the Malcolm and Muriel Barrow Bell Award from the Georgia Historical Society, and the Douglas Southall Freeman Award, which gave me the wherewithal to abandon outside employment long enough to turn history into a full-time occupation. A lean livelihood it has been, but it was the career I always wanted to follow, and I consider myself wealthy for the freedom to do what I love. That I am able to do so is attributable in part to a number of professional historians who have always been very kind with advice and assistance for the struggling amateur, among them James M. McPherson of Princeton, George Rable of the University of Alabama, Gary Gallagher of the University of Virginia, Stephen Sears of Norwalk, Connecticut, Robert K. Krick of Fredericksburg, Virginia, and especially A. Wilson Greene of Petersburg, Virginia.

Will Greene did me the incalculable favor of reading my entire manuscript, as did Jeff Wieand, of Concord, Massachusetts. Those two devotees of Civil War history once again rescued me from countless errors of fact and reasoning. Any cognitive blunders that remain after their faithful and thorough attention reflect only my own obstinacy. My copyeditor, Melissa Dobson, has now ushered me through three books, somehow managing to find legions of stylistic and bibliographic mistakes that crept magically into my letter-perfect manuscripts — apparently after I packaged them up for shipping. Her discriminating eye and her persistence in running down details have engendered my admiration and gratitude. Nor shall I ever forget the kind advice and assistance of the late Harry Foster, of Houghton Mifflin, who first proposed and encouraged the series of which this marks the penultimate volume.

Also deserving of my thanks is that battalion of curators and archivists at dozens of manuscript repositories around the country. These include David Emerson, of my own Conway Public Library; Paul Carnahan and Marjorie Strong at the Vermont Historical Society; Jan Albers, director of the Sheldon Museum in Middlebury, Vermont; Nick Noyes and Jamie Kingman Rice at the Maine Historical Society; Heather Bilodeau, director of the Camden Area History Center in Camden, Maine; Bill Copeley and Peter Wallner, at the New Hampshire Historical Society; Peter Drummey and the reading room staff at the Massachusetts Historical Society; Jackie Penny, Nigel Gully, and Elizabeth Pope, at the American Antiquarian Society, in Worcester; Karen Eberhart at the Rhode Island Historical Society; Ellen Schwanekamp, at the Chatauqua County Historical Society in Westfield, New York; Betsy Caldwell at the Indiana Historical Society; Nelson Lankford (in addition to the library staff) at the Virginia Historical Society; Ann Sindelar of the Western Reserve Historical Society, in Cleveland; Gwen Mayer, at the Hudson Library and Historical Society in Hudson, Ohio; Lisa Long and John E. Haas at the Ohio Historical Society; Anne Shepherd, of the Cincinnati Historical Society; Steve Nielsen, at the Minnesota Historical Society; Andrea Faling, at the Nebraska State Historical Society; Lin Fredericksen and Darrell Garwood, at the Kansas State Historical Society; Thomas Miller, of the Western Historical Manuscript Collection at the University of Missouri; Nan Card, at the Rutherford B. Hayes Presidential Library in Fremont, Ohio; Yolanda Ray, interpretive specialist at the Natchez Trace Parkway; Joanne Nestor of the New Jersey State Archives; Frank Mevers of the New Hampshire Division of Archives and Records Management; George Rugg, at Notre Dame; Brian Dunnigan, Barbara DeWolfe, Bethany Anderson, and Janet Bloom, of the Clements Library, as well as Malgosia Myc and Marilyn McNitt of the Bentley Historical Library, all at the University of Michigan; Cynthia Ostroff and Kathryn James, of Yale University; Thomas D. Hamm, at Earlham College; Tanya Zanish-Belcher and Melissa Gottwald, at Iowa State University; Kathryn Hodson, of Special Collections at the University of Iowa; Richard Clement and Kathy Lafferty, at the University of Kansas; Mary Huth, at the University of Rochester; Brenda Gunn and Adam Kohleffel, of the Center for American History at the University of Texas; Bill Ross at the University of New Hampshire; Jeff Marshall and Prudence Doherty at the University of Vermont; Sarah Hartwell, of the Rauner Library at Dartmouth College; Phil Weimerskirch at the Providence Public Library; Sean P. Casey at the Boston Public Library; Kathy Curtis of the Stanstead Archives in Stanstead, Quebec; Dwane Wilkin, executive director of the Quebec Anglophone Heritage Network; Jeffrey Flannery, Bruce Kirby, Jennifer Brathovde, and Patrick Kerwin, in the manuscript reading room at the Library of Congress; and, as always, Richard Sommers, David Keough, and Art Bergeron, of the U.S. Army Military History Institute.

This book and those that preceded it would never have been written were it not for the relative seclusion that allows me to concentrate for weeks on end. For this I will be forever thankful to my grandfather, who chose to live in this relatively isolated location nearly a century ago, and to my father, who decided to return here. I am also obliged to the new neighbors who now live within sight of my family home, both of whom have shown the kindness to keep continually out of carbine range. Most of all, however, I am grateful to Ellen Schwindt, who is responsible for almost all of the peace that I enjoy.

Index